Understanding the Political World

Understanding the Political World

A Comparative Introduction to Political Science

Eleventh Edition

JAMES N. **DANZIGER**

University of California, Irvine

PEARSON

Boston   Columbus   Indianapolis   New York   San Francisco   Upper Saddle River
Amsterdam   Cape Town   Dubai   London   Madrid   Milan   Munich   Paris   Montréal   Toronto
Delhi   Mexico City   São Paulo   Sydney   Hong Kong   Seoul   Singapore   Taipei   Tokyo

Senior Acquisitions Editor: Vikram Mukhija
Associate Editor: Corey Kahn
Editorial Assistants: Isabel Schwab,
  Beverly Fong
Executive Marketing Manager:
  Wendy Gordon
Senior Digital Media Producer: Paul DeLuca
Production Manager: S.S. Kulig

**Project Coordination, Text Design, and
  Electronic Page Makeup:** Integra
Cover Designer/Manager: Wendy Ann
  Fredericks
Cover Photo: © Pedro Ugarte/AFP/Getty Images
Senior Manufacturing Buyer: Roy Pickering
Printer/Binder: Quad/Graphics-Taunton
Cover Printer: Lehigh Phoenix Color Corp.

Credits and acknowledgments borrowed from other sources and reproduced, with permission, in this textbook appear on page 485.

Library of Congress Cataloging-in-Publication Data
Danziger, James N.
   Understanding the political world : a comparative introduction to political science/
James N. Danziger.—11th ed.
      p.   cm.
ISBN 978-0-205-85492-9
1. Political science.   2. Comparative government.   I. Title.
JA66.D36 2012
320—dc23

                                        2011051037

10 9 8 7 6 5 4 3 2 1—QGT—15 14 13 12

www.pearsonhighered.com

ISBN 13: 978-0-205-85492-9
ISBN 10:   0-205-85492-3

TO LESLEY, NICK, AND VANESSA

BRIEF CONTENTS

DETAILED CONTENTS

PREFACE

I was in Cairo with Semester at Sea less than two months before the events in Tahrir Square began to unfold in Spring 2011. My 50-plus students were tasked to discuss politics with the locals and, to the extent possible, assess Egyptians' views on who would replace Hosni Mubarak, Egypt's authoritarian ruler for three decades. I was having similar discussions. When we shared our insights, not one of us suggested that very soon there would be a massive populist uprising, let alone that it would topple the regime. Our theories and research findings in political science did not see it coming. Yet that did not frustrate me or embarrass me on behalf of political scientists everywhere. One of the things I love about this enterprise is that there always seem to be occurrences that challenge our understanding. That is one of the things that makes politics fun.

Albert Einstein commented that the study of politics is more difficult than the study of physics. The political phenomena that we attempt to study and to explain include so many variables and can spin in unexpected directions, especially while unpredictable humans try to control them. Yet all is not chaos. There are patterns. Some actions and outcomes are much more likely than others. A central goal of political scientists is to identify and communicate what happens and why it happens, and then to offer generalizations that capture the broad processes and underlying dynamics of politics. This is how political science attempts to enhance our understanding of the political world. Hence, the title of this book. It is an effort to provide you with some of the tools—key concepts, research findings, explanations—to help you better understand politics and also how political science approaches its subject matter.

The book offers you a path. After a brief consideration of how we decide what we know, the book explores what we know about the political beliefs and actions of individuals. It then advances to the country level of analysis, examining political institutions and political processes. This is followed by a consideration of politics at the level of the global system. The final chapters draw all the themes of the book together while examining the politics of three broad clusters of countries around the world.

I hope the events that are unfolding in the political world have persuaded you that it is essential to understand it and to act sensibly within it, because politics is arguably the most critical domain in which our futures are being shaped. You will be encouraged to consider whether the information, insights, and concepts of political science are useful. Can they help us understand the political world? Can they inform our value choices and normative judgments about public policies? Can they guide our policies and actions in ways that improve the quality of our lives, individually and collectively?

NEW TO THIS EDITION

The difference in this edition that should be obvious to loyal readers is the use of "four-color" printing, which is not only colorful and engaging, but also provides for the addition of eight full-page maps and many more visual cues to facilitate the reader's understanding of the underlying structure of content.

And of course, given the extraordinary rate of change in the political world, there is a systematic and thorough update of the quantitative data in almost every figure and table and well as extensive updates to almost all of the examples that are richly embedded throughout the text. Special attention has been paid to the implications of the "Arab Spring" and the policy implications of the global recession. Here are some additional significant differences from the previous edition:

- Among the country vignettes that open every chapter by introducing a major theme of that chapter are new ones exploring the struggle in Iraq to establish a democratic political regime, the attempts of the indigenous Mapuche people of Chile to persuade the government to return their land, how Ireland rapidly shifted from being the Celtic Tiger of high economic growth and prosperity to a country requiring a massive bailout, the remarkable transformation of China under communism, and the cooperative efforts of the Europeans to overcome their historical animosities and create a powerful union.

- Among the Debates that occur in every chapter are new ones on such topics as whether money dominates all other resources in influencing public policy decision making, whether the model of European social democracy is now unsustainable, and whether the new information and communications technologies are dramatically transforming our political beliefs and political actions.

- Among the Compare and Focus features in every chapter are new ones examining the obstacles to development in Nigeria and the Philippines and the levels of political knowledge among people of different age cohorts.

- A new section in Chapter 8 focuses more explicitly on the ways in which the financial actors in the political economy powerfully influence the government and those who make and implement public policy.

- The analytic framework employed to classify the world's countries in Chapters 13–15 has been modified to add new variables to the social development index as well as updating all the data forming the framework.

- Chapter 14 on the developing countries has been substantially rewritten to tighten the themes and clarify the arguments.

- Chapter 15 , on the transitional developed countries, has been significantly revised to emphasize the recent evolution in both the newly industrializing countries and the postcommunist developed countries.

- More data are presented in graphical form to improve their capacity to illuminate the issue being explored.

- On the Web, a list of useful and relevant Internet sites, and For Further Reading suggestions at the end of each chapter have been updated and expanded.

FEATURES

The eleventh edition of *Understanding the Political World* retains the conceptual framework of previous editions, focusing on politics at every level, from that of the individual person to the level of the global system. To enrich the reader's understanding, it employs a comparative perspective, considering evidence and examples from many countries in all regions of the world. This approach is guided both by Aristotle's wise observation that all thinking begins in comparison and by a recognition that the political world is now truly global.

As noted above, the book is organized to provide the reader with a brief characterization of how political scientists study politics in a comparative framework. It then uses such a framework to focus on how to understand politics at the level of the individual and the group, the different ways in which political institutions are organized, the dynamics of important political processes, and the key patterns of politics in major clusters of countries.

Chapter 1 and the Appendix introduce the logic of political science and the methods of comparative political analysis.

Chapters 2–4 examine both normative political theory and also the empirical study of political behavior at the individual and group levels, describing and explaining the causes of political beliefs and actions.

Chapters 5–8 emphasize the structural and institutional elements of political systems, offering concepts and examples that characterize the different ways in which people organize themselves politically.

Chapters 9–12 analyze crucial political processes, such as public policymaking and the exercise of power, political and economic development, politics across national borders, and political violence.

Chapters 13–15 explain in detail how important groups of countries try to achieve their broad goals of prosperity, stability, and security within the complex international environment. These chapters provide specific analyses of the developed countries, the developing countries, and two sets of transitional developed countries—the postcommunist developed countries and the newly industrializing countries.

In addition, the eleventh edition retains the following key features:

- Many discussions and debates provide memorable applications of key concepts such as power, authority, political violence, equality, and globalization and key issues such as whether terrorism is ever justifiable and whether interest groups are good for democracy.
- Continual use of country-based examples ground every topic in relevant, specific realities.
- Numerous presentations of current data, often in graphical form, facilitate analysis and comparisons on many topics.
- The use of captioned photographs and political cartoons illuminates themes in a manner that complements the textual discussions.
- A recurring focus on political economy emphasizes the significance of linkages between the political system and the economic system.
- An engaging, readable style draws the reader in.

MYPOLISCILAB FOR *UNDERSTANDING THE POLITICAL WORLD*

The moment you know

Educators know it. Students know it. It's that inspired moment when something that was difficult to understand suddenly makes perfect sense. Our MyLab products have been designed and refined with a single purpose in mind—to help educators create that moment of understanding with their students.

MyPoliSciLab delivers *proven results* in helping individual students succeed. It provides *engaging experiences* that personalize, stimulate, and measure learning for each student. And it comes from a *trusted partner* with educational expertise and a deep commitment to helping students, instructors, and departments achieve their goals.

MyPoliSciLab can be used by itself or linked to any learning management system. To learn more about how MyPoliSciLab combines proven learning applications with powerful assessment, visit **www.MyPoliSciLab.com**.

MyPoliSciLab delivers *proven results* in helping individual students succeed

- Pearson MyLabs are currently in use by millions of students each year across a variety of disciplines.
- MyPoliSciLab works, but don't take our word for it. Visit **www .pearsonhighered.com/elearning** to read white papers, case studies, and testimonials from instructors and students that consistently demonstrate the success of our MyLabs.

MyPoliSciLab provides *engaging experiences* that personalize, stimulate, and measure learning for each student

- *Assessment.* Track progress and get instant feedback on every chapter, video, and multimedia activity. With results feeding into a powerful gradebook, the assessment program identifies learning challenges early and suggests the best resources to help.
- *Personalized Study Plan.* Follow a flexible learning path created by the assessment program and tailored to each student's unique needs. Organized by learning objectives, the study plan offers follow-up reading, video, and multimedia activities for further learning and practice.
- *Pearson eText.* Just like the printed text, highlight and add notes to the eText online or download it to a tablet.
- *Flashcards.* Learn key terms by word or definition.
- *Video.* Analyze current events by watching streaming video from major news providers.
- *Mapping Exercises.* Explore interactive maps that test basic geography, examine key events in world history, and analyze the state of the world.
- *Comparative Exercises.* Think critically about how politics compare around the world.

- *PoliSci News Review.* Join the political conversation by following headlines in *Financial Times* newsfeeds, reading analysis in the blog, taking weekly current events quizzes and polls, and more.
- *ClassPrep.* Engage students with class presentation resources collected in one convenient online destination.

MyPoliSciLab comes from a *trusted partner* with educational expertise and an eye on the future

- Pearson support instructors with workshops, training, and assistance from Pearson Faculty Advisors so you get the help you need to make MyPoliSciLab work for your course.
- Pearson gathers feedback from instructors and students during the development of content and the feature enhancement of each release to ensure that our products meet your needs.

To order MyPoliSciLab with the print text, use ISBN 0-205-85492-3.

SUPPLEMENTS

Pearson is pleased to offer several resources to qualified adopters of *Understanding the Political World* and their students that will make teaching and learning from this book even more effective and enjoyable. Several of the supplements for this book are available at the Instructor Resource Center (IRC), an online hub that allows instructors to quickly download book-specific supplements. Please visit the IRC welcome page at www.pearsonhighered.com/irc to register for access.

Passport Choose the resources you want from MyPoliSciLab and put links to them into your course management system. If there is assessment associated with those resources, it also can be uploaded, allowing the results to feed directly into your course management system's gradebook. With MyPoliSciLab assets like videos, mapping exercises, *Financial Times* newsfeeds, current events quizzes, politics blog, and much more, Passport is available for any Pearson political science book. To order Passport with the print text, use ISBN 0-205-20851-7.

Instructor's Manual/Test Bank This resource includes learning objectives, chapter overview and lecture suggestions, multiple-choice questions, essay questions, and discussion questions for each chapter. Available exclusively on the IRC.

Pearson MyTest This powerful assessment generation program includes all of the items in the instructor's manual/test bank. Questions and tests can be easily created, customized, saved online, and then printed, allowing flexibility to manage assessments anytime and anywhere. Available exclusively on the IRC.

PowerPoint Presentation Organized around a lecture outline, these multimedia presentations also include photos, figures, and tables from each chapter. Available exclusively on the IRC.

Sample Syllabus This resource provides suggestions for assigning content from this book and MyPoliSciLab. Available exclusively on the IRC.

Longman Atlas of World Issues (0-205-78020-2) From population and political systems to energy use and women's rights, the *Longman Atlas of World Issues* features full-color thematic maps that examine the forces shaping the world. Featuring maps from the latest edition of *The Penguin State of the World Atlas*, this excerpt includes critical thinking exercises to promote a deeper understanding of how geography affects many global issues.

Goode's World Atlas (0-321-65200-2) First published by Rand McNally in 1923, *Goode's World Atlas* has set the standard for college reference atlases. It features hundreds of physical, political, and thematic maps as well as graphs, tables, and a pronouncing index.

ACKNOWLEDGMENTS

Many sources of ideas and information constitute the basis of *my* understanding about politics. Broadly, you should know that I was born and have primarily been educated in the United States. I have also studied, lived, and/or spent significant periods in more than 70 countries in Western and Eastern Europe, Central and South America, Asia, the Middle East and North Africa, and Sub-Saharan Africa. I have circumnavigated the globe twice on Semester at Sea. The people I met and the events I experienced in all these places have certainly influenced my perceptions about politics.

More direct contributions to this book have come from the work of my colleagues in political science and from the many students and others in the political world with whom I have interacted. I have drawn deeply and often from the ideas of these groups.

By the publication of the eleventh edition, the layers of contributions and ideas to the construction of this book are deep, rich, and indescribable. In every edition, there is a list of people who added positively to that edition, and I continue to be grateful to them all. Explicit guidance and advice regarding the writing of this particular edition have come from several valuable sources: Vikram Mukhija at Pearson Education; scholarly colleagues who have offered useful suggestions, and especially Richard Coldwell, C.B.E, Lesley Danziger, and Keith Topper; and students who have provided feedback on the book, including those who provided specific material and worked with me on the revision process, undergraduates Tyler Hunt, Margaret Liao, Aaron McCullough, Madiha Shahabuddin, Neil Thakore, and Kerry Wakely. The reviewers, who offered very thoughtful and constructive commentaries for this edition, include Lynda Barrow, Coe College; David Darmofal, University of South Carolina; Erik Root, West Liberty College; and David Yamanashi, Cornell College.

I am very grateful for the help provided by all these (and many unnamed) sources. Regarding the roads not taken and the missteps in this book, the responsibility is mine.

JAMES N. DANZIGER

TO THE READER

The aim of this book is revealed by its title: It is meant to help you understand the political world. It assumes that you are willing to think about politics. It does not assume that you have substantial knowledge about politics or political science, or even that you know the difference between politics and political science. I hope that when you complete the book and any course in which you are reading it, you will feel that you have increased your knowledge about the contemporary political world.

The study of politics is full of fascinating questions. First are the questions about *what is*, such as: Who exercises political power, and what values and purposes guide them? Why do people accept political authority? How do people organize themselves politically? What factors are associated with political violence? A second set of questions concerns *what ought to be*: Who should exercise political power, and what values should they pursue? Why should people accept political authority? How should political structures be organized? When is political violence justifiable?

People disagree sharply about answers to both these descriptive (what is) and normative (what ought to be) questions. In addition, the study of politics provokes a third set of questions regarding *what we can actually know* about the political world. Here also there are major disagreements about the appropriate methods for describing and understanding politics.

Although this book cannot resolve the underlying disputes, it offers you the basis for making sense out of politics at all three levels. As author, I make some basic assumptions: that you can think systematically about politics and make general statements about how politics works; that you will learn more about politics by considering the politics of many different places; that every observer of politics (certainly including you and me) has biases, only some of which can be understood; that you need a variety of sources of ideas and information before you can make informed and sensible decisions about the value disagreements pervading politics; and that this book is one such source that can be helpful to you. My efforts will be successful to the extent that *you* ultimately judge my assumptions to be correct (especially the last one...).

It is inevitable that you will be frustrated with the treatment of politics at some (many?) points in this book. I would say: Reader, be merciful! The study of politics is very complex. Gather bits of understanding where you can find them.

MAPS

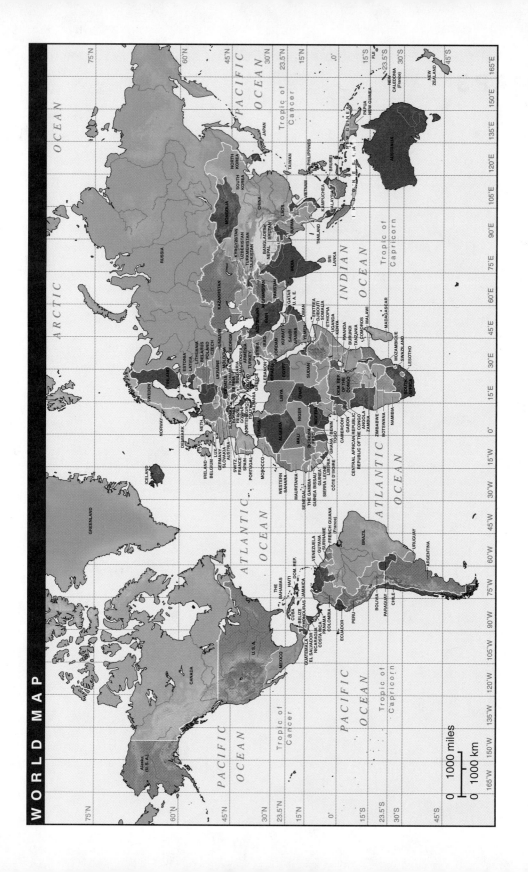

W O R L D   M A P

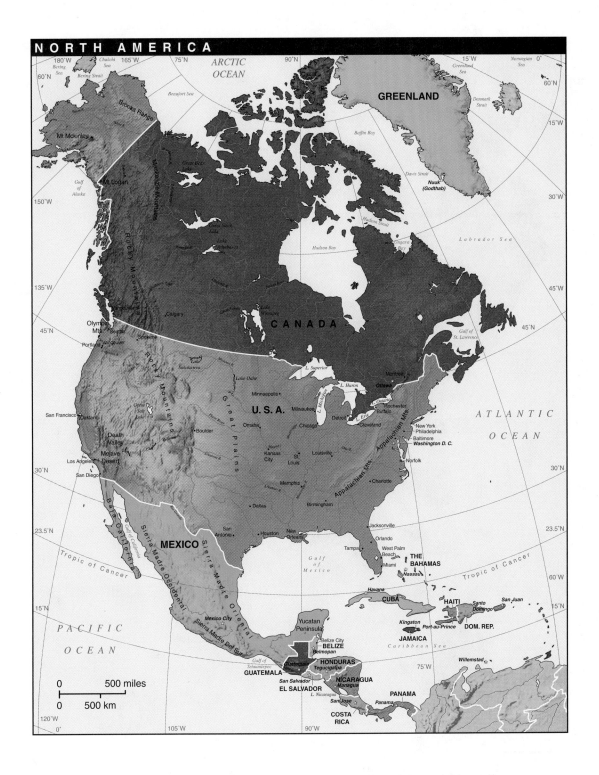

NORTH AMERICA

GREENLAND

ARCTIC OCEAN

180°W
Chukchi Sea
165°W
Bering Sea
Bering Strait
60°N
75°N
90°N
15°W
Greenland Sea
0°
Norwegian Sea
60°N

Beaufort Sea

Brooks Range

Mt Mckinley

Baffin Bay

15°W

Denmark Strait

Mt Logan

Mackenzie Mountains

Great Bear Lake

Davis Strait

Nuuk (Godthab)

30°W

Gulf of Alaska

150°W

Great Slave Lake

Labrador Sea

45°W

135°W

Lake Athabasca

Rocky Mountains

Hudson Strait

Ungava Bay

Hudson Bay

Vancouver Is.

Calgary

Lake Winnipeg

C A N A D A

Gulf of St. Lawrence

45°N

Olympic Mts
Seattle
Portland
Vancouver
Spokane

Rocky Mountains

Lake Sakakawea

Columbia R.

Lake Oahe

L. Superior

L. Huron

Montreal
Ottawa

45°N

San Francisco
Oakland

Great Salt Lake

Minneapolis

Milwaukee

Chicago

Detroit

L. Michigan

L. Ontario
Buffalo
Rochester

New York
Philadelphia
Baltimore
Washington D. C.

ATLANTIC OCEAN

Death Valley

Mojave Desert
Los Angeles

Boulder

Omaha

Kansas City

St. Louis

Louisville

L. Erie
Cleveland

Ohio R.

Appalachian Mts.

Norfolk

30°N

San Diego

Memphis

Charlotte

30°N

Baja California

Gulf of California

Sierra Madre Occidental

Dallas

Birmingham

Appalachian Mts.

Jacksonville

23.5°N

San Antonio

Houston

New Orleans

Orlando

Tampa

West Palm Beach
Miami

THE BAHAMAS

Nassau

Tropic of Cancer

60°W

Tropic of Cancer

15°N

MEXICO

Sierra Madre Oriental

Gulf of Mexico

Havana

CUBA

HAITI
Santo Domingo
San Juan

15°N

PACIFIC OCEAN

Mexico City

Yucatan Peninsula

Kingston

Port-au-Prince

DOM. REP.

75°W

JAMAICA

Caribbean Sea

Sierra Madre Del Sur

Belize City
BELIZE
Belmopan

Willemstad

Gulf of Tehuantepec

Guatemala

HONDURAS
Tegucigalpa

GUATEMALA

San Salvador

NICARAGUA
Managua

PANAMA

EL SALVADOR

L. Nicaragua

San Jose

Panama

120°W

0°

COSTA RICA

105°W

90°W

0   500 miles

0   500 km

SOUTH AMERICA

Caribbean Sea

Barranquilla

Maracaibo
Barquisimeto
Valencia

VENEZUELA

GUYANA

SURINAME

Georgetown
Paramaribo

Cayenne

Medellín

Bogotá

**FRENCH
GUIANA
(France)**

COLOMBIA

Quito

ECUADOR

Guayaquil

*Gulf of
Guayaquil*

Río Orinoco

*Amazon
Basin*

Manaus

Marajó
Island

Belém

Río Negro

Amazon R.

Fortaleza

Teresina

Andes Mountains

PERU

Lima

Río Madre de Dios

Lake
Titicaca

La Paz

BOLIVIA

Sucre

Río Madeira

Río Purus

Río Juruá

Río Tapajós

Río Teles Pires

Río Xingu

Río Araguaia

Río Tocantins

BRAZIL

Recife

Salvador

*Mato Grosso
Plateau*

Goiânia

☆ *Brasília*

Río São Francisco

Belo Horizonte

Atacama Desert

Campinas

Rio de
Janeiro

São Paulo

Cabo Frio

Curitiba

PARAGUAY

Asunción

Río Paraná

Río Pilcomayo

Porto
Alegre

Río Uruguay

Rosario

URUGUAY

Montevideo

CHILE

Tropic of
Capricorn

*Cerro
Aconcagua*

Santiago

ARGENTINA

Pampas

Buenos Aires

Río Paraná

Andes Mountains

Patagonia

Isla Grande
de Chiloe

*Gulf of
San Matias*

Valdes
Peninsula

*Gulf of
San Jorge*

Taitao
Peninsula

**FALKLAND
ISLANDS**

Port
Stanley

*Strait of
Magellan*

Tierra Del Fuego

**SOUTH
GEORGIA
ISLAND**

*PACIFIC
OCEAN*

*ATLANTIC
OCEAN*

*ATLANTIC
OCEAN*

Tropic of
Capricorn

0   500 miles

0   500 km

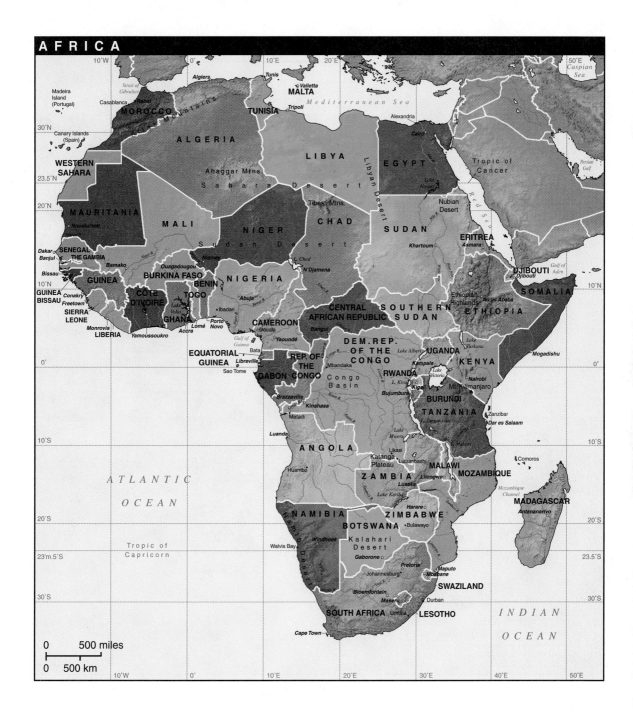

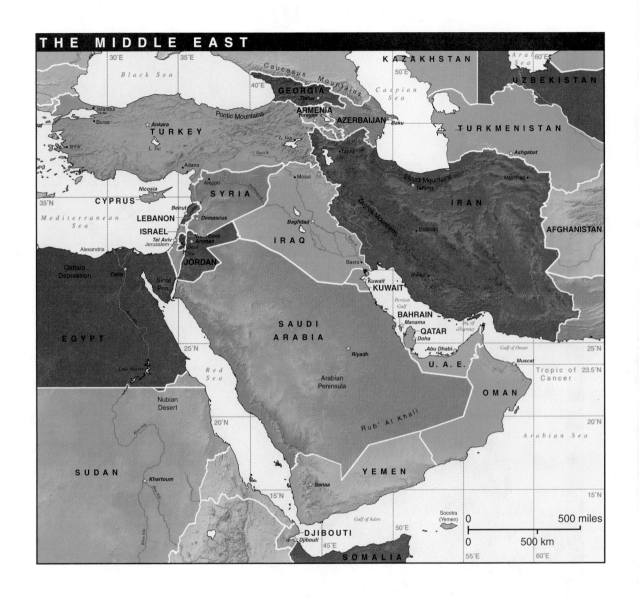

THE MIDDLE EAST

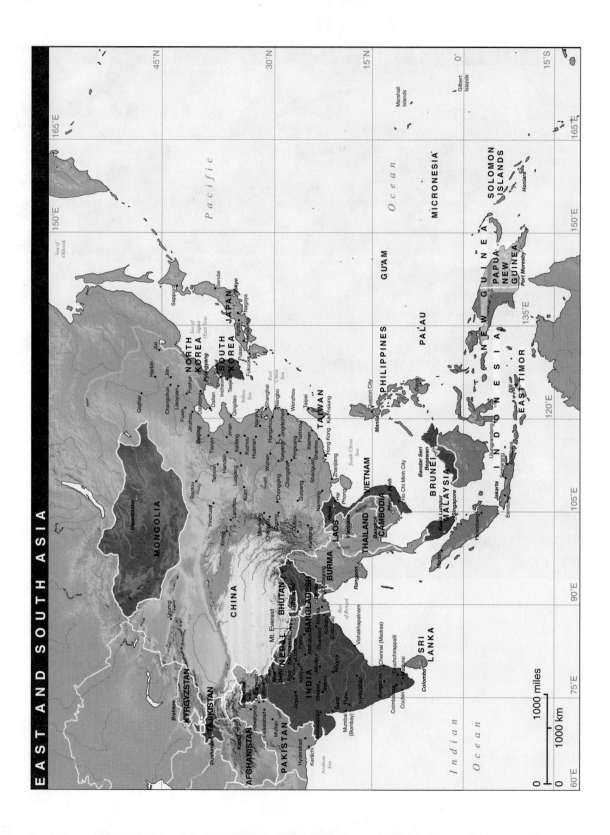

EAST AND SOUTH ASIA

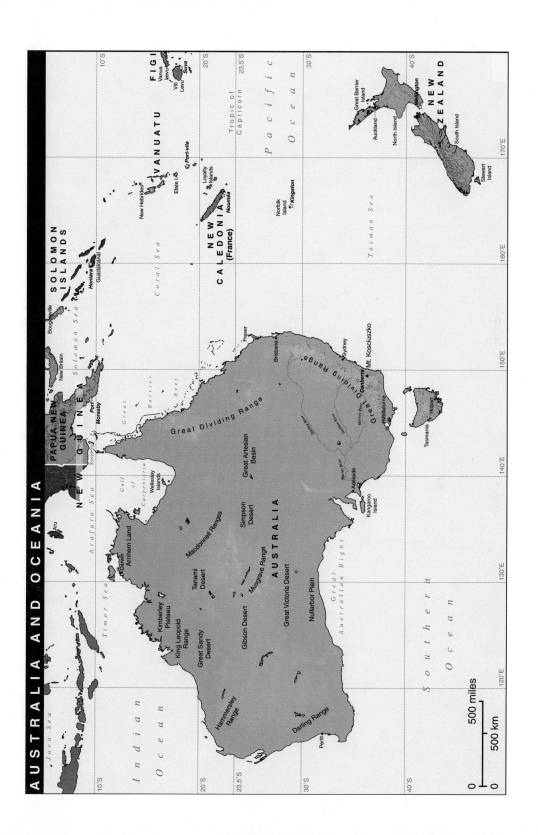

AUSTRALIA AND OCEANIA

AUSTRALIA

Indian Ocean

Southern Ocean

PAPUA NEW GUINEA

NEW GUINEA

SOLOMON ISLANDS

VANUATU

NEW CALEDONIA (France)

FIGI

NEW ZEALAND

Java Sea

Timor Sea

Arafura Sea

Gulf of Carpentaria

Coral Sea

Solomon Sea

Pacific Ocean

Tasman Sea

Great Barrier Reef

Great Australian Bight

Aru

Darwin

Arnhem Land

Wellesley Islands

Torres Strait

Port Moresby

Bougainville

New Britain

Honiara

Guadalcanal

New Hebrides

Port-vila

Etate I.

Loyalty Islands

Noumea

Norfolk Island

Kingston

Vanua Levu

Viti Levu

Suva

Tropic of Capricorn

Kimberley Plateau

King Leopold Range

Great Sandy Desert

Tanami Desert

Macdonnell Ranges

Simpson Desert

Musgrave Range

Gibson Desert

Great Victoria Desert

Hammersley Range

Darling Range

Nullarbor Plain

Great Dividing Range

Great Artesian Basin

Fraser

Brisbane

Sydney

Canberra

Mt. Kosciuszko

Melbourne

Adelaide

Kangaroo Island

Perth

Tasmania

Hobart

Murray River

Darling River

Lachlan River

Norman River

Flinders River

Great Barrier Island

Auckland

North Island

Wellington

South Island

Stewart Island

10°S

20°S

23.5°S

30°S

40°S

120°E

130°E

140°E

150°E

160°E

170°E

500 miles

500 km

0

Politics and Knowledge

Search me? Are there fundamental *political* issues when a school searches its students?

LEARNING OBJECTIVES

1.1 Define politics within a public context.

1.2 Analyze three types of political knowledge.

1.3 Evaluate the strengths and weaknesses of different sources of political knowledge.

1.4 Identify techniques and approaches used to gain political knowledge and assess whether they constitute a science.

1.5 Describe the purpose and the outline of the text.

◻▶ **Read**
and **Listen** to
Chapter 1 at
mypoliscilab.com

✓• **Study**
and **Review** the
Pre-Test &
Flashcards at
mypoliscilab.com

Imagine you have a 13-year-old sister in eighth grade. She has quite the day at school: The vice principal comes into her math class unexpectedly and asks her to bring her backpack and accompany him to his office. In his office, she sees a planner, a knife, a lighter, and some white pills on his desk. The vice principal lectures her about the importance of telling the truth, then asks which of the items belong to her. She tells him that she had lent the planner to another girl a few days earlier, but that the other items are not hers. The vice principal responds that the other girl had reported your sister for giving her the pills, which students are not allowed to possess at school.

The vice principal asks if he can look through your sister's backpack, and she agrees. A female secretary enters the office and searches the backpack. Your sister is then told to follow the secretary to the nurse's office, where she is asked to remove her jacket, socks, and shoes. She follows their directions. They next ask her to take off her pants and shirt, and again she follows their directions. These clothes are searched, and when nothing incriminating is found, they order your sister to stand up, pull her bra away from her body and shake it, then pull her underwear loose and shake it. No pills drop out when she complies. She is allowed to put her clothes back on and sits outside the principal's office for several hours. Finally, she is sent back to class.

What do you think of the events just described? Is this situation *political*? Do the actions of the vice principal seem appropriate? What about the actions of the school's secretary and nurse? Did your sister do the right thing by complying with each of their requests? Did she have a choice? What would you do in a similar situation?

Stop and think about these questions briefly before you continue reading. You will be asked many such "reflection questions" as you read this book. Your attempt to answer them, either with a quick note in the margin or at least a mental note, will help you better grasp your own understanding of issues that are raised. As E. M. Forster commented: "How do I know what I think until I see what I say?" So, what do you think *about this situation?*

Of course, this did not happen to your little sister (if you have one), but it did happen to 13-year-old Savana Redding of Safford, Arizona, in 2003. Here are some additional "facts" in this case. This public school has a responsibility to ensure the safety and health of all its students. The previous year, a student nearly died from drugs taken without permission at the school. The school district has a zero-tolerance policy for all drugs—no student is allowed to possess any drugs at school, whether over-the-counter, prescription, or illegal. The vice principal acted on information from another girl who reported that Savana had given her pills that day. It was not really a "strip search" because Savana never took off her underwear. All of these considerations seem to justify the actions that occurred.

However, there are valid points on the other side of the issue. The Fourth Amendment to the U.S. Constitution seems to protect Savana from this kind of search unless significant evidence indicates that something illegal is occurring ("probable cause"). The vice principal's action was taken based on questionable information from another girl who was already in trouble for possessing the pills. And the search occurred despite Savana's claim that she had no pills, without parental approval, and before any further investigation of the situation was attempted. Then there is common sense: The pills are merely extra-strength ibuprofen (pain killers). Is this really a legitimate reason for adults in authority positions to force a 13-year-old girl to submit to a humiliating strip search?

Savana's mother was outraged. With the assistance of a lawyer from the American Civil Liberties Union (ACLU), she sued the school officials on the grounds that they had subjected her daughter to an "unreasonable search." Savana's lawyer argued that, while a search of her backpack might be reasonable, a strip search was not, given the flimsy evidence of guilt and the minimal threat associated with ibuprofen. The school district's officials responded that the vice principal's actions were justified and consistent with numerous court cases that uphold the rights and responsibilities of schools to prevent dangerous behavior among its students, including searches for drugs or weapons.

Initially, a judge in Tucson ruled in favor of the actions by the school officials; however, on appeal, the circuit court reversed the decision by the narrowest of margins (6–5). The court concluded that the strip search of an eighth grader while looking for prescription drugs was a violation of her constitutional rights and it held that the family could sue the school officials for damages. The school's lawyers then appealed the case to the U.S. Supreme Court. In 2009, the Court majority (8–1) held that the search of Savana was unconstitutional. The majority reasoned that the particular drugs suspected in this case were not sufficiently threatening to justify the search. However, the Court did not allow the family to sue school officials, leaving open the question of how it might rule if school officials suspected a student of possessing something more dangerous than ibuprofen.

TOWARDS A DEFINITION OF POLITICS

The first step in our journey towards a better understanding of the political world is to establish what we mean by politics. The Savana Redding search captures some of the crucial themes related to politics:

1.1 Define politics within a public context.

> Politics is the competition among individuals and groups pursuing their own interests.
>
> Politics is the exercise of power and influence to allocate things that are valued.

👁—[**Watch** the
**Video "Conflict
Diamonds and
the Kimberley
Process"** at
mypoliscilab.com

Politics is the determination of who gets what, when, and how.
Politics is the resolution of conflict.

All of these definitions share the central idea that politics *is the process through which power and influence are used in the promotion of certain values and interests.* (The **bold** type indicates a Key Concept; these terms are listed at the end of the chapter and are included in the Glossary beginning on page 457.) Competing values and interests are clearly at the heart of the search of Savana Redding. The values that guide a zero-tolerance policy regarding drugs at the school are balanced against values that protect a student against an illegal search. Other groups might have a stake in this conflict, as did the ACLU, which intervened to promote its views about individual liberty, and the courts, which asserted their responsibility to interpret the laws.

As individuals, groups, and governmental actors make decisions about what is good or bad for society, and as they try to implement their decisions, politics occurs. Every individual holds an array of preferred values and interests, and that individual cares more about some of those values than others. What values is each individual willing to promote or yield on? If the values of different individuals come into conflict, whose values and rights should prevail? And, if people cannot work out their conflicting values privately through discussion and compromise, must the government intervene? How does the government exercise its power to resolve the conflict? Who benefits and who is burdened by the policies of government? These are all *political* questions.

For our purposes, politics is associated with those aspects of life that have *public* significance. Other aspects of life, in contrast, are understood to be private and thus are beyond the domain of politics. However, what is considered "private" in one country may be considered "public" in another. It is relevant that the search of Savana occurred in the United States. There are many other countries (e.g., Cuba, Iran, Zimbabwe) where the kind of search conducted on Savana would be well within the standard practices of government authorities and few, if any, citizens would publicly challenge the action.

In the political context of the United States, the school board—a political body elected by the citizens—has the right to establish policies regarding which behaviors will be unacceptable by the students (e.g., possessing drugs, using profane language) and by its employees (e.g., using corporal punishment, teaching creation science). The vice principal, as a public employee, exercises power when he implements those policies. The courts—another political institution—are active in the case as its judges, also public employees, attempt to resolve the conflict in values and interests between Savana's family and the school's employees. The court's judgments are based on interpretations of politically-created rules, including the U.S. Constitution, which ensures each citizen of certain rights but also grants government certain powers.

Even your choice about the job you take, the religion you practice, or what you read on the Internet can be either a private choice or one within the public domain. Can you see why a government might conclude that each of these choices have public significance and are thus political? Within each country, there is a constant debate about the appropriate areas for governmental action and the domains of life that should remain private and unrestrained by political action. Sometimes the term *politics* is used even more broadly than in this book to refer to competition over values in domains that are not truly public, such as the "politics of the family" or "office politics."

In almost every contemporary society, the domains that are subject to politics are very large. Politics, usually via government, determines how much education you must have and what its content will be. Politics establishes the words you cannot utter in a public place, how much of your hard-earned income you must give to government, and how various governments spend that money to provide different groups with a vast range of benefits (e.g., education, roads, fire protection, subsidized health care, safe food, national defense, aid to another country, etc.). Politics determines whether you are allowed to use a certain drug; the amount of pollutants that your car can emit; how secure you feel against violence by others within your neighborhood and within the global system; and whether you receive unequal treatment in the allocation of benefits because of your ethnicity, gender, ideology, or some other factor.

ON POLITICAL KNOWLEDGE
Types of Political Knowledge

Clearly, politics can affect your life in many ways. Yet people differ greatly in their understandings about the nature of politics, the uses of political power, and the distribution of political benefits and burdens. If you have discussed politics with your friends, you probably have noticed that they differ, both in how much they know about politics and in their opinions about what constitutes good and bad political actions. Your understandings about politics and your decisions about whether to undertake specific political actions are grounded in your knowledge of politics. Every individual's understanding of politics is composed of three general types of political knowledge: (1) *descriptions* of political facts, (2) *explanations* of how and why politics occurs as it does, and (3) *prescriptions* of what should happen in the political world.

1.2 Analyze three types of political knowledge.

Description

Many bits of political knowledge offer a ***description,*** which focuses on *what* questions and is usually based on one or more "facts." (The **bold *and italic*** type indicates a Key Concept; these terms are listed at the end of the chapter but are not in the Glossary at the back of the book.) Descriptive political knowledge is mostly composed of relatively straightforward political facts such as these:

> The date Hosni Mubarak resigned as President of Egypt: February 11, 2011
> The number of states in Nigeria: 36
> The country with the highest GDP (gross domestic product) per capita in the
> world in 2011: Qatar

But on many questions about the political world, there are no indisputable answers. On some questions, it is difficult to get precise information. Suppose you want to know which countries have operational nuclear weapons. Six countries acknowledge having operational nuclear devices: France, India, Pakistan, Russia, the United Kingdom, and the United States. However, the precise number of such weapons in each country is a state secret. China clearly has nuclear weapons but claims that none are "operational." Experts conclude that Israel has nuclear weapons, although Israel does not confirm this. North Korea claims to have operational nuclear weapons but there is no publicly available evidence about this capability, and Iran is suspected of having a secret nuclear weapons program. Twenty other countries, including Algeria, Argentina, Belarus, Brazil, Kazakhstan, Libya, South Africa, and Ukraine, are "potential proliferators" that had or were close to having nuclear weapons but are now assumed to have backed away from nuclear ambitions (Federation of American Scientists 2012). Thus, even the experts cannot reach consensus on the straightforward issue of which countries belong to the so-called nuclear club.

On other questions about politics, description requires assessments that raise complicated issues about power, interests, and values, making it difficult to reach agreement about the facts. Here are two examples:

Do nonwhites and whites in the United States experience equal treatment before the law?
Can a country legally invade another country that has not used military force against it?

This discussion on "Description" briefly refers to 21 countries on five continents. Do you have a clear sense of where they are? There will be detailed discussions of many countries in this book. Knowing the location of a country and its geographic relationship to other countries in its region is sometimes extremely important for understanding its political choices and actions. When a country is discussed and you are not sure where it is, you are strongly encouraged to locate the country on a map. For this purpose, a set of maps is included in this book. Several recent studies have shown that American students are more ignorant of world geography than students in most other countries. If that applies to you, help change the situation by referring frequently to the map.

Explanation

A lot of political knowledge is more complicated than just description because it is in the form of *explanation,* which attempts to *specify why something happens* and to *provide the reason or process by which the phenomenon occurs.*

Why is one in eight people "poor" in the wealthy United States? What causes a country (e.g., Zimbabwe) to have inflation higher than 10,000 percent in a single year? Why does a popular uprising rapidly overthrow the government in one country (e.g., Egypt) but not in another (e.g., its neighbor, Syria)?

Responses to these kinds of questions require explanation, not mere descriptive facts. Such questions can be among the most fascinating in politics, but adequate explanation is often difficult because patterns of cause and effect can be extremely complex.

Prescription

Statements about politics often include claims or assumptions that certain choices and actions are more desirable than others. These represent a third form of political knowledge: prescription. A *prescription* is *a value judgment that indicates what* should *occur and* should *be done*. Thus, a prescription deals with answers to questions about what ought to be, not merely description and explanation of what is.

For example, there are many possible prescriptive responses to this question: What should the government's role be in the provision of health care? Answers vary from the viewpoint that government should take absolutely no action that interferes with the private provision of health care, to the viewpoint that government should meet the full range of health care needs at no direct cost to patients. You can probably think of many positions between these two extremes.

The prescriptive position that you select on a political issue is an element of your **normative political knowledge**—*your value judgments*. Notice that normative political knowledge combines three types of understanding: (1) your descriptive knowledge of certain facts (e.g., the alternative ways that health care could be provided in a particular society); (2) your explanatory knowledge about why certain outcomes occur (e.g., the reasons why people don't receive equal health care); and most important, (3) your priorities among competing values (e.g., your preferences regarding equality, lower taxes, and limited government).

Throughout this book, you will be encouraged to clarify your own understandings about politics. You will be offered a variety of descriptive, explanatory, and prescriptive knowledge claims. It is hoped that as you absorb more of this information, you will become more knowledgeable about politics! Let's explore some of your views about politics by means of a thought experiment I term "the acid test:"

Assume you were born 20 years ago in either the country of Gamma or Delta. You do not know about your personal situation: whether you are male or female; your ethnicity; education level; social class; your parents' wealth; whether you reside in a city or a rural area; your religion; your mental or physical skills; and so on. Table 1.1 provides a variety of indicators of some *current* conditions in Gamma and Delta with regard to each country's prosperity, security, and stability. Here is the "acid test" question: *Now that you know the current conditions in Gamma and Delta, into which country would you prefer to have been born 20 years ago?* The Compare in 1 [there will be a Compare box in each chapter] considers some of the issues regarding this acid test. Make your choice from the data in Table 1.1 *before* you read Compare in 1!

TABLE 1.1

The Acid Test I

	Gamma	Delta
Governmental type	Nondemocracy	Liberal democracy
Political rights (1–7; 1 = most extensive)	7 (very low)	2 (high)
Civil liberties (1–7; 1 = most extensive)	6 (low)	3 (moderately high)
Press freedom (among 194 countries)	181st: Not free	72nd: Partly free
Economic freedom (among 141 countries)	82nd: Partly free	87th: Partly free
Religious freedom	Not free	Partly free
% women in national legislature	21%	11%
Political stability	High	Medium
Rate of crimes against the person	Low	Medium
Life expectancy	75 years	67 years
Literacy rate (adults)	92%	61%
Infant mortality/1000	16	48
% population with access to essential drugs	85%	35%
Internet users/100	22.5	4.5
% below the national poverty line	2.8%	25%
Unemployment rate	4.3%	11%
Wealth (GDP: gross domestic product) per capita	$7,600	$3,500
GDP per capita annual growth: 2000–2009	10.9%	7.8%
Inflation (annual, 2000–2009)	4%	5%
Public debt as % of GDP	17.5%	55.9%

COMPARE IN 1 | The Acid Test I

As you examined the indicators in Table 1.1, you perhaps noticed significant differences between Gamma and Delta. The economic prosperity (indicated by measures such as the country's wealth per capita and its economic growth rate) is noticeably higher in one country. The probability you would be poor, uneducated, and live a shorter life is higher in one country. Your likely freedom of action, in domains such as politics, religion, and access to information, varies considerably. There also seem to be differences in gender equality between the two countries. What differences are most striking to you?

The acid test asks you to decide, after considering all the data provided about Gamma and Delta, into which country you would prefer to be born. Which one did you choose?

Gamma and Delta are pseudonyms for two real countries, and the data are recent. In fact, both countries have a variety of broad similarities—population, climate variability, social history, period of time since independence, violent interactions with neighboring countries, and so on. These are arguably the two most important countries in the developing world. Each country has a rich history, including a remarkable ancient culture; extensive colonial exploitation; a fickle climate; deep social cleavages, especially those based on religion, gender, and class/caste; and each has more than 1 billion people.

(Continued)

However, since the independence of India in 1947 and the communist victory in China in 1949, the two countries have followed very different paths. Under the long and tumultuous rule of Mao Zedong (in power from 1949–1976), China (Gamma) attempted to implement a pervasive system of communism with a command political economy and totalitarian one-party government. The Chinese leadership after Mao engaged in a steady introduction of market economics, transforming China into a global economic power while still retaining tight Communist Party rule over the government. Initially, India (Delta) attempted to implement strong government control of key sectors of the economy, and it introduced democratic politics, although one party was quite dominant. Eventually, both experiments evolved in India as the economy shifted much more to private firms and the political system became more competitive with multiple parties.

Some results of these two different approaches to government and policy are reflected in the measures in Table 1.1. The strong commitment under Mao to egalitarianism and providing benefits to all citizens led to public policies that reduced the inequalities based on gender and social class with broad improvements in literacy and health for most of the population. The Indian government did not provide extensive policies to address inequalities based on caste, gender, and urban–rural differences; thus, these inequalities have altered much more slowly in India, resulting in continued disparities in domains such as literacy and health. India's economic growth has been sporadic, although strong in the last decade. China has sustained remarkable levels of economic growth for several decades as it became a global power. India proudly proclaims itself the "world's largest democracy" with a rough-and-tumble political system characterized by broad political rights, a relatively free media, a professional apolitical military, and an independent judiciary. In contrast, China's leadership continues to use a combination of state military and security forces, political socialization, severe censorship, and rewards to those who conform in order to sustain its oppressive Communist Party domination of political and social life.

Despite many similarities in their resources and history, China and India have significantly different current profiles. While many explanations can be offered for these differences, it is reasonable to claim that the most powerful explanation is *politics*—the decisions and actions taken by those with political power and authority in each country. As you develop your understandings of politics in this book, some of the key points underlying this acid test will be persistent themes.

First, a people and its government can pursue numerous desirable goals. While every country (and you) might like to have very positive scores on every indicator in Table 1.1, you will discover that the reality is more stark: Most countries cannot have it all. Various trade-offs must be made due to limited resources, the incapacity of people and their institutions to control their environment fully, and other factors related to human failures and impacts of the global system.

Second, the acid test challenges you to decide what aspects of political, social, economic, and personal life are more important to you. The book will assist you in clarifying your own thinking about what you value and what role you think government should play in helping you achieve those values.

And third, your choices and your values will not be the same as everyone else's—even among your peers and certainly among people around the globe. You will gain greater awareness of the different mixes of approaches and values that are part of the debate about how government can assist individuals and societies pursue a variety of desirable life conditions such as security, prosperity, stability, freedom, equality, justice, democracy, and well-being. Disagreements about ends and means are at the heart of politics in every country.

FURTHER QUESTIONS

1. Which broad value seemed to most influence your choice between Gamma and Delta?
2. Did your knowledge of the actual identities of Gamma and Delta change your evaluation at all?
3. What assessment(s) might cause another person to select the country that you did not select? ▶

SOURCES OF POLITICAL KNOWLEDGE

1.3 Evaluate the strengths and weaknesses of different sources of political knowledge.

This chapter has already made many knowledge claims—statements about what is accurate or correct. Table 1.1 and the Compare in 1 are loaded with such claims. When you are confronted by such claims, how do you decide what you know and what you believe? That is, where does your political knowledge—your unique combination of descriptive facts, explanations, and prescriptions about politics—come from? This section describes three important sources of your knowledge: (1) authority; (2) personal thought; and (3) science.

Authority

The method of authority involves *the appeal to any document, tradition, or person believed to possess the controlling explanation regarding a particular issue.* Knowledge about politics can be based on three kinds of authority sources: (1) a specific authority; (2) a general authority; or (3) "everyone."

Watch the Video "The Media in a Free Society" at mypoliscilab.com

Explore the Comparative "Public Opinion and Political Culture" on mypoliscilab.com

Specific Authority Sources   A particular individual (but few others) might place great confidence in the knowledge he derives about politics from a specific authority source such as a parent, teacher, friend, or famous person. Young people and those minimally interested in politics are especially likely to rely on specific authorities for much of their political knowledge. Chapter 4 will argue that specific authority sources powerfully influence some important political beliefs of most individuals. Can you think of a significant piece of your own political knowledge that you derived primarily from a parent, an influential teacher, or a public figure you admire?

General Authority Sources   A general authority source is one that has substantial influence on a large proportion of people in a society. Examples include constitutions, revered leaders, widely respected media or books, and religious teachings. General authorities are especially evident as a basis for normative political knowledge. Consider, for example, the issue of the role of women in politics. While this can be a descriptive issue, how do we determine the normative question of what the role of women should be? In some societies, there is disagreement about this question, and many look to an authority source to provide the answer.

- In the United States, the crucial source of authority for such questions is a *legal document*—the Constitution. Despite the claim that "all men... are endowed by their creator with certain inalienable rights ...," not every citizen was allowed to vote in 1787. Indeed, women were not granted this fundamental political right until the 19th constitutional amendment in 1920—fully 130 years into the American Republic. Advocates of women's rights argue that women still do not have full and equal political rights and have proposed another constitutional amendment, the Equal Rights Amendment; but since 1972, only 35 of the 38 states necessary have voted for its passage.
- In Iran, the key source of authority on women's political rights is also a document, but it is a *religious document*, the Koran. During the political regime of Shah Reza Pahlavi (1941–1979), women were encouraged to participate much more fully in politics than what Iran's religious conservatives

My Little Red Book: Young girls recite and memorize sayings from Chairman Mao Zedong during China's Cultural Revolution (circa 1968).

thought was consistent with the Koran. When the Ayatollah Khomeini (in power 1979–1989) replaced the shah, he insisted on a strict interpretation of the Koran that significantly limited the political roles of women. The political rights and activities of Iranian women remain a contentious issue between those who advocate an expanded role and those, like the current top leader, Ayatollah Khamenei, who insist on enforcing a more conservative interpretation of the Koran.

- In contemporary China, the political rights of women were established by the authoritative pronouncements of a *person*, Mao Zedong (who ruled from 1949–1976). Prior to the revolution of 1949, the role of women in China was defined by the traditions of Confucianism. Most women were essentially the property of men, and they had few political rights. As part of Chairman Mao's efforts to transform Confucian tradition, he granted women full equality under the law, and women were encouraged to participate actively in all aspects of political life. (The conflict between Mao's views and those of Confucianism are explored further in the Focus in 4).

"Everyone" as Authority   Sometimes we are convinced that something is true because it is a belief strongly held by many other people. If almost everyone (i.e., the reference group to which you look for information and knowledge) seems to agree on a "fact" about politics, there is little reason for you to disagree or challenge that fact. One reason to place confidence in a belief which is strongly held by many people is the assumption that it is unlikely so many people will be incorrect. Such knowledge has stood the test of time because it could have been challenged and repudiated in the marketplace of ideas. For example, you will probably find that almost everyone you know agrees that political terrorism is bad.

Problems with Authority as a Source of Knowledge   There are fundamental problems with using authority as a way of knowing. This should be most obvious with *specific authorities*. You might think that your parent or best teacher or favorite celebrity has the correct view on an important political issue, but few of the other 7 billion people in the world have any confidence in this source of your political knowledge.

And even though "everyone knows that X is true," there is no guarantee that everyone is correct. First, as "Honest Abe" Lincoln observed, you can fool all of the people some of the time. Indeed, a political belief that is widely held might be particularly immune to careful assessment. Experiments in psychology have revealed that some of a person's beliefs can be altered by the beliefs of others. For example, if a subject hears several respondents (collaborating with the experimenter) all give identical wrong answers to a question, the subject can usually be persuaded to change his mind about what he knows—even when he is correct. Second, "everyone" often consists mainly of people whose cultural background we share. If you reexamine the above example about terrorism with a different "everyone," it is unlikely that almost everyone living under an oppressive political regime believes that political terrorism is bad. It is common for citizens in most political systems to believe that the citizens of rival political systems have been brainwashed. We know that some beliefs of our rivals are incorrect. Isn't it likely that they are equally convinced that some of our strongly held beliefs are wrong?

There are even problems with *general authorities*. Sometimes even the most competent general authorities might not have access to crucial information or might rely on inaccurate data, as when they list the countries with nuclear weapons. And sometimes, despite a group's acceptance of a single authority, there are still ambiguities and problems of interpretation.

Consider again the normative issue of the political role of women. In interpreting gender equality, all branches of government in the United States continually debate and interpret the rather limited framework outlined in the Constitution. The appropriate role of women in Iran's politics remains a highly contested issue, despite the Koran. Indeed, there is considerable difference of opinion within the broader Muslim world regarding how to interpret the Koran's authoritative prescriptions regarding women's roles in political life. In some Muslim countries, such as Saudi Arabia and Sudan, women's roles are greatly restricted. Yet Bangladesh, Indonesia, Pakistan, and Turkey are Muslim-majority countries that selected female heads of government (prime ministers) in recent years. And in China, Mao Zedong's pronouncements on many topics, especially on economic matters, are now rejected by the leadership, even as his general views about gender equality remain a key authority source.

Woman power: Secretary of State Clinton and Supreme Court Justices Kagan (right) and Sotomayor (center) have key roles in defining the evolving role of women in American politics.

In short, it is common, and perhaps inevitable, for authority sources to offer inconsistent or conflicting knowledge claims about the political world. It is extremely difficult to differentiate between alternative authorities or even to establish widespread agreement on precisely what political knowledge a particular authority source provides.

Personal Thought

Have you ever insisted that some fact is correct because it seemed so obvious to you? It is possible to feel confident that you know something on the basis of personal thought—your own reason, feelings, or experiences. This second source of knowledge does not rely on outside authorities; rather, it assumes that the individual can use his own rationality or intuition or personal experience to assess a knowledge claim.

Rationality On occasion, you probably have decided that a certain claim is true because it is logical or obvious—it just "makes sense." The available information fits together in a coherent framework that, it seems, would lead to agreement among all people who think clearly. Or it is assumed that the knowledge claim is verified because it is self-evident to reasonable people and needs no further justification. For example, the Preamble to the U.S. Declaration of Independence claims that there are "self-evident" truths—that all men are created equal and that they have inalienable rights to life, liberty, and the pursuit of happiness.

Intuition   Another form of personal thought is intuition. Here, one's knowledge is based on feeling, on a sense of understanding or empathy, rather than on reason. You have probably been convinced that something is correct because it *feels* right. For example, the key slogan of Barry Goldwater, the Republican presidential candidate in 1964, was an explicit appeal to intuition: "In your heart, you know he's right!" And Barack Obama's 2008 campaign incantation "Change we can believe in!" was essentially an appeal to feeling and hope.

Personal Experience   You can also be convinced that something is true because of your own personal experiences. For example, you might be convinced that government bureaucracies are inefficient because a specific agency handled your inquiries so ineptly. Or you might believe that different ethnic groups can live together in harmony based on your own positive experience in a multiethnic setting. Personal involvement in a dramatic event, such as witnessing a handgun murder or being physically harassed by the police, can have a particularly powerful impact on one's political beliefs.

Problems with Personal Thought as a Source of Knowledge   There is a major problem with all three forms of personal thought as a source of knowledge: there is no method for resolving "thoughtful" differences of opinion among individuals. This is most obvious with personal experience: Because people have quite different personal experiences, they are unlikely to reach the same conclusions about what is true. Similarly, there is no reason to assume that different people will share the same intuitive feelings regarding what is true. Goldwater's poor electoral showing (he received only 39 percent of the vote) suggests that many people concluded (intuitively?) that he was not right, or perhaps they decided (rationally?) that he was too far right—too conservative ideologically. And, after a few years of Washington's rough-and-tumble politics, many of Obama's supporters had lost confidence in "change you can believe in."

Even rational thought will not necessarily enable people to agree on political facts. We do not all employ the same logic, and it is rare to find a knowledge claim that everyone agrees is obviously correct. Consider again the key knowledge claim cited earlier: "We hold these truths to be self-evident—that all men are created equal." This seems a clear appeal to rationality, a political fact that is self-evident to all thinking people. But what exactly does this claim mean? Do all men have equal physical or mental traits at birth? Do they grow up with equal opportunities? Are they equal before the law, regardless of the quality of legal help they can purchase? And we have noted the historical disagreement about how women's equality is to be interpreted. Many legal and political struggles in the United States during the more than two centuries since this "self-evident" truth was proclaimed have concerned precisely what equal rights *are* assured to every person in the American political system, with particular regard to race, gender, and age.

Science

In contrast to the two other sources of knowledge, science uses explicit methods that attempt to enable different people to agree about what they know. The goal of any science is to describe and explain—to answer *what, why,* and *how* questions. There are four essential characteristics of the **scientific method**:

1. Science is *empirical* in the sense that it is concerned with phenomena that can be observed, or at least measured.
2. Science entails a *search for regularities* in the relationships among phenomena.
3. Science is *cumulative* because it tentatively accepts previously established knowledge on a subject as the foundation for development of further knowledge. One can challenge existing knowledge, but it is not necessary to reestablish the knowledge base every time.
4. The method of science is *testable*. Its practitioners, "scientists," specify the assumptions, data, analytic techniques, and inference patterns that support their knowledge claim. Other scientists look for some analysis or evidence that would invalidate (falsify) the claim. They evaluate all aspects of the claim and can repeat the analysis to ensure that the claim should be part of the accumulated knowledge.

These four characteristics are supposed to give the scientific method some major advantages over the methods of authority and personal thought in determining whether we can agree on a knowledge claim. This can be helpful because you are surrounded by competing claims regarding the political world. There are many sources of statements about politics—family, friends, television, books, newspapers, teachers, politicians. When you hear or read any claim about politics, you might take one of the following actions:

Ignore it.
Accept that it is correct.
Reject it.
Try to assess it.

If you decide to assess it, you would probably ask questions such as: Is it based on accurate information? Is it consistent with other things I know about politics? Does it influence any political actions I might take? When you begin to ask assessment questions, and especially when you try to answer them, you are engaged in political analysis. At its core, **political analysis** is *the attempt to describe (to answer the* what *questions) and then to explain politics (to answer the* why *and* how *questions).* This book attempts to enhance your ability to engage in political analysis—to answer the *what, why,* and *how* questions about politics.

POLITICAL SCIENCE

Political science is one approach to political analysis. As you will discover in reading this book, **political science** applies *a set of techniques, concepts, and approaches whose objective is to increase the clarity and accuracy of our understandings about the political world.* That is, it is an attempt to apply the logic of the scientific method to political analysis. You will learn how some political scientists try to think systematically about political phenomena in order to describe "political reality" and explain how politics works. You will also be introduced to some of the findings about politics that have emerged from the work of political scientists and other social scientists.

1.4 Identify techniques and approaches used to gain political knowledge and assess whether they constitute a science.

Doing Comparative Analysis

Aristotle observed: All thinking begins in comparison. This book is called "a *comparative* introduction to political science" because it emphasizes how to utilize comparative thinking to enhance our understanding of politics. Comparisons will guide many of the discussions throughout the book, and each chapter will also have a specific feature called "Compare in…" to illuminate the comparative method in action. You were introduced to some aspects of the comparative method in the "acid test" that was the focus of the Compare in 1.

Political Science and Political Knowledge

Not everyone agrees that it is appropriate and desirable to apply the scientific method to politics. Some insist that a "real" science must utilize strong applications of the four elements set out in Thomas Kuhn's book *The Structure of Scientific Revolutions* (1996): (1) central **concepts**, which *identify and name crucial phenomena* (specifically, such as "the Iraq War," or generally, such as "war"); (2) **theories**, which are *sets of systematically related generalizations that provide explanations and predictions about the linkages between certain concepts* (in the form "If A, then B under conditions C and D"); (3) *rules of interpretation*, which indicate the methods that will establish whether the explanations and predictions posited by the theory are right or wrong; and (4) a list of questions or *issues* that are worth solving within the area of inquiry.

Few would claim that political science is fully developed on any of these four elements. Thus, is it possible to engage in political "science"? Each chapter in this book will offer you a debate about an issue relevant to the attempt to understand the political world. Where better to start than with the Debate in 1: Is political *science* possible?

The discussion about the value of political science raises important questions that you should assess throughout this book. In general, this book will make the case that, despite the complexity of politics, generalizations are possible—each political phenomenon is not unique. If political "science" means the attempt to apply the scientific method in order to understand the political world better, it seems desirable to use such systematic and analytic thinking. And, if we are to share *any* knowledge about the political world, we need methods to reach some interpersonal agreement about political facts. Although political science lacks precise concepts and theories, it does enable us to develop better concepts, improved methods, and sounder generalizations, and thereby it makes the study of the political world an exciting intellectual challenge.

This book assumes that understanding politics is extremely important. As Austrian philosopher of science Karl Popper (1963: 227) suggests, "We must not expect too much from reason; argument rarely settles a [political] question, although it is the only means for learning—not to see clearly, but to see more clearly than before." In the face of fundamental value conflicts and the potential for massive political violence among individuals, groups, and countries, enhanced political knowledge might reduce our misunderstandings and misconceptions. It can also be the grounds for greater tolerance and wiser value judgments about normative political issues. Enhancing *what* we know about politics and what we *value* should make us more effective in knowing *how* to behave politically—as

THE DEBATE IN 1 | Is Political *Science* Possible?

SCIENCE AND POLITICS DO NOT GO TOGETHER WELL

- The analysis of politics cannot be objective and unbiased in the way assumed by the scientific method. The issues chosen for study and the manner in which variables are defined, measured, and analyzed are all powerfully influenced by the analyst's social reality (e.g., by his own culture, ideas, and life experiences). In this view, no person—whether Sunni Muslim or agnostic, rural Nigerian or cosmopolitan Parisian, international lawyer or migrant farm worker—can be totally objective and unbiased in the way he tries to analyze political phenomena.
- The subject matter of politics defies generalization. The political world is far too complex and unpredictable for systematic generalizations. Politics is based on the actions and interactions of many individuals, groups, and even countries. Politics occurs in the midst of many changing conditions that can influence those actions. The range of variation in what people might do and in the conditions that might exist is so vast that clear "if A, then B" statements about politics are impossible.
- Political science is not a "real" science, in comparison to natural and applied sciences (e.g., chemistry, physics, engineering). The four key elements described by Kuhn (as listed above) are well developed and widely shared within the research communities of every natural and applied science. In contrast, researchers in political science (and other social sciences) have not agreed on a coherent set of concepts, theories, and rules of interpretation. As you will discover throughout this book, many different methods are used in political science. There is disagreement regarding the important issues that ought to be solved, little consensus on what theories or generalizations have been proven, and even great difficulty in operationalizing key concepts such as power or democracy.

- The "scientific" study of politics cannot adequately address the most crucial questions about politics, which are normative. Since the time of Aristotle (384–322 B.C.E.), classical political theorists have insisted that the ultimate aim of political analysis is to discover "the highest good attainable by action." In this view, political analysis is a noble endeavor because it helps determine what government and individuals *should* do so that valued goals (e.g., democratic politics, a good life, a just society) can be achieved. Max Weber (1864–1920), the influential German social scientist, approvingly quoted Russian novelist Leo Tolstoy's assertion that science can provide no answer to the essential question, "What shall we do, and how shall we arrange our lives?" (1958a: 152–153).

POLITICAL SCIENCE IS POSSIBLE AND WORTHWHILE

- Every person, including those who study politics, has biases. But the scientific method encourages individuals to be very aware of their biases and to counteract those biases by making their assumptions as transparent as possible. The method of science requires the analyst to be extremely clear in describing his assumptions, in characterizing how evidence is gathered, in displaying the techniques used to analyze the data, and in exploring threats to the validity of the knowledge claims that are made. This transparency limits bias and exposes the analyst's thinking to scrutiny. (As the author, I have attempted to be aware of my own biases—as an American, a man, a baby boomer, etc.—that influence every aspect of this book. As you read, try to become more conscious of *your* biases, which will affect your assessments of claims about the political world.)
- While the political world is complex, few events are truly random—there are patterns and linkages among political phenomena. The

(Continued)

challenge for the political scientist is to specify these patterns. Rather than assuming that all is chaos and nothing is related, the political scientist assumes that, by employing systematic techniques of gathering and analyzing empirical data, it is possible to present knowledge claims that help clarify that complex reality. Tendency statements—"if A, then a tendency to B"—might seem imperfect, but they can significantly increase our confidence regarding what we know to be true or untrue about politics.

■ Although some "real" sciences come closer to Kuhn's ideal than others, no science is pure. Scholars who study the way in which a scientific community operates conclude that every scientific discipline can be characterized by disagreements over concepts, methods, and theories and that the theories of every science include subjective elements. It is certainly true that political science is less scientifically pure than astronomy or chemistry, but this does not negate the value of applying the scientific method to make our thinking more precise and our knowledge claims more transparent, testable, and reliable.

■ Even those who use the scientific method to study politics do not assume it can provide a compelling answer to every important normative question. However, if it does provide more reliable knowledge, it enhances our capacity to reason about the questions of what should be done. Whether at the individual level or at the national government level, decisions about what actions should be taken in the political world will be improved if they are informed by empirical evidence and sound knowledge claims that are based on the scientific method.

MORE QUESTIONS...

1. Can you identify any of your own biases about political issues? What might be the main sources of those biases?

2. Can you think of examples where you have gained useful political knowledge from nonscientific sources such as literature, music, personal experience, or general authorities? ◢

voters, political activists, and political decision makers. The study of the political world is of crucial importance to the creation of humane social life. Ultimately it is up to you, as you read this book, to decide what can be known about politics and whether you think political "science" is feasible.

The Subfields of Political Science

Political science is composed of certain subfields that are usually defined by their specific subject matter, rather than by their mode of analysis. While there are different ways to categorize the subfields, four are prominent:

1. **Comparative politics.** This subfield *focuses on similarities and differences in political processes and structures* (Laitin, 2002). As noted above, much of empirical political science is comparative. Thus, comparative politics covers a huge domain within political analysis, and it has many sub-subfields (e.g., public administration, political parties, development, individual political behavior, and public policy). Comparison might be cross-national (e.g., comparing the legal systems of Iran and Italy or comparing the voting patterns in 40 countries), or it might compare actors within a single country (e.g., comparing the political beliefs about democracy among different ethnic groups in Nigeria).

2. **American politics.** To the rest of the world, the study of American politics is merely a subfield of comparative politics. While this is quite sensible (and appropriate), American politics is treated as a separate subfield in the United States. In terms of issues and approaches, American politics covers the same types of topics as comparative politics.

3. **International relations.** The *focus is on the political relations between countries, the behavior of transnational actors, and the dynamics within the worldwide system of states and groups.* Subjects within international relations include war, interstate conflict resolution, international law, globalization, neocolonialism, regional alliances (e.g., the European Union), international organizations (e.g., the United Nations), and transborder political organizations (e.g., Amnesty International). The study of foreign policy is also within this subfield.

4. **Political theory.** More precisely called political philosophy, this subfield *focuses on the ideas and debates dealing with important political questions.* Some of this work attempts to characterize and interpret the writings of major political theorists (e.g., Plato, Thomas Hobbes, Karl Marx, John Rawls), whereas other works are original explorations of the political questions themselves (e.g., What is the nature of a just society? What is the appropriate relationship between the citizen and the government?). Political theory is *the source of many of the normative knowledge claims made by political scientists.* Much of the work in political theory is based on the methods of rationality or authority or on an appeal to moral truths rather than on the scientific method.

Boundary-Spanning Hybrids   Political science is an eclectic field that often links with other fields of inquiry or, at least, borrows and adapts ideas from other disciplines. Some work actually spans the boundary between political science and another discipline. While the subject matter of this work fits within one of the preceding four major subfields, these hybrids would include political anthropology, political economy, political psychology, political sociology, and biopolitics.

WHERE IS THIS BOOK GOING?

Just as there are different approaches to political science, there are different ways to introduce you to the political world. This book is organized to lead you along one route to understanding. It uses a comparative approach; it builds from the politics of the individual to the politics of countries and the international system and concludes with chapters that bring all the topics together for each of three large groups of countries. Fundamentally, the book aims to help you create an increasingly sophisticated analytic framework for the study and analysis of the political world that surrounds you.

   The book is organized in five parts, each with its own chapters. You have nearly completed Part One, which has offered an initial discussion of the nature of political knowledge and the approach political scientists take to understanding, analyzing, and evaluating that knowledge. Each chapter includes a Debate on

1.5 Describe the purpose and the outline of the text.

✓⁃Study and **Review** the **Post-Test & Chapter Exam** at **mypoliscilab.com**

a political topic, a Compare analyzing two or more political actors, and a Focus on a chapter-relevant topic for a single country. Since this chapter has focused on political knowledge, the Focus in 1 shows you how the scientific method has been applied to explore whether political knowledge varies across age groups within the United States.

The remaining four parts of the book build from studying the individual in the political world to analyzing countries in the global system. "Man is the measure of all things," observed ancient Greek philosopher Protagoras (ca. 490–421 B.C.E.). In that spirit, Part Two begins its exploration of the political world at the most personal and individual level. It initially examines what individual men and women think about politics and how they act politically. After Part Two, the book moves on to the politics of large collectivities of people that we call states and that are organized politically as governments. Thus, Parts Three, Four, and Five offer perspectives and explanations from political science regarding how states and governments are organized for political action, how political processes occur, and how countries are attempting to fulfill their political goals in the challenging conditions of the global system.

Part Two, "Political Behavior," begins in Chapter 2 with an assessment of the kinds of *political beliefs* that people hold and with a description of normative political theories. It continues in Chapter 3 with a consideration of the *political actions* that people and groups undertake. Chapter 4 moves from description to explanation: Can we explain *why* people think and act politically in certain ways?

Part Three, "Political Systems," is about the politics of large numbers of people—about how the political world is organized and about the *structures of government*. Chapters 5 through 8 address questions such as: What is a state? How are the political system and the economic system linked? What features distinguish democracies from dictatorships? What are the responsibilities of political structures such as the judiciary or the legislature?

Part Four, "Political Processes," emphasizes the *key dynamics of politics*. Chapter 9 characterizes the public policy process and details three major explanations for how political power is distributed and how policy decisions are made. Chapter 10 explores the processes of political change and development. The vital issues of politics across borders and the manner in which states and other transnational actors cooperate and compete are central to Chapter 11. The various forms and causes of political violence are analyzed in Chapter 12.

Part Five, "Politics Among States," focuses on the actions and challenges facing *countries in the contemporary political world*. Chapters 13 through 15 consider countries at different levels of development as they pursue the general goals of prosperity, security, and stability in the complicated global system. Finally, the Appendix explains some major concepts in political science, including four important frameworks for engaging in political analysis: taxonomic, formal, functional, and relational.

My hope is that, by the time you complete reading and studying this text, you will think more like a political scientist in the sense that *you will have more confidence in your knowledge about politics and you will have developed a more informed and systematic approach to understanding the political world.*

FOCUS IN 1 | The Political Knowledge of Different Age Groups in the United States

You might have heard the knowledge claim that younger adults have less political knowledge than older adults. Cliff Zukin and his colleagues (2006) apply the methods of political science to analyze this claim in their book, *The New Engagement? Political Participation, Civic Life, and the Changing American Citizen*. To illustrate how the scientific method is used to explore a political question, this Focus very briefly describes the steps they utilize as well as a few of their results and conclusions.

1. *Examine existing evidence* that is relevant. Initially, you should look at existing research by political scientists or other social scientists that offers evidence and conclusions on the topic. The Zukin group used the available research on age and political knowledge as the foundation for designing and conducting the study.
2. With this background, *state the issue* in a precise manner. This particular issue can be stated in the form of a *hypothesis* (i.e., a proposition about a political fact): Younger people have less political knowledge than older people.
3. *Operationalize key concepts* by specifying exactly what each concept means and how it will be measured. In this study, operationalizing the concept of "political knowledge" begins with the recognition that it could cover many things. Political knowledge could be defined in terms of descriptive, explanatory, and/or prescriptive information about various aspects of politics such as policies, institutions, events, or people. It could include information-seeking behavior as well as how-to knowledge, such as how to vote or how to circulate a petition. For simplicity, the analysis by Zukin's group focuses on a few basic aspects of "cognitive engagement." Specifically, they examine (1) the descriptive knowledge people have about aspects of political life, including facts such as the names of key

political leaders and (2) people's exposure to key sources that transmit political knowledge, such as newspapers and the Internet. While cross-national comparisons are interesting, their analysis looks only at people in the United States and only at a single point in time (2004). Another key concept in this research is "age." Zukin's research group uses a simple taxonomy of four age groups among adults, as listed in Table 1.2. (If you don't know what a taxonomy is, consult the discussion of this concept in the Appendix.) They offer plausible reasons for these age boundaries (such as the political and social era in which people grew up), although, as with most variables, this variable could have been operationalized in other ways.

4. *Gather appropriate data.* You need a strategy for collecting evidence that is *valid* (i.e., it measures what it is supposed to measure) and *reliable* (i.e., it is accurate). You also decide what specific cases you are going to examine. In the empirical work by Zukin's group, the data were collected from a U.S. national sample of adults, selected randomly and interviewed by means of a telephone survey. Respondents were asked a series of questions about their political knowledge and about certain personal characteristics (including age). The responses of all the individuals were recorded and compiled into a digital file so that different variables for each respondent could be analyzed in various ways. (In any scientific research, you should consider whether there might be problems with the validity of the data. In this case, for example: Was the set of individuals selected for study a reasonable one? Were the questions well constructed, minimally biased, properly asked, and accurately recorded? Was sufficient data gathered to explore the core question?)

(Continued)

TABLE 1.2

Political Knowledge among Adults in the United States, by Age

Group Name: (birth year) Issue:	DotNet (since 1980)	GenX (1966–1980)	Boomer (1947–1965)	Dutiful (before 1947)	All
Majority party in U.S. Senate?[*]	51%	63%	64%	70%	63%
Name of U.S. Secretary of State?[*]	28	42	57	54	48
Is North Korea developing nuclear weapons?[*]	46	62	69	69	64
Follow public affairs "most of the time."[†]	25	37	50	60	45
Political information from newspapers at least 5 days/week.[†]	30	32	48	66	46
Political information from national television news at least 5 days/week.[†]	38	47	63	85	60
Political news from the Internet at least 3 times/week.[†]	28	32	24	14	24

[*]Percentage providing the correct answer.
[†]Percentage answering yes.
Source: Zukin et al. (2006), Table 3.9.

5. *Analyze the evidence.* The data in Table 1.2, based on a computer-based statistical analysis, report the percentage in each age group who correctly answered three questions about political facts and the responses of those in each age group to four questions about the frequency with which they are exposed to key sources of political knowledge.

6. *Decide what, if any, inferences and conclusions can be made* about the issue on the basis of your evidence. This is where your analytic skills become especially active. The Appendix in this book discusses some of statistical techniques that can be utilized to help you judge whether the age-group differences in the data are greater than might be expected by chance. In the absence of such statistics, what do you think from assessing Table 1.2? Do these data indicate differences in political knowledge across the age groups? The data do suggest that a considerably smaller proportion of the youngest group knows each of the three political "facts" in the study. And those in the younger group also seem much less interested in public affairs and less connected to traditional sources of political information such as newspapers and television;

(Continued)

but more of them obtain political news from the Internet, compared to the two oldest cohorts.

Is this evidence sufficient to conclude whether younger adults are less politically knowledgeable? Can you have confidence in a generalization about age and political knowledge in the United States based on only these seven questions in a single study at one point in time? Defensible conclusions often require extensive data, thorough analysis, and consideration of several alternative explanations. Sometimes the phenomena are so complicated or the evidence is so mixed that no generalization is possible. Any conclusion based only on Table 1.2 would be very tentative.

The book by Zukin's group contains extensive data analyses, not just the data in Table 1.2. They conclude that there is a positive relationship between higher age and greater political knowledge. Their study, like most good research, attempts to address the deeper questions and the ultimate goal of the scientific method, explanation, and broader generalization (theory). Does increased age *cause* increased political knowledge? If so, why and how does this occur? In trying to explain the relationship between age and political knowledge, has some other important variable been overlooked? To deal with this possibility, they identify and analyze factors other than age that might affect political knowledge. Among other explanatory factors that seem relevant are: the individual's education level; interest in politics within the individual's family and peer group; the political issues that matter most to each age group; the political climate at the time of the study; and so on. Do you understand why these types of factors might provide a better explanation than age does for the cause of variations in political knowledge?

Political phenomena are rarely straightforward and they can change—sometimes quite rapidly. These are among the reasons that the study of politics is so fascinating (and perhaps frustrating). For the political analyst, this means that generalizations must be made with care. If you wanted to establish a broad generalization about age and political knowledge, you would want data on more measures of political knowledge, from several time periods, and probably not just from the United States. In the spirit of the scientific method, *every* aspect of the analysis is open to criticism by other analysts. And the conclusions would stand only as long as other analysts were unable to challenge successfully any aspect of stages 1–6 in this analysis. In exploring political questions, further analyses are always appropriate to strengthen our knowledge claims.

FURTHER FOCUS

1. What political knowledge would you measure if you did a comparative analysis across different age groups? Why? (Always assume there is an implicit "why" question when these questions are raised in the book.)

2. What do you think is the most compelling explanation for the apparent differences in political knowledge across age groups in the United States? Would this differ in another country? What countries come to mind? ▲

KEY CONCEPTS

FOR FURTHER CONSIDERATION

1. What do you think is the most serious obstacle to a "science" of politics?
2. Which authority have you relied on most extensively as a source of your knowledge about politics? What is the biggest shortcoming of this source?
3. What is the most important question that political science should attempt to answer? What might prevent political scientists from answering this question adequately?
4. Many people insist that most of their political knowledge is based on their own rational thought processes. What might be wrong with this claim?
5. Do you think political scientists can play an important role in government, or are they just intellectuals who should only stand on the sidelines and analyze politics?

FOR FURTHER READING

Almond, Gabriel. (1989). *A Discipline Divided: Schools and Sects in Political Science.* Newbury Park, CA: Sage. One of the major scholars of comparative politics assesses the diversity of approaches to political science and the possibility of a science of politics.

Brians, Craig, Lars Willnat, Richard Rich, and Jarol B. Manheim. (2011). *Empirical Political Analysis: Research Methods in Political Science.* 8th ed. New York: Longman. A very effective and understandable presentation of the primary methods that political scientists utilize in the attempt to understand politics and develop defensible generalizations, focusing on a full range of qualitative and quantitative approaches.

Katznelson, Ira, and Helen Miller, Eds. (2004). *Political Science: State of the Discipline.* Centennial ed. New York: W. W. Norton. In only(!) 993 pages, a diverse group of political scientists offers essays (sponsored by the American Political Science Association) on the current insights and debates on central issues related to core concepts in the discipline such as the state, democracy, political institutions, participation, and modes of political analysis.

King, Gary, Kay L. Scholzman, and Norman Nie, Eds. (2009). *The Future of Political Science: 100 Perspectives.* London: Routledge. One hundred mini-essays (in 304 pages), many by distinguished political scientists, that explore a broad array of interesting questions about politics and political science.

Kuhn, Thomas. (1996). *The Structure of Scientific Revolutions.* 3rd ed. Chicago: University of Chicago Press. A short, understandable, and enormously influential discussion of how sciences develop and overturn paradigms; first published in 1962.

Kurian, George, James E. Alt, Simone Chambers, Geoffrey Garrett, Margaret Levi, and Paula D. McClain. Eds. (2011). *The Encyclopedia of Political Science.* Washington, D.C.: CQ Press. This five-volume reference resource provides helpful essays on more than 1,200 concepts that are significant in the study of politics as well as hundreds of valuable overview essays.

Pollack, Philip H. (2008). *The Essentials of Political Analysis.* 3rd ed. Washington, DC: CQ Press. Using many interesting examples, the book explains how to use empirical data and quantitative analysis (especially the use of the Statistical Package for Social Sciences—SPSS) in the study of political phenomena.

Popper, Karl R. (2002). *The Logic of Scientific Discovery.* London: Hutchinson. A major and widely respected statement of the philosophy and application of the scientific method; first published in 1959.

ON THE WEB

http://www.apsanet.org

This Web site for the American Political Science Association, the major organization for political scientists in the United States, provides links to a variety of activities and opportunities associated with political science professionals, including online papers from the national conference and articles from *PS: Political Science and Politics*.

http://www.psqonline.org

Political Science Quarterly is America's oldest, continuously published political science journal and brings you the world of politics.

http://www.etown.edu/vl

The rich and extensive set of links on this Web site, "WWW Virtual Library: International Affairs Resources," includes numerous sites for each region as well as links to many key international topics as varied as international organizations, environmental issues, world religions, media resources, health, and human rights.

http://www.realclearpolitics.com

A daily compendium of many of the most interesting stories about politics available on the Internet, including blogs, with a primary focus on U.S. politics.

http://www.politicsresources.net

Richard Kimber's Political Science Resources page includes an extensive listing of sites on topics such as political theory, political thought, constitutions, elections, political parties, international relations, and British politics.

Political Theory and Political Beliefs

What do you think? These college students express their strong political beliefs on an important issue.

2.1 Compare conservatism, classical liberalism and socialism.

2.3 Compare belief systems of the mass and the elite.

2.2 Distinguish cognitive, affective, and evaluative beliefs.

2.4 Determine the extent to which political culture explains political behavior.

O n your way to campus one day, you stop by Burger King for lunch. As you get your food, you notice a group of your classmates engaged in a very heated debate over the recent war in Afghanistan, a topic that hasn't interested you much. You decide to sit with them.

As you eat, Julie says, "The U.S. invasion of Afghanistan was totally immoral. The United States has no right to cause all that suffering, and it's costing America eighty billion dollars a year that should be spent dealing with issues at home, like poverty and education! This is even worse that what we did in Iraq! Don't you agree?"

She looks directly at you, searching for support. As you stare at your cheeseburger, you realize you are in the hot seat. You think, do I support the U.S. action? Did the U.S. "invade"? Is it costing $80 billion?

When you do not respond, Glen interjects, telling Julie, "You have no right to say that. Those in power are our most politically knowledgeable decision makers. As citizens, we shouldn't question their authority on issues such as deciding when to go to war!"

Julie replies, "It is not fair that I work so hard every day of the week so that the government can funnel my tax dollars into buying more tanks, guns, and airplanes to fight a war I do not support. Our government should focus on our own poor people and should do more to create jobs for us. I have every right to protest government action." You see Julie's point when you think about problems at home while your family's tax money is being used for a costly, distant war.

"I sort of agree," says Byron. "The U.S. is in a huge budget crisis. Our government is way too big. We should be cutting way back on spending on everything. Cut taxes. Give the money back to people!"

Frustrated with Julie's challenges to the government, Glen says, "By not supporting our leaders and criticizing their actions, you are threatening our country's political stability with your lack of patriotism. For your information, that money has not been wasted. By expanding our military power, we make our country more secure from people who threaten our way of life, and we are able to promote positive values such as democracy and freedom." Supporting democracy and U.S. military strength does seem worthwhile to you.

Then Elene joins in: "You both miss the point. The real reason America went to war is because of the men who led the countries in the conflict. Obama decided

⬚ **Read** and **Listen** to **Chapter 2** at mypoliscilab.com

✓ **Study** and **Review** the **Pre-Test & Flashcards** at mypoliscilab.com

to risk many lives in Afghanistan, just like Bush did in Iraq, because he wanted to demonstrate his manliness and power. If women had more authority in these countries, they might have figured out a solution without so much violence and death. I'm not saying it's all about gender, but a lot of women do see things differently than many men do, and if women had more political authority, they might come up with less violent approaches."

Amir, whose family is from the Middle East, cannot resist speaking. "I agree with Julie. American leadership has caused great pain and suffering for many innocent Muslim families. It started in Iraq. The reports of weapons of mass destruction were just a sham to allow the United States to force its values upon the Iraqis. George Bush even called the war a crusade! Then Obama caused more mass destruction in Afghanistan! We are marching in protest tonight on campus. Join us!"

You decide that everyone has made some good points. You wonder if you should spend more time gathering knowledge about political issues like the war. This discussion has made you reflect on your own values: When are war and violence acceptable? What should the government spend money on? Should your country push other countries to adopt American values? Should you attend the protest rally?

How would you (the real you!) react to this conversation? What are your views on these questions?

This conversation is richly political—full of many knowledge claims. Some of the comments seem factual, while others mix fact, feeling and evaluation. Some include strong prescriptive statements about what should be. There is a call for action. Your responses to this incident and to the questions it raises offer interesting evidence about your reactions to the political world. Some of your responses might involve what you think (your political beliefs and your political ideology), and others might involve what you do (your political actions). This combination of *an individual's beliefs and actions* is the essence of the domain of political science called **political behavior.** It is also sometimes called **micropolitics** because *the key object of study is the smallest political unit*—the individual as a thinker and actor in the political world. Micropolitics can also include the study of the political beliefs and actions of small groups such as families, committees, and juries.

Part Two of this book develops your understanding of the political world by examining major themes in the study of political behavior. This chapter explores individual's political views, ranging from *core values to specific beliefs.* Initially, it examines normative political theory—the assumptions and broad beliefs that guide political ideologies. The primary focus is on three political ideologies prevalent in Western political thought, conservatism, classical liberalism and socialism. The chapter then details what empirical analyses reveal about the basic elements of an individual's *political beliefs.* Third, the chapter considers the configuration of beliefs held by an individual—a cluster of beliefs called a *political belief system.* The final section explains attempts to characterize the dominant patterns of political behavior for an entire society—its *political culture.* The two other chapters in Part Two will extend our exploration of political behavior. Chapter 3 examines the political actions taken by individuals and groups. Chapter 4 assesses alternative explanations for the sources of people's political beliefs and actions.

NORMATIVE POLITICAL THEORY

Should an individual resist a government policy on drug use with which she disagrees? Why? By what means? With what goals? Should government provide for the poor? Why? By what means? With what goals? As each of us attempts to answer such questions, we must grapple not only with the facts and realities of the situation, as we understand them, but also with our underlying beliefs about topics such as the appropriate role of government and the rights and duties of the individual in society. Political questions are often very difficult to resolve because they can be embedded in underlying values and core beliefs that are subject to deep disagreement.

2.1 Compare conservatism, classical liberalism, and socialism.

Watch the Video "David Cameron on Corporate Social Responsibility" at **mypoliscilab.com**

Notice that the preceding questions are essentially *should* questions. The subfield of political science called **normative political theory** *offers explicit arguments and proposes answers to the significant "should" questions in the political world*, based on fundamental claims about the individual, the society and the state. Normative political theorists develop their ideas about the "should" questions by blending their observations about the world with the detailed articulation and defense of one or more basic values, principles or norms that shape their viewpoint. So, for example, a normative theorist's response to whether the government should provide for the poor would require an elaboration on several key issues, such as whether society has a political or moral obligation to others, how this applies to the particular case of poverty, and how government is implicated in any such obligation. Such theorizing usually invokes fundamental themes like justice, fairness, equality, and freedom.

Although there are overlaps between the two general approaches, normative political theory can be broadly contrasted with **empirical political theory**, which *relies upon observation and analysis of real-world data as it attempts to apply the methods of science in order to develop descriptive and explanatory knowledge claims about the political world*. Later sections of this chapter offer information and generalizations about people's cognitive, affective, and evaluative beliefs based explicitly in an empirical approach. But the formulation of an evaluative belief or a prescriptive knowledge claim will also draw upon normative thinking. Thus this chapter about political beliefs initially explores some key themes in normative political theory and describes several major political ideologies.

Some of the core issues of normative political theory are associated with the basic question: Why do we need a government? Theorizing about this can provoke further questions about human nature, about why and how people associate with each other, about how government should function, and about how people and government should interact. Plato, Aristotle, Confucius, Thomas Hobbes, John Locke, Karl Marx, and John Stuart Mill are among the many important thinkers who have offered profound, provocative, and influential ideas about these basic normative questions regarding the relationships among individuals, the state, and society. Such political questions remain important and fascinating. This section describes some of these questions and a few of the many answers that are proposed.

You will notice that many of the knowledge claims made by normative political theorists are based on more than their values. Most political theorists include descriptive statements (claims of how things actually are) as part of their arguments regarding what should be and why it should be. As they articulate their normative claims about the political world, they are influenced by the same factors that surround those engaged in empirical political analysis—their personal experiences, education, the nature of the time and place in which they live, and other key forces in their lives. Focus in 2 briefly considers how the socioeconomic context contributed to the hugely influential writings of three major political theorists.

FOCUS IN 2 | **Great Britain as a Context for Some Great Political Theorists**

What influences the thinking of the great political theorists? Of course, the answer is complex and variable. Chapter 4 will suggest that most people's political beliefs are influenced by an array of factors, including their own personal experiences and upbringing, their teachers and other individuals whose ideas engage them, and the sociopolitical contexts that provide evidence guiding their assumptions and inferences about human nature, the role of the state, and other key topics. It is probably not surprising that most of the great political theorists of the last four centuries selected for major English-language anthologies were substantially influenced by their lives in the sociopolitical context of Great Britain (see, for example, Ebenstein and Ebenstein, 2001; Goodin and Pettit, 2006; Love, 2010). Even many modern thinkers who did not live in the British Isles were substantially influenced by Britain's unique institutional innovations and political culture in the 17th–19th centuries. Here are very brief examples of three major theorists directly affected by their lives in Britain.

Thomas Hobbes. Englishman Thomas Hobbes (1588–1679) studied classics in school and at Oxford. After traveling in Europe, Hobbes became embroiled

in the social turmoil, civil war, and serious succession problems in England after the death of Queen Elizabeth, as several different hereditary lines claimed the throne. One king (Charles I) attempted to reign absolutely over a resistant Parliament through two civil wars and then was executed for high treason in 1649, as Cromwell's Puritans took over government. The chaos in England certainly influenced Hobbes's ideas about the brutal behavior of humans in the "state of nature." In 1640, Hobbes had written a tract to lawmakers urging that the sovereign (king) must exercise absolute power to reduce such disorder. He then fled England, fearing that he would be executed for his support of the monarchy. While abroad, Hobbes wrote his masterpiece, *Leviathan* (1651), in which he elaborated on his ideas, arguing that a powerful monarch should be established and obeyed. Recognizing the growing political influence of business in England, he also suggested that the "voice of the people" should be heard through representatives of the business class. However, no one has any right to challenge the complete power of the monarch to make and enforce laws, as long as the monarch preserves social order.

(Continued)

Adam Smith. Adam Smith (1723–1790) left his small village in Scotland to study in Edinburgh and then Oxford, where he focused on philosophy and European literature. Smith served as chair in logic and moral philosophy in Glasgow and then traveled in Europe as tutor to a wealthy English duke. Smith had developed a strong opposition to the British government's interventions in its economy—a view reinforced when he saw similar problems in France. He retired to Scotland to write his classic *An Inquiry into the Wealth of Nations* (1776). Shaped by his training as a philosopher, his work explored how humans could best interact to produce the most efficient economic system. He emphasized the benefits of a division of labor, where economic actors—generally unhindered by government—pursue their own rational self-interest while the "invisible hand" of the market guides the economy (see Chapter 8 of this book). However, Smith's life in Britain and his work as a customs agent persuaded him that there were some limitations to the free market, and he began to advocate certain important roles for government in the economy, such as enforcing contracts, protecting intellectual property rights, and acting in areas where the decisions of private economic actors would not produce necessary goods (e.g., roads and bridges). He also entered a contemporary policy debate, arguing that Britain should abandon its American colonies due to the high costs of sustaining imperialism.

Karl Marx. Although Karl Marx (1818–1883) was born in Germany, he lived the entire second half of his life (34 years) in England, where he researched and wrote his major work, died, and was buried. The moral and philosophical bases of his theories (especially French socialism and German philosophy) were established during his time as a student, journalist, and political agitator in Germany, France, and Belgium. His activism led to his expulsion from all three countries, and thus in 1849 he moved to England and found refuge in London. His earlier ideas were blended with his experiences in England: a detailed study of English corporate records and other research in the British Museum; his projections of the future of capitalism based on his analysis of English capitalism, the world's most sophisticated economic system; and his observations of the hardships of the English working class. Indeed, Marx's own life was substantially shaped by the severe hardships suffered in London by his own family, which lived in poverty and disease and included the painful deaths of three of his children. His writing in England culminated in his monumental work, *Das Kapital: A Critique of Political Economy* (1867). As stated by his disciple, Wilhelm Liebknecht, "[I]n England Marx found what he was looking for, what he needed: the bricks and mortar for his work. *Capital* could only have been written in London. Marx could only become what he did become in England" (McClellan 1983).

FURTHER FOCUS

1. Based on these brief discussions, which of the three theorists seems to have been most influenced by the context of life in Britain?
2. Could you make a case that most major political theorists would probably have developed their ideas regardless of the country in which they lived? ▸

Political Ideology

The political theories of Thomas Hobbes, Adam Smith, and Karl Marx are among the several dozen most famous and widely studied in the Western world. Some would describe the work of each of them as a political ideology. We can define a political ideology as *a comprehensive set of beliefs about the political world—about desirable political goals and the best ways to achieve those goals.* Thus, a political ideology characterizes what is and what should be in the political world, and it might also offer strategic ideas about how to make changes in the direction of that preferred situation. Many relatively coherent belief systems in the contemporary world might be classified as political ideologies.

This section characterizes three of the fundamental concerns that are addressed by most political ideologies and help us distinguish analytically among them—their assumptions and value judgments about: (1) individual human nature; (2) the proper relationship among the individual, state, and society; and (3) the desirability of establishing equality among individuals. Then it details three broad ideologies that are widely discussed in contemporary Western societies: conservatism, classical liberalism, and socialism. There are short explanations of the ideologies of fascism and political Islam as well as brief characterizations of some other "isms."

The Individual   The "nature versus nurture" debate centers on disagreements about whether a person's fundamental beliefs and behaviors are determined primarily by innate needs and values with which she is born or are mainly a product of her environment and experiences. Chapter 4 provides an empirical assessment of the implications of nature and nurture for political beliefs and actions. Here, our focus is on key assumptions that a political ideology makes about an individual's innate nature (e.g., the extent to which individuals are selfish or sharing, violent or nonviolent, emotional or rational) and about the adaptability of individuals (the extent to which they can be taught or induced to act and think in a way that is against their innate nature). For example, Thomas Hobbes grounds his theories in the assumption that people are essentially motivated to serve their own interests, and that they will use whatever means necessary, including violence, to protect themselves.

Individual, State, and Society   What is the proper relationship among the individual, the state, and society? One view is that the highest value in social arrangements is to maximize individual liberty and freedom of action. A different view is that the collective good of society is most important, and individual freedom must be constrained by the state (the government, broadly understood—see Chapter 5) to achieve the results that most benefit the overall society. For example, Adam Smith emphasizes the benefits to both individuals and to the "wealth of the nation" from allowing economic actors to operate with a very high level of freedom from government controls, because their pursuit of enlightened self-interest will result in a good society with an efficient and effective economy.

Equality   To what extent should there be equality in terms of what individuals do and the benefits they acquire? One position is that there should be legal equality—that every person should be equal before the law, have equal political rights, and enjoy equality of opportunity. An alternative position is that there should be material equality—that every person should enjoy a comparable level of benefits and goods. This second position places a high value on equality of conditions, adding social and economic equality to legal equality. A third position posits that people and situations are intrinsically unequal and that it is neither possible nor desirable to legislate any kind of equality. Karl Marx is among those who argue most fervently that a good society is achieved only when there is substantial equality in the material conditions of all individuals.

Three major Western ideologies are described below—conservatism, classical liberalism, and socialism. Although there is broad agreement about the core beliefs within an ideology, it is subject to varying interpretations across individuals and across cultures. And an ideology can have distinct versions, as in the differences within socialism between its Marxist-Leninist form and its democratic socialist form.

Conservatism

Conservatism *attempts to prevent or slow the transition away from a society based on traditional values and the existing social hierarchy.* As the word suggests, the essence of conservative ideology is to conserve the many valued elements of the system that already exists. What the conservative wishes to preserve depends on the time and place, but certain underlying elements are highly valued. Particular importance is placed on stability, tradition, and loyalty to God and country. The relationship of the individual to society and an antipathy to egalitarianism (i.e., equality of conditions) are at the core of conservatism.

The Individual   Conservatism makes two key assumptions about human nature. First, individuals are not consistently rational. In many situations, people are emotional and are unable to reason clearly. Thus, tradition and religion, rather than reason, are viewed as the most reliable sources for guiding society because they support stability and moderate change. In the words of one British conservative, "The accumulated wisdom and experience of countless generations gone is more likely to be right than the passing fashion of the moment" (Hearnshaw 1933:22). Second, individuals are inherently unequal in intelligence, skills, and status. Some individuals and groups are superior to others, and those who are superior should be in positions of power in society and in government.

Individual, State, and Society   Individuals have a basic need for order and stability in society. They belong to different groups that are unequal in power, status, and material possessions. Social harmony is maintained when these various groups work cooperatively together. Traditional values and ethics provide the guidelines for group cooperation as well as individual behavior. And it is the role of societal institutions such as the family and the church, as well as government (the state), to communicate and enforce these values.

Individual liberty is valued and individual rights should be protected, but only within a framework of mutual responsibility. No individual or group has absolute freedom to do whatever it wants; rather, each should behave in a manner consistent with society's traditional values. The superior groups should be allowed to enjoy the benefits and exercise the responsibilities associated with their position, but they should also protect the weak from severe hardships, a responsibility that the French call *noblesse oblige*—"the obligations of the nobility." And government should use its power to maintain social order; to preserve traditional values, especially regarding family life, religion, and culture; and to protect private property rights. State military and economic power should also promote the country's interests abroad and defend against intervention by other states.

Equality Because inequality is a natural aspect of society, it is foolish and even dangerous to seek egalitarianism. Forced equality is unwise because it disrupts the natural, cooperative hierarchy among groups, causes social conflict, and endangers the fundamental goal of order and stability. Attempts to force equality are also unacceptable because they directly undermine individual liberty, which is of greater importance than equality.

Thomas Hobbes, Plato (427–347 B.C.E., who proposed rule by philosopher-kings), and Confucius (551–479 B.C.E., who celebrated rigid social hierarchy; see Focus in 4), all reflect core values of conservatism. Other important advocates of conservatism include Edmund Burke, a British member of Parliament; British prime ministers Benjamin Disraeli and Winston Churchill; and, to a lesser extent, American Founding Fathers James Madison and Alexander Hamilton. In the conversation at Burger King at the beginning of this chapter, Glen's views were generally consistent with conservatism.

Most contemporary conservatives are pragmatic. They are less concerned about the form of government than about the use of government to promote order and stability. The conservative perspective is sympathetic to government intervention when the objective of the policy is to maintain or return to traditional values such as patriotism, family, morality, piety, and individual responsibility. In every era, conservatives resist current threats to the traditions they value. Today, those threats often include multiculturalism; expansion of the welfare state; and forced equality across class, race, and gender. A conservative government might actively support a state religion, expand its military power to influence other countries, suppress disorderly protest, provide minimal relief to those in poverty, or make abortion illegal. Some new policies are supported, but the rationale is always "to change in order to preserve," as the British Conservative Party has put it. Many of the contemporary political leaders who come closest to the spirit of conservatism are in certain countries in Asia and the Middle East (e.g., Brunei, Kuwait, and Saudi Arabia) where social hierarchy, order, and traditional values are celebrated.

Classical Liberalism

The ideology of classical liberalism *places the highest value on individual freedom and posits that the role of government should be quite limited.* In part, this ideology emerged in the 16th through 18th centuries as a response to rigid, hierarchical societies, such as those in feudal Europe. Intellectuals and those in commerce, among others, desired to be free from the constraints imposed by the dominant political, economic, and religious institutions in their society. They posited that each person should live responsibly but also should be allowed to live in the manner dictated by her beliefs and to enjoy fully the benefits of her efforts, with minimal limitations from these stifling, conservative institutions.

The Individual John Locke (1632–1704), a primary theorist of classical liberalism, describes individuals in a "state of nature" prior to the existence of government (see his *Second Treatise of Government*, 1690). Each person enjoys natural rights to life, liberty, and property. Each person is rational and has the ability to use reason to determine the sensible rules (the "laws of nature") that shape how she should live in pursuit of her own needs and without harming others. Notice two important contrasts with conservatism for classical liberalism: (1) the freedom of each individual to pursue her natural rights is the highest value; and (2) each individual is rational and responsible, and is the best judge of what is in her self-interest. (Notice also that the classical liberal's view of the state of nature is far more benign than the one described by conservative Hobbes as "solitary, poor, nasty, brutish and short.")

Individual, State, and Society   A person's full capabilities can be realized only if she is not limited by a conservative social order in which tradition and hierarchy are dominant. The social order celebrated in conservatism not only restricts individual freedom but also stifles progressive change and growth. In the classical liberal view, no one is forced to accept the authority of the state (government). Individuals can consent to be governed—choosing to "contract" with a minimal government, the main roles of which are limited to clarifying the laws of nature and enforcing the occasional violations of those laws. The state should mainly be a night watchman, a low-profile police officer who ensures the basic safety and freedom of every individual. Thomas Paine's (1737–1809) slogan captures this perspective: "That government is best which governs least."

For similar reasons, classical liberals celebrate a laissez-faire economy, a view particularly associated with the writings of Adam Smith noted briefly in Focus in 2. Each person should be free to pursue her economic goals by any legal activity and to amass as much property and wealth as possible. Individual actors are guided by enlightened self-interest, and the overall economy is structured by the "invisible hand" of the market and free trade. There are only a few circumstances where the state should act to constrain this freedom of economic action. This vision of a market political economy will be further explored in Chapter 8.

Equality   Equality before the law (equality of opportunity) is important, but government should not attempt to create material equality (equality of outcomes). People pursue their interests in different ways and with different levels of success. Even in situations of hardship, government action is undesirable because it undermines individual initiative and independence. Thus, government should have no significant role in addressing inequalities.

Among the many political thinkers associated with classical liberalism, in addition to John Locke and Adam Smith, are Jeremy Bentham (1748–1831) and John Stuart Mill (1806–1873). More contemporary advocates of classical liberalism (some of whom are labeled "neoconservatives") include economists F. A. Hayek (1899–1992) and Milton Friedman (1912–2006) and political commentator William F. Buckley (1925–2008). At Burger King, Byron was most aligned with this perspective. Part Five of this book will reveal that many contemporary political regimes are powerfully influenced by classical liberalism. Its emphases on limited government, individual liberty, and laissez-faire economics are among the central themes in many ongoing debates about public policy and government action.

A brief aside: If you are an American, you might be confused by these characteristics of liberalism because, in the United States, a "liberal" is someone who supports substantial government intervention and public policies that increase equality of outcomes. This confusion of terminology emerged during Franklin Delano Roosevelt's tenure as U.S. president (1933–1945). Faced with a devastating economic depression, Roosevelt argued for a "New Deal" in which the national government had a clear duty and responsibility to assist actively in economic recovery and in social action. This expanded government would regulate business, create jobs, and distribute extensive welfare services to the citizens, including cash payments and increased public provision of education, housing, health care, and so on. Roosevelt's political opponents labeled his policies "socialism." He knew this was a very negative label in the United States, so he called himself and his policies "liberal," contrasting them with the "conservative" policies of others (mainly Republicans, such as the previous president, Herbert Hoover) who emphasized limited government, laissez-faire economics, and individual freedom. Notice that, in the general language of political ideologies, what Roosevelt was calling conservatism was mostly classical liberalism, and what he was proposing as liberalism was a very modest version of democratic socialism (described below). Roosevelt's meanings of liberals versus conservatives were adopted in the United States, but not in most other countries. In this book, the traditional ideology of liberalism will be called classical liberalism to distinguish it from the American understanding of liberalism as an ideology of extensive government and reduced inequality.

Socialism

For socialism, *the most important goal is to provide high-quality, relatively equal conditions of life for everyone, with an active state assisting in the achievement of this goal.* Many people were still impoverished and exploited in the 19th-century world, despite the emergence of industrialization and democracy. Socialism evolved as a distinctive ideology among theorists concerned about the plight of people who had relatively little economic, social, or political power. They were dissatisfied that neither conservatism nor classical liberalism revealed much concern for improving the conditions of these groups. Socialism articulated a vision through which economic and political power could be directed to benefit all groups in society.

The Individual   In the socialist perspective, people are social and caring by nature. They are not innately selfish and aggressive, although negative social conditions can produce such behavior. Every individual's attitudes and behaviors are largely determined by the environment of family, community, and work. Thus, it is crucial to create an environment that encourages individuals to place the highest value on cooperation and sharing and to act in ways that increase the collective good of all.

Individual, State, and Society   Because the good of the society as a whole is the most important goal, some of an individual's interests must be subordinated to, or at least coordinated with, the overall interests and needs of everyone in the society. All groups, from national organizations (e.g., trade unions) to local organizations (e.g., workplaces, social clubs) to the family, must encourage everyone to act in ways that result in cooperation and service to the common good. The state has a crucial role, both through policies that provide every citizen with good material living conditions and through education and civic training. Thus, government must take an expansive role in society, ensuring that every citizen has access to high-quality education, shelter, health care, and jobs, as well as financial security against economic uncertainty. The state is also much more active in controlling powerful actors and self-interested groups whose behavior will harm the collective good of the society, and thus it engages in extensive regulation of both the economic sphere and the social sphere. When everyone enjoys comfortable material conditions, there is much greater willingness to work for the common good and to subordinate one's acquisitiveness and greed.

Equality   Both the organic, hierarchical world of conservatism and the individualistic, self-serving world of classical liberalism result in societies with huge disparities of material conditions, wealth, status, and power. From the socialist perspective, these disparities and inequalities cause misery, deep alienation, and pervasive conflict in the society. Thus, the ideology of socialism centers in a deep commitment to use the power and policies of the state to increase the material, social, and political equality of all its members. It is assumed that such equality transforms people into fulfilled, happy citizens and creates a society in which alienation and conflict are greatly reduced.

There are significant variations within the ideology of socialism. Among these, two major variations should be distinguished: Marxist-Leninist socialism and democratic socialism.

Marxist-Leninist Socialism   Marxist-Leninist socialism is a variant of socialist ideology that begins with three assumptions regarding the *forceful actions necessary to produce equality and social justice*. First, the entrenched socioeconomic elite, supported by the state that it controls, will resist change by every means available, and thus change will require violent overthrow of the existing order. Second, the transformation to socialism will be complex and face many obstacles in the existing system. Thus, a powerful government must be established and allowed total control of the process of change. Among the government's most important tasks is the restructuring of the economic system, with public ownership of all the major resources in the society and the production and distribution of goods and services for human need. And third, a small, dictatorial leadership group must be empowered to manage the government and to effect the complex changes in the economy and society. Once relative equality is achieved, both this leadership group and the powerful government supporting it can be eliminated. They will, in the words of Marx, "wither away" and be replaced by decentralized, citizen-run politics and an efficient administration. (See Chapter 9 on the class approach and Chapter 8 on the command political economy for a more complete discussion of these points.)

The core elements of this version of socialism are the theories of Karl Marx and its modified practical applications by V. I. Lenin in the Soviet Union and by Mao Zedong in China. These variations of socialism are often called communism, Marxism, or revolutionary socialism as well as Marxist-Leninist socialism. In the last 70 years, this version of socialism has been attempted in more than 60 countries, ranging from A (Albania, Angola, Algeria) to Z (Zimbabwe). Most of the major regimes that implemented Marxist-Leninist socialism have since abandoned it (see especially Chapter 15 on postcommunist developed countries). Some conclude that the Marxist ideology of communism has been totally discredited. Debate in 8 will consider whether communism is, in fact, dead.

Democratic Socialism   The other major variation within socialist ideology is democratic socialism. This variant also *treats egalitarianism as its primary goal, and assumes that the changes can be effected by a government that comes to power and rules by democratic means*. It rejects the idea that a society based on justice and equality can be created only through violence and repression. This government's authority is democratic, derived from consent of the governed in fair elections. In democratic socialism, the state's policies emphasize the substantial reduction of inequalities in material conditions, power, and status, but the state does not attempt to achieve complete equality of material conditions. The approach to change is gradual, placing continued importance on the protection of individual rights and freedoms, even as it transforms the socioeconomic order. The government might own some of the major economic resources in the society and it strongly regulates much of the economy, but it does not attempt to plan and control all aspects of the economic system (Przeworski 1985, 1993).

The ideology of democratic socialism is rooted in utopian socialists such as Thomas More (1478–1535), Robert Owen (1771–1856), and Claude-Henri St. Simon (1760–1825), who envisioned voluntaristic communities based on cooperation. Twentieth-century variations include the Fabian socialists such as George Bernard Shaw, Sydney Webb, and Beatrice Webb, who were convinced that the people would elect democratic governments that gradually created socialist societies, and the revisionist Marxists such as Karl Kautsky, who argued that violence and repression by the state was not a legitimate means for achieving lasting change. At Burger King, Julie was probably the person closest to this ideology.

One vision of democratic socialism was articulated by the British economist Sir William Beveridge in a major policy statement commissioned by the British government in 1941. This statement was prompted by the dismay among British leaders regarding the very poor education and health of many young British working-class men who were drafted for World War II (hence, another British example of political ideas shaped by socioeconomic conditions). In response to these circumstances, Beveridge argued that in a society operating according to the tenets of classical liberalism, there are five tragic effects on some people. Thus, the government should act as a "welfare state" (Castles 2004), implementing policies to overcome each of these five effects:

1. **Disease:** to be combated by public provision of subsidized or free health care services, including doctors, treatment, hospitals, and medicines.
2. **Want:** to be eliminated by public provision of sufficient money and other services to raise people above poverty.
3. **Squalor:** to be reduced by state provision of publicly owned and subsidized housing affordable to all.
4. **Ignorance:** to be eliminated by universal, free public education.
5. **Idleness:** to be overcome by government policies that ensure meaningful work for every person.

The principles of democratic socialism have substantially shaped the current governance, social life, and material conditions in some contemporary social market systems present in countries such as Denmark, Germany, and Sweden (see Compare in 13). This socialist ideology is also advocated by some of the political elites in the postcommunist countries of Central and Eastern Europe (see Chapter 15).

Some Further Points About "Isms"

To advance your knowledge regarding particular belief systems, you might take a course in political theory, political ideology, or world cultures, or pursue the "ism" of interest at the library or via the Internet. The preceding section identified three major political ideologies that influence the political belief systems of many citizens in Western countries. There are many other significant political ideologies in the contemporary political world, at least some of which are "isms." Table 2.1 briefly characterizes the essence of some of the political "isms" that you might encounter. Broader systems of religious-social beliefs also have great political importance, including Christian fundamentalism, Islamic fundamentalism, Confucianism, and Hinduism. Chapter 4 will indicate that it is almost impossible to understand politics in the contemporary world without considering the influence of these religious "isms" on beliefs and actions.

TABLE 2.1

A Brief Primer on Political "Isms"

In politics and political theory, there are many "isms"—systems of beliefs that address how societies should function, how people should live and what they should value, and how political systems should operate. Entire books are devoted to each of the "isms" below, but here they are characterized in 40 words or less to give you an orienting (dangerously simplified?) idea about the core vision regarding any "ism" with which you are unfamiliar. The references in parentheses indicate the chapters in this book where some of these "isms" receive greater attention.

Anarchism—a moral–political ideal of a society that is untouched by relationships of power and domination among human beings; there is an absence of organized government.

Authoritarianism—a system in which the political rights and interests of individuals are subordinated, usually by coercion, to the interests of the state (see Chapter 7).

Capitalism—linking politics to the political economy, it is a system dominated by a (laissez-faire) market economy in which economic actors are generally free from state constraints (see Chapter 8).

Collectivism—a doctrine holding that the individual's actions should benefit some kind of collective organization such as the state, a tribe, or the like, rather than the individual.

Communism—based on the theories of Karl Marx, the essential goal of this system is the socialization of societal resources with the state owning land, labor, and capital and using them to promote the equal welfare of all citizens (see Chapters 8 and 15).

(Continued)

TABLE 2.1

Conservatism—a belief in the virtue of preserving traditional values and social institutions and of promoting loyalty to country, reliance on family, and adherence to religion.

Corporatism—a political economy in which there is extensive economic cooperation between an activist state and a few groups that represent major economic actors such as large industry, organized labor, and farmers.

Environmentalism—advocacy of the planned management of a natural resource or of the total environment of a particular ecosystem to prevent exploitation, pollution, destruction, or depletion of valuable natural resources.

Fascism—a system in which the unity and harmony of government and society are of central importance and forces that might weaken that unity are repressed; a top leader is usually viewed as the embodiment of the natural will, and all individuals are expected to obey the leader's will.

Feminism—a diverse social movement promoting equal rights and opportunities for women and men in their personal lives, economic activities, and politics; it is also an influential analytic perspective on political science topics from the perspective of feminist theory.

Islamism—guided by a rigid and conservative interpretation of Islam, this "political Islam" encourages active, even violent opposition against any who undermine its beliefs about the appropriate way of living, both public and private.

Liberalism—an emphasis on the primacy of the freedom and rights of the individual, relative to any constraints imposed by the state.

Libertarianism—an extreme version of liberalism, advocating the right of individuals to act freely and unconstrained by the state as long as they do not harm other people.

Marxism—a set of ideas based on the writings of Karl Marx, who argued that society is composed of competing classes based on economic power, that class struggle and change are inevitable, and that the desired goal is the equal distribution of welfare in the society (see Chapter 8).

Nationalism—a deep commitment to the advancement of the interests and welfare of the core group (based on location, ethnicity, or some other crucial factor) with which an individual identifies powerfully (see Chapter 5).

Pacifism—a belief that the highest political and social value is peace and the absence of violence.

Socialism—a system committed to utilizing the state, the economy, and public policy to provide a high-quality, relatively equal standard of living for all and, usually, to support democratic political processes (see Chapters 8 and 13).

Totalitarianism—a system in which the state possesses total control over all aspects of people's lives, including their economic, social, political, and personal spheres (see Chapter 7).

Some "true believers" adhere almost totally to a particular ideology, and these people are the genuine ideologues. But only a few individuals have a complete grasp of the details and subtleties of any ideology, and even fewer are prepared to accept without reservation every element of an ideology. A larger set of people are substantially influenced by one or more ideologies. They have developed their own system of political beliefs, in which they combine basic principles from particular ideologies with ideas from other sources. And it will be suggested later in this chapter that many people have only rudimentary and inconsistent political beliefs.

Yet a particular "ism" can be a powerful force influencing people and shaping history. In the twentieth century, for example, both communism and fascism had particularly strong impacts. The role of communism will be explored later, especially in Chapters 8 and 15. Table 2.1 provides a basic definition of fascism. Fascism is antisocialist—it emphasizes an organic social order and thus opposes the idea of class struggle among groups—and it is antidemocratic—it views competitive, multiparty politics as divisive and destabilizing. While several twentieth-century regimes included strong elements of fascism, it is most closely associated with Italy under Benito Mussolini (1922–1943) and Germany under Adolf Hitler (1932–1945). In Germany, Hitler's particular version of fascism was driven by several key ideological elements. First, it held that the top leader is the embodiment of the national will and must be obeyed. Second, it inspired nationalistic fervor, with powerful loyalty to the homeland. The German leadership combined these ideas with a celebration of the superiority of the German race. This produced a virulent racism that became a justification for the brutal treatment of Jews, gypsies, homosexuals, and other "undesirable" groups, including the extermination of more than 6 million in the concentration camps of Europe. All of these ideological elements, under Hitler's charismatic leadership, resulted in Germany's expansion beyond its borders, provoking a war (World War II) that spread across three continents and caused more than 51 million deaths. Groups or political parties that embrace core ideas of fascism, especially nationalism and ethnic purity, continue to be active in many contemporary societies.

In the early twenty-first century, considerable attention has focused on the rising political importance of *Islamism*, also known as political Islam (and less accurately characterized as Islamic fundamentalism). Islam is one of the world's great religions, with more than 1.3 billion adherents across its many variations. Chapter 1 noted that there are deep disagreements within *dar al Islam* (the world of Islam) about how to interpret its crucial authority sources, especially the Koran, the teachings of Mohammed, and the analyses of Islam by venerated scholars of an earlier era. Islamic fundamentalists tend to embrace the most rigid and assertive beliefs regarding the interpretation of their holy authorities and the guidelines for their way of life, both personal and public. The political implications of this perspective can include an intolerance for what is viewed as deviant behavior by other Muslims, antagonism among different sects of Islam (e.g., Shi'a and Sunni), and hostility towards those non-Muslims who appear to challenge Islamic rule or to practice other religions within Muslim countries. Most Islamic fundamentalists participate in personal, social, and political activities to further their beliefs. However, a minority of this population (the Islamists) believes it is necessary to engage in violent struggle against those other groups

Sieg heil! Fascism under Adolf Hitler, with its extreme nationalism, antisocialism, and leader veneration, became one of the most effective and destructive mass mobilization ideologies in modern history. Here, Hitler prepares to speak to 700,000 farmers in 1934

to protect the *Umma*, the community of all Muslims. Some of these Islamists have gained considerable notoriety for their violent actions and terrorism (see Chapter 12), including such groups as al-Qaeda, Hamas, Hezbollah, Jemaah Islamiyah, and the Taliban. The death and suffering associated with communism, fascism, Islamism, and other extreme ideologies during the last 100 years are compelling evidence that political ideologies can be much more than bundles of ideas debated by intellectuals.

INDIVIDUAL POLITICAL BELIEFS

Types of Political Orientations

2.2 Distinguish cognitive, affective, and evaluative beliefs.

Can you describe your thought process when you were asked how you would respond to the issues raised at Burger King? Your reaction might have been determined by fundamental and consistent principles you have about society and government—what has been characterized above as a "political ideology." But if you are like most people, your thought processes in reaction to such political phenomena are probably best described in terms of a less structured combination of your factual knowledge, your feelings, and your assessments. These components of your political beliefs are termed cognitive, affective, and evaluative orientations.

Cognitive orientations are *an individual's knowledge about the political world*—what the person believes are political "facts." Cognitive orientations include descriptive knowledge such as: the names of political leaders; the policies supported by particular politicians, political groups, or countries; events in political history; the features of a constitution; or the procedures and actions of a governmental agency. They also include explanatory ideas, such as why the United States is fighting in Afghanistan or why the stability of the euro zone is linked to the Greek economy. A person's cognitive orientations might be correct and accurate, or they might be totally wrong. (Recall the survey questions about facts in Compare in 1.)

Affective orientations include *any feelings or emotions evoked in a person by political phenomena*. For example, what (if any) feelings are stimulated in you when you come across the following?

> You see someone burning your national flag.
> You read about a deadly terrorist attack in an area where you have friends.
> You are faced with the option of voting in an election, and you don't like any of the candidates.
> You are present at a political demonstration supporting a policy you strongly support.

The nature and intensity of your feelings in reaction to each of these situations are instances of your affective orientations.

Finally, an *evaluative orientation* involves your *synthesis of facts and feelings into a judgment about some political phenomenon*. For example, you might decide whether to vote for a candidate. You might determine whether an individual has a free speech right to make negative comments on the Internet about a racial group. You might assess whether Palestine should be granted full member status in the United Nations General Assembly.

A particular situation might generate a variety of political beliefs. For example, if your government has proposed a policy that restricts the right of a woman to have an abortion, this might stimulate many different thoughts and feelings—your knowledge about the constitutional rights of an individual to freedom of action and of the state to limit those rights; your religious, moral, or scientific beliefs about the status of a fetus; your personal knowledge of the experiences of people who have made decisions about abortions; your emotional response to the idea of abortion; and your judgment of what you conclude should be government policy on abortion. In short, on any topic, you can hold a variety of cognitive, affective, and evaluative political beliefs. It is likely that many of the attitudes that you might identify as your "fundamental political beliefs" are based on evaluative orientations grounded in cognitive and affective orientations.

Identifying Specific Beliefs

When employing the methods and assumptions of empirical political theory, we build our conceptual understanding of political beliefs in several stages. If we want to understand *one* person's political orientations, we might begin by collecting empirical data by means of an interview or questionnaire. A telephone interview was the basis for the data in Table 1.2, for example. There are hundreds of politically-relevant questions that enable us to identify some of the specific beliefs that a person holds: Does she know the name of the country's chief executive? How does she react to news that her state's governor has just prevented the

◉—Watch the Video "Is Torture Ever Justified?" at mypoliscilab.com

execution of a convicted murderer? Does she support the use of foreign troops in Afghanistan?

A similar analytic strategy can be used to determine what *many* people think about a specific issue. When *the attitudes of many people are gathered, aggregated, and summarized,* they constitute the most widely available data about people's political orientations: ***public opinion polls*** (also known as ***survey research***). Almost every day, the media provide data on the percentage of people who hold a certain opinion regarding a political issue. For example, a public opinion poll might report data about how Canadians respond to the question, "On the whole, should your government be responsible to reduce income differences between the rich and poor?" On the basis of this survey research data, you might decide you know what Canadians think about the issue. This information seems to be a stronger basis for a knowledge claim than a discussion with a few Canadian friends or even a statement by a Canadian political leader. Table 2.2 provides examples of the types of political questions that appear on such polls, offering comparative data on the responses from Canadians, Japanese, Russians, South Africans, Swedes, and Americans (from a major comparative survey research project conducted by political scientists in more than 80 countries). According to these data, about 67 percent of Canadians say that government should reduce income differences.

TABLE 2.2

Selected Political Beliefs of People in Six Countries*

Country	On the whole, should your government be responsible to reduce income differences between the rich and poor?		How successful is the government in your country in controlling crime?		Suppose your government suspected a terrorist act was about to happen. Do you think the authorities should have the right to stop and search people in the street?		How often do public officials deal fairly with people like you?	
	Definitely	Probably	Very	Quite	Definitely	Probably	Always	Often
Canada	36%	31%	4%	30%	13%	26%	11%	34%
Japan	34	32	2	16	11	36	2	22
Russia	53	33	2	9	6	21	3	10
South Africa	41	43	4	12	30	28	5	21
Sweden	37	31	1	11	26	32	25	36
United States	27	24	5	31	17	24	11	22

* Source: World Values Survey (2006).
* Only the two most positive of the four or five possible responses are indicated, so the totals do not equal 100 percent.

Public opinion polls should be interpreted with care. In assessing the information, you should consider questions such as these: Did those who conducted the poll have a bias towards a particular result? Were the questions or the possible responses worded in a way that might distort people's opinions? Did those who responded seem a representative sample of the entire group to whom the opinion is attributed? Are different interpretations of the data possible? Even when the survey researchers are unbiased, there are numerous reasons why their findings might be somewhat inaccurate. For example, there can be errors in their predictions, based on public opinion polls, of how the population will vote in an election. Why might this happen?

BELIEF SYSTEMS

Beyond the identification of specific beliefs of individuals, other interesting analyses can focus on the array of their political beliefs. The term **political belief system** refers to *the configuration of an individual's political orientations*. This network of cognitive, affective, and evaluative beliefs serves as a basic framework (also termed an opinion schema), guiding a person as she organizes her existing political knowledge and processes new information in order to establish a viewpoint on a particular subject (Dalton, 2008:28; Niemi and Weisberg, 2001).

2.3 Compare belief systems of the mass and the elite.

To examine a person's belief system, you can ask a series of analytical questions:

1. What is the *content* of the beliefs—that is, the subject matter and the nature of the beliefs?
2. What is the *salience* of the beliefs—that is, the importance or significance the person attaches to the beliefs?
3. What is the level of *complexity* of the beliefs?
4. Is there a *consistency* among subsets of beliefs that suggests a series of general principles from which specific beliefs are derived?
5. How *stable* are the beliefs over time?
6. Do the beliefs *motivate* the person to undertake any political action(s)?

The early empirical research on the nature of belief systems was particularly influenced by the analyses of Philip Converse (1964), who focused particularly on people in the United States. In general, Converse argues that a belief system has two levels of information. One level includes relatively straightforward *facts or opinions* such as a person's opinion that American public schools should not allow Christian prayer during class time. The second level is *constraint knowledge,* in which more abstract and overarching concepts (such as one's ideological or religious values) operate to shape and link ideas. In the school prayer example, a person might base her opinion on constraint knowledge about the constitutional separation of church and state or about free speech issues.

Studying the beliefs of individual Americans in the 1950s, Converse concluded that only about 15 percent of the population had a sophisticated, "elite belief system" characterized by extensive political knowledge and abstract ideas that were well organized by constraint knowledge. The rest of the population lacked detailed political knowledge, operated with minimal constraint knowledge, and thus had a belief system that lacked coherence. He termed this the belief system of the "mass public." Converse reported that almost half of the U.S. public revealed either a set of "simplistic political beliefs" or "political ignorance."

More recent research has challenged some of Converse's conclusions, particularly the distinction between belief systems of a mass public and an elite. Many empirical studies reveal that the extent of individuals' political knowledge ranges in a more normal curve from the highly informed to the uninformed (Delli, Carpini, and Keeter, 1996). Other studies conclude that even those with a modest level of political knowledge *are* able to fashion reasonable political opinions and make good judgments about politics (Sniderman, Brody, and Tetlock 1991; Zaller, 1992). In this view, members of the mass public use simple rules of thumb to make sense of issues, particularly in issue areas that interest them (Dalton, 2008: Ch. 2; Lupia and McCubbins, 1998; see also Chapter 4). Another perspective argues that individuals develop structured ways of thinking about the world, but that these ways are not similar for everyone. Thus, if the analyst studies how a particular person structures her thoughts—rather than merely asking questions about specific beliefs—her political attitudes might be generally consistent and coherent within this structure (Rosenberg, 1988, 2002).

Despite continuing debate regarding the precise nature of political belief systems across the full range of people, most researchers agree on certain generalizations that are broadly accurate for most people in most countries. Like nearly every generalization about politics, these are subject to many qualifications and some exceptions.

1. Political issues have low salience compared with other concerns in people's lives. Although Aristotle called the citizen *homo politicus,* or "political man," most people do not locate political issues in the center of their interest and attention space.
2. People tend to focus attention on concrete issues and have minimal grasp of the abstract political concepts that serve as constraint knowledge.
3. Interest and knowledge are greater on immediate, short-term issues than on longer-term ones.
4. While people's fundamental beliefs are relatively stable, there can be considerable volatility in their short-term political opinions, which tend to shift when subjected to modest changes in political information. This volatility might be due to limited interest or to the sheer difficulty of trying to understand complicated political questions.
5. Significant inconsistencies can exist across political beliefs, in the sense that a person can hold contradictory positions. For example, an American might express support for the First Amendment right to free speech but deny the right of an Islamic fundamentalist to speak at a public meeting or the right of the Knights of the Ku Klux Klan to hold a public rally in a predominantly African-American community.
6. The content of beliefs is often inaccurate. In one survey, for example, half the Americans questioned did not know how many U.S. senators serve their state.

Individuals with more sophisticated belief systems tend to differ on all six of these factors. Their belief systems are generally characterized by high levels of salience, abstraction, breadth, stability, consistency, and accuracy. While they employ constraint knowledge extensively to inform their beliefs, they do not share the same core beliefs (Higley and Burton, 2006; Rosenau and Holsti, 1986, 1993). For example, some might have a coherent system of beliefs that supports the protection of an individual's civil liberties, while other people's constraint knowledge and specific opinions consistently support the right of the government to limit individual liberties substantially in the protection of social order (Sniderman, et al. 1991).

While the political beliefs of every person can affect the political world, those who have more sophisticated belief systems are particularly significant. First, the most sophisticated and active political thinkers can influence the views of many others. They absorb and analyze complex events and issues in the political world and then communicate them to a broader audience. This "two-step communication" flow is viewed by some to be crucial in shaping the understandings of many people. And second, many of those with more sophisticated belief systems hold positions of power and authority in society, and thus the actions they take on the basis of their political views can have substantial impact.

POLITICAL CULTURE

2.4 Determine the extent to which political culture explains political behavior.

Some analysts attempt to identify broadly shared patterns of political orientations that characterize a large group of people. The objective is to develop generalizations about the political culture of the group. **Political culture** is normally defined as *the configuration of a particular people's political orientations*—that is, the generalized belief system of many. For this reason, political culture is not precisely a topic in *micropolitics*, but it is examined here because it is embedded in individual-level analyses.

The composition of the group whose political culture is studied depends on the interests of the researcher. It might be the people of a geographic community (e.g., Londoners, English, British, or Europeans) or of a community of shared identity (e.g., Sikhs in the Indian state of Punjab, Sikhs in the Indian subcontinent, or all Sikhs in the world) or of a community of shared meaning (e.g., French Canadians or all French-speaking peoples). Most studies have focused on the political culture of a country or of a major (ethnic or religious) community within a country.

✴—[**Explore** the Comparative "Political Cultures" on mypoliscilab.com

National Character Studies

Some research, generally termed *national character studies*, *attempts to capture the essence of a people's political culture* in terms of broad adjectives (Inkeles, 1997). When someone is described as being "soooo French," you might think of her as sophisticated, romantic, and volatile. At one level, we recognize immediately that such a characterization is a stereotype that does not fit the majority of individual subjects. Yet most of us, including people in the political world, use these kinds of labels (at least occasionally) as a shorthand method of describing groups or nations. Indeed, Franklin Delano Roosevelt (U.S. president from 1933–1945) observed that "the all-important factor in national greatness is national character."

Some political analysts have tried to specify the "national character" of a certain country and then to predict or explain the population's political behavior on the basis of such characteristics. Typically, these studies do not claim that everyone fits the national character profile, but they maintain that the profile is generally accurate for the politically-relevant strata. For example, Jorge Castaneda (2011:xi) analyzes how "the very national character that helped forge Mexico as a nation now dramatically hinders its search for a future and modernity." He defines a bundle of traits that includes a mistrust of others, fear of outsiders, and resistance to change. These combine with an unwillingness to engage in a vigorous debate on current political and economic issues, especially among the more powerful groups in Mexican society. Most importantly, the Mexican national character is dominated by "a premodern individualism" that, he argues, results in a fundamental rejection of collective action and collective solutions that must occur for Mexico to evolve into a vigorous democracy and respond effectively to the challenges of the global economy (Castaneda 2011:32).

A controversial analysis based on a very broad notion of supranational character is Samuel Huntington's (1998) description of nine global "civilizations." These civilizations are the highest level of cultural identity among humans, with the nine groups differing in history, language, culture, and especially religion. The groups, which are also somewhat regionally based, are African, Buddhist,

Confucian, Hindu, Islamic, Japanese, Latin American, Orthodox (Russian), and Western. Huntington predicts that clashes among these civilizations are now the fundamental source of international political conflict and are the most likely cause of the next global war. The Debate in 2 considers Huntington's claims.

Many analysts criticize national character studies as impressionistic and loaded with gross generalizations that greatly oversimplify political reality. Consequently, most scholars dismiss national character studies as caricatures with little capacity to account for the complex actual political behaviors within a country. However, the more thoughtful analyses of national character, based on dominant patterns of beliefs and behaviors, can provide fascinating insights into both the political culture and the political actions taken in a society, and such culture-based explanations are quite evident in recent research (Compton, 2000; Moisi, 2009).

THE DEBATE IN 2 | Is There a "Clash of Civilizations"?

Although national character studies are no longer in vogue, Samuel Huntington's (1993, 1998) controversial analysis is based on the concept of broad differences across supranational character types. Huntington defines nine distinct "civilizations." He then predicts that tensions and conflict are more likely to occur *among* these nine civilizations rather than within them, and he specifies which civilizations are most opposed. Huntington's claims about the crucial impact of these supranational character groups on current global affairs have been a source of heated debate among policymakers and academics. Is there a clash of civilizations?

A "CLASH OF CIVILIZATIONS" EXISTS

- There is considerable empirical evidence that fundamental differences exist between civilizations. For example, analyses from the World Values Survey indicate that Muslims and Westerners disagree profoundly on numerous social issues like gender equality and homosexuality (Norris and Inglehart, 2004).
- While ideologies and political regimes may change, underlying civilization identities are the product of centuries and will not disappear. Most people can choose to embrace or shed a particular political ideology, but few reject the fundamental

ethnoreligious identity of their birth. These broad ethnic and religious identities have a major and growing significance in a global society where violent conflicts over ideas and resources are unavoidable.

- The empirical evidence also reveals that since the end of World War II, there has been a continual rise in the number of ethnoreligious conflicts within states where the cleavages are related to the civilizations described by Huntington (Eriksson et al., 2003). Examples include the struggles between: the Christian and Muslim groups in Sudan; the United States' Western alliance and Muslim groups in Afghanistan, Iraq, and Pakistan; Tamils (Hindus) and Sinhalese (Buddhist) in Sri Lanka; the Tibetans (Buddhist) against the Chinese; and Israelis and regional Muslim groups.
- The humiliation and lack of respect experienced by many in the Islamic culture and the fears of danger and decline experienced by many in the Western culture have resulted in increasing hostilities between these two civilizations, which generally blame each other for these conditions (Moisi, 2009).
- The resurgence of Russia has generated strong clashes with those within and adjacent to its borders who identify with other civilization groups. This includes the Chechens, the Kazakhs,

(Continued)

and the Central Europeans. Similar clashes motivated the violence in the Balkans.

- Leaders of many Latin American countries have expressed open opposition to the ideology, policies, and values that guide the United States, as the leader of the Western bloc of developed countries. While major conflict is unlikely, there is clearly a volatile clash between the West and Latin American opinion leaders such as Hugo Chavez in Venezuela and Evo Morales in Bolivia.

THERE IS NO "CLASH OF CIVILIZATIONS"

- Like other discredited national character studies, "civilizations" as an organizing principle vastly oversimplifies reality. Each category collapses countless cultures, languages, and histories (Said, 2001). For example, there are substantial differences within the "Islamic" civilization, like those between Shi'a and Sunni; among Saudi, Indonesian, and Turk; and so on. Such differences are also clear among the many ethnic groups within the "African" civilization's Congo, Ghana, South Africa, and so on. Overall, there is as much variation *within* each civilization as there is between civilizations.
- The argument of value differences among civilizations on issues like gender ignores the compelling empirical evidence of deep divisions within Western countries, for example, on issues such as gay marriage, abortion, and the need for an equal (gender) rights amendment.
- More broadly, the empirical facts show no evidence of a systemic clash of civilizations. Statistical analyses demonstrate that "pairs of states split across civilizational boundaries are no more likely to become engaged in disputes than

are other states" (Russett et al. 2000: 583). Even disputes arising between the West and Islam (a friction point predicted by Huntington) are no more likely than conflicts between any other two states, *ceteris paribus*.

- For civilizations to exist as Huntington describes them, they must resist the penetration and influence of other civilizations. Yet globalization has dramatically increased the penetration across cultures, the convergence in values and behaviors, and the blurring of differences.
- Individuals and thus societies are not solely defined and motivated by their religious and ethnic identities (Sen, 2006). National and regional identities that crosscut Huntington's civilizations can also create powerful ties that bind. Indians' national pride, for example, is a strong counterbalance to Hindu–Muslim distinctions within India.
- Stephen Walt (1997) argues that the clash of civilizations argument is merely an attempt by some in the West to build up a new "bogeyman"— to find a new set of enemies after the fall of the Soviet Union and the end of the Cold War. If policymakers behave as if civilizations will inevitably clash, it will provide political leaders on both sides with justifications for certain military and foreign policy actions and might even result in an artificially induced civilizational conflict.

MORE QUESTIONS...

1. Which of Huntington's nine "civilizations" seems most plausible to you? Which seems the least plausible?
2. What empirical evidence would you find sufficient to resolve the question of this debate? ▶

Survey Research Analyses

The section above described how survey research is used to gather empirical data about individuals' political beliefs, as in Table 2.2. Thus, a more systematic and scientifically acceptable method for establishing the nature of a political culture is the use of carefully gathered empirical data on individuals' political beliefs and actions. Such *survey research analyses* then *aggregate these empirical data, searching for patterns or configurations that profile the political culture* of the sample and, by inference, that characterize the political culture of the population from which the sample is taken.

The first major study of this type is *The Civic Culture* by Gabriel Almond and Sidney Verba (1963). Lengthy interviews were conducted with a large sample of citizens in each of five countries. The data were then aggregated and analyzed in a diversity of ways to provide rich descriptions, as the study contrasted the quite different political cultures of Italy ("alienated"), Mexico ("alienated but aspiring"), the United States ("participant"), the United Kingdom ("deferential"), and (West) Germany ("detached"). Another of the notable early studies found widespread similarities in the social and political concerns among citizens in many democratic countries. Personal desires for a happy family life, a decent standard of living, and good health were most important, and political concerns centered on fears about war and political instability (Cantril 1965).

The most comprehensive recent comparative surveys of political culture are the World Values Survey (WVS). Ronald Inglehart and collaborating scholars have conducted five "waves" of this survey (in 1981, 1990, 1995, 2000, and 2006), and the survey now includes individuals from more than 80 countries which contain more than 85 percent of the world's population. Large samples of adults in each country are asked many questions about their opinions regarding politics, societal needs, personal values, and so on. Table 2.2 presented a few examples of the questions on the survey. Do you think the data in Table 2.2 are evidence that there are differences in the citizens' political beliefs across the selected countries? Compare in 2 describes recent research from the WVS that attempts broad crossnational comparisons of political orientations.

▶ COMPARE IN 2 | Value Differences Across Countries

The World Values Surveys are a major attempt to compare social and political values in more than 80 countries. The surveys attempt to measure an extensive array of each individual's political orientations. The researchers then aggregate those beliefs for the respondents in each country to specify "people's prevailing value orientations" (Inglehart and Welzel, 2005). One of their most ambitious efforts to map the values across countries is Figure 2.1. The responses to numerous questions were combined to create individual-level and then country-level values on two broad dimensions. The *self-expression versus survival* value dimension measures the priority placed on subjective well-being

values such as tolerance versus security values. The *secular-rational versus traditional* value dimension reflects how strongly individuals embrace the norms associated with religion, family, and country. Figure 2.1 is one of the comparisons that can be made using the country-level scores on these two dimensions. A brief look at several countries suggests how these collective value scores seem reflected in each country's actual politics. We focus in particular on the issues of homosexuality and obedience to authority, which, according to Inglehart's group, are especially significant reflections of the level of tolerance and propensity to democracy in a society (Norris and Inglehart, 2004; Inglehart and Welzel, 2005; 2010).

(Continued)

Switzerland's population scores very high on both secular-rational values and self-expression values. The Swiss value personal freedom and independence, with minimal state control over their actions and lives. Theirs is one of the most orderly and nonconflictual societies in the world. It is a wealthy country that has generally avoided many of the economic fluctuations that have plagued many other advanced countries, and most of its citizens enjoy considerable prosperity and have less immediate concerns about economic insecurity. Religion's lack of influence on Switzerland is also a factor regarding the views of the Swiss on individual rights, including homosexuality and divorce. Although some in Switzerland disapprove of homosexuality, the general population is tolerant of the gay community. In fact, Switzerland remains one of the most progressive countries regarding gay rights. Homosexuality was decriminalized as early as 1942 and, in 2007 Switzerland began recognizing same-sex partnerships with the Partnership Act. Switzerland actively encourages its homosexual citizens to reveal their homosexuality with the annual "Coming Out Day."

Uganda, on the other hand, has been torn apart by political instability, poverty, and conflict among social groups. These conditions are consistent with a political culture characterized by survival values and a very clear orientation to traditional values. Traditional values and a low level of tolerance are evident in Uganda's approach to homosexuality. Since its colonial era, Uganda has outlawed homosexuality and conviction currently carries a 14-year prison sentence. Indeed, in 2009 an Anti-Homosexuality Bill was proposed to punish homosexual behavior with the death penalty. The bill was openly endorsed by Uganda's President, Yoweri Museveni, as well as many other political and religious leaders. In the face of harsh criticism from the global community, the bill's provision of the death penalty for homosexuals has been altered to life in prison.

In another example, Morocco has a population that generally exhibits strong traditional and survival values. Most Moroccans live in tight-knit extended families and identify strongly with their kin group. The emphasis on obedience and acceptance of authority seems linked to both the power of the hereditary king and a somewhat repressive regime and also to the influence of the Muslim religion over the lives of most Moroccans. It is perhaps not surprising that the country was not among the first or the second wave of countries in rebellion against their leaders during the "Arab awakening" that began in the summer of 2011.

In contrast, the citizens of the Czech Republic are particularly high on secular rational values. Nearly 60 percent of the Czechs report they are atheists—one of the world's highest proportions. Both their break with religion and also the harsh experiences under communism from the late 1940s to the late 1980s seem associated with their skepticism regarding those in authority and the value of obedience. While there is some Czech nationalism, their identities are diluted by regional ties and residual links to the Czechoslovakia prior to 1989, as well as their growing identity as Europeans within the EU.

While you might find the blobs of countries in Figure 2.1 a bit odd, the researchers claim that most countries can be grouped, based especially on region and/or religion, into the eight political cultures that are labeled in Figure 2.1 (Welzel 2007). This is an admirable attempt to use solid empirical data to compare the broad value systems of people in many countries. While the analyses are more sweeping than many other studies, most scholars of political behavior conclude that the citizens of different nationality groups have social and political orientations that can be measured and compared.

FURTHER QUESTIONS

1. The location of which country in Figure 2.1 most surprises you? Why?
2. Do the clusters in Figure 2.1 make sense to you? Can you suggest a different way to categorize the countries?
3. Where do you think *you* might be located in Figure 2.1?
4. Does the analysis in Figure 2.1 seem to provide any support for Huntington's ideas about a clash of civilizations? ▲

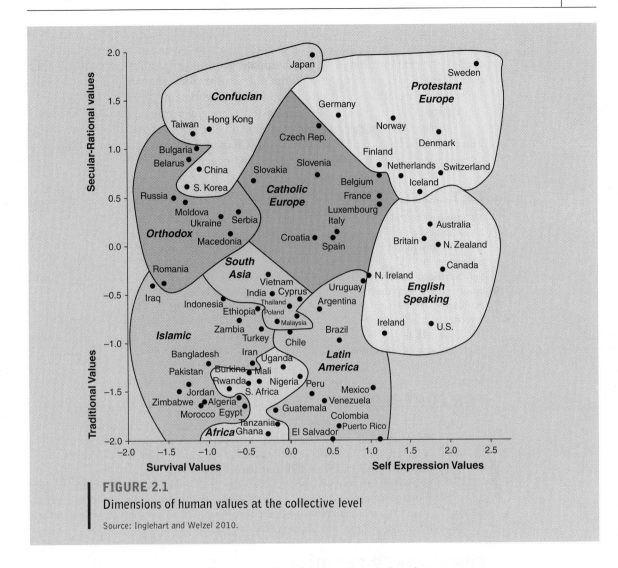

FIGURE 2.1

Dimensions of human values at the collective level

Source: Inglehart and Welzel 2010.

The extensive empirical research on political culture—as it has become more precise in its methods and more cautious about cultural biases—has revealed the considerable variability in political culture within a country, across individuals, between groups, and over time. Chapter 4 will examine some of the factors that might account for differences in the political beliefs of individuals within a society. But it is also evident from the survey research that many countries have a political culture that can be distinguished from the political cultures in some, perhaps most, other countries.

LOOKING AHEAD

Chapter 2 has introduced you to the systematic analysis of political behavior. This chapter describes key topics in the empirical study of political beliefs—what individuals know, feel, and think about politics. Analysis can focus on a single

✓•⫗**Study**
and **Review** the
Post-Test &
Chapter Exam at
mypoliscilab.com

person, a group, or even a culture, and it can assess a single belief or an array of beliefs across many issues. The chapter has also examined normative political theory—the exploration of how individuals, government, and society *should* operate. Normative theory is arguably the oldest subfield in the study of politics, and its perennial questions about the good society and the appropriate role of government remain as intriguing and as contested as they were during the time of Plato.

The next step in the analysis of political behavior is to move our focus from political beliefs to political actions. Thus, Chapter 3 explores the array of political actions in which an individual or group can engage.

KEY CONCEPTS

affective orientation   43
classical liberalism   34
cognitive orientation   43
conservatism   33
democratic socialism   38
empirical political theory   29
evaluative orientation   43
fascism   41
Islamism   41
Marxist-Leninist socialism   37
micropolitics   28

national character studies   48
normative political theory   29
political behavior   28
political belief system   45
political culture   48
political elite   39
political ideology   31
public opinion polls   44
socialism   36
survey research   44

FOR FURTHER CONSIDERATION

1. What are your general beliefs about human nature? Are these beliefs consistent with your most important beliefs about how people ought to behave and do behave politically?
2. What do you think is the most sensible assumption and the most questionable assumption of conservatism? Of classical liberalism? Of socialism?
3. Can you characterize your own political belief system? For example, what are your three to five most salient political beliefs? Do they deal with the same general content area?
4. If you were to analyze the political belief system of another person on the basis of five questions, what questions would you ask?

FOR FURTHER READING

Almond, Gabriel, and Sidney Verba. (1963). *The Civic Culture.* Princeton, NJ: Princeton University Press. This is a landmark empirical, comparative study of the political cultures of different countries.

Bryson, Valerie. (2003). *Feminist Political Theory: An Introduction.* 2nd ed. New York: Palgrave Macmillan. This provides an accessible introduction to some of the variations in the complex set of theoretical approaches and debates in this increasingly influential set of perspectives on analyzing politics at all levels.

Carlisle, Rodney, Ed. (2005). *Encyclopedia of Politics: The Left and the Right.* Newbury Park, CA: Sage. This clever and comprehensive (1,100 pages) two-volume set (the "left" volume examines progressive/socialist thinking and the "right" examines conservative and classical liberal perspectives) contains more than 450 readable and interesting articles that concentrate on the "isms" and many, many other interesting themes, as elaborated by historical and contemporary thinkers from many parts of the world.

Fromm, Erich, Ed. (1965). *Socialist Humanism.* New York: Doubleday. Prominent social scientists and political philosophers expound the virtues of socialism.

Griffin, Roger, Ed. (1998). *International Fascism: Theories, Causes, and the New Consensus.* London: Bloomsbury Academic. A diverse and thorough selection of writings on fascism, by both fascists and antifascists, exploring the strong appeal of this ideology to many individuals and groups during the mid-twentieth century and also at the beginning of the twenty-first century.

Huntington, Samuel P. (1998). *Clash of Civilizations and the Remaking of the World Order.* New York: Simon and Schuster. As described in this chapter (see Debate in 2), the author offers a sweeping and controversial analysis of major cultural groupings at the global level, where identity, especially religious and cultural, is the dominant force shaping both the beliefs and actions of individuals and also the patterns of world politics.

Inglehart, Ronald, and Christian Welzel (2005). *Modernization, Cultural Change and Democracy: The Human Development Sequence.* New York: Cambridge University Press. Building on his important earlier work (Inglehart 1989, 1997), the author and his co-author further develop detailed analyses based on the World Values Survey that characterize the nature of and shifts in political culture across more than 75 countries (see Compare in 2).

Love, Nancy S., Ed. (2010). *Dogmas and Dreams: A Reader in Modern Political Ideologies.* 4th ed. Washington, DC: CQ Press. A solid reader that includes important writings by many key theorists of the three major "isms" as well as others including anarchism, fascism, and feminism.

Mayer, Lawrence, and Erol Kaymak. (1998). *The Crisis of Conservatism and the Rise of the New Right in Western Democracies: Populist Revolt in the Late Twentieth Century.* Armonk, NY: M. E. Sharpe. An interesting exploration of the activities of ideologically driven and rather alienated populist groups that have their roots in traditional conservatism but have diverged substantially from it in both their attitudes and their political styles.

McLellan, David, Ed. (2007). *Marxism after Marx.* 4th ed. New York: Palgrave. An excellent set of readings exploring the many versions of Marxism that have continued to wield great significance in the field of political theory.

Moisi, Dominique. (2009). *The Geopolitics of Emotion: How Fear, Humiliation and Hope are Reshaping the World.* New York: Random House. In a variation on the clash of civilizations perspective, Moisi argues that there are broad, regionally-based cultures that differ. He claims that the driving emotion of the Western cultures is fear, of the Islamic cultures is humiliation, and of the Asian cultures is hope, and that the evolution and interplay of these patterns will have critical impacts on global society.

Murray, Charles. (1997). *What It Means to Be a Libertarian.* New York: Broadway Books. A brief, readable application of libertarian ideology to many contemporary issues (e.g., abortion, education, drugs, economic regulation, free speech), written by one of America's most controversial social critics.

Nisbet, Robert. (2001). *Conservatism: Dream and Reality.* Piscataway, NJ: Transaction. A short, illuminating discussion that traces the development of conservative thought and its significance in contemporary politics.

Putnam, Robert D. (1993). *Making Democracy Work: Civic Traditions in Modern Italy.* Princeton, NJ: Princeton University Press. Using communities in northern and southern Italy as his cases, the author develops a significant and widely cited argument about the role of political culture in sustaining democracy, and especially about the crucial importance of "social capital"—the citizens' willingness to engage and interact with each other.

Sabet, Amr G. E. (2008). *Islam and the Political: Theory, Governance and International Relations.* London: Pluto Press. A serious attempt to explore ideas such as development, human rights, and democracy from the perspective of Islam and to compare those views to political theories dominant in Europe and the United States.

Tucker, Robert, Ed. (1978). *The Marx–Engels Reader.* 2nd ed. New York: Norton. An extensive selection of the important writings, with commentaries, from the major theorists of revolutionary socialism, Karl Marx and Friedrich Engels.

ON THE WEB

http://www.nationalgeographic.com

National Geographic has offered rich information and photographs from locations around the world for nearly a century. Some of this material is informative about culture and society in many places, including insights about political culture.

http://www.americanprogress.org/issues/2009/03/progressive_quiz.html

One of several online sites where you can respond to a series of questions about your political beliefs and receive an analysis of your political ideology. Try it!

http://turnabout.ath.cx:8000

This site offers an interesting, quirky, and very diverse array of links to materials associated with "traditionalist conservatism worldwide." Links range across political perspectives from various countries, from conservatism in many of the world's religions to extreme-right fringe groups.

http://www.intellectualtakeout.com

The site promotes individual freedom and limited government and targets college students.

http://www.libertarianism.com

This portal for the libertarian belief system provides clear policy positions and many sources guided by this ideology.

http://internationalsocialist.org

The site of the International Socialist Organization, an association promulgating the Marxist-Leninist perspective, and publisher of the *Socialist Worker* newspaper and the *International Socialist Review* journal.

http://socialist.org

The site of the international democratic socialist movement, it contains information about the people, ideas, and events important to the movement.

http://www.keele.ac.uk/depts/por/ptbase.htm

This rich website hosted by Keele University in England provides many links to key political theorists and political theories.

http://www.independent.org

The Independent Institute, a libertarian organization, provides access to a comprehensive list of various online opinion articles, policy analyses, and book reviews tied to political ideology.

http://www.fordham.edu/halsall/mod/modsbook.html

The Internet Modern History Sourcebook includes numerous links related to important works on major political philosophies as well as key historical documents.

http://www.liberal-international.org

This Web site serves as the electronic home of Liberal International, a worldwide federation of liberal and progressive political parties.

http://www.feminist.com

Feminist.com is an online community designed to promote feminism and women's rights. The site contains a number of articles and speeches related to feminist thought.

Political Actions

Fearless activist, Aung San Suu Kyi has consistently been a strong voice promoting democracy and

LEARNING OBJECTIVES

3.1 Classify the modes of conventional and less conventional individual political action.

3.2 Distinguish between interest groups and political parties.

3.3 Summarize interest group strategies.

3.4 Identify the types of interest groups and the constraints under which they operate.

3.5 Analyze the roles of political parties.

Read and **Listen** to **Chapter 3** at mypoliscilab.com

Study and **Review** the **Pre-Test & Flashcards** at mypoliscilab.com

Imagine that you are walking in a crowd of peaceful protesters. Your group is asking for the basic political right to vote for the candidate of your choice for national office. Ahead of you is a line of heavily armed troops who are blocking your march. Although you are engaged in a nonviolent protest, you know that brutal force has been used against groups like yours in similar situations. What is *your* next step?

In this politically charged instant, one tiny woman moves forward. She walks alone up to the armed troops who aim their weapons directly at her. But no one is ordered to fire or to seize her, and she walks through the troops. You and the others are emboldened to follow her. Do you step forward?

In a country with a repressive and abusive military regime, one person stands tall, although she is only 5 feet 4 inches and weighs less than 100 pounds. Aung San Suu Kyi is a powerful voice for human rights and democratic freedom in Myanmar (some, including the United States, still call it Burma), a country of 54 million in Southeast Asia. This woman is classified as a national security threat by the military junta that has controlled the government of Myanmar since 1962. How can one woman stir up so much anxiety within a military leadership that seems all-powerful and uses extensive violence to subjugate its citizens?

Suu Kyi's first major public speech occurred in 1988 when she addressed nearly 500,000 protesting citizens who had begun a prodemocracy movement that year. Thousands of students participated in these protests, and many citizens risked their jobs and personal security to join her party, the National League for Democracy. When the party won control of the legislature in a 1990 election, Suu Kyi was designated as the prime minister–elect. However, the military dictatorship refused to turn power over to her and the democratically elected representatives. Suu Kyi was awarded the 1991 Nobel Peace Prize for her efforts, although the government would not allow her to travel from Myanmar to accept it.

To intimidate and weaken the members of the opposition movement, the military placed Suu Kyi under house arrest. She has been confined to her own house and prevented from making public speeches or meeting other political leaders for most of the last two decades. Suu Kyi has been attacked by a mob of government goons and accused of tax evasion, leading to brief imprisonment. But she remains visible and refuses to give up the struggle for political and human rights.

Others in Myanmar have been inspired to resist the regime. The prime minister was arrested in 2004 after proposing a "road map to democracy" and allowing Suu Kyi to speak in public.

Many citizens in Myanmar live quietly, intimidated by the ruthless actions of the military and hoping to go unnoticed. But others continue to engage in courageous actions. The Karen people, an ethnic minority, have resisted violently for 60 years, demanding autonomy in eastern Myanmar. Opposition politicians speak out for change and call for fair elections. Massive demonstrations for democracy were held again throughout the country in 2007, drawing more than 100,000 peaceful protesters, which included large numbers of Buddhist monks. The government responded with troops who arrested, beat, and bullied those who were demonstrating, even raiding pagodas to arrest monks. Some protesters were sentenced to 65 years in prison. The regime put Suu Kyi on trial again in 2009 and sentenced her to 18 months of house arrest, after an American swam to her riverfront home to talk with her. Again free, she continues to be an outspoken advocate of democracy. The international community observes the political activities of Myanmar's dictators with concern but takes little direct action.

Most political actions by individuals and groups have complicated and complex motivations. The political actions of the military junta, Aung Sun Suu Kyi, and other prodemocracy protesters in Myanmar are prime examples of attempts to control or shape agendas and events in a society. If you were a citizen in Myanmar, would you have the commitment and courage to stand up against a repressive system? More realistically, have you taken *any* meaningful political actions within the last year? What is the most risky political action you have ever taken?

In Chapter 2, we began our analysis of political behavior by examining the political beliefs of individuals and groups. The next step in our understanding of political behavior is to consider what people *do* politically—not merely what they think. For those people opposed to the regime in Myanmar, political beliefs must be converted into action before they will have any meaningful effect. And in the discussion at Burger King described at the beginning of Chapter 2, the most relevant questions from the perspective of the political world, even more than what you knew or what you thought, are: What did you *say*? What did you *do*?

In this chapter, we examine political participation—*all of the political actions by individuals and groups*. The explicit objective of most political participation is *to influence the actions or selection of political rulers* (Nelson 1993:720). We focus on the prominent modes of actual political behavior in which people engage, and we consider groups as well as individuals because many individuals, such as Aung San Suu Kyi, realize that they can be more effective politically if they act with others rather than alone. Thus, instead of engaging in a lonely act of protest, a person could join a huge demonstration; instead of writing a letter requesting a change in public policy, a person could join an organization that speaks for thousands of people.

What is the range of behaviors that a person might undertake in the political world? At one extreme are people who are obsessed with politics, see political implications in most of life's actions, are constantly involved in political discussion and action, and want to make political decisions for others. At the other extreme are people who have absolutely no interest in politics, pay no attention to political phenomena, and engage in no politically relevant actions. (In some instances, such as not voting in an election to indicate dissatisfaction, not doing something can also be a type of political participation.)

In the first half of this chapter, we examine this full range of individual political actions. In the second half, we analyze the nature and activities of two major forms of political groups: interest groups and political parties. Both individuals and groups share some modes of activity, but the actions of groups can also be analyzed by some additional dimensions because of their size and structure.

INDIVIDUAL POLITICAL ACTIONS

Modes of Political Activity

3.1 Classify the modes of conventional and less conventional individual political action.

👁 Watch the Video "Anti-Globalization Protests" at mypoliscilab.com

There are various ways to classify the modes of individual political action. Empirical studies of political participation consider both the more conventional forms of activity, such as voting, campaigning, contacting officials and participating in civic groups, as well as the less conventional actions such as protesting and even terrorism (Dalton 2008; Verba, Nie, and Kim 1978).

Figure 3.1 classifies the modes of individual political action in terms of two dimensions. The vertical dimension reflects the extent to which the individual engages in the political action, ranging from never to occasional to frequent to pervasive engagement. The second (horizontal) dimension considers the extent to which the political action is more or less conventional. While there are differences in what various people would consider conventional, there is clearly variation across an array of actions. Figure 3.1 suggests labels for those associated with certain domains of political actions. At the four (corner) extremes are those who are totally apathetic about politics, those who have made a full-time vocation of politics as elected officials,

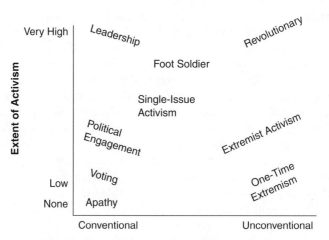

FIGURE 3.1

Some modes of individual political action

those revolutionaries who are passionately committed to transforming the existing political system, and those who are provoked into a rare but highly unconventional action. While we will explore some of these types of political actors and actions throughout this book, we can characterize a few of the main types here. Although most individuals can be labeled by their dominant activity, a particular individual might operate in different action domains at various times (Dalton 2008: Chs. 3, 4; Rueschemeyer, Rueschemeyer, and Wittrock 1998; Verba, Schlozman, and Brady 1995: Ch. 3). For example, an elected official will almost certainly vote, while a revolutionary might vote; and a conventional voter might at some point be mobilized to participate in an unconventional action such as a violent demonstration.

The categories in Figure 3.1 are elements of a *taxonomy*. When you attempt to classify units by some criteria, you are engaged in taxonomic analysis (as discussed in the Appendix). Recall Aristotle's comment that all thinking begins in comparison. In political science, many comparisons begin in taxonomies. Developing a taxonomy is often the first stage in political analysis because it sorts cases into a small number of groups in order to reduce complexity, facilitate comparative analysis, and aid the development of generalizations. Because the categories in a strong taxonomy do not overlap, Figure 3.1 is only a loose taxonomy. You will find numerous taxonomies in this book (e.g., the types of party systems, democracies versus nondemocracies, the Global North and Global South). No single taxonomy is used in all political analyses because each taxonomy emphasizes different aspects of the political world. It will be your decision whether any particular taxonomy seems useful.

Political Activists

Although the more routine modes of political action (listed in the middle and bottom of the left side of Figure 3.1) constitute the vast majority of actual political behavior, many of us are particularly interested in the extraordinary actions of the *political activists, who seem to "live politics"*. Political activists might hold government office, or spend many hours furthering a political goal or leader, or even risk their freedom and life in the pursuit of a political objective. At least three different types of political activists can be identified: foot soldiers, extremist-activists, and political leaders.

Foot Soldiers *Foot soldiers* are *activists who do the basic work of politics.* They link the masses to the government and the top political leadership by performing tasks such as communicating with citizens to promote an issue or a political leader, volunteering in a campaign, or regularly attending political rallies. In most countries, many foot soldiers are members of political parties or groups with a political mission. And most political organizations could not function effectively without foot soldiers.

Single-issue Activists There is another group of political actors who engage in political behavior more sporadically than foot soldiers. These people normally do not participate very actively in the political world, but an issue emerges that mobilizes them into a period of high-level action. For example, some residents in a neighborhood might become agitated when they oppose a plan for a new development that will have negative impacts on their community. They might spearhead a petition drive or organize a disruptive activity such as picketing or a protest march. In an increasing number of settings, people who are dissatisfied with the existing leaders or regime gather in public spaces for what are initially peaceful protests. However, if the regime responds with repression rather than policy change, these individuals can become more mobilized and more aggressive in their demands and their own actions. In recent years, these "people power" movements, primarily composed of individuals who normally engage in very conventional political behaviors, have become more frequent. As in the Myanmar example, many individuals in such countries as Egypt, Ivory Coast, Peru, Syria, Tunisia, and Zimbabwe have recently "taken it to the streets" in modes of political action that, for most of them, are exceptional. Such actions often last for only a short period, and then most return to more conventional modes of political action.

Extremist-activists   *Extremist-activists* are *those who are willing to engage in extensive, unconventional political action in pursuit of their vision of an ideal political outcome* which is substantially different than the existing situation. "Extremism" is a subjective and relative concept—a person is politically extreme only in comparison with some standard position, typically the broad center of the existing political order. Like foot soldiers and single-issue activists, extremist-activists might participate in conventional political activities. However, what distinguishes them is their willingness to engage in very intensive modes of unconventional political action and to sustain their actions over a long period of time. Some individuals can be classified as extremist-activists if their political goals or tactics locate them on the margins of the existing political culture. For example, members of the Earth Liberation Front are linked to violent acts promoting environmentalism in many countries. Another example is the Libyans who mobilized to fight for the overthrow of Muammar Qadaffi—during their armed insurrection, fewer than 1,000 of the thousands who fought Qadaffi's regime had ever fired a weapon before they participated in the armed rebellion.

Political analysts have focused considerable attention on individual extremist-activists who are the most unconventional and fully engaged: the revolutionaries. A *revolutionary* is a person who attempts to overthrow the existing political order and to replace it with a very different one, using political violence if necessary (see Chapter 12). Some well-known revolutionaries, such as Mao Zedong (China), Fidel Castro (Cuba), Ayatollah Khomeini (Iran), and Nelson Mandela (South Africa), eventually attained leadership roles in their political system after years or even decades of struggle. (Two other examples are featured in Compare in 4.) Others, including Che Guevara (Cuba, then Bolivia) and Steve Biko (South Africa), died in the struggle and became martyrs to those committed to revolutionary change.

Many extremist-activists are radical versions of foot soldiers, serving as the members of organizations such as the Revolutionary Armed Forces of Columbia (FARC); the worldwide al-Qaeda ("the Base") network; and ETA, the Basque separatist group in Spain and France. But an increasing proportion of the extremist-activists operate as members of small, relatively independent groups, and occasionally as a "lone wolf" extremist who acts almost completely alone (Sageman 2008). There is strong contemporary interest in extremist–activists who are willing to use *any* tactics and *any* level of violence to achieve their goals. These individuals are often labeled as terrorists because of their extreme tactics, and particularly their willingness to direct violence against those who are not

A youthful and charismatic Enrique Peña Nieto campaigns in 2004 for a Mexican state governorship, which he won. By 2012, he emerged as a top leader and major presidential candidate of the powerful PRI Party.

actively engaged in political struggle (for more details, see Chapters 4 and 12). Most extremist-activists operate in relative obscurity. Eventually, they burn out and drop out, or are captured by the state, or die as a result of political violence.

Political Leaders   Many of us are fascinated with ultimate political activists such as Angela Merkel, Robert Mugabe, Barack Obama, and Vladimir Putin. These top political leaders are distinctive because they succeed in capturing supreme political power within a government and using it with extraordinary energy and effect (whether good or bad). Their titles vary by country and level of government and include chairman, chancellor, dictator, governor, king, mayor, president, prime minister, and supreme leader, among others. A top political leader might put his substantial political power and position to admirable purposes, might implement reprehensible policies, or might accomplish almost nothing. These political leaders have been the subject of more descriptions, analyses, and evaluations than any other type of actors in the political world. They will frequently be the subjects in this book.

Political Participation Studies

After categories of political action are established, a basic research question is: How many people participate in each category, both within and across various national political contexts?

The most reliable comparative empirical data on political participation across many countries measure voting in national elections. Table 3.1 provides these data for selected countries. A striking observation about these figures is the huge variation in voting levels, ranging from a reported 99 percent in Vietnam to only 35 percent in Algeria. Notice the very high voter turnout in countries such as Vietnam, Cuba, and North Korea. In such countries, voting is primarily a symbolic act that is supposed to express support for the existing political leadership, not an action in which citizens select their leaders. In some countries, voting is mandatory (e.g., Argentina, Australia, and Singapore). In some, those in power either engage in election fraud to ensure victory (Afghanistan, Zimbabwe) or repudiate the vote if the outcome is not favorable (as in Myanmar when Aung San Suu Kyi won). These variations in voting alert

TABLE 3.1	
Voting Participation in Selected Countries: Percentage of Eligible Adults Voting in Most Recent Major National Election	
Percentage Turnout	**Countries**
95–100	Australia, Cuba, Vietnam
90–94	Singapore
85–89	Chile, Denmark, Iran
80–84	Brazil, France, Italy, Sweden, Turkey
75–79	Belarus, Cambodia, Malaysia, Palestine (territory), South Africa, Spain, Taiwan
70–74	Argentina, Germany, Ghana, Indonesia, Mongolia, Philippines, Ukraine
65–69	Costa Rica, Finland, Japan, Russia, United Kingdom
60–64	Canada, Iraq, Israel, Swaziland,
55–59	India, Poland, Portugal, Syria, Uganda
50–54	Nigeria
45–49	Hungary, South Korea, Switzerland
40–44	Colombia, Mexico, Pakistan, United States, Zimbabwe
35–39	Algeria, Morocco, Romania
30–34	
25–29	
20–24	
15–19	
10–14	
5–9	
0–4	

Source: International Institute for Democracy and Electoral Assistance, www.idea.int/vt

us to a general problem in cross-national analyses of individual-level political data—the same action or belief might have quite different meaning and significance in different settings.

It is even more difficult to do empirical, cross-national comparisons for modes of individual political participation other than voting. The same act can vary in meaning in different political and cultural environments. For example, the significance and potential personal risk of a public political protest are far greater for a person in North Korea than in South Korea and greater in both those countries than for someone in Sweden.

The most consistent finding in recent comparative research on participation is clear: Apart from voting, which *is* a political act done by many/most citizens, high levels of persistent political activity tend to be uncommon in most political systems. Research reveals that less than 10 percent of the population (and in many countries, considerably less) are political activists who engage in a high level of the more demanding forms of political action such as top leadership, protest, or extensive partisan political work (Dalton 2008: Tables 3.3–3.5; Rueschemeyer, Rueschemeyer, and Wittrock 1998; World Values Survey 2006). In contrast to these political "gladiators," even in an open democracy like the United States, about one-fifth of the adult population engages in no political activity and another one-fifth do little more than vote (Verba, Schlozman, and Brady 1995: 50–54, 72–74).

A second broad finding is that some citizens are willing to engage occasionally in more activist modes of political participation. While very few citizens participate in violent protests against people or property, there is evidence that a significant number of people do perform certain less-conventional political acts, including some actions that require considerable effort or risk. For example, in about half of the countries for which World Values Survey (2006) data are available, 15 percent or more of the citizens have engaged in at least one "challenging act" (e.g., a lawful demonstration, boycott, or building occupation). Compare in 3 and Table 3.2 examine the levels at which the citizens of 10 countries engage in at range of more and less conventional forms of political participation.

Although systematic, comparative data on less democratic and nondemocratic countries are limited, it seems that the reliance on nongovernmental channels and the incidence of unconventional political behavior are greater (and vary more substantially) in those countries than in democratic systems. In some less-democratic countries, state repression deters the great majority of citizens from participation. And there are also countries characterized by "departicipation" because the political leadership has weakened or even eliminated the mechanisms that enable citizens to engage in political actions (Nelson 1987: 116–120). But in recent years, a combination of encouragement from the actions in other countries, use of the new social networking technologies, and coverage by global media has increased the willingness of individuals to join in public protests against unpopular regimes, leaders, and policies (Schmidt and Cohen 2010).

TABLE 3.2

Recent Political Actions by Citizens in 10 Countries

Country (Number of Respondents)	Discuss Politics Often	Often Attempt to Convince Friends on Political Issues	Contact a Politician or Civil Servant to Express Views[*]	Donate Money to Politician or Issue[*]	Boycott or "Buycott" Products for Political or Ethical Reasons[*]	Attend Political Meeting or Rally[*]	Took Part in a Demonstration[*]
Brazil (2,000)	8.0%	17.3%	3.7%	2.3%	3.2%	7.3%	3.6%
Canada (1,211)	10.7	6.7	19.0	27.5	32.4	11.2	5.6
Chile (1,505)	7.0	5.5	6.1	17.0	3.2	2.5	2.9
Mexico (1,201)	10.4	11.3	10.6	23.3	8.5	12.6	7.4
Philippines (1,200)	11.3	9.8	6.5	3.5	2.4	14.3	3.0
Poland (1,277)	9.0	6.3	2.5	12.2	3.0	1.0	0.8
Russia (1,789)	13.0	8.1	3.7	3.9	3.0	3.3	2.8
South Africa (2,784)	5.0	4.5	3.0	5.2	2.8	10.9	4.0
Sweden (1,295)	9.6	7.4	7.2	24.6	36.1	8.2	6.7
United States (1,472)	15.6	12.3	21.9	30.8	24.1	12.5	5.3

[*] Respondent reports behavior within the last 12 months.

Source: International Social Survey Programme (2004).

COMPARE IN 3 | Extent of Political Actions in Mexico and Poland

An individual might engage in a variety of political actions, and Figure 3.1 suggests that these actions range in frequency and conventionality. How much do individuals engage in various political actions? Are there differences in levels of participation across different countries? Table 3.2 presents comparative data on such questions from the International Social Survey Programme, in which 1,200–2,800 individuals in each of 37 countries reported their recent political actions to survey researchers. What observations do you think are supported by the data? Let's briefly assess the political actions of people in Mexico and Poland.

The proportion of individuals engaging in politics in Mexico is greater than the proportion in Poland for every type of political action in the table. Compared to the Poles, Mexicans are nine times more likely to take part in a political demonstration, twelve times more likely to attend a political rally, and four times more likely to contact a politician to express their views. It seems clear that Mexicans engage in political actions at substantially higher levels than Poles. Why do you think this is? While the data in the table cannot explain differences, might this be a reflection of their recent histories?

(Continued)

Even before the Mexican Revolution that began in 1910, Mexicans had a history of political uprisings against their rulers. In the years following 1910, there was a complex set of armed struggles for control of the government. Under activist leaders such as Pancho Villa and Emiliano Zapata, ordinary citizens were encouraged to take part in demonstrations and political violence, with a promise of social and economic justice. Political action was widespread, with civil war and force replacing six governments in just the period from 1911–1928. These uprisings mobilized diverse social classes from both rural and urban areas. The ideas of resistance and revolution became a powerful part of most Mexicans' understandings about governance. Indeed, the dominant political party for seven decades—and still a major party—is called the Institutional *Revolutionary* Party (PRI), and the other two major parties are called the Party of the Democratic *Revolution* (PRD) and the National *Action* Party (PAN).

While Poland also had a tradition of regime change in the 20th century, the situation is different than Mexico. Despite recurrent resistance movements, most Polish regimes were established by outside powers which, especially after 1930, did not allow the Poles much freedom of political action or dissent. The borders of Poland were drawn by the great powers after World War I and substantially redrawn by the victors of World War II. Germany and Russia (and then the Soviet Union) were particularly repressive in controlling the Polish government's policies and ensuring that any serious political opposition by citizens was crushed. After the Communists took control in 1944, political dissent and any forms of anti-government activism were dealt with harshly by the Polish regime. There was a notable three-day protest in Poznan in 1956, but it was quickly crushed by authorities, with support from the Soviet Union. When an independent trade union movement (Solidarity) emerged, martial law was declared in 1981, thousands were jailed, and the extent of activism was limited considerably. In general, the citizens' calculus for anti-regime activism through this period was high costs with minimal benefits.

As noted above, these data cannot prove the reasons for higher or lower levels of participation.

However, it is notable that the three countries that seem least participatory in Table 3.2 (Russia, South Africa, and Poland) all have recent histories as highly repressive regimes that punished political dissent ruthlessly. In contrast, the three countries that seem the most participatory (United States, Canada, and Mexico) all have a strong tradition of rebellion, protests, and activism. It is also interesting that the data suggest that Americans are more politically active than might be expected from recent discussions of the low level of political participation in the United States. The United States is one of the top three countries on the level of participation for six of the seven modes of political activity in Table 3.2. These data about the United States recall a conclusion in the classic book, *The Civic Culture* (Almond and Verba 1963), which termed the United States the most "participatory political culture" in the study.

Like many studies using comparative political data, the data in Table 3.2 can be analyzed in different ways and can lead to somewhat different knowledge claims. For example, Table 3.2 only reports those who *often* discuss politics, but it might also consider those who occasionally discuss politics. In another example, the table focuses only on a single year instead of several years or another year in which the political dynamics in certain countries might be different. Also, might the cross-national differences be greater or smaller if other countries were selected for analysis? The analyst makes a variety of decisions about how data like these are selected, presented and interpreted. This does not mean that the data can be manipulated to produce any conclusion you want; but it should caution you that it is important to evaluate the data and consider multiple alternative interpretations.

FURTHER QUESTIONS

1. Do the data in Table 3.2 seem to support the generalization that most people in these countries are *not* very active in politics?
2. What types of political actions seem to be the best measures of the level of political participation by average citizens? ▲

GROUP POLITICAL ACTIONS

3.2 Distinguish between interest groups and political parties.

✷ Explore the Comparative "Interest Aggregation and Political Parties" on mypoliscilab.com

The actions of Aung San Suu Kyi offer a compelling example of the impact that one extraordinary person can have on the political world. However, even this totally dedicated political activist understood that there is power in numbers. Thus, she worked with many other citizens to establish and build the National League for Democracy, a movement that steadily gained supporters and organized into a political party that stands up against the military dictatorship. College students and Buddhist monks are among the other individuals in Myanmar demanding change, emboldened by the willingness of their peers to join them in the streets. In almost every situation, a political agenda is furthered most effectively when many people form a group.

As an analytic concept, a *group* can be defined as *an aggregation of individuals who interact in order to pursue a common interest* (see also Chapter 9). It is the pursuit of a common interest that is most crucial to this definition because the individuals do not necessarily interact directly with one another. The factor that distinguishes a *political* interest group from other groups is that *the common interest the group pursues is a political objective*—an interest in a particular area of public policy where action might be taken.

A distinction is usually made between political interest groups and political parties, although both types fit under our general definition of political group. A political group enters the special category of political party when the group seeks not merely to influence political decisions, but also to place its members in the actual roles of government such as chief executives and legislators. Although this distinction can become rather fuzzy among the most politically active groups, we shall treat political parties as a category different from other types of political interest groups.

Most people tend to feel that they are relatively powerless in politics when acting alone. But if a person joins with many others in a political group, it is possible that the group can exercise influence in the political world because of the group's numbers, organization, and capabilities. This chapter has provided examples of the impacts on a country's politics when many individuals join in unconventional political behavior, as in the recent populist uprisings in Egypt and Libya. And extremist groups, such as al-Qaeda, might have few members but can generate major effects as they pursue extensive, radical agendas. Group political action in more conventional modes can also have significant consequences. The mobilization of individuals into the "tea party" movement in the United States has enabled this loosely structured array of groups to use the ballot box to elect many new members to national and state office and to pressure most elected officials to shift their policy positions in the directions advocated by the movement.

Groups are also extremely important in politics because they are often the major mechanism through which individuals are linked to the political system—hence their label as "linkage institutions." Some political groups, such as Mothers Against Drunk Driving (MADD) or the German Farmers Association, are narrowly focused in their objectives and have limited membership. Other groups, such as a major political party like Myanmar's National League for Democracy, can have wide-ranging goals and a huge membership. The rest of this chapter describes the nature and activities of various kinds of political groups and political parties.

POLITICAL INTEREST GROUPS
Activities of Political Interest Groups

All political interest groups share the common objective of attempting to influence the allocation of public values. But such groups can employ a variety of strategies to achieve this purpose (Baumgartner and Leech 1998).

3.3 Summarize interest group strategies.

⊙―[**Watch** the **Video "Banking Interests and Regulatory Reform"** at **mypoliscilab.com**

Political Action   The most direct methods to achieve political objectives involve some form of political action. Such action might be taken by all group members or by some members who formally or informally represent the entire group. Depending on the political system, this might entail voting and campaign activities to influence the selection and action of political authorities. Or the group might attempt to communicate its interest to political actors by techniques such as letters, personal contacts, petitions, rallies, or political violence.

Provision of Material Resources   Political interest groups can also provide goods or services to political actors. Such a strategy assumes that providing goods and services will influence decision makers to be more favorably disposed towards the interests of a group. Each political system develops its own rules about the methods and amounts of money or goods that can be given legitimately to political actors. The line between legal and illegal provision of money and goods varies dramatically across political cultures. In some political systems, all it takes to shock people is the revelation that an interest group has given a political actor a small gift, but in many political systems, it requires a multimillion-dollar kickback to a politician to upset citizens and provoke action.

In most countries where there is some transparency in political contributions by private groups, the amount of money involved is substantial. In 2010, for example, interest groups contributed $3.5 billion to lobby government officials and candidates in the United States (Center for Responsive Politics 2011). Most such contributions are legal, although some are problematic; for example, in 1997, the Democratic Party returned more than $1 million to questionable donors, and President Clinton was widely criticized for "renting the Lincoln bedroom" for overnight visits in the White House by big contributors. In South Korea, it is estimated that legislative candidates in contested seats spend 10 times more money on their campaigns than is allowable under the law (Plasser 2002: 149).

The ethics of a system in which political interest groups can make huge contributions is increasingly questioned. It is obvious that interest groups give money in the expectation of influencing public policies. Although cause-and-effect relationships are hard to establish, there are striking linkages between groups' campaign contributions and beneficial legislation (Phillips 2003). In the 1996 election in the United States, for example, tobacco companies contributed $11.3 million; soon after, legislation was passed directing a 15-cent-per-pack cigarette tax to a fund offsetting lawsuits—a $50 billion benefit to the tobacco companies. The broadcasting industry contributed $5 million to members of Congress and soon gained digital TV licensing rights worth $70 billion (Parenti 2010: 200–203). Oil, energy, and natural resource firms contributed $18.3 million and then gained $18 billion in exemptions from the passage of an alternative minimum tax law (O'Connor and Sabato 2007: Figure 16.3).

No one knows the amount of illegal resources that are distributed, although in most countries, scandals regarding bribes and kickbacks seem to be reported with increasing frequency (Johnson 2006). In 2007, for example, former Philippine president Joseph Estrada was found guilty of taking more than $85 million in bribes during his presidency. Among other recent top leaders linked to corruption are Alberto Fujimori of Peru, in prison for embezzling $600 million, and Hosni Mubarak of Egypt, under investigation for accumulating as much as $30 billion in illegal wealth during his administration (Rubenfeld 2011). Evidence surfaced that Samsung executives distributed $205 million in payoffs to South Korean government officials and journalists in 2008 (Bloomberg.com 2009). Halliburton and associated companies are charged with paying more than $180 million in bribes to Nigerian officials for oil and gas contracts (Bala-Gbogbo 2010). In addition, the Chinese government reported more than 9,000 bribery cases involving public officials in the first six months of 2010 (Yan 2010). This is not a new phenomenon. In a wry comment on American politics, humorist Will Rogers once observed that "our Congress is the best that money can buy."

Exchange of Information   Providing data and information to those within the government is another activity performed by some interest groups. The interest group may have specialized information that policymakers would find difficult or impossible to obtain from other sources. These private groups are stakeholders with a vested interest in the public policies that emerge, and so most actively provide data that support their own interests. For example, in the early 1980s, the U.S. Congress began considering a law requiring mandatory air bags as a safety restraint in automobiles. In determining whether to pass such a law, legislators were particularly influenced by information provided by automobile manufacturers (whose data indicated that air bags were costly, would reduce fuel economy, and would not substantially reduce overall injury levels in automobile collisions). This critical information, from a highly interested party to the decision, was an important reason behind the refusal of Congress to require air bags (Reppy 1984). Later in the decade, a barrage of counterinformation from another powerful interest group, the insurance industry, persuaded Congress and the public that air bags could save lives and lower insurance premiums. This resulted in laws requiring air bags.

In many countries, as the scale of government and the reach of public policy have expanded, many organizations in society need detailed, inside information about what the government is doing or intends to do that might affect their organization. Thus, Salisbury (1990; Salisbury et al. 1991) has concluded that American interest groups in Washington, D.C. now spend more time gathering information *from* the government that is relevant to their organizations' interests (e.g., changes in rules or laws) than they do providing information *to* the government that might influence its policies.

Cooperation   Major interest groups can also exert influence through their compliance or noncompliance with the government policy process. In many countries, government actors understand that policy is implemented more successfully when it is acceptable to the affected interest groups. There are many countries (especially industrial democracies such as France, Japan, South Korea, and Sweden) in which government cultivates a special relationship with the interest group representatives of major economic organizations such as business, labor, and farmers. When such interest groups interact directly with the government to formulate and implement policy, they enjoy a privileged position. Governance based on *close cooperation between government agencies and these major sectoral interest groups* is called corporatism. For example, the shortcomings regarding the 2011 Fukushima (Japan) nuclear plant meltdown have been linked to the fact that the government regulatory agencies allowed the nuclear industry to establish and monitor its own safety procedures. Obviously, an organization benefits greatly when its interest group persuades the government to allow the organization to regulate itself.

CONSTRAINTS ON A GROUP'S BEHAVIOR

Each interest group must decide what mix of activities is most likely to serve its political agenda. This mix depends on many factors, including the nature of the group's political resources, the objectives it pursues, and the political environment in which it operates.

3.4 Identify the types of interest groups and the constraints under which they operate.

Explore the Comparative "Interest Groups" on mypoliscilab.com

Political Resources   A group's political resources are *those elements, controlled by the group, that can influence the decisions and actions of political actors.* The political resources that are most effective differ according to the situation and the political system. The preceding section emphasized the potential impact of financial resources and information, but certain other political resources can also be influential: control of factors of production, social status, legality, special knowledge or skills, ability to mobilize large numbers of people who pressure the government, capacity for social disruption, and access to decision makers. Various groups usually have dramatically different levels of all these political resources. An interest group's behavior depends on the kinds of resources it has available and its decision to use a particular mix of resources.

Objectives   The *objectives* that interest groups pursue in the political world are as diverse as the different policy issues on which the government might act. One group might want one specific goal, such as a subsidy for growing wheat, while another group might have very broad objectives, such as a set of policies to eliminate poverty. An interest group's strategies and the probability that it will be successful are related to the group's political objectives. In general, an interest group has an advantage to the extent that its objective (1) is similar to existing policy, and (2) is a decision that the political system has the capacity and motivation to make. For example, the Greenpeace groups in France and Germany are more likely to influence government policies on safer disposal of nuclear wastes than on stopping the development of new nuclear power stations, and these groups have little chance of achieving their broader goal of worldwide nuclear disarmament.

Political Environment   At the most basic level, the demands that groups can make and the actions they can take depend on the boundaries of acceptable political action within the particular *political environment*. Every example of interest group action given thus far in this chapter has focused on a group operating in a democratic political system. An essential feature of democratic systems is that interest groups have extensive rights to make political demands and engage in political actions. Yet there is some disagreement about the extent to which interest groups contribute to healthy democratic processes (see Debate in 3).

In democracies such as Great Britain, Italy, and Japan, professional representatives of interest groups (lobbyists) are as much a part of the accepted set of governmental actors as are elected legislators and their staffs. In Japan, it is common for a senior government official to "descend from heaven" (*amakudari*), leaving his position for a high-paying lobbyist's job for a major corporate interest. In the United States, 13,000 full-time professional lobbyists are registered in Washington, D.C., and one analyst contends that the total number of people engaged primarily in lobbying activities is more than 80,000 (that is, more than 140 lobbyists per member of Congress) (Birnbaum 2005; Center for Responsive Politics 2011).

In contrast, repressive political systems tolerate only a very narrow range of interest group activities that are in opposition to the leadership. In general, however, one of the key factors insuring the survival of a repressive political system is its capacity to stifle or crush opposition interest groups. In these environments, such groups operate on the margins of the political system, and they range from small revolutionary cells such as FARC in Columbia to organized groups such as the Buddhist monks in Myanmar, to mass movements such as the recent democracy demonstrations in Syria and Yemen. Such groups, and especially their leaders, usually face extensive harassment and punishment from the authorities, especially when they "go public." In 2011, for example, the Syrian government killed more than 5,000 and arrested tens of thousands who publicly protested against the Assad regime.

Nonetheless, groups periodically emerge to articulate demands for political, social, and economic changes. Sometimes, the state responds positively to these demands, and occasionally the group protests become so extensive that they drive the regime from power as occurred in the "velvet revolutions" in Europe in 1989 and the uprisings in Tunisia and Egypt in 2011 (see Chapter 12 for more examples). Some interest groups are eventually granted a major role in the political process. This happened in South Africa to the African National Congress, which began in 1912 as an interest group to promote the human rights of black South Africans, was later a government opposition movement, and then an outlawed violent protest group (in 1961); finally, it became the country's major political party whose leaders (from Nelson Mandela to Jacob Zuma) have become presidents of the country.

Types of Interest Groups

A relatively simple taxonomy distinguishes four types of political interest groups: (1) associational, (2) institutional, (3) nonassociational, and (4) anomic (Powell et al. 2012)

THE DEBATE IN 3 | How Interested Are Interest Groups in Democracy?

For as long as democratic governments have existed, there has been ambivalence about political interest groups. On the one hand, democratic theory is grounded in the idea that individuals can and should form political interest groups to influence the selection of officials and to promote public policies that serve their goals. On the other hand, the press, the public, and even some governmental officials are often heard blaming a country's problems on "special interests," which are effective in influencing government to enact policies that serve the interests of specific groups but are not in "the public interest." Do interest groups hinder the democratic process or facilitate it?

INTEREST GROUPS FACILITATE DEMOCRACY

- Interest groups are fundamentally important actors in a democratic system because they enable citizens to organize into groups of sufficient size to communicate their concerns and demands in a clearer, more amplified voice to policymakers (Baumgartner and Leech 1998).
- Interest groups are especially valuable in representing and supporting those groups whose views are not effectively represented by any of the political parties (Berry 2000).
- In a single country, thousands of interest groups can operate at the same time, representing the interests of different groups of people. Because there are so many groups whose voices are heard, no one interest group will go unchecked and become too powerful and influential relative to the others (Dahl 1971).
- Financial contributions from interest groups enable candidates to purchase the expensive media that allow them to communicate their ideas to many citizens and thus enhance the citizens' capacity to participate knowledgeably in the democratic process.
- Interest groups play a very beneficial role in the public policy process. They provide public officials with an enormous amount of relevant, specialized information that public agencies might not be able to gather efficiently and that supports improved policymaking.
- Interest groups serve as an expert watchdog over legislation or policies that public officials might try to implement but that are based on error or are self-serving. By articulating such concerns, interest groups add a valuable level of accountability and monitoring to the process of democratic governance (Berry 2000).

INTEREST GROUPS HINDER THE DEMOCRATIC PROCESS

- Most interest groups work to garner support for a single or narrow set of goals, often at the expense of the interests of the broader society.
- Many interest groups have large professional staffs that work 24/7 to promote their goals. Ordinary citizens rarely have this level of expertise and time commitment for political action, and thus the interests of these ordinary citizens are not as well promoted in the policy process as those of special interests (Parenti 2010).
- Interest groups have specialized information and data that they provide to government officials. Such information can be influential in the policy process, but it also tends to be heavily biased in favor of the interest group's position on issues (Baumgartner et al. 2009).
- Interest groups are the major supplier of personal resources to many political actors. Campaign contributions and other "goodies" can be the source of considerable corruption because they purchase special access to and influence with public officials (Johnson 2006).
- Interest groups form an unnecessary layer that insulates citizens from their government and discourages citizens from engaging in direct democracy (Barber 2004).

(Continued)

MORE QUESTIONS...

1. Can you think of any effective interest groups whose actions are a positive force in making your government work in a more democratic manner? Can you think of any effective interest groups that actually undermine democracy? Are your choices closely linked to *your own* interests and values?

2. Does a system of strong and active interest groups increase or decrease the effectiveness of political parties?

3. Can you imagine an effective political system that has no organized interest groups? ▲

Associational Interest Groups The first type, the associational interest group, is *organized specifically to further the political objectives of its members*. One example is the British Medical Association (BMA), a professional organization promoting public policies that support the goals of its members, 137,000 doctors. The BMA makes major contributions to political parties, provides expert information to government agencies, and guides the doctors' willingness to cooperate with government health policies. Another example is MADD, a primarily volunteer organization whose central goals are to stop drunk driving and underage drinking and to support the victims of drunk drivers. It utilizes its Web site, its network of more than 3 million members in five countries, and a professional lobbying staff to persuade policymakers and judges to impose stringent laws and harsh penalties on drunk drivers. It has trained 1,400 victim-advocates to provide counseling and legal support to victims of drunk drivers.

Institutional Interest Groups This type of group has been formed to achieve goals other than affecting the political system, but it also pursues political objectives. Most occupational and organizational groups recognize that the decisions of the political system sometimes have major impacts on their own interests. Thus, they have a formal or informal subunit whose primary purpose is to represent the group's interests to the political system. For example, the University of California is a large institution of higher education, but its interests are strongly affected by local, state, and national policies on educational funding, research funding, regulation of research, discrimination in admissions and hiring, tax law, patent law, collective bargaining, and many other policies. Consequently, the university has full-time professional and student lobbyists on each campus, in Sacramento (the state capital), and in Washington, D.C.

Nonassociational Interest Groups These groups are fluid aggregates of individuals who are not explicitly associated with a permanent organizational entity but who share some common interest regarding certain issues and become politically active on an issue. A loosely structured organization might temporarily emerge to plan and coordinate political activities, but the group is temporary and relatively informal and, once the issue has lost its immediate salience, the group disappears. If an interest group emerges in your community to stop a building development, or to recall a public official, or to promote a particular law, it can be categorized as a nonassociational interest group. Such an interest group can be also termed a *social movement* when its *activities on an issue of social change become more sustained*, its supporters increase in number and loyalty, and its form becomes more of *an organized campaign spread over a broader geographic area*. Examples include the women's rights movement, the civil rights movement, the indigenous peoples movements, the pro-choice and anti-abortion movements, and the U.S. tea party movement (Givan, Soule and Roberts 2010; Smith 2007).

Anomic Interest Groups These groups are short-lived, spontaneous aggregations of people who share a political concern. These people participate in a group political action that emerges with little or no planning and then quickly stops after the action is completed. A riot is the clearest example of an anomic interest group—the participants tend to share common political interests or grievances that they express through a generally disorganized outpouring of emotion, energy, and violence. A political demonstration is a somewhat more organized version of this type of interest group activity, and this characterizes the initial period of many of the recent "people power" actions described above.

Many taxonomies, like these four types of interest groups, present what Max Weber called ideal types. An ideal type is *a set of distinctive forms of a phenomenon defined in order to reveal the different ways in which key characteristics can be combined*. There are usually no actual, real-world cases that are precisely like

No GMO! Greenpeace activists demonstrate against genetically modified papaya outside the Thai Ministry of Agriculture. In most countries, thousands of interest groups engage in political action in the attempt to influence public policy decisions.

one of the ideal types, and most actual cases blend elements of the different ideal types. Ideal types are analytic constructs that are pure forms meant to facilitate our comparative thinking and our understanding. There will be many sets of ideal types offered in this book, in addition to the four ideal types of interest groups, including types of legislative-executive relations, administrative systems, party systems, political economies, public policies, and political violence.

POLITICAL PARTIES

3.5 Analyze the roles of political parties.

Watch the Video "Party Politics in Scotland" at mypoliscilab.com

Explore the Comparative "Political Parties" on mypoliscilab.com

An interest group is transformed into a **political party** when *the group attempts to capture political power directly by placing its members in governmental office.* The political party is the broadest linkage institution in most political systems because most parties are overarching organizations that incorporate many different interests and groups. While countries can have thousands of political interest groups, most have only a handful of political parties.

Activities of Political Parties

Political parties in most countries engage in six broad activities, functioning to: (1) broker policy ideas, (2) engage in political socialization, (3) link individuals and the political system, (4) mobilize and recruit activists, (5) coordinate governmental activities, and (6) organize opposition to the governing group.

Brokers of Ideas The first, most central activity of political parties is to serve as major brokers of political ideas. Many individuals and political groups have interests and demands regarding the policies of government. A crucial function of political parties is to aggregate and simplify these many demands into a few packages of clear policy alternatives. To the extent that political parties are effective in this activity, they dramatically reduce the complexity and scale of the political process for the decision maker, who must perceive and respond to the individual and group demands, and for the voter, who must select political leaders whose overall policy preferences are closest to his own.

While all political parties are brokers of ideas, parties can be differentiated into two broad categories—ideological and pragmatic—on the basis of their intensity of commitment to those ideas. *Ideological parties* hold major programmatic goals (e.g., egalitarianism, ethnic solidarity, Islamic fundamentalism) and are deeply committed to the full implementation of these goals. Ideological parties are usually extreme within the context of their particular political culture. The German Green Party, described in Focus in 3, is an example of an ideological party. Others include the Islamic Salvation Front (FIS) in Algeria, the North Korean Communist Party, Sínn Fein in Northern Ireland, and the American Libertarian Party.

In contrast, *pragmatic parties* hold more flexible goals and are oriented towards moderate or incremental policy change. To achieve electoral success, pragmatic parties might shift their position or expand the range of viewpoints they encompass. Parties of the center are characteristically pragmatic parties. Examples include the Christian Democrats in Germany, the Congress Party in India, the

FOCUS IN 3 | Let's Party! The Rise of the Green Party in Germany

Few political interest groups transform into successful, modern political parties. The Green Party in Germany has achieved this transformation. It began as a diverse set of loosely affiliated interest groups in the 1960s and declared itself a political party in 1980. Its electoral fortunes in the national legislature have gone up and down (starting with 3.7 percent of the seats in 1983, dropping as low as 0 percent of the seats in 1990, and currently holding 10.9 percent of the seats).

Where did the Green Party come from? Like all political groups, it began with people who wanted to influence politics. In the late 1960s, some West Germans were displeased with their government's support of U.S. actions in Vietnam and Southeast Asia. Some believed that their government, and the entire "establishment" in their society, had been corrupted in its quest for ever-expanding power and wealth. And some had other policy concerns, including the huge inequalities in wealth and welfare within their society and among countries, the discrimination against certain groups such as women and ethnic minorities, the frightful build-up of nuclear weapons by the superpowers, and the degradation of the environment.

People with these various political beliefs, energized mainly by young countercultural Germans, demonstrated, marched, and formed local protest groups. These groups began to elect some of their members to local office, especially in larger cities. The most dynamic people in these local groups developed a national network, and in 1980 they formed a national political party, *Die Grünen* (the Greens).

The common concern that attracted many individuals to the Green Party was its commitment to preserving the environment. In Europe, the Greens became the first important party representing the "self-expressive, postmaterialist values" discussed in Chapter 2.

The Green Party remains an ideological party, and its party platform includes strong anti-establishment elements. The party ideology emphasizes the transformation of Germany: from a leading postindustrial society to one that uses only those technologies that do not damage the environment; from elite domination to broad democratic participation; from capitalism to a system in which workers own and control industry; from a militaristic, NATO-based country to one that becomes neutral, eliminates nuclear weapons, and stops preparing for war.

The Green Party had a substantial impact on German politics in the 1980s but struggled for electoral support in the early 1990s. In 1993, it merged with three East German progressive parties and is now called Alliance 90/The Greens. This merged party was a somewhat uneasy junior partner in a governing coalition with the large Social Democratic Party (1998–2005). It opted to remain outside the conservative-led "grand coalition" of parties (2005–2009) and the current government, both under Chancellor Angela Merkel.

The future of the Alliance 90/Green Party at the national level remains uncertain. Germany is both the largest economy and the political leader within the European Union. Although the country is still attempting to improve the economic conditions in the formerly communist East Germany, which merged with West Germany in 1990, the German population is generally prosperous and enjoys a high standard of living. Recent economic problems associated with the global economic slowdown and hostility towards the large immigrant population are among the policy issues that have created electoral swings towards more conservative political parties. However, the German citizenry is one of the world's most secular and self-expressive in terms of political culture (recall Figure 2.1),

(Continued)

and thus a portion of the electorate might continue to support the progressive policies of the Alliance 90/Green Party. Will it be outflanked by the more radical Left Party or absorbed by the large Social Democratic Party in the left center? Can it avoid self-destruction caused by the strong ideological differences among its moderate and more radical factions? Some analysts suggest that this party is too wild to last much longer.

FURTHER FOCUS

1. What condition(s) might substantially increase or decrease the support for Germany's Green Party?
2. What policy positions are most likely to benefit and harm electoral support for "green" parties in most countries? ▲

Institutional Revolutionary Party (PRI) in Mexico, and the Democratic Party in the United States.

Agents of Political Socialization   A related activity of political parties is their socialization of people into the political culture (see Chapter 4). In some countries, most people develop a clear "party identification," which means that a person has a strong attachment to one political party he trusts to represent his political interests. The person's political beliefs and actions are influenced by information that a political party provides or by the person's perceptions of what the party supports. Even if a person does not have a strong party identification, political parties can be an important source of his political knowledge because they provide easily understood reference points regarding politically relevant information.

Links between Individuals and the System   In its role as a linkage institution, a political party connects individuals and the political system. Most individuals rely on political groups to represent their interests within the political system. More than other groups, political parties function in a general manner to formulate, aggregate, and communicate a coherent package of demands and supports. If the party gains political power, it can attempt to implement those demands on behalf of the individuals whose interests it serves. Thus political parties greatly facilitate the individual's sense of integration into the political process.

Mobilization and Recruitment of Political Activists   The political party offers a well-organized and obvious structure within which a person can direct his political interests. It is a source of political information, of contact with other politically relevant individuals and groups, and of effective access to the political system. In many political systems, involvement with a political party is the primary mechanism through which individuals are drawn into roles as political foot soldiers and, ultimately, as political leaders. Often, political parties select the candidates for political positions or have the power to place people directly in positions within the political system. Whether one is considering a highly democratic polity such as Great Britain or an extremely nondemocratic one such as China, most individuals in key executive and legislative positions have achieved these positions through recruitment and selection by a political party.

Coordination of Governmental Operations   The fifth major activity of political parties is to coordinate the actions of the government. The political party can encourage or require its members to work together to achieve shared policy goals. It can establish an internal hierarchy, with party leaders (e.g., in the U.S. Senate, majority and minority leaders, whips, and committee chairs) controlling the actions of party members in the conduct of government. The parties can also provide mechanisms for facilitating cooperation and regulating conflict among different parties. Leaders of several parties might form a coalition to secure majority support for certain policies. Such coalitions are especially important in legislatures in which no single party commands a majority. Political parties can also establish forms of power sharing in the conduct of government business. For example, the parties can agree to formulate executive or legislative committees in a manner that reflects the political strength of the various parties.

Organized Sources of Opposition   Finally, where the political system has more than one party, the parties not participating in the governing group can serve as an explicit and organized source of opposition. The function is fully institutionalized in Great Britain, where the major out-of-power party in Parliament is explicitly designated as "Her Majesty's Loyal Opposition." This party should oppose, but never obstruct, the actions of the governing party because the opposition party remains loyal to crown and country. In Britain, the opposition party is guaranteed control of a specified amount of time during legislative sessions. The opposition leaders receive salaries to serve as a "shadow government," with a member of the opposition serving as the alternative and potential future replacement for each top official in the government. Hence, there is a shadow prime minister, a shadow minister of defense, and so on, who articulate what they would do if they held ministerial positions as the governing party.

DOING POLITICS

Politics comes alive when people engage in political action. Participation in a protest march, the attempt to persuade a friend to share your political perspective, and even the act of voting can be a moment of heightened experience. Acting alone or with others, the individual who takes political action might seek to serve his own crass self-interest, or a national goal such as democratic governance, or an altruistic goal such as global peace.

   This chapter should increase your awareness of the diverse modes of political action as well as the rather modest levels of such actions usually reported by most people. Some people are shocked that so many citizens do not even bother to vote in a country such as the United States. Others are surprised that anyone really thinks that one person's involvement in politics, whatever the level of commitment, will make any difference in the grander scheme of things. Yet events, such as recent ones in the Middle East, might challenge some assumptions about the limited impact of group political action. Political participation is a crucial topic in our developing understanding of the nature of the political world because people's actions are at the heart of the political process.

✓•⟮**Study** and **Review** the **Post-Test & Chapter Exam** at **mypoliscilab.com**

In this chapter, you have been introduced to methods and findings from the study of individual and group political actions. To this point, our treatment of political behavior has focused mainly on description and taxonomy—on what people believe about politics and on what political actions people undertake. For a richer analysis, however, we must at least attempt to answer the *why* questions: Why do people engage in a particular political action? Can we explain the apparent differences in people's political beliefs? Explaining political beliefs and actions is the central topic in Chapter 4.

KEY CONCEPTS

associational interest group 74	political activists 61
corporatism 71	political environment 72
extremist-activists 62	political participation 59
foot soldiers 61	political party 68
group 68	political resource 71
ideal types 75	pragmatic party 76
ideological party 76	social movement 75
(political) interest group 68	taxonomic analysis 61

FOR FURTHER CONSIDERATION

1. Why might the absence of a political action be viewed as an act of political participation?
2. Apart from voting, what political action do you think is most important?
3. Imagine that you could engage in a conversation with the political activist—contemporary or historical—who most fascinates you. Whom would you choose? Why? What would you ask him or her?
4. Should there be any limits on a group's actions to influence political decision makers? What principles can you offer to justify any such limitations?
5. What is the most unconventional political action in which you have engaged? If the same circumstances arose now, would you behave any differently? Why?

FOR FURTHER READING

Ackerman, Peter, and Jack DuVall. (2001). *A Force More Powerful: A Century of Non-Violent Conflict.* New York: Palgrave. A series of engaging case studies set in many countries (e.g., Chile, Denmark, Poland, Serbia) reveals how political activism grounded in strategies of nonviolence (e.g., strikes, protests, boycotts) has achieved major political change in the face of repressive regimes and dictatorial leaders.

Ahmed, Shamima and David Potter. (2006). *NGOs in International Politics.* Bloomfield, CN: Kumarian Press. A sensible description of the actions and impacts of major NGOs (nongovernmental organizations) that operate as global citizen activists and service providers, as they work with and around national governments.

Aung San Suu Kyi and Alan Clements. (2008). *Aung San Suu Kyi: The Voice of Hope: Conversations.* Updated and rev. ed. New York: Seven Stories Press. Former Buddhist monk Clements presents moving conversations secretly recorded in Myanmar with Aung

San Suu Kyi (recall the chapter opener). Her extraordinary blend of spirituality, love, courage, and defiance are reflected in her approach of activist Buddhism.

Baumgartner, Frank, Jeffrey Berry, Marie Hojnacki, David Kimball and Beth L. Leech. (2009). *Lobbying and Policy Change: Who Wins, Who Loses and Why.* Chicago: University of Chicago Press. Based on an extensive study of cases, the authors argue, that most lobbies, even well-funded ones, tend to be less effective in shifting U.S. policy than most people assume.

Beah, Ishmael. (2007). *A Long Way Gone.* New York: Farrar, Straus and Giroux. A dramatic and remarkable autobiography of a Sierra Leone boy who is captured and trained as a child soldier. He describes his violent world and how he escapes it and establishes a new life for himself.

Bohlen, J. (2000). *Making Waves: The Origins and Future of Greenpeace.* Montreal: Black Rose. The fascinating history, written by one of its founders, of an international interest group committed to fighting governments and huge corporations in order to protect the environment.

Chan, Stephen. (2011). *Southern Africa: Old Treacheries and New Deceits.* New Haven, CN: Yale University Press. Richly textured analyses are offered for five men who have dominated the politics of South Africa and Zimbabwe in recent decades: Mandela, Mbeki, Mugabe, Tsvangirai, and Zuma.

Cigler, Allan J., and Burdett Loomis, Eds. (2011). *Interest Group Politics.* 8th ed. Washington, DC: CQ Press. Thoughtful essays on how interest groups operate in the American political context during an era characterized by a huge infusion of money into the policy process, single-interest politics, social movements, and the Internet.

Givan, Rebecca Kolins, Sarah Anne Soule and Kenneth Roberts, Eds. (2010). *The Diffusion of Social Movements: Actors, Mechanisms and Political Effects.* New York: Cambridge University Press. A series of studies explore how social movements regarding such issues as creationism science, human rights, and genetically modified foods emerge, spread, and affect the public policy domain.

Greenwood, Justin. (2011). *Interest Representation in the European Union.* 3rd ed. Basingstoke, England: Palgrave Macmillan. An exploration of the roles, behaviors, and impacts of various types of interest groups (e.g., business, "the public," professional groups, and labor) in the context of the European Union (EU) as a supranational policy-making body that also must link with national governments and a multitude of interest groups.

Hoffman, Abbie. (1989). *The Best of Abbie Hoffman.* New York: Four Walls, Eight Windows. A selection of the funny, irreverent writings on radicalism and revolution by one of the key leaders (now deceased) of the student radical movement of the late 1960s and a member of the Chicago 7, tried for conspiracy after the riots at the 1968 Democratic Party convention in Chicago.

Jensen, Jane. (2008). *Women Political Leaders: Breaking the Glass Ceiling.* New York: Palgrave Macmillan. The pathways to power and the challenges facing 60 women (e.g., Benazir Bhutto in Pakistan, Michelle Bachelet in Chile, Kim Campbell in Canada, and Ellen Johnson Sirleaf in Liberia) who have achieved the highest positions in their governments are explored.

Loader, Brian D., Paul G. Nixon, Dieter Rucht, and Wim van de Donk, Eds. (2004). *Cyberprotest: New Media, Citizens, and Social Movements.* London: Routledge. A useful set of essays exploring how the new information and communication technologies (ICTs) are utilized in Europe by activists (citizen groups and social movements) in an attempt to mobilize other citizens and pressure governments to respond to their demands.

Lowi, Theodore. (1979). *The End of Liberalism: The Second Republic in the United States.* 2nd ed. New York: Norton. An incisive critique of the shortcomings of politics dominated by interest groups.

Ma Bo. (1995). *Blood Red Sunset: A Memoir of the Chinese Cultural Revolution.* New York: Viking. A harsh, gripping autobiography of a young person drawn into the fervor of Mao Zedong's Cultural Revolution. A Red Guard working on a hopeless program to create farmland in Mongolia, Ma Bo is transformed from a true believer into an embittered man fighting to clear himself from charges that he is a reactionary.

Meisner, Maurice, and Gareth Schott. (2006). *Mao Zedong: A Political and Intellectual Portrait.* London: Polity Press. An illuminating biography of one of the most remarkable leaders of the 20th century, emphasizing both his personal qualities and his enormous impact on the evolution of politics and economics in China.

Rueschemeyer, Dietrich, Marilyn Rueschemeyer, and Bjorn Wittrock. (1998). *Participation and Democracy East and West: Comparisons and Interpretations.* Armonk, NY: M. E. Sharpe. The patterns of citizen participation and activism are compared and analyzed, grounded in studies of the Czech Republic, Germany, Hungary, Norway, Poland, Sweden, and the United States.

Till, Brian Michael. (2011). *Conversations with Power: What Great Presidents and Prime Ministers Can Teach Us About Leadership.* New York: Palgrave Macmillan. Till, a recent U.S. college graduate, manages to interview many of the most fascinating top leaders of our era, including Gorbachev, de Klerk, Carter, Musharraf, Barak, Havel, and Clinton. The book includes his narratives about each leader and their answers to his pointed questions.

Volgy, Thomas J. (1999). *Politics in the Trenches: Citizens, Politicians, and the Fate of Democracy.* Tucson: University of Arizona Press. A political science professor offers a brief, highly readable and revealing description of the challenges and actual experiences of political leaders in American local politics, based on his many years as a local government elected official and his interviews with more than 300 elected officials.

Zaeef, Salam. (2010). *My Life with the Taliban.* New York: Columbia University Press. A fascinating inside look at the thinking and actions of the leadership in the Taliban through the eyes of an Afghan who became a top official in their movement.

ON THE WEB

http://www.politics1.com/parties.htm
   This site offers a directory and description of U.S. political parties.

http://www.ifex.org
   The International Freedom of Expression Exchange represents more than 80 organizations in 50 countries committed to human rights and civil liberties and describes current situations of concern.

http://www.idea.int
   The International Institute for Democracy and Electoral Assistance (IDEA) provides information about current democratic practices and various relevant databases for more than 100 countries, including comparative data on voter turnout for both presidential and parliamentary elections covering the period since 1945.

http://www.greenpeace.org/usa
   Greenpeace's U.S. Web site describes some of the key initiatives taken by this global, action-oriented interest group.

http://www.uschamber.com/default
   This Web site of the U.S. Chamber of Commerce, the world's largest business federation, representing more than 3 million large and small businesses and, according to some, the most powerful lobby group in the United States.

http://pol.moveon.org

The site for a progressive citizen action group in the United States that mobilizes its 3.3 million members to engage in political activism.

http://www.protest.net

This Web site provides a comprehensive calendar of upcoming protests and political rallies taking place around the world. The site lists upcoming protests by both geographic region and political issue.

http://www.internationalanswer.org

This Web site serves as the electronic home of International ANSWER, a coalition of antiwar and antiracism groups, providing information about movements taking place throughout the international community.

http://www.sociosite.net/topics/activism.php

This site, developed by Washington State University, provides a number of links and articles related to both American and global social movements.

http://www.amnesty.org

Amnesty International has been dedicated to human rights causes for more than 40 years, with 2.2 million members in 150 countries. The site provides information on a variety of topics ranging from refugees to arms control.

http://civicyouth.org

The Center for Information and Research on Civic Learning and Engagement (CIRCLE) promotes research on the civic and political engagement of Americans between the ages of 15 and 25. The organization's Web site offers a variety of interesting data and studies on this topic, including research papers on youth participation and strategies for mobilizing young adults into political participation.

Influences on Beliefs and Actions

Our hero! Belarus children (literally) sing the praises of their President. Schools provide the state with a powerful setting in which to teach (indoctrinate?) children about the state's version of appropriate political beliefs and actions.

LEARNING OBJECTIVES

4.1 Assess how the context in which individuals live impacts their political beliefs and actions.

4.2 Characterize the different agents of political socialization.

4.3 Illustrate how personal characteristics are linked to political beliefs and actions.

4.4 Distinguish normative from empirical approaches to understanding political personality.

The following five excerpts are from school textbooks used in different countries. In each, what subject is being taught, and from what country might each textbook come?

1. Add "not" to the following sentence: "The Iranians are brave."
2. Our forefathers believed, and we still believe today, that God himself made the diversity of peoples on earth.... Interracial residence and intermarriage are not only a disgrace but also forbidden by law. It is, however, not only the skin of the Betas that differs from the Alphas. The Beta stands on a much higher plane of civilization and is more developed. Betas must so live, learn, and work that we shall not sink to the cultural level of the Alphas. Only thus can the government of our country remain in the hands of the Betas.
3. Imperialism knows no other type of relations between States except domination and subjugation, the oppression of the weak by the strong. It bases international relations on abuse and threat, on violence and arbitrariness. Between January 3 and June 10, 1961, Gamma military airplanes violated Delta airspace 3 times in the month of January, 15 in February, 17 in March, 9 in April, 8 in May, and 10 in June. What was the average monthly number of violations of Delta airspace by Gamma military airplanes?
4. Which of the following descriptions of the United States is incorrect?
   a. The world's leading arms-exporting country.
   b. The world's most heavily nuclear-armed country.
   c. The world's leader in chemical weapons research.
   d. The world's most peace-loving country that never once was at war with other countries.
5. The instinctual state of the ants corresponds to the leadership state among mankind...the principles of a perfect insect state give people cause to think. They have preserved bees and ants in the struggle for survival and thereby proved their validity. We earlier noted the following truths...:

   ■ The work of the individual has only one purpose: to serve the whole group.
   ■ Major accomplishments are possible only by the division of labor.

Read and Listen to Chapter 4 at mypoliscilab.com

Study and Review the Pre-Test & Flashcards at mypoliscilab.com

- Each...risks its life without hesitation for the whole.
- Individuals who are not useful or are harmful to the whole are eliminated.
- The species is maintained by producing a large number of offspring.

It is not difficult for us to see the application of these principles to mankind:...The ethnic state must demand of each individual citizen that he does everything for the good of the whole, each in his place and with his abilities. And if a person acts against the general interest, he is an enemy of the people and will be punished by the law. A look at our history proves that we as a people must defend our territory to preserve our existence.

Many factors can influence an individual's political beliefs and political actions. The educational system certainly can be one of those influences. To most observers, each of the examples above might be characterized as a crude form of indoctrination. In each case, those controlling the state also controlled the content of the educational system. And that content is created and taught in certain ways in the attempt to shape the behavior of the people raised in that society.

Do you have an idea of the source of any of the textbook excerpts above? Example 1 is from a recent Arabic-language arts textbook for sixth-grade Iraqi students (Robinson 2003). Example 2 is from a South African high school textbook on race relations during the era of apartheid (1948–1988, substitute "whites" for "Betas" and "nonwhites" for "Alphas") (Thompson 1966: 100). Example 3 is mathematics as it is framed for Cuban middle school students (substitute "Cuban" for "Delta" and "North American" for "Gamma") (Fagen 1964: 68). Example 4 is an item on a 2003 history test for South Korean eighth graders (Demick 2003). And Example 5 is from a biology text for fifth-grade German girls during World War II (Harm and Wiehle 1942).

The textbook examples above lack subtlety. Even as a young child, you would have recognized and resisted such manipulation...right? Is it possible that your own education presented you with ideas that manipulated your thinking about politics—even if in much more subtle ways? Who or what shaped your ideas and actions in the political world? The attempt to answer that question is the central theme of this chapter and the next step in our journey towards becoming more informed political thinkers.

In analyzing political behavior in Chapters 2 and 3, we focused on *describing* the political beliefs and political actions of individuals and groups. In this chapter, we explore some of the interesting *why* questions in this analysis of political behavior. Can we *explain* why individuals hold particular political beliefs and why they engage in certain political actions? Figure 4.1 indicates four broad types of explanatory factors that might account for individual political behavior: (1) the environment, (2) agents of political socialization, (3) personal characteristics, and (4) personality and human nature. This chapter considers these four types of influences on the political beliefs and actions of individuals, from the apathetics to the activists.

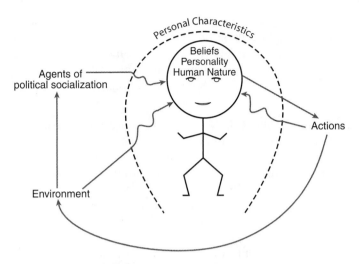

FIGURE 4.1
A framework for explaining individual political behavior

THE ENVIRONMENT

In the national election in Vietnam in 2011, it was reported that 99.5 percent of the adults voted, whereas in the United States, 41.6 percent of the citizens voted in the 2010 national election. What best accounts for this difference? In Vietnam, voting is an obligatory act, a required gesture of support for the current political leadership, rather than a genuine selection among candidates—indeed, there is no choice. Most Vietnamese vote because someone who does not vote risks unwanted scrutiny by Communist Party authorities. In the United States, voting has always been a voluntary act, and there are no sanctions for not voting. Thus, the citizen decides whether her sense of civic responsibility or her desire to affect the outcome on ballot choices merits the effort of going to vote.

The example of voting in Vietnam and the United States is suggestive of how a person's *environment—the broad context in which an individual lives*—can powerfully influence her political behavior. In its most comprehensive form, the environment includes literally everything outside the individual. It obviously includes political elements (e.g., governmental procedures, public policies, specific political events, and actors), but it also includes elements of the social and cultural system (e.g., religious foundations and attitudes towards ethnicity, gender, and class), elements of the economic order (e.g., level of economic prosperity and development), and the physical features of the environment (e.g., topography and natural resources).

For any particular political belief or action, there are various possible effects from an environmental stimulus. An element of the environment might activate, repress, transform, or amplify a person's political behavior. Most elements of the environment are likely to have little or no effect at any given moment, so

4.1 Assess how the context in which individuals live impacts their political beliefs and actions.

Watch the Video **"Deforestation in the Brazilian Amazon"** at **mypoliscilab.com**

the task of the political analyst is to identify those few environmental elements that do have especially significant effects on political belief or action and to explain how these effects occur. Because the environmental context is—at least in theory—of enormous scope, it is helpful to consider different ways in which the environment might affect behavior. Here are two examples regarding the *political environment*:

1. **Effects on information about politics.** In Myanmar, the government strictly limits the information available about politics, so many citizens have only minimal knowledge of the current politics, even of their own country. In the United States, the interested citizen has access each day to information about worldwide political events from hundreds of hours of television and radio programming and even more Internet sites and other reading materials.

2. **Effects on individuals' political party involvement.** From the late 1940s to the late 1980s, Bulgaria had only one legal political party, the Communist Party. Party membership, open to only about 10 percent of the population, was essential for any citizen who wanted to hold political office or gain major advantages in the society, such as quality housing (see Chapter 15). Currently, Bulgaria has 18 active political parties, and six parties hold seats in the parliament. Party membership and opportunities to run for public office are now open to all Bulgarians. However, party membership no longer provides the advantages that it did during the communist period, and thus the proportion of Bulgarian adults who are active party members of *all* political parties is actually lower now under multiparty democracy than it was during one-party communism.

The broader *cultural, social, economic, and physical environments* can have indirect but no less powerful influences on a person's political behavior than the political environment. For example, if the dominant religion in the cultural environment has traditionally relegated women to a secondary role—as in countries such as Saudi Arabia that adhere to the sharia laws of Islam—it is likely that few women will be political activists. If the social environment has an undercurrent of racism, this will affect the voting behavior of both the majority and minority racial groups. If the economy has very high unemployment, this will influence policy decisions about job creation. Can you think of ways in which even a country's physical environment could influence politics? (Read the Compare in 11 if you cannot).

The impact of the environment on political behavior is sometimes hard to predict. If poverty is widespread in an economic system, will this influence the probability of political rebellion? On the one hand, such poverty might produce a frustrated population that will be responsive to a revolutionary movement promising future prosperity, and it might inspire a particular person to become very active in such a movement. On the other hand, the people might be too concerned about basic survival to have the time and/or energy to engage in political action.

It should be evident from these examples that many aspects of the environment might influence political beliefs and actions. The analyst must be sensitive to possible environmental effects when attempting to provide an adequate explanation for a particular political behavior.

AGENTS OF POLITICAL SOCIALIZATION

Each person has a complex blend of political beliefs—of cognitive, affective, and evaluative orientations regarding political phenomena. (These three kinds of orientations were defined in Chapter 2.) Even individuals who live in the same environment can hold very different political beliefs. Political socialization research attempts to explain the sources of individuals' political beliefs.

Political socialization can be defined as *the processes through which individuals acquire their beliefs and values about the political world*. An understanding of how this process works is of obvious importance not only to political analysts but also to those who wish to influence people's political beliefs and actions, especially political leaders. Plato (ca. 428–347 B.C.E.) observed that society's most important function is civic training and instructing citizens regarding the nature of their social and political world and their proper roles in that world. The appropriate content and style of such political socialization are subject to debate because one person's vision of proper civic training might be viewed by another person as indoctrination and brainwashing.

Political scientists attempt to analyze the **agents of political socialization**—the *major sources of political training and indoctrination shaping an individual's political beliefs and values*. The main focus has been to explain the processes through which the key agents of socialization affect political beliefs. There has been considerably less attention, and very limited empirical success, in demonstrating a link between the activities of a specific agent of socialization and individuals' actual political actions. In this section, we discuss some of the most important agents of political socialization: the family, schools, peer groups, the media, religion, culture, and events.

4.2 Characterize the different agents of political socialization.

Explore the Comparative "Identity" on mypoliscilab.com

The Family

The family is the first—and often most powerful and lasting—agent of political socialization. The political orientations of most individuals are deeply influenced by the behaviors and beliefs they experience in the family environment. Before individuals are capable of making judgments for themselves, they have absorbed perceptions about the political world from conversations overheard within the family. For example, most 7-year-old children in the United States already identify with one political party and have affective orientations towards both major parties (Jennings, Markus, and Niemi 1991).

Even the pattern of interactions between parents and children can have political implications. If the family is very hierarchical—with the father or mother ruling with an iron hand, preventing discussion, and using strong sanctions for disobedience—the child might conclude that this is the appropriate pattern of authority relationships in the society. If the family tends to discuss issues before it makes rules or decisions, the child might feel more strongly that she has the right to participate actively in decisions, even in the political world. The political leadership usually has minimal control over the political socialization that occurs in the family. Indeed, the family can transmit values that are at variance with those preferred by the state and its leaders. The Focus in 4 describes how Mao Zedong used the other agents of political socialization to counteract the influence of the family in China.

FOCUS IN 4 | Political Socialization in China

Contemporary Chinese political culture is shaped by many forces. Historically, the most critical influence on the cultural norms in China is Confucianism. Based on the teachings of a fifth-century B.C.E. Chinese intellectual, *Confucian culture* stresses that *individual action must be based on what is best for the group and for society as a whole*. Harmony and cooperation are always to be sought, and disunity and conflict must be avoided. Confucianism places the highest value on *order, stability, and discipline* within a framework of hierarchical authority. Society is shaped by a series of superior–subordinate relationships in which obedience must be offered: by subject to ruler, by child to parent, by younger to elder, and by female to male.

Such principles powerfully support a political system in which authoritarianism is natural and acceptable. The political elite is justified in taking any action that maintains harmony and order or that serves the broader interests of the society—regardless of the costs to individuals or groups (e.g., political parties, unions, and students).

When Mao Zedong came to power in China in 1949, his commitment to egalitarianism and a revolutionary restructuring of Chinese society placed him in direct conflict with Confucian values. He deeply opposed the Confucian ideals valuing tradition over change, males over females, and older people over younger people. To transform China into a new society associated with his interpretation of Marxism, Mao dealt aggressively with all the key agents of political socialization.

Mao attacked all forms of *religion*—including Confucianism—and used the power of the state to suppress religious practices and to force all the people to embrace atheism. He viewed the *family* as the most important agent of socialization in Confucian norms. He tried to eliminate the nuclear family through collective child-rearing. When that failed, he demanded that the family must "revolutionize itself," but he soon concluded that families would continue to be a "citadel of oppression." Thus, he emphasized other agents of

political socialization to shift cultural norms from Confucianism to communism.

He utilized the *schools* as the primary agent of socialization. Students were relentlessly drilled on the values of the new communist social order and taught that the norms of Confucianism constituted reactionary, unacceptable thinking that would be harshly punished. Every aspect of the curriculum and textbooks were grounded in Marxist thinking, whether it was history, literature, or science. Students were also given a book of Mao's political comments, *The Little Red Book*, that many memorized completely and recited at school, at home, and in public marches.

Mao altered *peer relations*. He promoted gender equality, placing women in positions of authority within the Communist Party, major organizations, and government councils. He enacted the Marriage Law of 1950, which gave a woman rights to take legal recourse against bodily harm by her husband, to initiate a divorce, and to own property. These rules were a direct repudiation of Confucian norms, in which a wife was the property of her husband, who could exploit or dispose of her as he wished. He outlawed foot binding, a practice in which many young girls had their feet wrapped tightly with cloth every day so that their toes did not develop properly, preventing them from walking freely (and making them more dependent on males).

Mao also mobilized young people as active participants in the revolution. They were encouraged to report any counterrevolutionary action, even by their parents or friends, and many did so. He established the Red Guards, a grassroots organization composed primarily of teenagers. The Red Guards were empowered to attack "the four olds" of society—old ideas, cultures, manners, and customs. For example, the Red Guards destroyed 5,000 of China's 7,000 temples. They would parade "capitalist roaders" (anyone accused of lacking enthusiasm for the revolutionary changes in society) through the streets, ridicule them, and beat or kill them.

(Continued)

Mao used Communist Party membership to grant power and authority to those loyal to his ideology. At every level in society—whether a large collective farm, a factory, a school, or a village—real power was held by members of the party who enforced the "mass line" on all others. Those who deviated from Mao's vision were subjected to intense criticism from their peers and, if peer pressure and "re-education" failed to make them recant and behave properly, they would lose privileges (like good jobs and housing), be tortured and imprisoned, or executed.

Also, the *media and modes of cultural expression* became instruments of absolute support for Communist Party viewpoints. Television, newspapers, and other media were all owned by the state. No independent perspectives were allowed. Plays, music, art works, and all other forms of culture were required to reflect "socialist realism"—a celebration of the glorious revolution, of the heroic struggle of the workers and peasants in overthrowing the feudal regime under the emperor and the privileged classes, and of the new utopia of communist egalitarianism and abundance shared by all. The state engaged in extensive censorship, destroyed counterrevolutionary cultural works, and punished any who used artistic expression to criticize the party or the state.

Few modern societies have controlled the agents of political socialization with such intensity and pervasiveness as in Mao's China. In the face of extensive coercion and socialization, very few were willing to challenge the new norms publicly. Most behaved in accordance with those norms and some became true believers—political activists in support of the revolution. However, there was always some resistance to the new values, especially in villages, and Confucian values were never fully extinguished. Indeed, one of the dominant explanations for the recent explosion of economic development and productivity in China—as well as in other East Asian countries such as Singapore, South Korea, and Taiwan—is the norms of order, hard work, education, and financial acquisitiveness associated with Confucianism (Compton 2000).

FURTHER FOCUS

1. What can a state do to try to counter the influence of the family or religion as an agent of political socialization?
2. Which agent of political socialization has had the biggest influence on you? Why? ▶

Schools

The excerpts from textbooks that opened this chapter are extreme examples of the use of schools for political socialization. From the perspective of political authorities, schools can be the state's most valuable agent for political socialization. Schools offer the opportunity for sustained and highly controlled contact with youth at the extremely impressionable age when many political beliefs can still be molded. Apart from the family, the classroom is the most important microcosm of society that most young people experience. The teacher is the authority figure who rewards thinking and behavior that conform to what is deemed desirable by the society and who sanctions or withholds rewards from those who fail to conform. In most societies, students are taught to accept the authority of the teacher, to control their behavior, and to value the symbolic rewards offered by the education system. Every school system has rituals that support the political system. These might include songs, chants, or activities that express allegiance to political leaders or symbols. The photo on page 84 shows students in Belarus singing a daily song that celebrates the virtues of their country's president.

The school curriculum can be extremely powerful in shaping the student's understanding of the political world. Educational authorities control what subjects are taught, what textbooks contain, what content is tested, who teaches, and even what teachers say and do. An extreme form of this central control over education was achieved during the French Fourth Republic (1946–1958). It was said that the minister of education in Paris could look at her watch and specify exactly what chapter in what textbook the children of a certain age were studying at that moment all over France. While most subject matter in the schools of most countries is not openly political, school systems in *every* country present materials that are supportive of that country's politics and dominant cultural norms. All textbooks and all lessons in school are selective and thus contain biases in what is emphasized, what is ignored, and how meaning and value are established.

Have you noticed anything unusual about the use of the pronouns *he* and *she* in this book? To counter the male dominance in the language of many American textbooks, I alternate masculine and feminine pronouns in odd and even chapters, respectively. If you were aware of the gender pronouns in Chapter 2 and this chapter, your reaction may be indicative of the subtle ways in which you have been affected by cultural norms that are reinforced by language and education

Peer Groups

Persistence is the rule for the political attitudes and behaviors an individual learns from parents and schooling–that is, what you learn early tends to have deep and long-lasting effects. However, according to the *life cycle* interpretation of political socialization, learning never stops entirely. As the importance of parents and formal schooling diminishes, peer groups become an increasingly significant influence on many people's political socialization. *Peer group* is a general term that includes friends and colleagues from social networks such as work, school, church, and clubs. A person tends to be influenced by what "people like me" think. People bring their ideas and values into closer conformity with those of their relevant peer groups, since this makes the relationship more comfortable (Agnew 2003; Jennings, Markus, and Niemi 1991).

In many cases, peers and others influence a person's political views via a *"two-step" communication flow* (Bennett 2012; Katz and Lazarsfeld 1955). People with greater interest in and knowledge of politics absorb new information from various sources (*step one*). Then they relay what they have learned to others (*step two*), especially those in the mass public whose political beliefs are less salient and developed (recall Chapter 2). Direct communications from peers allow for a rich exchange of political information because such political messages have the immediacy, credibility, and power of personal interaction. Focus in 4 describes how China has used the peer group as a major mechanism for political socialization, especially during the period under Mao Zedong.

Peer influence can also be a powerful factor in the radicalization of the "homegrown" terrorists who are becoming a significant threat in many countries. There is considerable evidence that individuals, especially young adult males who feel alienated and alone as part of a cultural and religious minority, find encouragement and direction from a small group of peers who gather informally. As they share their ideas and frustrations, they begin to radicalize each other and to discuss how they could strike out at those in their country who antagonize them. In some cases, these ideas move from imagination to action, usually by committing violent acts. Some analysts refer to this peer political socialization resulting in terrorist thinking and action as the "bunch of guys" (BOG) theory (Sageman 2008). These small peer groups, which usually have no direct connection with larger, known terrorist organizations such as al-Qaeda, are emerging in many countries, from Europe and North America to Asia, North Africa, and the Middle East. An example of terrorists who emerged from such groups is the two Anglo-Indians who rammed an automobile filled with explosives into the Glasgow Airport terminal in the summer of 2007 (Meyer 2007).

The Media

Very few of us directly experience the great majority of political phenomena about which we claim knowledge. For most adults, *the media*—especially television, radio, the press, and the Internet—are the major sources of political information. Dan Nimmo and James Combs (1990: xiii) argue: "Few people learn about politics through direct experience. For most persons, political realities are mediated through mass and group communication, a process that results as much in the creation, transmission, and adoption of political fantasies as it results in independently validated views of what happens." They claim that each of us creates a personal vision (a "fantasy") of political reality based mainly on what is communicated to us by information sources such as other people, the mass media, and popular culture. Regardless of how fantastic our political visions are, it is important to understand that the media can be a crucial agent of political socialization for either stability or change.

These information sources really do *mediate* between the individual and most political reality. While most media content is not explicitly political, much of it does contain subtle information that influences how one thinks about politics and society. Exposure to television and radio is extensive in most countries. Thus, the individual is bombarded with messages about values, lifestyles, and so on. While sweeping generalizations about the impacts of the media on people's political beliefs and actions are not possible, two broad observations can be offered.

First, there is considerable evidence that the media are especially significant in *drawing people's attention to some political phenomena rather than to others*—an impact called *agenda setting*. The media signal what is important by their selection of what topics to cover and the depth of coverage, and the media influence the individual's interpretation of political phenomena by the manner in which information is presented. In general, the media (over?)simplify political topics by personalizing stories, focusing on single events, and glossing over the complex nature of most political issues (Bennett 2012; Iyengar and McGrady 2006).

Secondly, however, the research also concludes that few people absorb media information in a way that significantly changes most of their political attitudes or actions. Rather, people interpret and retain media information selectively to reinforce their existing attitudes. Many people, especially those with less-sophisticated political belief systems and minimal political knowledge (see Chapter 2), do not pay much attention to the media that provide explicit political information. The media-based information for such people often comes indirectly from a politically knowledgeable peer through the two-step communication flow described on page 92.

Newspapers are still credited with having the greatest effect on knowledge about politicians and issues among the most educated people (Graber 2009). However, television is now regarded as the most important source of political information for the largest number of people in Western democracies (Dalton 2008: Table 2.1). In the more technologically developed societies, the many forms of Internet content—which includes not only online television and news media but also search engines, blogs, and online videos—have become a key source of political information (Brookings 2011; Chadwick 2006). An increasing amount of this digitized political information is actually transmitted in peer-to-peer networks, enhancing its power. There is some debate whether the shift from broadcasting to narrowcasting, especially via the Internet, social media, and partisan media sites, will enable individuals to focus almost exclusively on sources that reinforce their existing political viewpoints, and this "selective exposure" is dangerous for a healthy democracy (Sunstein 2002, 2009). The Debate in 4 assesses whether the new ICTs (information and communications technologies) are dramatically altering the impact of media on political beliefs and political actions.

| THE DEBATE IN 4 | Do the New ICTs Substantially Change Our Political Beliefs and Actions? |

With the enhanced global communication through cell phones, satellites, and the Internet, many societies have become "information-rich and communication intensive" (Bimber, 2003; Chadwick and Howard 2009). From the globalized 24/7 news to the extensive political blogging to the tweets reporting revolution in the streets of repressive regimes, the impacts of all these information and communications technologies (ICTs) seem extraordinary (Cropf and Krummenacher 2011). Thus, some argue that these ICTs are dramatically changing the nature of individual political beliefs and actions. Others insist that these ICTs are important, but merely add incrementally to the existing array of agents of political socialization that influence political behavior. Are these new social media truly game changers?

New ICTs Are Powerfully Shaping Political Beliefs and Political Actions

■ As the impacts of parents and schools as agents of political socialization fade by an individual's

teenage years, the media often become the critical agent. For younger generations, the Internet is increasingly the primary platform for acquiring and sharing knowledge about the political world. The unique diversity, speed, anonymity and shrill nature associated with political information circulated on these ICTs have substantially altered the content and impacts of this information on both citizens and political officials (Barbour 2008; Pew 2011; Sunstein 2009).

■ While collective norms might still be shaped by mainstream broadcast media outlets, the Internet and new social media are critical in the creation of the individual's identity. Through the Web, people rely on themselves and their own resources to solidify an identity and self-awareness, including the formation of their cognitive, affective, and evaluative political beliefs (Bimber 2003).

■ Information is power. ICTs such as search engines, online news, and political Web sites allow individuals to access far more information than in

(Continued)

the past. Not only is access easier and less costly, but the user can also rapidly explore multiple sources and control her analysis of information and knowledge claims about politics (Brookings 2011).

- Social media ICTs such as YouTube and blogs enable those with minimal resources to reach a large, possibly global audience, giving expression and potential influence to those who previously had no capacity to communicate their political messages to a broad audience (Hands 2011; Jensen 2010).

- These social media and digital technologies such as cell phones have become critical tools providing political activists with new modes for cooperation, mobilization, and coordination of their political actions, as in the Arab Spring 2011 uprisings in Egypt and Tunisia (Hands 2011; Ritter and Trechsel 2011).

New ICTs Have Not Dramatically Changed Political Beliefs and Political Actions

- While the utilization of online sources of political information has increased dramatically, most people primarily seek this information from online modes of traditional, dominant news sources (e.g., CNN, BBC, Al Jazeera). The mere digitizing of information from conventional sources will not result in major changes in the content or even the impact of these agents of political socialization (Garrett and Danziger 2011).

- More broadly, most empirical research has concluded that ICTs in the political world are essentially power reinforcing. Those elites and groups who already exercise substantial political power and influence have been able to capture a disproportionate share of the power and benefits associated with the use of ICTs (Bimber 2003; Schmidt and Cohen 2010).

- Despite the presence of all these ICTs, most citizens exhibit no greater knowledge about

or interest in the political world, and political participation has not increased significantly as a result of these technologies. Most research on participation has not yet found a positive correlation between the greater use of ICTs and increased levels of citizen engagement in politics (Boulienne 2009; Garrett and Danziger 2011).

- Social media seem mainly to facilitate "slacktivism" instead of activism (Gladwell 2010). That is, many casual participants and bandwagoners seek social change through low-cost activities such as joining a digital social movement (e.g., a "Save Darfur" Facebook group). Such forms of virtual political action translate into minimal effects in the real world of political action (Shirky 2011).

- Those who use ICTs to focus and narrow their exposure to sources consistent with their existing political views experience little more than a modest strengthening of those views (Sunstein 2002). Those who expose themselves to the multiplicity of perspectives and the huge number of contradictory knowledge claims about politics from the nonmainstream ICTs tend to be overwhelmed. As with other agents of socialization in conflict, the dominant effects are to increase uncertainty and reduce political action.

MORE QUESTIONS...

1. As governments are increasingly unable to control the information that citizens access through the new ICTs, will there be generally positive changes in pursuit of the goals of democracy, tolerance, and a shared community of meaning in a society?

2. Are you persuaded that the content of political information that most individuals are influenced by will change as they become more reliant on ICTs as a crucial source?

Much of what you know about the political world from the mainstream media is contingent on what topics the media choose to cover and what content the media select to report. Like textbooks, the media are not neutral; someone has selected the subjects and content. In many countries, the major media are owned and controlled by the government or by members of the wealthy, dominant class in that society (Bagdikian

2004). The print and broadcast media are free of substantial government censorship in slightly more than one-third (35 percent) of all countries, and these countries include only 15 percent of the world's population. Governments severely censor the media for fully 43 percent of the world's people (Freedom House 2011). Through their ability to control the media, most governments have a significant resource for political socialization, exposing people to "news" and information that reinforce the government's view of the political world. And there is empirical evidence of a global decline in freedom of the press for nine straight years (Freedom House 2011).

Of course, you are not completely passive in the process. In most countries, people can choose among alternative media sources and can attempt to evaluate the truth of what they read, hear, and see in the media. And the recent explosion of telecommunications technologies (such as satellite television transmissions and the Internet) has made it increasingly difficult for a government to control all the sources of information reaching its citizens. Consequently, most governments are becoming less effective in shaping people's political beliefs through the media, even as the media are an ever-more-important source of people's political "reality."

Religion

For some individuals, religion is a powerful agent of political socialization. First, political beliefs and actions can be influenced by religious beliefs that individuals should act to correct the failures of secular society and should promote religious views on issues where the government has enacted unacceptable public policies, such as abortion, school curriculum, gender relations, and homosexuality. Secondly, people in some environments are so disillusioned with the conditions of their society that they look to religion for a framework of beliefs and actions to improve those conditions. This is especially the case in societies where people perceive substantial negative effects due to the shift from traditional to modern life (Haynes 2007, 2010). And third, some religious belief systems make no distinction between religious life and public life, and thus it is natural that religious values—not public policies—always have precedence. This acceptance of the dominance of religious prescriptions over secular authority is evident in certain "fundamentalist" groups within all the major religions, particularly Christianity, Judaism, and Islam.

In all these situations, religious authorities—whether texts or the pronouncements of religious figures—can guide and motivate their followers. Arguably more than any of the other agents of political socialization, it is possible to link the content communicated by religion as a socializing agent with both political beliefs and political actions. In many instances, one person's piety can be another person's intolerance and bigotry. The current era is one in which there are huge differences in the impacts of religion as an agent of political socialization on those who are generally unaffected by religious beliefs, those who separate their religious beliefs from their political beliefs, and those whose political views are substantially shaped by their religious values.

Culture

In every country, most mainstream culture, which ranges from product advertisements to cinema to music to public monuments, is supportive of the society's dominant values, including its political values. (Consider, for example, whether there is variation in the main ethnicities of villains in films produced in your country over the past seventy years.) Moreover, culture—like the media—can be extensively controlled by the dominant political order in a society and can be used to reinforce the state's view of the political world. Cuba, like many of the communist states in the past, has generally insisted that culture must meet the standards of "socialist realism," which means that no art, theater, or cinema should be allowed if it fails to celebrate the virtues of socialism—Cuban style.

However, culture does not necessarily reinforce the dominant order. Culture can inform and criticize subtly, by means of metaphor and symbol, in ways less likely to be interpreted as a direct challenge to the established authorities. This is especially true in societies where there is considerable censorship of the media and state control of most sources of public information. During the 1980s, for example, an extensive body of fiction, cinema, poetry, theater, art, and music emerged with political content critical of the state's views in countries such as East Germany and Poland that were still communist (Larkey 1990). Culture can also be openly subversive, directly attacking mainstream values or advocating opposing values. For example, Jamaican reggae music offers a revolutionary vision of an alternative social and political world for its people. While most contemporary Anglo-American music has little explicit political content, strong political content can be found in some hip-hop music and in songs by performers such as Charlie Daniels, Rage Against the Machine, U2, and Bruce Springsteen (Coles 2003).

Events

The general effects of the environment on political beliefs and action have already been discussed. While the context of everyday life has slow, evolutionary effects on a person's political behavior, a specific event can act as a sudden and powerful agent of political socialization. For example, Sarah Brady shifted from being a politician's wife to being a tireless political activist on behalf of gun control legislation after her husband, James Brady, President Reagan's press secretary, was shot and paralyzed in a 1981 assassination attempt on the president. Another example of mobilization after a dramatic event is the transformation of Sonia Gandhi, an apolitical spouse, into the leader of the Congress Party in India after the assassination of her husband, Prime Minister Rajiv Gandhi. It is also suggested that many recruits for extremist movements such as political Islam are motivated to avenge a traumatic experience in which a family member or close friend is injured or killed by the domestic or foreign military.

PERSONAL CHARACTERISTICS

In our explanation of political beliefs and actions, we should also analyze the influence of an individual's *personal characteristics*. Sometimes called *demographic characteristics*, these include both visible characteristics, such as age, gender, and ethnicity, and less visible ones, such as education, income, social class, and occupation. What underlying dynamic might link personal characteristics with political behavior?

Personal characteristics can be thought of as *filters* that influence how the environment and the agents of political socialization affect an individual's political behavior. For example, the current impact of parents as agents of political socialization is likely

4.3 Illustrate how personal characteristics are linked to political beliefs and actions.

◉─[Watch the
Video "The
Zapatista
Rebellion" at
mypoliscilab.com

to be far greater for their offspring of age 4 than those of age 44. Similarly, an environmental context of Islamic fundamentalism in Saudi Arabia will have very different effects on the political beliefs and behaviors of Saudi men and women.

Much of the empirical research on political behavior attempts to establish and clarify the relationships between personal characteristics and specific political beliefs or actions. No single personal characteristic is a certain predictor of political behavior, but empirical research (based on relational analysis) in many countries indicates that some personal characteristics are associated with certain political beliefs and actions. And when key personal characteristics seem to reinforce each other, you might have greater confidence in a correct prediction about a particular political behavior.

For example, can you think of any personal characteristics that might inform your prediction of whether a particular person voted for John McCain or Barack Obama in the 2008 U.S. presidential election? Table 4.1 uses relational analysis (like Table A.4 in the Appendix) to explore those linkages. Do any personal characteristics seem to be associated with a tendency to vote for either candidate? In addition to comparing the overall percentage of voters in a category (e.g., high school graduates) for each candidate, another useful technique for answering this question is to determine whether there are instances where the candidate's percentage for a category is noticeably different from the candidate's percentage of the total vote.

While most of the differences are not dramatic, some demographic characteristics do seem to correlate with support for McCain or Obama. Notice, for example, that the probability of voting for Obama was substantially higher among those who had any of the following characteristics: 18- to 29-year-old; African American, Chicano/Latino, or Asian American; Jewish or "other" religion; not a high school graduate; and family income below $50,000. People's probability of voting for McCain was especially high among Caucasians, Protestants, and those over age 65.

Although there are some clear associations among variables, we cannot conclude that any personal characteristic actually *caused* a person to vote for a particular candidate (see the distinction between correlational and causal analysis in the Appendix). And when several personal characteristics are associated with voting choice, we also cannot determine which of them are the most powerful predictors of candidate choice without statistical analysis (such as regression analysis, a statistical technique that identifies how much variance in the dependent variable—vote choice, in this case—can be attributed to each subject's level on various independent variables). Nonetheless, Table 4.1 provides reasonable support for our assumption that personal characteristics are sometimes associated with political behavior.

While generalizations are always difficult, there is some consistency in the empirical research on the personal characteristics of those who do vote (in political systems where there are genuine voting choices). In general, a higher probability of *voting* is correlated with characteristics such as membership in organizations that have explicit interests in politics (e.g., political parties and unions), higher education, higher income, higher social class, greater age level, and male gender. Incidence of voting is also associated with the person's political beliefs, especially a strong identification with a party; a greater sense of personal capacity to influence the political world (political efficacy); and deeper knowledge about the available political choices.

TABLE 4.1

Voting Choices in the 2008 U.S. Presidential Election, by Personal Characteristics

			Obama 52%	McCain 48%
Gender	Male	47%*	49%	48%
	Female	53	56	43
Ethnicity	Caucasian	74	43	55
	African American	13	95	4
	Latino	9	67	31
	Asian American	2	62	35
Age	18–29	18	66	32
	30–44	29	52	46
	45–64	37	50	49
	65+	16	45	53
Family Income	less than $50K	38	60	38
	$50–100K	36	49	49
	more than $100K	26	49	49
Education	Not high school grad	4	63	35
	High school grad	20	52	46
	Some college	31	51	47
	College grad	28	50	48
	Postgraduate	17	58	40
Religion	Protestant	54	45	54
	Catholic	27	54	45
	Jewish	2	78	21
	Other	6	73	22

*Percentage of total electorate
Note: Due to rounding, not all categories total 100 percent.
Source: *CNN* (http://www.cnn.com/ELECTION/2008/results/president/)

Research findings on *other modes of political behavior* are less extensive and less consistent. As in the taxonomies of participation, the cross-national studies by Verba and his colleagues (Verba, Nie, and Kim 1978) remain among the most influential in identifying the individual characteristics that correlate with each mode of conventional political action. Participation in campaign activities is especially linked with higher education, higher income, and male gender. Communal activities are generally associated with higher socioeconomic characteristics and with identification with a particular social group (religious, ethnic, or linguistic) that has a political perspective. Contacting government officials personally is least clearly related to personal characteristics, and some research suggests that the decision to engage in personal contacts depends more on whether the person

COMPARE IN 4 | You Go Your Way, I'll Go Mine

The two young men have some common roots. Both are born into societies grounded in traditional social systems of hierarchy and male domination and strong, fundamentalist religion. Both are sons of prosperous professional fathers who are deeply religious. Each young man displays high intelligence and receives an excellent education.

As young adults, each trains successfully for a professional career and enters that career. Each is shocked when he witnesses religious or racial discrimination and the severe deprivation that characterizes the lives of the great majority of people in his society. Each becomes a deeply devout follower of his religion. Each develops a powerful commitment to the independence of his people from foreign powers, which are seen as the source of oppression and injustice. Each chooses a life of political activism and decides to engage in extreme political acts, as necessary, to achieve his vision of social justice. But the two men follow very different paths.

The first man travels to another country to join the revolutionary struggle against a major colonial power. He is trained and supported in guerrilla warfare tactics (see Chapter 11) by the U.S. Central Intelligence Agency and becomes an effective leader. After successfully defeating the foreign power, he returns home to Saudi Arabia to work in the family business. However, he is deeply offended by the presence and influence of foreigners in his religion's holiest lands. His open demands to expel the foreigners and establish a pure religious state result in conflict with the authoritarian regime in his homeland. He is harassed by the regime, his citizenship is revoked, and he is forced to leave the country. He eventually returns to the country where he had fought on behalf of the revolution.

By this time, he is convinced that his righteous cause can be advanced only by extreme acts of violence. He uses his considerable personal wealth ($300 million) to organize a loosely connected international network of highly trained extremist-activists living in more than 60 countries. He calls on all his followers to use whatever means necessary to free their lands from foreign rule. Members of his network commit many acts of international terrorism, including a massacre of tourists in Luxor, Egypt, in 1995 and the bombings of the U.S. embassies in Kenya and Tanzania in 1998. Many plots are unsuccessful, including an attempt to fly a hijacked airplane into the Eiffel Tower and assassination attempts on the leaders of Egypt, Jordan, and Pakistan. His network commits the most brutal terrorist attack ever undertaken in the United States, with two hijacked passenger airplanes crashing into the twin towers of the World Trade Center and another into the Pentagon on September 11, 2001. These attacks resulted in more than 3,000 deaths as well as worldwide fear and disruption of both travel and financial markets. In response to criticism that he targets "innocents" and supports terrorism, he comments:

> American history does not distinguish between civilians and military, and not even women and children. Americans are the ones who used the bombs against Nagasaki. Can these bombs distinguish between infants and military?... Your situation with Muslims in Palestine is shameful.... [T]he American-led sanctions resulted in the death of over 1 million Iraqi children. All of this was done in the name of American interests. We believe that the biggest thieves in the world and the terrorists are the Americans. The only way for us to fend off these assaults is to use similar means. We do not differentiate between those dressed in military uniforms and civilians; they are all targets in this fatwa [death decree]. (*Source:* http://abcnews.go. com/sections/world/ dailynews/terror_980609.html)

The Central Intelligence Agency (CIA) labels his al-Qaeda organization "the most dangerous terrorist organization in the world," and he becomes the prime target in the "war on international terrorism" initiated by then-U.S. president George W. Bush. He is hunted relentlessly for nearly a decade and is finally killed in 2011 by U.S. special forces in a raid of the home where he had been hiding.

(Continued)

The second man witnesses the whites' racism against Indians while serving as a lawyer in South Africa. To resist such injustice, he develops a strategy of civil disobedience inspired by Henry David Thoreau as well as by his own religious beliefs. His fundamental principle is *ahimsa*—nonviolence in thought as well as in action. He advises his followers: "Not to submit; to suffer." He is repeatedly jailed for his nonviolent resistance to laws that he believes are unjust. He assumes that the opposition will discredit itself by its repressive responses to nonviolent protest.

Returning to his native India, he begins to organize protests demanding independence from the British imperialists. His protest techniques continue to be based on nonviolence and *satyagraha*—soul force. In contrast to brute force, soul force produces constructive change through positive action and reconciliation, not through harming and angering the enemy. He observes, "My experience has shown me that we win justice quickest by rendering justice to the other party." He becomes an extraordinarily powerful and inspirational leader through his theatrical acts of civil disobedience and his personal sacrifices, including extended fasts, lengthy marches, and sexual abstinence. His nonviolent activism captures world attention, and his Indian followers

expand to the tens of thousands. His supporters call him *Mahatma*—great soul. His tireless political activism over three decades contributes greatly to Britain granting independence to India. His life of struggle is not a complete success, however. He fails to prevent the division of India into separate countries dominated by Hindus and Muslims, a struggle bloodied by 1 million deaths. He fails to persuade Hindus to repudiate the divisive and unjust social caste system, and he is assassinated by a Hindu extremist within months of India's independence.

Despite their early similarities, Osama bin Laden (1957–2011) and Mohandas K. Gandhi (1869–1948) diverged onto nearly opposite paths of extreme political activism in the pursuit of their personal visions of social justice and human liberation.

FURTHER QUESTIONS

1. Given the similar upbringings of Osama bin Laden and Gandhi, how might you explain their different paths of activism?
2. Is it ironic that both died violently?
3. Which of *your* personal characteristics has had the biggest impact on your political beliefs and actions? ▲

Osama bin Laden and Mohandas Gandhi are two extraordinary extremist-activists who had similar backgrounds but chose fundamentally different paths of political action.

has an effective private means to gain her objective or must rely on contacting public officials to achieve this objective. Contacting officials might be the type of political action that has increased most during recent decades and it is increasingly facilitated by e-mail and other digital communications innovations (Chadwick and Howard 2009).

In studying *extremist-activists*, many analyses attempt to specify the personal characteristics that typify a particular type of activist relative to the general population. For example, many of the Muslims who have engaged in terrorist acts are young adult males who are well-educated, married with children, and come from middle-class families (Berrebi 2007; Sageman 2008). The rural extremist-activists engaged in a struggle for control over land in Asia and Latin America tend to be male, poor, and of limited education. Urban activists who promote leftist ideologies (e.g., Marxism, environmentalism) are generally characterized as well educated, middle class, mainly young, and only slightly more likely to be male than female. Right-wing urban activists are more varied. Those promoting an ethnic or racist position (e.g., neo-Nazism) tend to be young, male, working or lower class, and somewhat lower in education (Schain, Zolberg, and Hossay 2002). Those promoting conservative causes such as the antiabortion movement are more middle aged, female, middle class, and relatively well educated (Dalton 2008:Ch. 4).

Overall, what do you expect to be the personal characteristics most likely among *top political leaders* in a given society? Perhaps the broadest generalization is that leaders' personal characteristics tend to be quite consistent with the characteristics of the socially dominant groups within their society. Why do you think this occurs? Among the most common shared characteristics, across many societies, are high education, upper-middle-class or upper-class background, association with the society's dominant religion and ethnicity, and male gender.

Given our general fascination with extraordinary political actors such as presidents, charismatic leaders, and revolutionaries, it is interesting to assess whether particular environments, socialization experiences, or personal characteristics seem to account for the political behavior of these individuals. Compare in 4 briefly describes the environment, socialization, and personal characteristics of two remarkable political activists. Do these factors seem relatively similar for the two men? Do these factors seem to produce similar political behavior?

POLITICAL PERSONALITY

4.4 Distinguish normative from empirical approaches to understanding political personality.

The three types of explanatory factors we have discussed to this point are either outside the person (the environment and agents of political socialization) or are surface characteristics (e.g., age, ethnicity). However, you might find yourself agreeing with those political scientists who insist that an adequate explanation of political behavior requires analysis of the *political personality—the deeper psychological dynamics inside the individual that affect that person's response to political stimuli.*

Personality

Personality can be broadly defined as the propensities within an individual to act in a certain way, given a particular context. If someone is usually cheerful or aggressive or thoughtful under a variety of circumstances, this style of behaving could be called a *personality trait* of that individual. The cluster of basic personality traits that dominates an individual's attitudes and behavior is what most people mean when they talk about someone's personality type. It seems plausible that personality could influence the political beliefs and actions of any individual. Most of the empirical research examining political personality has focused on the beliefs and actions of political activists. Political personality analyses are found in biographies, in opinion pieces in the media, in our conversations about top political leaders, and even in leaders' own speeches and writings.

Normative Approaches   People have always had strong opinions about the kind of personality that a political leader *should* have. What personality characteristics do you think are desirable in a political leader? Perhaps no one is better known for advice about the kind of personality a political leader needs than Niccolò Machiavelli (1469–1527), author of *The Prince* (1517/1977). Machiavelli believed that society tends towards disorder, in part because events are substantially dependent on *fortuna*—a combination of chance, fate, luck, and unpredictable circumstances. The political leader must act decisively to overcome *fortuna*. She must think strategically, suppress moral judgments, and act with fierce resolve.

"Everyone sees what you seem to be," Machiavelli (1517/1977: Ch. 18) observed; "few know what you really are." Thus, the leader must combine the qualities of the lion (aggression, bravery) and the fox (cleverness) and must make the citizens completely dependent on her every decision and action. In the pursuit of the good society, the leader must be single-minded and, if necessary, ruthless to achieve her desired ends. Machiavelli insisted that the effective political leader will face many situations where the ends justify the political means, even if ethical behavior must be sacrificed: "To preserve the state, he often has to do things against his word, against charity, against humanity, against religion....[H]e should not depart from the good if he can hold to it, but he should be ready to enter on evil if he has to" (Machiavelli 1517/1977:Ch. 18). Few contemporary politicians want to be characterized as "Machiavellian;" most politicians work hard to project certain personality traits that they think will appeal to their followers (e.g., honesty, responsiveness, compassion, and thoughtfulness).

Empirical Approaches   While some studies offer normative perspectives on political personality, most contemporary studies are empirical and try to explain the actual behavior of top political leaders and activists. These studies attempt to identify leaders' key personality traits (such as idealism, aggressiveness, decisiveness, and so on) and then link those traits to specific political beliefs and actions.

Political personality approaches can delve quite deeply, explaining the psychological needs, drives, or experiences embedded in the person's psyche that are the underlying forces resulting in her political behavior. In this perspective, activist political behavior is seen as a response to a person's psychological life history. For example, Harold Lasswell (1960), one of the intellectual founders of behavioral political science, argues that the activist political personality is motivated primarily by the drive to overcome a low sense of self-esteem. However, the systematic empirical evidence suggests that most top political leaders actually rank higher than the average adult on measures of self-esteem and psychological well-being (Sniderman 1975).

One personality-based analysis has posited that the behavior of political leaders can be explained by their responsiveness to some combination of seven incentives that they connect powerfully with political action: (1) the urge to solve public problems, (2) the need to be accepted by others, (3) the search for fame and glory, (4) the desire to follow their conscience in serving society, (5) the pleasure derived from competition and manipulation of others, (6) the satisfaction from commitment to a grand mission, and (7) the desire for praise and adulation (Woshinsky 1995:Ch. 11). Empirical research also documents the more Machiavellian motivations and strategies that cause some political leaders to lie about their actions, especially to their own citizens (Mearsheimer 2011).

Some of the most detailed analytic work develops an extensive *psychobiography* of the individual political activist. Such analyses attempt to provide information about political activists' personalities and to explain how such information helps us make better sense of how, and especially why, they act as they do. Erik Erikson (1958, 1969), among the most influential scholars in this tradition, adopts a Freudian framework to reveal the crucial importance of child-rearing and early socialization through adolescence in determining the activist's later political behavior. (See Erikson's psychobiographies of Martin Luther [1958], Mohandas Gandhi [1969], and Lucian Pye's [1962] application of Erikson's approach to analyze an entire class of political leaders in postcolonial Myanmar.)

Empirical, personality-based approaches have also been used to account for the behavior of other types of political activists such as student radicals. What do you hypothesize about the student-radicals? Are student extremists different from other students in their intelligence or idealism or independence? Are student radicals of the left different from student radicals of the right? The limited empirical research generally concludes that student radicals tend to be more intelligent, creative, idealistic, and independent than the nonradicals. It also has been shown that these qualities apply to those student radicals whose ideology is extremely progressive or extremely conservative (Fendrich 1993; Kerpelman 1972).

Recently, there has been particular interest in analyzing the psychology of those who engage in terrorist acts. While the backgrounds and even the personalities of terrorists vary, it has been suggested that many do share some traits. They can be troubled by high levels of loneliness, alienation, and isolation. As noted above regarding the impact of peers, they can seek to overcome this through the sense of belonging provided by a small, strong network of friends (BOGs). These

individuals can also be very frustrated because they feel that the political and social conditions they value have been denied them by others whose actions are illegitimate and against whom they are willing to retaliate with violence. Some recent terrorists also have very strong religious convictions and are prepared to engage in any necessary actions to protect and promote their religion (Post 2008; Sageman 2008; Smelser 2007; Victoroff 2005).

Biology and Human Nature

Some analysts who offer a psychological explanation for political behavior do not focus on individual personality; rather, they emphasize even deeper drives. There has been recent interest in how the human brain functions and whether this can account for certain types of political behavior. Some theorists claim that political beliefs and behavior are based on essential biological/genetic foundations. For example, John Hibbing and his colleagues present experimental evidence that individual genetic factors and brain biology are connected with the predisposition to certain ideological orientations (Hibbing et al. 2008; Hibbing and Smith 2007; see also Fowler and Dawes 2009; Wilson 1978). New research technologies will continue to expand our understanding of the systematic connections between brain function and political behavior.

A more generalized explanation is grounded in *human nature—innate motivations and invariant drives shared by all people.* Some analysts ask whether there are innate human motivations that affect political behavior. At some time, most of us have engaged in a discussion about the possibility of a utopian society. Typically, someone takes the position that a benign utopia is not possible because humans are imperfect—men and women are intrinsically selfish or violent. The person who makes such an argument is linking the political behavior of individuals and groups with notions about innate (and possibly universal) human nature. From an opposing perspective, it can be argued that people's social values and behavior, if not their basic nature, can be shaped via proper socialization and enlightened institutions. Such shaping of people into a cooperative society is the theme of *Walden Two*, a novel by behavioral psychologist B. F. Skinner (1948). However, the power and danger of such pervasive socialization are a central theme in Aldous Huxley's (1932) classic novel *Brave New World*.

The links between biology, human nature, and political behavior raise fascinating issues. Are there fundamental elements of humans that cannot be significantly altered by socialization and institutions? To what extent are we the product of our environment? Empirical social science has yet to provide decisive answers to these questions about nature and nurture in relation to political behavior.

CONCLUDING OBSERVATIONS

✓•⌐**Study**
and **Review** the
Post-Test &
Chapter Exam at
mypoliscilab.com

Our exploration of political behavior has continued with a consideration of primary explanations for individuals' political beliefs and political actions. The research and theories that attempt to answer the *why* questions about political behavior emphasize four types of explanatory factors: the environmental context, the agents of political socialization, personal characteristics, and political personality. The basic assumption is that some combination of these factors influences the kinds of political stimuli to which people are exposed, the manner in which they interpret these stimuli, and their responses to the stimuli.

The *environment* presents the individual with stimuli and opportunities as well as with obstacles to certain political beliefs and actions. While a person can ignore or misperceive these broad environmental constraints, they do constitute a framework that guides, and to some extent determines, political behavior. In most political behavior research, the analyst can (and should) identify the major features of the environment that might affect the probability that an individual will manifest certain political beliefs or actions.

In a similar manner, an individual's *personal characteristics*, such as age, gender, social class, and education, can have a powerful cumulative influence. First, they can serve as a set of filters that influence the kinds of political phenomena to which the person is exposed. Second, they can influence the expectations that others have regarding how the person ought to think and act politically. The empirical evidence is sometimes quite clear (as are the data on voting in the 2008 U.S. presidential election) that certain personal characteristics (in a given environmental context) correlate significantly with particular political beliefs and actions. Personal characteristics, rather like the environment, are best understood as a set of forces that influence the nature and intensity of individual political behavior but do not determine that behavior.

The inadequacy of either the environment or personal characteristics as a complete explanation for most individual political behavior is reflected in the fact that people with comparable personal characteristics or people who operate in a similar environment do not necessarily manifest identical political beliefs or actions. For example, of two sisters, one might be an activist deeply involved in Democratic Party politics and the other might be politically apathetic. Similarly, consider the divergent paths of political activism pursued by Mohandas Gandhi and Osama bin Laden, despite notable similarities in their characteristics and environments. While the environment and personal characteristics might not provide a total explanation, a strong case can be made that these factors do tend to set the boundaries within which much political behavior occurs.

The attempt to build an empirically validated causal theory of the effects of *political socialization* on political behavior is intriguing. A major analytic shortcoming in most of the political socialization research has been the difficulty in demonstrating empirically that there is a clear causal linkage from a specific agent of socialization to a particular belief, and then to a politically relevant action. In most instances, researchers lack the methodologies and the data-gathering instruments to measure how the messages of various agents of political socialization are absorbed, interpreted, and responded to by people. Rather, the researchers must attempt to infer what socialization agents have been important by asking individuals to recall the major sources of their own political beliefs.

Despite these empirical difficulties, the study of political socialization is a useful tool/strategy in increasing our understanding of the major forces that influence how people learn about and evaluate political phenomena. In their attempt to use the agents of political socialization, political regimes display their own belief that these socialization processes can either create and preserve popular support for the existing political order or create a new political consciousness. Research suggests that where the agents of political socialization are ineffective or provide contradictory messages, a person's political behavior will tend toward apathy or, in a few cases, towards producing the totally committed political activist. While the precise linkages among agents of political socialization, political beliefs, and political behavior have yet to be empirically verified, this area of inquiry remains an important one for political scientists.

The explanation of political behavior by *political personality* is perhaps the most intriguing of the four sets of factors. Most of the personality-based work has examined the political psychology of activists, such as radicals, terrorists, and top leaders, while the emerging work on the biological bases of political behavior focuses primarily on the political beliefs and political actions of the mass public. Personality-based approaches have been the least fully explored means to explain political behavior, although they typically use some of the same evidence as the other approaches. For example, this approach might explain political personality in terms of the relationship of the individual to a social group, as would an explanation based on the peer group as an agent of political socialization. Thus, personality is difficult to isolate from other forces—the environment, personal characteristics, and political socialization and learning—that intervene between human nature and political behavior and that shape personality. At this point, the recent research linking political beliefs and actions to biological mechanisms is mainly based on laboratory experiments whose results are intriguing but far from conclusive.

We began this chapter by asking whether it is possible to explain political beliefs and actions. In general, analyses can rarely prove that any of the four types of explanatory factors we examined is almost always *the* basic causal factor for a particular individual's political belief or action. Nonetheless, the evidence we explored in this chapter suggests that relevant knowledge about each of these four sets of explanatory factors can provide significant insights that can further your understanding of political behavior.

KEY CONCEPTS

agenda setting   93

agents of political socialization   89

Confucian culture   90

environment   87

human nature   105

personal characteristics   97

political personality   103

political socialization   89

FOR FURTHER CONSIDERATION

1. Which agent of political socialization has been strongest in influencing *your* key political beliefs? Which of your key beliefs have been least influenced by this agent? What accounts for the agent's minimal influence on these beliefs?
2. Under what conditions are personal characteristics likely to have particularly powerful effects on an individual's political beliefs or actions?
3. To what extent are people either a blank page on which political beliefs can be written ("nurture") or genetically determined actors ("nature")? In what ways is this overall assessment valid for *you*?
4. Can you identify any examples where your own schooling might be viewed as politically biased by someone from another culture?
5. What is your assessment of Machiavelli's advice to the leader that ethics, the leader's promises, and even "the good" must sometimes be sacrificed to achieve desirable ends?

FOR FURTHER READING

Calderisi, Robert. (2007). *The Trouble with Africa: Why Foreign Aid Isn't Working.* London: Palgrave. A controversial explanation, which focuses particularly on a "national character" analysis, for the difficulties that most African countries have faced in achieving economic development.

Erikson, Erik. (1969). *Gandhi's Truth.* New York: Norton. Applying his rich psychobiographical approach, Erikson explains the crucial points of development shaping the personality and political style of Mohandas Gandhi.

Gobodo-Madikizela, Pumla. (2003). *A Human Being Died That Night: A South African Story of Forgiveness.* Boston: Houghton Mifflin. A psychologist who was a member of the Truth and Reconciliation Commission in South Africa explains the importance of this public acknowledgment process in creating a new peace and reducing the likelihood of future ethnic and racial atrocities.

Hayhoe, Ruth. (1992). *Education and Modernization: The Chinese Experience.* New York: Pergamon. An insightful analysis of the effects of education on the political socialization process and on culture and modernization in China, from Confucianism to Marxism.

Hibbing, John, and Kevin Smith (eds.). (2007). *The Biology of Political Behavior. The Annals of the American Academy of Political and Social Science,* 614 (1). A series of articles explaining the current research attempting to utilize biological, genetic, and brain behavior approaches to explain political beliefs and actions related to topics such as leadership styles, tolerance, aggression, and racial attitudes.

Huxley, Aldous. (1932). *Brave New World.* London: Chatto and Windus. A chilling vision of a society in which the state effectively uses socialization and material conditions to control the thoughts and actions of citizens.

Khadra, Yasmina. (2007). *Sirens of Baghdad*. Trans. John Cullen. London: Heinemann. A compelling novel that describes the conversion of a gentle, idealistic Iraqi college student into a disillusioned survivor in war-torn contemporary Iraq and then into a violent, nonreligious radical activist.

Lawrence, Bruce, Ed. (2005). *Messages to the World: The Statements of Osama Bin Laden*. London: Verso. The known commentaries by the late leader of al-Qaeda provide insights into his worldview and strategies.

Mandela, Nelson. (1995). *Long Walk to Freedom*. Boston: Little, Brown. In his autobiography, Nelson Mandela provides a compelling narrative of his extraordinary life of political activism against racial injustice and apartheid, culminating in his election as president of South Africa.

Mearsheimer, John J. (2011). *Why Leaders Lie: The Truth about Lying in International Politics*. New York: Oxford University Press. In an interesting bridge to Machiavelli's ideas, this always controversial political scientist examines the different strategies and motivations when top leaders lie about the reasons for their foreign policy actions.

Nixon, Richard M. (1962). *Six Crises*. New York: Doubleday. Richard Nixon, one of the most controversial U.S. presidents, provides a revealing self-assessment of his reactions to six critical events in his early political career.

Post, Jerrold. (2008). *The Mind of the Terrorist: The Psychology of Terrorism from the IRA to al-Qaeda*. London: Palgrave Macmillan. A compelling exploration of how "normal" many terrorists are, given their context, based on numerous interviews and thorough research on those who engage in terrorism, whether their goal is separatism, fundamental social change, or religious purity.

Sears, David O., Leonie Huddy, and Robert Jervis, Eds. (2003). *Oxford Handbook of Political Psychology*. New York: Oxford University Press. This award-winning book employs the insights of psychology to examine issues in the political world such as the impact of personality, political socialization, information processing in opinion formation, emotion and politics, gender and political behavior, and styles of conflict resolution.

Skinner, B. F. (1948). *Walden Two*. New York: Macmillan. A renowned behavioral psychologist presents his conception of a setting in which socialization is used to create a benign and cooperative community. An intriguing counterpoint to Huxley's *Brave New World*.

Thomassen, Jacques. (2006). *The European Voter*. New York: Oxford University Press. A thorough comparative analysis and explanation of the changing voting behavior of citizens in many European countries.

Wattenberg, Martin. (2008). *Is Voting for Young People?* New York: Pearson Longman. This short book uses empirical data from the United States in comparison to other democracies to assess the political inactivity of young Americans, relative to their European peers and older Americans, and to argue for more political activism.

Wolfenstein, E. Victor. (1967). *The Revolutionary Personality: Lenin, Trotsky, Gandhi*. Princeton, NJ: Princeton University Press. A classic study of three major revolutionary leaders from a psychoanalytic perspective.

Zimbardo, Philip. (2007). *The Lucifer Effect: Understanding How Good People Turn Evil*. New York: Random House. A distinguished psychologist explores why behaviors such as organized genocide and the abuses at the Abu Ghraib prison in Iraq occur. His central argument is that it is not one bad person enticing others into highly unacceptable acts, but rather that groups collectively turn to such behavior in response to their social environment and the organizational system in which they function.

ON THE WEB

http://www.americanrhetoric.com/informationindex.htm

The News and Information Index from American Rhetoric is an extremely rich set of links to newspapers from around the world and other online news sources, magazines, search engines, polling databases, and legal databases.

http://www.electionstudies.org

Data (which can be downloaded) and analyses from the American National Election Study, the major survey of U.S. political opinions and behavior (1948–2008). The material on the Web site addresses topics such as the role of personal characteristics, ideology, and partisanship in relation to political beliefs and actions.

http://www.cddc.vt.edu/feminism

The Feminist Theory Web site, hosted by the Center for Digital Discourse and Culture at Virginia Tech University, provides a large number of links to information on beliefs as well as groups and movements inspired by a feminist perspective on political and social issues in many countries.

http://culturalpolitics.net

This site offers numerous links that explore the role of culture in shaping our political, economic, and social lives.

http://www.cnn.com/WORLD

The site for CNN, the 24-hour, U.S.-based international news organization.

http://www.itn.co.uk

World news and British news from Independent Television News, based in London, are provided.

http://www.nytimes.com

This is the site for key articles and information from one of the premier newspapers in the United States.

http://wn.com

WorldNews provides an extensive electronic news portal with international sites in multiple languages categorized by geographic region, country, and subject.

http://news.bbc.co.uk

The Internet home of the British Broadcasting Company, this site offers world political, business, scientific, and entertainment news from a British perspective.

http://news.google.com

Using the same technology as in the Google Internet search engine, this site provides access to thousands of different news sources.

Political Systems, States, and Nations

A stateless nation. Kurds in Iraq protest, demanding greater regional autonomy for their group

LEARNING OBJECTIVES

5.1 Characterize the alternative definitions and goals of the state.

5.2 Compare and contrast the concepts of nation and state.

5.3 Outline the key components of the political system.

📖 **Read**
and **Listen** to
Chapter 5 at
mypoliscilab.com

✔ **Study**
and **Review** the
**Pre-Test &
Flashcards** at
mypoliscilab.com

They inhabit a region of 74,000 square miles, most living inside the current borders of Turkey, Iraq, and Iran. But they are not Turks, not Arabs, not Persians (Iranians). These kin-based, mountain nomads have always had their own language, a distinctive culture, and a powerful sense of shared identity. They want to be recognized as their own country; instead, they have experienced centuries of discrimination, cultural destruction, massive violence, and even genocide.

They continue to dream of Kurdistan—the land of the Kurds. Kurdistan was briefly recognized by a few other countries (e.g., the former Soviet Union) after World War I, but their land was successfully claimed by other countries. Great Britain held colonial control of some of the area, where substantial oil deposits were discovered in 1920. The British gave most of the oil-rich areas inhabited by the Kurds to Iraq, whose new leaders the British installed and assumed they could control. At the same time, Atatürk was establishing the modern state of Turkey (see Focus in 10). Atatürk launched a major military and cultural offensive against the 19 million Kurds inside Turkey. He insisted they were not Kurds, but "mountain Turks." Kurdish language, names, schools, and cultural traditions were forbidden, and when the Kurds resisted, the Turkish military killed 250,000 of them.

In Iran, Shia Muslims took power after the Iranian Revolution of 1979. They have extensively persecuted the Kurds within Iran's border because the Kurds are Sunni Muslims. Then, Iraq's Saddam Hussein—frustrated by the Iran–Iraq War (1980–1988) and the defeat in the Gulf War (2003)—turned his wrath on the Iraqi Kurds. In the military campaign known as *Al Anfal*, meaning "The Spoils," the Iraqi military were given orders to kill every Kurdish male between the ages of 18 and 55. Between 1986 and 1988, *Al Anfal* included mass executions of tens of thousands of noncombatants; the destruction of more than 4,000 villages; the use of chemical weapons, such as mustard gas, in more than 60 villages; the destruction of civilian buildings like schools and mosques; and the arbitrary jailing of tens of thousands, including women, children, and elderly people accused only of sympathizing with the Kurdish cause. More than 100,000 Iraqi Kurds were killed during this genocide.

Although as many as 35 percent of the Kurds have fled the area to escape the violence, about 36 million Kurds still live in the region, including about 19 million in Turkey, 9 million in Iran, 6.5 million in Iraq, and 1.5 million in

Syria. The granting of partial autonomy to the Kurdish region in Iraq after the fall of Saddam Hussein has raised the hopes of Kurds throughout the region that—through negotiation, political activism, and armed resistance—Kurdistan will one day become a reality.

The desire of the 36 million Kurds for a state of their own highlights one of the most significant causes of conflict in the modern world: the existence of nations—groups of people with a powerful, shared sense of identity—who live in areas that are not coterminous with the boundaries of states, which are the legal political entities in the international system. Sometimes, as in the case of the Kurds, as well as the Masai in Kenya and Tanzania, and the Palestinians in Israel and Jordan, the nation spills over across the boundaries of two or more states. Other times, the nation is a subgroup that exists within a single state but wants autonomy or independence. This is the situation of groups such as the Quebecois in Canada, the Tamils in Sri Lanka, and the Basques in Spain, among many others.

In Part II (Chapters 2–4), we focused on improving our understanding of the political beliefs and actions of individuals. In Part II, we substantially expand our level of analysis, examining the politics and political behavior of very large collectivities of people. This chapter explains and distinguishes two crucial concepts characterizing these large groupings: *state* and *nation*. States are arguably the most important actors in the international system. However, nation-based identities are powerful, and the disjunction between state boundaries and peoples with shared identities might the greatest cause of violence and death in the contemporary political world. The chapter concludes with a focus on a more abstract model that can help us grasp how these large groups operate as a political entity—the concept of the *political system*.

THE STATE

In discussing the politics of large groups of individuals, one of the core concepts is "the state." Anthropological evidence suggests that early social organization among humans was probably based on small living groups of family. As suggested by humanistic psychologist Abraham Maslow (1954), human groupings formed so that people were better able to meet their physiological, safety, love, and belonging needs. As groupings became larger, tribes or bands were formed on the basis of more extensive kinship and economic ties. It might be argued that the "state" emerged in ancient times, when a large collectivity had distinctive leadership roles, accepted rules for social interaction, and a set of organizational arrangements that identified and served collective needs.

5.1 Characterize the alternative definitions and goals of the state.

Watch the Video "Somalia's Pirates" at mypoliscilab.com

A Legal Definition of the State

However, the social scientific concept of the state is a relatively modern one. It is based on the legal notion that the state is *a territorially bound sovereign entity*. The idea of sovereignty emerged in the 16th and 17th centuries. In current interpretations, **sovereignty** is *the premise that each state has complete authority* *and is the ultimate source of law within its own boundaries.* Sovereignty is the key element in the legal concept of the state. It is a basic assumption of international politics and is reflected in a fundamental principle of the United Nations–the sovereign equality of all member states. This means that, before the law, Cambodia is equal to China, Bolivia is equal to Brazil. While sovereignty has legal standing and moral force in international law, the reality of international politics is that a state's sovereign rights depend ultimately on whether the state has sufficient power to enforce its position (Sassen 1996). Thus, it is not likely that, when major national interests are at stake, China will yield to Cambodia merely on the basis of Cambodia's sovereign rights.

State is among the most extensively used concepts in political science, and it has various meanings. Notice that in the general language of political science, the word *state* usually refers to the set of organizational units and people that performs the political functions for an entire national territorial entity, such as France, Indonesia, or Nigeria. In some countries, including the United States, the concept of state also refers to subnational governmental units (e.g., the state of Alabama). In this chapter and throughout this book, the term *state* will normally denote the full array of governmental units that act on behalf of a sovereign country.

You should also be aware that the language of political science often treats the state as though it were a single actor. For example, consider the statement that "each state has complete authority...." In reality, the state is composed of many people who behave as individuals but whose combined behaviors are characterized as if they were performed by a single actor. This book also examines other collectivities of individuals (e.g., the group, the political party, the judiciary) that are discussed as though they operate as a single actor.

Associated with the idea of sovereignty in the legal definition of the state is the doctrine of **territorial integrity**, which holds that *a state has the right to resist and reject any aggression, invasion, or intervention within its territorial borders.* As with the more general notion of sovereignty, a state's actual protection of its territorial integrity depends on the state's capacity and political power.

It might seem that there are many relatively clear examples of a state's territorial integrity being violated, such as the Iraqi army's invasion of Kuwait in 1990; but there is often considerable disagreement over claimed violations of territorial integrity. First, territorial integrity is a fuzzy concept when there is a *dispute over borders.* There are numerous current disputes between countries regarding ownership of offshore waters and their resources (e.g., Canada, Denmark, Russia and the U.S.). Such disputes are sometimes settled by adjudication by an international agency. But border disputes can precipitate fighting, as a land border dispute did recently between Cambodia and Thailand.

Second, attempts to exercise sovereignty can be disputed when there is *disagreement about who the legitimate rulers are.* In Angola, for example, three contending groups each claimed to be the legitimate ruling group of the resource-rich country at independence in 1975. Each group controlled parts of the country, and each had outside assistance (money, arms, troops) from actors such as Cuba, South Africa, the former Soviet Union, the United States, and the United Nations.

This struggle over sovereignty resulted in a devastating civil war that ravaged the country for more than 25 years (1975–2002). The toll included complete collapse of the economy, 4.5 million refugees, tens of thousands who lost limbs to millions of land mines, and the death of more than 1.5 million Angolans. Similar conflicts over sovereignty have arisen recently in Ivory Coast, Somalia, and the Spanish Sahara.

Third, the international community has become less sensitive to the protection of sovereignty when there is strong evidence that the government is committing *serious human rights violations* against its own citizens. This can lead to intense controversies about whether sovereignty has been violated. One recent example is Libya. After substantial numbers of Libyans openly protested against the rule of Muammar Qaddafy in 2011, opposition groups seized control of considerable territory, especially in Eastern Libya. Qaddafy responded aggressively, sending his military forces against the rebels. Some major actors in the international community, including the United Nations, Britain, France and the United States, insisted that Qaddafy stop the violence against his own people. A NATO-led coalition then intervened, claiming its goal was a humanitarian intervention to prevent Libya from using its troops to engage in widespread, deadly violence against the regime's opponents. Airplanes and missiles destroyed some of Libya's military capabilities, but also attacked Libyan troops and other sites, including Qadaffy's residence. Qaddafy claimed that these actions were a clear violation of Libya's sovereignty. Whose claim is most compelling? Similar disputes over sovereignty versus intervention are becoming more common as the international community embraces the doctrine of R2P—the "responsibility to protect." This issue is explored in the Debate in 5.

A Structural–Functional Definition of the State

As an alternative to the legal definition, the state can be defined by the key organizational *structures* that operate as "the government" and the key *functions* that the state performs. In this structural–functional perspective, the **state** is defined as a country's *organized institutional machinery for making and carrying out political decisions and for enforcing the laws and rules of the government.*

Max Weber (1864–1920), the great political sociologist, emphasizes one specific function that distinguishes the state from all other organizations: the state has a monopoly on the legitimate use of force and coercion in the society. That is, only the state has the right to use violence to enforce the society's laws and decisions.

In the broader "state-centered" definition, the state is an autonomous actor, composed of public officials making decisions. The state's essential functions are to maintain order and to compete with other actual or potential states (Levi 2002). In this view, the state pursues "the national interest," which it attempts to achieve against resistance from both domestic and international actors (Morgenthau 2005; Kahler 2002). The particular way in which a state's structures are configured is crucial in shaping the content of public officials' policy preferences and the state's effectiveness in implementing those policy preferences in the society.

THE DEBATE IN 5 | Does Humanitarian Intervention Violate State Sovereignty?

A controversial issue in recent years is whether it is acceptable for states and international actors to use force (or the threat of force) against a state that is suspected of or is abusing the human rights of its own citizens. This is sometimes justified as humanitarian intervention by those taking the actions (Holzgrefe and Keohane 2003). However, the state that is the target of such an intervention can object that this is a clear violation of its sovereignty and hence of international law (Jackson 2007). Indeed, this policy has been termed "the most significant adjustment to national sovereignty in 360 years" (Gilbert, quoted in Pattison 2010:4). Disputes over the clash between these principles have recently been serious issues regarding countries such as China, Congo, Libya, and Sudan. Is humanitarian intervention an acceptable action if it violates a state's sovereignty?

PROTECTING HUMAN RIGHTS TAKES PRECEDENCE OVER STATE SOVEREIGNTY

- The international society of states now defines sovereignty in terms of a bundle of both rights and obligations. Respect for human rights to "life, liberty, and security of person" is among those obligations, by virtue of the Universal Human Rights Declaration (adopted by the United Nations in 1948) and other treaties. Thus, a state that inflicts gross and widespread atrocities on its own population has forfeited some of its rights, including its claim that humanitarian intervention violates its sovereignty (Pattison 2010).
- In 2005, the United Nations General Assembly explicitly asserted its collective "responsibility to protect" (R2P) people by humanitarian intervention when a government does not safeguard its own peoples' lives, particularly in cases of large-scale state violence against its population such as ethnic cleansing, violent

At what level of human suffering can outside powers legitimately intervene within a sovereign state over the objections of the state's leaders, as occurred in Sudan?

repression of peaceful protest, or extensive use of imprisonment without due process (Evans 2008).
- The global community of states has a clear responsibility to take whatever actions are necessary to prevent any state from abusing individuals' human rights because this demonstrates the states' willingness to act beyond national self-interest.

(Continued)

- Outside states, acting in concert, also have a responsibility to intervene in situations of a severe humanitarian crisis, including actions to prevent a deepening of the crisis, to direct reactions to it, and to engage in rebuilding efforts in the aftermath, regardless of objections from the "sovereign" state (Pattison 2010).
- If no outside group intervenes to stop a state from serious violations of human rights, the state might engage in even more extensive and unacceptable acts of violence against its own citizens. Similarly, in the absence of such action by interveners, other states might be emboldened to violate the human rights of their own citizens.

STATE SOVEREIGNTY TAKES PRECEDENCE OVER OUTSIDERS' CONCERNS ABOUT HUMAN RIGHTS

- State sovereignty is a central premise of international law. This core principle provides a state with almost complete authority to implement policy decisions within its own borders. A state's right to this exclusive internal jurisdiction is violated if another state or group intervenes within its borders without its consent. In accordance with international law, the state can respond by any means necessary to defend its territory (Jackson 2007).
- Despite the idealized notion of universal human rights, different cultures have significantly different interpretations of individual rights and the conditions under which such rights have been violated. It is not appropriate that a predominantly Western conception of human rights should necessarily take precedence over a country's own standards.
- It can be very difficult for outside actors to determine the precise level of the purported violations of human rights within another country.

Even more important, there are no universally accepted standards regarding the level at which human rights violations become so gross (that is, so extensive, severe, and persistent) that outside intervention is justified (Evans 2008).

- States accept the principle that, in the absence of full procedural support from the UN, external actors cannot intervene within a state that opposes such an action. Yet such interventions do occur (e.g., NATO in Kosovo and Libya). Such actions are often better understood as an assertion by powerful states of the right to intervene (R2I) in the affairs of weaker states that they wish to control—even if under the cover of UN support.
- Humanitarian intervention, when associated with severe economic sanctions and military invasion, can cause more harm to the population than the human rights violations that prompted these actions. This problem is compounded when intervening states do not follow international norms that require an intervention to be proportional to the human rights violation (Pattison 2010).

MORE QUESTIONS...

1. How severe and extensive must a violation of human rights be in order to justify the intervention of other countries in the internal affairs of a sovereign state? Who can legitimately judge the level of violation?
2. Is R2P any more compelling if there appear to be human rights violations by several groups within a country, not just the government?
3. Is it acceptable for external interveners to cause widespread suffering and destruction within a country in the attempt to end the perceived human rights abuses?

A widely used structural-functional approach, based on the work of the late Gabriel Almond and his colleagues (e.g., Powell, Strom and Dalton 2012), centers on two questions:

1. What *functions* must be performed if the state is to persist?
2. What *structures* perform these necessary functions within a given state?

Chapters 6 and 7 will detail many of the major political structures and institutional arrangements (e.g., legislatures, judiciaries, and electoral systems) that handle the various political functions. The classic version of Almond's structural–functional approach identifies eight functions that must be performed in every state:

1. *Political socialization* is the processes through which individuals acquire their cognitive, affective, and evaluative orientations towards the political world.
2. *Political recruitment* is the processes through which people are drawn into roles as political actors.
3. *Political communication* is the mechanisms by which political information flows through society.
4. *Interest articulation* is the low-level communication, by individuals and groups, of what they need or want from the state.
5. *Interest aggregation* is the transformation of all these political needs and wants into a smaller number of coherent alternatives.
6. *Policymaking* is the process by which the state establishes laws, policy decisions, and value allocations.
7. *Policy implementation* is the actual application of such laws and policy decisions.
8. *Policy adjudication* is the interpretation and resolution of disagreements regarding what the policies mean and how they should be implemented.

While it might seem obvious at first glance that a certain structure always performs a particular function, more reflection (and later chapters) will suggest that the situation is usually more complex. In most contemporary societies, almost every political function is performed by a variety of structures. Many of these structures are part of the state, but others are nonstate actors such as interest groups, religious organizations, media, social groups, private businesses, and international organizations. For example, it is not simply the case that Congress performs the policymaking function in the United States. Many policy decisions are also formulated by the president, by cabinet departments, by the bureaucracy, by the courts as they both interpret and reshape laws, by structures at the local levels of government, by special interest groups, and by citizens through electoral initiatives. Thus, the central focus in structural–functional research is to illuminate the key processes performed by each important structure and the subtle interrelationships among structures as they contribute to a given function.

Major Goals

Another core question is: What major goals does a state pursue? Each state assigns different levels of relative importance to a wide variety of goals; however, most can be subsumed under three overarching goals: security, stability, and prosperity. Each of these goals includes component goals that the political system might act to serve. The significance of each component goal and the capacity of the state to achieve each goal depend on many factors such as the state's resources, strategic location, history, political culture, leaders, political structures, and the behavior of actors outside the political system. While many of these factors depend primarily on dynamics inside to the state's borders, others are substantially affected by the actions of other global actors. Figure 5.1 illustrates this framework of basic goals.

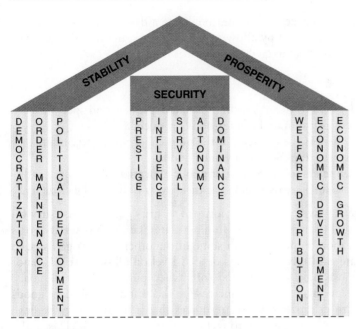

FIGURE 5.1
Basic goals of states

In the descriptions that follow, the major components of each overarching goal are presented in the general order of their priority for most states.

Security

1. *Survival* is the fundamental element of security. It entails the very existence of the state, such that other states do not conquer it and that internal forces do not destroy it.
2. *Autonomy* refers to the capacity of the state to act within its own boundaries without intervention into or control of its affairs by external actors.
3. *Influence* involves the state's ability to alter the actions of external actors in desired ways by means of persuasion or inducements.
4. *Prestige* is the desirable situation wherein external actors admire and respect the state.
5. *Dominance* is the use of power or violence to enable the state to impose direct control over external actors.

Stability

1. *Order maintenance* is the capacity of the state to ensure social peace for its citizens through the prevention of individual and group violation of societal norms, especially those involving violence.
2. *Political development* refers to the concentration of political authority in a state that has strong capabilities to make and enforce effective policies and to gain support from its citizens.

3. *Democratization* is the process of institutionalizing a democratic system of governance, which is achieved by allowing free elections, limiting the actions of the rulers, and guaranteeing civil and political rights.

Prosperity

1. *Economic growth* refers to the increasing scale, complexity, and specialization of the productive system and of the goods produced.
2. *Economic development* is the capacity of the political economy to obtain, manage, and transform resources into valued goods.
3. *Welfare distribution* refers to the private or public allocation of adequate and increasing levels of valued goods to enhance the quality of life of the citizenry.

Notice that Figure 5.1 gives particular priority to security goals because survival must be an essential goal of every country. In most states, certain prosperity goals and stability goals are more important than some of the other security goals, such as dominance. No state can fully achieve its desired level on all of these 11 major goals. Thus, a state must make difficult trade-offs when pursuing multiple goals. For example, when a state makes a costly increase in the amount of welfare goods and services allocated to its citizens, it uses resources that it might otherwise have reinvested in the state's economic system to facilitate economic growth. This trade-off is often referred to as the fundamental policy choice of *growth versus welfare*. In another example, resources that the state allocates to the military for major security goals are not available for either welfare or the production of consumer goods. This policy trade-off is characterized by the phrase *guns versus butter*. Of the 11 major goals listed in Figure 5.1, which ones do you think are most complementary? Most incompatible?

Throughout this text, we will frequently examine the pursuit of the goals of security, stability, and prosperity through the state's actions within its own boundaries and the state's interactions with actors outside its borders. There are crucial normative questions that each state confronts regarding how much priority to give to each goal, what strategies it should employ in the pursuit of its goals, and how extensive state action should be. Moreover, there are strong disagreements within each state regarding how expansive its domain of action should be. Everyone agrees that the boundaries of state activity should be limited to *res publica*, a Latin phrase meaning *"things of the people."* But what "things" should be included? And how expansive should the state's involvement with these things be? For example, each of the major "isms" outlined in Chapter 2—conservatism, classical liberalism, socialism, fascism, Islamism—has a fundamentally different prescription for the extent of legitimate state action. And the role of the state in the economic system is a key topic in Chapter 8.

We shall see throughout this book, and especially in Part Five, that some states are active in almost every aspect of their citizens' lives, while other states intervene in only limited spheres and to a limited extent. One state might provide a total health care delivery system to all citizens, with no direct charges for doctors, hospitals, or treatment, whereas another state might subsidize only hospitalization for the very poor. One state might require schools to provide daily religious instruction, while another state might forbid schools from engaging in even the general discussion of religious philosophies. In every society, there are persistent, and sometimes very contentious, political debates about the appropriate boundaries of state action and about the best means to achieve a particular aspect of one of the 11 major goals.

THE NATION

In the political world, the concept of the nation has a psychological and emotional basis rather than a legal or functional basis (as the concept of the state does). A **nation** is defined as *a set of people with a deeply shared fundamental identification*. Different factors might be the basis of such identification: shared descent (belief in a common kinship or history), shared culture, shared geographic space, shared religion, shared language, or shared economic order. The nation is a community of understanding, of communication, and of trust (Connor 1994). The Kurds are an example of a nation that fulfills all these conditions.

Most people feel some identity with a variety of different reference groups or communities such as a religion, local community, ethnic group, social club, and sports team. In the usage here, what distinguishes a nation from other reference groups is that the nation is a major group, beyond the family group, with whom a person identifies very powerfully. It is an essential division between "us" and "them." The strength of a person's primary national identity depends on the relative importance he places on various identities and the extent to which the most important identities reinforce this basic conception of "us" versus "them." Thus, **nationalism** is *a powerful commitment to the advancement of the interests and welfare of an individual's own nation*, with minimal concern about the conditions of those outside the nation.

A related concept is ***identity politics***. This means that some key shared trait(s) lead a significant group of people to see themselves as being distinctive, with a shared political agenda that might shape their political beliefs or motivate their actions (Hoover, Marcia and Parris 1997). Identity politics characterizes a group defined by one of the major nation-based factors described above, such as ethnicity or religion. However, some suggest that the concept of identity politics particularly applies to groups that perceive themselves to be marginalized or oppressed within their social order. In this sense, it has been applied to groups based on markers such as ethnic minority status, caste, gender, sexual orientation, or disability.

Another broad class of nation-based groups that is sometimes given special consideration is ***indigenous peoples***—a term for more than 370 million people in about 70 countries. Each of these 5,000 distinct nations is understood to be a "first people" who originally inhabited a geographic area as "natives," but who were then subjugated by an invading nation. In nearly every case, these nations have almost no political or social power and their culture is marginalized or suppressed by the dominant culture. Since the early 1970s and most recently with the Declaration of Rights of Indigenous Peoples (2007), the United Nations has been concerned about protecting such groups against discrimination and against efforts to destroy their nationality identity and culture. Some of these nations have become more politically assertive, demanding autonomy, although most countries resist providing their indigenous peoples with special political rights.

5.2 Compare and contrast the concepts of nation and state.

Watch the **Video "The South Ossetia Crisis"** at **mypoliscilab.com**

Nation and State

The best situation for effective governance is a ***nation–state***, which is *an area that has both the territorial borders of a single state and a citizenry who all share the same primary national identity.* Only a few modern states have the combination of common culture, history, ethnicity, religion, and language that results in a strong sense of shared nationality among nearly all the citizens governed by the state. Japan is an example of a relatively homogeneous nation–state.

However, the most common situations are what might be termed "stateless nations." Occasionally, one nation is split into two states, such as North and South Korea. In such cases, the citizens often dream of reunification, even when their governments and ideologies differ fundamentally. This occurred in Germany, which was split into communist East Germany and capitalist West Germany after World War II. In 1990, citizens of the German nation were reunited in a single country after nearly half a century of antagonistic separation into two very different states. The example of the Kurds at the beginning of the chapter illuminates the more severe form of a stateless nation, with one nation distributed across multiple states.

The reality of the contemporary world is that most countries are ***multinational states***, which *include significant groups whose fundamental identities are associated with different nations.* When these nation-based identities are very strong, they can produce intense animosity and violence between groups within (and between) states (Laitin 2007; Miller 2007; Taras and Ganguly 2010). These problems have been particularly evident in many of the states that gained independence after 1945 with borders that were based on the arbitrary administrative decisions of colonial powers, not nationality differences. But in many multinational states, nation-based conflicts have not been permanently resolved, regardless of the age of the country.

When identity and region are relatively similar, it is possible to provide greater autonomy to major groups or to reorganize states and borders. So, for example, Scotland and Wales have been given far greater regional political autonomy within Great Britain. When the former Soviet Union—the world's most multinational state—collapsed in 1991, it was replaced by 15 states that were generally organized on nationality grounds. The recent split into Sudan and South Sudan was another attempt to better align borders and nationality identities.

However, there are far more instances where the problems in multinational states persist. The agitation by the Quebecois in Canada, the Basques in Spain, and the Irish Catholics in Northern Ireland are testimony to the possibility that even centuries-old states can struggle with nationality conflict. There are reports every day of struggles such as those of the Israelis and Palestinians, the Tibetans in China, the Tamils in Sri Lanka, and the South Ossetians in Georgia. The bloody nationality violence in Eastern Europe during the 1990s was based on devastating ethnic battles among the Bosnians, Croatians, Serbs, and others in the former Yugoslavia. Even this carnage is overshadowed by the horrendous ethnic conflict in Rwanda and Burundi between the Hutus and the Tutsis. More than 100,000 (mostly Tutsis) were slaughtered in Rwanda in only 100 days in 1994, and more than 300,000 Hutus and Tutsis were killed in ethnic conflict in Burundi between 1994 and 2006.

Some scholars predict that the current reorganization of states based on nationality identities will produce more than 50 new states and that nation-based conflicts might remain the world's major cause of violence and instability (Barber 1995; Miller 2007). The example of the Indian subcontinent in Focus in 5 illustrates many of these issues regarding the challenges of balancing states and nations.

▶ FOCUS IN 5 | State and Nations: The Indian Subcontinent

The problem of discontinuities between nations and states is often most severe in states that have gained independence since 1945. The Indian subcontinent exemplifies these problems. The vast Indian subcontinent was a feudal society divided into many small kingdoms ruled by kings (*maharajahs*). Starting in the 16th century, the riches of India were pursued—and often exploited—by many traders, including the British, Dutch, French, and Arabs. The states from which these traders came began to struggle for dominance over the Indian trade, and the British finally gained hegemony in the 18th century after defeating the French. From that time until 1947, the Indian subcontinent was the major jewel in the British imperial crown, treated as a single territory under colonial rule.

After a lengthy and often violent campaign of political and social action by Indian nationalists, the British granted the subcontinent independence in 1947. Despite the desires of the British and the efforts of some Indian leaders, such as Mohandas Gandhi (recall Compare in 4), the subcontinent was deeply split on the basis of religion between Hindus and Muslims. Because it seemed impossible to fashion a single state out of these two nations, two states were formed in 1947: India, which was predominantly (82 percent) Hindu; and Pakistan, which was predominantly (90 percent) Muslim.

Many Hindus in Pakistan and Muslims in India were forced to leave their homelands and migrate to the new state sharing their religion. The hostility and bloodshed associated with the partition resulted in one million deaths. There have been periodic violent boundary conflicts ever since. The ownership of nuclear weapons by India and Pakistan since 1998 accentuates the need to resolve the conflicts between the two states.

While the major religious difference on the Indian subcontinent was generally resolved by this partition, many other nationality problems remained. For example, since 1947, India and Pakistan have disagreed about which country should control the region of Jammu and Kashmir. At independence, India was given control of the region, although the majority of the population was and remains Muslim. Disputes over control of the region have resulted in more than sixty years of military conflicts and intermittent guerrilla war, despite persistent United Nations involvement.

The situation was further complicated by the concentration of Muslims in two geographically distinct areas in the northeast and northwest regions of the subcontinent. As a consequence, Pakistan was composed of two parts at independence, separated by more than 1,500 miles of rival India's territory. The two parts of the country engaged in a protracted nationality dispute between the two major ethnic groups, the Punjabis, who were dominant in West Pakistan, and the Bengalis, who were dominant in East Pakistan. The Bengalis felt discriminated against both economically and culturally by the Punjabis, who controlled the government and the military. When the Bengalis won a national election in 1970, the Punjabis in West Pakistan attempted to retain political power and refused to allow the elected Bengali leaders to take the reins of government. The Punjabis launched a brutal military operation to suppress the Bengalis, who decided that victory in the struggle would enable them to form their own independent nation–state. After a brutal civil war in 1971, which resulted in 3 million deaths from

(Continued)

violence and starvation and 10 million refugees fleeing Pakistan, the Bengalis of East Pakistan won the civil war and created a new sovereign state, Bangladesh.

Major nation-based cleavages continue to plague India, creating substantial barriers to forging a single identity as a nation–state. There are 21 official languages in addition to the two "national" languages, Hindi and English, each understood by only about one-third of the population. In all, there are about 1,650 different dialects spoken in India, most of which are mutually unintelligible.

India has at least five major religious groupings: Hindu, Muslim, Sikh, Christian, and Buddhist. Hindu nationalism has increasingly been expressed through a political movement, resulting in the growing power at the regional and national levels of Hindu parties, particularly the Bharatiya Janata Party (BJP). The BJP, which dominated the government from 1998 to 2004 and is now the main opposition party, is the most serious threat to a secular Indian government since independence. With the increase in Hindu nationalism, violence against Christians and Muslims has risen significantly.

Another religion-based nation that has been a source of political unrest in India is the Sikhs, who are concentrated in the northwest part of India called the Punjab. The Sikhs have a very strong identity as a religious community and an ethnic group. Their sense of nationality is heightened by their belief that they are discriminated against politically by the Hindus. The Sikhs have occasionally been militant in demanding greater political autonomy, and since the early 1980s, some have insisted on full independence to create the nation–state of Khalistan. Prime Minister Indira Gandhi was assassinated in 1984 by two Sikhs among her private guard in retaliation for an Indian army attack on rebels inside the Sikh's holiest shrine.

Rajiv Gandhi succeeded his mother as prime minister, only to be the victim of another nation-based dispute. The Indian army had intervened on the neighboring island-country of Sri Lanka in an attempt to limit the extremely violent, ethnically-based civil war between the native Sinhalese and the Tamils, who had migrated to Sri Lanka from southern India. Tamils in Sri Lanka were angry that India did not support their independence struggles and by the treatment they received from the Indian army. In 1991, Rajiv Gandhi was assassinated by a Tamil woman who had strapped a bomb to her body.

In sum, the many deep cleavages on the Indian subcontinent, based on religion, ethnicity, culture, and region, have exposed the (now five) states to persistent instability, conflict, and nation-based carnage.

FURTHER FOCUS

1. What strategies can a state like India use to overcome the many nation-based cleavages?
2. Might the current problems in the region have been even greater if Gandhi's vision of a single state had been fulfilled, rather than the split into Bangladesh, India, and Pakistan? ▲

THE POLITICAL SYSTEM

5.3 Outline the key components of the political system.

As the Appendix explains, formal models are abstractions that can sometimes be very helpful in enabling us to better visualize how something works. A formal model that has influenced the way many political scientists (including me) understand the dynamics of politics is based on a concept called "the political system." You might also find it useful, perhaps as a metaphor, for thinking about politics.

The political system concept was developed in the work of David Easton (1965), whose idea was to adapt "general systems theory" from biology. Any "system" is a series of components that operate together and are interrelated, such that change in any one component can affect other components. For example, an engine is a mechanical system composed of such interrelated components as pistons, carburetor, spark plugs, and so on. A jazz band is an example of a human system whose components can be more improvisational but no less interrelated. And a political system is also a system of human behavior with multiple components. The political system model identifies these components and the linkages among them as they perform certain activities.

For Easton, the unique nature of the political system is that it performs a particular function: *the authoritative allocation of values for the collectivity*. This means that the political system makes policy decisions (allocations) that are binding (based on its authority) with regard to things that have importance (values) to the people it serves (the collectivity). Each part of this definition is important for our general understanding of politics, and so the next few paragraphs elaborate on each.

Explore the Comparative "Political Landscapes" on mypoliscilab.com

Values *Values* are those *things that have great significance and importance to people*. **Political values**, *those within the domain of res publica*, have a variety of other forms. They can be *broad ideals* like liberty, equality, freedom, and justice. They can be *material goods,* such as a decent house or road system; they can be *services,* such as quality health care or a good education; they can be *conditions,* such as clean air or security from national enemies. Values can also be *symbolic goods,* such as status. In addition to positive values, there are negative values such as coercion or imprisonment, polluted water, epidemic disease, and so on. (Notice that this social scientific concept of values is broader than the notion of values as moral judgments that people use to guide their actions.)

Most values are scarce resources—either there is an insufficient amount of a given value to satisfy everyone, or the enjoyment of one value by some requires a loss of value to others. For example, a state's vast arsenal of nuclear weapons may make one person feel secure while at the same time it makes another person feel extremely insecure. One person might favor more government expenditures to fight global terrorism, while another would prefer the government to spend more resources on providing quality health care, and a third might prefer lower taxes rather than either of these forms of government spending. Every possible value distribution entails trade-offs among different values as well as some inequality in the benefits and burdens linked to each person. Thus, there are always disagreements, competition, and even violent conflict over whose values will be served and whose will not. What are *your* top two values for your society? For yourself?

Allocation Pierre Mendes-France, a distinguished French premier (1954–1955), observed that "to govern is to make choices." *Allocation* refers to such choice making—to the process by which decisions and actions are taken to grant values to some and deny values to others. Value allocations occur at every moment when decisions are made to alter or even to sustain the existing distribution of values. Making these decisions and actions in the face of competition and conflict over values is a central aspect of politics.

Authoritative Value allocations are *authoritative* when the decisions are accepted as binding by those people affected by the decisions. One of the most fascinating questions in political analysis is: Why do people accept the authority of the political system to allocate values in a manner that is not to their direct advantage? That is, why do people accept the imposition of taxes, policies, and laws that they judge to be undesirable for themselves? Compare in 5 suggests some of the reasons people accept the decisions of the political system, comparing authority relations with the exercise of power.

COMPARE IN 5 | Power and Authority

Few discussions about politics can occur without direct or indirect reference to power or authority. Both concepts imply the capacity of A (one actor) to control the behavior of B (another actor). What is the difference between power and authority?

Power. *Coercive power is exercised when A induces B to behave in a manner in which B would not otherwise behave, based on the use of force or the threat of force.* In some cases, A actually does inflict direct bodily harm on B using an instrument of force (e.g., guns, bombs, torture), or A imposes undesirable conditions on B (e.g., imprisonment or discriminatory treatment). However, there are many cases of power exercise where B's behavior is controlled when B believes there is a credible threat that A will administer coercive power.

Some scholars distinguish a second form of power, economic power (Boulding 1993). In *economic power,* A manipulates the control of resources that B wants or needs, in order to alter B's behavior. A might refuse to sell or give to B an important resource (e.g., oil, economic aid, or military protection) that B wants, unless B meets A's demands. Alternatively, A might promise to provide B with a resource (e.g., a trade agreement or a bribe) only if B does what A desires.

Of course, A is not necessarily successful in the threat or use of coercion or the manipulation of economic resources. B could decide not to alter its behavior in the way that A wants by ignoring a threat, by refusing the economic resources offered by A, or by responding with its own coercive power, which could result in violence between A and B. When actors have competing values, the option of employing coercive power or economic power is always a possibility.

A third form of power is "soft power" (Nye 2004). Soft power is evident when B is persuaded to accept what A wants because B greatly admires A's virtue and qualities, and because B believes that it shares important values with A. Thus A exercises its soft power when B accepts A's demand, even if not in B's evident self-interest, without any explicit threat or the promise of the provision of a resource. (For other views of power, see Bachrach and Baratz 1962; Boulding 1989; Dahl and Stinebrickner 2003; Lukes 2005; and Wrong 1996.)

Authority. B's compliance in an authority relationship with A is not based on power. B behaves in the manner consistent with A's demands on the basis of authority when *B willingly accedes to what A wants because of B's belief that A has a legitimate right to demand compliance.* Authority is voluntaristic. B accepts the decision or demand of A because it is "the right thing to do," not because of coercive, economic, or soft power. The judgment of B that A's authority is legitimate might be grounded in one or more of the following (see Weber 1958a: 295–301):

- *Law.* B believes that the laws or rules enforced by A are rationally established, purposeful, and enacted by a legitimate process, and thus compliance with those laws is proper behavior.
- *Tradition.* B is influenced by a long-standing habit among most people to accept patterns of authoritative action by A. Socialization is typically an element in this form of convincing (indoctrinating?) B to accept the authority of A.
- *Charisma.* B accepts the actions of a dynamic leader whose personal qualities are so extraordinary that the leader wins B's trust and unquestioning support. This seems an extreme form of soft power.

(Continued)

Source: © *The New Yorker* Collection 1977 George Booth from cartoonbank.com. All Rights Reserved.

■ *Contract.* Acceptance of A's authority is based on B's belief that there is a contract between A and B in which A enforces a social order that protects B's interests. When actor A is the state, a broad version of this is the concept of the social contract proposed by classical political theorists such as Thomas Hobbes (1588–1679; recall Chapter 2) and John Locke (1632–1704).

Notice that the dynamics of power and authority relationships cover a vast number of situations that involve competing values and agendas and thus are political. There are many instances where the behaviors of both actors A and B are a complex mix of power and authority patterns. As with other actors, even the power and authority of the state can be challenged. Consider: Antigone, in Sophocles' (496–

(*Continued*)

406 B.C.E.) classic play, who challenges a law by the king, her uncle Creon; Mohandas Gandhi's campaign of resistance to British rule in India; the civil rights movements in South Africa and in the United States; the citizens' resistance to tainted political leadership in many countries, such as the 2011 challenge to Libya's Qadaffy. Of course, not all challenges to a state's power and authority are legitimate and desirable. Creon tries to persuade Antigone that a danger of defiance is social disorder: "He whom the State appoints must be obeyed to the smallest matter, be it right or wrong.... There is no more deadly peril than disobedience" (Sophocles 1967: 144). The balance between compliance and resistance to power and authority is at the heart of politics.

FURTHER QUESTIONS

1. In general, is it more sensible for the state to rely on power or authority to achieve its goals of security, stability, and prosperity?
2. Consider Lord Acton's cynical aphorism that "all power corrupts." Do you agree with this gloomy appraisal?
3. American philosopher Henry David Thoreau (1817–1862) writes: "If [the law of the state] is of such a nature that it requires you to be the agent of injustice to another, then I say, break the law" (Thoreau 1849: 92). What injustice would persuade you to break the law? What law would you be willing to break? ▰

For a Collectivity The domain of activity for the political system is all those areas where it makes authoritative decisions that affect people's lives. In Easton's classic definition, a political system functions "for a society." His definition serves the purposes of this book well because the book focuses primarily on states—country-level political systems. But a political system can exist at any level. This concept could certainly apply to subnational political systems (including such U.S. examples as states, counties, and municipalities). It could also apply to a supranational political system that encompasses more than one country (e.g., the European Union, which includes 27 separate countries). Thus, this book offers a more generalized definition of the political system as "the authoritative allocation of values *for a collectivity.*"

Conceptualization of the Political System

In Easton's (1965) conceptualization, the political system can be viewed as a gigantic processing mechanism that converts "inputs" into "outputs" (Figure 5.2). The political system exists within a larger environment that includes other systems, such as the economic system, the cultural system, the physical resource system, and many others. This broader environment generates many inputs, called demands and supports, which the actors in the political system consider. The political actors then produce outputs, the decisions and actions that allocate values. If these outputs have an effect on the environment, this might produce new demands and supports. This processing system becomes a continuing cycle.

The *environment of the political system* is the name given to *all those activities that are not part of the political system's activity domain.* Do not think of the environment as a separate physical area, but rather those things that occur around the political system and provide both opportunities and constraints

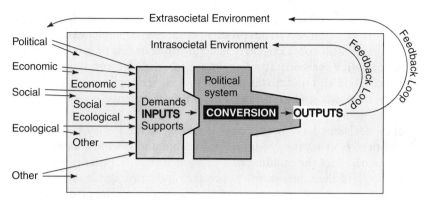

FIGURE 5.2

Conceptualization of the political system

Source: Based on Easton 1965:31.

on its functioning. This environment could include anything, anywhere in the world, although most of the global environment has little direct relevance to any action by a particular political system. So, for example, if the physical resources environment inside the country (or the relevant parts of the physical resources environment outside the country) contain few energy resources, that has an effect on the challenges facing those making political decisions. If the internal cultural environment is permeated by religious conflict, that matters. If a neighboring country is taking actions perceived as a threat to security, that will affect the demands and supports that the political system must deal with. You can see that many aspects of the environment can shape the inputs to the political system's actions.

Demands are *wants or desires for particular value allocations.* Demands might come from individuals, groups, or systems either within the society or outside of it. For example, when a citizen or interest group expresses a preference for lower taxes, or more expenditure on health care, or greater regulation of corporations, this becomes a demand on the political system.

Supports are *actions by individuals or groups that indicate either favorable or unfavorable orientations towards the political system.* These actions can be directed towards any actor in the political system, from a major figure like the president to a low-level bureaucrat to a governmental body like the legislature to a political symbol like the country's flag. Support can be positive, as when a person pays taxes, serves in the state's military, salutes the flag, or votes. Support can also be negative, through actions that criticize or oppose the political system such as a person refusing to pay taxes, avoiding military service, burning the flag, or defacing the ballot.

At the heart of the political system framework is *conversion*—the process by which political actors assess demands and supports within the context of the relevant environmental forces and then determine what values will be allocated to whom. Many political analysts have been especially interested in studying this process. Chapter 9 will describe an analytic model of the public policy process that defines a series of key stages, from problem definition to implementation and evaluation. Chapter 9 also compares three general explanations of how the political system makes policy decisions: the *class approach,* the *elite approach,* and the *pluralist approach.* You will find that in each of these three approaches, a different mix of groups wield power and influence as the political system converts demands and supports into policy decisions.

Once policy decisions have been made and implemented, they become **outputs** of the political system. Some outputs are visible and obvious, as when the political system authorizes the building of a new nuclear power plant, spends the money to build it, and then puts it online producing energy. But it is sometimes difficult to identify the decisions (outputs) because they might involve subtle actions, secret policies, or even "nondecisions" that perpetuate the existing value distribution or bury issues. For example, if some people demand new government subsidies for small farmers and the government does nothing, there has been an allocation decision—even though no visible policy action can be identified. A policy might also be implemented in multiple ways, making it difficult to specify the exact policy output. For example, the state might have a law that a person cannot kill another person, yet the state does not mete out identical punishment to all those who do kill.

Most analysts distinguish outputs from **outcomes**—*the impacts of the decisions taken and implemented by the political system.* Ultimately, it is the impacts of the political system's policy choices that really affect people's lives. The essential question is: What difference did that policy choice (that value allocation) make? How does the implemented policy affect people's health, welfare, security, freedom, knowledge, self-worth, or other values? Even more than in the analysis of outputs, it can be extremely difficult to identify with precision the overall outcomes of a policy and its effects on particular individuals and groups.

The final component in the systems approach is the feedback loop. Decision outputs result in outcomes that alter aspects of the environment and thus affect the next round of demands and supports reaching the political system. *Feedback* is the dynamics through which information about those changes in the environment are monitored by the political system. As changes alter both the environment and the demands and supports, political actors might decide to revise the value allocations they have previously made. As Figure 5.2 indicates, feedback is drawn as a loop to emphasize the continuous circular process among components in the system.

For Easton (1965), a crucial question is: How does a political system persist in a world of challenges and change? Political decision makers must maintain a delicate balance of forces: The environments must be prevented from constraining or overwhelming the political system and must be exploited for the resources and opportunities they present; political actors must be sensitive and accurate in their perceptions and policy decisions; demands must be managed so that they are not irreconcilable and do not overload the resources available; positive support must be nurtured and negative support discouraged or suppressed.

In short, the actors in the political system must operate with political skill and political will. If the political system's performance is poor, there can be serious consequences: a substantial decline in the quality of citizens' lives; major social disorder as in Libya in 2011; a "failed state" such as Somalia; even the "death" of the political system, as occurred in the Sudan in 2011 (when it broke into two countries). Later chapters, especially Chapters 10 and 12, will develop these themes more fully.

THREE MAJOR CONCEPTS: A REPRISE

This chapter has furthered our understanding of the political world by exploring three major concepts that characterize large political entities: state, nation, and political system. First, *state* emphasizes the legal standing and power of sovereign entities, the necessary functions that they perform, and the domain of their actions. The discussion also identified an array of goals that most states pursue, centering on the core goals of security, stability, and prosperity.

Second, *nation* indicates a mental state characterized by a sense of shared identity among a set of people, distinguishing "us" from "them" in the sociopolitical world. Multinational states face particularly strong challenges from the instability that can result from different nation-based identities. The Indian subcontinent is among the many examples of the problem of disjunction between state and nation.

And third, *political system* attempts to provide political scientists with a basic analytic concept for building a general theory of political entities and processes. It is useful as a metaphor for thinking about the dynamic processes among the crucial components in an open, dynamic, and adaptive system whose essential function is the authoritative allocation of values for its collectivity. In Chapters 6 and 7, our discussion of political units will become more concrete as we examine the actual political institutions and structures in contemporary states.

✓•–⟦**Study**
and **Review** the
Post-Test &
Chapter Exam at
mypoliscilab.com

KEY CONCEPTS

authority   126
demands   129
environment of the political system   128
feedback   130
identity politics   121
indigenous peoples   121
inputs   128
multinational state   122
nation   121
nationalism   121
nation-state   122
outcomes   129
outputs   129

political system   125
political values 125
power   126
prosperity   118
res publica   120
security   118
stability   118
sovereignty   113
state   113
supports   129
territorial integrity   114
values   125

FOR FURTHER CONSIDERATION

1. Do you think there are circumstances in which a country's sovereignty should be violated? What is the most serious problem with your position on this question?
2. Do you identify with more than one nation? Is there any conflict between these identities? Under what types of circumstances might a person's multiple nationality identities produce serious internal conflicts?
3. To what extent is it possible to align states and nations in the contemporary world? Would doing this be desirable?
4. Develop a dialogue between person A, who believes that the authority of the state must be obeyed under almost all conditions, and person B, who believes that the authority of the state can be disputed in any situation in which B substantially disagrees with the state's decision.
5. Describe several situations in which the decision-making capacity of the most powerful actors in the political system is almost completely constrained by factors in the extrasocietal or the intrasocietal environment.

FOR FURTHER READING

Barber, Benjamin R. (1995). *Jihad versus McWorld.* New York: Random House. An incisive analysis of current world trends, in which there is a simultaneous globalization of culture and economics and a breakdown of peoples into distinct and hostile nationality groups.

Connor, Walker. (1994). *Ethnonationalism: The Quest for Understanding.* Princeton, NJ: Princeton University Press. A detailed analysis of the nature of and the imperatives driving a people's strong identity with nation as opposed to state, enriched by many illuminating examples.

Evans, Gareth. (2008). *The Responsibility to Protect: Ending Mass Atrocity Crimes Once and For All.* Washington DC: Brookings Institution Press. Linked to the Debate in 5, this is a vigorous justification of the obligation of a state to protect its own citizens from atrocities and, if it fails, the necessity (R2P) for international intervention.

Hutchinson, John, and Anthony Smith, Eds. (1995). *Nationalism.* New York: Oxford University Press. Hutchinson, John, and Anthony Smith, Eds. (1995). *Ethnicity.* New York: Oxford University Press. These two "Oxford Readers" offer an exceptional selection of short excerpts relevant to understanding each concept. Each book includes perspectives from a wide variety of social scientists, historians, social theorists, and others.

Jackson, Robert. (2007). *Sovereignty: The Evolution of an Idea.* Malden, MA: Polity Press. A thoughtful exploration of the concept of sovereignty, including its historical development and its contemporary implications for interstate relations, human rights, and global society.

Kaufman, Stuart J. (2001). *Modern Hatreds: The Symbolic Politics of Ethnic War.* Ithaca, NY: Cornell University Press. The manipulation of ethnonationalist sentiments to serve the political goals of leaders is described in a set of intriguing case studies.

Kesey, Ken. (1962). *One Flew Over the Cuckoo's Nest.* New York: New American Library. A funny, gripping novel (also made into a film) that, at its core, considers the virtues and costs of defying institutional authority.

Marx, Anthony W. (2003). *Faith in Nation: Exclusionary Origins of Nationalism.* New York: Oxford University Press. This study emphasizes the way in which nation-based identity is created mainly by excluding groups, especially based on religious differences, as an intentional strategy to establish nationalism and consolidate governmental power.

Miller, Benjamin. (2007). *States, Nations, and the Great Powers: The Sources of Regional War and Peace*. New York: Cambridge University Press. The explanation of why some regions are peaceful and others are war prone is based on different patterns of balance or imbalance between nations and states in the region, using case studies from Europe, South America, and the Middle East.

Paul, T. V., John Ikenberry, and John Hall, Eds. (2003). *The Nation-State in Question*. Princeton, NJ: Princeton University Press. These essays explore the continuing power and central importance of the state, despite the enormous forces undermining the state from both nation-based identities and globalization.

Rashid, Ahmed. (2002). *Jihad: The Rise of Militant Islam in Central Asia*. New Haven, CT: Yale University Press. Author of the widely discussed *Taliban* (2000, Yale University Press), Rashid offers a rich account of the rapid emergence of religious nationalism in the "stans" of Central Asia (e.g., Tajikistan and Kazakhstan), driven particularly by poverty, corruption, and a reaction to the suppression of Islam in the region.

Snyder, Jack. (2000). *From Voting to Violence: Democratization and Nationalist Conflict*. New York: W. W. Norton. In exploring four different types of nationalism (civic, ethnic, revolutionary, and counterrevolutionary), the author examines the relationship between nationalism and other dynamic forces, especially democratization, political leadership, and political violence.

Sorensen, Georg. (2001). *Changes in Statehood: The Transformation of International Relations*. New York: Palgrave. A useful taxonomy of states (modern, postmodern, and postcolonial) is the basis for an exploration of how states attempt to achieve their security goals as they respond to pressures from external and internal forces.

Taras, Raymond, and Rajat Ganguly. (2010). *Understanding Ethnic Conflict: The International Dimension*. 4th ed. New York: Longman. In addition to a helpful conceptualization of the nature of ethnic conflict, revealing case studies discuss the problems of nation and state in settings such as Canada, Eritrea and Ethiopia, Sri Lanka, and the former Yugoslavia.

Thoreau, Henry David. (1849/1981). *Walden and Other Writings*. Ed. J. W. Krutch. New York: Bantam. These essays, especially "On Disobedience," constitute one of the most influential arguments in English for resisting authority.

ON THE WEB

http://www.atlapedia.com

Atlapedia provides diverse statistical information and various maps for each country as well as recent political history.

http://cwis.org

The Web page of the Center for World Indigenous Studies, an independent, nonprofit organization emphasizing the distribution of knowledge about the issues and status of indigenous peoples (nations not coterminous with states) and promoting greater autonomy of power to such peoples.

http://www.ipl.org

The Internet Public Library provides links to numerous reference books, newspapers, and magazines about various countries.

https://www.cia.gov/index.html
    The Web site of the U.S. Central Intelligence Agency includes the CIA World Factbook, a detailed and relatively up-to-date compilation of information about the political, economic, geographic, and demographic characteristics of every country.

http://www.un.org/esa/socdev/unpfii
    The official site of the United Nations Permanent Forum on Indigenous Issues.

http://www.state.gov
    Operated by the U.S. Department of State, this site has country reports and information on international organizations, human rights, and numerous other topics related to foreign policy and international relations.

http://www.countryreports.org
    Country Reports provides comprehensive reports for most countries and includes access to international news and reference maps.

http://www.un.org/Pubs/CyberSchoolBus/infonation/e_infonation.htm
    Infonation, developed by the United Nations, provides the latest statistics for all UN member states.

http://www.nationsonline.org
    This site offers an encyclopedic array of portals with details of states and many aspects of their governmental, cultural, and economic forms.

http://www.economist.com/countries
    This site, produced by the publishers of *The Economist,* a respected British newsmagazine, contains detailed country profiles and links to international news resources.

Political Institutions I:
Institutional Structures

There was trouble on the Korean peninsula. Troops from communist North Korea had invaded noncommunist South Korea in 1950. U.S. President Truman authorized a "police action" and sent U.S. troops to South Korea to stop the invasion. As the conflict escalated into a major war, the Truman administration concluded that a stable U.S. economy was important for the war effort. However, a wage dispute resulted in a major strike by the steelworker's union against the steel mill industry. Truman feared this strike would seriously disrupt the war-related production of many defense contractors as well as harm the U.S. economy as a whole.

Given these concerns, Truman seized the steel mill industry, placed it under the control of federal administrative agencies, and ordered the workers to end their strike. However, President Truman's bold steps to control the industry did not follow the proper procedures outlined in acts of Congress. The president argued, with the support of the steelworkers, that he had "inherent powers" to seize the steel mills, especially in a time of crisis. The steel companies, led by Youngstown Sheet and Tube Company, challenged Truman's justification and filed suit against President Truman and Secretary of Commerce Charles Sawyer. The companies claimed that the president did not have the authority to seize the steel mills without following the legislature's procedures.

After hearing the case, the United States Supreme Court supported the position of the steel companies by a vote of 6 to 3. In the majority opinion, Justice Black wrote that the inherent power to order seizure of the steel mills would need to be based on either the U.S. Constitution or a statute from Congress. The Court majority ruled that there was no such constitutional provision or statute. Chief Justice Vinson disagreed. In a dissenting opinion, Vinson argued that President Truman's actions were justified because Congress had not expressed explicit disapproval and because other presidents, including Abraham Lincoln, had taken similar actions in the past. Faced with the Supreme Court decision, Truman's administration withdrew its control of the steel mills, and the workers went back on strike. At that point, Congress became very concerned about the impacts of the strike on the Korean War. Congress quickly passed legislation providing the president with the legal grounds to seize the steel mills. In response, the workers ended their strike and the war effort went on.

In this famous case, all the major political institutions of the U.S. national government were actively involved: the executive (the president), the legislature (Congress), the judiciary (the Supreme Court), and the administration (federal government agencies). These four political institutions exist in every modern state. And every political system has grappled with serious questions regarding how to design, modify, and manage its set of political institutions and political arrangements to maintain an effective government that can achieve valued goals. As James Madison noted during the writing of the U.S. Constitution: "In framing a government which is to be administered by men over men, the great difficulty is this: You must first enable the government to control the governed; and in the next place, oblige it to control itself."

Studying the institutional structures of the state raises questions such as: What responsibilities are dominated by the political executive? How are representatives selected for the legislature? What are the relationships between the executive and the legislature? How powerful is the bureaucracy? Are the courts independent of the other branches of government? How do the political system and the economic system intersect? What is the role of the constitution?

Exploring these kinds of questions in Chapters 6, 7, and 8 helps us identify and compare the government structures and processes of political systems around the world. Initially, Chapter 6 provides an analysis of the four major structures that are the basic components of contemporary political systems: *executives, legislatures, administrative systems*, and *judiciaries*. Chapter 7 will compare differing forms of institutional arrangements regarding matters such as executive–legislative relationships, the party system, and citizen democracy. Chapter 8 will analyze the ways in which the political system and the economic system are linked. The discussions in these chapters will emphasize broad patterns and generalizations. The usual qualifications apply: There are exceptions and variations across political systems and even within each political system as it is influenced by many factors such as forces in the environment, personalities, political culture, policy area, and so on. Let's begin with a discussion of executives.

EXECUTIVES

The historical evidence indicates that as long as there have been political systems, there have been individuals or small groups who assume top leadership roles. Such leaders have the responsibility to formulate and especially to implement public policy, and they can be broadly called the *executive structure*. The word executive comes from the Latin *ex sequi*, meaning "to follow out" or "to carry out." Thus, the particular role of the executive is *to carry out the political system's policies, laws, or directives*.

One might be tempted to generalize that a few individuals emerge as the leadership cadre in *every* political order. But there are some historical counterexamples, especially from Africa and Asia, of societies that are *acephalous*—that is, "without a head." In such systems, many people in the community share power somewhat equally as a collective leadership. Nonetheless, in most systems, a few people do assume the positions of executive power.

6.1 Analyze the structure and roles of political executives.

Explore the Comparative "Chief Executives" on mypoliscilab.com

At the apex of the executive structure, there is usually an actor who can be called the chief executive. In a national political system, this might be a single person with a title such as president, prime minister, chief, premier, supreme leader, or queen. Or the top executive leader can be a role filled by two or more people. In this case, there might be a president and a prime minister (as in the French example described in Compare in 7) or a group exercising shared executive leadership (e.g., a junta).

A broader definition of the executive includes not only the chief executive but also the entire administrative system. Such a definition derives from the notion that the policy implementation function (the execution of policy) is shared by the chief executive and the administration. The top executive group cannot survive without the continuing support of an extensive system of people who interpret, administer, and enforce its policy directives. However, we examine the chief executive and the administration in separate sections of this chapter so that we can differentiate analytically among the major structures in most political systems.

Roles of Executives

Leadership Roles   In the contemporary political world, political leadership is almost always associated with chief executives. The leadership role entails taking the initiative in formulating, articulating, and implementing the goals of the political system. The effective chief executive becomes the spokesperson for the aspirations of the people, attempts to galvanize the people's support for these goals, and develops strategies that facilitate their accomplishment.

To a large extent, the chief executive takes the initiative in policy formation. Executive policy leadership is especially crucial during times of crisis because the executive structure has the potential for a level of coherence and unanimity of action that is often lacking in the legislature. In most political systems, the chief executive has the capacity to veto, either directly or indirectly, the bills that the legislature initiates. Increasingly, even the drafting of legislation is a function dominated by the executive because many major bills require the expertise and policy direction of the chief executive and its staff.

Symbolic and Ceremonial Roles   The actors in the executive role usually function as the unifying symbol of the entire society, becoming the ultimate mother/father figures for the people. This is especially true when the chief executive has a strong image, such as Thailand's King Bhumibol and King Mswati III in Swaziland (see Focus in 9). The executive's presence becomes central to many of the society's rituals and ceremonies, whether it is the Japanese emperor's wedding, the Kenyan president's official send-off of the national team to the Olympic Games, or the British queen's Christmas Day televised message to her subjects.

Supervision of the Administration   In almost all contemporary political systems, the executive has primary responsibility for implementing the policies and laws of the political order. At the apex of this administrative hierarchy, which might include millions of public employees in the state's departments, bureaus, and agencies, is the top group of the executive structure. Most systems have an executive cabinet, with each member directly and personally responsible for some major area of administration. Given the scale and complexity of the activities in each area, these top executive actors can neither know nor control all of the actions that occur within their domain. Nonetheless, they are supposed to set the broad guidelines for policy implementation, and in many political systems, they are accountable for any major failures that occur. In parliamentary systems, for example, the minister of a department will probably resign if there is a serious shortcoming or blunder in her area of responsibility.

Supervision of the Military and Foreign Affairs Given the state's monopoly of the legitimate use of force, the top political executive usually has direct control over the military (including internal security forces). In such cases, the top executive is the commander in chief of the entire military system of the state, including personnel and other resources (aircraft, nuclear weapons, military intelligence, and so on). The chief executive must set policy and supervise the organization and utilization of the state's military capabilities, a task that can have the most serious consequences for the security and well-being of the country.

Associated with control of the military is the executive's responsibility for foreign affairs—the state's relations with other states. As Chapter 12 will describe more fully, the relations between states involve complex patterns of cooperation and conflict as each state attempts to accomplish its goals in the international environment. The chief executive (or the chief executive's delegates) represents the state in its dealings with other countries. Particular significance is often attached to situations where the chief executives of different states meet directly, as in a state visit or a "summit conference." In fact, such meetings among heads of state typically are symbolic gestures of cooperation or occasions for ratifying agreements that have been reached by the chief executives' representatives. But the concentration of the states' political power in the chief executives is so great that such meetings can provide opportunities for major breakthroughs in the relations between the states.

Structural Arrangements

Fused versus Dual Executive Many political systems have a dual executive. One actor, the *head of state, performs the more ceremonial aspects of top leadership,* while another actor, the *head of government, is responsible for the more political aspects of governance.* The main advantage of the dual executive is that citizens can be angry or hostile towards the head of government while still remaining loyal to the nation and to the political system through their affection and support for the more ceremonial head of state.

Constitutional monarchies are obvious examples of political systems with a dual executive. In these systems, there is a ruling king or queen (e.g., Queen Elizabeth II in Britain, Queen Margrethe II in Denmark, or Emperor Akihito in Japan) and a prime minister or other head of government. The monarch has little or no power to make authoritative policy decisions and serves mainly symbolic or ceremonial functions, as an embodiment of the nation and the people. Monarchs

Queen Elizabeth II, the head of state, opens Parliament each year by delivering a speech written by the prime minister, the head of government. The speech outlines the legislation the prime minister's government will introduce. The queen comes to Britain's House of Lords, whose members sit behind the Law Lords (the highest judiciary group, wearing the wigs). By tradition, the now powerful House of Commons members, including the prime minister, symbolically "demand" entry into the chamber and stand in the back (not visible in the photo).

with limited powers also operate in some less democratic countries, such as King Norodom Sihamoni in Cambodia.

Some countries have attempted to create a dual executive without a monarch, establishing a second executive office as head of state (such as the presidency in Germany, India, and Ireland) that is typically insulated from the daily struggles of politics and thus can be a symbol of national unity. In countries where the culture is deeply grounded in a religious belief system, the head of the religion can function like a head of state, as in Iran, where the president (Ahmedinejad) and legislature lead the political system, but the religious leader, Ayatollah Ali Khamenei (the "Leader of the Islamic Republic and of the Nation"), has formidable power over most aspects of political life.

Most political systems have a *fused executive*. Here, *a single actor fulfills both the ceremonial roles associated with the head of state and the political functions associated with the head of the government*. In such cases, it can be difficult or impossible to distinguish (dis)loyalty to a partisan political leader from (dis)loyalty to the nation. Clever chief executives use this fusion of roles to their advantage, "wrapping themselves in the flag." Such executives criticize or even punish their opponents by claiming that they are traitors to the political society (even though the opponents are usually criticizing only the political actions of the leader). For example, Zimbabwe's President Robert Mugabe used this tactic very effectively to intimidate and eliminate his rivals.

Some political systems have two actors who perform parts of the chief executive role but are not really dual executives in the sense described in the preceding paragraphs. For example, there are countries (e.g., France and Russia) where both a prime minister and a president perform essentially political functions, although one usually has a stronger claim to the head-of-state role (see Focus in 7). Some political systems have a political executive but also have a monarch who, in addition to serving as head of state, is a powerful political actor. Bhutan, Kuwait, Morocco, and Swaziland are examples where the monarch is the head of state and has greater political power than the prime minister.

The Executive   While the term *chief executive* refers to the one person or small group at the apex of the executive structure, the executive is a broader term, including *all the people and organizational machinery that are below the chief executive in the executive structure*. Thus, the executive encompasses high-level decision makers in all the departments, agencies, and other administrative units that are in the chief executive's chain of command. As was noted earlier, a definition of the executive far broader than the one in this book might also include the entire administrative system.

In theory, and usually in practice, this is a hierarchical system of political control, in the sense that the actors in the executive structure are supposed to follow the directives of the chief executive. But the chief executive's power over the rest of the executive is rarely absolute. There are many reasons why the chief executive's directives might not be carried out:

- Units within the executive might be too disorganized or corrupt to act effectively.
- Units in the executive might lack the resources to carry out policies in the manner desired by the chief executive.
- Some units might be more involved in competing against other units than in coordinating their actions to meet the chief executive's policies.
- Units might misunderstand, resist, or defy the chief executive.

Can you think of other reasons?

The Age of the Executive?

Although chief executives have nearly always been evident, and usually ascendant, in political systems, some analysts call the 20th century the "age of the executive." This label reflects the apparent concentration of power in executives and the relative decline of legislatures' powers. What might account for this concentration of power? To some extent, this is a chicken-and-egg issue: The reduced capacity of many legislatures to take coherent and decisive state action is linked to the emergence of more coherent and decisive executives.

In comparison with legislatures, the executive structure tends to be more streamlined and less prone to stalemate and inaction. Also, the executive, centered in a single person or small group, can offer a unified focus for a mass public that either desires simplicity and clarity in an age of great complexity or wants a form of heroic leadership. The chief executive typically speaks with one voice and, when effective, can assure the people that political power will be exercised with purpose and efficiency to respond to the pressures and demands in the society and in the international environment. Even if a chief executive cannot deliver, she can at least promise decisive leadership in a manner that no other political structure can.

Can you suggest any conditions under which a state might be dominated by a structure *other* than the political executive?

LEGISLATURES

6.2 Summarize the roles of the legislature.

Watch the Video "The Problem of Party Discipline" at mypoliscilab.com

Explore the Comparative "Legislatures" on mypoliscilab.com

Most states (about 96 percent) have a legislature as one of their basic structures of governance (Derbyshire 2000). Among the names of legislatures (which can have one or two "houses") are the Senate and the House of Representatives (United States), the Senate and the Chamber of Deputies (Chile, Mexico, and Venezuela, among others), the Legislative Assembly (Costa Rica), the National People's Congress (China), the Majlis (Iran), the National Assembly (Egypt and Tanzania, among others), the Lok Sabha and the Rajya Sabha (India), the Knesset (Israel), the House of Representatives and the House of Councillors (Japan), and the House of Commons and the House of Lords (United Kingdom).

Roles of the Legislature

Legislatures have always been *structures in which representatives of the people discuss, assess, and enact public policies*. Indeed, the roots of the name of the first modern legislature, the British Parliament, suggest this crucial function—the French word *parler* means "to talk." Most early legislatures were created to provide advice to the political executive, typically a monarch, and to represent politically relevant groups. Legislatures also became responsible for enacting public policies. The roots of the word *legislature* are the Latin words *legis*, meaning "law," and *latio*, "bringing or proposing." Some of the earliest legislatures, such as the Roman Senate (ca. 500 B.C.E.–100 C.E.), had great power to discuss and enact laws. Thus, most modern legislatures have three broad roles: (1) enacting legislation, (2) representing the citizenry, and (3) overseeing the executive.

Enactment of Legislation   It might seem obvious that legislatures draft, modify, and then ratify public policy in the form of legislation. In some political systems, many laws are initiated and written by the legislature. However, most contemporary legislatures do not play the dominant role in the policymaking function; rather, this role has passed to the executive and the administration.

The essence of the legislature's power in the policymaking process is, in most political systems, a constitutional provision that a majority vote of the members of the legislature is required to authorize the passage of any law (legislative enactment). In some systems, legislatures have special committees that thoroughly assess and can amend all proposed legislation under the committees' jurisdiction. One of the most important responsibilities of the legislative majority is the power to enact laws that raise revenue and authorize its expenditure on public policies ("the power of the purse").

Representation of the Citizenry   A second major role of the legislature is to represent the opinions and interests of the citizenry. Most legislators are elected by some set of voters, and it is assumed that a key responsibility of a legislator is both to reflect and to serve the interests of those voters. One of the many institutional puzzles for every political system is how to convert the votes of citizens into a legislature that reflects the voters' preferences. Focus in 6 explores these issues of the electoral system and representation with a case study of South Africa.

The concept of *representation* is not straightforward because there are at least five different views of the broad "interests" that a legislator might attempt to represent: (1) all of the citizens in the legislator's constituency (geographic area); (2) the group that is most dominant in the legislator's constituency, possibly a social class, religious group, or ethnic group; (3) the political party to which the legislator owes loyalty; (4) the country as a whole, whose broad interests might transcend those of any area, group or party; or (5) the legislator's own conscience, which provides moral and intellectual judgment about appropriate political action (a position made famous in a brilliant justification by British parliamentarian Edmund Burke in his 1774 "Address to the Electors of Bristol" [1790/1955: 219–222]).

Is it possible for a legislator to represent all five interests simultaneously? Most contemporary legislators do not do so, for reasons such as:

- In the Burkean ideal, a legislator could act against the views of her constituents or her party to follow a policy she believes is in the country's best interest.
- A legislator could deliver specific benefits to her own constituents (e.g., "pork barrel politics"), even though these are not the best use of resources to meet the needs of the country as a whole.
- The legislator could vote for a policy that is not the preference of her constituents but is part of a vote trade with other legislators to gain support for another policy she prioritizes.
- A legislator could vote on an issue primarily in exchange for financial or other support from a particular interest group.

Even before South Africa began dismantling the system of apartheid in 1990, there were extensive discussions about how to transform the political system into an effective democracy. Given the deep social cleavages and widespread citizen mistrust in the government, one critical issue was how to establish an **electoral system** that *translates the citizens' votes into a fair and representative legislature.* During apartheid, South Africa had elected its legislature by a form of **plurality voting**: *the candidate who receives the largest number of votes is elected* in each constituency. The plurality system is most often used in single-member districts, where just one legislator is elected to represent each region.

To ensure that each nation-based group in South Africa received legislative seats that approximated the group's electoral strength, the 1994 constitution implemented a system of **proportional representation (PR)**: *The seats are allocated to a party's candidates in close proportion to a party's share of the total votes.* Thus, when the African National Congress Party received 65.9 percent of the votes in 2009, it was allocated 264 (66.0 percent) of the 400 seats in the National Assembly. Although there are nearly 50 countries that utilize plurality voting for their legislatures (including Great Britain and the United States), the majority of countries now utilize some form of PR (Reynolds, Reilly and Ellis 2005: 31). The box (on page 145) offers a simple example of how plurality and PR would work in the mythical countries of Zeta and Theta.

The PR system requires that legislative districts be "multi-member," meaning that two or more legislators are elected to represent a region. South Africa is divided into nine multi-member regions, which each send between four and 46 representatives to the National Assembly. Two hundred (of the 400) seats are distributed proportionately, based on the votes in each of these nine regions. The other 200 seats are filled with candidates elected for the entire country. For both these groupings of seats, the South African electorate chooses from "closed lists." This means that each party determines its own priority list of candidates, indicating to voters the order in which candidates will be elected if the party wins seats.

South Africa differs from most PR countries that have large districts because there is no minimum threshold of votes that a party must win nationally in order to win seats in the legislature. Thus, South Africa currently has seven small parties that received less than 1 percent of the national vote but have one to three members in the National Assembly. In other PR systems, minimum electoral thresholds are implemented (for instance, a party gets no seats unless it receives at least 5 percent of the national vote in Germany). The higher the minimum threshold requirement, the more difficult it is for smaller parties to obtain seats (Klingemann 2009).

There is an active debate in South Africa about whether to modify this electoral system. Some argue that the problem with PR in general, and especially with closed lists, is that the parties have too much control over the specific candidates who will be elected because the parties produce candidate lists. Some countries (e.g., Finland) utilize an "open list" PR system, which allows the voters to select (from the parties' lists) the specific candidates they want to elect. Others object to the multi-member districts, arguing that there is very little connection between the individual voter in a particular district and the numerous legislators who represent the district. For instance, South Africa averages more than 20 legislators per district. This limits the direct representational link between a legislator and a specific constituency of people to whom she provides services. Thus, some South Africans propose that some or all of the members of the National Assembly should be elected in single-member districts with plurality voting.

The debate in South Africa mirrors the discussion in many countries about how to establish an electoral

(Continued)

Zeta and Theta each have a 250-member national legislature. Zeta uses a plurality electoral system. Assume that in each of the 20 individual legislative seats in one region of Zeta, the candidate for Party A garners 31 percent of the votes, more votes than the candidate of any other party. Party A wins all 20 seats. In Theta, the same region utilizes PR and has the same 20 seats. Here, Parties A and B would each send six legislators, D would send four, B would send three, and E would send one. While the example for Zeta is probably unrealistic (some other party might get the plurality of votes in some of the individual seats), it is not uncommon in a plurality system that the largest parties win far more seats than their share of votes in the election, and small parties tend to get few or no seats.

	Percentage of Votes	Zeta: Plurality (of 20 single seats)	Theta: PR (of 20 seats in district)
Party A	31%	20 (wins in every constituency)	6
Party B	15%	0	3
Party C	29%	0	6
Party D	19%	0	4
Party E	6%	0	1

system that blends several goals. Plurality systems have the virtue of increasing the electorate's control over the legislator that serves them, increasing *accountability*. In contrast, PR systems generally produce a distribution of seats across parties that is a close approximation to the overall distribution of votes, increasing *fair representation*. Regarding *effective governance*, plurality systems tend to reduce the number of significant parties in the legislature, resulting in a more adversarial democracy—a system of majority government and minority opposition. In contrast, PR produces multiple active parties and the survival of small parties, encouraging a more consensual democracy because more parties usually must cooperate in order to produce a legislative majority (Norris 2003: Ch. 2). South Africans continue to debate changes in their electoral system to increase its effectiveness for both representation and governance.

FURTHER FOCUS

1. Which aspect of the South African electoral systems seems least desirable? How would you alter it?
2. What would guide your decision about whether to implement a plurality or PR electoral system in a particular country (given your specification of conditions relevant to that decision)? ▲

- A legislator holding office in some systems must follow the dictates of the political leadership and acts as little more than a "rubber stamp." This position characterizes the behavior of a legislator in an undemocratic regime like North Korea, for example.
- Some legislators are deeply committed to adhering to their political party's line, or they must obey the party to survive politically. Such party discipline is usually the situation for members of the British House of Commons, for instance.

Voting matters. In a township near Johannesburg, South Africans wait for hours to cast votes for their representatives to the national legislature.

- Some legislators have such deep loyalty to a particular ideology or group that they rarely feel obligated to consider how they might represent other groups among the electorate. Members of religious parties, such as Shas in Israel, can have this perspective, as do members of extremely ideological factions, including some "tea party" Republicans in the U.S.

Thus it is a huge challenge for a legislator to balance all five competing views of representation.

Oversight of the Executive and Administration   The third major role of legislators concerns their interactions with the executive and the administration. In general, the legislature is responsible for overseeing the political executive's actions. The legislature might have the constitutional right to select the executive, to approve the chief executive's selection of key appointments, and to authorize major policy decisions by the executive. In the steel industry case, for example, the U.S. Congress resisted presidential action that went beyond executive powers they had authorized. In parliamentary systems, the cabinet and prime minister hold office and make policy only if they have the "confidence" of the majority of the members of the legislature (see Chapter 7). In some systems, such as in India, the president is actually chosen by the legislature (although it is the prime minister, not the president, who is the most powerful executive officer).

Many legislatures have the right to approve the executive's selection of major appointments. The Israeli legislature must approve the cabinet as a whole. The U.S. Senate has the right to "advise and consent" on presidential appointments such as cabinet members or Supreme Court justices. The Senate's 1987 rejection of Judge Robert Bork, President Reagan's nominee for the Supreme Court, is an example of a legislature asserting its power over a top-level executive appointment.

A second area of legislative oversight involves the right of the legislature to scrutinize executive performance. Many political systems have regular procedures by which the legislature can question and even investigate whether the executive has acted properly in implementing public policies. At a minimum, the legislature serves as a discussion and debating chamber. Subjecting the political executive's plans and actions to public debate serves as a modest check on executive power. Many legislatures have a regular opportunity, during their legislative sessions, to question the specific plans and actions of key members of the executive. In Britain, Italy, and South Africa, for example, ministers in the executive cabinet must appear before the legislature and respond to legislators' questions or criticisms about any actions taken by their department.

Most legislatures also have formal investigatory powers on a continuing or a case-by-case basis. The 2003 parliamentary investigation of British Prime Minister Tony Blair regarding the basis of his claims that Iraq had weapons of mass destruction and whether this justified Britain's military intervention is an example of such oversight. In addition, some legislatures have followed Sweden's innovative idea, setting up an *ombudsman—an independent agency that investigates complaints regarding the actions of the executive branch and its administrative units.* If legislative questioning, committees, or the ombudsman discover inappropriate behavior by an administrative unit, the legislature can usually oblige the unit to alter its behavior. If the problem is with the executive, significant political pressure is exerted on the executive to correct it. Of course, if the executive resists such pressure, the ultimate resolution of the dispute entails either legal adjudication or, in most cases, a power struggle between the executive and the legislature.

The most fundamental power of oversight held by some legislatures is their capacity to overturn the government. In a parliamentary system, the legislature can require or pressure the executive to resign from office by a vote of censure or of no confidence, or by defeating a major bill put forth by the executive (see Chapter 7). In Italy, for example, the legislature forced the executive to resign about once a year—on average—between 1951 and 1994. Even in presidential systems, the legislature has the power to overturn the executive by means of the extraordinary process of impeachment, though this is rare. In 1992, Brazilian President Fernando Collor de Mello resigned after being impeached by the National Congress on corruption charges. And in 2008, Pakistan's President Musharraf resigned as the legislature began impeachment proceedings for treason. In the United States, no president has been removed from office because of impeachment and conviction. However, in 1868, President Andrew Johnson was acquitted on the House of Representatives' impeachment charge by only one vote in the Senate, Richard Nixon avoided an impeachment trial in 1974 only by resigning, and Bill Clinton was acquitted by the Senate on two articles of impeachment brought by the House in 1998.

Legislative Structures

Number of Houses   There is one very visible difference in the structural arrangements of various legislatures—the number of houses (often called *chambers*). There are **unicameral** (*one-chamber*) **legislatures** in more than half of the countries that have legislatures (Derbyshire 2000). The presumed advantages of a unicameral system are that political responsibility is clearly located in one legislative body and that risks of duplication or stalemate between parallel bodies are eliminated. More than two-thirds of the countries with a strong central government (see Chapter 7 on these "unitary states") have unicameral legislatures, including Algeria, Bulgaria, China, Costa Rica, Denmark, Finland, Greece, Hungary, Israel, Kenya, New Zealand, South Korea, Sweden, Taiwan, and Tanzania.

Since 1990, there has been a considerable increase in the proportion of countries that have *bicameral legislatures*—those with two separate chambers. Bicameral systems are especially prevalent in countries that are federations (states in which a central government and regional governments share power). Bicameral federations include Australia, Brazil, Canada, Germany, India, Mexico, and the United States. There are bicameral systems in one-third of the unitary states, including France, Great Britain, Italy, and Japan (Derbyshire 2000).

Given the apparent advantages of a unicameral system, what is the justification for two chambers? There are two main arguments. First, two legislative houses ensure more careful deliberation on issues and laws. Second, the two houses can be based on two different and desirable principles of representation. In about two-fifths of the bicameral legislatures (e.g., Germany and the United States), one house represents the regional governments and the other house more directly represents the numerical and geographic distribution of citizens. A few upper houses also represent functional groups in the society, as in the Republic of Ireland, where members are appointed as representatives of sectors such as agriculture, labor, industry, culture, and public services.

Over time, some bicameral systems have evolved towards unicameral systems, especially in cases where the need for extensive checks and balances within the legislative branch has not seemed compelling and where the problems of overlap and stalemate between the two chambers have become severe. Some political systems, such as those of Sweden and Costa Rica, have constitutionally abolished one chamber. In others, such as Norway and Britain, the powers of one chamber have been so reduced that it can only delay, but cannot veto, the decisions of the more powerful chamber. In fact, the United States is now the only bicameral political system in which the regional upper chamber (the Senate) is more powerful than the popularly-based lower chamber (the House of Representatives) (Derbyshire 2000).

Size of Legislatures   The number of members in legislatures varies enormously, with some houses having fewer than 10 members and others having thousands of members (e.g., the National People's Congress in China has 2,987 members). The single house, or the lower house, typically represents "the people." Each legislator is elected from a constituency of roughly the same size. In general, there is a positive correlation between a country's population and its number of legislators (a ratio defined mathematically as a "cube root law" by Taagepera and Shugart 1989: 174–179). Among the more populous countries, however, there is no obvious principle for determining the optimal number of legislators. In the U.S. House of Representatives, 435 members are elected, a ratio of 1 member per 717,000 people. Of the 165 countries with a legislature, only India has a higher ratio of population to members than does the United States. The United Kingdom, with less than one-third the U.S. population, has 650 elected members in its House of Commons, a ratio of 1 member per 96,000 citizens. More than half of all countries have a ratio of fewer than 65,000 people per representative (Derbyshire 2000).

Can you think of an appropriate criterion for deciding the number of members in a country's legislature? For example, are there good reasons why the upper house in the United States (the Senate) has two rather than three—or four or more—representatives from each state?

The Decline of Legislatures

Many observers claim that for more than 100 years, there has been a general decline in the power of legislatures relative to executives and administration. While it is very difficult to measure power relations over time with precision, several types of circumstantial evidence suggest legislative weakness. To begin with, the legislature is essentially a rubber stamp for the actions of a powerful political executive in about one-sixth of contemporary political systems. Among other political systems, several factors, related to the strengths of the executive identified above, point to the relative weakness of legislatures.

First, most legislatures do not provide a coherent structure within which power can be concentrated and exercised effectively. Many legislatures have relatively slow and cumbersome procedures for the lawmaking function, especially where there are regular legislative committees that amend legislation. This complexity in the legislative process is even more evident in bicameral systems because there is often disagreement between the two chambers.

Second, most legislatures react to policy initiatives from the executive more than they create policy. The legislatures almost never have the level of support services that is available to the executive. Their budgets, facilities, staff sizes, and even the legislators' own salaries are significantly lower than those of top members of the executive and administrative structures. Similarly, the technical expertise and knowledge resources available to legislatures are far less than those available to the executive and administrative structures, a major liability when legislators attempt to deal with the complex subjects facing governments in modern societies.

Some analysts suggest a third, more social–psychological weakness of legislatures: Most citizens desire clear, dynamic, and singular political leadership, but legislatures are typically composed of many people, and most citizens feel the legislators are either indistinguishable, where party discipline is very strong, or offer too many different identities. In the United States, for example, it is usually possible to answer this question: What does the president think about issue Y? But how does one answer the corresponding question: What does the legislature think about issue Y? Not only are there two chambers and two parties, but there is also a great diversity of opinions among the individuals and factions within the legislature. In a sense, even though legislatures usually have spokespersons and leaders, no one can truly speak for the legislature. One might even conclude that the legislature in a democratic society tends to fulfill one of its roles *too* well: Its members too accurately represent the diversity of political beliefs among the society's population, and thus they speak with many voices.

Although the power of legislatures has not kept pace with that of other institutions, especially the executive and the administration, not all legislatures are impotent or dying institutions. Certain national legislatures remain extremely powerful political structures, such as those in Italy, Japan, Sweden, and the United States. In most other relatively democratic political systems, legislatures have significant impacts on the governing process through their roles in enacting legislation, in representation, and in oversight. And in almost all societies that have a legislature, its members can exercise political power in many subtle ways. At the least, members of the legislature have dramatically more political power than most other citizens.

ADMINISTRATIVE SYSTEMS

6.3 Compare the functions and powers of political administrative systems.

✷⊣Explore the Comparative "Bureaucracies" on mypoliscilab.com

Administration is the general term used to describe *the machinery and the processes through which the state's rules and policies are applied and implemented.* While the executive (discussed above) denotes the top managers of the policy implementation function, the administrative system consists of the thousands, or even millions, of public employees who do the ongoing business of interpreting and implementing the policies enacted by the state. These employees are divided into organizational units called departments, ministries, agencies, and bureaus. Administrative units perform important activities such as providing publicly-provided goods and services (e.g., national security, roads, education, solid-waste disposal, health care, monetary aid for the needy), maintaining order, collecting revenues, keeping records, and regulating or controlling the aspects of the economy (e.g., the power grid, provision of transportation, finance system, growth and distribution of food).

Administrative Functions and Power

The scale of activity of a state's administrative structure depends on the political system's definition of *res publica* (recall page 120). In political systems that penetrate a larger sphere of the society and economy, there is a corresponding need for more extensive administrative structures because the administration is the basic apparatus through which the state interprets, implements, and monitors all of its policies and activities. The administrative structures in contemporary political systems perform five broad functions:

1. **Provision of public goods and services.** The essential work of the actors in the administrative structure is the constant interpretation and application of policies that provide public goods and services to individuals and groups.
2. **Regulation and enforcement of behavior.** Administrators are also responsible for interpreting and applying many public policies that set guidelines for the behavior of individuals or groups. These can vary greatly, from monitoring collusion among corporations to enforcing traffic laws, to protecting the civil rights of ethnic minorities.
3. **Provision of knowledge.** Many administrators develop great expertise within their specialized areas. This knowledge can be of enormous utility for almost every decision and action undertaken in that area by the political system.

4. **Information management.** Administrators are responsible for the collection, storage, and analysis of huge amounts of information about the people and processes in the society. This information provides a crucial database—for recording activities and conditions in the society and for providing information relevant to every stage of the policy process (see Chapter 9).
5. **Resource management.** In roles such as collector of revenues from citizens and businesses or operator of state-owned companies producing goods and services, the administrative structure is in charge of many tasks that extract and utilize resources for the political system.

This brief list of functions suggests the enormous breadth and depth of the administrative structure and its activities. Some observers argue that in the complex, extensive, and knowledge-based political systems of the early 21st century, the power of administrative institutions is supreme. Although the administrators are, in theory, "servants" of their political masters and their clients, it might be that, in reality, these roles are reversed. Civil servants have such unmatched knowledge and experience in their specialized domains that generalist politicians rarely have sufficient expertise to question their information, recommendations, or actions (Weber 1958a). Also, their power to grant or withhold benefits provides them with considerable leverage over clients. And most administrators are career employees who have quasi-permanent tenure, while politicians and clients come and go. The modern administrative structure has such wide-ranging power and competence that it is typically credited with keeping the political system functioning when executives and legislatures are ineffective, as in the Third and Fourth Republics in France and in many modernizing states in Africa and Asia. Indeed, Max Weber, the great German sociologist, observed that "in the modern state, the actual ruler is necessarily and unavoidably the bureaucracy" (Weber 1958a: 211).

Bureaucracy as One Form of Administration

Weber's quote about bureaucracy is a reminder that administration and bureaucracy are often treated as synonymous concepts; but in the attempt to clarify our language of political analysis, it is helpful to distinguish them. Weber provided the definitive definition of bureaucracy, as a particular structure and set of processes through which the administration can operate. Structurally, bureaucracy is an *organization that is hierarchical and specialized, by means of an elaborate division of labor.* Weber also defined the concept of bureaucracy by a key process: its members (1) apply *specific rules of action* to each case; therefore, the resulting treatment of each case is (2) *rational, (3) nondiscretionary, (4) predictable, and (5) impersonal* (Weber 1958a: 196–244).

In some countries, most governments have deeply incorporated this rational bureaucratic style of administration. But there are also many contemporary political systems, and even more examples historically, where public administrators often treat people unpredictably or with clear biases. Compare in 6 characterizes five different forms of administration.

In complex societies, calling an organization "bureaucratic" is not usually intended to be a compliment. Some criticisms of bureaucracy are really directed

COMPARE IN 6 | Five Styles of Administration

For many people in the most advanced democracies, the words *bureaucracy* and *bureaucratic* have a negative connotation, as in "that is so bureaucratic!" Bureaucracy is only one style of the administrative function. While its rigid, rule-following approach can seem mechanical and inefficient, let's compare it to four alternative styles of administration by exploring variations on a single scenario:

You are driving in another country and are given a ticket for speeding—driving 80 kilometers per hour (kph) in a 40 kph zone. You plead your case to the traffic officer: You are unfamiliar with the metric system, you don't understand how to read the traffic signs, you can't figure out the speedometer in this rental car, you are sorry, and you are a friendly tourist! What happens next? Five alternatives:

1. The officer listens patiently. Your pleading makes no difference. She explains that Rule 3.207 of the Vehicle Code governs this case— you are traveling more than 10 kph over the posted limit. The rules state that you must follow her to the local judge's office, pay a fine of 125 rupesas, and you will then be free to continue your journey. The judge is also unmoved by your arguments, repeating that the law is clear. You pay the 125 rupesa fine and you leave. This is a classic case of *Weberian bureaucracy* in action: There are explicit rules, and you are merely a case in which all the representatives of the organization apply the rules exactly, with no consideration of your personal circumstances.

2. When you plead your case, the officer seems sympathetic. She says that she understands how tourists might be confused by the rules in her country and that she will reduce the reported speed on the ticket from 80 kph to 60 kph, which will result in only a 50 rupesa fine. You try your pleas again with the judge, promising to obey the all the country's laws. The judge senses your contrition and suspends the fine, after giving you a stern warning. You leave quickly, before anyone

reconsiders. This is *humane administration* because those with authority do not merely apply the rules—they try to understand your personal circumstances and adjust their actions to be responsive to your particular situation. Humane administration seems preferable to the bureaucratic style; but the problem is that, once the rules are no longer applied impersonally and predictably, other styles (numbers 3–5 below) are much more likely.

3. When none of your arguments work with the officer, you point out that other cars were passing you just before you were stopped. Why you? The officer just shrugs. At the judge's office, your arguments again are ineffective. The judge then announces your fine is 200 rupesas. You are shocked and say that the traffic officer said that the fine would be about 125 rupesas. The judge looks sternly at you, and responds that the fine is whatever she decides it should be. Did you want to question her decision? If so, she might have to increase the fine even further. Or perhaps you'd like to spend the night in jail, thinking about your dangerous driving? You flinch, pay, and get out of the building as fast as you can. This is *arbitrary administration.* You are singled out for ticketing among others who are equally guilty. Why? You are given a higher fine than stated in the rules. Why? The answer is that those with authority can use their discretion to decide when and how to administer the rules. Discretion worked in your favor under humane administration, but in arbitrary administration, you are just as likely to be placed at a disadvantage by flexible, unpredictable and non-rule-following actions.

4. When you try your arguments on the traffic officer, she notices your foreign accent. Where are you from, she asks? You say, I am from the United States! She frowns and mutters that Americans need to be taught a lesson. In

(Continued)

front of the judge, you are asked your religion, and reply that you are a Protestant. The judge responds: "Do you know this is a Catholic country and we believe in following the rules? Your fine is 175 rupesas." You have a sense that if you had been from a different country or were Catholic, you might have gotten off easier. In this situation of *discriminatory administration,* you might be right. People are treated differently by the authorities on the basis of their ethnicity, religion, gender, social class, or some other marker that distinguishes among groups. Unfortunately, in this situation, you are in groups that are not favored.

5. After the officer listens impassively to your pleadings, she tells you that things will not go well with the judge. You will pay a very big fine of about 250 rupesas and might go to jail because you were traveling over 150 kph. You are stunned by these "facts" and scared, but decide to take a risk. As you hand your license

to the officer, you also fold a 50 rupesa note underneath the license. The officer examines your license and hands it back to you, but the 50 rupesa note is gone. She says if you pay a 60 rupesa fine on the spot, you will not need to go before the judge. You hand over another 60 rupesas. She returns to her motorcycle and drives off. This is *corrupt administration.* There are many ways in which bribes are solicited, collected, and distributed in such systems. If you are lucky, you'll handle the bribe transaction successfully and not end up in jail.

FURTHER QUESTIONS

1. How could a non-Weberian bureaucracy operate like number 2 above without significant risk of becoming one of the less desirable approaches (3, 4, or 5)?
2. Why is corrupt administration probable in many countries, especially those with lower levels of individual wealth? ◣

---

at all large administrative structures that exercise increasing control over people's lives and that seem too large and too powerful. But at its heart, the bureaucracy label has come to connote a system that is too inflexible and impersonal. And the bureaucrats themselves are seen to be relatively free of political accountability because they are protected by professional norms and employment rules that give them job security and insulate them from political pressure. Despite criticisms of its occasional excesses in practice, most people conclude that they would prefer a Weberian bureaucracy rather than one that is arbitrary, discriminatory, or corrupt. Every country is a mix of the five styles described in the Compare in 6, but the variations in that mix are huge. Personal contacts and bribes (in various societies called *chai, baksheesh, mordida,* or *dash*) are still essential for success in dealing with the administrative system in many countries.

JUDICIARIES

In a Hobbesian state of nature (see Chapter 2), disputes among people would normally be resolved by force or the threat of force. In such a setting, "might makes right." Thus, a primary reason for the social contract is to authorize the state to intervene in the potential and actual disputes among individuals and groups by creating and enforcing rules regarding proper forms of behavior. Every society holds that those who violate its rules and laws (i.e., its policies) must be sanctioned. The specific rules in a given society emerge from its unique culture, history,

6.4 Outline the major elements within judicial systems.

Explore the
Comparative
"Judiciaries" on
mypoliscilab.com

and politics. However, a commonality within all legal systems is that there are usually ambiguities regarding the rules:

What does the rule mean?
Has a rule been violated?
Who are the "guilty" actors?
How serious is the offense?
What sanctions are appropriate?

These kinds of ambiguities are resolved through the adjudication function in every political system. Most political systems have established judicial structures whose primary role is adjudication.

Aspects of Adjudication

The **adjudication** function attempts to *interpret and apply the relevant rules or laws to a given situation,* addressing the five questions above. There are several different types of laws. When the issue involves *civil law*—the rules regarding relations between private actors (individuals or groups)—the main objective of adjudication is to *settle the dispute.* Examples include the rules dealing with divorce, contracts, and personal liability litigation.

The situation involves *criminal law* when an individual or group behaves in a manner interpreted as an offense against the social order. Here, adjudication can be an important mechanism of *social control.* Examples of offenses are murder, substance abuse, theft, bribery, extortion, and environmental pollution. The state represents the public interest and enforces the social contract, ensuring that the relations among actors are within the boundaries of "acceptable social behavior." Just as the definition and scope of *res publica* differ greatly across political systems, the definition of acceptable social behavior varies dramatically. In some countries, social control entails little more than regulation of violent behavior between people. In contrast, other countries might enforce rules that prohibit spanking one's child or wearing certain clothing.

Adjudication can also consider cases involving *constitutional, administrative,* or *statutory law.* Here, the activities center on *arbitration regarding the behavior of the political system itself.* The main issues for adjudication involve questions about the legitimate domain of action by a governmental actor in its relations with other governmental units or private actors. Such a dispute might concern a highly technical disagreement over the implementation of a specific policy (e.g., is a person with vision correctable to 20/400 qualified to receive state-subsidized services intended for the "visually impaired"?), or it might raise fundamental constitutional questions about the distribution of political power (e.g., can the chief executive seize control of an industry in the absence of authorization from the constitution or legislature?).

Finally, **international law** is the *rules that attempt to prevent and resolve disputes between states or other global actors.* Adjudication entails interpreting written agreements about interactions that cross state borders or laws formulated by international legal bodies such as the International Court of Justice within the United Nations. As Chapter 11 will detail, there are substantial difficulties in enforcing international law, especially when a state determines that the law is not in its national interest.

Judicial Structures

Most political systems have specialized structures of the **judiciary**—*the system of courts and personnel that determines whether the rules of the society have been transgressed and, if so, whether sanctions ought to be imposed on the transgressor.* (Some broad definitions of judicial structures even include agencies of law enforcement, such as police and security forces, as well as agencies that apply sanctions against rule breakers, such as prisons, although in this book, these are considered administrative structures.)

While there are significant cross-national variations, most political systems have a hierarchical system of judicial structures, with appeal processes possible from lower- to higher-level courts. The United States has one of the world's most complex judicial structures, with its Supreme Court and extensive system of federal, state, and local courts, including judges, prosecuting attorneys, defense attorneys for the indigent, court clerks, and so on. Most judicial systems also have subsystems that are responsible for different aspects of adjudication. For example, the French judicial structure separates the criminal and civil law system from a second system that handles administrative law. In Ukraine, one major system handles criminal and civil law, and a second major system is composed of special prosecutors who monitor actions in all types of cases and who can challenge, retry, or even withdraw cases from the regular courts. In Great Britain, one major judicial system is responsible for criminal law and a second handles civil law.

Among the contemporary countries that do not have judicial structures as part of the government are the Islamic countries that adhere to sharia law. Sharia is the divine law, detailed in the Koran and further elaborated in the *hadith*, the teachings of Muhammad. It is sharia, not the laws of humans, that is the dominant judicial framework in countries such as Iran, Saudi Arabia, and Sudan. The Koran prescribes all aspects of social, spiritual, and moral life. As part of that prescription, the sections on law provide the details of what in Western jurisprudence includes criminal law, civil law, and administrative law. Sharia is applied by religious courts, and the punishments for many violations of the law are specified in the Koran.

The constitutions of many states include provisions meant to create an independent judiciary. The notion that a judicial system is independent means that the judicial actors are not under the statutory control of any other political structure. It does not mean that the judiciary is *apolitical*. The legal system and the set of judicial structures in *every* political system are political. Adjudication, by its very nature, entails crucial decisions that distribute values and shape meanings for a society. Also, the judicial officials in most systems are either appointed by those with political power or are elected in a political process by the voters.

The judiciary in some political systems have the substantial power to exercise **judicial review,** whereby *judicial structures establish the final interpretation of what the constitution and the laws mean,* including the right to reinterpret or even revoke the policy decisions of the other political structures. About one in 10 states

THE DEBATE IN 6 | Is Judicial Review Democratic?

In essence, judicial review means that the judiciary has the right not only to interpret what a particular rule means but also to assess the constitutional legitimacy of any law enacted by the legislature or any policy action implemented by the executive or the administration. The judiciary can uphold the authority of the government regarding the policy, or it can rule that the government's action violates fundamental laws, especially the constitution. Currently, more than half the world's democratic countries have some form of broad judicial review. It can be a key method of ensuring there is a strong countervailing power that prevents the legislature, executive and administration from overstepping their authority. However, some critics argue that essential features of judicial review are actually inconsistent with the basic values and principles of a democratic society. Is judicial review democratic?

JUDICIAL REVIEW IS UNDEMOCRATIC

- The hallmark of representative democracy is that those who have great power over the laws of the society should have a direct mandate from the people by means of election. Yet in most countries, the judges who exercise the extraordinary power of judicial review are not elected by the people. Thus, Alexander Bickel, a distinguished professor at Yale Law School, argues that judicial review is undemocratic because "it thwarts the will of representatives of the actual people of the here and now; it exercises control, not on behalf of the prevailing majority, but against it."

- High court judges making these decisions cannot be held accountable because they usually serve for life and cannot be removed from office except in extraordinary circumstances (i.e., impeachment). Thus citizens have almost no capacity to replace the judges who make fundamentally important decisions about the restraints on the rulers or the rights of the ruled, a hallmark element of democracy (see Chapter 7). Indeed, "the people" have no significant

influence on either what cases the judges consider or the decisions that the judges make.

- Crucial interpretations and decisions can hinge on a bare majority vote by a tiny number of people. The highest constitutional court in most countries makes decisions by simple majority, with fewer than 15 judges. In the United States, for example, fundamentally important judicial rulings are made by only five members of the Supreme Court, even when four of their colleagues on the Court completely disagree with them.

- Even if the judges truly are independent (questionable), the grounds for a decision in cases of judicial review can be highly subjective. There can be deep disagreements among the judges about how the basic legal documents of the society should be interpreted and applied to specific cases.

- In short, crucial rulings about actions by the government are made when a handful of unelected and unaccountable individuals use their own subjective reasoning to offer a contested interpretation of documents and statutes that can be generations old. And "the people," the elected chief executive, and the elected national legislature have no recourse but to accept this judgment (Waldron 2006). What could be more undemocratic in a democratic society?

JUDICIAL REVIEW SUPPORTS DEMOCRATIC PROCESSES

- In representative democracies, supreme power rests with the citizens, who then exercise that power to elect officials to serve them. Those officials, in turn, appoint many others to play important roles in governance. Even in countries where top judicial officials are appointed, their authority is derived directly from the elected officials, whose power is based on popular consent. Thus, empowering appointed judges is fully consistent with democratic principles.

(Continued)

- Once appointed, high court judges are independent of those in other powerful roles in the political system. Unlike most other political actors in a democracy, judges engaged in judicial review do not need to curry favor in order to raise money for reelection and they have no need to compromise their positions in order to make deals with others in the political system. Thus, they are able to make reasoned interpretations of the fundamental laws of the land, as well as rule on specific actions by the other branches of government, based solely on the constitutional merits of the case.

- A just democracy must be guided not only by majority rule but also by a commitment to protect the rights of the individual and minorities against a "tyranny of the majority." An independent judiciary, including judicial review, is a key element in such protection. In making decisions on constitutional rights of the weak as well as the strong, these judges are not pressured or constrained by the current whims of the electoral majority because they do not need to stand for reelection.

- In *Federalist Paper No. 78*, Alexander Hamilton (2007) explains that judicial power does not "by any means suppose a superiority of the judicial to the legislative power. It only supposes that the power of the people is superior to both; and that where the will of the legislature, declared in its statutes, stands in opposition to that of the people, declared in the Constitution, the judges ought to be governed by the latter rather than the former. They ought to regulate their decisions by the fundamental laws."

- In most democracies, the judges engaged in judicial review are highly qualified legal experts. They generally have years of experience in the legal system and their judicial decisions are bound by the statutes and by precedent. While they might occasionally disagree on the interpretation of a constitutional issue, most of their decisions are by clear and unambiguous majorities and reflect shared analyses.

MORE QUESTIONS...

1. In a democracy, is it acceptable to have powerful decision makers who are neither elected by nor directly accountable to the citizens?
2. Might there be any serious problems if the binding interpretation of the constitution is made by elected officials?
3. How does the considerable distance between the people and the highest judges in the judicial branch serve as an advantage? A disadvantage? ▶

has a strong system of judicial review, including Canada, Colombia, Germany, India, Israel, Italy, Mexico, Norway, Switzerland, and the United States. Research has revealed that judicial structures in many advanced democracies have exercised increasing power to redefine and overturn the actions of the other branches (Koopmans 2003: Ch. 4; Stone Sweet 2004). The Debate in 6 questions whether such judicial review is actually consistent with democratic premises.

However, even when judicial structures do strive to maintain some political independence, they still might respond to external pressure. First, the judiciaries in nearly all contemporary states are ultimately dependent on other political structures, especially the executive and the administration, to enforce their decisions. Second, when judicial officials displease the dominant power group, they can often be ignored, replaced, or even eliminated. In an extreme example, more than 150 high-level Argentine judges "disappeared" during the 1970s, and it is speculated that the Argentine government ordered their executions. In the United States, President Franklin D. Roosevelt became frustrated with decisions by the U.S. Supreme Court in the 1930s when it blocked his New Deal legislation expanding government policies in response to the Great Depression. He threatened to add additional members to the nine-member Supreme Court to get favorable decisions, but Congress did not support his threat. However, the Court did begin to rule favorably on his legislation. While it cannot be proven empirically that Roosevelt's threat to increase the size of the Court changed the judicial reasoning of the justices, it was punned at the time that "a switch in time saved nine."

Third, because the people in top judicial positions have usually been socialized by those in the culture's dominant socioeconomic groups, they are likely to share the values of those groups when they make judgments. Thus, one key consideration regarding an *independent* judiciary is assessing the extent to which the judicial structures make decisions and take actions that are *not* substantially influenced by their shared political orientations with and dependence on other powerful social, economic, and political structures in the society. While the rituals of the judicial structures offer the appearance of protecting impartial justice, the reality is that the judicial structures in many, perhaps most, countries serve the interests of the political and economic elite and that a truly independent judiciary is a rarity.

Styles of Adjudication

Among the many styles of adjudicating disputes, several are prevalent. The common law tradition is grounded in the general laws and rules that have been enacted by legislatures and have evolved over time. The key goal of the legal system is to interpret existing precedents from previous judicial rulings. Innocence is presumed until evidence indicates guilt. The court system is adversarial, with the disputing sides making their points and the judge acting as a referee to insure that the proceedings are fair. The common law style emerged in England and was generally adopted in countries strongly influenced by Britain or the United States.

In the civil law tradition, the key goal is the precise application of extremely detailed legal documents to the specific case. The court system is more inquisitional, with the judge asking critical questions under the assumption that the party on trial is guilty of violating the law unless innocence can be proven. This system is associated with the legal approaches of ancient Rome and also France, with its development of the Napoleonic code. It is generally adopted in Continental Europe and the countries emerging from their colonial influence as well as many communist countries. It is arguably the case that Sharia law is very similar to civil law in its style of adjudication, although the laws of Sharia, as noted above, were promulgated by religious authorities, not legislatures and administrations as in civil law.

A third style of adjudication might be termed *dispute resolution.* Here, the goal is to find a ruling that is generally acceptable to all sides. Such an outcome might be based on negotiations led by a third party arbitrator who works to develop a satisfactory compromise between the disputants. This third party might be appointed by the political system or might be respected members of the community. This style has been especially effective in some Arab and sub-Saharan African societies, and many countries attempt to handle some legal cases through dispute resolution approaches.

CONCLUDING OBSERVATIONS

Traditional political science assumed that a detailed description of political structures is the best way to explain how politics works. But empirical research revealed considerable diversity in the roles of particular political structures. Key political functions might occur in a wide variety of structures inside and outside the formal governmental arrangements. In response, there was a period during which political structures were viewed as so malleable that most analyses treated them as secondary elements, merely forming one of the contexts where various political, economic, and social groups maneuver as they pursue their interests. More recently, many scholars have reemphasized the importance of institutional arrangements. For the "new institutionalists," the particular configuration of political structures and rules can powerfully shape political actions and outcomes (March 2006). And for the "neostatists," the structures of the state—its institutional arrangements, the actors who have major roles in its institutions, and its policy activities—are autonomous and have fundamental impacts on political, economic, and social processes.

Thus, precise, behaviorally-oriented and process-based analyses of politics now treat political structures more richly. A full understanding of the political world requires a clear grasp of the essential features of executive, legislative, administrative, and judicial structures. Institutional structures are the skeleton and organs of the body politic. Just as one could explain certain biological functions and processes of the body without explicit reference to the skeleton and organs, so one could explain certain functions and processes of the political system without reference to structures. But such an abstract description of a biological organism would be incomplete without indicating the way in which the structures constrain and shape the functions. Similarly, attempts to describe or explain politics, especially in actual settings, are much richer and more complete if they include a characterization of how key political institutions constrain and shape the political process (March and Olsen 1989). The next chapter will take us further in understanding political institutions as it analyzes how some of the key institutional structures interact to produce different forms of the body politic.

✔•⌐**Study** and **Review** the **Post-Test & Chapter Exam** at **mypoliscilab.com**

KEY CONCEPTS

adjudication 154
administration 150
bicameral legislature 148
bureaucracy 151
civil law 158
common law 158
dispute resolution 158
dual executive 139
executive 141
fused executive 141
head of government 139

head of state 139
international law 154
judicial review 155
judiciary 155
legislature 142
ombudsman 147
plurality voting 144
proportional representation (PR) 144
representation 143
unicameral legislature 147

FOR FURTHER CONSIDERATION

1. Whom should a legislator represent on policy decisions? Develop an argument justifying the order of importance you attribute to representing the following entities: those groups who voted for the legislator, the constituency, the legislative coalition, the political party, the party leader, the nationality group, the country, the legislator's own best judgment.

2. Evaluate whether, on balance, it would be desirable to have an administrative system that is flexible and is sensitive to unique, individual circumstances in the handling of each case (that is, does not follow the principles of a Weberian bureaucracy).

3. The discussion of the judiciary asserts that every set of judicial structures is political. Is the notion of an independent judiciary a sham?

4. What are the benefits and shortcomings of a political system that has a weak chief executive? A fused chief executive?

FOR FURTHER READING

Bell, John. (2006). *Judiciaries Within Europe: A Comparative Review*. Cambridge: Cambridge University Press. An exploration of the interplay between the cultural context within which individual judges operate and the judicial system processes in England, France, Germany, Spain, and Sweden.

Derbyshire, Denis, with Ian Derbyshire. (2000). *Encyclopedia of World Political Systems*. New York: M. E. Sharpe. A useful inventory (circa 2000) of the forms of contemporary political institutions, as well as detailed descriptions of each national political system.

Ginsburg, Tom and Rosalind Dixon. Eds. (2011). *Comparative Constitutional Law. Northampton, MA: Edward Elgar.* This comprehensive (780 pages) and costly volume offers thoughtful essays on the nature of constitutional law, including current debates regarding such topics as constitutional design, human rights, and judicial review.

Koopmans, Tim. (2003). *Courts and Political Institutions: A Comparative View*. Cambridge: Cambridge University Press. Koopmans, a former law professor and judge in the European Union, offers a persuasive analysis of the increasing power of the courts to engage in judicial decision making and to exercise influence and control over the actions of other political structures. The cases of Britain, France, Germany, and the United States are at the center of the study, but other constitutional court systems are also examined.

Morgenstern, Scott, and Benito Nacif, Eds. (2002). *Legislative Politics in Latin America*. Cambridge: Cambridge University Press. This lengthy book includes illuminating comparative studies of the different styles of legislatures and the alternative strategic behaviors of legislators in numerous Latin American countries.

Norris, Pippa. (2004). *Electoral Engineering: Voting Rules and Political Behavior*. Cambridge, England: Cambridge University Press. A creative scholar considers the impacts of the various electoral systems with survey data and other empirical evidence from 32 countries in order to assess whether, given political culture, such engineering of institutional arrangements can influence political behavior, from voting to the building of social capital, to democratic accountability

Osborne, David, and Ted Gaebler. (1993) *Reinventing Government*. New York: Penguin. An influential critique of large bureaucratic government and a framework (using examples from the United States) of how to make government (and especially the administrative system) more responsive and entrepreneurial.

Peters, B. Guy. (2009). *The Politics of Bureaucracy: A Comparative Perspective*. 6th ed. New York: Routledge. A rich, analytic comparison of the behavior and power of bureaucracies in many countries.

Pitkin, Hannah F. (1972). *The Concept of Representation*. Berkeley: University of California Press. A thorough descriptive and normative exploration of political representation.

Sparrow, Malcolm K. (2000). *The Regulatory Craft: Controlling Risks, Solving Problems, and Managing Compliance*. Washington, DC: Brookings Institution. Writing as much for those who work in the public service as for scholars, Sparrow offers a positive and persuasive argument in support of administrative regulation, detailing the role of regulators as important innovators and protectors of the public interest within the policy process.

Stone Sweet, Alec. (2004). *The Judicial Construction of Europe*. Oxford: Oxford University Press. The author characterizes the considerable expansion of power of the European Union (EU) court system in shaping the political behavior of individual actors, the nature of the political system, and the functioning of the EU itself.

Von Mettenheim, Kurt, and Bert Rockman, Eds. (1997). *Presidential Institutions and Democratic Politics: Comparing Regional and National Contexts*. Baltimore, MD: Johns Hopkins University Press. Essays in a comparative perspective, as well as ones focused on a single country, that examine the behaviors and institutional frameworks of top executives.

Wilson, James Q. (1990). *Bureaucracy: What Government Agencies Do and Why They Do It*. New York: Basic Books. An interesting analysis of the performance of the American national administration, identifying both the value and the flaws of the system.

ON THE WEB

http://www.gksoft.com/govt/en

Governments on the Web provides a comprehensive database of governmental institutions on the Internet. The site contains 17,000 entries from 220 different countries. Most of the information is accurate, although there have been no updates for a decade.

http://www.usa.gov

The U.S. government's Official Web portal provides a wealth of government-related material, including access to the Internet sites of every major U.S. government agency.

http://www.direct.gov.uk/en/index.htm

Directgov is the official Web portal of the government of the United Kingdom, and it provides extensive details about all the major political institutions and government agencies. The majority of the world's countries now have an official Web portal like this. They can usually be located by entering "Countryname" and "government portal" on a search engine. [For another example, Canada is: http://www.canada.gc.ca/home.html]

http://thomas.loc.gov/home/legbranch/cis.html

http://www.loc.gov/rr/news/fedgov.html

http://www.uscourts.gov

These three Library of Congress sites provide information about the legislative, executive, and judicial branches of the U.S. government, respectively.

http://www.fedworld.gov

This site provides a huge central information network of the U.S. federal government, with searchable access to agencies and departments, documents, databases, and so on—a comprehensive site for searching for, locating, ordering, and acquiring government and business information.

http://www.thisnation.com

This electronic textbook provides an in-depth look at American politics and includes links to other American government-related Internet resources.

http://www.usa.gov

The U.S. government's official Web portal provides a wealth of government-related material, including access to the Internet sites of every major U.S. government agency.

http://lcweb.loc.gov/rr/news/extgovd.html

This site allows you to browse through Library of Congress electronic government resources.

Political Institutions II: Institutional Arrangements

Meet and greet. To build support among Iraq's diverse groups, Prime Minister Nuri-al-Maliki talks

LEARNING OBJECTIVES

7.1 Assess the impact of written constitutions on regimes.

7.2 Distinguish between democratic and nondemocratic political systems.

7.3 Compare and contrast unitary, federal, and confederal systems.

7.4 Differentiate between parliamentary, presidential, and other types of executive-legislative systems.

7.5 Characterize the different types of political party systems.

Read and **Listen** to **Chapter 7** at mypoliscilab.com

Study and **Review** the **Pre-Test & Flashcards** at mypoliscilab.com

Thomas Jefferson once observed that true democracy can only grow on fertile soil. The "soil" needs to be enriched with certain elements. There needs to be tolerance (and ideally cooperation) among different factions in the country; there needs to be an effective structure of authority and governance; and perhaps most importantly, the people need to trust in government and in each other. It might be that a reasonable level of economic prosperity is also an important nutrient. Without these elements—without a fertile soil—a democracy cannot thrive. Iraq is among the countries currently struggling to find that mix of elements.

Iraq was fashioned out of parts of Mesopotamia and Kurdistan by the British, who faced an immediate rebellion and implanted an outsider from Mecca to be King in 1921. Deeply split into three nations (the Shias, the Sunnis, and the Kurds), Iraq was the first Arab state to overthrow its leader by a military coup, in 1936. Despotic political leadership continued during the brutal rule of President Saddam Hussein, from 1979–2003. When the United States led an invasion into Iraq searching for "weapons of mass destruction" and overthrew Hussein, Iraq was left without a government. The United States insisted that the Iraqis establish a democratic government. But could a country with a history of nationality differences and tyranny be rapidly transformed into a democracy?

Having no recent experience with government transparency, free elections, competitive political parties, or peaceful turnovers of power, the Iraqis floundered. The United States asserted its own vision, establishing a transitional government in 2003 and pressuring the Iraqis to move forward by offering substantial aid and military support. Despite continued violence and volatile relations among different groups in Iraq, a constitution was ratified by a national vote in October 2005. The new Iraqi government is defined in the constitution as a parliamentary democracy, with a legislature elected by proportional representation. The executive branch is a hybrid headed by a prime minister, a president, and a presidency council. Iraq is a federation with 18 provinces and a system of local governments. There is a national judiciary guided by both civil law and sharia law (since Islam is the state religion).

In the most recent election in March 2010, four major parties and five small parties competed for the 325 member legislature. However, more than 450 candidates were not allowed to run in the election because they were linked to the banned Ba'athist (Sunni) Party and the election was tainted by considerable voter fraud. It then took eight months to fashion a governing coalition due to continued disagreements among the major parties. Underlying these difficulties was the fact that the main Iraqi factions did not trust each other. During the Hussein regime, a genocidal campaign had been waged against the Kurds, who now demanded substantial regional autonomy. The Hussein government had been dominated by the minority Sunnis, who subjected the majority Shias to discrimination and repression. The Shias now aimed to control the government, marginalizing the Sunnis; but there are also deep divisions among different sects among the Shias.

The tensions among these different groups in Iraq and the presence of the United States "occupation" military has resulted in continuing political violence. Iraq became a battlefield of guerrilla warfare, suicide bombings, IEDs (improvised explosive devices), executions, kidnappings, and other forms of intergroup brutality. Neither the coalition forces nor the Iraqi security forces have been able to stop the violence. At the same time, the efforts by the new government to rebuild the country's economic infrastructure, to provide stable jobs, and to enable most Iraqis to enjoy a decent standard of living have had only limited success. In this complex "soil" of distrust, widespread human suffering, and new political institutions with little depth of support, the growth of democracy has struggled.

Most see a half-full, half-empty glass of democracy in Iraq. On the one hand, the Iraqis have a sound constitution and have implemented all the appropriate political institutions for democratic governance. On the other hand, the government lacks credibility with most citizens, has not been particularly effective in enacting and implementing policies, and intergroup violence continues to (literally) explode in Iraq on almost a daily basis. The combination of instability, difficult living conditions, and poor government performance has not resulted in the levels of trust, tolerance, or well-being that seem necessary to nurture the young democracy in the near future.

Chapter 6 provided us with a clearer grasp of each of the four major institutional structures in political systems. While all are in place now in Iraq, they have not yet delivered prosperity, stability, or security. It is evident that it is valuable to seek a deeper understanding of how these institutions and other structural elements interact in the pursuit of fundamental goals. Thus, this chapter takes us further in exploring the various ways in which these structures and other key elements of governance are arranged across different countries. Thus we will examine the role of the constitution, the continuum from democratic to nondemocratic regimes, the distribution of power between central and peripheral governments, the various patterns of executive-legislative relations, and the types of party systems.

CONSTITUTIONS AND CONSTITUTIONAL REGIMES

Constitutions

7.1 Assess the impact of written constitutions on regimes.

◉ Watch the Video "Venezuela's Constitutional Referendum" at mypoliscilab.com

✴ Explore the Comparative "Constitutions" on mypoliscilab.com

In Iraq, a central element in framing the government's "institutional arrangements" is a constitution, *a set of statements describing the fundamental rules of the political system.* The constitution declares the existence of the state, and it expresses three crucial sets of rules. First, the constitution allocates governmental activities, defining what actions are within the domain of *res publica* and what political structures will perform these various functions. Second, it establishes the formal power relationships among the major political structures, indicating the conditions under which each is independent or dependent on the actions of the others. Third, the constitution limits the power of the rulers and guarantees the rights of the ruled, by defining the maximum extent of the state's authority over its citizens and by enumerating citizens' freedoms and benefits from the state.

The actual drafting of every constitution is either directly or indirectly controlled by those with political power in the society. Many groups in a society might offer interpretations of what the constitution means and how it ought to be applied to particular circumstances—leaders, courts, political parties, interest groups. Ultimately, the force of the constitution depends on the will of those with political power to enforce its provisions.

Most constitutions are a single written document, like Iraq's Constitution. However, a few political systems do not have such a document; their fundamental rules are embedded in major statutes, precedents, and legal decisions, as in Great Britain's "unwritten constitution" or in Israel's "basic laws." While early constitutions tended to be relatively short and general, some postcolonial constitutions are quite detailed. The Nigerian Constitution has 245 articles, and the Indian Constitution has 395 articles. The language of constitutions is also becoming increasingly similar because drafters liberally borrow ideas and even specific language from other countries. For example, more than three dozen countries have borrowed Abraham Lincoln's felicitous phrasing regarding government "of the people, by the people, and for the people."

Although the idea of a constitution has a certain timeless quality, the constitutions of political systems are always changeable. Most countries periodically alter their constitutions. For example, India has added more than 100 amendments to its constitution since 1950. And at some point, many countries have abandoned their existing constitutions and ratified new ones in an attempt to rejuvenate their political systems. Among the countries adopting new constitutions since 2005 are Angola, Bolivia, China, Colombia, Congo, Dominican Republic, Ecuador, Iraq, Kenya, Kyrgyzstan, Montenegro, Myanmar, Swaziland, Thailand, and Zimbabwe. The process does not always succeed. In 2005, Kenyan citizens rejected a new constitution proposed by then-President Mwai Kibaki. In 2007, Venezuelans rejected a bundle of 33 major amendments to the Constitution proposed by President Hugo Chavez. And, although the parliament of the European Union adopted a new constitution in 2004, some key member states (e.g., France and the Netherlands) have subsequently voted against ratification.

A country's constitution does not necessarily provide a description of how the political system actually works. As you will read below, the reality of politics in many countries is dramatically at odds with the vision in their constitutions. Yet a constitution can be a very significant document. In the turbulent debate over the creation of Spain's new constitution in 1978, the distinguished historian Julian Marais insisted, "If the constitution does not inspire respect, admiration and enthusiasm, democracy is not assured." Even if the state makes major diversions from its constitution's provisions, the constitution remains a moral yardstick against which to measure actual performance, and it is a persistent reminder of the high ideals and goals that have been set for the political system.

Constitutional Regimes

It is useful to analyze the extent to which a political system does generally abide by the provisions in its constitution. A constitutional regime *operates in terms of the rule of law and ensures effective restraints on the power holders,* as defined within the constitution. The defining feature of a constitutional regime is that the state attempts to fulfill the provisions of its constitution. A political system becomes more fully a constitutional regime to the extent that it abides by the three sets of crucial rules described above. In the short run, at least, those who have political power in the society greatly influence the interpretation of the constitution and how the constitution's provisions will be implemented. In constitutional regimes, these interpretations are generally reasonable and judicious, and the implementation is fair (Sunstein 2001).

Among constitutional regimes, it is not always the case that compliance with the rules is complete. Disagreements over interpretation of the constitution occur, practice and precedent can result in a gap between the rules and standard practice, and political actors sometimes willfully bend the rules to serve their agendas. Even the limits on the rulers and the rights of the citizens are not absolute and are not absolutely implemented. For example, Article 10 of the French Constitution guarantees freedom of religious practice, but the courts have ruled that current legislation preventing French (Muslim) women from wearing a burqa in public is an acceptable limit on their rights. Also, some states implement a "temporary" suspension of major constitutional provisions in response to circumstances that seriously threaten the stability of the society.

Thus, regimes range on a continuum and are less constitutional when the disparity becomes larger between the provisions in the constitution and the actual politics of the society. In theory, at least, a state could scrupulously follow a repressive and undemocratic constitution imposed by the political leadership and be labeled a constitutional regime. Saudi Arabia might be an example of this, given its adherence to authoritarian "basic laws" and sharia.

Nonconstitutional Regimes

Hence, in a nonconstitutional regime, *the structural arrangements of the constitution are not generally upheld and there are few restraints on those with political power.* Almost every political system occasionally violates or ignores some principle in its constitution. But the regime can be called *nonconstitutional* when there is persistent nonenforcement of constitutional provisions, especially those regarding the rights of the ruled or crucial limits on the rulers.

Various sets of conditions can result in a nonconstitutional regime. First, leaders in some political systems simply ignore with impunity the basic rules in the constitution (e.g., Myanmar, Vietnam). Second, in some countries (e.g., Congo, Somalia), the rule of law collapses because the social order disintegrates through severe political violence or natural catastrophe. And third, there are instances when either the entire constitution or major constitutional rights are suspended "temporarily" but then are not restored for a lengthy period. In Israel, for example, this temporary suspension of constitutional rights (there is no written constitution) has persisted since its independence in 1948.

DEMOCRACIES AND NONDEMOCRACIES

7.2 Distinguish between democratic and nondemocratic political systems.

Another taxonomy for classifying political systems is to specify the extent to which their institutional arrangements are democratic. "Democracy" is arguably the most ideologically-loaded concept in any discussion about politics and governance. How do we define democracy? Here is a multiple-choice question version:

Watch the Video "Reforming the House of Lords" at mypoliscilab.com

Democracy is:

a. an agreeable, lawless . . . commonwealth, dealing with all alike on a footing of equality, whether they be really equal or not.
—(Plato, ca. 427–347 B.C.E., Greek philosopher)

b. the theory that the common people know what they want, and deserve to get it good and hard.
—(H. L. Mencken, 1880–1956, U.S. journalist)

c. a system where no man is good enough to govern another man without that other's consent.
—(Abraham Lincoln, 1809–1865, U.S. president)

d. the substitution of election by the incompetent many for appointment by the corrupt few.
—(George Bernard Shaw, 1856–1950, Anglo-Irish playwright)

e. all of the above.
f. none of the above.

We know that all political systems are not democracies. But what does constitute a democracy? From our education, as well as from our other socialization and experiences, most of us have an intuitive sense about which countries are democracies and which are not. However, the concept can become slippery when we try to apply it. North Korea calls itself the *Democratic* People's Republic. Is it? Sri Lanka calls itself the *Democratic* Socialist Republic. Is it? Egypt, France, Kenya, and Venezuela also consider themselves democracies. Are they? Democracy has become such a highly valued label that most states, except a few systems ruled by a hereditary monarch, claim that they are democratic. Is almost every contemporary political system to be called a democracy? If not, what general label do you give to countries that are not democratic? Dictatorship? Tyranny? Totalitarian regime? Authoritarian system?

Suppose you were to determine which of a group of countries were democracies. How would you proceed?

One approach is to distinguish democracies from nondemocracies. While we work towards acceptable definitions and labels, let's start by considering "dictatorship" as the opposite of democracy. To begin to clarify your thinking, use your current understanding of democracy and dictatorship to classify these seven political systems: Algeria, Cuba, Japan, Kuwait, Singapore, the United States, and Zimbabwe. If you have been raised in the United States or Western Europe, you might view Japan, the United States, and possibly Kuwait and Singapore as democracies and Algeria, Cuba, and Zimbabwe as run by dictators. Why might it matter where you were raised? Recall that Chapter 4 attempted to persuade you that how one understands and uses political labels depends on one's own political socialization and political environment. It might be argued that this problem regarding interpersonal differences in assessments underscores the virtue of the scientific method. The scientific method requires the analyst to specify what a particular concept means with great precision and in an empirically measurable manner. This method might be the only way in which people with fundamentally different ideological views could agree on which states are democracies and which are dictatorships. The discussion in this chapter will proceed in the spirit of the scientific method, although the author acknowledges his own lifetime socialization, which is grounded in the political conceptions of the American and Western world.

How might individuals with dramatically different political worldviews attempt to agree on the accuracy of the classifications suggested earlier? For example, consider these issues:

- In Cuba, a far greater proportion of the citizens vote in elections than in either Japan or the United States. The government provides far more extensive social benefits to all its citizens than either Japan or the United States. Aren't those the best features of a democracy?

Algeria calls itself the "Peoples' Democratic Republic." Elections for the president were held in 2004 and 2009 and Abdelaziz Bouteflika was elected each time by substantial majorities. Elections for the national bicameral legislature occurred in 2002 and 2007, with 22 different parties winning seats. Under these conditions, is Algeria a dictatorship?

- By what criteria is Zimbabwe not a democracy when President Robert Mugabe defeated other candidates in four straight elections (in 1990, 1996, 2002, and 2008) and his party won less than half of the seats in a 2008 legislative election?
- By what criteria is Singapore a democracy when almost every member of the national legislature and every prime minister has, in every election since its independence in 1959, been from a single political party?

In asking and responding to such questions, you begin to establish the standards that must be applied when you attempt to distinguish between democracy and dictatorship. These kinds of questions also underscore the importance of defining with precision the concepts that we use in political analysis.

Defining Democracy

What are the necessary and sufficient conditions for democracy? In its classic sense, true *direct democracy* (also known as participatory democracy) is government of and by the people—*all the citizens are active, direct participants in making public policy decisions.* Realistically, there is no such political system; indeed, Jean-Jacques Rousseau (1712–1778) claimed that only a society of gods could be a true democracy. If our definition is less stringent, democracy might entail the relatively equal capacity of *every* citizen to influence the policy process. It would be difficult to make a persuasive case that this condition holds in *any* political system, including Japan or the United States. In every political system, "some are more equal than others." In every political system, some make public policy decisions and others observe.

An alternative concept is representative democracy, a system in which the *citizens periodically elect people who represent them in the political process and make policy decisions on their behalf.* Another general term used to describe a representative democracy is a *republic.* In fact, the majority of the countries in the world, in their formal title, call themselves republics (examples, from the A's: Republic of Albania, People's Democratic Republic of Algeria, People's Republic of Angola, Argentine Republic, Republic of Armenia, Republic of Austria, and Republic of Azerbaijan). You might think some of these A "republics" are not particularly democratic.

Kuwait seems to meet this criterion for representative democracy because its citizens periodically elect representatives. Yet few would classify it as a democracy because about half of its resident adult population (those who cannot trace their Kuwaiti ancestry to 1920) are not allowed to vote in legislative elections, and the chief executive, the emir, is appointed from the ruling Al-Sabah family. Thus, the definition needs to be refined to specify that the elections for representatives must be held under conditions of *universal (adult) suffrage.*

Cuba meets all these conditions, but few would consider it a democracy because, among other reasons, there are very limited choices for governmental office. There is only one candidate per district, and this person is chosen by a local committee based on "patriotism" and "revolutionary history" as well as merit. In practice, nearly every candidate is a member of the single (Communist) party. Thus, an adequate definition of democracy should also stipulate that the elections provide voters with *alternative choices.*

Even with this clarification, there are cases, such as Singapore, where numerous parties offer candidates, but more than 95 percent of legislators are always elected from one party. Thus, even the notion of a contest among alternative candidates can be ambiguous. However, these conditions do seem to define an *electoral democracy: a political system in which virtually all citizens periodically vote to select political leaders from among alternative contenders.*

Additional conditions might seem appropriate in refining our definition of democracy. It is also important that the people have the genuine capacity to retain or reject those serving as their political leaders. This additional condition, called the *limited mandate,* means that the electorate grants the authority to govern (the mandate) for only a short, fixed (limited) period of time, and then the electorate has the opportunity to select representatives again. And, it means that if political leaders do not gain sufficient votes, they relinquish office voluntarily and peacefully. This condition can be harder to demonstrate because it is not clear if the top leaders in several of these countries would peacefully step down if they lost an election. This is problematic in Singapore, and there are instances in both Algeria and Zimbabwe where an election that would have turned out the leaders was ignored. It is hard to imagine that the leaders in Cuba or Kuwait would step down even in the unlikely situation they were outvoted.

Are we there yet? Perhaps. But shouldn't a full democracy not only ensure voting rights among alternative choices and a limited mandate, but also allow the citizens and the media to exercise freedoms such as freedom of speech, assembly, and political opposition at all times? Zimbabwe, for example, loosely meets the conditions for electoral democracy, but opposition groups and media are harassed, arrested, and subjected to violence by those loyal to President Robert Mugabe. Thus, scholars classify a political system as a liberal democracy when *citizens enjoy not only electoral democracy but also substantial political rights and civil liberties regarding participation, personal freedoms, and opposition.* And if a country is *an electoral democracy, but its citizens' political rights and civil liberties are significantly limited*, some analysts describe that country with yet another term, ***illiberal democracy*** (Zakaria 2007).

Now we have established one possible set of sufficient, as well as necessary, conditions for a democracy: *governance by leaders whose authority is based on a limited mandate from a universal electorate that selects among genuine alternatives*

Zimbabwe's President Robert Mugabe is very popular with his supporters, whom he rewards; but most observers inside and outside of the country judge him to be a ruthless and corrupt dictator who suppresses opposition and rigs the elections.

and has some rights to political participation and opposition. This is a modest notion of democracy because it guarantees the people little more than political rights and the occasional opportunity to select among the competing elites who govern them. Some scholars include even more elements, such as an electoral system that does not substantially skew the conversion of votes to seats (recall Focus in 6 on electoral systems), an independent and neutral judiciary, and civilian control of the military (Diamond and Plattner 2009).

Our definition is clearly less than a full participatory democracy, where there would be active, direct rule by all the people, who would be empowered to make policy decisions themselves by referenda or some other means (see Barber 2004; Dahl 1971, 2006; Schumpeter 1950). Even with our modest definition, only two (Japan and the United States) among the seven political systems are clearly classified as democracies. Singapore is more problematic because the extent to which there is genuine contestation is unclear. Not only does one party win nearly all the legislative seats and control the government, but also the last several presidents of Singapore have been elected by "default" because a governing panel declared that only one candidate was qualified to run. While all seven systems encourage some forms of political participation and allow some political opposition, the authority of the political leadership in Cuba and Kuwait is not based on its electoral selection, by universal suffrage, among genuine alternatives, or for a fixed period of time. And the leaders in Algeria and Zimbabwe have so manipulated the electoral process (harassing and arresting opponents, controlling the media, engaging in electoral fraud) that neither country meets the spirit of the definition.

Most definitions of democracy focus on the *process*, as discussed above. However, some analysts go even further, arguing that a genuine democracy must guarantee not only appropriate processes of empowering and replacing leaders but also must deliver desirable *policy outputs*. In such a process-plus-output conception of genuine democracy, the political system might ensure that all citizens have access to quality education, employment, good health care, and decent housing, and enjoy such conditions of life as a sense of personal safety and a healthy environment. While it might seem reasonable that a democracy should "deliver the goods," there is substantial disagreement about the nature of this package of goods, and thus the policy decisions about these goods are part of the political process but do not define democracy (see Chapter 9).

This extensive discussion might help you identify the criteria that *you* think are necessary for an adequate definition of democracy. (It is certainly possible that your definition will differ from any of those suggested here. You should, however, be able to justify your criteria.) Could you now articulate a conceptual definition of democracy and use it to classify a set of political systems? Do you think your friends will accept your definition and classifications? Would a Singaporean or Cuban student accept it? You might be surprised by how difficult it is to develop a generally accepted definition of this most widely used political concept.

Defining Nondemocracies

How about *nondemocracies*? What concepts can be used to characterize those political regimes that are not democratic? Several are widely employed.

Autocracy   One conventional concept for some nondemocracies is *autocracy.* A stringent definition might be that a single ruler exercises absolute power and authority (independent of any consideration of the process through which power was acquired). However, you might consider whether any one person could successfully exercise absolute power in the contemporary political world.

Dictatorship   Related to autocracy is the concept of *dictatorship.* A "dictator" might be a single individual or small group that has nearly absolute power and authority. Dictatorship might be better defined in terms of *rulers who hold power in the absence of a limited mandate*—a critical factor in our definition of democracy. That is, if the citizens have no regular and realistic opportunity to replace the political leadership, then the political system is a dictatorship. This applies to the military dictatorship in Myanmar. However, even a political leadership that has popular support from the majority but does not provide genuine opportunities for the population to renew the mandate in competition with alternative leaders could be defined as dictatorial. This definition might characterize the situation in Cuba under Raul Castro and perhaps for some hereditary rulers, such as the Emir of Kuwait.

Authoritarian Regime   A concept that political scientists often apply to a nondemocratic system is *authoritarian regime.* Many authoritarian regimes, like dictatorships, lack a limited mandate. But what distinguishes **authoritarianism** is another dimension: *the political actions and decisions of the ruler are not constrained, while the political rights and freedoms of the citizens are significantly limited.* In other words, an authoritarian regime places severe restrictions on the activities of individuals and groups who desire to understand and influence the political system. The flow of political information is strictly controlled by the government. And the great majority of the population is not allowed to participate in any political activities except those expressly encouraged by the regime, such as mass rallies and voting in support of the leaders (Linz 1993; Wiarda 2004).

Citizens are not permitted to question the political institutions, procedures, or public policies of an authoritarian regime. However, the nonpolitical aspects of people's lives, such as their occupation, religion, and social life, are not generally under the direct control of the political system. Singapore, as well as Algeria, Kuwait and Zimbabwe, could be characterized as authoritarian regimes.

Totalitarian Regime   In a *totalitarian regime,* the definition of *res publica* becomes total. Thus, under **totalitarianism,** *the political system's decisions and its control penetrate into almost every aspect of its people's lives.* The totalitarian regime demands complete obedience to its extensive rules regarding culture, economics, religion, and morality. The state attempts to dictate the behavior and even the thoughts of its population in almost every domain of existence. Every political system intervenes occasionally in such domains, but the defining characteristic of the totalitarian regime is its constant and pervasive efforts to totally control the lives of its population.

All organizations are subordinated to the totalitarian state. Every activity of the individual citizen is subject to scrutiny by the state, which claims it is protecting what is best for the society as a whole. The state might define the acceptability of films and plays, determine what job each individual will have, prohibit the activities of organized churches, prevent families from moving without approval, and so on.

Totalitarian regimes, even more than authoritarian regimes, depend on the use of extensive coercion for their survival. The state employs its military, internal security forces, and other instruments of violence to suppress any citizen or group that challenges its authority. To sustain its pervasive control, the totalitarian regime also makes extensive use of the agents of political socialization, especially the media, the educational system, and cultural forms. Often the totalitarian state is dominated by a single leader, venerated in a cult of personality, and by a single political party. The people have no control over the policies or the mandate of the leadership. George Orwell's novel *1984* (1949/1967) is a literary vision of the totalitarian state, and other recent examples include Afghanistan under the Taliban, Cambodia under Pol Pot (1975–1979; see Compare in 10), and North Korea.

Most nondemocracies can be located on a continuum between totalitarianism and authoritarianism. That is, there are regimes which extend their control beyond basic authoritarianism into important nonpolitical domains but do not exercise the totality of control associated with absolute totalitarianism. Belarus, Congo under Mobuto Sese Seko (1965–1997; see Focus in 11), Indonesia under Suharto (1966–1998), Iran, Myanmar, and Saudi Arabia are examples along this continuum of countries that are not totalitarian regimes but do assert extensive control over culture, religious practice, and social life.

Not all political analysts are consistent in how they employ these concepts. In this book, at least, autocracy, dictatorship, authoritarianism, and totalitarianism will all be treated as modes of politics that contrast with democratic regimes. *Autocracy* will be applied if there is near-absolute one person rule. *Dictatorship* will especially emphasize the absence of a limited mandate for the political leaders. *Authoritarianism* will connote a more encompassing array of nondemocratic practices and significant controls over citizens' political behavior. And *totalitarianism* will be used to describe systems whose oppressive control goes far beyond the political sphere into personal and social life as well. Many authoritarian or totalitarian regimes are dictatorships. However, there are instances where people elect their leaders (electoral democracies) but the political system substantially limits the people's personal and political freedoms, as in Singapore and Iran.

A Democracy–Nondemocracy Measure

This discussion of democracy suggests that there are gradations along a democracy–nondemocracy continuum. Can we measure how democratic national political systems are? Can we identify the number of countries that are democratic? The precise number of countries in the current "wave of democracy" (a key theme in Chapter 10 and in Part Five of this book) ebbs and flows yearly as some countries establish democratic systems while others retreat or revert to nondemocratic systems (Diamond 2009; Schedler 2006).

Freedom House (2011) is an international organization that analyzes these questions. First, Freedom House identifies those countries that meet the minimal conditions for an electoral democracy. Second, those countries that do not meet these conditions can be classified as nondemocracies. Third, Freedom House analyzes the extent to which each country grants its citizens the *political rights* (e.g., to form political parties that promote genuine alternatives, to campaign and vote in free and fair elections) and *civil liberties* (e.g., religious and ethnic freedom, press freedom) that define a liberal democracy.

Freedom House has developed a widely-cited scale, with each country scoring from 1 to 7 points on political rights and from 1 to 7 points on civil liberties. A country's combined average score on the two measures can range from 1.0 points, the most extensive liberal democracies, to 7.0 points, the world's most repressive regimes. Based on actual conditions, a country is classified as "free" (1.0–2.5 points), "partly free" (3.0–5.0), or "not free" (5.5–7.0) (Freedom House 2011).

According to the analysis of Freedom House, 45 percent of all countries (and 43 percent of the world's population) are "free." However, 31 percent of the countries are only "partly free," and 24 percent are "not free." Even more striking, fully 35 percent of the world's population is not free, living under highly repressive political regimes. There are clear regional variations, ranging from fully 96 percent of Western European countries being classified as free, compared to only 6 percent of free countries in the Middle East and North Africa, where 78 percent are not free. Table 7.1 reports the Freedom House classifications of selected countries on both political rights and civil liberties, circa 2010.

AREAL DISTRIBUTION OF POWER

With the exception of small political systems serving only a few thousand citizens, most political systems have found it desirable or necessary to create governmental structures at several levels. Thus, another type of institutional arrangement is the *areal distribution of power*—the allocation of power and functions across the levels of government. National political systems are organized into one of three major forms: (1) unitary states, (2) federations, and (3) confederations.

7.3 Compare and contrast unitary, federal, and confederal systems.

Explore the Comparative "Federal and Unitary Systems" on mypoliscilab.com

Unitary State

In a **unitary state**, *a central government holds all legitimate power.* The central government has indivisible sovereignty, although it usually delegates some power to regional units such as provinces, departments, or counties. These subnational governments serve at the convenience of the central government, which can revoke their power or functions at any time. Currently, more than 70 percent of the countries are unitary states. Examples include most African, Asian, and Latin American countries and include China, France, Japan, South Africa, and the United Kingdom.

Why are most contemporary states unitary? The major advantage is that there is clear, hierarchical authority—all power is controlled by the central government. Even if there were a disagreement between the central government and the peripheral governments, the center's superior constitutional power is clear, and center–periphery stalemates are uncommon. Also, control from the center should provide a more uniform implementation of policy throughout the country. And primary citizen loyalty tends to be mainly attached to the national political system, reducing the risk of divisive regionalism.

TABLE 7.1

Classification of Selected Countries by Level of Freedom and Regime Type, Circa 2010

	Freedom Score	Liberal Democracy	Electoral Democracy	Nondemocracy
Free	1.0	Costa Rica 1,1*		
		Sweden 1,1		
		Poland 1,1		
		United States 1,1		
	1.5	Japan, 1,2		
		South Korea 1,2		
	2.0	South Africa 2,2	Argentina 2,2	
			Brazil 2,2	
			Serbia 2,2	
	2.5	India 2,3	Indonesia 2,3	
Partly Free	3.0		Mexico 3,3	
			Sierra Leone 3,3	
			Turkey 3,3	
	3.5			
	4.0		Nigeria 4,4	
	4.5			Thailand 5,4
				Singapore 5,4
	5.0			Venezuela 5,5
Not Free	5.5			Cambodia 6,5
				Egypt 6,5
				Russia 6,5
	6.0			Congo 6,6
				Swaziland, 7,5
				Vietnam 7,5
	6.5			China 7,6
				Saudi Arabia 7,6
				Syria 7,6
	7.0			Myanmar 7,7
				North Korea 7,7

*Scores: The first score is political rights, the second score is civil liberties, with 1 = the highest score and 7 = the lowest score. A country's Freedom Score is the average of these two component scores.
Source: Freedom House 2011.

Federation

A federation has *a constitutional division of power and functions between a central government and the set of regional governments*. In contrast to a unitary state, the central government and the regional governments share power in a federation. Each level has primary control of certain functions and neither level has legal power to dominate the other level in all policy domains. At least, the center government usually controls policy in such areas as national defense, finance, commerce, and foreign affairs. The essence of a federation is coordination, not hierarchy. Federations require a complex balancing of the power between the central government and the regional governments and thus are more prone to disagreements, power struggles, and stalemates than a unitary state. Nonetheless, there are five major rationales for a federation:

1. **Large size.** Many states become federations to distribute governmental power where there is a huge area to be governed. Fewer than 25 states are federations today, but this group includes nearly half the land area of the world. Most of the largest states are federations, including Brazil, Canada, India, Mexico, Nigeria, Russia, and the United States. During the constitutional debate in the United States, Thomas Jefferson observed, "Our country is too large to have all its affairs directed by a single government."

2. **The prior existence of strong states.** A federation can be an acceptable compromise when strong peripheral governments create a central government. In the formation of the United States, for example, the already strong state governments were unwilling to give up all of their power to a central government, as in a unitary state. Rather, they agreed to delegate certain functions to the new central government while retaining all other "residual" powers for themselves.

3. **The attempt to create unity or accommodate diversity.** Chapter 5 described the serious problems of conflict between states and nations, especially in the newer states. Federations attempt to bond diverse nations into a unified state while still recognizing the different nations' diversity and desire for power at the regional level. The regional governments can represent a major ethnic, linguistic, religious, or other nation-based characteristic dominant in the region. India is a federation with 28 states, most of which are related to the linguistic, ethnic, or religious majority in the area.

4. **The desire to disperse political power.** A federation can be established to prevent the overconcentration of power in the central government. After the trauma of Hitler's rule, West Germans formed a federation to prevent the emergence of another overly powerful central government. The bulk of legislative power was granted to the central government, but most power to administer and adjudicate the laws is held by the Länder (regional) governments.

5. **The desire to concentrate power and resources.** In contrast to the preceding rationale, a federation can be created to combine several states into a stronger political system. For example, in the effort to create Arab unity and to expand the political and economic power of the state, Egypt has several times formed federations with its neighbors: Syria, Yemen, Iraq, and Jordan.

Confederation

A confederation is *an association in which states delegate some power to a supranational central government but retain primary power*. It is a loose grouping of states in which each state's membership, participation, and compliance with the supranational central government are conditional, depending on the state's perception of its own national interest. Confederations are usually created when states decide that the performance of certain functions is enhanced by structured cooperation with other states. To facilitate such cooperation, the states establish permanent supranational machinery. The United Arab Emirates is a confederation of ministates, and the United Nations is a confederal structure containing more than 190 member states. Confederations can emphasize economic cooperation, such as the European Union (EU), or military cooperation, such as the North Atlantic Treaty Organization (NATO).

Although confederations can serve many useful functions for member states, their activities and even their very survival are always contingent on the members' continuing support. A member state might refuse to comply with confederation policies that conflict directly with the state's definition of its own national interest. Disagreements among the members can necessitate negotiation and compromise, as in the periodic adjustments within the EU regarding issues such as farm subsidies to member states and a common monetary policy. A confederation can wither if the supragovernment is ineffective, as in the case of the Articles of Confederation in colonial America, or if members refuse to support its directives, as in the League of Nations after World War I.

Table 7.2 summarizes some of the major advantages and shortcomings of each approach to the areal distribution of power. While each has relative advantages under certain conditions, none is without considerable drawbacks, and none can ensure the effective functioning or even the survival of a political system. The

TABLE 7.2

Relative Strengths and Weaknesses of Areal Distributions of Power

Form of Areal Distribution	Strengths	Weaknesses
Unitary state	Clear authority Decisive control No stalemates between center and periphery	Hyperconcentration of power Weak representation of diversity and minorities
Federation	Representation of diversity Checks on center's power Creates unity	Duplication and overlap of power Conflicts over ultimate power Sluggishness; compromises
Confederation	Facilitates cooperation Power retained by subunits	Conditional compliance Instability

general trend towards the centralization of political power within states has meant that the distinctions between unitary states and federations are less clear than in the past and that confederations have become particularly fragile.

FORMS OF EXECUTIVE–LEGISLATIVE RELATIONS

Another conventional method of classifying and especially of describing political systems is by defining the pattern of power and interaction between the executive and legislative structures. The taxonomy in this section emphasizes the three most common patterns through which these two structures interact to perform the functions of policymaking and policy implementation: the presidential, parliamentary, and hybrid forms of government. Two other types of executive–legislative arrangements are also briefly examined: the council and assembly systems.

7.4 Differentiate between parliamentary, presidential, and othe types of executive-legislative systems.

Presidential Government

The crucial feature of presidential government is the *separation of executive and legislative structures*. Figure 7.1 portrays the electoral chain of command that is supposed to define the relationships between citizens and these major political structures. In separate electoral decisions, the citizens select the chief executive (usually called the president) and the members of the national legislature. This electoral process provides both the president and the legislature with independent mandates to represent the citizens in the governing process. The term length of each is predetermined, and thus the tenure in office of each is not dependent on the other (except in the rare case of impeachment of the chief executive).

The separation of executive and legislative powers is explicit and intentional to ensure a system of checks and balances in the policymaking and policy-implementation processes. Primary responsibility for policymaking (debating, modifying, and enacting policies as law) resides in the legislature. Although the chief executive can veto legislation, the legislature can override that veto.

Watch the Video "Parliamentary Democracy in Ireland" at **mypoliscilab.com**

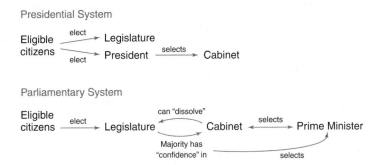

FIGURE 7.1
Presidential and parliamentary systems of government

Primary responsibility for the implementation of policy is with the president, who has control of the government's administrative departments. The president also appoints a cabinet, whose members are responsible for overseeing policy in the government's administrative departments and who are controlled directly by the president.

In practice, it is common to find considerable interdependence and blurring of functions between the executive and legislative structures and especially for the president to have substantial involvement in policymaking. The United States is the model example of presidential government, and it is also found in many Latin American and some African and Asian states, including Brazil, Ivory Coast, Kenya, Mexico, Sri Lanka, Venezuela, and the Philippines.

Parliamentary Government

In contrast to the presidential system, the crucial element of parliamentary government is the *fusion of executive and legislative functions and structures*. As is indicated in Figure 7.1, the people elect the legislature (the parliament), whose majority empowers a cabinet, which then empowers one of its members to be the chief executive, typically called a prime minister or premier. The maximum length of the legislature's mandate is often five years, but its term can be shorter under the circumstances described next. The complex relationships among cabinet, legislature, and prime minister merit further detail.

Cabinet and Legislature   The cabinet is a collective leadership group of 6 to 30 people who are, in most systems, also members of the legislature. The cabinet is "responsible" to the legislature. This means that the cabinet serves only as long as it can retain the confidence of the majority of the members in the legislature. The cabinet has primary responsibility for both the policymaking and policy-implementation functions. Although policies must be voted into laws by the legislative majority, it is the cabinet that devises, drafts, and implements most policies.

In an intriguing manner, the cabinet and the legislature are at each other's mercy. At *any* time, the legislative majority can pressure the cabinet to resign, either by a negative vote on a major piece of legislation proposed by the cabinet or by a general motion of "no confidence" in the cabinet. Also at *any* time, the cabinet can "dissolve" the legislature, requiring immediate new elections. In the subsequent election, voters select a new legislature, whose majority then identifies a cabinet it will support, and the process begins anew. Thus, the cabinet and the legislature are rather like two gunfighters standing gun-to-gun in a spaghetti Western: Each has the power to eliminate the other, but each might also be destroyed in the exchange. In 2011, Canada, Portugal and Slovenia were among the countries where a coalition government fell on votes of no confidence.

Legislature and Prime Minister   In the parliamentary system, the prime minister (or premier or chancellor or whatever the chief executive is called) is not directly elected by the citizens. The prime minister is the member of the legislature who is supported as chief executive by the majority of the legislature. The prime minister can be removed at any time by a no-confidence vote of the legislature, and he might also be obliged to resign if the legislature defeats a major legislative initiative he proposes. The prime minister directs the overall thrust of decision and action in the legislative process.

Cabinet and Prime Minister   The balance of power between the cabinet and the prime minister can be subtle, although both depend on majority support of the legislature. Traditionally, a cabinet that had legislative support could select one of its members to serve as prime minister. The prime minister was *primus inter pares*—"first among equals"—in the cabinet. The prime minister exercised broad policy leadership within a collective decision-making body. If a cabinet majority no longer supported a prime minister, the prime minister either resigned or attempted to reconstitute a cabinet that did support him and was supported by the legislative majority.

In many contemporary parliamentary systems, however, there has been a substantial shift of power from the cabinet to the prime minister. In these systems, the electorate selects legislative candidates from a party committed to support a particular prime minister. If a legislative majority can be formed, its leader becomes prime minister. The prime minister then appoints the members of the cabinet and clearly dominates the cabinet in the governmental process. In Figure 7.1, the two-headed arrow between cabinet and prime minister indicates these alternative patterns of power.

Thus, the parliamentary system is characterized by the fusion of executive and legislative functions because the cabinet and prime minister formulate policies, guide their passage through a legislature that they control, and administer policy through the administrative departments. However, the actual policy process in a parliamentary system depends on whether there is a coherent majority group in the legislature. There are both "stable" and "unstable" parliamentary systems.

In a stable parliamentary system, there is a clear majority in the legislature. Such a majority could be composed of either one party or a coalition. This majority provides the prime minister and cabinet with sufficient legislative support to enact their policy program, without the problems of stalemate and confusion of accountability that can result from the separation of powers in the presidential system. Australia, Denmark, Great Britain, and Japan are examples of parliamentary government systems that are usually stable. Great Britain currently has a somewhat unstable government due to the uneasy coalition between the Conservatives and the Liberal Democrats.

In contrast, an unstable parliamentary system often emerges when there is no coherent legislative majority. Instead, policymaking requires agreement within a coalition composed of multiple parties that tend to disagree on some important policy issues. If the legislature votes no confidence in the cabinet or defeats it on a major bill, the cabinet usually resigns. Then the media report that a parliamentary government has "fallen" or that there are efforts to form a new government (a new cabinet, actually). The new cabinet might have almost all the same people as members, or it might have a quite different set of people from the legislature. In general, prime ministers in unstable parliamentary systems are weaker than those in stable parliamentary systems. Unstable parliamentary systems have been prevalent in contemporary legislatures that have strong ideological differences and multiple political parties, such as Israel and Italy.

Hybrid Systems

An increasing number of political systems attempt to blend desirable aspects of both the presidential and parliamentary systems. These **hybrid systems** *have a prime minister and an elected legislature that can both enact and implement policies, but they also have an independent president*, who is elected for a fixed term, has some executive functions, and can act with decisiveness (Elgie 1999; Shugart and Carey 1992).

Some hybrid systems function more like parliamentary systems: The president has limited power, and the prime minister and cabinet exercise most of the control. In India, for example, the president is elected by the legislature for a five-year term and has notable responsibilities, including the appointment of state governors and the right to take over governance of the states during emergencies. However, the prime minister is the dominant political power in the system, while the president performs mainly ceremonial roles, such as appearances on national holidays. Germany, Austria, Iraq, and Ireland are other examples of this style of the hybrid.

Who's on first? Vladimir Putin (right) has dominated Russia's hybrid political system since 2000, moving from president to prime minister to president again, while Dmitry Medvedev is second in command, holding the other position.

In other hybrid systems, there is a more balanced sharing of power between the president and the parliament. In Finland, for example, the president controls the administration, has oversight powers and must cosign legislation. However, the prime minister, cabinet and legislature are in charge of most policymaking. Finally, there are some hybrids where the president is the most powerful political actor. While the prime minister and the cabinet have primary responsibility for day-to-day policymaking and administration, the president tends to dominate the policy process when he chooses to do so, and he is the main focus of public attention and expectations regarding the leadership function. Focus in 7 describes the French hybrid system, which is one where the president is the key actor. Hybrids with a strong president have been implemented in almost all the postcommunist countries that emerged from the Soviet Union and Central and Eastern Europe.

Council Systems

In council systems, *a small group shares collective leadership and is responsible for both executive and legislative functions.* Although one member of the group might be deemed the leader for symbolic reasons, all members of the council are equal in constitutional terms, and they make decisions and actions based on the will of the council majority or, ideally, on council consensus. In American local government, the weak-mayor–council system and the boards of commissioners/supervisors (prevalent in many counties, school districts, and special districts) are council systems. Also, many tribal societies in Africa were traditionally ruled by a council of elders who collectively made decisions that were binding on the members of the tribe.

▶ FOCUS IN 7 | A Hybrid System in Action: France

Many recent constitutions establish a hybrid model in which both a president and a prime minister have significant political power. A central issue for hybrids is whether two independent executives can share power effectively. An early example of this system is the French Fifth Republic, established by the "de Gaulle Constitution" of 1962. France created this hybrid to overcome the highly unstable parliamentary system of the Fourth Republic, where governments averaged less than one year. In the hybrid, the premier (prime minister) and cabinet are responsible for the day-to-day functioning of the government, as in a parliamentary system, but the president (an office Charles de Gaulle fashioned for himself as a condition for his return to government) has extensive power and the freedom to exercise it. The president is elected popularly for a fixed term, and he selects a premier, who selects a cabinet. The cabinet controls the budget and legislative agenda as in a normal parliamentary system; however, the president can dissolve the legislature while retaining the cabinet. And Article 16 in the constitution provides that the sweeping powers of the presidency may be exercised whenever the president *alone* deems the political situation to be dangerous for the country.

De Gaulle served as the first president of the Fifth Republic from 1958 to 1969. He was an extraordinarily powerful man, and he demanded

(Continued)

extraordinary power. He established a precedent that the president can act far more extensively than the constitution allows. He dominated every premier who served during his presidency. The presidents after de Gaulle (from Pompidou to Sarkozy) have continued to follow the de Gaulle precedent, exercising considerable power. The president is so strong that the French hybrid is also termed a "semi-presidential" system.

Many people felt that the French "dyarchy" (dual rule) would lead to a constitutional crisis as soon as a premier and cabinet challenged the president's extensive power. The first strong test of the French hybrid occurred between 1986 and 1988, when Socialist President François Mitterrand was faced with a legislative majority dominated by conservatives. But Mitterrand accepted the situation, appointing the conservatives' leader, Jacques Chirac, as premier. Despite strong ideological differences between the president and the premier-cabinet-legislature majority, there was a reasonable sharing of power and authority, which the French call *cohabitation*. President Mitterrand continued to be very active in foreign policy but allowed the premier to control the domestic policy agenda. From 1993 to 1995, a conservative legislative majority produced a second period of cohabitation. A weakened Mitterrand acknowledged that "it is not the task

of the president of the Republic to govern" (Safran 2008).

In 2000, the French shortened the presidential term from seven years to five years, ostensibly to increase the political accountability of the president. The shorter term also makes it considerably more likely that the elected president will be from the same part of the political spectrum as the legislative majority that empowers the premier and cabinet.

Since 2002, there has been no cohabitation because both the president and the prime minister are from the coalition of conservative parties. After several periods of cohabitation, the power relationships between the president and the premier in the French hybrid system seem to be sufficiently limited and institutionalized to survive the conflict inherent in dyarchy and in a future situation where strong ideological differences exist between the two executives.

FURTHER FOCUS

1. What seems to be the greatest benefit of the French hybrid, in comparison to a parliamentary system?

2. If the president and prime minister are from opposing parties in a hybrid, would this usually be a desirable check-and-balance feature? ▲

In many situations in which a small collective group forcefully removes the top leader, the group initially shares power. When the group that has taken power is from the military, this council-type group is called a *junta*. There were numerous juntas in Latin America and Africa in the latter half of the 20th century (e.g., in Algeria from 1992 to 1999; in Argentina from 1976 to 1983), although Myanmar is one of the few current juntas. In most cases, council rule evolves into more dictatorial rule as a single political leader increasingly dominates the others.

Assembly Systems

In assembly systems, *collective leadership is exercised by a large group, usually constituted as a legislature.* There might be an executive officer, but the legislature is clearly dominant. Switzerland has an assembly system in which the legislature dominates the collective seven-member executive council that it elects. Most confederations, such as the United Nations and the European Parliament (the elected legislative wing of the EU), are assembly systems in which legislatures delegate administrative power to an appointed executive. The New England town meeting, a form of U.S. local government, is an extreme version of the assembly system because all citizens directly participate in key decisions and oversee the administration of policy.

In theory, most communist states are assembly systems because the constitution grants most power for policymaking to the legislative body. In reality, however, the legislatures in such states have traditionally rubber-stamped the policies and administration of a single leader or a small collective leadership group, as in China and North Korea. In fact, few, if any, national political systems operate as true assembly systems because power for policymaking and policy implementation rarely remains dispersed among a large group of relatively equal rulers.

Which Form Is Optimal?

Which form of executive–legislative relations is best? If there were agreement on this question, we might reasonably expect most states to have adopted the same form of government. In fact, however, each form has its strengths and weaknesses, as reflected in the Debate in 7.

THE DEBATE IN 7 | Which Form of Government Is Preferable: Parliamentary, Presidential, or Hybrid?

A central normative question regarding government institutions is: Which arrangement of executive–legislative relations is preferable? Countries vary in the manner in which they organize executive–legislative relations. Initially, most modern countries established either the parliamentary form or the presidential form, yet many of the countries that have dramatically transformed their governmental structures in the last several decades have opted for a hybrid. The current diversity suggests that no one form is clearly preferred in all cases. Moreover, other factors such as the nature of the party system and the electoral system can be crucial in shaping the effectiveness of any of the forms (Cheibub 2007; Mainwaring and Shugart 1997). Nonetheless, it is useful to consider the key arguments regarding the strengths and weaknesses associated with each of the three major forms of executive–legislative relations.

THE PARLIAMENTARY FORM IS THE MOST EFFECTIVE INSTITUTIONAL ARRANGEMENT

■ The fusion of executive and legislative powers eliminates potential executive–legislative conflicts that can result in deadlock in presidential or hybrid systems. This singular authority structure ensures that, as long as the governing majority (party or coalition) maintains its cohesiveness, this group is responsible for every stage of the policy process, and there are few roadblocks to the passage and implementation of any policy (Strom 2004).

(Continued)

- This concentration of political control also ensures that there is a clear system of accountability. The successes or failures of policy can be associated directly with those who are part of the governing coalition. If citizens are dissatisfied, they know which parties to vote against in the next election, and the citizens know whom to reelect if they are satisfied (Linz 1994).
- The chief executive position does not concentrate such a dangerous level of power as in the presidential system. And if the chief executive loses the support of the governing majority, he can be replaced at any time and in a relatively rapid political process that does not require a national election or the trauma of an impeachment trial.

THE PARLIAMENTARY FORM HAS SERIOUS PROBLEMS

- A coherently organized majority exercises great, unchecked power: it can streamroll policy through almost all opposition because it controls both the legislative process and the agencies that administer policy. Even in its most benign form, the system is not well structured to encourage compromise, to protect against a tyrannical majority, or to ensure that minority concerns are represented in the public policy process (Horowitz 1990).
- The electorate does not directly choose the chief executive because he can be selected and changed by a vote of the legislature at almost any time, without any direct input from the citizens. It is possible for the citizens to be stuck with a chief executive that they did not vote for and that the majority does not support.
- Parliamentary systems are often plagued by uncertainty and instability, which stems from the chief executive's capacity to dissolve the legislature at any time and the legislature's ability to vote no confidence in the executive at any time. This perpetual vulnerability of the executive and the legislature can result in extensive strategic game-playing, despite the apparent fusion of executive and legislative actors (Tsebelis 2002).

THE PRESIDENTIAL FORM IS THE MOST EFFECTIVE INSTITUTIONAL ARRANGEMENT

- In presidential systems, citizens have the power to elect their top executive leader directly. The voters explicitly choose a president, who serves for a fixed term in office without legislative intervention (except in the extraordinary circumstances of impeachment).
- This directly elected president can act as a singular leader and an embodiment of the political will of the national majority, and is not someone who emerged from a backroom deal in the legislature. And the president can take strong positions, even in the face of short-term disfavor in public opinion.
- Presidential systems are more stable because presidential and legislative elections occur in regular, fixed intervals, so everyone knows exactly when the next election will occur and new mandates for power will be given.
- The separation of executive and legislative power provides a healthy system of checks and balances, preventing abuse of power and ensuring more careful consideration of policy before it is adopted and implemented (Horowitz 1990).

THE PRESIDENTIAL FORM HAS SERIOUS PROBLEMS

- Presidential systems often obscure which policymaking structure is responsible for the impact of a particular policy. Executive and legislative power can be exercised by different groups who can, rightly or wrongly, accuse each other of policy failures. Thus, accountability is often unclear, even if the executive and legislative majorities are from the same political parties, and especially when there is a partisan split between the two branches.
- The separation of power enables the legislature and the executive to block each other's actions if they do not fully share a political agenda. The legislature can refuse to pass executive-supported legislation, while the executive can veto policies adopted by the legislative majority and can use its control over all administrative agencies to distort or even block the intent of legislative policy. Such

(Continued)

circumstances can produce interbranch conflicts, policy stalemates, and governmental paralysis (Tsebelis 2004).

- The fixed terms of both the executive and the legislature provide predictability at the cost of flexibility and responsiveness. An ineffective legislature cannot be forced to face the electorate until the end of its term. And, short of a traumatic impeachment, a highly unpopular chief executive cannot be replaced before the end of his lengthy, fixed term and can hold onto power with minimal support from either the legislature or the citizenry (Linz 1994).

THE HYBRID FORM IS THE MOST EFFECTIVE INSTITUTIONAL ARRANGEMENT

- The hybrid combines the best of both the parliamentary and presidential systems. It takes advantage of the parliamentary form's fusion of executive and legislative power to ensure greater policy coherence, from conception to adoption, to implementation.
- The hybrid also provides an independently elected presidential-type executive who can represent the national will and can act decisively when the cabinet and legislature fail to respond to a critical situation (Elgie 2004).

THE HYBRID FORM HAS SERIOUS PROBLEMS

- As with presidential systems, a significant risk with hybrids is the potential for major power

struggles, especially between the cabinet and prime minister on one side and the president on the other side. The situation is made worse by the fact that the constitution is usually ambiguous about the conditions when one or the other is dominant in the policy process.

- The hovering presence of the president does not usually reduce the inherent problems of the parliamentary form, such as excessive concentration of power in the majority and the uncertainty and instability due to the constant threat of dissolution.

AND IN CASE YOU WERE WONDERING . . .

A *council system* has the virtue of distributing power among a manageable number of people, but there is a strong tendency for collective leadership to result in persistent internal power struggles as one or a few members attempt to assert their dominance. And while *assembly systems* are the best approximation of a genuine representative democracy, they lack the clear and decisive executive leadership that people in most contemporary states seem to want and that complex modern political systems seem to need.

MORE QUESTIONS . . .

1. Which system makes most sense to you?
2. Can you think of any conditions (e.g., the party system, aspects of the political culture, etc.) that might make different forms preferable? ▲

POLITICAL PARTY SYSTEMS

The system of political parties is another institutional arrangement that can be explored. Party systems are generally classified according to *the number of political parties* and *the interactions among the parties in the governing process*. In the comparative study of political parties, there are usually four main types of party systems: (1) two-party systems, (2) multiparty systems, (3) dominant-party systems, and (4) one-party systems. The distinguishing features of each type are described in this section, and representative examples are identified in Figure 7.2 and discussed in Compare in 7.

7.5 Characterize the different types of political party systems.

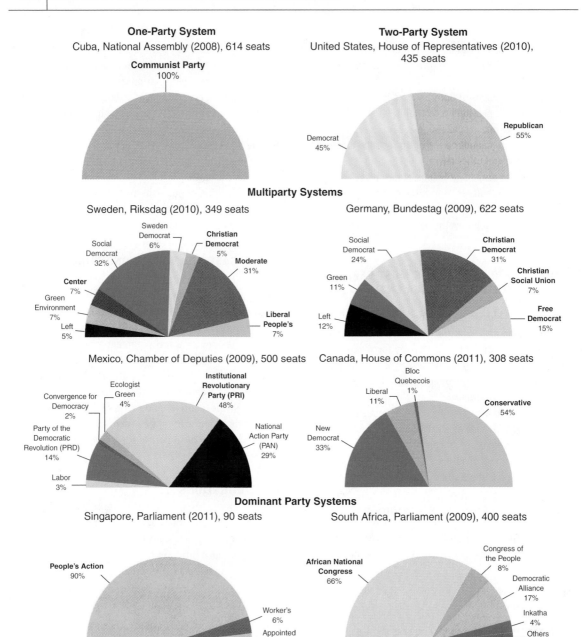

FIGURE 7.2

Examples of party systems (governing parties in bold)

Two-Party Systems

A *two-party system* is characterized by two major political parties that alternate in governmental power. Each party has a realistic possibility of forming a governing majority, although the electoral success of each party varies over time. Minor third parties exist in a classic two-party system like Honduras, but these parties have limited power. At the moment, there are only a few countries, such as Jamaica and the United States, where only two parties hold virtually all of the seats in the national legislature. Although either the Conservative or Labour Party had been a majority party in Great Britain for many decades, neither won a legislative majority in the 2010 election. Regional parties (e.g., the Scottish Nationalist Party) won some seats, and the Liberal Democratic Party held enough seats to become a necessary coalition partner, aligning with the Conservatives to achieve a parliamentary majority. And as in Spain in 2011, some essentially two-party systems seem to be shifting from two party control of nearly all the seats. When a country has two large parties, but third parties consistently prevent either party from achieving an outright majority, it is termed a "two-plus party" system.

Explore the Comparative "Voting Systems and Elections" on mypoliscilab.com

Multiparty Systems

As you might expect, a *multiparty system* has more than two parties who can win enough seats to be potential partners in creating a legislative majority and enacting legislation. In parliamentary systems, this means that a coalition of two or more parties might be necessary to form a government. Most contemporary political systems have some form of multiparty system.

Working Multiparty Systems In some "working" multiparty systems, a cluster of parties usually cooperates to form a governing majority. For example, several center- and right-oriented parties might form one group, with social democratic and socialist left parties constituting another. This is the case in Denmark, which has a stable system of seven major parties with coalitions of the left and the right. Currently, the Social Democratic Party leads a multiparty center-left coalition.

There are also some multiparty systems where parties have organized themselves into two blocs that compete for power. Citizens are reasonably confident that, even when they vote for a party that cannot win a majority of seats, their party is committed to cooperating with particular parties to form a governing group. Italy, which had experienced decades of highly volatile multiparty government, introduced a new electoral system in 1996 in an attempt to create more party coherence. After some initial turbulence (ironically, a total of 251 parties put forth candidates in the 1996 election), the system seemed to stabilize with two major alliances, each led by the major party in the bloc: the People of Freedom group (victors in the 2008 election) and the Democratic Party group. Chile is another example, where six parties each have a substantial proportion of seats, but these parties have formed two blocs that currently operate almost like a two-party system.

It is also possible, although uncommon, to have a working multiparty system in which parties across the ideological spectrum cooperate in a long-standing governing coalition. A notable example of this situation is Switzerland, where four major parties, ranging from right wing to center left, have shared governing power in every election since 1959, and the general viewpoint is that it is undesirable for any one of the parties to govern independently. A more unique form of this broad array of parties was Germany's "grand coalition" from 2006 to 2009. When neither multiparty coalition gained a majority of seats, the leading parties of the two blocs agreed to create a governing cabinet including nearly all the major rival parties (the two leftist parties refused to participate) under the leadership of Angela Merkel, leader of the Christian Democrats. The 2009 election resulted in a more traditional center-right coalition between the Christian Democrats, Christian Social Union, and Free Democrats (Figure 7.2).

Unstable Multiparty Systems   Multiparty systems are often unstable. In these cases, no party is close to a majority and differences in party ideology prevent temporary coalitions from forming long-term blocs. In such party systems, there is usually a point where the government's policy on an issue induces a coalition partner to withdraw its support, in turn causing a crisis for the government. In parliamentary systems, such a crisis often leads to the resignation of the government or the dissolution of the legislature. In presidential or assembly systems, this situation tends to produce paralysis in the legislature. Clearly, the difficulty of forming a governing majority among multiple parties increases because different parties are more firmly committed to their unique ideological orientations. Smaller parties often demand more influence than their vote total merits if they are crucial to the coalition majority. Instability is especially high in multiparty systems with a minority governing coalition, controlling less than half the seats.

Israel presents an extreme example of the challenges in some multiparty systems. In the 2009 election, the 120 seats in the Knessset were shared among 12 parties, and no party had as many as one-fourth of the seats. The largest party, Kadima, was unable to form a governing majority, and the current government is a complex coalition of parties of the right, including ultrareligious parties that might bolt at any point if their views are not supported by the government.

New democracies seem especially prone to a proliferation of political parties. In 2005, more than 300 parties competed for votes in Iraq. And in the initial years (after 1989) of democratic politics in the postcommunist states of Central and Eastern Europe, as many as 200 parties ran candidates. While there has usually been a significant reduction in the number of effective parties in the postcommunist states (Hungary, for example, now has only three), many are still dealing with somewhat unstable multiparty systems. When many parties win representation, it has been difficult to form the stable coalitions necessary for coherent policymaking. Even more established political systems grapple with the challenges of achieving stability in situations with multiple competing parties. Canada has multiple parties and minority governments in four of the prior five elections, but elected a Conservative Party majority in 2011 (Figure 7.2).

Dominant-Party Systems

In a *dominant-party system*, the same party repeatedly captures enough votes and seats to form the government, although other parties are free to compete.

In Figure 7.2, South Africa and Singapore are clear-cut examples of a dominant party. In Singapore, the People's Action Party wins nearly all the contested seats in the legislature in every election (since the first full general elections in 1959), although as many as 20 other parties put up candidates. Typically, a dominant party eventually loses support and becomes a competitor in a multiparty system. This happened to Japan's Liberal Democratic Party (LDP), a dominant party in Japan for more than 40 years after the ratification of the 1947 constitution. But scandals involving LDP leaders and changing attitudes among the Japanese electorate are among the reasons that the LDP lost its legislative majority in 1993 and has been less dominant since then, suffering a major defeat in the 2009 election. Other parties that lost their overwhelming electoral dominance after decades in power include the Congress Party in India and Mexico's Institutional Revolutionary Party (PRI).

One-Party Systems

In a *one-party system*, a single party is controlled and protected by the government elite. Some authoritarian regimes do not tolerate the existence of any political parties other than the single party that represents the state and its vision of political order, as in North Korea and Sudan. Any party that expresses opposition to the ruling party is viewed not as the "loyal opposition" but as disloyal or even seditious (in other words, it is seen as stirring up resistance or rebellion against the government). There are currently few absolute one-party systems in a technical sense, given the high ideological premium associated with the appearance of democratic processes. Thus, some form of party competition is introduced, although the ruling party maintains near-total control. In Cuba (Figure 7.2) and China, for example, the Communist Party allows other parties to elect a few representatives.

▶ COMPARE IN 7 | Party Systems in Four Countries

As indicated in this chapter, party systems can range from multiparty systems to one-party systems. Figure 7.2 displays the distribution of parties in eight countries, reflecting the various types of party systems. While each country's situation is unique, this comparison focuses on four of the examples to reflect how different party systems function.

The political elite in *Cuba*, a *one-party system*, attempts to sustain the total domination of the Cuban Communist Party. Unlike some one-party states, candidates can run for the National Assembly without the direct approval and support of the party. The party was created under Fidel Castro's leadership in 1965 through the merger of several revolutionary groups. Although other political parties are banned, some of the members of the Cuban legislature are not members of the party when they are elected. But because all candidates are selected by bodies (e.g., trade unions, women's groups) dominated by the party, all candidates are approved by the party. To offer at least the appearance of popular control, if the proposed candidate in a district does not win a majority of votes (almost everyone 16 or older votes), a new candidate must be proposed.

(Continued)

South Africa is a *dominant-party system.* Numerous parties put up candidates for the parliament, and seats are distributed through a mix of single-member and multimember PR districts (Focus in 6). Since the end of apartheid, the African National Congress (ANC) has won a clear majority of seats in every election. Other parties try to challenge the dominance of the ANC, but no combination of parties has yet made a serious dent in the ANC's huge majority of parliamentary seats. However, the first serious split within the ANC occurred before the 2009 election, over a rancorous conflict between current President Jacob Zuma and the man he outmaneuvered within the ANC, former President Thabo Mbeki, whose followers have now created a breakaway party.

The *United States* is a clear example of a *two-party system.* While candidates from other parties are usually on the ballot in most districts, it is rare that the individual winner by plurality will be from any party other than the Democratic or Republican parties. And this produces a legislature in which only the two parties have a major role. In 2010, the Republicans won 242 seats in the House of Representatives, the Democrats won 193 seats, and not a single member was from any other party. Only two of 100 Senate seats are held by "independents." Why are other parties unsuccessful? It is partly a tradition among the large majority of voters to select either a Democrat or a Republican. Even more importantly, the electoral system is based on plurality voting in single-seat districts, making it extremely hard for a third-party candidate to win. This leads many voters to conclude that a vote for a third party is either a wasted vote or serves only as a "protest" vote because such a vote will not influence the outcome.

Like almost all *multiparty systems,* Mexico has a proportional representation (PR) electoral system with more than one member elected from each district. The Mexican system is similar to the mixed PR system in South Africa, which was described in Focus in 6. There are 300 single-member districts, which elect the person with the highest vote total, and 200 PR seats based on party lists. To prevent a proliferation of small parties in the legislature, a party must get at least 2 percent of the national vote to get any seats from the PR lists. Only in the 1990s did Mexico's Chamber of Deputies become a true multiparty system. Two parties (PAN, a conservative party, and PRD, a leftist party) began to garner enough votes to prevent the centrist PRI (the Institutional Revolutionary Party) from winning the majority of seats, as it had done for five decades. Since the 2000 election, there has been active competition among the three major parties and considerable change in the composition of the legislature in each election. During this period, no single party has had a majority in the Chamber of Deputies, even in the 2009 election when PRI nearly doubled its seats. Because the three major parties are always competing with each other and do not share a common political agenda, it is often difficult to fashion a majority to pass legislation.

FURTHER QUESTIONS

1. If multiparty systems are more prone to instability, why are they present in so many countries?
2. Can you explain why PR electoral systems tend to produce multiparty systems? ◣

No-Party Systems

The taxonomy should have a category for those political systems that have no political parties. Historically, many political systems had no organized parties. But only a few contemporary political systems do not allow political parties. Countries such as Kuwait, Oman, and Swaziland have banned political parties, either because the rulers do not want any organized bases of opposition to their authority or on the grounds that parties divide people's loyalty and do not focus on what is best for everyone. The latter argument is a primary justification given for the nonpartisanship (lack of political party affiliations or organization) of candidates for public office in many U.S. local governments.

CLASSIFICATION AND CLARITY

Most theorizing about political systems begins with some classification scheme. Classifying political systems into a taxonomy can be straightforward, especially when the categories are based on clear institutional characteristics (e.g., federations, confederations, and unitary states). But many of the most interesting classifications (e.g., democracies and dictatorships) are challenging because political systems tend to be complex mixtures of characteristics that do not fit tidily into any category. In addition, any classification is time-specific because evolutionary and revolutionary processes can change the nature of a political system.

✓•⎡Study
and **Review** the
**Post-Test &
Chapter Exam** at
mypoliscilab.com

There are at least three important reasons for classifying political systems. First, such classification can provide us with useful descriptive information about political systems. Most people have a vague sense that other political systems are different from their own, and by describing how various political systems are organized between central and peripheral units or by the alternative pattern of interactions between the executive and legislative functions, we expand our grasp of alternative forms of governmental structures.

Second, the classification of political systems helps us to undertake political analysis—to identify patterns of similarities and differences among the political systems of the world. Rather than positing that every political system is unique, the analyses in Chapters 6–8, as well as throughout this book, assume that some generalizations can emerge from comparative analysis. Sets of political systems that share important characteristics can be compared with each other or compared with sets that do not share those characteristics. Such comparisons provide us with a basis for thinking more clearly about the kinds of generalizations that we can articulate and can then increase our confidence regarding what we know about the political world.

Third, the taxonomies in this chapter might encourage us to specify with greater precision what we mean by value-laden terms such as *democracy* and *dictatorship*. In this manner, the analytic study of political institutions improves our understanding of how these terms are most appropriately used as thoughtful descriptors rather than as mere rhetorical labels.

Ultimately, developing greater precision in our use of key political concepts and increasing our knowledge about the political world can do more than clarify our thinking. They can also enhance our ability to evaluate the nature and desirability of the political structures in our own nation and in other countries, and to decide whether there is a "best" form of government.

Would you argue that one form of areal division of power and one form of executive–legislative relations and the same constitution are best for *all* states? Or might the best institutional arrangements be contingent on the major goals and key characteristics of the particular political society? As a closing puzzle, if your country were to convene a constitutional convention now, would you argue in favor of retaining all of the governmental forms that currently exist in your political system? Why or why not?

KEY CONCEPTS

assembly system   184
authoritarian regime   173
authoritarianism   173
autocracy   173
confederation   178
constitution   166
constitutional regime   167
council system   183
democracy   171
dictatorship   173
direct democracy   170
electoral democracy   170
federation   177
hybrid system   182

illiberal democracy   171
liberal democracy   171
limited mandate   170
nonconstitutional regime   167
nondemocracy   172
parliamentary government   180
participatory democracy   170
party system   187
presidential government   179
representative democracy   170
totalitarianism   173
totalitarian regime   173
unitary state   175

FOR FURTHER CONSIDERATION

1. What is your definition of a democratic political system? What are the minimal conditions necessary for a country to be classified as a democracy? If you opt for the definition used in this chapter, explain which elements of the definition are the most essential and the least essential for democracy.
2. In the late 18th century, the United States opted for a federal, presidential, bicameral, two-party system with plurality elections. Given the situation at the beginning of the 21st century, what are the major shortcomings of each of these decisions? Speculate what politics in the United States might be like if the country became a unitary state with a parliamentary government or a multiparty system based on proportional representation.
3. Some analysts argue that democracy is not possible unless there are at least two political parties. Provide a critical evaluation of this viewpoint. In theory, might we expect any relationship between the number of parties and the extent to which the political system is democratic?

FOR FURTHER READING

Arendt, Hannah. (1973). *The Origins of Totalitarianism*. New York: Harcourt. The classic study of the forces underlying totalitarian regimes.

Barber, Benjamin. (2004). *Strong Democracy: Participatory Politics for a New Age*. Berkeley: University of California Press. A 20th anniversary edition of an important book offering a persuasive argument that democracy can and should be based on active and extensive participation by the citizenry.

Chhibber, Pradeep, and Ken Kollman. (2004). *The Formation of National Party Systems: Federalism and Party Competition in Canada, Great Britain, India and the United States*. Princeton, NJ: Princeton University Press. The evolution of party systems in the four countries are examined over three centuries to illuminate the importance of the areal distribution of governmental power in shaping the party systems, despite similar electoral systems.

Cheibub, Jose Antonio. (2007). *Presidentialism, Parliamentarianism, and Democracy*. New York: Cambridge University Press. Using many cases over several decades, the author analyzes whether the presidential or parliamentary form is more likely to be successful in achieving stability and in sustaining democracy.

Collier, Paul. (2010). *Wars, Guns and Votes: Democracy in Dangerous Places.* New York: Harper. The always controversial Collier argues that democracy has been pushed with the wrong incentives in many of the developing countries, generating more violence and instability. He suggests that the key promises given to countries engaging in democratization should be security from coups and aid that goes to NGOs, not government agencies.

Dahl, Robert, Ian Shapiro, and Jose Antonio Cheibub, Eds. (2003). *The Democracy Sourcebook.* Boston: MIT Press. This very strong collection of readings covers critical topics, from the definition of democracy to issues of representation, constitutional regimes, and the impacts of democracy on individual countries and the global system. The (generally short) excerpts include both major historical thinkers (Locke, Rousseau, Madison) and important contemporary scholars (Dworkin, Pzeworski, Sen).

Diamond, Larry. (2009). *The Spirit of Democracy: How to Build Free Societies Throughout the World.* New York: Holt. A compelling, highly readable (and optimistic) exploration, full of engaging examples, of the strategies that can help countries in all areas of the world establish and sustain democracy.

Elgie, Robert, Ed. (1999). *Semi-Presidentialism in Europe.* New York: Oxford University Press. An exploration of how similar forms of executive–legislative structures (hybrids with a directly elected president and a prime minister responsible to the legislature) can result in different patterns of politics and power.

Lawson, Kay and Peter H. Merkl. Eds. (2007). *When Parties Prosper: The Uses of Electoral Success.* Boulder, CO: Lynne Reinner. The dynamic activities and the impacts on their political system of major political parties in more than 15 countries, mainly from Europe and Latin America, are examined in interesting case studies.

Obinger, Herbert, Stephan Leibfried, and Francis Castles, Eds. (2005). *Federalism and the Welfare State: New World and European Experiences.* Cambridge, England: Cambridge University Press. Scholars explore the evolution of federal states (Australia, Austria, Canada, Germany, Switzerland, and the United States) to assess the interplay between this form of power distribution and the patterns of social welfare policies that emerge.

Sorensen, Georg. (2008). *Democracy and Democratization: Processes and Prospects.* Boulder, CO: Westview Press. A useful exploration of central issues associated with the diffusion of democracy to many countries, including the attempts at promotion by outside powers, the rise of electoral authoritarianism, and the consequences for the international system of the trends towards democratization.

Wheare, K. C. (1980). *Modern Constitutions.* 2nd rev. ed. London: Oxford University Press. Although first written in 1951, this description of the content and impacts of constitutions is arguably still the best.

ON THE WEB

http://confinder.richmond.edu

Constitution Finder at the University of Richmond provides links to the constitutions and other key documents for most countries.

http://www.constitutionmaking.org/default.html

This site provides the texts of more than 700 national constitutions written since 1789 as well as rich discussions of many of the issues and themes addressed in constitutions.

http://www.servat.unibe.ch/law/icl

> The International Constitutional Law (ICL) Project provides English translations of constitutions as well as other textual material related to constitutions from more than 90 countries. It also cross-references those documents for quick comparison of constitutional provisions.

http://freedomhouse.org

> The site of Freedom House, which includes current ratings for every country, along with topical discussions regarding the levels of political rights and civil rights as well as press freedom and religious freedom, in those countries.

http://www.systemicpeace.org/polity/polity4.htm

> The Polity IV Project provides current and longitudinal trend data and generates scores for each country, which is classified along a 21-point continuum ranging from "consolidated democracy" to "hereditary monarchy."

http://mirror.undp.org/magnet/Docs/parliaments

> This site explores a variety of issues regarding the functioning of legislatures and their relations with other branches of government and covers governing systems and executive–legislative relations within presidential, parliamentary, and hybrid systems, along with information about political parties.

http://www.politicalresources.net

> This is a very useful and accessible site with information on many countries, including current data on party systems and the Web sites of most parties from each country.

https://www.cia.gov/library/publications/world-leaders-1/index.html

> This part of the U.S. Central Intelligence Agency Web site presents the World Leaders database that lists the chiefs of state and cabinet members of all foreign governments.

http://m.state.gov/mc36886.htm

> A site sponsored by the U.S. State Department provides basic details of the governments of every country.

Political Economy

This is no game! On the (river) Liffey in Dublin, an artist's installation of Monopoly hotels and houses provides an ironic commentary on the collapse of Ireland's housing bubble.

LEARNING OBJECTIVES

8.1 Explain the role of the state in a nation's economy.

8.2 Determine the relationship among the separate elements that make up the political economy.

8.3 Assess the different measures of economic prosperity.

8.4 Compare the ideal-type political economies.

8.5 Identify the challenges faced by market, command, and mixed economies.

8.6 Contrast real world examples and ideal-type political economies.

□•[**Read** and **Listen** to **Chapter 8** at mypoliscilab.com

✓•[**Study** and **Review** the **Pre-Test & Flashcards** at mypoliscilab.com

In the early 1970s, Ireland was primarily an agrarian economy and had one of the lowest levels of GDP per capita in Europe. The Irish government moved decisively to implement policies that would energize and transform the Irish economy. Most importantly, the government took steps to gain membership into the European Union (EU) in 1973. Among its other policies to reshape the economic sector, the government set the Irish corporate tax rate at an extremely low level of 12.5 percent to attract global companies and foreign direct investment. In addition, the government offered large government grants to encourage major global companies like Microsoft, IBM, and Ryanair to locate extensive operations in Ireland. Government agencies also provided financial incentives to stimulate the growth of small businesses and to encourage them to market their goods in the broader EU market.

The Irish government emphasized to national and global firms that Ireland had a well-educated and disciplined labor force that worked at low wages, compared to other EU members. It took advantage of EU grants to improve its educational system and to modernize its infrastructure. Ireland's National Development Plan vastly improved the transportation system, including enhancement of the roads and extension of fixed rail services. Deregulation of the financial sector made it considerably easier for the Irish to borrow money for purchasing consumer products and housing.

These strong government initiatives resulted in two decades of dramatic expansion and growth in the Irish economy. By the mid-1990s, the international business community, especially the high-technology sector, was substantially invested in the Irish economy, which was now known as the "Celtic Tiger." Between 1995 and 2000, the economy continued to expand at a very high rate, averaging 9.4 percent growth per year. Disposable income among the Irish soared and unemployment fell to 4.5 percent by 2007. Ireland shifted from a net emigration state to a popular destination for immigrant workers. Ireland was rated as the world's number one country in *The Economist's* quality of life index. In less than three decades, Ireland had blossomed from being one of the poorest countries in the EU to one of the wealthiest.

Then, in 2008, the Irish economic bubble burst. Many of the government policies that had spurred economic growth now contributed to a serious economic collapse. The government's deregulation of the financial sector, low interest rates, and lowered income taxes had stimulated an investment and buying spree. Public spending had increased 48 percent, there had been far too much borrowing, housing had become hugely overvalued, and many people, as well as the government, were now in serious debt. The government tried to cut back on its own spending to reduce its deficit and protect its credit in the Euro zone.

By September 2008, Ireland was the first EU country to fall into recession. Demand for goods kept dropping from both domestic and global consumers. Ireland's debt was judged to be the riskiest in the EU, worse than the debt in Greece. As the recession deepened, unemployment rose to 14 percent in 2010, and the IMF (International Monetary Fund) projected that Ireland's economy would contract by more than 10 percent. Under pressure to meet EU guidelines about deficits, the government was forced to reduce its spending even further. After bailing out its failing banks and cutting back on many popular programs such as subsidies for medical services and higher education, the Irish government negotiated a $90 billion bailout package funded by the IMF and the EU. Despite the aggressive policies of the Irish government to heal the economy, business and consumer spending continued to languish.

If one needed evidence that the economic system and the political system are completely intertwined in a modern society, the recent history of Ireland offers a compelling case. Both the period of Celtic Tiger economic growth and the serious economic problems now facing Ireland are extensively linked to the policies of the Irish government. Indeed, both the economic difficulties and the economic policy challenges currently facing many countries, including Great Britain, Greece, Portugal, Spain and the United States, are directly associated with their governments' policies. Thus, the distinguished scholar Charles Lindblom (1977: 8) observes: "In all the political systems of the world, much of politics is economics and most of economics is also politics. …For many good reasons, politics and economics have to be held together in the analysis of basic social mechanisms and systems."

This book is about the *political* world. But if Lindblom is correct, your understanding of contemporary politics requires an understanding of its pervasive linkages with economics. This *combination of politics and economics* is called political economy. This chapter explains this concept. First, it describes the connections between the economic system and the political system. Then it characterizes three different types of political economies: (1) the *market economy*, (2) the *command economy*, and (3) the *mixed economy*. Finally, it examines how these political economies are related to major "isms" in the political world, especially capitalism, socialism, and communism.

POLITICS AND ECONOMICS

Many decisions made by the political system have significant impacts on the economy. Can you think of how the following government policies might affect the economy?

8.1 Explain the role of the state in a nation's economy.

- The government does not construct or repair any highways and roads.
- The government owns all factories producing cars.

Watch the Video "Preventing Stagflation in the Global Economy" at mypoliscilab.com

Explore the Comparative "Economic Policy" on mypoliscilab.com

- The government collects very high taxes on the profits of businesses.
- The government fully finances the provision of all medical services for all citizens.
- The government places no restrictions on the right of foreigners to enter and work in the country.
- The government controls the prices of all basic foods.

Similarly, the actions of major economic actors and the performance of the economic system can have major impacts on the political system, which depends on the economic system to generate income, goods, and services for the survival and prosperity of its citizens. For example, what policy responses might you predict from the U.S. government to the following economic situations?

- A lengthy nationwide strike by air traffic controllers
- Exceptionally high unemployment over many months
- The proposed sale of the country's largest automaker to a Chinese corporation
- The discovery that there is less than five years' worth of oil reserves within the country's boundaries
- Bankruptcy filings by two of the country's largest financial institutions

The more one reflects on modern societies, the clearer it becomes that "much of politics is economics and most of economics is also politics."

Understanding political economy requires a grasp of some basic economic concepts. This chapter describes a conceptual framework for the economic system that is similar in spirit to Easton's framework for a political system (see Chapter 5). The framework presents only some core ideas that have been simplified considerably. However, this discussion does involve complicated abstractions, so hang in there! (If you want the full treatment, take an introductory economics course, or read an introductory economics book such as Heyne, Boettke, and Prychitko [2010]. For a political science perspective, see Wilensky [2002: Ch. 2]).

A POLITICAL-ECONOMIC FRAMEWORK

8.2 Determine the relationship among the separate elements that make up the political economy.

The abstract model presented in Figure 8.1 is our starting point for understanding the idea of a political economy. The figure offers an extremely simple characterization of the way in which extraordinarily complex systems of production and exchange operate (see Baumol and Blinder 2011: Ch. 8; Miller 2011: Ch. 8).

Factors, Firms, and Households/Consumers

Explore the Comparative "Civil Societies" on mypoliscilab.com

In the beginning (according to this model), there are three kinds of important productive resources—the three major *factors of production* (A) (see Figure 8.1). *Land* means the ground plus any raw materials (commodities such as coal and bananas) on or in the ground. *Labor* is human productive input (our common understanding of "work"). *Capital* is the nonhuman productive input from other resources (especially financial resources, machinery, and technology). Each factor of production is controlled by an owner who, in the language of economics, is referred to as a *household* (B).

Some actor called a *firm* (C) attempts to acquire a combination of these productive resources (factors of production) in order to produce a *good* (D1). A good

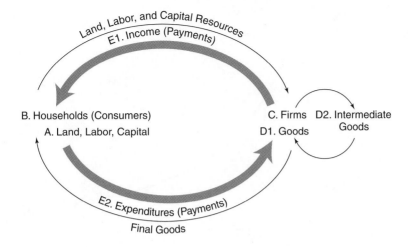

FIGURE 8.1
An economic system framework: the income-expenditures model

can be a product (e.g., a pencil, a nuclear missile) or a service (e.g., a massage, transportation on an airplane).

A firm (in this book, the terms *firm* and *producer* are used interchangeably) might be a single person who produces a good from her own resources. For example, a masseuse (massage giver) provides a massage through her own labor skills. Or a firm might be a large organization that uses many productive resources (of land and commodities, workers and capital). For example, a firm that produces something as simple as pencils needs productive resources such as wood, graphite, rubber, machines, and workers. The firm transforms these factors of production into the final good—here, pencils. Often some *intermediate goods* (D2) are acquired in order to make more complicated goods. The pencil firm, for example, has probably acquired intermediate goods such as graphite (which it acquires from another firm that has mined and refined this chemical element) and wood (which has come from a firm that owns, cuts, and mills trees).

A household has a second role, as a *consumer*, when it wants to acquire a final good (e.g., a pencil, a massage, whatever). A consumer offers something of value to the firm in exchange for the good that the consumer wants. What emerges between the household/consumer and the firm is a system of *payments* (E1 and E2 in the figure). A firm must pay something to a household that controls a productive resource necessary for the firm to produce goods. And a household, in its role as a consumer, must pay something to the firm to get a final good that it wants. Notice that any individual or group can act as a household, a consumer or a firm, depending on whether the individual or group is selling a factor, transforming productive resources into goods, or is acquiring a final good.

The size of a payment (the price) is established when there is an agreement between a consumer who is willing to exchange (give up) something to get the good and a firm who is willing to give up the good for what the consumer offers. In the language of economics, each actor increases her **utility** (her overall happiness) in such an exchange because each has higher utility after the exchange than before it.

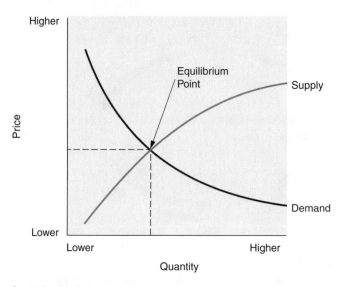

FIGURE 8.2
The relationship between the supply of a good and the demand for the good

So, for example, the actor who has grown a dozen tomatoes might have a higher utility when she exchanges them with someone who will give her something she values enough to give up the tomatoes.

In every system, there are some good-for-good exchanges, called *barter trading* (e.g., the dozen tomatoes are traded for a massage). But most economies are dominated by good-for-money exchanges, where the consumer gives the producer some amount of money in exchange for the final good (e.g., a tomato might be exchanged for $1, or a massage might be given for $50).

If firms want to sell more massages than customers want to buy, the price of a massage is likely to come down. This is how **supply and demand** operate: If demand is low relative to supply, the price comes down; if demand is high relative to supply, the price goes up. In theory, with enough producers and consumers making exchanges, the price of a good reaches a perfect balance point between supply and demand, known as the *equilibrium point* (see Figure 8.2).

The payment by a consumer to a firm (E2) is usually a different amount than the payments by the firm for the productive resources used to produce that good (E1 in Figure 8.1). A firm is successful if it can sell the good for more than it paid to produce the good. This excess of payments over costs is **profit**. If the firm must sell the good for less than the cost of producing it, the firm suffers a *loss*. Obviously, firms normally try to increase their profit and to avoid loss.

Getting and Spending

This system of exchanges goes around and around. Households expend their resources on goods, and firms provide the households with income as they pay for productive resources. Ideally, everyone is exchanging things of value for other

The richest merchant in a Bedouin market in Morocco displays the goods she is selling, proudly wearing the chains of gold coins that attest to her entrepreneurial skills as a "firm" in a market economy.

things that they value even more. As the system becomes more complex, many actors are involved in the production and distribution of goods. Some additional actors operate as brokers, organizing and facilitating exchanges. For example, the grower of tomatoes might sell them to a broker, who then markets the tomatoes to other consumers. If more and more goods are produced, bought, sold, and consumed by all the actors in the economic system, there is *economic growth*.

The complexity of the actual exchanges in most economic systems is beyond comprehension. As an example, see how long a list you can quickly develop of the different people who contributed some fraction of the value (the one dollar) that you pay for a can of tomatoes at the supermarket. (Think about all the actors involved in the production and distribution to you of that can of tomatoes) With sufficient time, you could probably identify hundreds of people who share in the dollar you paid.

Presumably, you (like every other actor) attempt to pursue a strategy that maximizes your utility (i.e., that results in your most preferred mix of goods and resources) and hence enhances your life. Individuals (and groups) have very different sets of preferences. One person might want to hoard money or food or precious metals; another might want to spend everything on consumption for personal pleasure. One person might work hard to gain the resources to own a mansion and a

Mercedes-Benz, while another person might be happiest with minimal work and no possessions other than the bare necessities she carries in a backpack.

Of course, it is a tough world, and all people are not equally capable of maximizing their value preferences. A person's success in getting her preferred mix of goods and resources can be affected by realities such as the types and amounts of resources she already controls, her skills in producing goods, the demand for her goods, the actions of other producers, and even luck. Over time, there are likely to be huge differences in the mix of goods and resources controlled by different individuals and groups.

The State Joins In

We now have our first approximation of an abstract model of the economic system. One very important addition to this simplified model is the political system. As noted at the beginning of the chapter, the modern economic system is inextricably connected to the political system. Why might the state decide to intervene in the economy? Here are a few of the most important reasons:

- there is a certain good that is socially important but no firm can produce it for a profit;
- there is a good that requires a scale of production beyond any firm's capacity (e.g., national defense);
- the state is needed to enforce legal behavior by households and firms (e.g., contracts);
- the state must protect people from dangerous or illegal goods or production techniques;
- the state has a policy goal of providing a good to some individuals who cannot afford it (e.g., health care);
- the state's goal is to redistribute goods and wealth from some individuals to others.

Notice that each subsequent rationale for state intervention on the previous list is driven more fully by a political value relative to an economic necessity (Lindblom 2003).

Thus, the state (F) is added in Figure 8.3, and these interactions between the economy and the state result in the dynamic processes we call the *political economy*. The state can powerfully affect the economic system in the six general ways, labeled F1 through F6 in Figure 8.3. The state can:

- be a consumer, purchasing any good from a firm. (F1)
- replace (that is, be) a household, in the sense that it controls certain factors of production. (F2)
- replace (that is, be) a firm, producing a good. (F3)
- regulate the manner in which either households or firms operate by enacting policies that encourage or prevent certain behaviors by those economic actors. (F4)
- tax (extract resources from) the payments to any actor. (F5)
- transfer payments or goods to any actor. (F6)

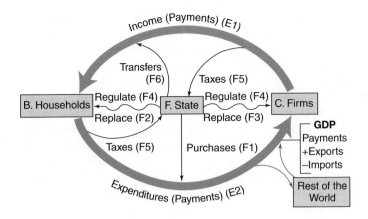

FIGURE 8.3
A political economy framework

The state's patterns of action on these six dimensions distinguish different types of political economies.

The World Joins In

The second important addition to our simplified model of political economy is nothing less than "the rest of the world." While Figure 8.3 could represent an economy at any level (e.g., a city), it is most commonly understood as the national economy of a state. It is quite likely that there are exchanges of goods and factors of production that cross the boundaries of the state. *All those goods and factors of production that are sold to actors outside the state's boundaries* can be considered *exports*. Thus, if the tomatoes or automobiles produced in the United States are sold to households in Mexico, these exports generate revenue for U.S. firms (hence the plus sign in Figure 8.3). Exports are generally viewed as a positive for the economy, assuming the goods are sold for a profit, because they inject additional money into the system. Conversely, *the goods that a country's actors purchase from firms in another country* are *imports*. Thus, if the United States imports tomatoes or automobiles produced in Mexico, these imports result in money leaving the U.S. economy (although the U.S. households and firms do get the goods).

Each country has major policy choices as it decides whether to influence the economic transactions that cross its borders. The state might be genuinely committed to "free trade" and thus make no effort to influence import and export activity. However, many countries do intervene in economic transactions that cross their borders in an attempt to serve their own national interests. Thus, the state can discourage imports by taxing them on entry (tariffs) or by limiting how much of an import is allowed (quotas). In some cases, the state might even encourage certain imports. Similarly, the state can implement policies that either facilitate or obstruct exports by its own firms. Can you think of reasons why a state might restrict certain exports or encourage certain imports?

There have always been economic exchanges the cross state borders. In the last few decades, however, the scale and complexity of interstate exchanges have become extraordinary. There is now a vast "global economy," and it is possible that there is more economic value in the economic exchanges that cross borders than in those that occur within countries. Chapter 11 will detail the forces of globalization, but the key point here is that states find it increasingly difficult to control their own economy. First, many firms now operate "multinationally," that is, they operate in multiple countries and can move their production from country to country, often very rapidly. Second, even more firms utilize factors of production and intermediate goods they have acquired from other countries. And third, most large firms now sell their goods in multiple countries. Thus, many consumers purchase goods whose productive factors are not primarily from their home country. For example, consider whether the clothes you are wearing or your electronics gear are goods in which the majority of components were produced by firms inside your country. Probably not.

The global economy has many consequences for the national political economy. States have much less capacity to regulate the behavior of firms, to control the balance of imports and exports, and even to tax many economic transactions. Thus, for most countries, the actions of firms and households outside the state's borders are very significant for the functioning of their political economy. The key impacts of such external actors will be particularly emphasized in Chapters 13–15.

The Economy Strikes Back

The previous discussion described how the state can implement a variety of policies that affect the economy. It is equally important to consider how the economy affects the state. A fundamental goal of every country is prosperity, and a healthy economy is the essential provider of resources to serve that goal. The state depends on the economic system to generate the goods and revenue that enable the state to function and its citizens to prosper. More than any other policy domain, governments flounder and fall when there are serious problems with the economy.

In most political economies, a substantial proportion of the activity in the economic system is not under the direct control of the state. Rather, there are many economic actors whose behaviors are of fundamental importance to economic health. The political economy is in trouble if unemployment is high, or a major firm is struggling, or state regulation is stifling economic growth, or high taxes are discouraging investment. Thus, those private sector actors with economic power can wield substantial, sometimes massive influence on the decisions and actions of the state. Moreover, some of those actors are among the most active and well-funded political groups, and they contribute money and employ lobbyists to shape public policies in ways that benefit their operations (Parenti 2010).

Who are the major sets of economic actors? First, there are the large corporations operating in the country. These firms are especially concerned about such policies as taxation, regulations on business practices and labor relations, and investment incentives. This group includes the flagship companies in the national economy, and their prosperity is directly linked to the prosperity of the country, psychologically as well as financially. There are also the multinational corporations with significant activity in the country. They have particular leverage with government officials because they can threaten to shift their productive activities outside the country if policies do not favor their operations. A second group is the country's small businesses. In most economies, these firms are the source of most job growth and are the heart of the overall functioning of the economic system, as they produce and distribute the bulk of the goods. A third set of actors is the interest groups that represent these various business communities and engage in substantial lobbying on their behalf. These interest groups are well funded and highly influential with government in almost every country, and in some countries (described below as "corporatist political economies"), the representatives of these organizations are actually direct participants in the policy process.

A fourth group of economic actors that are very powerful is composed of organizations in the global financial community. Some operate within a country—the banks and a broad array of institutions that have been termed the "shadow banking system" and that control financial capital (Lanchester 2010). Others are international financial institutions like the International Monetary Fund, the European Central Bank, and the World Bank, who can force major policy decisions on many governments, particularly those in the developing world, or in countries that are struggling financially, like Ireland. During the recent global recession and the financial crises in countries from Greece to the United States, these global financial actors, in concert with the banks, insurance companies, and brokerage houses, have been increasingly visible as the players whom governments placate and protect. In analyzing the collapse of bubble economies, the extent to which governments have allowed these actors to operate in dangerous ways and the willingness of governments to offer them protection (e.g., bailouts) has become much more evident than usual (Nouriel and Mihm 2011). Some critics argue that in almost every country, some combination of these powerful economic actors dominates governments far more than they are controlled by governments and by the economic policies of the state (Blustein 2006; Ritholtz 2009). At least, the deep intertwining of the economic system and the political system are indisputable.

MEASURING ECONOMIC PROSPERITY

Many analyses require a measure of the economic prosperity of a country. The most widely used indicators are usually based on one of two monetary figures that summarize "gross product"—the total value of all the final goods produced by a state's economic actors during a certain time period, adjusted for exports minus imports. *Gross domestic product (GDP)* is the total value of all final goods produced by all people within a state's boundaries, whether or not they are citizens (see Figure 8.3). The *gross national income (GNI)* includes the production of all citizens of the state, whether they are inside the state's boundaries or not. For cross-national comparisons, these amounts are typically measured in U.S. dollars. International economic actors have mainly utilized GDP as the primary indicator of a country's economic vitality, but in recent years, some have begun to emphasize GNI. Each has certain strengths as a measure of a country's prosperity in a

8.3 Assess the different measures of economic prosperity.

global economy where there are increasing numbers of noncitizen workers and multinational firms.

Because both measures are greatly influenced by the size of the country, attempts to compare the relative prosperity of the people in different countries typically divide the productive total by the number of citizens (as "per capita"). However, as measures of a country's prosperity, both GDP per capita and GNI per capita have at least three important flaws:

1. They do not measure how the prosperity is distributed among the country's economic actors, and thus many citizens have an individual level of prosperity that is sharply different from their country's average production per capita. The level of wealth inequality *within* countries is a perennial hot topic, with some analysts claiming that it is a critical problem and others viewing it as an inevitable condition of a vibrant economic system. Compare in 8 and Figure 8.4 examine the level of inequality in selected countries.

2. Only the goods that actually enter the society's monetary sector are measured, while many other valued goods are ignored. These unmeasured goods include both household work and goods in the "underground economy," particularly trade in illegal goods, barter trade, and the black market. In some countries, GDP and GNI are particularly misleading because such unmeasured goods are a significant proportion of total economic activity.

3. GDP per capita and GNI per capita are often used to compare the prosperity of one country versus another. However, there are huge between-country disparities in the exchange value of money. In two different countries, the same amount of money (converting local currencies into an international exchange currency, usually dollars) can buy much more or much less of the same specific goods (e.g., a pound of rice in Japan might cost 20 times as much as in India).

Due to these cross-national disparities in the value of money, there is increasing use of a third prosperity measure that attempts to establish equivalent value across countries, an index based on *purchasing power parity (PPP)*—that is, *correcting monetary indicators to reflect the amount of currency required in that country to buy certain standard goods.*

An understanding of the "average wealth" of citizens in a country, especially in comparisons between richer and poorer countries, is somewhat different depending on which measure is presented. If we use PPP indexing, Vietnam's GDP per capita of only $1,113 per year equates to $3,097 per capita in "purchasing power," nearly three times higher. In some countries, PPP lowers the wealth measure because the cost of living is high. The level of the GDP corrected for purchasing power in Denmark, for example, is actually only 2/3 of its GDP level. In purchasing power dollars, the economic gap between the wealthier countries and the poorer countries usually decreases. Thus in the case of Denmark and Vietnam, the ratio drops from about 50:1 to 11:1 when corrected for PPP. Indeed, for many of the poorer countries, GDP per capita (PPP) dollars are more than double the GDP per capita dollars. However, it is important to note that when a country attempts to participate in the global economy, and especially when it attempts to

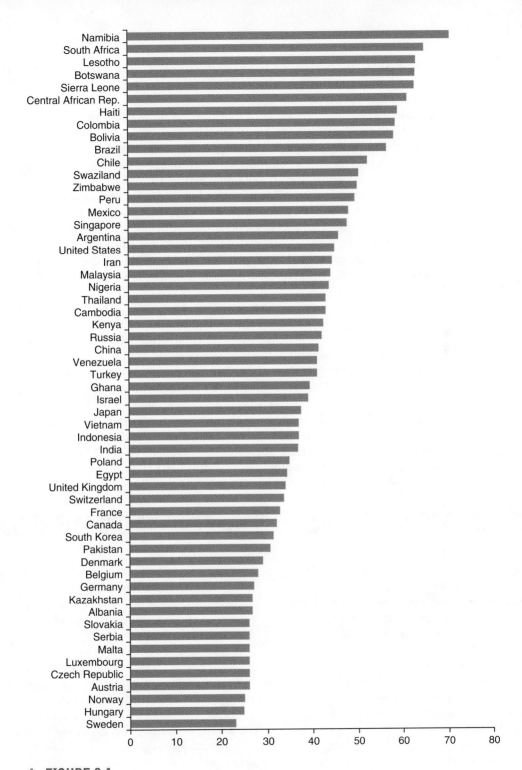

FIGURE 8.4

Wealth inequality/equality in selected countries (Gini index)

Source: CIA (2011)

import goods, the purchasing power of its currency is directly tied to international exchange rates, not to the price of rice at home (or PPP dollars), and its relative wealth or poverty remains.

More broadly, is there a better measure of the general prosperity in a society than GDP per capita (PPP)? Some scholars now argue that GDP-type measures give value to many economic activities in our collective lives that should not be valued, such as the cost of cleaning up environmental damage (e.g., oil spills) and expenditures on crime (e.g., maintaining prisons) and that GDP does not account for many things that do provide us with a higher quality life, such as volunteer service and environmentally sustainable activities. They also cite the recent findings of economists and other social scientists who conclude that beyond a limited level of wealth, human well-being correlates much more with conditions such as physical and mental health, quality of social life, and level of education rather than with increases in GDP per capita and material consumption (Easterlin 2006; Layard 2005; Frank 2001).

Thus, some propose an alternative measure, such as the "Genuine Progress Indicator" (GPI). The GPI adds the economic value of those things that enhance our quality of life and increase environmental sustainability and it subtracts the costs of those economic activities that reduce quality of life. While GDP per capita in the United States has risen about 240 percent during the period from 1950 to 2005, the Genuine Progress Indicator per capita has risen only about 25 percent. (Costanza 2008; www.rprogress.org). Another group proposes the "Happy Planet Index" (HPI), a measure for each country which combines individuals' reported satisfaction with their lives, longevity, and the country's ecological footprint (to protect resources for future generations) (Abdallah et. al. 2009). Do you think there is a case for a different measure of prosperity than GDP?

COMPARE IN 8 | Wealth Inequality

Chapter 2 identified the normative disagreements, especially between conservatives and socialists, about the desirability of equality. Many discussions focus on the inequalities in wealth between the "rich" countries and the "poor" countries. However, others focus on the wealth inequalities *within* countries. These can be masked by general measures of national economic prosperity per capita, such as GDP per capita (PPP). Are there significant inequalities within many countries? How are we to make sense of this?

Economic inequality (or equality) can be measured in various ways. One widely used measure is a statistic called the "Gini index." When used as a measure of income inequality, the Gini index computes a score in which a perfectly equal distribution of wealth in the population would equal 0.00, and a completely unequal distribution would have an index score of 100. As the Gini index is higher, and especially where it is greater than about 45, the wealth distribution is very unequal. The index also provides a way to compare the relative inequality across countries. Another form of measuring wealth within a country is the ratio of the country's personal income that is held by the top X percent of the population relative to the lowest Y percent.

(Continued)

Figure 8.4 provides Gini index score for selected countries among the 135 countries for whom there are data. Inequality in the distribution of family income ranges from the most unequal country, Namibia, with a Gini index score of 70.7, to the most equally distributed, Sweden, at 23.0. There are considerable cross-national differences in the extent of wealth inequality. About 28 percent of the countries have Gini indices of 45 or higher. Only 4 percent of the countries have scores above 60.0, 12 percent score in the 50s, 27 percent are in the 40s, 39 percent are in the 30s, and 15 percent are below 30 (CIA 2011). Of the ten most unequal income distributions, six are in sub-Saharan Africa and four are countries in Latin America. Of the ten countries with the most equal distributions, eight are in Europe and two are in Scandinavia.

It is generally the case that the rich countries (discussed as the "developed countries" in Chapter 13) have relatively *less* inequality in the distribution of wealth than most of the poorer countries (the "developing" countries in Chapter 14).

Most of the countries with the greatest wealth inequalities are extremely poor countries. And most of the countries with the greatest equality in wealth distribution are countries that are European social democracies or European countries that were under communism until 1989 (Castles 2004). There are exceptions to this general pattern. Two rich countries (Singapore and the United States) have high inequality scores, while some poor countries (e.g., Ethiopia, Kazakhstan, and Pakistan) do have substantial equality in income distribution. An important issue to be addressed in later chapters is what general factors might account for greater or less equality in income distributions.

FURTHER QUESTIONS

1. Does the location of any country in Figure 8.4 surprise you? Why?
2. Why might there generally be more wealth inequality in poorer countries than in richer countries? ◣

TWO IDEAL-TYPE POLITICAL ECONOMIES

Based on the framework in Figure 8.3, we can distinguish two ideal-type political economies: *market economy* and *command economy*. Remember that an *ideal type* is a description of what a certain phenomenon might be like in its pure form, but it does not necessarily correspond exactly to any real-world example.

8.4 Compare the ideal-type political economies.

◉─[**Watch** the Video "China's New Rich" at **mypoliscilab.com**

In distinguishing the market economy from the command economy, it's useful to consider five fundamental questions:

1. Who controls the factors of production?
2. Who determines what goods are produced?
3. Who establishes the value attached to different resources and goods?
4. Who decides how resources and goods will be distributed?
5. What is the role of the state?

The next two sections consider these questions for each ideal-type political economy. Table 8.1 summarizes the responses to each of these key questions. The table also provides answers for a "mixed" economy, which is less an ideal type than a real-world compromise between the two. (For other approaches that explain political economy, see, for example, Heyne, Boettke, and Prychitko [2010] and Lindblom [1977, 2003].)

TABLE 8.1

Comparing Command, Market, and Mixed Political Economies

	Command	Market	Mixed
Who controls the factors of production?	The state owns all significant factors (land, labor, and capital).	Every private actor (household) controls her own factors.	The state and private actors each control some factors.
Who determines what goods are produced?	The state devises a detailed economic plan that specifies what level of each good will be produced.	All actors (firms) make their own separate decisions about production in an attempt to maximize their own utilities.	Some firms are under direct state control, but most make decisions in the market. The state regulates some actions of many firms and households.
	The system is supply-oriented.	The system is demand-oriented.	The system is mainly demand-oriented.
Who establishes the value attached to different productive factors and goods?	The state sets the value (price) in all exchanges.	The market (via the "invisible hand") sets the value based on the equilibrium of supply and demand.	The market sets the value. The state regulates some prices to serve national priorities.
Who decides how factors and goods will be distributed?	The state's plan indicates who will receive which goods and in what amounts.	Distribution is based on a summation of the actions of all consumers and producers in the market.	The market is the main decision maker. The state intervenes in some cases to ensure that certain actors have access to particular goods.
What is the role of the state?	The state is dominant, controlling almost all aspects of the political economy.	The state plays a minimal role in the political economy. The state enforces the "social contract," protecting all from violence or from law breakers.	The state attempts to strike a balance between: • competition and state control • private profit and a sharing of societal resources

The Market Economy: Total Private Control

1. **Who controls the factors of production?** In the ideal-type market economy, there is *total private control.* The state has almost no significant role in the political economy. Thus, every actor has direct, personal control over the use of all the factors of production that she owns. The laborer, the landowner, or the owner of capital decides who, if anyone, she will exchange her resources with and the amount of resources she will accept in that exchange. And each

firm acts to maximize its profits through acquiring productive resources and then producing goods that can be sold to consumers (Lindblom 2003).

2. **Who determines what goods are produced?** All the firms' decisions about what goods to produce are based on their own assessments of how they can achieve maximum profit. If one thinks of an economy in terms of the supply and demand for goods, the market economy is demand-oriented. The most important consideration for a firm that is deciding what to produce is this: What good can I offer that others will demand and that will generate the highest profit for me? Overall, production is guided by what the famous Scottish economist Adam Smith (1723–1790, Compare in 2) called the "invisible hand" of the market. This invisible hand is a summation of the self-serving actions of every household and every firm regarding their uses of the factors of production.

3. **Who establishes the value attached to different factors and goods?** Similarly, the invisible hand of the market establishes value. Every factor of production and every good that is produced is valued at its *opportunity cost*—the resources that someone will give to acquire it. Value is determined in the competitive market of supply and demand (recall Figure 8.2) as every household and firm tries to gain the maximum payment from others in exchange for its productive factor or good. Competition is particularly intense where supply and demand are quite unequal. For example, if a firm needs five workers who can program in C++ (demand) and only two workers are available with this skill (supply), the workers can bid up the resources that the firm will offer (this is usually a wage rate, but it can also include other resources such as work conditions, benefits [e.g., housing, health care], or shares of the firm's profits). Conversely, if five workers offer the skill and the firm needs only two workers with this productive factor, the firm can lower the resources it must pay for the work.

   A basic economic assumption in a market economy is the continual adjustment of supply and demand towards an equilibrium point. For example, some workers might move to a different place or offer a different labor skill if the wages for programming get too low or there are too few jobs. And a firm might find a substitute for the labor it needs if the labor is too expensive or too scarce to enable the firm to make a profit (e.g., outsourcing). Can you think of other supply–demand adjustments that the workers or the firm might make?

4. **Who decides how productive factors and goods will be distributed?** Again, it is the invisible hand of the market, rather than anyone in particular, that determines who gets which factors and goods. As each person pursues her own private utility, economic actors accumulate dramatically different bundles of factors and goods, depending on their preferences, the resources they control, and their skill and luck in exchanging and transforming resources in the market.

5. **What is the role of the state?** The state is passive in the productive system, allowing private actors to operate in a relatively unconstrained manner. The state's primary obligations, under the social contract, are to prevent private actors from doing violence to each other, to protect private property rights, and to defend the state's sovereignty. In meeting these responsibilities, the

state might purchase some goods and productive factors, might levy minimal taxes, and might affect firms' import and export activities. Otherwise, state intervention in the economy is extremely limited.

The Command Economy: Total State Control

1. **Who controls the factors of production?** In the ideal-type command economy, *the state assumes total control of almost all the significant factors of production.* The state eliminates private ownership of labor, land, and capital. The state owns the land, the natural resources, the factories, the machines, and so on. The state even owns labor, in the sense that the state decides the form in which all individuals will provide their labor.

2. **Who determines what goods are produced?** The state devises a detailed *economic plan* that specifies what goods will be produced, how much, and from what combination of productive factors. The production decisions in the state's plan are supply-oriented (in contrast to the demand orientation of the market economy). The state-as-firm attempts to use all productive factors optimally to maximize the supply of goods that it has determined are most appropriate to produce.

3. **Who establishes the value attached to different factors and goods?** Because the state controls all the factors of production and is the firm producing all the goods, it can also set the values (i.e., establish the payments) for all exchanges within its boundaries. Competition is eliminated because the state, rather than the market, establishes the payments for every factor of production and every good in the society. Thus, the state tells a group of farmers to produce 1 million tomatoes and then sets the exchange value of those tomatoes. Similarly, the state decides which individuals will have jobs programming C++, and it establishes the wages and benefits they receive for their work.

4. **Who decides how productive factors and goods will be distributed?** The state is particularly active in the decisions about the distribution of goods to the population. The state's plan aims to distribute an optimal bundle of goods to every citizen, given the resources available. Thus, the plan indicates who will receive which goods in what amounts. The plan could specify, for example, that automobile-producing factory X will receive 46 tons of steel each month, and that town A will receive three tomatoes per family per week. The plan can even indicate where these goods will come from (i.e., steel from factory Y and tomatoes from farm B).

5. **What is the role of the state?** Clearly, the answers to the preceding four questions indicate that the state has a dominant, even an overwhelming role in this ideal-type political economy. The state controls almost all the important factors of production, plans the manner in which they will be utilized in the production of goods, establishes the official value of all resources and goods, and decides how the resources of the society will be distributed among individuals. In the command economy, profit is accumulated by the state, not by individuals. The state then determines how this profit will be used to serve its objectives of prosperity, security and stability.

KEY PROBLEMS OF EACH IDEAL-TYPE POLITICAL ECONOMY

Table 8.2 lists several of the most important virtues of each of the two types of political economy. These benefits stem from the logic of each approach. In theory, the market economy is efficient and dynamic because profit-driven, self-serving behavior in a highly competitive environment encourages high levels of productivity and innovation. In theory, the command economy is effective and humane because society's resources are managed and distributed so that everyone benefits from the most desirable set of goods and services possible. These virtues are valid, at least in theory. However, there are significant potential shortcomings in the functioning of either the market economy or the command economy. These problems are also summarized in Table 8.2 and are characterized below.

8.5 Identify the challenges faced by market, command, and mixed economies.

Market Economy

Resource Inequality and Hardship Substantial resource inequalities tend to emerge in a market economy. Competition is everywhere, and it tends to become ruthless. In the economic marketplace, some are extremely successful and others

TABLE 8.2

Benefits and Problems of Market and Command Economies

	Benefits	Problems
Market Economy		
Competition	Energetic and efficient production	Ruthless interactions; huge inequalities in wealth and resources
Demand orientation	Goods' cost and quality responsive to consumers' desires	Creation of demand for and proliferation of goods that have limited social value
No central plan	Local decision and "invisible hand" stimulate innovation, facilitate freedom	Economic cycles of boom and bust, inflation and recession
Command Economy		
No competition	Work for common good; relative equality of wealth and income	Little initiative; shoddy products; low productivity; limited innovation
Supply orientation	Production and distribution for social and individual needs	Oversupply and shortages; lack of coordination
Central plan	Rational use of societal resources	Overcentralized control; lack of responsiveness to changing circumstances

are complete failures, and the market system is indifferent to the hardships of those who do not succeed. Neither the successful actors nor the state intervenes to protect those who have minimal success. Over time, the rich tend to get richer (especially if they cooperate with each other), while the less successful increasingly lack the resources for a secure and decent life.

Production for Profit, not Need   A demand-oriented system of private production does not necessarily produce goods that best meet human needs. Rather, production decisions are dominated by actors who produce those goods that they believe will result in maximum profit ("greed is good"). Such goods might be inessential or extravagant or even dangerous. The state does little to regulate the economic actors or provide for those who cannot afford important goods, like health care. More broadly, the aggressive pursuit of profit in the absence of state regulation can result in economic behavior that is unethical or dangerous. And short-term profitability trumps longer-term considerations of societal benefits, such as environmental sustainability.

Severe Economic Cycles   A third problem is that a market economy can experience major economic cycles. There is no guarantee that the very large number of private decisions about production and consumption (the "invisible hand") will mesh in a manner that ensures steady growth and prosperity for the economic system as a whole. The economy is prone to large swings towards either hyperactivity (causing inflation and scarcity) or serious economic slowdown (causing recession or depression), and the state does not intervene to counteract these swings. Fluctuations between boom and bust, even if infrequent, can be deeply disruptive to the productive system and the bad times can result in substantial hardship.

Command Economy

Limited Incentives for Efficiency   The absence of competition in the command political economy can result in problems as serious as those resulting from excessive competition. First, if the state controls wages and prices, there are no major economic incentives for firms to be efficient, for managers to be innovative, or for individual workers to work hard. Second, if there is no competitive market of alternative goods, there is minimal incentive to produce goods of high quality. People are obliged to accept goods that are unexciting or poorly made.

Unresponsive Production   The state's emphasis on a supply orientation means that production decisions are not directly responsive to consumer demand. The central planners' ideas of what people should want are not necessarily what consumers actually do want and will purchase. Thus, the plan typically results in substantial oversupply of some goods and severe shortages of others.

Overcentralization and Inflexibility   Command economies are so centralized that they lose touch with the differences and complexities of individual firms and consumers. The central planners usually do not receive and react effectively to information regarding miscalculations and mistakes in either the development or the implementation of the state's overall plan. Such rigidity and unresponsiveness make

In many countries, inequalities result in slums and shanty towns packed with the poor that are often adjacent to the housing and office buildings of the prosperous, as in this *favela* in Rio de Janeiro, Brazil.

the efficient use of productive resources unlikely. In short, the political economy that combines minimal competition, a weak demand mechanism, and inflexibility is prone to low productivity, inferior goods, and inefficient use of resources.

The Mixed Economy

Given the potential shortcomings of the ideal-type market and command political economies, is there an alternative? The mixed economy can be understood as *an attempt to combine the strengths of these two ideal-type economies while also minimizing their shortcomings.* As a hybrid, the mixed economy is not a "pure" ideal type. It compromises on each of the five major issues considered earlier (see Table 8.1).

1. **Who controls the factors of production?** Control of the means of production is shared between the state and private actors. The state owns or directly controls some of the major factors of production, such as those relating to key commodities (e.g., coal, oil, steel), key infrastructure systems (e.g., transportation,

telecommunications), and key financial resources (e.g., banks). However, many firms are private and private actors (households) control a substantial share of the factors of production.

2. **Who determines what goods are produced?** Production decisions are primarily demand-oriented, driven by the market mechanism. Half or more of all production is done by private firms. Most public-sector firms (those owned and managed by the state) must interact and even compete with many private firms when acquiring productive resources and when selling goods to consumers. However, private firms and households are constrained by the state, which regulates the behavior of private actors and can implement an economic plan that specifies broad guidelines for all actors in the economic system.

3. **Who establishes the value attached to different productive factors and goods?** The value of most goods is established, as in a market economy, through the processes of supply and demand. But the state does intervene to ensure that national priorities are protected. For example, the state might set guidelines to control the prices of key goods (e.g., basic foods, energy) and of certain factors of production (e.g., wages); it might regulate the manner in which firms and households collaborate and compete; and it might employ taxing and expenditures (purchases [F1] in Figure 8.3) to influence the economic system.

4. **Who decides how factors and goods will be distributed?** Decisions on the distribution of productive factors and goods are the most complicated element of the mixed economy. Private actors are allowed to take actions that maximize their profits. The state then intervenes through taxation mechanisms (F5 in Figure 8.3), extracting resources from firms and households. The state uses these taxes to purchase goods (F1) or to provide transfer payments (F6), both of which the state redistributes to certain actors in the social order. The state undertakes only a partial redistribution of resources, leaving private actors with considerable resources and freedom to make their own decisions about production and consumption.

5. **What is the role of the state?** The mixed economy, the state is far more active than in the market economy, but far less in control than in the command economy. The system blends a demand orientation and a supply orientation. The state's actions are to facilitate some competition while also mitigating the effects of ruthless competition, and to allow private actors and the economy to benefit from their skillful use of resources while also ensuring a certain level of necessary material well-being for the less successful actors. The great challenges for the state in a mixed economy concern striking a proper balance between competition and control, between a free market and a managed economy, and between private property and a sharing of society's resources.

All real-world political economies are mixed, as each attempts to find the best balance of market forces and state interventions. The search for such a balance is continual and in some cases impossible. Focus in 8 describes some of the challenges facing the Mexican political economy.

▶ FOCUS IN 8 | Mexico's Political Economy

Since the Mexican Revolution of 1917, the economy of Mexico has experienced dramatic highs and lows as it has transformed from an agrarian system to a more diversified economy. Currently, about 63 percent of the Mexican labor force is engaged in the provision of services, 23 percent are in manufacturing, and 14 percent are in agriculture. The economy now generates about $13,900 per person (in PPP), ranking 70th among all countries (CIA 2011). The evolution of the economy is shaped by many forces, but two have been most critical.

The first force is Mexico's "geopolitical" situation—its natural resources and its geographic location (on geopolitics, see Compare in 11). Mexico has discovered abundant oil and other minerals, has considerable land suitable for farming, and has a long coastline on two oceans. Also, Mexico's economy operates under the looming presence of the United States, which is the largest and most influential economic system in the world, as well as being a political and military superpower. And to Mexico's south are the small countries of Central America, which have lower GDP per capita than Mexico and more commodity-based economies.

The second critical force shaping the economy has been the policies of the Mexican national government. Policy was dominated by a single party (PRI, recall Chapter 7) from the Revolution of 1917 until the 2000 election of Vicente Fox. PRI policies shifted the Mexican economy from a reliance on agriculture towards more balance and diversification through industrialization and then provision of services. State control and intervention in the economy were relatively high. The government owned large shares in major industries (e.g., energy, telecommunications) and regulated most key economic sectors. Its policies of high tariffs and subsidies to domestic firms protected both agriculture and industry from external competition. Labor was controlled to keep wages low, although some PRI leaders did promote state

spending on social programs for the poor as well as some redistribution of land to the peasants. PRI was accused of extensive corruption that funneled considerable wealth from the economy to its members and to wealthy Mexicans. During the 1980s and 1990s, the government shifted away from state control and ownership of the economy, and towards more market-based policies, encouraging private entrepreneurs and opening the economy to foreign capital and imported goods. These policy changes were driven by severe economic crises in Mexico, including the near collapse of the peso, and by the general trends in the global economy.

The evolution of the Mexican political economy was accelerated when Mexico joined Canada and the United States in the North American Free Trade Agreement (NAFTA) in 1994. Mexico gained much greater access to the huge market for goods in the United States. More than 80 percent of its exports go to the United States. This includes oil, vegetables and fruits, and manufactured goods, many of which are produced in plants (*maquiladoras*) located near the U.S. border. Most of these plants import components (intermediate goods) from the United States and then complete the assembly of final goods that are exported, such as automobiles and televisions. The Mexican economy has grown in most recent years, with increasing rates of job creation, home ownership, and business start-ups, and with many families rising to the middle class. Greater prosperity has been associated with reduced birth rates and improved tax collection by the government.

NAFTA has also resulted in some negative effects in Mexico. For example, many agricultural products are now imported from the United States because they are cheaper (due to more efficient technology and U.S. government subsidies to its producers). This has increased unemployment and poverty among Mexican farmers. Also, the Mexican economy has become so dependent on the health of the U.S.

(*Continued*)

economy that the recent economic problems in the United States have generated even deeper problems in Mexico, in areas such as job losses, obtaining financial capital, and currency value.

Illegal immigration, high levels of violent crime, and a burgeoning drug trade are also linked to Mexico's stronger economic ties to the United States. And while the areas close to the U.S. border have enjoyed most of the benefits from trade within NAFTA, many people in central and southern Mexico have experienced a decline in their living standards. Inequality has grown in Mexico with the market-based economy of the NAFTA period. But the recent national governments led by fiscally conservative presidents Fox (2000–2006) and Calderon (2006–) have not promoted increases

in government aid to the poor and others affected by the economic decline. PRI might direct more resources to the less advantaged groups now that they have regained power in the Chamber of Deputies (recall Figure 7.2). The evolution of Mexico's political economy will be a key factor in its progress as a transitional developed country (see Chapter 15).

FURTHER FOCUS

1. What seems to be the most serious problem for the Mexican political economy? How might it be dealt with?

2. Does it seem more beneficial or harmful for Mexico to have the United States as its neighbor? ▲

POLITICS PLUS POLITICAL ECONOMY: THE OTHER "ISMS"

The Three "Isms"

8.6 Contrast real world examples and ideal-type political economies.

◉━[**Watch** the **Video "Zimbabwe's Economic Crisis"** at **mypoliscilab.com**

One set of great "isms" in political analysis includes the Western ideologies of conservatism, classical liberalism, and socialism (see Chapter 2). Another set of "isms" explicitly links politics to political economy: capitalism, communism, and socialism. In 20th-century politics, these were extremely emotive labels, endowed with powerful ideological content. In their most straightforward form, capitalism, communism, and socialism correspond loosely to market economy, command economy, and mixed economy, respectively.

Capitalism is *a system in which private economic actors are quite free from state constraints, private property rights are fundamental, and the state engages in few actions that might shift resources among private actors.* It is founded on the philosophy of laissez-faire economics celebrated by Adam Smith, and it imposes the severe limitations on government activity that are associated with classical liberalism and the market political economy. The freedom of private economic actors is paramount, and the state should not intervene to benefit either winners or losers in the economic competition. There is no assumption that capitalism requires any particular form of political processes (e.g., on the democracy-nondemocracy continuum) to function efficiently (Thurow 1997). Singapore and Switzerland are examples of mainly capitalist systems.

Communism has as its centerpiece *the socialization of resources—the notion that the state must control society's land, labor, and capital to achieve substantial equality for all citizens.* Consistent with the command political economy model, the state guides the utilization of all these major means of production with a central plan so that the production and distribution of goods serve the best interests of the entire population. However, communism also emphasizes a strong ideological commitment to economic and social equality among all its citizens. And it typically posits that government and politics, like the economic system, must be guided powerfully by a unified leadership, at least until equality is achieved. Communism is generally associated with the theories of Karl Marx and with the economic systems that were developed in countries such as China (1949 to about 1990), Cuba (since 1959), North Korea (since the early 1950s), and the former Soviet Union (1917–1991).

Socialism is in the middle of the three "isms," and thus it is not precisely differentiated from the other two. It seeks *a complex balance between state involvement and private control of the economy and a key policy goal is a relatively equitable distribution of benefits to all citizens.* In common with the mixed political economy, some major productive resources are owned or controlled by the state, and the state actively intervenes in planning and regulating the economy; but most production decisions are private, and value is established primarily by supply and demand (Przeworski 1985). Sweden and Denmark are examples of what are known as democratic socialist systems (or "social market" systems; see Chapter 13) because they blend socialist economics with democratic politics. Socialism is distinguishable from communism because it only controls a few important factors of production in the society, allows private actors considerable freedom of action, and does not aim to achieve total economic equality among all citizens.

Socialism can be a confusing term because Karl Marx (recall Chapter 2) and most Marxist theorists use the terms socialism and communism in a different manner than either most contemporary Western commentators or the political economy approach of this book. In Marxist theory, communism is a higher stage of political economy that follows socialism. Marxists posit that during the socialist stage, the state strives to achieve social control of resources (the means of production) by eliminating private property. As private property is eliminated, the substantial inequalities between different classes of citizens are reduced. (A detailed description of the class approach to explaining politics will be provided in Chapter 9.) Communism emerges only when multiple classes (and the inevitable conflict between those classes) cease to exist. In the classless society, everyone works for the good of all, not to gain private value. Thus, most Marxists acknowledge that no "socialist" state (e.g., Cuba) has yet completely eliminated classes and the class struggle; in this sense, communism remains a goal.

This book employs the common Western usage: A society is termed communist if a state has nearly total control over the major factors of production and the politics tend towards totalitarianism. Given the recent shift away from communism (see Chapter 15), only a few contemporary states (e.g., North Korea) meet this criterion. Indeed, given all the failures of communist systems in recent decades, some suggest that communism is dead. The Debate in 8 considers this proposition.

The Real World

No contemporary country has a political economy that corresponds exactly to either the market economy or the command economy. Because these are ideal types, this fact is not surprising. While it is possible to locate countries generally along

THE DEBATE IN 8 | Is Communism Dead?

In the decades after World War II, many thought that Marx's prediction of the inevitable success of communism was correct because more and more countries adopted its main guidelines for their political economies. Soviet Union leader Nikita Khrushchev famously announced in 1956 that communism would bury capitalism. However, the Cold War between the communist Soviet bloc and the capitalist bloc led by the United States ended in the late 1980s with almost every country abandoning the command political economy, even the Soviet Union. While many note the triumph of capitalism over communism (Fukuyama 1992; Heilbroner 1994), the global economic meltdown has revitalized the Marxist perspective (Panitch 2009). Is communism, as a model for a political economy and a society, dead?

COMMUNISM IS DEAD . . .

- The command political economy that drives communism has stifled the incentives for productivity, innovation, and flexibility, in every country that has implemented it. These fundamental weaknesses resulted in failure and abandonment of this approach almost everywhere, from the Soviet Union and Eastern Europe to wherever it was attempted in Africa, Asia, or Latin America.
- Even most countries that are still "nominally" communist actually practice capitalism. For example, China protects its one-party political system, but it has freed its markets and many of its firms in order to benefit economically from global trade. In a radical departure from Marxist ideas, the Chinese "Communist" Party protects property rights and promotes wealth accumulation. Of more than 180 countries, the only countries that still practice something close to communism in political-economic terms are a very few small, economically backward states like Laos and North Korea.
- The attempt to create a population that truly believes in the communist ideology of collective

sharing of societal resources and the equal distribution of benefits has repeatedly failed. Despite massive efforts at political socialization and substantial use of coercion by the state, human nature seems to prevent people from genuinely embracing the ideals of collectivism and egalitarianism.

- In retrospect, it is clear that the viability and spread of communism during the cold war (1945–1990) occurred primarily because communist countries could wield extensive coercion against their own populations and possessed formidable military power to promote communism abroad.
- Consider the well-known European aphorism: If you are not a communist at 20, you have no heart; if you are still a communist at 40, you have no brain (an observation even repeated by Russia's top leader Vladimir Putin in 2007). Political and economic power in the world is clearly dominated by older and wiser people who, almost without exception, completely reject communist ideas.

COMMUNISM IS ALIVE AND WELL . . .

- Numerous countries still operate under the general principles of a command political economy. The strong, one-party state controls the political economy and opens it to the market only to the extent that the market furthers the key communist aims of using society's key resources to increase the broad sharing of benefits. This is the case in countries in European Central Asia (e.g., Belarus, Tajikistan, Turkmenistan, Uzbekistan), Asia (e.g., Cambodia, Nepal, North Korea, Laos, and Vietnam), and Latin America (e.g., Cuba).
- In countries that have "abandoned" communism, a substantial proportion of the population still prefers their circumstances under communism to those in the postcommunist period. In Russia, for example, four-fifths of those surveyed in 2001 said that they wished the old Soviet Union still existed (Peterson 2001). Similarly, some

(Continued)

of China's rural population not only opposes capitalism's exploitation, but supports equal property distribution (Nadiri 2007).

- Democracy and communism are not incompatible. In fact, several democratic countries have or recently had majority communist party governments—Cyprus, Moldova, and Nepal. In democratic India, three states have recently been dominated by the communist party, including 34 straight years in West Bengal (Williams 2008).

- The key principles of communism, especially the collectivization of major societal resources and redistribution of wealth towards the less advantaged, are very evident in the political philosophies of leaders such as Evo Morales in Bolivia, Daniel Ortega in Nicaragua, Jacob Zuma in South Africa, and Hugo Chavez in Venezuela, as well as some European leftist parties with solid electoral support.

- Insurgency movements inspired by communist ideals are still active in some countries that suffer from economic underdevelopment and severe inequalities. This includes movements in Colombia, India, Peru, the Philippines, and Turkey.

- Reconsider: If you are not a communist at 20, you have no heart. . . . The majority of the world's population is young, poor, and suffering from the severe inequalities in their own societies. It is not surprising that many of them are attracted to the fundamental values of an ideology that promises economic and social justice.

MORE QUESTIONS . . .

1. Is it possible that the ideals of communism will always appeal to at least a minority of people in countries experiencing high levels of poverty and inequality?

2. Is the repeated failure of the command political economy due to "clumsy implementation" or its inherent flaws?

3. Is a relatively classless society possible, or will there always be inequality?

a continuum from a "pure" market economy to a "pure" command economy, all actual political economies are mixed. This does not mean that all political economies are basically the same—the mix of elements varies a great deal from country to country. Every state engages in some activities as a firm, some regulation of economic actors, and some redistribution of resources. Politics and values play a powerful role in establishing exactly what kinds of interventions the state will undertake and what values and interests the state will serve. Thus, understanding the mixed nature of actual political economies entails more than simply comparing the proportion of the GDP controlled by private actors versus the state or even measuring the bundle of state-provided goods and services.

In contemporary political discourse, the labels of capitalism, socialism, and communism are often presented in an ideological context. To their advocates, each represents the best mix of political and economic strategies to achieve a desirable society. To their critics, they describe undesirable *sociopolitical* orders. Communism, for example, is disparaged as an inefficient economic system with a nondemocratic government that denies individual freedom and rights. And capitalism is maligned as a system of self-interested individualism that denies the need for collective action to protect the disadvantaged or to nurture society as a whole, to promote social values and culture, or to protect the ecology (Heilbroner 1994).

Every "ism" considered in Chapter 2, from anarchism to totalitarianism, includes assumptions about appropriate forms of political economy. One "ism" that is explicitly linked to many contemporary political economies is *corporatism*, a system characterized by *extensive economic cooperation between an activist state and large organizations representing major economic actors*. The corporatist state attempts to consult, cooperate, and coordinate with the representatives of several key groups that control major productive resources in the society. These "peak associations" (organizations that represent these big groups) usually include large industries, organized labor, farmers, and major financial institutions. The peak associations have some autonomy from the state, but they are supposed to work together for common national interests. Thus, corporatism blends features of capitalism (e.g., private ownership, private profit) and socialism (e.g., extensive state economic planning, coordination of major factors of production with the state's conception of the national interest). Brazil, France, Japan, Peru, Portugal, and Spain are among the contemporary states that still have significant corporatist tendencies (see Crouch and Streeck 2006; Schmitter 1993; Wiarda 1997, 2004).

The four examples that follow—Switzerland, South Korea, Denmark, and Cuba—briefly suggest some of the features of actual political economies, relative to the ideal types grounded in the major "isms" presented above (Data sources are CIA 2011; Heritage Foundation 2011; Transparency International 2011; UNDP 2011).

Generally Market and Capitalist: Switzerland The fourth wealthiest major country in the world (measured as GDP per capita in purchasing power parity), Switzerland has a relatively weak central government. This decentralization of political power is linked to a political economy that strongly emphasizes private control and limited government involvement. Switzerland is ranked fifth among 178 countries on a measure of freedom of the economy from state regulation (Heritage Foundation 2011). Nearly all factors of production are privately owned, and most decisions and actions regarding the use of those resources are in private hands. Apart from defense expenditures and education, relatively few resources are allocated to the provision of public goods, given the wealth of the society. Central government spending is less than 15 percent of GDP, and total expenditure by all levels of government is 32 percent of GDP, among the lowest of all developed countries. Although still low, welfare spending rose substantially in the 1990s, generating a national debate about limiting public expenditure on social programs.

Generally Mixed and Capitalist: South Korea In South Korea, the state has little commitment to use the political economy for direct improvement of its citizens' quality of life. Apart from education, the state does not provide many welfare goods and services to its citizens. Government expenditures (by all levels) are only about 28 percent of GDP, the lowest among all relatively developed countries. It is not a purely capitalist system, however, because the state is extremely interventionist in promoting economic development. The state bureaucracy works very closely with firms to implement a comprehensive, collaborative strategy for economic growth, helping it to rise to thirty-second in the world on GDP per capita. This strategy has particularly favored the development of a few major Korean companies. Government loans, tax credits, and other subsidies are channeled to these companies, which are expected to operate and diversify in directions suggested by the government. In turn, the government has assured the companies that they will enjoy high profits and a labor force that is well educated, disciplined, and unable to organize effectively for higher wages. The state has also used many hidden subsidies and import restrictions to provide competitive advantages in the international market to its export-oriented firms. Thus, South Korea ranks only thirty-fourth on the measure of economic freedom. (This "developmental-state" approach, another political economy mix of state and private sector, will be discussed further in Chapter 10.)

Generally Mixed and Socialist: Denmark   Denmark is ranked sixteenth among major countries in terms of GDP per capita (PPP). The great majority of productive resources in Denmark are privately owned, and the state allows entrepreneurs considerable freedom of action, with a ranking of eighth on the economic freedom measure. However, the state is very active in guiding the Danish political economy. First, it enforces strong policies that regulate private economic actors in a generally corporatist approach, especially policies that control working conditions and environmental quality. Second, the state provides an extensive array of welfare services to the population, including: income supplement programs; a comprehensive, free health care system; state-subsidized housing for the elderly and for low-income groups; free child care; free education from infancy through university; and an extensive public transportation system. Third, it has one of the world's most equal income distributions and is ranked the world's least corrupt country. More than 51 percent of GDP is spent by all levels of government, the second highest among developed countries. To finance these programs, the government collects various forms of taxes equal to more than 50 percent of the GDP.

Generally Command and Communist: Cuba   In response to the global movement towards more market-oriented systems, Cuba has reduced its level of centralized state control over the economy. However, the state still owns and controls Cuba's major means of production, and there is a detailed central economic plan. Cuba is ranked 176 among the 178 countries on economic freedom. Agriculture and manufacturing operations remain collectivized, and the state controls many prices. The state promises work for all (although there is unemployment), and it sets workers' wages. Consistent with the ideals of communism, the state retains a fundamental commitment to control and allocates societal resources to serve human needs. There has been a strong emphasis on state spending on education and health care and on policies to equalize the distribution of land and income in order to increase equality among races, between genders, and between urban and rural citizens. Despite its rather low GDP per capita (it ranks 93 in the world), government policies result in Cuba ranking in the top 15 countries in the world on the UN "nonincome" measure of quality of life that emphasizes health and education (Human Development Index) (see Chapter 13).

CONCLUDING OBSERVATIONS

✓•―⌈Study
and Review the
Post-Test &
Chapter Exam at
mypoliscilab.com

This chapter has introduced you to an approach to political analysis that classifies and characterizes countries in terms of their political economies. These concepts are abstract and require the fusion of political science and economics. They are important concepts because the linkages between the political system and the economic system are fundamental and pervasive in the contemporary world. Indeed, the two systems have become so interrelated in most states that it is difficult to separate them, except in an analytic sense. There is substantial variation in the extent to which the state intervenes in the economy. In some countries, the state's role is limited, while in others the state is deeply involved in most aspects of the production and distribution of goods. Regardless of the form of the political economy, the health of its economy is crucial to every state and the impacts of the economy and economic interests on government and politics are enormous.

In considering communism or capitalism, you might find it difficult to avoid strong normative judgments due both to your political socialization and to your tendency to identify an "ism" with particular states for which you have definite positive or negative feelings. In the United States, "tea party" activists are outraged by the "socialist" policies of President Obama. In Bolivia, President Morales claims that "(t)he worst enemy of humanity is U.S. capitalism." It is certainly reasonable that you will make both analytical *and* normative judgments about the virtues and shortcomings of every form of political economy and every "ism."

Indeed, assessing the appropriateness of a country's political economy might be the most crucial issue in understanding its effectiveness in the contemporary political world. In recent years, the support for communism and the command political economy has substantially declined among the leaders and citizens in many countries. As you will see in Part Five, however, that decline has not necessarily led countries to adopt a full implementation of a market economy. It has not even meant that most political leaders and most citizens have abandoned their support for all of the principles associated with a more command-oriented political economy or more extensive redistribution of wealth.

Despite your own political socialization, you might reflect on a fundamental question: Is *every* state, regardless of its current economic and political development, best served by exactly the same political economy? If you allow for variations in the most appropriate form of political economy for countries in the current global system, you leave open many challenging and important questions about political choices, questions that will be considered from a variety of perspectives in the remainder of this book. This exploration will begin in Part Four, with chapters that examine crucial issues associated with political decision making; political, social, and economic change; and political violence.

KEY CONCEPTS

FOR FURTHER CONSIDERATION

1. The economic productivity of command political economies has always been inferior to that of market political economies in comparable countries. What, then, might have been the attraction of this approach to many groups and to many countries between the 1950s and 1970s?
2. What would be the greatest benefit to individuals if the state played almost no role in its political economy? What would be the most serious problem with such a system?
3. Are there measures, other than the growth in GDP per capita, that might indicate the success of a political economy? Why are leaders in most states so worried if there is no growth in GDP per capita?
4. Do you agree with those who contend that capitalism is so individualistic that it fails to protect the collective good?

FOR FURTHER READING

Courtois, Stephane, Nicholas Werth, Jean-Louis Panne, Adrzej Paczkowski, Karel Bartooek, and Jean-Louis Margolin. (1999). *The Black Book of Communism: Crimes, Terror, Repression*. Trans. Jonathan Murphy and Mark Cramer. Cambridge, MA: Harvard University Press. A detailed and profoundly critical analysis of the history of communism in the 20th century. Its core argument is that a series of regimes and ruthless dictators (e.g., Lenin and Stalin in the Soviet Union, Mao Zedong in China, Pol Pot in Cambodia, Kim Il Sung in North Korea) have led communist regimes that engaged in brutal "class genocide" in their societies, resulting in as many as 100 million deaths.

Friedman, Milton. (1981). *Capitalism and Freedom*. Chicago: University of Chicago Press. The major contemporary explication of the classical liberal preference for a strong market economy with only limited state intervention.

Garson, Barbara. (2003). *Money Makes the World Go Around*. New York: Penguin. The controversial social critic offers a wonderfully readable exploration of the global economy by tracking the money in two small investments and revealing how that money has various effects on people around the world.

Heilbroner, Robert. (1994). *Twenty-First Century Capitalism*. New York: W. W. Norton. An economist and social critic outlines the challenges facing capitalism and the continuing need for the state to guide the market economy and serve the social good.

Judt, Tony. (2010). *Ill Fares the Land*. New York: Penguin Press. Writing to "young people," this major scholar of social history offers an eloquent argument for the values of social democracy—collective action for collective good—in contrast to the ideology of capitalism and self-interest that dominates current thinking in the most prosperous countries and is, he argues, dangerous and destructive.

Kristol, Irving. (1978). *Two Cheers for Capitalism*. New York: Basic Books. A leading U.S. neoconservative argues that capitalism is superior to alternative forms of political economy.

Levitt, Steven D., and Stephen J. Dubner. (2010). *Super Freakonomics: Global Cooling, Patriotic Prostitutes and Why Suicide Bombers Should Buy Life Insurance*. New York: William Morrow. And now for something completely different: Like the earlier Freakonomics (2008), this book offers a playful and interesting wander through microeconomics, revealing how economic thinking can explain the impacts of incentives and public policy on individual and group behavior and (often) generates unexpected outcomes.

Lindblom, Charles E. (1977). *Politics and Markets: The World's Political-Economic Systems*. New York: Basic Books. A rich, comparative analysis of the relative merits of the political economies of modern socialism and capitalism.

Reisman, George. (1998). *Capitalism: A Treatise on Economics*. A lengthy but powerful and readable defense of laissez-faire capitalism, debunking myths about its weaknesses and critiquing rival theories, from Keynesianism to communism. Available free online at www.capitalism.net/Capitalism/CAPITALISM_Internet.pdf.

Ritholtz, Barry. (2010). *Bailout Nation: How Greed and Easy Money Corrupted Wall Street and Shook the World Economy*. New York: Wiley. Blogger and money manager Ritholtz offers a scathing and highly controversial indictment of both government policy and the behavior of profit-driven financial actors that led to the recent global economic crisis.

Roubini, Nouriel and Stephen Mihm. (2011). *Crisis Economics: A Crash Course in the Future of Economics*. New York: Penguin. A reasoned analysis of the interplay between the economic system and the political system that explains how problematic behavior of actors in both domains caused recent financial crises in many countries and must be altered or there will be an even bigger crisis soon.

Royo, Sebastian. (2002). *"A New Century of Corporatism?" Corporatism in Southern Europe—Spain and Portugal in a Comparative Perspective*. Westport, CT: Praeger. Detailed case studies of the last three decades in Spain and Portugal are the basis of an exploration of how technological and postindustrial changes have created the conditions for a resurgence of corporatism in European settings.

Westoby, Adam. (1989). *The Evolution of Communism*. New York: Free Press. A thorough and illuminating history of the development of communist thought and practice.

Yergin, Daniel, and Joseph Stanislaw (2002). *The Commanding Heights: The Battle Between Government and the Marketplace That Is Remaking the Modern World*. Rev. ed. New York: Simon and Schuster. A sweeping, readable account of how major countries in Europe, Latin America, Asia, and North America embraced extensive state intervention in their political economies in the period after World War II and then shifted from the mixed economy towards a stronger form of market economics.

Yunus, Mohammed. (2010). *Building Social Business: The New Kind of Capitalism that Serves Humanity's Most Pressing Needs*. New York: PublicAffairs. Nobel Prize winner for his innovative microcredit strategy (see Focus in 14), Yunus offers his vision of a model of "social business" which blends free market entrepreneurialism with a focus on meeting social needs.

ON THE WEB

http://imf.org

The key documents and agreements among all states and for particular members of the International Monetary Fund (IMF), an organization that includes more than 180 countries that cooperate to sustain a smoothly functioning system of interstate trade and to provide loans and other financial assistance to countries.

http://freetheworld.com

A site containing reports and data from the Economic Freedom Network, a congeries of researchers "committed to bringing economic freedom and growth to all the countries of the world."

http://www.marxists.org

The Marxists Internet Archive offers links to numerous sources that make the case against capitalism as an economic system.

http://worldbank.org

The official site of the World Bank, an international consortium of banks and other major financial institutions, includes extensive economic data regarding the structure and performance of the economies of more than 180 countries.

http://www.wto.org

The World Trade Organization (WTO), which coordinates trade policy for about 150 countries, offers this Web site to provide key documents and agreements as well as sections that articulate and justify the WTO philosophy of open trade relations among countries.

http://globalexchange.org

Dedicated to a progressive agenda, this Web site includes links to articles and a section on the global economy that emphasizes fair trade, fair loan practices, and greater equality across countries and people.

http://www.cato.org

From the Cato Institute, this site offers evidence, including various online studies and articles, for the benefits of free trade and the costs of protectionism.

www.economywatch.com

Brief characterizations of many national economic systems are provided, including data and graphics, as well as links to other sites.

http://www.weforum.org

The site of the World Economic Forum, an organization designed to allow world leaders to address global issues, contains a substantial amount of information on a variety of international economic issues (e.g., sustainable development, globalization).

http://www.capitalism.org

This libertarian-inspired site describes the core principles of a system of unconstrained, free market capitalism, including a useful glossary, links to articles, a newsletter, banners, and the unique "Capitalism Tour."

http://www.economist.com

The electronic home of *The Economist*, a leading British-based news magazine, provides access to economic data and selected articles examining issues of political economy and world finance.

Public Policy, Power, and Decision

Outside Chile's Supreme Court, police arrest a Mapuche woman protesting the long sentences imposed on four Mapuche activists who had attacked police while asserting their land rights on a

LEARNING OBJECTIVES

9.1 Differentiate among the types of public policy and outline the stages of public policy.

9.2 Identify the common elements among the three major approaches to public-policy making.

9.3 Characterize the elite approach.

9.4 Characterize the class approach.

9.5 Characterize the pluralist approach.

9.6 Evaluate the simililarities, differences, and usefulness of the three major approaches to public policy-making.

"Mapuche"— their name means "people of the land." This indigenous people of Chile has sustained its nation-based identity for many centuries. They fought the Inca Empire to a standstill in the 1400s, and drove back the Spanish conquistadores from their land in the 1500s. But in the late 19th century, a substantial part of the land claimed by the Mapuche in southern Chile was acquired by outsiders, especially large agricultural barons, small farmers, and multinational logging companies.

Since the middle of the 20th century, the Mapuche have persistently urged the Chilean government to enact policies that respond to their claims regarding their land rights, the protection of their cultural identity, and their desire for greater political autonomy. The Mapuche do have some resources for influencing government policy. With 600,000 people, they hold some electoral clout. Chile is one of only 22 countries that have ratified the United Nations' Indigenous and Tribal Peoples Convention (1989), which pledges to promote the rights of groups like the Mapuche. Also, the center-left coalition that dominated Chilean politics from 1988–2010 expressed some sympathy for the Mapuche claims. And in 1998, the Mapuche established Coordinadora Arauco-Malleco (CAM), an interest group to coordinate their political actions.

However, the political forces lined up against the goals of the Mapuche are formidable. There are some elites in Chile who are directly opposed to the Mapuche's land claims. In particular, the wealthy landowners and multinational logging interests who currently hold Mapuche lands have considerable influence with key elected political leaders in the executive and legislative branches and with senior appointed officials in the administration. More broadly, the general Chilean population is not particularly sympathetic to the Mapuche claims that the national government should grant them political autonomy. Although they are a sizeable subgroup, the Mapuche constitute only 5 percent of the Chilean population, and most of them are poor, landless peasants who lack political skills or the will to mobilize into political action.

Thus, proposed legislation to expropriate land and return it to the Mapuche generated substantial opposition and was defeated in the legislature. Chile's

Read and **Listen** to Chapter 9 at **mypoliscilab.com**

✔ **Study** and **Review** the Pre-Test & Flashcards at **mypoliscilab.com**

president, who initially supported their claim, dropped his advocacy. As a concession, the government did purchase a small amount of land (8,000 hectares) which was distributed to the Mapuche. But the redistribution program was very limited, because most landowners demanded high prices to sell their land to the Mapuche, and the government was unwilling to pay that amount or to force them to lower their price. Similarly, the government allocated only a modest amount of funds to support the maintenance of Mapuche cultural traditions.

Then in 2010, the coalition that gained a majority of the seats in the national legislature shifted to include several conservative groups, including Alianza por Chile, that promote a single national identity for all Chileans and insist that the government should aggressively punish the illegal activities of the Mapuche. Thus, the Mapuche remain frustrated by their lack of success in persuading government to respond favorably to their policy agenda. Since their policy demands have not been achieved through normal political channels, some of their activists continue to engage in unconventional political actions. This has included hunger strikes, demonstrations, and some violence. For example, a group of Mapuche occupied a farm that was being minimally used. When they refused to leave, the government was pressured by local landowners to intervene, and its security forces were dispatched to reclaim the property. The confrontation became violent, and an unarmed 22-year-old Mapuche student was shot in the back by the police. Within the next year, more young Mapuche activists were killed as they engaged in several other political protests.

The Chilean government has attempted to calm the volatile situation. It has appointed special commissions to investigate the issues and develop new policy initiatives. The government has made decisions intended to satisfy the policy agenda of the Mapuche as well as those who oppose their demands. But the Mapuche simply do not have as much political clout as their opponents. Thus, the political goals pursued by the "people of the land" remain largely unfulfilled and unpromising.

Recall from Chapter 1 that the core definitions of politics focus on the competition among individuals and groups who utilize power and influence to pursue their interests on issues controlled by public authorities. The attempts by the Mapuche to regain their lands and preserve their cultural autonomy are clearly within the domain of *res publica* in Chile. As the Mapuche engaged in politics, other groups who had a competing agenda also mobilized. Policy decisions were made by the government. The Mapuche got some of what they sought, but not much. Other groups seem to have been more successful.

Considering the story of the Mapuche raises one of the most obvious yet fascinating general questions in political science: *How does politics actually work?* That is, how does a political system handle the incredibly difficult and complicated issues and the competing demands that are the stuff of politics? How and why do actors in the political system decide to deal in one way or another on issues like these? Who has political power and influence and how are they exercised?

If someone from another country asked you how major public policy decisions are made in your country, what would you say? What key points would you emphasize? Presumably, your response would include a discussion of certain important actors and how they utilize power and influence within the context of the key political institutions that make such public policy decisions.

Earlier chapters introduced many of these actors and institutions—political activists, interest groups, legislatures, legal systems, and so on. And they characterized concepts such as power and analytic models such as the political system framework. This chapter expands the discussion by focusing explicitly on several fundamental approaches for analyzing public policy and the exercise of political power. Initially, the chapter explicates the concept of "public policy," with a consideration of taxonomies and frameworks that characterize the public policy process. It then describes three basic theories (elite, class, and pluralist theories) that provide alternative explanations of how public policy decisions are made and how the distribution of power shapes that decision process.

PUBLIC POLICY

A public policy is *any decision or action by a governmental authority that results in the allocation of something that is valued.* Earlier chapters indicated that each political system establishes how extensively and in what forms its public policies will define *res publica* and impact its environment. These public policy decisions range enormously: in substantive area, in scale, in significance, in the number of people affected, and in the role of the policymakers. A national government can decide to declare war on a rival country or to commend a victorious sports team. A local government employee can decide to fill a pothole or to issue a building permit to a homeowner. The government representatives of many countries can hammer out a joint treaty to limit greenhouse gases. A security unit can arrest a suspected terrorist. A government can pass a law making sex among certain consenting adults illegal. The Chilean government can decide to allocate some land to the Mapuche or to use force to drive them off someone's private property. Each of these actions is an example of a "public policy."

Table 9.1 and Compare in 9 offer some representative examples of current public policy decisions made by seven national political systems. The Compare claims that there is considerable policy variation across these countries. Do you agree? Beyond these kinds of direct comparisons of public policies, there are several other approaches to the study of public policy. One approach is to classify and compare various *types* of public policies by means of a taxonomy. A second approach analyzes the various stages of the policy *process* and attempts to explain the dynamics at each stage. A third approach studies the *impacts* of a particular public policy because what matters, ultimately, is how (if at all) the policy makes a difference in the lives of individuals and groups. Finally, a fourth general approach is more *prescriptive*, evaluating what public policy ought to be implemented, given existing goals, conditions, and resources. We can start by considering the types of public policies.

9.1 Differentiate among the types of public policy and outline the stages of public policy.

Explore the Comparative "Health Systems" on mypoliscilab.com

Types of Public Policies

Several criteria are used to classify different types of public policies. For example, a straightforward classification of policies is based on the *functional area* that is served, such as education, health, transportation, trade, public safety, the environment, or defense. Alternatively, policies can be distinguished by the broad

TABLE 9.1

Selected Public Policies in Seven National Political Systems

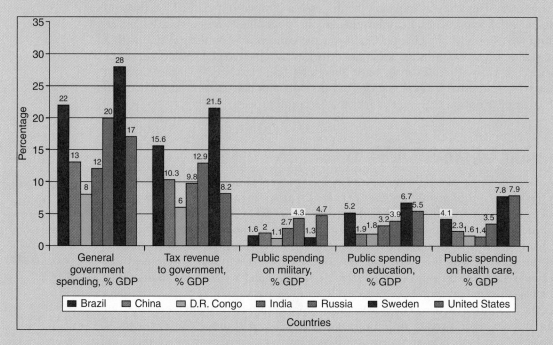

	Brazil	China	D.R. Congo	India	Russia	Sweden	United States
Policy on abortion	Only to save life or after rape	Yes, on multiple grounds	Only to save life	Yes, on multiple grounds	Yes, on multiple grounds	Yes, on multiple grounds	Yes, on multiple grounds; varies by state
Policy on death penalty	No, since 1889	Yes, for 60 crimes, ~2,000/ year	Yes, but few known recent cases	Yes, but few known recent cases	Yes , but moratorium since 1998	No, since 1921	Yes, in 36 of 50 states, ~50/ year
Mandatory military service	Yes	Yes, but not enforced	No	No	Yes	No	No

Sources: CIA (2011); UNDP (2009); WDI (2009); Tradingeconomics.com (2009); Amnesty International (2011); http://www.un.org/esa/population/publications/abortion/doc/unitedstates.doc

objective of the policy: (1) *distributive* policies provide particular goods and services (e.g., the building and maintenance of a system of streets and highways); (2) *redistributive* policies explicitly transfer values from one group to another group (e.g., a policy that provides subsidized housing to those with limited financial resources); (3) *regulatory* policies limit actions (e.g., a policy that prohibits

COMPARE IN 9 | Selected Public Policies in Seven Countries

Over time, do different political systems make substantially different public policy decisions? To explore this briefly, Table 9.1 provides examples of broad public policy decisions made by seven national political systems. The expenditure data are reported as the percentage of each country's total GDP (gross domestic product) that is allocated to a policy domain by all levels of government. This is an indicator of policy effort, given the country's overall wealth. The tax revenue measure is an extractive policy, while the other expenditure measures are distributive policies. The three nonmonetary policies are regulatory, regarding certain rights and freedoms of individuals relative to state power.

The broadest conclusion from these data is that there are considerable differences in public policy decisions across the seven countries. On every specific policy domain, the country with the highest proportion allocates at least three times as much as the lowest. Each country has developed its own distinctive pattern of public policies, which are particularly grounded in the country's needs, wealth, and dominant political ideologies. For example, Sweden is a wealthy country that has a long tradition of democratic socialism and the provision of social welfare goods to its population (see Compare in 13). Thus, Sweden allocates a substantially higher proportion of its societal wealth through government spending than any of the other countries, with a particular focus on education and health care. To pay for all these public services, Sweden also collects the highest proportion of taxes. Sweden has progressive policies on abortion and capital punishment and stopped requiring military (or community) service in 2010.

In contrast, Congo is a very poor country with an ineffective government, extensive corruption, and a postcolonial history of violence, both internally and across its borders (see Focus in 11). Thus, it is not surprising that its government is able to collect the smallest proportion of the nation's wealth in taxes and allocates the lowest proportion of the country's wealth to government spending. Given the

insecurity and political violence Congo experiences, a substantial proportion of available tax revenues is allocated to the military and there are very low levels of spending on education, health care, and many other public services. It is perhaps surprising that Congo does not have mandatory military service. However, the military is one of the few reliable, relatively well-paying jobs available to many Congolese men, and thus the government has not needed to resort to a compulsory draft. Because the capabilities of the Congo's central government are so weak, there is little enforcement of many public policies, such as the prohibition on abortions.

It is also interesting to compare Brazil, Russia, India, and China, the four "BRIC" countries that are potentially advancing towards global power status. Although each is attempting to project its military power within its region, India and Russia allocate almost twice as much of total societal wealth on their militaries as Brazil or China. Brazil places more emphasis on education and health, while China focuses on economic development and infrastructure.

The level of funds allocated is one way to compare policy decisions. It is also important to consider how the money is spent. For example, what are the key targets of health care spending (e.g., disease prevention, infant health, medical training, HIV-positive people, hospitals)? Is public spending on education emphasizing teachers' salaries or student-teacher ratios or educational technologies or . . .? The manner in which a public policy is implemented is also significant for policies that are not primarily measurable in terms of money. For instance, the Chinese government not only allows abortion, it has aggressively encouraged and facilitated abortion in an attempt to control population growth. In contrast, legal abortion is severely limited in Brazil and is a deeply controversial policy domain in the United States.

And while comparing policy outputs is meaningful, the most important comparisons might be of the *impacts* of policies. That is, what is the effect of public spending on health care on indicators

(Continued)

such as life expectancy and infant mortality rates? Does an increased level of military spending seem to increase a country's security? Which groups carry the burden of taxes and which do not? Does spending in one policy area (e.g., health care) provide indirect benefits to another policy area (e.g., education)? What is the effect of the policy of capital punishment if there is a moratorium on using it (as in Russia since 1998)? Table 9.1 and these kinds of questions should help you to see the rich and complex considerations that are relevant when you attempt to compare public policies within and across political systems.

FURTHER QUESTIONS

1. On what public policy do you think it would be most interesting to study cross-national differences in policy implementation? Why? What might you learn?

2. Which two countries in Table 9.1 seem to have the most similar configuration of policy allocations? ◣

a woman from having an abortion); (4) *extractive* policies take resources from some actors (e.g., a sales tax on purchases); and (5) *symbolic* policies confer honor or disrepute on certain actors (e.g., a medal awarded to a soldier for bravery).

Analysis of the Stages of the Policy Process

A different approach to policy analysis examines the *stages of the policy process— the sequence of actions from the inception of an idea for policy to the point where the policy ceases to exist*. A policy can be analyzed at each stage: what actors participate, how they interact, how the policy is defined, and so on. Many public policy analyses focus on one specific stage and explore the dynamics of that stage of policymaking in detail (Andersen 2010; Bardach 2008). Six stages are usually distinguished, as characterized in Figure 9.1, and described below. And to provide a concrete example of the policy process, Table 9.2 indicates how the issue of poor reading scores in a school district might evolve during the policy process.

1. **Issue identification.** Some actor decides that a condition in the environment requires a public policy response. For example, the national legislature decides that personal income taxes are too high, a group of residents complains to the county board of supervisors that traffic congestion has become a serious problem in their neighborhood, the defense department gets secret intelligence that a rival state is developing a new nuclear weapons system. If important policymakers push the policy issue forward at this point, it becomes part of the agenda for possible action. Alternatively, policymakers might decide to drop the issue at this stage.

2. **Problem definition.** Next, there is an attempt to explain why the problem exists, to determine what seem to be the causes of the problem, and to define desired outcomes. Expert staff as well as interested stakeholders with knowledge of the policy domain can have a major role at this stage, which emphasizes research and analysis.

3. **Specification of alternatives.** Policy analysts develop policy proposals that seem to respond to the problem, given the causes, the preferred outcome, and

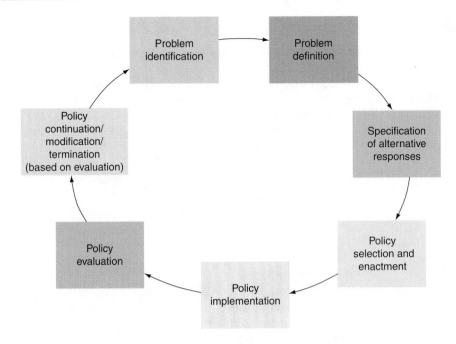

FIGURE 9.1
The stages of the public policy process

the likely obstacles. In addition, the resources necessary to implement each policy alternative are identified. The costs (e.g., financial, political, organizational) of each alternative policy must be estimated, as well as the level of expected benefits.

4. **Policy selection.** Decision makers assess the alternatives, trying to assess the possible costs and benefits from the options. At this stage, the process will be some mix of political, financial, and technical considerations. The decision might be to enact a particular policy, to delay, or to do nothing and see if the policy issue disappears from the public agenda. Considerable negotiations, lobbying, compromises, and adjustments to the proposed policy might occur during this stage.

5. **Implementation.** The policy is now interpreted and applied in specific contexts. Those in relevant administrative positions typically take the lead role, determining how to translate the new policy into actual programs and activities, organize the necessary resources, and then deliver those programs.

6. **Evaluation.** After some period of time (or never), new information is gathered to ascertain whether the policy has had any of the anticipated impacts, whether conditions (related to the policy domain or the political situation) have changed, and whether any unintended effects of the policy must be considered.

At any stage, but especially after implementation or evaluation, the policy might be continued, modified, or terminated. It is also possible that the circumstances might trigger another cycle of the policy process outlined above, possibly beginning with a new stage of issue identification.

> **TABLE 9.2**

An Example of Each Stage of the Policy Process: Reading Skills of Children

Stage	Action
Problem identification	Data indicate reading scores of children are too low.
Problem definition	Set goal: Raise mean reading scores of sixth-grade children by 10 percent in three years.
	Reading scores decline steadily in grades 2–5.
	Low reading scores are especially associated with families where English is not the first language.
	Seven schools where more than 20 percent of students come from such families have lowest average reading scores.
Specification of alternatives	Target: Seven lowest scoring schools or apply programs to all schools?
	Policy initiative:
	• Intensive reading instruction in grades 3–5.
	• Provide teachers with training in reading pedagogy.
	• Provide reading specialist teachers.
	• Provide computer-aided learning software.
	• Require an extra 30 minutes of reading instruction per day.
	• Or. . . .
Policy selection	Local school board decides:
	• Focus only on 7 lowest scoring schools.
	• Provide three new reading specialists to work with students.
	• Allocate funds to target schools for computer-based reading instruction software.
Implementation	School superintendent meets with principals of target schools and they decide how to distribute the time of the reading specialists across the schools and classrooms.
	Committee of principals will select and hire specialists.
	Interschool technology committee trains teachers to use reading software, principals require teachers to develop a plan for its use, and teachers implement it in the classrooms.
Evaluation	Changes in reading scores will be analyzed by district staff in each of the next three years.
	Teachers will provide written report on the effects of the new initiatives on the classroom.
	Continuation of the two policies will be reevaluated after year 2 and year 3.

Policy Impact Analysis

The last stage of the policy process described above, evaluation, is an especially significant mode of policy analysis. As noted in Compare in 9, a crucial question is: What difference did the policy make? This can be considered in different ways.

What have been the direct effects of the policy? Have there also been notable indirect effects? Who benefits and who experiences negative effects from this policy? What are the nature and extent of those benefits and burdens? What have been the actual costs compared with the anticipated costs? On balance, has the policy improved the overall situation? These questions about the impacts of a policy might be addressed by policymakers and their staffs or by various other actors, such as interest groups, affected publics, and political rivals.

Policy Prescription

Every public policy affects someone's interests. Thus, there are always actors (stakeholders) trying to influence and shape public policy decisions at every stage and to influence policymakers to make some decisions and not others. As actors define and then pursue a policy goal, they are also engaged in *policy prescription*. Their policy goal might be based on careful policy analysis and policy impact studies, or derived from ideological principles, or influenced by an agent of political socialization or an authority source such as a political party or political leader (recall Chapters 2–4). Whatever the basis of their policy prescriptions, policy advocates propose what public policies *should* be adopted and how policy *should* be implemented: the Chilean government should respond to the land claims of the Mapuche by policy A; the U.S. government should implement policy B to respond to job losses; the government of India should adopt policy C to improve the health of its millions of rural poor.

A key analytic question regarding the public policy process is: How does the process lead to certain decisions and not others? The next section explores this question from three very different perspectives that attempt to explain how political power is distributed and wielded by various groups who participate in the policymaking process.

EXPLAINING PUBLIC POLICY DECISION MAKING

The first part of this chapter described analytic concepts that specify the stages in the public policy process. This section details three "political" explanations of the public policy process: (1) the elite approach, (2) the class approach, and (3) the pluralist approach. Each approach provides a different explanation of how politics works, how influence is exercised, and what forces seem to shape the decisions that result in public policy. No actual country or political system is likely to operate exactly like any of these three approaches. Rather, each approach is a rich illustration of a pattern of power and decision making that is prevalent in some systems. The three approaches share two important analytic features:

9.2 Identify the common elements among the three major approaches to public-policy making.

1. All three are constitutive approaches (as a type of functional analysis; see the Appendix) in the sense that each attempts to define *the* fundamental unit of analysis that explains politics.
2. All three explain politics in terms of the interactions among aggregations of individuals who use the political system to pursue their own particular interests.

Our discussion begins with the elite approach.

THE ELITE APPROACH

Key Concepts

9.3 Characterize the elite approach.

Two key concepts are central to the elite approach. First, *politics* is defined as *the struggle for power to control policy.* Second, the political world is characterized by *political stratification;* that is, *the population is segmented into separate groups that are in layers (or "strata") with higher or lower amounts of power.* In the elite approach, there are only two major strata. The stratum that *does more of what there is to do* (in the public policy process) and that *gets more of what there is to get* (in valued impacts from policy decisions) is called the political elite. The stratum that *does less and gets less* is called the *mass.*

Elite theory can be visually represented by a power pyramid, as shown in Figure 9.2. Such a depiction emphasizes that the elite is composed of a relatively small number of individuals who are in a dominant position on top of the large mass. Notice that there is a third stratum between the elite and the mass. This is the *political understructure,* composed of *political officials and administrators who carry out the elite's policy directives.*

Major Theorists

The elite approach is particularly grounded in the writings of European political theorists of the late 19th century, especially the Italians Roberto Michels, Wilfredo Pareto, and Gaetano Mosca. In *The Ruling Class* (1896/1939), Mosca analyzes the political histories of a variety of political systems and concludes that they all

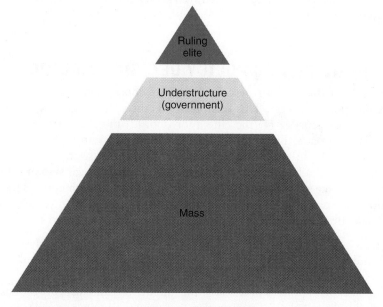

FIGURE 9.2
Characterization of an elite system

have two strata: the political class (the elite) and the nonpolitical class (the mass). The political class controls all political functions, holds almost all political power, and dominates the public policy process. The basis of elite power has varied across time and location, but Mosca identifies broad historical stages during which the primary basis of elite domination has been military power, then religious control, then economic power, and most recently, technical knowledge. According to Mosca, the major role of the political system is as an instrument of the political class, serving the elite's interests in making and implementing public policies.

A well-known U.S. application of the elite approach is *The Power Elite* (1956) by C. Wright Mills. Mills concludes that the power elite in U.S. society is composed of those who control society's most powerful institutions: (1) the "warlords" in the military establishment, (2) the "corporation chieftains" in the economic sector, and (3) the "political directorate" in the top positions in the political system. Mills observes that the members of the elite share crucial values about how society in general, and the political system in particular, ought to operate. The members of the elite tend to come from similar social and educational backgrounds, to circulate among major positions in each of the three key institutional structures, and to have long-standing personal relationships with each other. Like other elite theorists, Mills does not claim that the elite operates as a conspiracy that continually plots to retain control. But some of its active members do meet periodically to discuss common interests, and most of its members act in concert to protect their shared interests during times of crisis (see also Domhoff 2005, 2009).

Most elite theorists focus on the elite itself—the identity and socialization of elite members—and on how the elite maintains its domination through a variety of techniques, such as the manipulation of symbols, the strategic distribution of resources to various groups, control of the state, and the use of force. There is a normative element in the discussions of many elite theorists, indicating their disapproval of a system in which there is such a high concentration of political power serving only a small minority within society. But others respond that elite theory merely reveals the inevitable tendency for a few people to take control and to dominate the political order, while those in the mass willingly subordinate themselves to the few who are capable of giving coherence to political society.

The Public Policy Process

The process through which values are allocated is explained primarily in terms of the elite's actions. Some members of the elite decide that a particular public policy decision is in the elite's interest. They then discuss whether this policy should be enacted and how it should be implemented. When there is general consensus among those members of the elite who are concerned about the decision, representatives of the elite instruct the relevant members of the understructure (the government) to perform the policymaking and policy-implementation activities that serve the elite's interests.

In the elite explanation of the policy process, the active elites are subject to very little direct influence from the mass or even from the understructure of governmental officials. The mass is politically apathetic and impotent, and this large proportion of the population passively accepts whatever policies are imposed upon them. The members of the understructure follow the elite's directives because they believe that their survival in positions of authority depends on the power and support of the elite.

The Prevalence of Elite-Based Political Systems

How many countries have elitist political systems? As noted in Chapter 7, at least two-fifths of contemporary countries (containing more than half the world's population) are nondemocratic systems. It seems reasonable to infer that most of these systems are dominated by an elite in the manner described by the elite approach.

However, the issue might be more complicated. Is it true that all the key conditions of elitism are met in every nondemocratic country? This empirical question could be examined in specific political systems (e.g., Cuba, Saudi Arabia, and Zimbabwe) by assessing these kinds of analytic questions:

- Does the political leadership act with unanimity on all major issues?
- Is there active and effective political participation by nonelite groups?
- Are some major political decisions responsive to nonelite demands, even when the decisions are contrary to the elite's interests?
- Is there dramatic inequality in the distribution of resources between the elite and the mass?

▶ FOCUS IN 9 | Elite Politics in Swaziland

A contemporary example of elite politics is Swaziland, a small African country between Mozambique and South Africa. While Swaziland was a British colonial protectorate (1902–1968), a local king (Sobuza II) became a hero of his people by leading the movement for independence (starting in 1921). After independence in 1968, Sobuza became the ruling monarch of the new country. A British-style parliament with competing parties was installed. Parties competed in three parliamentary elections, although the king's party dominated in each election.

In 1973, the king banned all opposition groups and declared that European government forms were "un-Swazi." The king personally appoints two-thirds of the members of the Senate and one-fourth of the members in the House. Indeed, according to Swaziland's official publications, even the method for selecting the next king is "a secret," except it is stipulated that he must be a young, unmarried prince.

When Sobuza II died in 1982, the private power struggle among members of the royal family and the king's council resulted in the selection of King Mswati III. He has been termed "the world's last absolute monarch," and although a few concessions to opposition activities were made in recent years, political parties are still banned, and the nonpartisan parliament essentially affirms the king's decisions.

Everyone in Swaziland has always understood that real political power is concentrated in the king and his elite group of advisers, known as the National Council. Young King Mswati III quickly removed many of his rivals from positions of authority and elevated his own set of trusted advisers to positions of decision-making power. Under King Mswati III, as under King Sobuza, both policymaking and the major sectors of the economy (the mines and most farmlands) are directly controlled by a king's council. Thus, one

(Continued)

A day after being called back from high school in England and being crowned as the ruler of Swaziland, King Mswati III attends a party in the palace. The 18-year-old king moved quickly to establish rule under his personal control.

key criterion of elite politics is clearly met: Almost all major political decisions are made by a small group, and the mass of people in Swaziland have little direct impact on the policies or politics of the state.

Most of the benefits of policy are enjoyed by this elite, a second key criterion of an elite system. The richest 10 percent of the Swazi population have one of the world's highest shares of total income (41 percent), and the country has a high level of income inequality (recall Table 8.2). In contrast, fully 69 percent of the Swazi population are below the poverty line and 40 percent of adults are unemployed. Swaziland has the world's highest incidence (one in four) of adults with HIV/AIDS, and the average life expectancy is only 49 years, among the bottom five among 222 countries (CIA 2011).

FURTHER FOCUS

1. Is inequality or nondemocracy likely to be a more serious problem for maintaining stability in Swaziland?

2. Are there any reasons why a country might be better off if it is governed by a small elite?

While definitive answers to these questions are difficult, our knowledge of political systems suggests that many contemporary states are generally characterized by elite rule. (Consider the brief description of Swaziland in Focus in 9). The power to make crucial political decisions and most benefits from those decisions do seem predominantly concentrated in the hands of a small elite.

It is also possible to ask whether a country classified as a democracy is actually run by an elite. That is, even if a political system meets the basic criteria of democracy such as a limited mandate and freedom to criticize and oppose the leadership (recall Chapter 7), does this necessarily mean that the system is not elitist?

This question underlies a fierce debate among analysts regarding whether the elite approach best describes politics, even in many "democratic" political systems. Some, such as C. Wright Mills (1956; see also Parenti 2010), provide arguments and evidence that there is elite rule even in most democracies. In this view, a small proportion of the population dominates most significant political decisions and enjoys a hugely disproportionate share of the benefits from the truly important policy decisions made by the government.

Such empirical assessments of the elite approach, whether for a single city or an entire country, are highly controversial and ideologically charged because they represent a direct attack on whether the place is a democracy. Conclusive verification of the elite approach in most political systems would be a massive undertaking, requiring the documentation of systematic elite dominance on a large number of key decisions across a variety of issue areas.

THE CLASS APPROACH

9.4 Characterize the class approach.

Watch the Video "Contesting Political Cultures in Britain" at mypoliscilab.com

The class approach shares certain fundamental concepts with the elite approach, but it offers a very different explanation of the continuing dynamic processes of politics. The most important shared concept is *stratification*, the basic fact of *structured inequality* in the distribution of values in society.

The strata identified in the class approach are called classes, the second key concept. *Class* denotes *a large group of individuals who are similar in their possession of or control over some fundamental value*. The most fundamental value that distinguishes classes differs for different class theorists. Karl Marx (1818–1883), the best-known class theorist, differentiates classes primarily on the basis of a group's relationship to the major factors of production in the economic system (Marx 1867/1981: Ch. 52). At the simplest level, Marx divides society into two classes: (1) the *capitalist class*, which includes those who own significant amounts of the major factors of production (especially financial resources, raw materials, and capital—the elements to produce goods and accumulate wealth); and (2) the *proletariat class*, which includes those who own little more than their own labor.

Some contemporary analysts suggest various modifications to Marx's ideas about class. First, most class theorists identify more than two major class strata, with each class characterized by its particular levels of social, political, and economic power. Second, some argue that it is *control* (rather than ownership) of the means of production that is most important. Third, others observe that in certain social systems, the key elements that distinguish different class strata are status, kinship, ethnicity, religion, or tradition-based authority (rather than ownership of the means of production). And fourth, still others posit that possession of information resources and knowledge has become the crucial resource distinguishing classes in postindustrial, high-tech societies (Castells 2009). In general, these analysts assert that there is strong empirical evidence for the continuing prevalence of class politics, even in developed countries and even in the 21st century (see, for example, Poulantzas 1973; Shayo 2009; Wright 1998).

Figure 9.3 provides two models characterizing class systems. Part A shows a characterization similar to the elite approach in its hierarchical and pyramidal form, and it emphasizes a clear separation between multiple classes. Alternatively, part B highlights the overlap among classes. Here the boundaries between classes are permeable rather than distinct, there is more interdependence among classes, and some members of a "lower" class have as much or even more political power than those in the class above them. However, class domination continues to be the basic form of political and social relations (see Lenski 1966: 284).

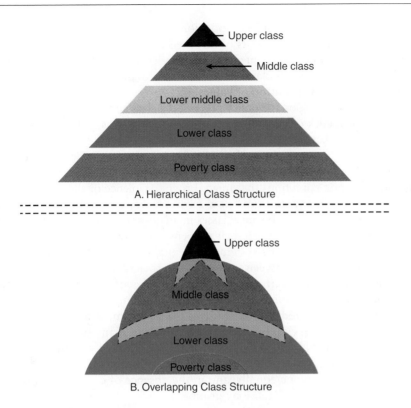

FIGURE 9.3
Two different characterizations of class structures
Source: Based on Bill and Hardgrave 1981: 181.

The third crucial concept of the class approach is ***class conflict.*** It is assumed that classes lower in the class system can increase their share of key values only at the expense of the classes above them. Given the fundamental inequalities in the distribution of values, struggle between classes is inevitable. The higher classes employ various strategies, and ultimately coercion, to prevent a significant loss of values (and of relative advantage) to the classes below them. Lower classes find that only violence enables their class to increase its relative share of values. Thus, class conflict is systematic and ubiquitous, although its most visible and violent manifestations (such as strikes, riots, and rebellion) might be suppressed for periods of time if the higher classes are effective in the ways they distribute benefits and use coercion.

The Public Policy Process

Most class analysts do not explain in detail how policy decisions are actually made. They assume that the common interests shared by members of a class will result in general consensus within that class regarding what public policy decisions should be enacted. Like elite theorists, class analysts view the political system as a set of structures that are subordinate to the dominant class. Thus, members of this dominant class either hold key positions of governing authority or directly control those who do. The interests of this class are well understood by those who can enact public policy. Consequently, the policies and actions of the state serve the interests of the dominant class, which attempts to maintain its domination and preserve the existing distribution of values.

Rather than focusing on the policy process, the class approach centers its analytic attention on the tactics of class domination and the dynamics of the class struggle. Not every public policy decision by the state is coercive or of direct benefit to only the dominant class. The state might implement policies to shorten the length of the working day or to increase health care benefits to the middle classes. Such policies either ameliorate the worst conditions that might provoke violence or they provide certain classes with advantages over classes below them. The goals of such public policies are strategic: to provide benefits to some classes in an effort to buy their support or their acquiescence, or at least to dampen their propensity for conflict.

Despite such strategies, the systematic inequalities in fundamental values generate continuing conflict between classes in the society. Periodically, this conflict explodes into class violence. In one of these episodes of class war, a lower class succeeds in overthrowing the highest class. At this point, a new class gains dominance in the system, including control over the government and the most of the benefits from public policies. In the view of Marx and many other class theorists, major class conflict will end only when the elimination of dominant classes reduces the system to a single class, and hence society becomes classless. The state's policies then serve everyone equally, and in the absence of class inequalities, there is no cause for further conflict among groups.

THE PLURALIST APPROACH

9.5 Characterize the pluralist approach.

Explore the Comparative "Governments and Public Opinion" on mypoliscilab.com

Pluralism offers a very different account of the political process, in which *multiple groups compete actively in the pursuit of their political interests.* The pluralist approach is grounded in the concept of the **group,** which is defined as *any aggregate of individuals who interact to pursue a common interest.* A political group, as an analytic concept, exists whenever individuals have a shared interest regarding some allocation of values by the political system.

The pluralist explanation of politics as a complex web of group interactions has many historical roots, but is particularly identified with American social scientists, especially political scientists Arthur Bentley (1908/1967), David Truman (1951), and Robert Dahl (1961, 1971, 1991), who is most strongly associated with the development and defense of pluralism (which is also sometimes termed polyarchy or the group approach).

Pluralism begins with the assumption that an individual's *group memberships are multiple and nonoverlapping.* That is, any particular individual can belong to many different groups. Individuals are not stratified into large, permanent groups as described by the elite and class approaches because the aggregation of people who share a common identity on one political interest is not the same as the people who are part of groups formed for other political interests. Table 9.3 shows six hypothetical people whose group memberships overlap in different ways, depending on the issue.

TABLE 9.3

Group Memberships of Six Hypothetical Individuals in the United States*

Groups	Person 1	Person 2	Person 3	Person 4	Person 5	Person 6
			Individuals			
Democratic Party	✓				✓	
Republican Party		✓	✓			
AFL-CIO union	✓					
Family Research Council			✓			✓
Mothers Against Drunk Driving		✓			✓	✓
NARAL Pro-Choice America	✓	✓	✓			
National Rifle Association	✓		✓			
Parent-Teacher Association	✓	✓				

*Each checkmark indicates a group with which the individual is affiliated. This distribution supports the concept of nonoverlapping (nonreinforcing) group memberships. An individual shares membership with different people across various groups and policy domains.

The second important assumption is that *many different political resources might influence those who make public policy decisions.* As discussed in Chapter 3, the kinds of resources that might be used to influence political decisions include money, numbers of supporters/voters, monopoly of expertise, political skill, access to information, legal rights, and status. It is also assumed that every individual (and hence every political group) has some political resources with which he can attempt to influence policy decisions.

In pluralism, politics can be understood as *the interaction among groups that are pursuing their political interests.* The role of the government is to manage the interactions within this giant system of interacting groups. Thus, public policy is defined as *the balance point of the competition among groups on an issue at the time when government makes a policy decision.*

The Policymaking Process

Figure 9.4 provides a visual model of how a policy decision is made according to pluralism, using health care policy in a country such as the United States as the example. There is a continuum of possible policies, ranging from free state provision of all health care services to every citizen at one extreme to total private provision based on fee-for-service to each recipient of health care at the other extreme.

The analytic framework of the policy process in pluralism can be summarized in five major steps:

1. Identify the key groups that have an active interest in decisions in this policy area.
2. On a continuum of possible policy outcomes, locate the preferred policy decision of each group.

In many societies, policy decisions are made through discussion and voting by local groups, as in this *jirga* (tribal meeting) in rural Pakistan.

3. Estimate the level of political resources each group employs to influence the decision regarding this policy (represented as a "weight" on the continuum, based on the total impact of the political resources that the group utilizes).
4. The government establishes the equilibrium point that balances the "weights" of the political resources mobilized by all groups.
5. This equilibrium point on the policy continuum is authorized by government as a public policy decision.

In the pluralist model, the particular functions of the government are to (1) establish rules of the game for the group struggle, (2) determine the interests of competing groups and the levels of political resources mobilized by those groups, (3) find a public policy that approximately balances the positions of all active groups in terms of their interests and resources, (4) enact these balance points as public policy decisions, and (5) implement the resulting policy. Government, as an analytic construct in pluralism, is best understood as a referee (a neutral arbiter) in the competition among groups.

In a more realistic interpretation, however, government is not merely an automatic weighing machine that totals the value of each group's influence resources. The government might have an ideological position and thus

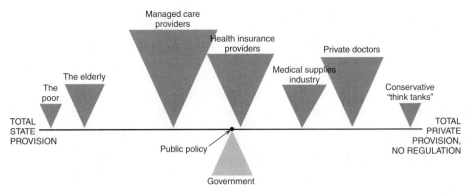

Symbols:

— = Continuum of possible public policies regarding health care policy

▼ = Interest group mobilized on this issue, with volume of triangle representing the group's political resources applied to the issue

▲ = Government, which determines the equilibrium point and ratifies that point as public policy

● = Public policy position, which is the equilibrium point in the competition among groups, given each group's political resources

FIGURE 9.4

A group approach model of the policy process: a hypothetical policy decision

place greater emphasis on some objectives rather than others. For example, the government might enforce rules that help or hinder some groups in using their political resources, it might value some political resources more substantially than others, it might allow certain groups greater access to important information, or it might be more or less willing to find the financial resources necessary to implement a certain policy. In addition, certain elected and career governmental actors have their own personal and institutional interests (e.g., for political support, for growth of their unit's power, for personal wealth). When such interests are relevant, these actors can become active as groups that participate in the decision process (with obvious advantages because they are inside "the system").

Like all models, Figure 9.4 substantially simplifies reality. But it should help you to understand the logic of pluralism. A policy decision can change at any time if a different distribution of group interests is mobilized and the issue is taken up by policymakers. Pluralism explicitly rejects the notion that a small elite or a single class dominates the public policy process. Rather, many different groups become active in politics, but only on the narrow range of issues relevant to their interests. Mobilized groups use their political resources to affect the decision. While a group might not always win, its participation can affect the policy decisions made in the area. In the case that opened the chapter, for example, it seems that although the Mapuche only got a small part of what they wanted, they did utilize their political resources and the Chilean government did grant them some land rights. And, pluralist theorists would argue, the Mapuche achieved some success against strong opponents and will have more opportunities to pursue their goals at the next round of policy making.

Critics of pluralism argue that some groups *are* likely to win almost every time they play the game of politics because they have a huge advantage in their political resources, such as wealth, access to decision makers, and political skill. Further, some challenge the pluralist assumption that no one resource always dominates, arguing that money trumps all other resources. This argument is the subject of the Debate in 9. The critics also claim that the government/state, far from being neutral, is guided by a strong ideology and is almost always responsive to those upper strata groups with most economic and social power in the society. Thus, even though "the little people" might occasionally win a particular episode, the powerful groups in the system are persistent winners, and big winners, and the system perpetuates very substantial inequalities in the distribution of benefits (Bachrach and Baratz 1962; Parenti 2010). While the relatively poor Mapuche were appeased with a small amount of land, the big winners were the rich and powerful landowners and logging companies, who continued to profit from land that should have been returned to its original owners.

THE DEBATE IN 9 | Does Money Dominate the Policymaking Process?

Some are convinced that money dominates politics, even in the most properly run democracies. Class theory is particularly pointed in its arguments that the power and actions of the dominant economic class ensure that government and policy decisions serve its interests (Domhoff 2009). In contrast, pluralist theory argues that while money is one important resource that can influence the policy process, no one resource dominates. Other key political resources that can shape policy decisions include large numbers of people who can use their votes, the media, and the legal system. Everyone can form interest groups to promote their political goals. Everyone can win in the competition over policy decisions, at least some of the time, and the wealthy do not get everything they want (Dahl 1961; 1991). If we consider the country celebrated as the inspiration and model of pluralist democracy, the United States, does money dominate policy making?

MONEY DOMINATES POLICYMAKING

- Most of those in positions of substantial power in the government, whether in the executive,

legislative or judicial branch, are among the wealthiest 3 percent of the society. Government cannot be understood as a neutral referee in the policy process when so many of those who make policy decisions are from and share the interests of the monied class (Parenti 2010: 197–200).

- Politicians at all levels depend on increasingly large amounts of money to finance their (re)-election campaigns. Those who contribute significant funds to elected officials have the greatest access to elected officials and can make successful demands on their decisions.

- Corporations and wealthy individuals far outspend others in society in hiring lobbyists, funding policy advocates, sponsoring think tanks, and purchasing media content that both promote their interests and also influence the beliefs and actions of government officials and voters (Bagdikian 2004; Phillips 2003).

- The ultimate test of public policy is: who benefits most? Whenever financial considerations are a key factor in a policy debate, it is almost always

(Continued)

the wealthy who enjoy the greatest benefits from the enacted policy. For example, between 1979 and 2007, the richest 10 percent of Americans gained 91% of all income growth, and favorable government tax policies are a key to this disproportionate distribution of benefits (Economic Policy Institute 2011).

■ Justice might seem blind, but seeking justice is not free. Most legal disputes on matters of public policy involve interpretation of laws and discretionary decision making. The balance is typically weighted in favor of those who can afford the best legal representation (Parenti 2010: Ch. 9).

MONEY DOES NOT DOMINATE PUBLIC POLICYMAKING

■ In a pluralist democracy, votes and elections count (Dahl 1961). As median voter theory posits, the policies of government officials will generally be responsive to the interests of those with sufficient votes to determine their electoral success. And it is voting coalitions of the numerous citizens from the middle and lower classes that determine the outcome of elections, not the votes of the relatively small number of rich people (Stone 1989).

■ Prolific spending in a campaign or in lobbying the government does not guarantee victory. There are a significant number of instances in every electoral cycle where a candidate or a ballot proposition is victorious despite being outspent during the campaign. Similarly, heavy spending by interest groups is not always correlated with policy success (Baumgartner et al. 2009; Edwards, Wattenberg and Lineberry 2008).

■ There are many political interest groups that are composed largely of members who are not part of the wealthiest 10–20 percent. But these groups organize, aggregate their political resources, and prevail on policy issues of major importance (e.g., education, equality, abortion, immigration, workers' rights, and social welfare programs) (Dahl 1991).

■ Many powerful elected and appointed policy makers, including seven of the last nine U.S. presidents, are from modest backgrounds. Some of them, as well as some political leaders with considerable wealth, have been powerful advocates for those with limited wealth and social standing (e.g., Clinton, L.B. Johnson, the Kennedys, Kerry, Obama).

■ In the U.S. legal system, justice is "money blind." The interpretation of law is based on the principles of justice and fairness. If an actor has legality on his side, he will usually prevail in protecting his interests, regardless of his economic situation. Litigation often protects the less advantaged against those with "deep pockets" in numerous policy domains (e.g., civil rights, environmental protection) (Robinson 2009; Schmalleger 2011).

MORE QUESTIONS . . .

1. Can you think of compelling examples of policy decisions where, as pluralist theory posits, groups utilize other political resources to defeat groups who deploy substantially more financial resources?

2. Is there any potent political resource that money can't buy?

THE THREE APPROACHES COMPARED
Which Approach Is Correct?

The three approaches offer compelling answers to the basic political questions of who gets what, why, when, and how. Which of these three approaches is correct? Is one the most accurate explanation of politics for all political systems? For most political systems at a given historical moment? Do different approaches best account for the politics of particular systems? For particular types of issues?

9.6 Evaluate the similarities, differences, and usefulness of the three major approaches to public policymaking.

✓•⌐**Study**
and **Review** the
**Post-Test &
Chapter Exam** at
mypoliscilab.com

⚹⌐Explore the
Comparative
"Social Welfare
Systems" on
mypoliscilab.com

Advocates of each position offer both theoretical and empirical evidence to show that the politics of actual systems correspond to the description provided in their approach. As an indirect method of providing support for their approach, advocates also cite considerable evidence indicating the inaccuracies and contradictions of the other approaches. As you might suspect, the debate has been most acrimonious between, on the one hand, supporters of pluralism and, on the other, supporters of the elite and class approaches, which both assume persistent stratification and deep inequality. Some scholars contend that almost all political systems, even "democratic" ones, are elitist in the sense that the policy process is guided by and generally supports the interests of a dominant elite (Domhoff 2009). In the United States, the debate has been most intense among those who study power at the local level, prompted by the dispute five decades ago between "elitists" such as sociologist Floyd Hunter (1953) and "pluralists" such as political scientist Robert Dahl (1961).

Political scientists and other social scientists have yet to establish a critical test that reveals which of the approaches best describes or explains politics. After hundreds of studies in various political systems at the local, regional, and national levels, the disagreements among the advocates of the three approaches remain as deep as ever. To decide which approach provides the greatest insight into the politics of a particular political system, you might consider numerous conceptual and empirical questions, a few of which follow:

- For the *elite approach*, look for: evidence of actual collaboration among the elite in the formulation of public policy; the frequency with which the elite seems to lose on policy decisions of significance to its members; whether there really is a mass of citizens who are uninformed, politically inactive, and impotent regarding policy choices.
- For the *class approach*, analyze: whether the state almost always operates to serve the interests of one dominant class group; whether most people's interests and behaviors can be defined in class terms; whether most significant social changes are attributable to violence grounded in class conflict.
- And for *pluralism*, assess: whether there are persistent winners and persistent losers on policy decisions; whether the state applies rules and policies fairly and equally to all groups; whether competition among groups can be fair if there are huge inequalities in the levels of political resources available to different individuals and groups.

Essential Similarities and Differences

The elite and class approaches share certain crucial premises. For both approaches, the fundamental feature of society is stratification—the unequal distribution of values across distinct groups. Also in both approaches, the government is one of the key mechanisms controlled by the dominant group, and the government's policy decisions are intended to maintain that group's domination.

But the elite and class approaches differ in their conceptions of the nature of the groups and of group interactions. For the elite approach, there are two broad groups: the elite and the mass. Elite theorists mainly focus on the elite—its membership, the basis of elite domination, and the strategies employed by the elite to maintain its control. The mass is assumed to be inactive politically and is rarely analyzed in detail.

In contrast, most class theorists identify more than two distinct class groups and emphasize the dynamic interactions among the classes. There is substantial political energy inherent in the lower classes, who are the active agents of major political change. The class approach attempts to explain why class conflict is inevitable, how it manifests itself, and how it produces transformations in the sociopolitical system. In short, the elite approach tends to provide a top-down perspective in a two-group system, whereas the class approach often takes a bottom-up perspective that emphasizes the dynamic processes of conflict and change among multiple groups.

Pluralism differs fundamentally from both the elite and class approaches, beginning with its rejection of the notion of social stratification. It conceptualizes a sociopolitical world composed of many groups, with each individual belonging to a variety of groups. Different groups emerge on each particular political issue, and each group has an array of resources that it can organize to influence decisions on that issue. As groups compete to shape a public policy decision, the government is a relatively neutral referee that ensures the competition is fair; it is not the instrument of any particular group or class. There is a dispersion of power, of resources, and of benefits from policy decisions, not a pattern of "structured inequality." Everyone wins some and loses some, but the losers can always win on the next issue.

Vigorous and often hostile debate has persisted among the advocates of these three conceptions of how politics works. This debate is deep and serious because it reflects fundamental disagreements about the very nature of society and politics. The elite and class approaches are based on a *coercive view of society*. Conflict is a fundamental feature of the relations among groups. Social coherence is maintained by means of power and constraint, evident in domination by the most powerful class and its agent, the state. In contrast, pluralism reflects an *integrative view of society*. Society is essentially stable and harmonious in the sense that there is a moving equilibrium maintained by a "fair" competitive game, refereed by the state and played by many groups who accept the rules and the outcomes. Social coherence is grounded in cooperation and consensus (see Dahrendorf 1959).

The analytic taxonomies and stage model presented in the first part of this chapter offer a different way of understanding the public policy process. Those approaches tend to focus on providing an in-depth, empirical account of the dynamics during a particular stage of the process (e.g., implementation of health care policy), or the analysis of a specific policy domain (e.g., the impacts of tax policy, the case for military action in a particular setting). There is an attempt to define how political institutions shape the process and to explore the behavior and interactions among various stakeholders.

The various approaches to public policy analysis presented in this chapter provide you with a rich set of alternatives for responding to Harold Lasswell's (1960) classic question about politics: Who gets what, when, how, (and why)? Public policy analysis provides some additional useful tools in the political science quest to better understand the actions of any particular political system, its power structure, and its decision-making processes. Policy analysis can also be employed to determine the most desirable response to a given problem, providing a prescriptive policy recommendation. These descriptive, explanatory and prescriptive insights about the public policy process will be helpful as we consider countries' pursuit of prosperity, stability and security in the remaining chapters of this book.

KEY CONCEPTS

class   244
class approach   244
class conflict   245
elite approach   240
group   246
mass   240
pluralism   246

political elite   240
political resources   247
political stratification   240
political understructure   240
politics   247
public policy   233
stages of the policy process   236

FOR FURTHER CONSIDERATION

1. What do you think is the single most important flaw in the assumptions or knowledge claims of the elite approach? The class approach? Pluralism?
2. How might someone who embraces the class approach and someone who accepts the pluralist approach debate the public policy decisions associated with the Mapuche presented in the chapter-opening case? How might the pluralist approach account for a case like Swaziland, described in Focus in 9?
3. In a sense, all political systems are elitist because a few govern and many are governed. Does this observation seem accurate? Is it a persuasive basis for confirming the validity of the elite approach?
4. List six groups that have a political agenda and with which you have a membership or a strong identity. Ask a variety of friends to provide you with a similar list. How much overlap is there in your group affiliations? Does this seem to support the pluralist tenet of nonoverlapping memberships? (To undertake a more complete test, you would need to survey many individuals from a variety of backgrounds.)

FOR FURTHER READING

Allison, Graham, and Philip Zelikow. (1999). *The Essence of Decision: Explaining the Cuban Missile Crisis.* 2nd ed. New York: Longman. This revised edition of Allison's seminal case study of the Cuban missile crisis in 1961 offers a superb presentation of three important models of the policy decision process that differ from those described in this chapter. These models emphasize: (1) "rational choice" by decision makers who engage in a dispassionate cost–benefit analysis of the expected utilities of different actions (see the Appendix); (2) "organizational processes" by which institutional routines shape policy due to actors' adherence to simple problem-solving strategies and standard operating procedures; and (3) "bureaucratic politics," whereby stakeholders' behaviors and choices are based on their personal values and the imperatives of their particular roles.

Anderson, James E. (2010). *Public Policymaking: An Introduction.* 7th ed. Boston: Wadsworth. A solid text introducing the field of public policy analysis, with chapters focusing on the stages of the policy analysis framework presented in the first part of this chapter.

Balulis, Joseph, and Vickie Sullivan, Eds. (1996). *Shakespeare's Political Pageant: Essays in Politics and Literature*. Lanham, MD: Rowman and Littlefield. These articles offer a rich exploration of how the interplay of politics, power, and human nature is illuminated in the extraordinary plays of William Shakespeare.

Burki, Shahid J. (1991). *Pakistan Under the Military: Eleven Years of Zia ul-Haq*. Boulder, CO: Westview. A detailed description of elite rule in Pakistan under an authoritarian regime.

Castles, Francis. (1999). *Comparative Public Policy: Patterns of Post-war Transformation*. Northampton, MA: Edward Elgar Publishers. A careful comparison of the development of 12 key public policy domains in many of the advanced democracies, spanning 30 years.

Chadwick, Andrew and Philip Howard, Eds. (2008). *The Routledge Handbook of Internet Politics*. New York: Routledge. An excellent selection of analyses regarding the interplay between politics and the Internet, considering the links of the Internet to political behavior, government institutions, public policy, and the law.

Dahl, Robert. (1961). *Who Governs?: Democracy in an American City*. New Haven, CT: Yale University Press. This remains the classic theoretical and empirical statement of pluralism as an explanation of politics and the policy process.

Domhoff, G. William. (2009). *Who Rules America?: Challenges to Corporate and Class Dominance*. 6th ed. Boston: McGraw-Hill. The author updates Mills's *The Power Elite*, using more data and an elaborated theoretical base and reaching similar conclusions confirming that an elite governs the United States. See also his interesting Web site at http://sociology.ucsc.edu/whorulesamerica/power/wealth.html

Evans, Geoffrey, Ed. (1999). *The End of Class Politics?: Class Voting in Comparative Context*. Oxford: Oxford University Press. In a series of revealing country-based studies, the contributors to this volume present a data-based case, grounded particularly in analyses of elections, that class politics continues to be a powerful force in certain developed countries and postcommunist developed countries.

Glazer, Amihai, and Lawrence S. Rothenberg. (2005). *Why Government Succeeds and Why It Fails*. Cambridge, MA: Harvard University Press. This readable analysis emphasizes the economic conditions that influence public policy in domains such as the regulation of personal behavior, welfare policy, and economic growth.

Ibsen, Henrik. (1882/1964). *Enemy of the People*. In *Six Plays by Ibsen*. Trans. Eva Le Gallienne. New York: Random House. A classic Norwegian play revealing the political processes by which self-interest and greed overwhelm the efforts of a good citizen to prevent his town from making a policy decision that will result in grave environmental damage and a risk to public health.

Kingdon, John. (2002). *Agendas, Alternatives, and Public Policies*. 2nd ed. New York: Longman. The classic work that most fully explains the idea of agenda setting: how an issue emerges from many and becomes an important item drawing attention and action in the policy process.

Moran, Michael, Martin Rein, and Robert Goodin, Eds. (2006). *The Oxford Handbook of Public Policy*. New York: Oxford University Press. A comprehensive (780 pages) treatment of public policy analysis, including all the major analytic approaches and all stages of the policy process.

Rothkopf, David. (2009). *Superclass: The Global Power Elite and the World They Are Making*. New York: Farrar, Straus and Giroux. In a supercharged version of elite theory, this lively book identifies the 6,000 members of the global elite and explains how they exercise enormous power and control over the economic and political systems of the contemporary world.

Wildavsky, Aaron. (1979). *Speaking Truth to Power*. Boston: Little, Brown. One of the most perceptive scholars of the public policy process, the late Aaron Wildavsky offers many insights in this exploration of policymaking and policy analysis.

Yang, Benjamin. (1997). *Deng: A Political Biography*. Armonk, NY: M. E. Sharpe. A compelling characterization of Deng Xiaoping, the shrewd leader who followed Mao Zedong to power in China. This book also provides an intriguing and illuminating account of an elite political system in action.

ON THE WEB

http://www.trinity.edu/mkearl/strat.html

This site provides a comprehensive look at the study of social inequality and contains links to many lively Web sites on inequality as well as information on related topics such as gender stratification and homelessness.

http://www.marxist.com

"In Defense of Marxism" is a comprehensive site that argues for the relevance of class theory and Marxism in the contemporary world, with essays and research on many political topics.

http://www.ncpa.org

The conservative National Center for Policy Analysis provides material, blogs, and links to many current policy issues on its Web site.

http://www.urban.org

The Urban Institute describes itself as a nonpartisan economic and social policy research organization that focuses on policy analyses in domains such as education, health, crime, the economy, and international affairs.

http://www.care2.com/causes/politics

The Care 2 Make a Difference Policy Network offers numerous links to ideologically progressive material, think tanks, and blogs that address current policy issues.

http://www.angelfire.com/or/sociologyshop/CWM.html

This site offers a variety of links that explore the works and theories of elite theorist C. Wright Mills.

http://www.publicpolicypolling.com

Details of current public policy issues in the United States, including current polls regarding proposed legislation and candidates.

http://www.ifpa.org

A site focusing on foreign policy issues, from the Institute for Foreign Policy Analysis, a nonpartisan group.

Change and Political Development

Deal! The leaders of the world's fourth and second (soon first?) largest economies (in PPP),
Prime Minister Manmohan Singh of India and Premier Wen Jiabao of China, sign a major trade

LEARNING OBJECTIVES

10.1 Compare alternative perspectives on social, political, and economic change.

10.2 Identify the attributes of development and summarize economic development strategies.

10.3 Outline the characteristics and stages of political development.

10.4 Analyze how political systems respond to environmental challenges through political institutionalization and system transformation.

⬚ᐧⵘ Read and **Listen** to **Chapter 10** at mypoliscilab.com

✓•⬚ **Study** and **Review** the **Pre-Test & Flashcards** at mypoliscilab.com

As you sail up the Huangpu River into Shanghai, you are struck by many things. The huge cranes loading container ships along both sides of the river seem to go on for miles. You enter a city of massive, modern skyscrapers and more construction cranes than any other city in the world. The roads suffer from such pervasive gridlock and the air is so thick with pollution and noise that you wonder why so many people stay in this huge metropolis. But what is perhaps most noteworthy is what this city represents—the rapid and extensive development of a country that was, until only three generations ago, weakened for centuries by internal conflicts, famines, corruption, and foreign intervention. And that within less than five years this country, whose recent development occurred under the iron hand of communism, will become the world's largest economy, surpassing the United States. What accounts for these remarkable changes in such a relatively brief period?

The transformation began in 1949, when communist forces under Mao Zedong gained power in China after a lengthy civil war. The next three decades under Chairman Mao were a blend of chaos and rapid development. Mao wanted to revolutionize the country by destroying the burdens of its feudal, rural, impoverished, and disorganized past. He established a strong, centralized political system between 1949 and his death in 1976, using harsh totalitarian controls over political and cultural life under the guardianship of the oppressive Communist Party. Mao directed his political power to transform China's economic and social systems. His regime implemented an extensive command political economy, with state ownership of almost all productive means. Population growth was aggressively limited, and there was a shift from rural to urban areas. The Focus in 4 described some of Mao's attempts to use the agents of socialization to undermine Confucian values.

Yet Mao's reign was also wracked by chaos and conflict. Mao's policies led to more than 30 million state-caused deaths through brutal treatment of opponents, "permanent revolution" movements, and recurrent famines. Despite the turbulence of Mao's reign, this period also laid the foundations for economic development. Among the many important changes were the establishment of an effective central government; land reform; weakening of the rigid Confucian hierarchy of gender, age, and class; great improvements in health and education; and the transformation from an agrarian to an industrial nation.

Under Deng Xiaopeng, Mao's successor (and China's top leader from 1978 to the 1990s), the political system remained authoritarian, firmly under the control of the Communist Party. However, Deng abandoned the statist approach to economic policy and quietly embraced many aspects of the free market. Chided that he had adopted capitalism, the pragmatic Deng mused: "It doesn't matter if a cat is black or white, so long as it catches mice." Profit became not only an acceptable motivation but also a highly desirable one (another of Deng's famous comments is "to get rich is glorious"). Under Deng, the share of industrial output under state ownership dropped from 78 percent to 26 percent, and almost the entire agricultural system shifted from state communes to private control. China moved aggressively into the global economy, including a rapid shift to manufacturing for export and to more sophisticated goods. China's total GDP and foreign trade each rose more than twelvefold, and both rural and urban income per capita increased more than tenfold.

Since Deng stepped down in the early 1990s, the political leadership has continued to manage the Chinese economy actively, and it has sustained a very high growth rate, due particularly to strong gains in labor productivity and great success in exporting goods. Overall, GDP has increased at an annual rate of 8 percent since 1978. China now accounts for one-fourth of all global economic growth. A larger proportion of Chinese enjoy a high standard of material living than at any point in the history of the country. Yet many millions of Chinese still live in relative poverty, especially in rural areas, and increasing urban–rural inequalities in the distribution of wealth are creating substantial tension. Citizen dissatisfaction with corruption is rising. Environmental degradation has been severe, especially in urban areas. As China has become "the world's largest . . ."—in terms of GDP, holder of foreign currencies, and purchaser of commodities (e.g., energy), many believe that the continuing path of development in China is the most significant factor in the evolution of the world's economy in the near future. (CIA 2011; Meisner 1999; 2006)

CHANGE

The recent history of China is dramatic example of social, economic, and political *change,* an array of processes that are occurring in every contemporary society. It illustrates that the political system is affected by the broader changes in society but also that political action can be a major source of change. Indeed, the study of politics is a moving target because there is typically a tension between continuity and change. Exploring the processes of change in the political world is the focus of this chapter.

10.1 Compare alternative perspectives on social, political, and economic change.

Even with the strong forces of globalization, some cultures are changing more slowly than others. For example, many of the Masai of the Serengeti Plain in East Africa live in a manner that is similar to the ways of their ancestors of 50 generations

Explore the
Comparative
"Welfare
States" on
mypoliscilab.com

ago. They continue to raise their cattle, ignoring the Kenya-Tanzania border and resisting the attempts of the Kenyan government to alter their long-standing cultural patterns of family and tribal life. But even the Masai have been affected by the modernization surrounding them. It has brought health care and disease, money from tourists and reduced land for grazing herds, education and cultural confusion.

There seems nowhere to hide from the forces of change. The Greek philosopher Heraclitus articulated this view in the fifth century B.C.E. His famous dictum, "You can never step in the same river twice, for fresh waters are ever flowing in upon you," is an extreme version of the viewpoint that everything is in constant flux, that change is inevitable. It is presumed that just as individuals undergo a developmental sequence of birth, growth, maturity, decline, and death, social organisms (groups, organizations, and societies) also have some form of evolutionary development.

On the opposite side of the debate about the inevitability of change is the wry French observation: *Plus ça change, plus c'est la même chose.* This translates loosely as "The more things change, the more they remain the same." Do you believe this? Is this a wise commentary about the human condition? An erroneous cliché?

There are ongoing disagreements about the desirability of change, as well as its inevitability. One normative position, most aligned with modern rationalism, is that change is generally a positive force in human society. Change is the mechanism of growth, development, and progress, all of which are assumed to increase knowledge, extend control over the environment, and thus improve the human condition. This view is reflected in the ideas of thinkers such as Isaac Newton (1642–1727), Immanuel Kant (1724–1804), and Charles Darwin (1809–1882). In the contemporary world, it is especially prevalent among those who believe in the benefits of science and technology.

A contrasting position is that change and development have significant negative effects, perhaps so many that change is undesirable. Plato (ca. 428–347 B.C.E.), Jean-Jacques Rousseau (1712–1778), and Sigmund Freud (1856–1939) are among those who argue that knowledge, civilization, and excessive control over the environment result in a loss of innocence, goodness, and happiness and create the capacity for great harm and destruction. In this view, humans have achieved material progress at the cost of moral and spiritual decline. Our capacity to increase our supply of food and material goods cannot be separated from our development of harmful behaviors and technologies (e.g., weapons, chemicals) that degrade the environment and eliminate certain species of life, including, possibly, human beings. Most people now recognize the paradox that change and development simultaneously increase *and* reduce the quality of life. And most accept the serious problems and dangers associated with progress in order to enjoy the material benefits that change brings.

10.2 Identify the attributes of development and summarize economic development strategies.

DEVELOPMENT

Characteristics of "More Developed" Human Systems

Contemporary changes of social, economic, and political systems are usually discussed in terms of development or modernization. While both of these concepts can be slippery, social scientific research often avoids the concept of ***modernization*** because it is particularly fuzzy. What is "modern" depends very much on the particular historical moment and even on the values and culture of the analyst. For example, in the world of rapid social and technological change, what seemed modern in the United States 40 years ago (a world without personal computers, mobile phones, the HIV-AIDS epidemic, the Internet, and so on) does not seem so modern today.

Watch the Video "Environment and Economic Growth in China" at mypoliscilab.com

The concept of *development* is also fluid, but more measurable. Development refers to the processes through which certain key characteristics become more pronounced. "More developed" human systems exhibit relatively high levels on three key dimensions that tap social, cultural, economic, political, and personal characteristics (Bill and Hardgrave 1981: 63):

1. The *organizational* dimension: behaviors and actions by groups, institutions, and societies that are based on specialization, interdependency, and differentiation of roles and functions.
2. The *technological* dimension: the use of increasingly complex and sophisticated artifacts to produce useful goods and services and to control the environment.
3. The *attitudinal* dimension: cognitive, affective, and evaluative orientations that are dominated by scientific knowledge, rationality, secular values, and individualism.

The *technological* dimension is the core driver of economic development, which is of great importance to every state (recall Figure 5.1). Thus, states attempt to identify and implement strategies that facilitate economic development, which they usually define by some measure of national economic production such as GDP per capita or the rate of growth in GDP (described in Chapter 8). The expansion of available goods and services in the society offers the promise of a life that is more secure and more comfortable for at least some citizens.

Advances on the *organizational* and *attitudinal* dimensions are reflected by social indicators such as greater urbanization, expanded communications, more extensive social networks, improved efficiency, higher education levels, higher literacy rates, and greater social mobility. Most people assume that there are also societal benefits associated with increases on each of these dimensions; but there are some individuals and social movements who argue that increases on these dimensions are not necessarily desirable. They believe that such changes can have negative effects on deeply revered social and cultural values. In some countries, these negative changes are referred to as **Westernization** and are evident in attitudinal changes that shift towards *greater secularism, individualism,* and *materialism.* Groups that are strongly committed to sustaining tradition and religious values, such as those of Islam or Hinduism, can be very concerned by these types of changes within their countries.

Indeed, even economic development is questioned by those alarmed about the negative effects on the environment of unrestricted economic growth. Concerns for the environment center on both the *depletion of the earth's resources* (e.g., the destruction of the forests, shortages of water, overfishing, and the overcultivation of the land to increase food production) and the *degradation of the environment* (e.g., the climate change and solid waste associated with industrial processes and consumerism).

There are no agreed-upon measures for distinguishing sharply between systems that are developed/modern and those that are not. However, there is a general distinction between the "developed countries" and the "developing countries," often based on a single measure of *economic* development—GDP per capita (recall Compare in 8). In Chapter 13 (e.g., Figure 13.1), this book will offer a broader set of criteria for categorizing levels of development, which measure economic development but also the three dimensions of social development discussed above. In this chapter, the more developed countries can be understood as those that are relatively high on productive output, urbanization, literacy, organizational complexity, specialization, and secularization.

The Process of Development

Stage Typologies   Scholars have attempted to define the process(es) through which development and modernization occur. One approach is to define a series of stages or phases that each society passes through (Rostow 1960). Best known are the simple typologies, many of which have only two stages, such as *traditional* and *modern, less developed* and *more developed,* or *mechanical* and *organic.* These labels are so broad that they do not provide much conceptual clarity.

Karl Marx proposed a more complex typology in which most societies pass through six stages of development, each based on how its major productive resources are controlled. Marx posited that there is an initial stage of *primitive communism,* in which all individuals jointly share control over any available productive resources. The development process then continues through a series of stages in which there are increasingly subtle forms of domination by some classes over others: *slavery,* then *feudalism,* and then *capitalism.* Eventually, capitalist systems are transformed into *socialist* and finally to *communist* systems, the ultimate stage of development in which all citizens blend into a single class that shares control of resources (recall Chapters 2, 8 and 9 on communism and class theory).

Response to Key Challenges   Most explanations of the process of development do not assume, as Marx does, that there is a single, inevitable sequence of stages. Rather, analysts identify a series of key challenges in the development process (Black 1966). These challenges include the tension between traditional values and modern ones; the transition from a rural, agrarian society to an urban, industrial society; the transfer of social and political power from traditional elites to modernizing ones; and the fit among geographical territory, nation-based identities, and state boundaries. A country's development process depends on the sequence in which the challenges occur, how the society responds to the challenges, and crucial features of the society and its environment.

For example, Barrington Moore (1966) uses detailed historical analyses of eight countries to define four different models of development based on how relationships evolved among key social groups, especially the landed aristocrats and peasants in the rural areas and the urban entrepreneurs and government employees. One of Moore's most powerful conclusions is that all forms of development are essentially revolutions from above, implemented by a ruthless minority and causing great hardship to the large majority of the population, which does not want these changes.

Individual-Level Change   Most analyses of development focus on the macrolevel—that is, on the organizational and technological dimensions of systems such as economic and political systems. But attention to the attitudinal dimension shifts the analysis to the social-psychological characteristics of individuals that might account for variations in rates and patterns of development (Inglehart and Welzel 2005; Inkeles and Smith 1999; Inkeles 1997). You might understand individual-level change intuitively if you think about what happens to people when their existing values are challenged by education, other religions, or different cultures. The Koran recognizes the importance of personal values in shaping society, noting, "Lo! Allah changeth not the condition of a people until they first change what is in their hearts." These analyses of individual attitudes and change are related to the political behavior studies described in Chapters 2–4, although the focus here is on a broader array of beliefs (not just political beliefs).

In the attempt to establish the attitudinal traits associated with modernity, the work of Alex Inkeles and his colleagues (Inkeles and Smith 1999) is noteworthy. This group gathered extensive survey data from men in six developing countries (Argentina, Bangladesh, Chile, India, Israel, and Nigeria). Statistical analyses produced a set of seven qualities that the researchers believe constitute a "syndrome of modernity"—that is, the general attitudinal traits of a modern person in a developing society:

1. Openness to new experiences regarding both people and behaviors.
2. A shift in allegiance from those individuals in traditional authority structures (e.g., parents, religious leaders) to those representing modern institutions (e.g., government leaders).
3. Confidence in modern technologies (e.g., science, medicine) and a less fatalistic attitude about life.
4. Desire for social mobility for oneself and one's children.
5. Belief in the value of planning and punctuality.
6. Interest in local politics and community affairs.
7. Interest in news, especially national and international affairs.

Inkeles and his colleagues conclude that there is remarkable similarity in these clusters of beliefs among the modern men in all six societies they studied, and perhaps among modern individuals in almost all cultures. Some posit that such an emerging commonality of beliefs is part of a broader set of forces that are homogenizing everyone into a global culture, a global information network, and a global economy (Barber 1995; Friedman 2007). However, it is unclear whether most people are equally exposed to and equally changed by global culture. In most developing societies, some people and groups enthusiastically embrace the new beliefs and new behaviors, while others cling tenaciously to the old ones. Indeed, in some cases of religious fundamentalism, it seems that leaders who display the activist and outward-oriented psychological traits associated with the syndrome of modernity are actually working to return the society to more traditional patterns of attitudes and actions.

Civil Society   The attitudinal changes in individuals are especially important when they result in new patterns of social interaction. Thus, one key consideration in assessing development is the extent to which a *civil society* has emerged. Attitudes particularly associated with the existence of civil society include tolerance of differences in opinions and behaviors, social trust, willingness to negotiate and to avoid violence in resolving differences, and a sense of shared identity with others. Some analysts conclude that, while a society can be "developed" without being a civil society, these values of civility are crucial for sustaining effective community and democracy (Diamond 2008; Linz and Stepan 1996; Putnam 1993; 2000).

Culture and Change   Some studies of development emphasize the importance of the culture in the processes of change. Since Max Weber's classic study (1958a) of the link between the culture of Protestant religions and the rise of capitalist political economies, there have been continuing efforts to clarify the relationship between broad cultural systems and economic development. Some, like Weber, argue that Protestantism motivated people to make substantial, even irrational, sacrifices of material consumption and the pleasures of life, inciting them to work extraordinarily hard and accumulate wealth rather than spend it. A society infused with such values is associated with the transformation to a modern society and economy (Davis 1987: 223–234).

Weber (1951, 1958b) also applied an analysis of culture and religion to India and China to explain the absence of development there. But since the 1980s, there has been a dramatic surge of economic development among the Asian newly industrializing countries (to be discussed later in this chapter). Because these Asian countries have had substantially higher levels of development than most other countries employing similar development strategies, more recent explanations have emphasized how Asian culture has *facilitated* development (Davis 1987; Fukuyama 2009; Huntington 1991; Pye 1985; and see Chapter 15).

The Dynamics of Economic Development

The actual economic development of a country is the product of a complex set of actions by both major players (e.g., the government, large corporations, and international banks) and small players (e.g., small businesses and individuals as consumers and workers) that is staggering in scale and almost incomprehensible in nature.

In the abstract, the discussion of political economy in Chapter 8 (look again at Figure 8.3) provides the key to understanding what is happening. Economic development occurs as more and more households and firms are engaged in ever-higher levels of production and consumption. More goods (and, ideally, more diverse and complex goods) are produced, more income and expenditures are exchanged, and thus the GDP gets larger relative to the number of people sharing in the carnival of production and consumption. And a political economy is normally healthier if it is not only growing but also bringing more income into the country via exports than it sends out to pay for imports.

Chapter 8 explored some of the general challenges facing every political economy in the quest for economic development. From a public policy perspective, the underlying puzzle is: What should the state do to facilitate economic development? In recent decades, three competing visions guided the answer to this question in many political economies: statism, neoliberalism, and the developmental state approach.

Statism   Many developing countries (e.g., Brazil, Mexico, India, and Tanzania) implemented versions of statism, especially between the 1950s and 1980s. Statism *emphasizes strong actions by the state to manage the system of production and distribution of goods.* The state extensively regulates the market and the actions of firms and households, and it protects firms from external competition. Many important areas of production (e.g., transportation, power, and banking) are publicly owned and are operated as state enterprises. The state also controls the prices of certain basic goods (e.g., foods, fuel), and it distributes free or subsidized goods and services (e.g., health care and shelter), especially to less advantaged groups. The political economies of many communist countries (e.g., Bulgaria, China, and Cuba) were extreme forms of the statist approach.

Neoliberalism   Alternatively, many countries applied variations of neoliberalism. Grounded in the market political economy model (see Chapter 8), the guiding principle of the neoliberal approach is to *maximize the economic freedom of firms, households, and individuals.* There is an attempt to limit severely the state's interventions in the economy, which are seen to undermine and distort the efficiency of the free market. Public expenditure is minimal, there is little government regulation of the economy, and direct foreign investment and free trade across state boundaries are encouraged. The state is mainly concerned with maintaining fiscal and monetary discipline (not taxing or spending much, keeping the currency stable) and facilitating the activities of firms in the national and global marketplaces. Since the mid-1970s, many countries have adopted versions of the neoliberal approach, especially due to two factors: the disappointing levels of economic growth achieved with the statist approach and strong pressure from the international financial community and the global economy to embrace neoliberalism (Rodrik 2003; Linz and Stepan 1996).

The Developmental State Approach   The third approach is a hybrid that combines elements of the statist and neoliberal approaches. This *developmental state approach* links an emphasis on a private, market-based system of firms with a state that actively intervenes to promote and protect the country's firms in the global economy. It is grounded in three broad strategies:

1. **State-supported, export-oriented capitalism.** As in neoliberalism, aggressive capitalism is favored, and there are minimal governmental constraints on firms. However, the state has a high profile in the political economy. The state enacts taxing, spending, and regulatory policies that promote the export of goods, encourage savings and investment, discourage high levels of domestic consumption, and produce a trained and docile labor force.
2. **Targeting market niches.** The state also works cooperatively with firms to identify and then produce particular goods that can be successfully sold in the

international marketplace. Government subsidies enable firms to sell goods at low or no profit while the firm captures a share of the market and gains consumer support. The state's policies (e.g., tariffs) also protect firms against imported goods.

3. **Agrarian support.** Government policy strongly supports efficient domestic food production. This element can include redistribution of land to small private farmers, subsidies on domestic food production, and tariffs on imported foods (Simone 2001; Woo-Cumings 1999).

As Chapter 14 will discuss in more detail, very few developing countries utilizing the statist approach achieved high levels of economic growth. Some developing countries employing neoliberalism have enjoyed periods of solid growth, but only a few have experienced sustained growth and prosperity. In general, most developing countries that have achieved solid and sustained economic growth during the last four decades have pursued some variant of the developmental state approach. Many of these success stories have been in Asia, particularly China, Singapore, South Korea, Taiwan, Vietnam, and to a lesser extent Malaysia and Indonesia. The most successful are sometimes called the *newly industrializing countries (NICs)* (see Chapter 15 for more details). Other developing countries that have attempted variations of the developmental state strategy have had mixed success, with some achieving relatively high levels of multiyear economic growth (e.g., Chile and Uruguay), others failing to sustain such growth (e.g., Brazil and Mexico), and still others having very little success.

Even most of the high-growth economies of Asia have not avoided some serious bumps. In the late 1990s, a severe economic slump began in Thailand and then spread to many of these countries, resulting in negative GDP growth, high unemployment, and a huge decrease in the value of assets such as property and stocks. These problems spread to other rapidly developing countries in Latin America and other areas (Franko 2003). The breadth and depth of these negative economic conditions resulted in recognition of the flaws as well as the potential benefits of the developmental state model. A variety of problems were identified, such as the state's overprotection of favored firms, inadequate regulation of the banking and credit systems, the unrestrained speculation in land and the stock market, and increased inequality of wealth. Most of these economies have regained their economic momentum, but there is now more debate about whether the developmental state approach is always the best strategy for broad economic growth and economic stability (Stein 2006).

Dependency within the International Political Economy Most developing countries have been unable to achieve high, sustained economic growth during the postcolonial period (since about 1960). Why is this? Some analysts offer a perspective known generally as the dependency approach, which argues that *the "late developers" face difficult challenges because of their subordination to and dependence on the more developed countries and the transnational institutions they control in the current world.*

According to the *ideological* framing of the dependency approach, the key problem for current developers is a long history of exploitation by the more developed "capitalist/imperialist" states. The developed countries have manipulated and controlled the political economies of the developing countries for decades or even centuries by means of their economic, military, and political domination of the "world system." Indeed, a major reason the developed countries have sustained their prosperity since the mid-20th century is that they still exploit and reap benefits from the developing countries, especially through their broad control of capital, markets and prices, and multinational corporations. In this view, the activities of the developed countries have not merely retarded the progress of the late developers, they have actually "deformed" (distorted and ruined) the efforts of the developing countries.

The *descriptive* version of the dependency approach provides a similar analysis but without heaping blame exclusively on the advanced states. It posits an economic hierarchy in which economic actors at every level take advantage of those below them in the global economic system. At the top of the heap is a core, composed of the powerful states, large firms (especially multinational corporations such as JPMorganChase, General Electric, and Exxon Mobil), and financial institutions controlled by the most developed countries. At the bottom of the heap on the *periphery* are the villages of the developing countries (Isbister 2006; Wallerstein 1974, 1980, 2004; Wiarda 2003).

In this version, many actors engage in exploitation. The resources of villages and the urban poor (raw materials, cheap labor) are exploited by local and regional economic actors, who are in turn exploited by national economic actors, who are exploited by the powerful core actors in the global economy. For example, analyses of Brazil identify an exploitive alliance composed of three key sets of actors: (1) the multinational corporations, (2) the Brazilian capitalist class, and (3) the Brazilian state apparatus. The groups in the alliance, and especially the multinationals, gain most of the benefits from Brazil's rich resources, whereas the great majority of the Brazilian population remains poor and backward (Packenham 1998).

Continuing Dependency?   It is clear that the process of development is substantially affected by the current global economy. However, three arguments are offered by analysts who dispute the validity of the dependency approach. First, serious internal problems in many developing countries, especially extensive corruption and conflicts among nationality groups, are major limitations on development (Calderisi 2007; Isbister 2006; Johnston 2006). Second, the economic success of some Asian developing countries, relative to those in Africa and Latin America, suggests that cultural factors are more crucial to development than is the level of dependence on foreign capital or foreign companies (Fallows 1995; Huntington 1991). Third, the low- and middle-income countries of the developing world, measured either as a group or by region, have actually achieved higher average annual rates of economic (GDP) growth since the early 1990s than the developed countries (World Bank 2011). In response, dependency theorists note that when income inequality continues to rise worldwide—the disparity between the top and bottom 20 percent has nearly doubled in the last three decades to a ratio of 50:1—the systematic subordination of those on the periphery cannot be dismissed (UNDP 2006).

POLITICAL DEVELOPMENT

10.3 Outline the characteristics and stages of political development.

✳️ Explore the Comparative "Media and Interest Articulation" on mypoliscilab.com

To this point, this chapter has broadly considered development in all spheres of human activity, particularly in the economic and attitudinal spheres. Let us now turn to the specifically *political* aspects of development. Political development refers to *the emergence of more extensive capabilities in the political system,* especially in the sense that political structures and processes become more specialized and more effective in managing internal operations and in responding to the environment.

Characteristics of Political Development

Political development is typically measured by the extent to which a political system exhibits relatively high levels on the following four dimensions:

1. **Concentration of power in the state.** Most power and authority are centralized in a single state-level governmental system, and traditional sources of political authority weaken. The citizens agree that the state has the right to make and enforce public policies and they accept those decisions as authoritative. The formal-legal aspects of government (e.g., constitutions and laws) are well established.
2. **Specialized political structures.** Most key political functions are fulfilled by complex, organized political institutions such as legislatures, executives, political parties, and political interest groups. The actions of these institutions are generally guided by bureaucratic principles such as rationality and efficiency.
3. **Political institutionalization.** The citizens value and support the political structures and processes, which become more stable, and the citizens fulfill their roles of conventional political participation, as voters, foot soldiers, and so on (recall Chapter 3).
4. **Extensive capabilities of the state.** The political system becomes better able to generate support, to respond to demands from its population, and to control the environment. Overall, its organization is more stable and coherent, its structures are more efficient, and its actions more effectively serve its goals and objectives. In a "capabilities analysis," a political system achieves a higher level of political development when it improves its effectiveness on any of five key capabilities (Powell, Strom and Dalton 2012):

   Extractive: using human and material resources from the environment.
   Regulative: controlling individual and group actions.
   Distributive: allocating values through institutionalized structures and procedures.
   Responsive: making decisions and policies that react to demands for value allocations.
   Symbolic: manipulating images and meanings and distributing nonmaterial rewards and values.

The Process of Political Development

Figure 10.1 presents one model of the process through which political development occurs. From this perspective, the elements of modernization (in the figure) provide the material and human resources that lead to the emergence of a developed political system. Greater economic capability produces goods that the political system can distribute. An urban population with increasingly modern beliefs is more willing to accept the authority of government and to participate meaningfully in politics. In essence, the political system develops more complex and specialized structures as a response to changes that are occurring in the society and the economy.

Conceptualizing political development as primarily a response to economic and social change is based on the historical analyses of political systems that developed in the 18th and 19th centuries. However, the power and impact of the political system itself, as a causal force for change, are more evident when one analyzes the societies that have undergone substantial development during the last 50 years (Wiarda 2003).

This leads to a second perspective in which the political system is the crucial force that causes development of the social and economic systems. Thus, Figure 10.2 emphasizes the central importance of the political system as an agent of change in relation to other societal characteristics. As Kwame Nkrumah (1909–1972), the first president of Ghana, observed: "Seek ye first the political kingdom, and all else shall be added unto you." This nearly religious invocation asserts that

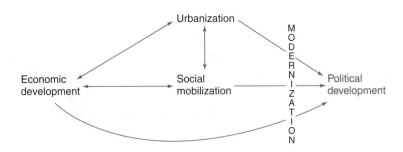

FIGURE 10.1
Model of development I

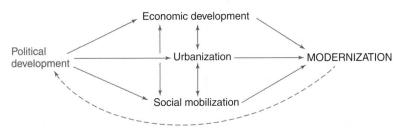

FIGURE 10.2
Model of development II

if the political system is developed first, it can then serve as the instrument through which social and economic development is achieved. Public policy decisions by an assertive political leadership can establish specialized political structures, expand the capabilities of the political system, and mobilize certain groups into the political process. The political leadership can then deploy these more developed political structures to enact public policies that empower governmental officials to perform new functions, assert state control over key human and natural resources, and allocate those resources in ways that result in social and economic development in domains such as the political economy, the educational system, the culture, national identity, the media, and religious practices.

Obviously, change and development in the political, social, economic, and other domains are interdependent; that is, they affect each other. But Figure 10.2 emphasizes the central role of politics and political choice as drivers of development. In this conception, overall development is shaped by the ideology, will, and actions of political actors rather than being driven primarily by economic growth. This was the case for China under Mao Zedong, the example that opened this chapter. Another compelling example of a leader's explicit use of the political system as a powerful instrument to change many aspects of the society is Kemal Atatürk's efforts to modernize Turkey, described in Focus in 10.

FOCUS IN 10 | Political Development and Modernization in Turkey

The modernization effort in Turkey is an example of "seeking the political kingdom first." Historically, the area of the Turkish nation was part of the large Ottoman Empire ruled by a sultan. After World War I, an army commander named Mustafa Kemal led a fierce military struggle for national independence. Victory resulted in the creation of the sovereign state of Turkey in 1922. Mustafa Kemal, who seized political power in the new republic, was committed to rapid modernization. At the time, Turkey had very traditional political, economic, and social systems, with Islamic law dominating the actions of the 98 percent Muslim population. The new leader decided that the key to modernization was to reduce the hold of Islam on the people.

In a stroke of symbolic politics, Kemal began his modernization drive at the personal level. He changed his name to Mustafa Kemal Atatürk, the addition meaning "father of the Turks." (Kemal was also a fortunate name because it means "perfect one.") Atatürk initially focused on political development, establishing a new state based on the principles of independence and democracy. A constitution was approved in 1924,

executive power was granted to a president, the sultan was exiled, a legislature was elected, and a single political party was established. Atatürk thus created a political system with modern structures of governance and modern forms of political participation. This political system then became the instrument for Atatürk's broader efforts to reform Turkey.

From 1925 until his death in 1938, Atatürk employed his great political power to implement three major sets of public policies that were meant to modernize Turkey and to separate it from the traditional Muslim world. First, he enacted laws that prohibited the wearing of religious garments in everyday life, abolished religious schools, and closed religious tombs as places of worship. Second, he encouraged the emergence and empowerment of a nationalist elite by steps such as creating a new Turkish language and banning the public use of other languages (recall his suppression of the Kurds described in Chapter 5); replacing the Ottoman script with the Latin alphabet; and establishing Turkish literacy programs, especially in urban areas. Third, he

(Continued)

established a new civil code (copied from Switzerland) to govern the legal relations between individuals and collectivities, relegating sharia law and the Koran to peripheral status in guiding public life. For example, he tried to eliminate the subordinate role of women, encouraging them to work, providing them with rights of divorce and inheritance, allowing them to vote and hold public office, and banning polygamy.

The effects of Atatürk's changes are evident in contemporary Turkey, whose 79 million people are 99.8 percent Muslim. While 70 percent of the population lived in villages in 1964, Turkey is now 70 percent urban. The economy, 75 percent agrarian in 1978, is 90 percent industrial and service-based. Turkey now has the most educated and modern women in the Muslim world, and Tansu Çiller was Turkey's first female prime minister (1993 to 1996). A 2004 constitutional amendment says "women and men have equal rights" and about one-fourth of Turkish professionals are women; yet substantial gender inequality remains due to a continuing gap between legal standing and social realities.

Politically, the attempt to create an effective multiparty democracy in Turkey remains unfinished. There have been periods of serious social instability and governmental corruption, and three periods of military rule since 1960, although the military returned the reins of government to civilians in each case, once order was restored. For the first time since Atatürk, an Islamist party (the Welfare Party) came to power in 1996. When the government began to promote numerous policy changes based on Islamic principles and practices, the military responded with warnings and then forced the party from office in a "soft coup" that revealed the continuing power of the military in what is perhaps best characterized as an illiberal democracy (see Chapter 7). A reformulated Islamist party (AK—Justice and Development) has dominated the last three elections (2002, 2007, and 2011). Despite continual attempts by Recep Erdogan, Turkey's first ever three-term prime minister, to reassure the military of his support for Atatürk's secular society, he also managed the selection of devout Islamist as president in 2007. This combination of political power and religious orientation has

Students carrying a portrait of Atatürk, founder of modern Turkey, chant slogans to protest the attempts by the government to reduce the secular orientation of education policies.

heightened the uneasiness among the military and secular elements of society, and there are continuing tensions over a drift away from secularism.

Thus, Atatürk's strong policies have not totally transformed Turkey. However, his legacy is an illuminating example of how a committed political leader can reform the political system and then use political power to achieve considerable social and economic development within a society, consistent with Figure 10.2.

FURTHER FOCUS

1. Which of Atatürk's policies do you think was the most important for overall development in Turkey?

2. As the leader of a developing country, if you had to emphasize economic development or political development, which would you choose? ▶

Political Development as Democratization

In contrast to the capabilities analysis described above, some scholars (e.g., Cutright 1963) define political development as the establishment of the rule of law, legitimate elections, and representative institutions. Others object that this conception of a "developed" political system is extremely biased. Can you see why? What concept do such characteristics seem to measure?

You might answer that the preceding paragraph describes a *democratic* political system (recall Chapter 7). If you agree that the essence of political development is the capability of the political system to handle basic functions, it is possible to have a political system that is quite developed but nondemocratic (e.g., China, Cuba, Swaziland, and Syria). However, it is certainly valid to conclude that one highly desirable outcome of political development is a system that is democratic. Democratization can be understood as those *changes that deepen and consolidate democratic processes* (Diamond 2008; Schneider 2009). Democratization was proposed as one of the pillars of the stability goal of states in Figure 5.1, although not every political system aspires to this goal.

Samuel Huntington (1991) suggests that there have been three long waves of democratization among modern states. The first occurred between the 1820s and 1926, when about 30 countries established liberal democracies. Some of these then "reversed" (democracy was abandoned), until a second wave produced 36 democratic governments between 1945 and 1962. After another period of reversal, the third wave began in 1974. In the early 1990s, the push towards democratization was strong in many of the postcommunist states that emerged from the former Soviet Union and in Central and Eastern Europe and in some former military regimes in Latin America, Asia, and Africa (e.g., Chile, Ghana, Panama, South Korea, Taiwan, and Uruguay). Then the Arab Spring of 2011 moved some countries in the Middle East (e.g., Egypt and Tunisia) towards democratic practices. While there are currently 115 electoral democracies, Freedom House notes that there has been a drop in electoral democracies in recent years and "a decline in global freedom" for five consecutive years (Puddington 2011). It is unclear at this point whether the third wave of democratization will be sustained by more popular uprisings or is now in significant reversal.

What might account for the broad expansion of democracies since the 1970s? Consider the following six explanations.

First, the level of *economic development* has long been presented as a crucial factor. As suggested by Figure 10.1, economic development can cause changes in the social system that facilitate democratization. Greater wealth and a credible commitment to distribute it with reasonable fairness reassures both citizens and leaders that the increased participation and demands associated with democratization can now be handled with less risk of instability (Acemoglu and Robinson 2009; Huntington 1991). The Debate in 10 explores whether economic development is a necessary prerequisite for democracy.

Second, *external actors* have been an important force in the shift towards democracy. Global actors such as the World Bank, the EU, and the United Nations, among others, have insisted that countries introduce democratic reforms as a condition for economic assistance. Countries have sometimes withdrawn their support for authoritarian leadership, as the Soviet Union did in Central and Eastern Europe during the late 1980s. And external actors sometimes intervene directly in another

DEBATE IN 10 | Is Economic Development a Necessary Prerequisite for Democracy?

Few research questions in political science attract more current interest than the attempt to identify the conditions that are most conducive to establishing democracy. Fifty years ago, the distinguished social scientist Seymour Martin Lipset (1959) argued that economic development is the crucial prerequisite for democracy. Supported by the fact that all the most developed countries at the time were democracies, Lipset's thesis became the conventional wisdom. However, as a much more diverse set of countries has attempted to introduce democracy during the "third wave" of democratization, there has been considerable debate about whether economic development really is a *necessary* precondition for establishing and maintaining a democratic regime.

ECONOMIC DEVELOPMENT IS A NECESSARY PREREQUISITE FOR DEMOCRACY

- The empirical facts support this linkage. Numerous comparative analyses indicate that there is a strong correlation between a higher level of economic development and stronger democracy (Acemoglu and Robinson 2009; Richards 2007). Most economically developed countries are democracies, while very few poor countries are democracies.
- As indicated in Figure 10.1, economic development typically results in greater urbanization, higher levels of education, and the development of a political culture with more trust and tolerance of diversity, all factors that are conducive to the emergence and maintenance of democracy (Spagnoli 2003).
- Economic development directly fosters the emergence of an educated and entrepreneurial middle class, whose members demand greater political voice and form the social-structural basis for effective democracy (Bueno de Mesquita and Downs 2005).

- Economic development results in more widespread prosperity, creating a larger proportion of the population who has the time necessary for active democratic participation. Conversely, in a society that lacks economic development, a substantial proportion of the population is so concerned with survival and economic advancement that people have little time or motivation to participate extensively in democratic life (Spagnoli 2003).
- The effects of economic development in raising education levels also promote greater political knowledge and awareness among the population, encouraging more extensive political participation and greater political tolerance.
- No democratic country with a GDP per capita of greater than $6,000 has ever abandoned democracy (Przeworski 2004). Thus, the prosperity that results from economic development is a crucial element in sustaining democracy.
- Economic development leads to greater access to a broader range of political information and more openness to global society. Such inputs reduce a nondemocratic government's ability to limit its citizens' exposure to ideas that promote the concept of democracy and undermine authoritarian control.

ECONOMIC DEVELOPMENT IS NOT A NECESSARY PRECONDITION FOR DEMOCRACY

- The empirical facts support this conclusion. A reasonable generalization from the hundreds of comparative empirical studies is that the conditions associated with the emergence of democracy are complex, multiple, and varied. No single condition, including a high level of economic development, must always be present for the successful transition to democracy (Spagnoli 2003; Tilly 2007).
- Economic development is not essential for establishing many of the critical preconditions

(Continued)

for democracy in developing countries: effective political institutions, a working political party system, and a civil society in which groups share trust and tolerance (Schneider 2009).

■ Many countries with high economic growth remain authoritarian regimes and have been very effective at resisting the demands for democracy, as cases such as China and Singapore clearly demonstrate. Indeed, high-income countries that are nondemocracies are actually *less* likely to transition to democracy than middle-income countries that are nondemocracies (Bueno de Mesquita and Downs 2005; Przeworski et al. 2000).

■ Many relatively poor countries have successfully implemented democracy. In fact, the proportion of countries that are democracies is substantially higher than the proportion that is at high levels of economic development (Freedom House 2011).

■ The spread of information and communications technologies (ICTs) and the Internet has reduced the significance of economic development in facilitating key preconditions of democracy such as mechanisms for interest aggregation, shared cultural identity, and a community of communication.

■ Some of the most durable democracies in the developing world maintained their high levels of political rights and civil liberties during long periods of limited economic development and negligible economic growth. Examples include Botswana, Costa Rica, and India.

MORE QUESTIONS . . .

1. Which argument (bullet point) on each side of the debate is least persuasive? Why?

2. What is your evaluation of the argument that every wealthy country will eventually become a democracy? ▰

country with the stated purpose of promoting democracy, as the United States and its allies did in Iraq and Afghanistan (Pickering and Peceny 2006; Robinson 1998).

Third, the *breakdown of authoritarian and totalitarian regimes* has provided a window of opportunity for democratization. In such cases, nondemocratic political systems have lost their capabilities to suppress the pressure for change. This seems to have been a particularly important factor in the states of the former Soviet Union and Central and Eastern Europe, as well as in countries such as Argentina, Egypt and Tunisia (Linz and Stepan 1996).

Fourth, *changing norms favoring democracy* is often a factor. As citizens perceive that democracy is a positive value and that other countries are making the transition to democracy, they become more insistent that their leaders implement democratic reforms (Diamond 2008).

Fifth, nonviolent *"people power" movements* have become a crucial force for change in almost three-fourths of the countries that have democratized. There is a clear relationship between the strength of such movements and the level of democratic freedom that is achieved and maintained (Karatnycky and Ackerman 2006). And recently, such movements have been significantly facilitated by the Internet and social media, as in the "Arab Spring" of 2011 (Ritter and Trechsel 2011).

Sixth, the presence of *political leadership* committed to democracy can be important. In many countries, new leaders attained power based on their promise to pursue democratization as a central goal (as with Vicente Fox in Mexico, South Africa's Nelson Mandela, and Ukraine's Viktor Yushchenko). Indeed, most current leaders declare allegiance to democratization, if only to maintain domestic and international support (Sorensen 2007).

WORLD OF CHANGES

Easton's model in Chapter 5 emphasized that the political system must attempt to respond to constant changes in its internal and external environments. Thus, Easton (1965) asked: How can a political system persist in a world of changes? His answer is that the political system must produce decisions and actions that increase the support for the political institutions and the authorities and that manage the complex demands and challenges from the environment.

Thus political systems, like the global environment in which they function, are constantly engaged in both system maintenance and adaptive change. Most political change is modest, resulting from the effects of (1) new policy decisions, (2) alterations in the way existing policy is implemented, or (3) variations in the inputs from the internal or external environments. We could probably identify thousands of small changes in a single week. Although political change usually results from the gradual accumulation of minor adjustments, it is more noticeable when there is a substantial shift. For example, there could be a major change from a dominant party to a multiparty system, from authoritarianism to electoral democracy, from social order to widespread rioting, from a statist political economy to a neoliberal one, from male-only to gender-neutral political rights, from an elected leader to a military dictatorship.

Even more *fundamental change in the nature of the political system or the political economy* can be called a **system transformation**. The emergence of a secular regime in Turkey under Atatürk, the destruction of the Saddam Hussein regime in Iraq, the abandonment of state socialism in Russia (see Compare in 15), and the dramatic alterations in Cambodia's political system that are the subject of the Compare in 10 are examples of system transformation. One striking feature of the political world in the last several decades has been the substantial number of such transformations. Chapter 15 will focus on political systems in which political and economic transformations have been particularly extensive in the past several decades: postcommunist countries and newly industrializing countries. In addition, coming chapters explore major transformations that seem to be occurring at the international level and are generally associated with *globalization*. System transformation is rare. Incremental change is the norm.

Change, when incremental and certainly when more dramatic, can generate both optimism and concern in any society. It might seem that key actors in most political systems would value political development as one desirable mode of change. This is probably the case if such development is understood as an increase in political institutionalization—*the depth of capabilities, stability, and citizen support for the existing political system.* And greater economic growth and development—the increased capacity to produce and distribute a broad array of goods—is a second change goal valued in almost all countries (Chapter 8).

However, change can be destabilizing. Thus there is more caution about what, if any, political and economic development will be encouraged in countries where the existing elites fear a loss of their advantaged position. For example, there are nondemocracies, such as Belarus, China, Myanmar, and Oman, where leaders aim to increase the capabilities of the economic system and the political system without substantially expanding the processes and institutions of democracy. And

10.4 Analyze how political systems respond to environmental challenges through political institutionalization and system transformation.

Watch the **Video "Global Food Prices and Changing Diets"** at **mypoliscilab.com**

COMPARE IN 10 | Six Political Systems in Cambodia?

The case of Cambodia illuminates a political system that has undergone six major changes in the relatively short time span of less than 50 years.

Cambodia I. The Cambodia of 1962 was a small, beautiful state in Indochina that had been granted its independence by France in 1953. It has been said that the most important activities in the lives of Cambodians were to dance, make love, and watch the grass grow. They were ruled under an authoritarian political system by Prince Norodom Sihanouk, a hereditary leader who attempted to balance the forces of the left and the right within Cambodia and to keep Cambodia on a neutral course. However, in the late 1960s, Sihanouk was unable to prevent Cambodia from being drawn into the increasingly widespread and intense war in neighboring Vietnam. Some Vietcong (the leftist guerrillas attempting to overthrow the South Vietnamese state) took sanctuary in Cambodia, but Sihanouk insisted that Cambodian sovereignty prevented the United States and South Vietnamese armies from invading Cambodia to attack these Vietcong. Sihanouk also attempted to direct international attention to the "secret bombing" raids in Cambodia conducted by the U.S. military but denied by the political leadership in the United States.

Cambodia II. Because of Sihanouk's resistance to their military objectives, the U.S. leaders supported (and perhaps directed) a March 1970 coup in which Cambodian army leaders overthrew Sihanouk and replaced him with General Lon Nol, a rightist dictator who was generally viewed as a puppet of the United States. There were dramatic changes in Cambodia's political structure and foreign policy under the new Lon Nol government (1970–1975), which was kept in power by the United States. In turn, the Cambodian government and military assisted the U.S. military in fighting the Vietcong as well as in battling an expanding internal civil war led by the Khmer Rouge, Cambodian communists who opposed Lon Nol and his U.S. allies.

Cambodia III. With the collapse of the U.S. military effort in Southeast Asia, Lon Nol's government was among the casualties. Thus, the Khmer Rouge came to power in April 1975 and created yet another political system, renaming the country Kampuchea. Under the communist regime of Pol Pot, Kampuchea experienced one of the most dramatic transformations in a political system during the 20th century. The new government immediately relocated everyone from urban areas to the countryside, organized the entire population into collective farms that were really forced labor camps, and implemented a massive reeducation (indoctrination) program. In a brutal reign of terror, about one-third of Cambodia's population of 7 million was either killed or died during a total restructuring of the society.

Cambodia IV. The Vietnamese exploited this time of disruption by invading and conquering the Cambodians, their centuries-old enemies. In January 1979, the Vietnamese army installed a puppet Cambodian government under Prime Minister Hun Sen (a dissident member of the Khmer Rouge). Thus, Pol Pot's barbaric regime was replaced with a new political system that operated as a satellite of Vietnam's communist government.

Cambodia V. After 13 years of guerrilla warfare against Hun Sen's government by groups loyal to the Khmer Rouge and Sihanouk, a treaty in Paris led to United Nations–supervised elections for a national legislature in 1993. The election and subsequent constitution created a fifth political system, an odd combination bringing together many of the old adversaries. Sihanouk became king, a constitutional monarch with mainly symbolic power. His anticommunist son, Prince Ranariddh, as "first" prime minister, shared political power with communist Hun Sen, the "second" prime minister. The Khmer Rouge, who refused to participate in the election, continued a punishing guerrilla war and controlled large parts of the countryside.

(Continued)

Cambodia VI. After another civil war, Hun Sen's forces were victorious in a 1997 coup that deposed Prince Ranariddh, who was exiled. Key supporters of the prince's political party either fled the country or were executed. Meanwhile, rival forces within the Khmer Rouge captured Pol Pot, who was imprisoned and soon died. In three subsequent national elections, most recently in 2008, Hun Sen has continued as prime minister and his party controls 75 percent of the seats in the lower house. Another son of Sihanouk (Sihamoni) is now king, but he lives abroad and has mainly ceremonial duties. Despite a multiparty system with open elections and some freedom of opposition, Cambodia is not an electoral democracy according to Freedom House. Corruption, abuse of power, and political violence are still so severe that the World Bank terms Cambodia a "fragile state."

A phrase in the Cambodian national anthem aptly describes the country's recent history: "The bright red blood ... spilled over the towns and over the plain." It is unusual for a political system to undergo six dramatic changes in about 50 years, several of which were system transformations. Has the fragile state of Cambodia now stabilized sufficiently so that the existing political system will persist, at least for a while?

FURTHER QUESTIONS

1. If you were to do a detailed comparative analysis of two of the six political systems in Cambodia, which two would you compare? Why?
2. How might a small country like Cambodia avoid being drawn into an intense conflict among major powers that spills over into its territory? ▰

Skulls of the victims of the brutal Khmer Rouge reign of terror (1975-1979) are on display in many villages around Cambodia as memorials to honor the dead and strengthen Cambodians' resolve to prevent a reoccurrence of such state violence against its own people.

there are some countries, such as Iran, North Sudan, and Saudi Arabia, where the current leaders have a very specific vision of what forms of political and economic development they will facilitate, since any change must serve religious and social values that might be undermined by the type of 21st-century development described above.

Regardless of the form of development envisioned by the political leadership, the elites in most countries recognize that it is very difficult to control the *directions* of change with precision. The recent economic turmoil in many countries is an ominous indicator of the extent to which economic systems are vulnerable to decline and disarray. Their extraordinary complexity, both internally and as part of the global economy, makes it increasingly difficult to understand how they are changing and how to control them.

Political systems are arguably even more vulnerable to decline and disarray. Samuel Huntington (1968) has described how some political systems that appear to have achieved a reasonable level of political development then experience a substantial deterioration of political structures, processes, and roles. He calls this situation political decay—*a significant decline in the capabilities of the political system and its level of political institutionalization, and especially in its capacity to maintain order*. Political decay is evident in high levels of civil disorder—strikes, violent crime, riots, nation-based conflict, and rebellion.

Political decay can have multiple causes, many of which are associated with the change processes discussed in this chapter. The development process is inherently destabilizing. Economic growth produces new resources over which to compete; urbanization concentrates heterogeneous groups into large, densely packed and volatile masses; expanded, globalized communications make the people aware of the many resources and values that they do not currently enjoy. Most people expect their political system to provide stability, prosperity, and security. If the political system does not adequately meet these expectations and if it lacks solid political institutionalization, citizen support and social order can decline. In response to political decay, several scenarios can evolve:

- The political system cracks down on disorder, limiting the rights of protest groups, opposition parties, the free press, and so on, and deploying its security forces (e.g., the police, the military) to suppress any antiregime activities.
- A charismatic leader emerges. The leader gains the support and obedience of the people but only by personalizing power and thus weakening the overall processes through which power and political structures are institutionalized.
- The military—the one organization in most societies that *is* institutionalized—forcibly takes over political power under the justification of restoring order.
- A popular uprising, typically supported by external actors, drives the old leadership out; but if the active groups are fragmented and do not rapidly provide a coherent governing alternative, extensive, widespread disorder is likely.

In each of the first three scenarios, there is usually a shift towards greater authoritarianism. If the country had been deepening its democratic practices, these scenarios of political decay can lead to "democratic breakdown" and illiberal democracy. Such trends are evident in most regions in recent years (Freedom House 2011; Schedler 2006; Wiarda 2004; Zakaria 2007). If the situation approaches the fourth scenario of widespread disorder, even the fundamental goal of state survival is under threat.

Almost 50 countries are currently under such severe pressures, relative to their level of political institutionalization, that they are classified as "highly fragile states" (Marshall and Goldstone 2009). When *a political system completely loses its capacity to maintain basic order*, it can be characterized as a **failed state.** Recent examples include Afghanistan, Congo (D.R.), Iraq, Somalia, and Zimbabwe (Foreign Policy 2011; Rotberg 2003). Such widespread disorder can be almost akin to Hobbes's notion of the "state of nature." Life for most citizens truly is nasty, violent, and short, and many people engage in behaviors that are brutish. A failed state also creates dangers for other states in its region, due to disruptions caused by displaced populations and economic hardships. And in some cases, a state actually does cease to exist, as occurred several times in the recent history of Cambodia described in Compare in 10.

CONCLUDING OBSERVATIONS

Ultimately, all political systems aim to increase their capabilities and thus achieve greater political and economic development. In general, most people assume that development in other countries should result in political systems and political economies that resemble those in their own country. It is debatable, however, whether all states should or even can follow the same developmental path. Some, perhaps most, developing countries might have characteristics that are not compatible with the patterns of development or the political structures and processes that "worked" in other countries, especially those that developed in earlier eras.

The leaders in most countries try to assess whether the prior experiences and strategies of some other state provide a model for their own change and development. Even if leaders do select a model that seems compatible with their goals and unique characteristics, achieving political development and political institutionalization and sustaining economic growth are extremely difficult for many countries in the contemporary world. The remainder of this book will continue to illustrate the extent to which the choices and actions of states are influenced and sometimes controlled by other actors in the global system and by limits on their own resources. This is a particular problem for states with low capabilities and minimal stability—that is, states that lack political institutionalization.

Huntington is certainly correct that the challenges to political development are great. There have been periods of major political instability even in some European and Latin American countries—and these countries had the advantage of a long period in which the structures of a modern state could evolve into more complex and effective forms and in which the citizens could come to accept and value their political system. In contrast to those countries, most other states began creating their own modern political systems in the last 60 years. While these systems have the appearance of modernity—specialized political structures,

✓•⌐**Study**
and **Review** the
**Post-Test &
Chapter Exam** at
mypoliscilab.com

widespread political participation, and so on—many lack the stability and value that come with a long evolutionary development.

The political elites in many of these states face many fundamental dilemmas in a world of changes. How much political participation and opposition should be allowed? Into what aspects of people's lives should *res publica* be extended? In what ways should the state intervene in the political economy? What benefits and what burdens should the state allocate to particular groups? What should government do to nurture civil society and social order? In essence, can the political system shape political, economic, and social change? All states continually deal with these challenging issues, which will be recurrent themes in the remainder of this book.

KEY CONCEPTS

change   259
civil society   264
core   267
democratization   272
dependency approach   266
development   261
developmental state approach   265
economic development   261
failed state   279
modernization   260

neoliberalism   265
newly industrializing countries
  (NICs)   266
political decay   278
political development   268
political institutionalization   275
statism   265
system transformation   275
Westernization   261

FOR FURTHER CONSIDERATION

1. Most people in Western societies have been socialized to believe that change is associated with progress and is generally a good thing. However, the ideology of conservatism (as outlined in Chapter 2) does not make this assumption. What are the conservative's views about change? More broadly, can you specify types of change that would not necessarily be positive for a given political system?

2. The success or failure of the developmental state strategy in certain developing countries is sometimes attributed to elements of culture. How important do you think a society's culture might be in shaping development? Why? What factors other than culture might affect a country's capacity for rapid development?

3. Many countries have recently established democratic political processes. Is political decay inevitable in most of these countries? Why or why not? What strategies, general and specific, seem most promising in the attempt to avoid serious political decay?

4. Write a dialogue between two analysts: One contends that the dependency approach offers the best explanation for the failure of many countries to achieve development, while the second analyst argues that other factors best explain why some countries have limited development.

FOR FURTHER READING

Acemoglu, Daron and James A. Robinson. (2009). *Economic Origins of Dictatorship and Democracy*. New York: Cambridge University Press. An economist and political scientist combine to offer a highly praised (partly mathematical) theory of the key determinants of democratization, with interesting cases from many countries. They emphasize how the structure of the economic system and policy commitments regarding equality in the distribution of resources are critical for whether a country consolidates democracy or entrenches nondemocracy.

Achebe, Chinua. (1959). *Things Fall Apart*. New York: Doubleday. In this highly acclaimed and moving novel, Achebe describes how the beliefs and lives of a virtuous leader and others in his Nigerian village are undermined by missionaries and the colonial administration, as modernization results in the disintegration of their cultural traditions.

Becker, Elizabeth. (1986). *When the War Was Over: The Voices of Cambodia's Revolution and Its People*. New York: Simon and Schuster. A gut-wrenching description of Cambodia under the Pol Pot regime (Compare in 10).

Collier, Paul. (2007). *The Bottom Billion: Why the Poorest Countries Are Failing and What Can Be Done about It*. New York: Oxford University Press. The author elaborates on four key reasons accounting for the development failures of the world's poorest countries: civil wars, abundant resources that others covet, poor geography, and bad governance.

Cornwall, Andrea, Elizabeth Harrison and Ann Whitehead, Eds. (2007). *Feminisms in Development: Contradictions, Contestations, and Challenges*. London: Zen Books. Case studies and broader analyses examine development theory from a feminist perspective and provide strong examples regarding both the crucial roles and the marginalization of women in development.

Diamond, Larry. (2009). *The Spirit of Democracy: The Struggle to Build Free Societies throughout the World*. New York: Holt. A leading scholar of democratization offers an analysis of how countries can deepen their democracies, how other countries can help, and the strategies necessary to avoid the "democracy recessions" recently evident in a number of countries.

Harrison, Neil E. (2000). *Constructing Sustainable Development*. Albany: State University of New York Press. This brief, useful exploration of the various meanings attached to the concept of "sustainable development" concludes that the core values associated with the concept are inconsistent but argues nonetheless that there are policy actions that could advance sustainable development.

Huntington, Samuel P. (1991). *The Third Wave: Democratization in the Late Twentieth Century*. Norman: University of Oklahoma Press. A wide-ranging assessment of transitions to democracy by one of the major scholars of comparative development. The general argument about political institutionalization and political decay discussed in this chapter is fully elaborated in his earlier sweeping study *Political Order in Changing Societies* (New Haven, CT: Yale University Press, 1968).

Johnson, Chalmers. (1996). *Japan: Who Governs? The Rise of the Developmental State*. New York: W. W. Norton. This book provides a broad framework characterizing the government–industry cooperation that produced the "Japanese miracle" and became the basis of the development approach taken by other Asian NICs.

Lipset, Seymour Martin. (1988). *Revolution and Counterrevolution: Change and Persistence in Social Structures*. Rev. ed. Rutgers, NJ: Transaction Books. Provocative essays on the processes of change and development, with a particular emphasis on the effects of culture.

Rotberg, Robert I., Ed. (2003). *When States Fail: Causes and Consequences*. Princeton, NJ: Princeton University Press. The first part of the book is a series of essays examining the conditions under which states deteriorate to the point of collapse; the second part offers analyses of what can be done to prevent failed states and how to rebuild such states.

Schneider, Carsten. (2009). *The Consolidation of Democracy: Comparing Europe and Latin America*. London: Routledge. A careful analysis of the conditions under which democratic consolidation (institutionalization) is more likely, placing particular importance on the fit between the political institutional arrangements and the dispersion of power in the society.

Sorensen, Georg. (2007). *Democracy and Democratization: Processes and Prospects in a Changing World*. 3rd ed. Boulder, CO: Westview. A wide-ranging discussion of the spread of democratic processes in many countries, defining the patterns and conditions under which democracy is viable and the likely evolution of various democratic systems.

Wiarda, Howard J. (2004). *Political Development in Emerging Countries*. Belmont, CA: Wadsworth. A sensible description of the major theories of development in the developing countries (see Chapter 14). It indicates how frameworks such as dependency theory, neoliberalism, globalization, and the developmental state approach apply to the situation in such countries.

ON THE WEB

http://hdr.undp.org/en/reports

This is the site for the United Nations Development Programme office, the source of the yearly Human Development Report, which provides an exceptionally comprehensive set of social and economic data about every country as well as detailed thematic explorations of topics regarding environment, health, human rights, economic development, and so on.

http://worldbank.org

At the official site of the World Bank, an international consortium of banks and other major financial institutions, extensive economic data are available, including selections from the annual World Development Report, as well as information on issues of development and trade.

http://www.iisd.ca

The Web site of the International Institute for Sustainable Development offers information and essays on this topic, ranging from policy statements and economic data to book-length studies.

http://w3.acdi-cida.gc.ca/home

This site from the Canadian International Development Agency provides links to many sources of information about development issues, such as aid, economic growth, environmental impacts, and human rights issues.

http://www.un.org/esa/dsd/index.shtml

The home page of the United Nations Division for Sustainable Development, this site provides access to a wide variety of relevant UN resolutions and publications.

http://www.ulb.ac.be/ceese/meta/sustvl.html

This section of the very comprehensive World Wide Web Virtual Library (http://vlib .org/) contains an extensive listing of Internet resources related to sustainable development and political change.

http://www.foreignpolicy.com/articles/2009/06/22/the_2009_failed_states_index

The Fund for Peace, an independent research organization, and the journal Foreign Policy use 12 indicators of state cohesion and performance to compute an annual "Failed State Index" for all countries and provide details of the challenges facing the 60 countries most at risk of failure.

http://www.crisisgroup.org/home

This is the International Crisis Group's "Crisis Web," which details the current crises within countries with serious levels of political decay and offers policy suggestions for conflict management and a return to political order.

Politics Across Borders

LEARNING OBJECTIVES

11.1 Compare realist and idealist perspectives of the state.

11.2 Classify the main actors in the global system and characterize the mechanisms of cooperation between states.

11.3 Analyze the types of interactions between states and evaluate the impact of globalization.

⬚•⬚ Read and **Listen** to **Chapter 11** at **mypoliscilab.com**

✓•⬚ **Study** and **Review** the **Pre-Test & Flashcards** at **mypoliscilab.com**

After being ravaged by the two bloodiest and most costly wars in modern history (World War I and World War II), bitter rivals France, Germany, and Italy, along with Belgium, Luxembourg, and the Netherlands, decided to create political and economic ties that would ensure their countries would cooperate rather than fight. In 1952, the six countries established an economic union and then, with the Treaty of Rome (1957), created the European Economic Community (the "Common Market.") Countries that had periodically fought now began an era of cooperation. Cultures that had clashed now attempted to blend and share common goals.

In 60 years, this competitive group of states has evolved into the European Union (EU) and grown to 27 member states and 500 million citizens, operating with 23 official languages. Greater economic integration has led to an efficient sharing of markets and labor across borders and the elimination of most tariff fights. The economy of the EU is currently the world's largest, characterized by diversity, growth, and prosperity.

The EU is governed by effective legislative, executive, administrative, and judicial branches, which operate on democratic principles and exhibit strong political institutionalization. The Lisbon Treaty of 2009, approved by all 27 members, increased coherence in collective policymaking by implementing a more integrated, majority-based political framework under a strong president. The EU has established a collective security pact that not only prevents these states from going to war against each other but also makes the EU a formidable military power, such that no country in the world is likely to challenge one of its members.

However, all is not perfect in the EU. While several countries, especially France and Germany, advocate increased integration and seek to create "pooled sovereignty" by establishing a federation, the EU is still a rather loosely connected confederation. Long-held cultural and national identities remain a major obstacle to complete integration. The broad voting consensus required for policymaking can be difficult to achieve when some of the 27 countries disagree or act on their own national interests. There are substantial challenges in sustaining a single economic policy; for example, only 16 countries in the EU have joined the euro zone, while countries like the United Kingdom and Sweden continue to use their own national currencies. And weaknesses, just like strengths, become a shared problem for all member states, as the euro zone crises in Greece, Ireland, and Portugal during the recent global recession have revealed. The fiscally-sound countries have been obliged to bail out the countries running high deficits, fostering distrust and resentment.

Critics argue that the EU does not have a coherent military policy or even a standing military. Some members have also refused to provide military forces to support EU security initiatives outside of the EU countries. Moreover, the EU's open borders allow unrestricted movement of people across all EU countries, including individuals who have entered any EU country illegally from the rest of the world. Thus, the native population of every EU country is attempting to adapt to the influx of many new cultures. This has generated considerable tension and a rise in popularity of nationalistic (and sometimes anti-EU) political parties and social movements. Some countries are now considering a return to controlled borders—a serious retreat from the vision of an integrated Europe.

Clearly, the European Union has a long way to go in terms of integrating and establishing a unified Europe, but the countries that make up the EU are generally more successful working together than they ever were as competing, independent states. The EU is one of the most remarkable recent efforts by states to establish institutions that overcome historical conflict and facilitate cooperation.

The states in the EU are among the millions of political actors whose interests and actions cross national borders. Many of the most important aspects of contemporary politics occur across borders. Mexico and the United States attempt to cooperate to reduce the flow of guns, drugs, and people across their shared border. India and Pakistan argue about who should control Jammu and Kashmir. UN forces are active in South Sudan to promote peace and security with Sudan. Multinational corporations such as Toyota work with and around government regulations to produce goods in many countries and then sell them in other countries. More than 100 countries discuss how to reduce carbon emissions in response to climate change. One billion people live in countries in which they are not citizens. Almost everyone now recognizes that no country can function within its own borders without extensive penetration by actors from beyond those borders.

Understanding how these kinds of political behaviors and institutions function across borders is the focus of this chapter. Some of the many important nonstate actors are highlighted in the discussions, although states are central to most of the topics because they are still crucial actors in the politics across borders. Globalization (discussed later in this chapter) is dramatically increasing the extent to which states are penetrated by outside forces, and many states expend much—and, in some cases most—of their political energy on their relations with other states and with transborder actors. *One state's decisions and actions in its relations with all actors operating outside the state's borders* are called **foreign policy**. The *politically relevant interactions among two or more actors from different states* are called international relations. Initially, this chapter details key perspectives and certain constraints that might guide states as they pursue their goals in the politics that occurs across borders. Second, it discusses the means by which states and transborder actors attempt to facilitate cooperation and resolve conflict. Third, it examines key forms of political competition across borders, such as balance of power and colonial domination. The causes and use of force and violence across state borders will be considered in Chapter 12.

PERSPECTIVES ON STATES' BEHAVIOR

Realist and Idealist Perspectives on the States' "Motives"

11.1 Compare realist and idealist perspectives of the state.

Chapter 5 identified three core goals that all states pursue: prosperity, stability, and security, as well as an array of key subgoals. All of these goals, and especially security, can be powerfully influenced by the politics across borders, politics in which states remain critical actors. While a state has sovereign rights to control what occurs within its territorial borders, it faces a security dilemma in the global system because the politics between and among states occurs in an international system that is generally assumed to be *anarchic*. This does not mean that the system is chaotic; rather, it means that *a state's security is always at risk because there is no overarching authority that can impose order and "good behavior" on all the states* in their relations with each other and with other actors outside their border.

Scholars attempt to explain how and why states interact in the ways that they do in the absence of such an authority. To understand how states behave in relation to other actors in the global system, it is helpful to identify what motivates them. That is, states can be analyzed, almost like individuals, as having motives and values as they pursue their goals in the international environment. Two perspectives have especially influenced international relations theory on this issue: political realism and political idealism.

Watch the Video "Nuclear Disarmament Under the INF Treaty" at mypoliscilab.com

Political realism assumes that *people are naturally disposed to base their behavior on self-interest*. This same self- (national) interest extends to the behavior of the states that people form. Because there is no supreme authority that protects the states from predatory behavior by other states in the international system, every state experiences the security dilemma—that no higher power will necessarily protect it. Thus, the fundamental goal of each state is to ensure its own security and survival. A state's security increases to the extent it maximizes its own power (e.g., political power, economic power, knowledge power, and especially military power) relative to the power of every other state. States are in constant competition for power, especially because power is a "zero-sum" commodity—an increase in power for one actor results in an equivalent decrease for others. There is no expectation that another state can be trusted, will avoid violence, or will act ethically. A state makes treaties or breaks them, makes war, or cooperates with other countries for only one reason: to maximize its security goals and serve its national interest.

In contrast, the crucial assumption of political idealism (also called *political liberalism*) is that *human nature is basically good. People, and the states they construct, can be altruistic and cooperative*. States have many goals, and aggressive, power-maximizing behavior is not inevitable. If a state's actions reduce the welfare of people in any country or increase interstate conflict and war, it is usually because of poorly designed institutions (e.g., governments, economic systems, and legal systems), not because people and states are evil or selfish. For the political idealist, it is possible to establish an international system in which well-designed institutions can facilitate cooperative behavior among states and create a situation that is a "positive sum"—some gain, no one loses.

It is obvious that realism and idealism (and their recent elaborations, neorealism and neoliberalism, respectively) lead to very different explanations of a state's behavior towards other states (Kegley 2011; Keohane and Nye 2011; Mearsheimer

2001). They also provide contrasting prescriptions about how a state should respond to the actions of another state. Your understanding of the political world will be influenced by your orientation to these perspectives. Are you more oriented to the realist or the idealist perspective?

There are other important perspectives on politics across borders that some scholars find illuminating. Two that are especially noteworthy are constructivist and feminist approaches to international relations. *Constructivism* suggests it is important to recognize that actors develop unique understandings of events, based on their knowledge, experiences, and habits. Thus, actors are less constrained by an anarchic world and concepts like national interest than realists assume; rather, actors interpret the structural conditions in which they find themselves, based on their own experiences, norms, and values. For similar reasons, constructivists conclude that idealists place too much reliance on the forms of institutions, since these will be perceived differently by various actors, depending on the orientations they bring to the situation. In this view, neither realism nor idealism is adequately sensitive to the "socially constructed" nature of the identities and norms that shape beliefs and guide actions taken by individuals, groups, and states in the international system (Barnett and Finnemore 2004; Wendt 1995; 1999).

As you might expect, *feminist IR* analyzes topics from the frames of reference and assumptions of feminist theory and gender studies. It posits that, in general, women have different political orientations than men, due to their socialization (and perhaps different brain biology). Thus, women are more inclined towards cooperative interactions and nonviolent solutions and, if more such women were in positions of power, states would interact somewhat less aggressively (Enloe 2001; Steans 2006; Tickner 2001). As you read the discussion of politics across borders, consider how the different assumptions of realism, idealism, constructivism, or feminism can alter one's interpretations of the topics in this chapter.

A Geopolitical Perspective

It is always the case that the state's pursuit of its goals is constrained by many factors, both within and outside its borders. The political systems model outlined in Chapter 5 reminds us that a state's actions can be very much influenced by many aspects of the extrasocietal environment, including the actions of other state and nonstate actors. And there are also influential factors within a state's intrasocietal environment, such as its history and political culture, the style of its major political leaders, and the nature of its political structures.

Geopolitical analysis emphasizes one set of critical factors that might constrain a state's behavior, especially in its relations with other actors in the international system. Geopolitics assumes that *the geography of a state—that is, its physical characteristics (e.g., strategic location, topography) and its natural and human resources (e.g., population size, fossil fuel resources, arable land, water)—might significantly affect both the internal and external politics of the state* (Cohen 2008). Few argue that "geography is destiny." However, it is reasonable to assume that a state's geography can be a significant source of both opportunities and constraints on its political actions in the international system (Dalby 2008; Kaplan 2009). Compare in 11 proposes how a geopolitical analysis might offer insights into the foreign policies of two states.

COMPARE IN 11 | Geopolitics in Two Countries

Imagine two island countries, Sigma and Theta. Each lies just off a (different) large landmass that is dominated by one of the world's most powerful countries. Unfortunately, this powerful neighbor is a major enemy and a threat. Each island nation has a well-educated, mainly, urban population. Each has a fickle, tropical climate, and one-fourth of the land is arable. Sigma has relatively abundant natural resources while Theta has fewer such resources, but both need to import sources of energy.

If you knew nothing more about either country, could you make any educated guesses about how these countries might pursue key political and economic goals and about the relations these countries might develop with other actors in the international system? This is the core of geopolitical analysis. For example, to enhance their security, each might look for an alliance with another country that is a powerful enemy of their neighbor. Each would probably establish a strong military. So that the hostile neighbor does not sense instability and weakness, the political system might be somewhat authoritarian to control its population and minimize internal conflict. Sigma might be able to rely on its fertile land and natural resources as a solid basis for exports. Theta might need to rely more heavily on its workforce to produce more sophisticated value-added goods and services to gain trading partners. Both would need to secure energy resources.

Sigma could be Cuba. Cuba achieved independence from its colonial master, Spain, in 1902. After nearly 50 years of corrupt, authoritarian regimes that left most of the population minimally educated and economically exploited, a successful guerrilla war led by Fidel Castro installed a communist regime in 1959. This antagonized Cuba's powerful neighbor and former best friend, the United States. As Cuba perceived numerous attempts by the United States to undermine its regime (some real, some imagined), its leadership increased Cuba's military readiness, with universal military service and constant political socialization regarding the threat from the United States (recall the

Cuban math problem at the beginning of Chapter 4). Castro and the Communist Party became increasingly authoritarian politically, suppressing almost all opposition voices. While its command political economy resulted in low productivity, the system did manage to provide good health care, universal literacy, greater social and economic equality, and Social Security for all citizens. Cuba forged a strong alliance with the major cold war enemy of the U.S., the Soviet Union, which served as Cuba's military protector and which provided it with $4 to $6 billion in subsidies each year, including energy resources. After the Soviets tried unsuccessfully to install missiles on Cuba pointing at the United States (the "Cuban missile crisis" in 1961), the U.S. intensified its pressure for an extensive trade embargo that has undermined the Cuban economy. Since the collapse of the Soviet Union (1989) and the loss of Soviet subsidies, Cuba has struggled even more because only limited trade bypasses the embargo. Recently, Cuba developed strong ties with Venezuela's Hugo Chavez, another leader antagonistic to the United States, who has exported energy resources to Cuba, in exchange for skilled Cuban professionals who work in Venezuela, especially in health care and education.

Theta could be Taiwan. An island extension of China, it was conquered by Japan in 1895 and subjected to harsh colonization until Japan's defeat in World War II. When the Nationalists under Chiang Kai-shek lost to Mao Zedong in the civil war on mainland China in 1949, the Nationalists fled to Taiwan and took control of its political and economic systems. The Nationalists were in fundamental opposition to Mao Zedong's government, insisting that they were the rightful rulers of China and would one day regain control of the mainland. In response, Mao's government insisted that Taiwan was a "renegade province" that would ultimately be reunited with China. The United States, deeply threatened by China's communist government, stepped in to become Taiwan's protector.

(Continued)

Taiwan took advantage of extensive military and economic support from the United States. It established a strong military presence, backed by U.S. arms. And it developed an aggressively capitalist political economy, following the developmental state approach, described in Chapter 10. Because it had limited natural resources, Taiwan became a manufacturing economy, importing materials and moving from the production of toys, textiles, and other less-sophisticated goods to the export of goods such as electronics components, armaments, chemicals, iron, and steel. It relied on the United States as its main target for exports and imports, including energy.

In 1971, the United Nations voted to deny Taiwan recognition as an independent sovereign state. Given concerns that instability in Taiwan would encourage China to intervene or invade, Taiwan's government was highly authoritarian, with strict limits on political opposition, and substantial democratization has emerged only in the last decade. Over time, Taiwan has managed its human resources very

effectively and created a strong economy within the global system. Because Japan and China are such juggernaut regional economies, Taiwan has slowly built trade relations with these historical enemies, and they are now its main trading partners. Tensions with China remain high, however, with China continuing to claim sovereignty over Taiwan, and Taiwan relying on its substantial military and the ongoing protection from the United States to retain its independence (CIA 2011).

While geography is not destiny, it is evident that the domestic and foreign policies of both Cuba and Taiwan have been significantly influenced by their geopolitical circumstances.

FURTHER QUESTIONS

1. How might Cuba and Taiwan have acted differently if their powerful neighbor was a strong ally instead of an intransigent enemy?

2. What are other countries for whom a geopolitical analysis might be especially insightful? ▲

Compare in 11 also reveals how the politics across state borders are usually characterized by a mix of cooperation and competition. For example, Taiwan interacts with the United States as a cooperative partner on security issues, and it both cooperates and competes with the United States regarding imports and exports. The rest of this chapter explores these two dominant patterns in international relations. In most instances, a state realizes more benefits and fewer costs if it pursues its goals by strategies of *cooperation* with other states and with transborder actors. However, *competition* is always a possibility, as states come into conflict with other actors as they pursue their goals. The final section in Chapter 12 will examine those crucial situations where conflict resolution fails and the competition escalates into violence across borders and into war.

MECHANISMS OF POLITICAL COOPERATION ACROSS BORDERS

Do you agree with the proposition that, under most circumstances, a state is likely to accomplish more of its goals at lower costs if it can develop mutually advantageous cooperative arrangements with other states? This section will consider the various ways in which states can cooperate. From the neoliberal (contemporary idealist) perspective, a state has an inherent preference to establish arrangements

11.2 Classify the main actors in the global system and characterize the mechanisms of cooperation between states.

Watch the Video "Global Governance and the ICC" at mypoliscilab.com

through which such cooperation can be nurtured. Realists are likely to be more cynical about such cooperation, viewing such arrangements as strategic actions to be made or broken as they serve the state's national interest.

Even in the absence of any formalized mechanisms of cooperation, there are several patterns of behavior that a state might adopt and that are noteworthy for their nonconflictual approach:

1. **Altruism:** A state acts in accordance with moral principles, not its national interest. Thus, the state might provide humanitarian aid to the population of another country with no expectation of direct benefits, or it might make a unilateral decision to reduce its military capabilities or its carbon emissions in order to improve the global environment.

2. **Accommodation:** A state willingly makes concessions on one or more values of importance in order to promote an acceptable outcome or a nonviolent resolution of a dispute with another actor. This might involve a compromise in which several states find "common ground," or one state might make a disproportionate level of concessions in an attempt to improve its relations or avoid conflict with another actor (e.g., a state, a multinational financial institution, or an international judicial body).

3. **Neutrality:** A state claims its right to be impartial among competing states and to refrain from supporting any states in a conflict. A key goal of a neutral state is to avoid being drawn into a dispute among other states. Thus, in recent decades, countries such as Austria, Finland, Sweden, and Switzerland have defined themselves as neutral states.

Diplomacy and Interstate Agreements

One of the most widely used mechanisms through which states communicate and enhance cooperation is *diplomacy*. Diplomatic practices enable a state's skilled representatives to engage in regular discussions and negotiations with the representatives of other states. Thus, most states maintain an array of actors (e.g., ambassadors, cultural attachés) and institutions (e.g., embassies, trade delegations) who attempt to further their state's interests and resolve potential problems with other states by means of "normal diplomatic channels" and informal communications. The essence of traditional diplomacy is strategic, face-to-face discussions between diplomats on behalf of their countries. However, modern communications technologies (e.g., videoconferencing) have provided new ways for leaders as well as diplomats to interact, allowing them to deal with each other directly, even if not in person. In the world of 24/7 news media, political officials are aware that every public utterance is being recorded and is accessible around the world to other political actors via some medium, ranging from Al-Jazeera to YouTube.

A special form of diplomacy is when the top leaders of countries meet to share views and seek common policy ground. In any given week, there are one-on-one meetings, such as when chief executives or foreign ministers travel to meet their counterparts. During a single week in November 2011, for example, U.S. president Barack Obama held private meetings with China's president Hu Jintao,

Germany's chancellor Angela Merkel, India's prime minister Manmohan Singh, and Turkish prime minister Recep Erdogan among others.

So many private meetings in such a short time were possible because the leaders of major countries (the "G-20") were holding a summit meeting in Cannes. The G-20 is a global group of key industrial and emerging-market countries (plus a representative from the European Union) that particularly focuses on financial issues. The leaders of an even more elite group of powerful industrialized countries, the "G-8," also meet periodically to discuss shared policy concerns. Table 11.1 lists the members of these two groups. There are numerous other regional groups that hold recurrent meetings in an attempt to cooperate on policy (e.g., Association of Southeast Asian Nations [ASEAN] in South Asia, MERCOSUR in Latin America, the Organization of African States [OAS]).

More explicit cooperation among states is usually established by bilateral (between two states) or multilateral (among three or more states) agreements. The two most prominent forms of these agreements are treaties and regimes. Treaties are *formal agreements between states that they will cooperate or assist each other,* usually in the domains of military, economic, or political interactions. They resemble a contract between states (or with an international organization) and there is an expectation that the agreement is binding on all signatories. Most treaties involve a limited set of countries. For example, the North American Free Trade Agreement (NAFTA) is a treaty among three states (Canada, Mexico, and the United States) to cooperate on a complex set of trade arrangements. The Strategic Arms Reduction Treaties (e.g., START II, 1993) are weapons-limitation pacts between the United States and Russia. The European Union (EU), described at the beginning of this chapter, is an example of a major multistate, multipurpose confederation based on treaties for economic, political, cultural, and military cooperation among its 27 member countries.

Some multistate agreements are called international regimes to signify *a set of norms, rules, and procedures accepted by many countries that guide their behavior regarding a particular issue area.* There are only a limited number of international regimes. They are treaty-like, but typically there is a very large number of signatories and compliance is somewhat less rigorously enforced. Current

TABLE 11.1		
Major Diplomatic Groupings of States		
G-8	**G-20 (adds to G-8)**	
Canada	Argentina	Mexico
France	Australia	Saudi Arabia
Germany	Brazil	South Africa
Italy	China	South Korea
Japan	India	Turkey
Russia	Indonesia	European Union
United Kingdom		
United States		

examples are in the area of arms control (e.g., the Nuclear Nonproliferation Treaty [1968], now including 189 countries) and environmental protection (e.g., the 1997 Kyoto Protocol on climate change and greenhouse gas emissions, accepted by 191 countries and the EU). Many international regimes establish a permanent organization through which the member states can enact, modify, and implement the agreements and facilitate cross-national cooperation (Drezner 2007; Keohane 2005).

The World Trade Organization (WTO) is one of the most powerful and controversial international regimes. Established in 1995, the WTO emerged from an international trading regime that had evolved over the prior 50 years. The WTO, which currently has 153 member countries, states that its main goal is "to ensure that trade flows as smoothly, predictably and freely as possible" among all countries. It works with member countries to establish and enforce policies that eliminate all barriers to global free trade (e.g., tariffs on imports, subsidies to producers, "dumping" strategies [selling goods abroad at below cost to cripple competitors]). Hence, the WTO claims that the primary result of its actions is "a more prosperous, peaceful and accountable economic world" (WTO 2011).

However, critics assert that, as elite theory posits (recall Chapter 9), WTO rules and agreements primarily benefit the financial elites and multinational corporations that dominate global trade. They claim that the free trade agreements implemented by the WTO increase the profits of multinational corporations (MNCs) but reduce the power of workers, are indifferent to violations of human rights, fail to protect the environment, and undermine the sovereignty of national governments, which must accept WTO regulations. To its detractors, the WTO is "one of the most powerful, secretive and antidemocratic bodies on Earth," and the main results of its actions are to "preside over the greatest transfer in history, of real economic and political power away from nation-states to global corporations" and to "run roughshod over the rights of people and nations, causing all manner of environmental and social harms" (Global Exchange 2009; Mander 1999).

The direct, day-to-day interactions among most states are substantially governed by a variety of formal and informal agreements, of which treaties and regimes are among the most important. Like other forms of international cooperation, such agreements are binding only as long as the participating states are willing to abide by the conditions of the agreement or are willing to submit disputes to some form of resolution. But such agreements can collapse for various reasons.

- Some participants might find that their national goals are not well served, so they ignore or violate the agreement. For example, countries sometimes conclude that their own national economic needs justify subsidies to their producers (e.g., farmers, steel producers), even if other countries object that such subsidies violate WTO agreements.
- Participants might have different interpretations of what actions are deemed acceptable under the agreement. For example, Iran is among the 189 countries that have signed the Nuclear Nonproliferation Treaty, but there is considerable dispute over whether Iran's ongoing uranium enrichment programs

Large groups march in Manila, demanding that the Philippine government withdraw from the WTO.

are in violation of the treaty. Iran insists its actions are within its rights to develop nuclear energy for peaceful purposes. As agencies of the UN continue to investigate, some countries such as the United States argue for stronger sanctions against Iran, while others such as China and India have opposed additional sanctions.

■ Fulfillment of the key objectives in an agreement might be impossible. For example, the Treaty of Locarno (1925) between Britain and Italy failed in its attempt to deter Germany from violating the borders of France and Belgium because Britain and Italy were not strong enough to counteract Germany's military power, and Italy's government eventually concluded that Italy's national interests were better served by becoming more pro-German.

International Law

The *broadest attempt to formalize and constrain the interactions among states* is international law. In 1625, Hugo Grotius, the "father" of international law, published *De jure belli et pacis* (*On the Laws of War and Peace*) (Grotius 1625/1957). This document emphasized natural law—*universal principles of behavior that are recognizable through human reason and human nature and that direct us to act with goodness*—and thus should guide the relations among states and restrain hostile or destructive interactions. Unfortunately, states often define reasonable behavior according to their own political interests rather than shared abstract moral rules. Thus, by the 19th century, natural law had been supplanted by positivist law—*explicit written agreements that define both appropriate and unacceptable behaviors between states*, in the form of international treaties or conventions. Positivist laws have attempted to adjudicate geographic boundaries (e.g., the 12-mile limit on the territorial waters of states), to regulate states' use of environmental resources (e.g., laws limiting whale hunting in international waters), and to establish states' rights and limits over non-national resources (e.g., the law of outer space).

The treaties and conventions of positivist law even attempt to distinguish acceptable from unacceptable behavior during conflicts between states. For example, the Helsinki Agreement binds combatants to use no glass-filled projectiles or other forms of violence that produce "unnecessary suffering." The Geneva Convention on "fair" war prohibits the use of poison gases and insists that captured soldiers be treated with dignity, although it does not preclude most of the terrible forms of suffering or death that a soldier can experience *before* he becomes a prisoner.

While positivist law has the great advantage of being formulated in explicit written agreements, the effectiveness of such agreements ultimately depends on the willingness of states to comply with them. Even if states sign a particular agreement, they sometimes openly violate the agreement and later deny accusations of such a violation. The International Court of Justice (also known as the ICJ or the World Court) at The Hague was established in 1946 to adjudicate violations of positivist international law and to offer advisory opinions on issues of international law.

Part of the United Nations, the International Court of Justice has occasionally served as a valuable mechanism for conflict resolution between states. However, the court has jurisdiction and binding authority only if both parties to the dispute accept its ruling. Less than one-third of the member states of the United Nations have agreed to accept automatically the ICJ's jurisdiction in matters affecting them. When the political or economic stakes are high or even when emotional elements of the disagreement are intense, states have often refused to accept the court's jurisdiction or to be bound by its judgments. The United States has taken cases to the court, but it is among the majority of states that rejects the court's automatic jurisdiction, as it did in a 1984 case brought by the Nicaraguan government, which objected to covert U.S. actions against it (such as mining Nicaraguan harbors).

Prior to the 1990s, the ICJ was not particularly active. Between 1946 and 1991, it considered only 64 cases, gave advisory opinions in 19 cases, and handled very few cases that actually concerned violent conflicts between states. However, the ICJ has averaged 14 cases per year since the mid-1990s, is dealing with more disputes involving political violence, and is now issuing numerous advisory opinions each year (http://www.icj-cij.org). Another important recent development is the expanded use of international law to arrest and prosecute political leaders and other individuals accused of extensive human rights violations. Such trials can be handled by the relevant country, as in the trial of Saddam Hussein in Iraq. Since 2002, a permanent International Criminal Court (ICC) at The Hague is a "court of last resort" that can take up cases of genocide, crimes against humanity, and war crimes if any of the 114 countries that support the court is not prepared to handle such a case in its national court system. In its early years, the ICC has tried cases of human rights violations involving top government leaders from Ivory Coast (Laurent Gbagbo) and the Sudan (Omar Bashir) and rebel leaders from the Democratic Republic of Congo and Uganda.

The increased activities of these international courts reflect a growing interest in using international law more aggressively, not only to adjudicate disputes between states but also to hold individuals accountable for the ultra-violence perpetrated by their states. Do you think political leaders should be legally responsible before an international court system for the actions of their soldiers? More broadly, is it acceptable for a state to refuse the court's jurisdiction? What do you think would happen to international politics if all states automatically accepted the jurisdiction of the International Court of Justice and the ICC?

International Organizations

International organizations is a broad term for many of the *transnational institutions whose core objectives include actions to influence the behavior and policies of states and other transborder actors.* (Transnationalism describes *institutions or actors who engage in a significant array of activities that cross state borders.*) A few international organizations attempt to prevent or resolve conflict among states. Most such organizations focus on specific issue areas that are of global significance in the economic, social, environmental, cultural, or political domain and, in their actions, tend to facilitate cooperation across borders. There are three major types of international organizations: intergovernmental organizations (IGOs); international nongovernmental organizations (NGOs); and multinational corporations (MNCs).

IGOs Intergovernmental organizations (IGOs) are *political institutions whose members are states,* not private groups or individuals. Although there are currently fewer than 300 permanent IGOs, they have vast potential to shape the politics across borders. States jointly establish IGOs for a variety of different purposes: to provide a forum for communication between states; to implement policies that respond to political, social, or economic problems transcending national boundaries; to enact international laws and treaties; and to intervene in disputes between states. Most IGOs are regional, such as the EU, the North Atlantic Treaty Organization (NATO), the Association of Southeast Asian Nations (ASEAN), and the Arab League. Others have a global membership and focus, such as the World Trade Organization (WTO), the International Monetary Fund (IMF), and the World Health Organization (WHO).

The most powerful and wide-ranging IGOs in the 20th century were two major international organizations: the League of Nations and the United Nations. The League of Nations was formed in 1921 (after World War I) as a mechanism for collective security against aggression. But Italian aggression in Ethiopia and Japanese aggression in Manchuria in the 1930s revealed that the League lacked the diplomatic, political, or military power to achieve its goal.

The United Nations (UN) was created in 1945 (after World War II) as an international organization dedicated to managing international security. In pursuit of this objective, the UN has five principal organs with specific functions:

1. The *Security Council* is the body within the UN that has the authority to directly manage international conflicts because it can pass binding resolutions that authorize the use of force, peacekeeping missions, and sanctions.

Its membership includes five permanent members with veto power (China, France, Russia, the United Kingdom, and the United States) and 10 rotating members.

2. The *General Assembly* has representatives from all 193 member states of the UN and serves as a forum for discussion of global issues. Although the General Assembly lacks the legal authority to pass binding resolutions, it oversees the entire UN budget as well as many specialized bodies.

3. The *Economic and Social Council* (ECOSOC) promotes economic and social cooperation and development. To achieve this goal, ECOSOC works with the General Assembly to coordinate and oversee most UN committees.

4. The *Secretariat* is the central bureaucracy, responsible for the UN's day-to-day operations. It is headed by the UN's most visible representative, the secretary-general (currently, Ban Ki-Moon).

5. The *International Court of Justice* is the UN's primary judicial body. It is responsible for interpreting international law (described in the previous section).

Figure 11.1 shows a number of the special units that function within the principal divisions of the UN.

While the United Nations has a mixed record of success and failure in its central objective of maintaining global peace, it *has* improved the international political climate. At the least, the United Nations has been a highly effective setting within which rivals can engage in continuing diplomacy. Particularly within the Security Council and the General Assembly, UN officials and representatives from various countries can attempt to mediate conflicts and prevent escalation to war. The UN can also pass resolutions that might constrain certain countries from acting in opposition to the moral force of international public opinion (Kennedy 2006; Weiss and Daws 2009).

Most directly, a UN *peacekeeping operation* can intervene between combatants. This is *an impartial, multinational military and civilian force authorized by the UN Security Council with the consent of the disputing parties.* The peacekeeping force literally stands between the combatants in an attempt to ease tensions, and it uses force only in defense. The United States and the Soviet Union used their veto power in the Security Council to block many potential peacekeeping initiatives during the cold war. In the post–cold war period (beginning in the late 1980s), the use of UN peacekeeping forces has expanded. Thus, 47 UN peacekeeping operations have been deployed since 1990, compared with only 18 in the preceding 42 years (United Nations Peacekeeping Operations 2011). By its various actions, the UN has contributed to what former UN Secretary-General Dag Hammarskjold (1953–1961) called "preventive diplomacy"—limiting the extensive political and military involvement of major powers during conflicts between other countries. In 1988, the UN peacekeeping operations were awarded the Nobel Peace Prize.

Significantly, most of the post–cold war operations differ from earlier ones in that their central objective is to establish *internal* peace among factions within a country. Of 15 peacekeeping missions active in 2011, for example, the primary objective in 13 (including the Democratic Republic of Congo, Haiti, Ivory Coast, Kosovo, and Lebanon) was to prevent political violence among groups within

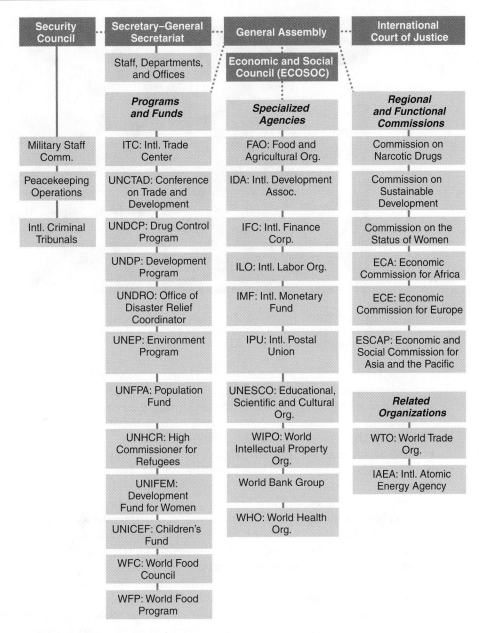

FIGURE 11.1

United Nations organization: principal organs and selected units

the country. It has been difficult for UN forces to end the violence in these internal conflicts where both borders and the identity of combatants are ambiguous. However, a study of 124 UN peacekeeping actions in internal conflicts concludes that they have generally been successful in ending the violence and increasing the likelihood of greater democratization (Doyle and Sambanis 2000).

The United Nations is active in diplomacy, peacekeeping, and providing services to enhance the quality of life of citizens in many countries, as in this distribution of food aid to children in Haiti.

The UN's other main goals concern improving the relations among states and helping countries improve the health, welfare, and human rights of their people. Coordinated by both the General Assembly and the Economic and Social Council, committees, agencies, and commissions, such as the World Health Organization (WHO), the United Nations Educational, Scientific, and Cultural Organization (UNESCO), and the United Nations Conference on Trade and Development (UNCTAD), attempt to mitigate global problems and enhance the quality of human life in areas such as human rights, agricultural development, environmental protection, refugees, children's health, and disaster relief.

The continuing level of political violence in the international system underscores the fact that the United Nations lacks the power to prevent all interstate conflict. Many states withdraw their support (financial and political) when UN actions are at variance with the states' perceptions of their national interest. However, through its agencies, its debates and resolutions, its continuous open forum for formal and informal communications between states, and its peacekeeping operations, the UN does contribute to greater cooperation, reduced human suffering, and reduced conflict among states. For such contributions, Nobel Peace Prizes were awarded to the UN and then Secretary-General Kofi Annan in 2001 and to the UN International Atomic Energy Agency and its then head, Mohammed Elbaradei, in 2005.

NGOs The second type of international organization is nongovernmental organizations. NGOs are composed of *nonstate actors (private individuals and groups) who work actively in a particular issue area* to provide information, promote public policies, and even provide services that might otherwise be provided by governments. *International* NGOs work with each other, with governments, and with IGOs to address problems that cross state borders. Between 1960 and 2000, the number of NGOs active in at least three countries rose from 1,000 to more than 30,000 and currently is more than 50,000. This includes about 5,000 major NGOs that are very active in a large number of countries (Union of International Associations 2011; Weiss 1996).

International NGOs are committed to furthering political and social issues with transnational dimensions. Although their issues tend to be regional or global, the actions and effectiveness of these NGOs can be analyzed in the same framework applied to the analysis of national interest groups (see Chapter 3). These groups encourage concerned individuals, groups, and even the governments of other states to write letters, organize demonstrations or boycotts, or engage in other political actions to pressure a government or transnational actor to change its practices (Smith 2007).

For example, you might be aware, from media, mailings, or other information sources, of the environmental protection actions of Greenpeace, the animal preservation goals of the World Wildlife Federation, or the lobbying by the Union of Concerned Scientists to limit destructive technologies. Amnesty International, another well-known NGO, is concerned with protecting human rights and is engaged in campaigns to focus attention and pressure on governments that are violating the rights of their citizens. It is one of the leading NGOs among an expanding group of transborder organizations that promote the protection of human rights. Often, local movements of human rights activists coalesce with others outside their state's boundaries to promote this issue.

The actions of some NGOs extend far beyond lobbying because they generate resources and actually deliver goods and services, such as the humanitarian medical services provided by *Medecins sans Frontieres,* winner of the 1999 Nobel Peace Prize. With the globalization of communications and greater mobility, many other groups, advocacy networks, and social movements are able to engage in a mix of persuasion and action, although most operate in only a limited set of countries. Overall, transnational NGOs enjoy higher public trust than either governments or business, and have a growing economic base (more than $1 trillion). They are "increasingly important in shaping national and international politics, governance processes and markets" and are "amongst the most influential institutions of the twenty-first century" (Elkington and Beloe 2003).

MNCs It is also clear that the actions of many *multinational corporations* (MNCs, also referred to as TNCs—transnational corporations) have significant impacts on the politics within and between states. From a political economy perspective, MNCs are *powerful firms that produce and sell a diversity of goods in many countries* in pursuit of private profit (e.g., Exxon, British Petroleum, Samsung, CITIC Group-China, Sumitomo). The global impacts of major MNCs are based on their sheer economic weight as some of the richest institutions in the world. In terms of comparative economic power (measured as gross economic product), only about half of the top 100 economic units in the world are countries, and half are multinational corporations (Kegley and Wittkopf 2004: Table 5.2).

Three other crucial features of MNCs add to their major importance in the global system. These features enhance the MNC's flexibility and bargaining power in dealing with the governmental institutions and the political economy in any state. First, a major MNC functions as a *globalized network*. Because its operations are spread across many countries, an MNC can rapidly move its activities to exploit opportunities and avoid problems in any host country and even in its home country. This enables the MNC to pressure governments into competing for a share of its operations by providing the MNC with large financial inducements (e.g., tax breaks, enhanced government services, bribes) and by minimizing the state's regulatory constraints on the MNC's undesirable activities (e.g., negative environmental impacts, labor practices, product safety). Secondly, the MNCs capacity for *product diversification* enables an MNC to shift its balance of production among a variety of different goods, further reducing its dependence on any single country or any particular source of land, labor, or capital. And third, an MNC can *transform itself,* breaking off units into independent companies, engaging in mergers, launching completely new areas of activity, or even shutting down entire divisions. These three strategic elements increase the MNC's autonomy, influence, and profitability at the expense of the host country's political economy and its government, which must continue to make costly concessions to compete for a share of the MNC's operation and are constantly vulnerable to the MNCs decisions.

Moreover, those MNCs that engage in financial services can shift assets in nanoseconds, since they operate primarily in the virtual world. When globalized financial institutions suddenly move in similar directions, such as speculating in a country's currency or dumping its bonds, the country's overall financial stability and strength can be quickly altered. Such actions by financial MNCs can result in a rapid credit crunch or a run on the currency. With all of this leverage, these financial MNCs are able to exert tremendous influence on government policy in ways that serve the goals of the MNC.

For all these reasons, some critics claim that MNCs challenge the very sovereignty and autonomy of the state because they can avoid most of the laws and taxes of any state and can pressure the state to enact favorable policies. Critics also argue that MNCs monopolize the production and distribution of important goods in the world marketplace, squeeze out many small firms, and widen the economic gap between the rich and poor countries (Keohane and Nye 2011; Russett, Starr, and Kinsella 2009). Hence, "the MNC remains one of the most controversial actors in the international political economy" (Jenkins 1993: 606).

POLITICAL COMPETITION ACROSS BORDERS

11.3 Analyze the types of competitive interactions between states and evaluate the impact of globalization.

Actors operating across state borders often look for mutually beneficial interactions. But when the divergent interests of states and other transborder actors are stronger than their mutual interests, competitive behavior is more likely than cooperation. From the realist perspective in particular, competition is a central feature of the international system.

Recall that power is exercised when one actor uses its actions or resources to cause another actor to do something that the other actor otherwise would not do (Compare in 5). In the relations between states, there are frequent examples of "power politics." Chapter 12 will examine the use of force across borders. But even without using force or even threatening to use force, any state can attempt to use its influence, trying to persuade another state to act in a certain way that it is not inclined to do, just because it is the right thing to do or because it will serve the other state's goals in ways it does not realize. Usually, however, it takes more than persuasion to cause a country to act against what it perceives to be its national interest.

Some analysts suggest that states can successfully use "**soft power**" (Fraser 2005; Nye 2004, 2011). This is a variation on the power/influence theme, positing that one state so admires another state's values, its policies, or even its culture that the first state agrees to go along with the demands of the admired state. For example, it is argued that the soft power of the United States (e.g., its political institutions, music, values, Barack Obama) has penetrated some other countries so deeply that it gives the United States leverage in interstate dealings with those countries. The concept has been applied to other countries like China (Kurlantzick 2007), although not all scholars are persuaded about the power of soft power (Berenskoetter and Williams 2007).

Compare in 5 also described "**exchange power**." This means a state can offer something of value to another state in order to cause the other state to do something it would not otherwise do. Or the state can threaten or actually act to withhold something of considerable value to another state in an attempt to induce compliance. States use such exchange power in many ways. If another state needs a good (a few of the thousands of examples are: oil, military protection, a trade agreement, a vote, a useful technology, a loan, sensitive information), the power-exercising state might be in a position to provide this good, thus forcing the needy state to comply with its wishes.

When *a group of states combine to withhold a desired good in order to pressure a state*, the strategy can be called *sanctions*. To avoid using violence, states or even the United Nations apply sanctions to a country whose behavior they want to alter. They might withhold food, loans, replacement parts, or any other good. Recently, there have been more attempts to apply "comprehensive" sanctions, a situation in which many important restrictions are placed on a state's acquisition or sale of goods. During the 1990s, for example, there were 20 cases in which the United Nations successfully applied comprehensive sanctions to drive a country's leader from power or to force regime change (Cortright and Lopez 2002).

Transnational Systems of Power

If soft power and exchange power approaches do not resolve the differences, a transnational system of power might still prevent major, direct conflict between competing states. One important system is a **balance of power**. This occurs when there is *a rough equality in the power resources (political, economic, and especially military) that can be exercised by sets of competing states*. An actor is prevented from taking advantage of others because of the power of other actors to retaliate. The term *balance of power* is widely used and has many meanings. In the broadest sense, it implies that there is a rough equilibrium of power between competing states, and this discourages any state from taking aggressive action against rivals

Watch the Video "Normalizing Sino-Japanese Relations" at mypoliscilab.com

Explore the Comparative "Foreign Policies" on mypoliscilab.com

because the state fears effective retaliation. This concept often refers to a regional or global balance of power that involves a number of states. Six key elements in this classic notion of balance of power, listed below, are especially associated with the political realist perspective (Morgenthau 2005; Little 2007).

1. It is an attempt to maintain a general stability in the relations among states and to preserve the status quo.
2. It assumes that peace can be maintained if potential aggressor states are deterred by overwhelming opposing power.
3. There are typically a few (usually four to six) major power states that are decisive in ensuring that the balance is sustained.
4. These states, and others, create shifting alliances based only on self-interest and system equilibrium, not on friendship or ideology.
5. One or more power states must intervene if the behavior of other actors threatens the overall balance of the system.
6. There will be periodic political violence and war because states must use force to preserve themselves and because the system is not always in such good balance that all conflict between states is deterred.

A relatively effective balance of power system functioned in Europe for about 250 years, until World War I in 1914. In describing Britain's role in this system, Winston Churchill (1948) observed, "For 400 years the foreign policy of England has been to oppose the strongest, most aggressive, most dominating power on the continent, in joining the weaker states." However, the growing importance of both ideology and nationalism and the permanent hostility among certain major powers undermined the logic of the balance of power approach after 1914.

After World War II, the classic balance-of-power system was replaced by a *bipolar* balance-of-power system, in which the United States and its allies were generally balanced against the Soviet Union and its allies. The groups associated with each superpower were rigid in their ideological antipathy to the other bloc and were inflexible in their alliance formation. Each bloc attempted to achieve hegemony—*sustained domination of the international system.* However, the formidable military power on each side deterred them from fighting each other directly during a 40-year "cold" war (see page 370 in Chapter 13).

From the early 1970s until the breakup of the Soviet Union in 1991, the international system of power became increasingly *multipolar*. The coherence of the U.S. bloc and the Soviet bloc declined, as powerful actors such as China, Japan, Western Europe, and groupings of "nonaligned" states began to act with greater independence. At the same time, the United States and the Soviet Union continued to be the preeminent global powers and to engage in a massive buildup of military capability and nuclear weapons. Each side attempted to gain an advantage in weaponry and was fearful that its rival would gain some form of technological superiority. The result was an arms race that produced nuclear arsenals capable of massive, even total, annihilation of humankind (see Figure 11.2). In this situation of *mutually assured destruction (MAD)*, a form of balance-of-power politics evolved that was, and still is, a dangerous and, possibly, irrational mechanism for regulating the relations among powerful states in the nuclear age.

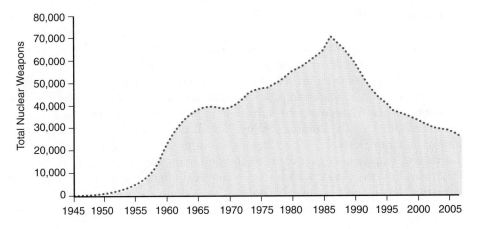

FIGURE 11.2

Total number of operational nuclear weapons, 1945–2006

Source: Federation of American Scientists (2007).

In the post–cold war era (since the early 1990s), the state system continues to have multipolar elements, especially through the United Nations. However, the military and economic dominance of the United States has provided some characteristics of a *unipolar* period, in which the international system is generally controlled by a single "hegemon." The United States has often taken the lead in spearheading collective military action through the United Nations (e.g., the 1991 Persian Gulf War) or through NATO (e.g., the 1999 actions against the Serbs in Kosovo; the opposition to Kadaffi's forces in Libya in 2011). In some cases, the United States has operated somewhat unilaterally (e.g., the military campaign against Afghanistan beginning in late 2001) or dominated a military "coalition of the willing" (the war against Iraq in 2003).

Domination and Dependence

While all states enjoy sovereign equality, it is obvious that some states are far more powerful than others. Students of the contemporary, and increasingly globalized political world, must understand how and in what situations one state exercises substantial power over another. The capacity of one state to alter the actions of another state can be based on different forms of leverage; the primary three are:

1. *Economic* leverage is based on the advantageous trade relations, financial interactions, or economic aid that the state can provide (or withhold from) another state.
2. *Military* leverage can be applied either negatively, via the use or threat of military action against a state, or positively, via military assistance in the form of protection, provision of military resources, or training.
3. *Political* leverage is derived from the ability of a state to affect the actions of another state through the use of its political resources, such as its negotiating skills, its effective political institutions, or its influence in interstate relations.

Colonialism/Imperialism During the 20th century, particular attention focused on colonialism or *imperialism*, which is characterized by *one state having extensive dominance over another state, including manipulation or control of key economic and military structures for the benefit of the dominant state.* A state might have a variety of reasons for attaining mastery over another state. First, the subordinate state can provide resources, both human and physical, for the dominant state. Second, the subordinate state can be a controlled market for the products of the dominant state. Third, the subordinate state can serve important strategic functions, either as a buffer between the dominant state and its rivals or as a staging area for the dominant state's political or military objectives. Fourth, a state with a missionary zeal might dominate another state to ensure that its values (usually political or religious) guide the subordinate state. Fifth, a state might want to dominate another state to gain international prestige.

While all forms of colonial domination entail a mix of economic, military, and political control, dominant states have employed three different styles:

1. In the *segregationist* style of colonialism, the interaction is pure exploitation. The dominant state makes little or no attempt to improve the economic, political, or social systems in the subordinate state. This style generally characterized the relations of Belgium, Germany, and Portugal with their African and Asian colonial territories.

2. In the *assimilationist* style, the dominant state makes some attempt to transform the subordinate state into an external extension of itself. While the subordinate state is still being exploited, the institutions, knowledge, and culture of the dominant state are introduced to the elite of the subordinate state and become a basis for political, economic, and cultural development. This style is particularly associated with French colonialism in Africa and Asia and the extensive colonialism of the former Soviet Union.

3. In the style of *indirect rule*, the dominant state works with the traditional leaders and institutions of governance and culture in the subordinate state as intermediaries in its control, but it also introduces the modern forms of the dominant state that will eventually supplant traditional forms. The British approach to its vast empire is the classic example of indirect rule, and this mode of colonialism also characterizes the style of the United States in some Latin American and Pacific Rim states.

Neocolonialism In the decades after World War II, most states willingly or reluctantly granted independence to their colonial holdings. But political independence does not necessarily end a state's subordination to a strong state. The label neocolonialism is given to *new, more indirect forms of domination and dependence that are nearly as powerful as those under colonialism.* Although the dominant state may officially withdraw its direct political and military presence, it can maintain domination, primarily by economic leverage. Through foreign aid, loans, technology transfer, military support, and economic intervention, the dominant state can continue to control many actions of a supposedly independent state. The dominant state's manipulations become relatively invisible, and its interests are served by a subtle alliance among a small elite within the subordinate country, MNCs, and other transnational actors (such as the IMF) (Maxfield 1997). These new forms of domination were described in the discussion in Chapter 10 of the dependency approach, which posits that the patterns established under colonialism have evolved into a *world system* of dominance and dependence that is global and systemic (Wallerstein 2004, 2005). The recent history of the Democratic Republic of Congo, described in Focus in 11, exemplifies how colonialism and neocolonialism can contribute to the plight of vulnerable states on the periphery.

◤ FOCUS IN 11 | The Faces of Colonialism: Congo

The Democratic Republic of Congo is a large, resource-rich state (one-fourth the size of the United States) located in the center of the African continent. It encompasses 72 million people and 250 ethnic groups. King Leopold of Belgium claimed the area as his own private kingdom in 1879 and placed it under Belgian colonial administration in 1908. As they extracted Congo's natural resources with ruthless efficiency, King Leopold's companies and Belgian-led military forces treated the local people with brutality, forcing the men into virtual slavery as workers in the mines and on the plantations. The colonial regime provided only minimal education to the people and encouraged Catholic missionaries to teach the great virtue of obedience to authority.

The Belgians exploited the resources of the Congo until internal resistance and the widespread liberation of African colonies made it clear that continued colonial rule was not acceptable. The Congo was granted its independence on June 30, 1960, and Belgium rapidly withdrew its military and administrative personnel and most of its financial and technical support.

Unprepared for self-rule, the Congolese elite broke into competing factions, and the country collapsed into political decay and civil war. A faction under soldier Joseph Mobutu and assisted by Western countries (and the U.S. Central Intelligence Agency) was victorious in the civil war and then assassinated the pro-Soviet prime minister.

In 1965, Mobutu, now army chief of staff, led a coup that overthrew the civilian government. Mobutu installed himself as the leader of a one-party, authoritarian regime. He "Africanized" his society, changing the country's name to Zaire and his own name to Mobutu Sese Seko ("all powerful one"). Despite Mobutu's repressive rule, several civil wars, the persistent failure of the economy, widespread corruption, and the massive diversion of funds to Mobutu and his cronies from state-owned mines, he remained in power for more than three decades.

Mobuto's long tenure in office was completely dependent on neocolonialism—the foreign aid, loans, technology transfer, and military support he received from Western countries, especially the United States (which appreciated his staunch anticommunism). Zaire relied heavily on foreign corporations to build and maintain its mines, factories, and infrastructure. The IMF (the consortium of Western banking institutions) loaned Zaire enormous amounts and repeatedly restructured Zaire's debt (the largest in Africa). In return, the IMF demanded "conditionality"—that Zaire implement strong economic policies, including devaluation of the currency, lowering real wages, and drastically reducing social welfare programs. There were extended periods when the IMF sent in European citizens to directly manage Zaire's national banking system.

The combination of internal corruption, exploitation by foreign corporations, and IMF's

(Continued)

conditionality left few resources for the people of Zaire. The level of education declined, the country could no longer feed itself, and the infrastructure (e.g., roads, water supply, telecommunications) was in shambles. The real wages of urban workers fell to less than one-tenth of what they were at independence. Surrounded by the appalling poverty of most of the population, Mobutu was rumored to be the wealthiest person in sub-Saharan Africa, with holdings of more than $10 billion.

When the cold war ended, the United States found Mobutu to be an embarrassment and tried to pressure him to make democratic reforms. Mobutu finally allowed elections in 1993, but when his own candidate for prime minister was defeated, he ordered the armed forces to prevent the winning candidates from taking office, and he installed a puppet government. Multinational corporations continued to exploit Zaire's resources.

After years of political decay, Mobutu's demise came suddenly in 1997. After a Zairean guerrilla group (composed mainly of Tutsis) expelled 1.2 million Hutu refugees who had escaped the ethnic chaos in Burundi and Rwanda, they turned on Mobuto. When Mobuto's army deserted him, he fled. The guerrilla army's leader, Laurent Kabila, declared himself president and renamed the country the Democratic Republic of Congo. Not all Congolese accepted Kabila's rule, and there was a destructive civil war. When Kabila was assassinated in 2001, his son, Joseph Kabila, took power.

From 1998 to 2003, military groups from eight countries engaged in vicious fighting in Congo in what became known as "Africa's World War." This complex mix of civil war, ethnic conflicts, refugee issues, and exploitation of Congo's resources by all groups was the bloodiest conflict since World War II, with at least 4 million deaths and millions of refugees. Joseph Kabila has manipulated the electoral system to win elections in 2006 and 2011; but there have been coup attempts in 2003, 2004, and 2011, and turmoil continues (Turner 2011). Congo ranks fourth among "failed states" worldwide.

After 90 years under a brutal and exploitative colonial system, 50 years of "independence" have brought no blossoming of democratic politics, no sharing of the Congo's abundant resources among its people, and no economic development. Rather, contemporary Congo is a tragic product of colonialism and neocolonialism, as well as its own internal failings—a state characterized by poverty, corruption, oppression, economic chaos, political decay, and continuing dependence on foreign states and foreign economic actors.

FURTHER FOCUS

1. Which of the specific foreign interventions in the Congo described above might have done the greatest long-term damage?
2. Are there any benefits that a developing country might gain from a lengthy period under neo/colonialism? ▲

Globalization?

According to Thomas Friedman, "[a] new international system has now clearly replaced the Cold War: globalization. That's right, globalization—the integration of markets, finance and technologies in a way that is shrinking the world from a size medium to a size small and enabling each of us to reach around the world farther, faster and cheaper than ever" (Friedman 1999: 110). The new conventional wisdom is that the forces of globalization are reshaping everything, from international politics to national economies, to our individual values.

What is globalization? As a working definition, globalization can be viewed as *the increasing integration of diverse economic, sociocultural, military, and environmental phenomena by means of dense networks of action and information that rapidly span vast distances around the world.* This definition is guided by the suggestion of Keohane and Nye (2000: 105) that we first define *globalism* as "a state of the world involving networks of interdependence at multicontinental distances." Two defining characteristics of such networks affect globalism: (1) the networks are increasingly dense and (2) they involve extremely rapid transmission of phenomena across substantial distances. These networks allow the movement of people, goods, ideas, information, financial capital, and even biological substances. *Globalization* refers to an increase in the level of globalism (Keohane and Nye 2000).

What aspects of human existence are affected by globalization? It is particularly associated with economic factors: a worldwide market political economy with private economic actors minimally constrained by states or borders, open capital markets, vigorous competition, and a reduction of state control over the economy. However, the linkages associated with globalization can affect many important aspects of our world. Thus, Keohane and Nye (2000) suggest four major domains of globalism: (1) *economic globalism*: the long-distance flows of goods, services, capital, and information that shape market exchanges (e.g., less costly imports, instantaneous transfers of financial capital); (2) *social and cultural globalism*: the movement of people, ideas, information, and images, which then influence the individuals, societies, and cultures into which they flow (e.g., MTV, international tourism); (3) *military globalism*: the long-distance networks of interdependence, in which the threat or exercise of force is employed (e.g., mutually assured destruction, international terrorist networks); and (4) *environmental globalism*: the long-distance transport of materials and biological substances via natural movement (e.g., ozone depletion, bird flu) or via human agency (e.g., the intercontinental spread of HIV-AIDS).

There is heated debate about the overall impacts of globalization on individuals, countries, and the international system. The Debate in 11 summarizes a few of the central claims. As is often the case, there is considerable truth as well as substantial hyperbole associated with the assertions of both the advocates and the foes of globalization. It is clear that the extraordinary increases in the speed, distance, and density of networking have altered the global economic and sociocultural systems, facilitating capitalism and markets and richly connecting some peoples and groups. Yet most of the world's population continues to live, work, and experience life on the margins of those systems. There are powerful and contradictory forces at work. Some forces create enhanced interactions and shared identities across vast spatial and political boundaries, while other forces, reacting against globalization, intensify the importance of local activities and particularistic identities.

Even as states are increasingly penetrated by outside forces, the states remain formidable actors in the international system. Thus, it is possible that globalization could be substantially limited by the policy actions of the most powerful states. This might occur if such states conclude that their national interest (especially their prosperity and stability) is being undermined by globalization or if states enact policies that support resistance from powerful, well-organized domestic actors harmed by globalization. Alternatively, states might cooperate with each other to coordinate their national policies in ways that limit the most negative effects of globalization. In this case, the calculus of the states would be, as in other

THE DEBATE IN 11 | Is Globalization a Positive Development?

Human society has evolved from small groups of self-sufficient hunter-gatherers to huge urban populations who rely on others for almost every aspect of existence. Many observers suggest that globalization—with its powerful forces that integrate economies, spread knowledge, and mix cultures—is shifting us to a new stage of human development. The global availability of more diverse goods and services, the vast worldwide communications network, and the widespread sharing of technological capabilities are presented as evidence that globalization is a positive force enhancing the quality of life for nearly all countries and peoples. However, others argue that the current forms of global integration have had extensive negative impacts on many countries and individuals. On balance, is globalization a positive development?

GLOBALIZATION BENEFITS MOST SOCIETIES AND INDIVIDUALS

- A unified global market and free trade create a more efficient system for the production and distribution of goods that results in lower prices and improved product quality. Financial capital flows quickly to the places where it will produce the highest, most effective return on investment.
- Greater integration increases the transfer of technology and expertise across borders, resulting in the diffusion of best practices, more extensive innovation, and increased global productivity (Friedman 2005).
- Higher productivity, higher-quality goods, and lower prices will generally "raise all boats." That is, these improvements will raise the level of material living standards and the prosperity enjoyed by large numbers of people in many countries (Baghwati 2007; Wolf 2004).
- Globalization results in greater sharing and homogenization of culture and values across borders, creating a world with more shared understandings. This leads to a reduction in the

kinds of nation-based differences that cause conflict (Fukuyama 1999).
- Global communication enables individuals who share political interests but are dispersed geographically to engage in effective cooperation and mobilization, thus enhancing their political power (Shirky 2011).
- As trade and economic interdependency increase in a global system, powerful economic and political actors view war and major armed conflict as disruptive and undesirable, and thus they will act to prevent them. Even more positively, these powerful actors have strong incentives for cross-national cooperation (Mandelbaum 2004).

GLOBALIZATION RESULTS IN MANY NEGATIVE EFFECTS ON SOCIETIES AND INDIVIDUALS

- Globalization encourages production, capital, and jobs to move wherever costs are lowest and profits are highest, resulting in considerable economic instability from country to country and hardship for many workers whose jobs are "outsourced" (Smick 2008).
- Similarly, as production shifts to countries with the fewest regulations on labor and the least restrictive environmental standards, the results include a "race to the bottom" characterized by more hazardous working conditions, dangerous products, and environmental degradation.
- A large share of the benefits of globalization are captured by the most powerful economic actors in the world (Stiglitz 2006) and thus the system is best understood as the newest form of neocolonialism.
- With globalization, the distribution of wealth grows even more unequal between core countries in the Global North and most countries in the Global South that are at the periphery of the international system (Klein 2008) (recall dependency theory in Chapter 10).

(Continued)

- As globalization produces more interdependency and mobility of goods, local problems spread quickly and can have global consequences, whether they are economic problems (e.g., the global economic crisis that spread from East Asia to many countries in the late 1990s) or dangerous pathogens (e.g., the H1N1 virus).

- In response to the destruction of their culture and their economic stability from globalization, many groups (e.g., nation-based, religious) become mobilized, resulting in political disorder and violence as groups attempt to protect their identities and economic interests. Thus, there is greater local and global instability.

- As national governments lose control of MNCs and economic activities, they will be weakened and less able to respond effectively to the growing negative impacts on their people and their economy. This will expose each country to more social turbulence and increase hostilities and conflicts between states (Rodrik 2011).

MORE QUESTIONS . . .

1. On balance, is globalization a positive development for you personally? For your country? For most people in the world?

2. If globalization is the current general stage in human development, is it the "final stage"? If not, what might be the next stage after globalization? ▶

forms of interstate cooperation, that collaborative approaches are the best means to serve their goals.

However, most analysts conclude that state policies will not stop current globalizing trends. They emphasize that states have less and less capacity to control their participation in or insulation from the globalizing international system. Borders become more permeable to goods, people, capital, and ideas. There is also considerable skepticism that states can sustain sufficient cooperation with other states in the brutally competitive system. Indeed, almost all analysts assume that the forces of globalization are transforming the international system in ways that are probably not controllable and are certainly not understood (Baghwati 2007; Friedman 2007; Rodrik 2011; Stiglitz 2003; 2006).

Competition in the Globalizing World

The disintegration of the Soviet Union in 1991 is regarded as the crucial event ending the bipolar, cold war era. The nature of the current era is subject to debate (Betts 2010). One conception is that the United States will continue to dominate as a hegemon in a generally unipolar international system (Posen 2003). Another conception anticipates that the rising power of China or perhaps of all the "BRIC" (Brazil, Russia, India, China) countries as well as the EU will generate a multipolar system (Ikenberry 2011). A third scenario anticipates that the United States has punched itself out by overextending its global military activities and that the emerging system will have features of international anarchy that have always been a core assumption of the realists (Szabo 2011). Or perhaps a variety of global actors will manage to create effective transnational institutions that will fulfill the idealists' ideal of a world in which cooperation is the dominant style. Or??? Three

✔•⌐**Study** and **Review** the **Post-Test & Chapter Exam** at **mypoliscilab.com**

major trends are likely to be particularly important in shaping the near-term evolution of politics across borders in the globalizing world.

First, *military power* remains a significant factor in the relations among states. The lessening of cold war tensions has been balanced by the rise of new forms of militarism in every region. Military spending is now more than $1 trillion per year worldwide, and it increases every year (SIPRI 2011). Despite the presence of multilateral military forces and multistate alliances, most military power remains under the control of individual states. If powerful and politically effective groups are increasingly threatened by globalization, it is possible that they will pressure their governments to be more active in protecting their citizens, their economies, and even their cultures. And leaders might become more assertive in response to the breakdown of borders and challenges to state sovereignty.

This might produce protectionist and isolationist policies towards other states and the use of the state's military to protect and project the state's interests. It is likely that conflicts will be more frequent if globalization and ethnonationalism are rampant. Empirical research suggests that in the 20th century, unlike the 19th century, aggressive competition and military conflict became more likely as the international system became highly diffuse and multipolar—rather like the system that seems to be emerging (Brecher and Wilkenfeld 2000; Mearsheimer 2001; Russett, Starr, and Kinsella 2009). As was discussed earlier in the chapter, it is not obvious that the United Nations or any other actors have the will and capacity to prevent such conflicts.

Second, intense *economic competition* could split the countries that were allies during the cold war. In fact, competition among the major powers will pivot more on economic issues than on military or ideological issues (Rodrik 2011). In the global economy, regional groupings have formed as states coordinate their policies with similar states ("harmonization") in order to protect their group of states from outside pressures. The EU might become this type of coordinating mechanism for its member states. The major economic competition might be among three groups: North America under leadership from the United States, the European Union, and an East Asian group under Chinese leadership. Other regional economic groups have formed around Russia, in South America, and among the Muslim states of Central Asia. As the competition for increasingly scarce goods like energy resources, minerals, water and food becomes ever more intense, how will states organize to gain more than their fair share?

Third, the state-centered system is evolving towards one in which *transnational entities* are extraordinarily important. The dynamics of globalization seem to be generally beyond state control, as does the extensive and growing power of the MNCs, described above. States might actually be willing accomplices of these transborder actors because the most powerful elites controlling these states could reap substantial benefits from a globalized international order structured by the MNCs. IGOs such as the WTO and the IMF could become the tools to facilitate further globalization (Sassen 1996).

Alternatively, states might continue to lose power to transborder, global actors and, as a consequence, lose their central role in structuring the international system. State borders have little significance for transnational actors. IGOs and NGOs pursue international agendas that are not shaped by the goals of individual states or negated by state sovereignty. MNCs can shift their resources and their operations from country to country in single-minded pursuit of profit maximization within the global economy. Although located in a home country, MNCs have operations in other host countries as well. The MNC's loyalty to the prosperity and security goals of its home country can become limited or nonexistent.

Thus it might be that the emerging international order will soon be dominated by "imperial corporations," whose globalized systems of production and distribution of goods, finance, technologies, and communications enable them to transcend sovereign states and shape the global system (Barnet and Cavanagh 1994). For these reasons, some predict that a key conflict in the early twenty-first century will be between the MNCs or between MNCs and states (Heilbroner 1993). Do you think it would be desirable to have an international system dominated by transnational actors rather than by states? Would the relentless pursuit of profit produce a more peaceful or a more just world than the relentless pursuit of national interest and state power? Will there be a decrease or an increase in international political violence? This last question is among those that are addressed in Chapter 12.

KEY CONCEPTS

balance of power   301
colonialism   304
diplomacy   290
foreign policy   285
geopolitics   287
globalization   306
hegemony   302
intergovernmental organizations
   (IGOs)   295
international law   293
international organization   295
international regime   291
international relations   285
multinational corporations (MNCs)   299
mutually assured destruction (MAD)   302

natural law   293
neocolonialism   304
nongovernmental organizations
   (NGOs)   298
peacekeeping operation   296
political idealism   286
political realism   286
positivist law   293
sanctions   301
security dilemma   286
soft power   301
transnationalism   295
treaty   291
world system   305

FOR FURTHER CONSIDERATION

1. The chapter suggests that a new pattern will emerge to structure politics across borders. What is the most desirable pattern for the international system in the early decades of the twenty-first century? What is the least desirable? What seems most likely?
2. Can the United Nations, or *any* multinational body, be so effective in imposing an international order that major conflict between states becomes highly unlikely?
3. What is the most effective strategy to produce increased cooperation among key actors in the international system?
4. Is globalization likely to change the distribution of power among states and other transnational actors in significant ways? Who is likely to benefit most from globalization?

FOR FURTHER READING

Baghwati, Jagdish. (2007). *In Defense of Globalization*. New York: Oxford University Press. An elegant argument for the benefits of globalization, in developing countries as well as developed countries, as well as thoughtful rebuttals of the main critiques.

Barnet, Richard J., and John Cavanagh. (1994). *Global Dreams: Imperial Corporations and the New World Order*. New York: Simon and Schuster. A rich, insightful, and often scathing analysis of the enormous power and impacts of major MNCs on the international system and the lives of citizens in many countries.

Cohen, Saul Bernard. (2008). *Geopolitics of the World System*. 2nd ed. Rowan & Littlefield. A thorough explanation of the geopolitical perspective on analysis (the subject of the Compare in 11), grounded in numerous examples of all regions in the current globalized world.

Drezner, Daniel. (2007). *All Politics Is Global*. Princeton, NJ: Princeton University Press. A persuasive argument is developed that strong states remain the most powerful actors in the international system, despite globalization, through their leadership in international regulatory regimes.

Friedman, Thomas. (2007). *The World Is Flat: A Brief History of the Twenty-First Century: Release 3.0*. 2nd revised ed. New York: Farrar, Straus and Giroux. The author offers his second engaging exposition of globalization (following *The Lexus and the Olive Tree*, published in 1999). He argues that new technologies, especially information and communications technologies (e.g., the Internet, wireless mobile communication, integration software), are reducing both global productive inequalities and the obstacles to transborder activities in ways that are transforming the global political economy as well as political, social, and individual power.

Fukuyama, Francis. (2004). *State-Building: Governance and World Order in the 21st Century*. Ithaca, NY: Cornell University Press. The scholar famous for predicting "the end of history," due to the triumph of global capitalism, revises his views to focus on how it is legitimate for the international community to intervene in the attempt to establish viable political institutions in weak and failed states where the emergence of liberal democracy is not occurring naturally.

Goldstein, Joshua and Jon Pevehouse. (2012). *International Relations*. 10th ed. New York: Pearson Longman. A readable and comprehensible explanation and assessment of the major theories of international relations, of key topics such as conflict, international organization and violence, and of international political economy.

Gruber, Lloyd. (2000). *Ruling the World: Power Politics and the Rise of Supranational Institutions*. Princeton, NJ: Princeton University Press. The author argues that, although countries decide voluntarily to transfer power to supranational institutions such as the EU and NAFTA, many of the countries, and perhaps the international system itself, do not benefit from the increasing power of these supranationals.

Ikenberry, G. John. (2011). *Liberal Leviathan: The Origins, Crisis and Transformation of the American World Order*. Princeton, NJ: Princeton University Press. An argument that the international system will continue to build on the rules norms and power relations in the current liberal regime led by the U.S., even as new powers emerge.

McCormick, John. (2006). *The European Superpower*. New York: Palgrave. A persuasive analysis of the emergence of the European Union as the major superpower in the new global system, where its multifaceted "soft power" will be more potent than the military approach that has empowered the United States.

Nugent, Neill. (2010). *The Government and Politics of the European Union*. 7th ed. New York: Palgrave McMillan. A thorough description of the most significant regional alliance in the global system.

Pastor, Robert A., Ed. (1999). *A Century's Journey: How the Great Powers Shape the World*. New York: Basic Books. Noted scholars explore the twentieth century foreign policy behavior and resulting international impacts of each of seven major powers—China, France, Germany, Great Britain, Japan, Russia, and the United States. The authors illuminate the pervasive influence of these powers on the relations between states, the international political economy, and the international system.

Rodrik, Dani. (2011). *The Globalization Paradox: Democracy and the Future of the World Economy*. New York: WW Norton. An economist's readable argument that democracy cannot be sustained in a world of "hyperglobalization," particularly given its reshaping of financial institutions, plus suggestions of policy remedies.

Steans, Jill. (2006). *Gender and International Relations*. 2nd ed. Malden, MA: Polity Press. A comprehensible and thoughtful explanation of feminist perspectives on international relations theory, an important approach that particularly challenges the key assumptions and interpretations of realist theory on core topics such as war and peace, international political economy, development, and human rights.

ON THE WEB

http://www.unsystem.org

The official Web site for the United Nations, including detailed information about many of its major agencies and programs.

http://www.smartbrief.com/un_wire

An independent news service, the "UN Wire," partnered by the United Nations focusing on issues of global political concern.

http://europa.eu/index_en.htm

The official Web site of the European Union, with extensive information about the workings of the EU and its major institutional elements.

http://www.icj-cij.org/homepage/index.php?lang=en

The official website of the International Court of Justice provides details of current cases as well as a history of the court.

http://www.people.virginia.edu/~rjb3v/rjb.html

This wide-ranging "Foreign Affairs Online" Web site provides many links regarding matters of international relations, international law, and foreign policy.

http://www.aseansec.org/index.asp

The official Web site of the Association of Southeast Asian Nations includes information and documents relevant to ASEAN and news about countries in the region as well as somewhat self-serving Web pages constructed by each member state.

http://www.nato.int/

This Web site focuses on military, strategic, and policy issues of importance to the North Atlantic Treaty Organization, a collective security association of 28 partner countries dominated by the United States and West European powers.

http://www.theglobalist.com

The Globalist, a "daily online magazine on the global economy, politics, and culture," offers a strong set of links to think pieces by many interesting commentators as well as relevant articles on issues in the global society.

http://www.globalissues.org

This site explores a variety of global issues, including globalization, environmental issues, international law, and population.

http://www.globalpolicy.org

Global Policy Forum is an independent policy watchdog that monitors the work of the United Nations and scrutinizes global policymaking, especially in such areas as the UN Security Council, the food and hunger crisis, and the global economy.

http://www.g7.utoronto.ca

The G-8 Information Centre, developed by the University of Toronto, provides a wealth of information on the G-8 (a cooperative institution with representatives from the major developed countries—the G-7 plus Russia = G-8), ranging from academic journal articles to recent summit information.

http://osce.org

The official Web site of the Organization for Security and Cooperation in Europe (OSCE), the largest regional security organization in the world, with 55 participating states from Europe, Central Asia, and North America, active in conflict prevention, crisis management, and postconflict rehabilitation.

http://www.apecsec.org

The electronic home of Asia-Pacific Economic Cooperation (APEC), an organization focusing on economic growth, cooperation, trade, and investment among 21 governments in the Asia-Pacific region, including Canada, China, Japan, Russia, and the United States.

http://www.oas.org/en

The home page of the Organization of American States provides a comprehensive database of information regarding the group's activities and policies.

http://www.coha.org

The Council on Hemispheric Affairs is a progressive NGO that monitors and provides analyses of events in the Western Hemisphere.

http://www.unhcr.org/cgi-bin/texis/vtx/home

The United Nations High Commissioner for Refugees is the agency that attempts to document the scale and details of the movement of populations across borders and to suggest appropriate policy responses to deal with the challenges of coping with the large numbers of dislocated people.

Political Violence

Three months of bombing by Serbian forces destroyed the city of Vukovar, Croatia in 1991, during the Balkans War. A Serbian soldier celebrates the devastation as he cycles past a burning house.

LEARNING OBJECTIVES

12.1 Define political violence.

12.2 Relate the use of violence to the formation and maintenance of political society.

12.3 Classify the major types of political and nonpolitical violence.

12.4 Analyze the nature and causes of war.

12.5 Evaluate the normative implications of political violence.

Read and **Listen** to **Chapter 12** at mypoliscilab.com

Study and **Review** the **Pre-Test & Flashcards** at mypoliscilab.com

Bojan awoke from a deep sleep when three masked men entered his home. They dragged him and his wife outside, and he was forced to watch the men rape his wife. They announced they were extracting revenge for the bombing in a local bar the previous night where three members of their paramilitary group were killed. They then shot Bojan in the head.

During the 1990s, the Balkans area in Central Europe was the site of brutal violence among its major ethnic groups. More than 250,000 were killed, often in house-to-house fighting and in cold-blooded executions of men, women, and children, and more than 700,000 were displaced from their homes. The key protagonists were military and paramilitary forces drawn from the 9 million Serbs (generally Greek Orthodox, procommunist), 4.5 million Croats (Catholic, noncommunist), 2 million Slovenes (Catholic, noncommunist), 4.5 million Bosnians (Muslim), 2 million Macedonians (Greek Orthodox, with strong links to northern Greece), and 600,000 Montenegrans (Greek Orthodox, pro-Serbian).

Given its geopolitical location at the crossroads of Western and Eastern Europe, the Balkans have historically been a site of conflict, and its peoples had been conquered by imperial powers such as the Romans, the Austrian Hapsburgs, and the Ottoman Turks. When not engaged in resistance to the imperial invaders, the ethnic groups lived in uneasy tension and occasional fighting with each other. Even during World War II, when the Nazis invaded, these ethnic groups killed more of each other than were killed by the Nazis. A charismatic leader, Josip Broz Tito, held these groups together as a single country (Yugoslavia) between the end of World War II and the late 1980s. However, the breakup of the Soviet empire in Central and Eastern Europe after Tito's death reopened old ethnic animosities, leading to a resurgence of violence.

When the Croats declared independence in the early 1990s, the dominant Serbs resisted the breakup of Yugoslavia, and the Serbian military engaged in a bloody, if sporadic, conflict with Croatian forces until 1995, despite international recognition of Croatia and a United Nations-arranged cease-fire. Bosnia also declared independence but did not gain immediate recognition. Serbs, about one-third of the population within Bosnia, launched a civil war to secure as much of the region of Bosnia-Herzegovina as possible for Serbia. In a devastating town-to-town fighting, Serbian and Bosnian paramilitary groups murdered and brutalized civilians as well as each other. Eventually, the United Nations and the European Union (EU) imposed a settlement, based on a complex federation representing all key ethnic groups.

The next explosion of violence was in Kosovo, an impoverished southern province in Serbia. About 90 percent of the Kosovo population are ethnic Albanians, whose desire for autonomy resulted in a separatist guerrilla war in the late 1990s. While the United Nations attempted to intervene, Serbian president Slobodan Milosevic encouraged the local Serbs to engage in ethnic cleansing. Within months, the Serbs had either killed or exiled the great majority of ethnic Albanians. In response, massive North Atlantic Treaty Organization (NATO) airstrikes against Serbian forces enabled the ethnic Albanians to return to their homes in Kosovo. The Kosovars than executed many local Serbs and driving most of them from their homes and communities. In 2010, two years after Kosovo declared its independence, the International Court of Justice ruled its declaration was legal, although Serbia and Russia are among the majority of countries that still do not recognize Kosovo's sovereignty.

The recent history of the Balkans is an example of the complex forms of political violence that occur in the contemporary political world. The people have experienced extensive and brutal civil war, ethnic violence, terrorism, war, foreign military intervention, systematic rape, arson, and government violence against its own citizens. Our awareness of such violence is usually high. On a given day, the media rarely report that the great majority of countries and billions of people experienced no bombings, kidnappings, riots, or violent acts with a political motivation. Rather, the media are likely to report on the few settings that do experience armed conflict, riots, assassinations, terrorist incidents, and so on.

In part, this selective reporting reflects our general fascination with the horror of violence. In part, it indicates our underlying sense that such political violence is extraordinary—an aberration from politics-as-usual. But unfortunately, the reality is that there is considerably more political violence in the world than most of us recognize, violence that occurs below the few headlines that grab our attention.

Violence is excluded from some definitions of politics, such as the pluralist approach, because violence is viewed as a breakdown of politics, which is understood as consensus building, compromise, and conflict resolution. However, other definitions, including the class approach, treat conflict and violence as one possible, and perhaps even inevitable, form of politics. Indeed, in some approaches, political violence is portrayed as a positive force, producing necessary change and constructive outcomes. Given its omnipresence in the political world, it is important for students of political science to have a better understanding of the nature and dynamics of political violence.

VIOLENCE

Initially, we need to consider the concept of violence itself. The most common notion is that *violence* entails *the use of physical force, usually with the purpose of injuring or damaging the target of the violence.* In the political world, the tools of such violence can range from flying fists and bullets to nerve gas and nuclear missiles.

12.1 Define political violence.

But some analysts take a much broader view of violence. First, the *threat* of violence might be understood as a form of violence, even if the violent act is not committed. If someone points a gun in your face and you hand over your money, you will probably view this interaction as a violent one, even if the person does not fire the gun. Similarly, if a state points nuclear missiles at the state across its border but does not launch any, would you classify this as an act of violence? Is it a violent act if a group threatens to blow up a public building unless its demands are met? Is it a violent act if a group shouts down a speaker at a public rally? Do you think that such acts of intimidation and threat of force have a violent element, even if there is no actual physical injury or damage?

Second, an even broader view of violence includes various forms of subjugation and manipulation that do not involve even the threat of direct physical harm. For example, consider a group that is an "underclass" within a society. The group is subjected to discrimination in education, in health care, in jobs, and in housing. This intentional pattern of systematic deprivation continues over time. The group is not targeted for any specific physical violence, but the economic and cultural systems provide the group with minimal opportunities to gain a significant share of the values in the society. Some would classify such oppression as a form of violence by the dominant group(s) against the fundamental rights of the deprived group to life, liberty, and the pursuit of happiness.

This chapter defines **political violence** as *the use of actual physical violence or very serious threats of such violence to achieve political goals.* As you assess the role of violence in politics, however, consider the other ways in which the world of politics generates actions and impacts that "do violence" to many people. Although to the use of physical force is evident in politics, the more subtle forms of coercion and manipulation are more extensive, if less visible.

POLITICAL SOCIETY

12.2 Relate the use of violence to the formation and maintenance of political society.

👁—[Watch the Video "Tiananmen Square"* at mypoliscilab.com

Chapter 2 described the claim by Thomas Hobbes (1588–1679) that the formation of **political society** is an attempt to overcome the frequent reliance on force and violence in human interactions. As individuals use whatever means necessary to pursue their self-serving interests, interpersonal violence is inevitable. To overcome such violence, Hobbes observes, individuals accept the *social contract* in an attempt to submit force to reason—to ensure that force becomes the *ultima ratio* (final resort), not the *prima ratio* (first resort). In political society, *individuals accept the authority of the state and cede to the state a monopoly over the legitimate use of violence,* sacrificing their own right to use violence in exchange for a similar sacrifice from others.

Even if most people accept the social contract, some individuals and groups do not, arguing that the existing political society and its social contract have no authority over their actions. They believe that they have the right to engage in "justifiable" violence, which is based on motives such as self-defense, the restoration of order, the promotion of fundamental values, or retribution. They might further claim that they have never accepted the right of the current government to command their obedience or that the political system is illegitimate (because it lacks a democratic mandate or because it has failed to deliver security, stability, and prosperity).

TYPES OF POLITICAL VIOLENCE

A simple taxonomy of political violence can be based on specifying the *source* of the violence and the *target* of that violence. Either party may be a state or an individual/ group. Figure 12.1 distinguishes four categories of political violence. Although these categories help organize and clarify our discussion, this taxonomy is imperfect and the boundaries between categories are imprecise (hence the dashed lines) because the states, groups, or individuals who engage in political violence are usually motivated by multiple objectives, can operate in fluid groupings, employ complex strategies, and focus on multiple targets.

12.3 Classify the major types of political and nonpolitical violence.

Explore the Comparative "Civil Rights" on mypoliscilab.com

State Violence Against Individuals or Groups

Given the state's monopoly of the legitimate use of violence, there are many instances in which the state's application of political violence seems justifiable. The state typically characterizes its own use of violence as an *order-maintenance* activity. The state's agents act as security forces, judges, and executors of punishment when individuals or groups seem to have violated the society's legal system. Thus, the state might arrest, try, and punish an actor who breaks a criminal law, as in actions such as robbery, or a civil law, as in actions such as tax fraud. In such matters, most citizens are likely to support the state's efforts to create and maintain public order.

But some uses of violence by the state are more problematic. V. I. Lenin (1870–1924) defined the state as "a body of armed men, weapons, and prisons." Because the state has the capacity to define the nature and severity of all "crimes," it is possible for the state to be highly repressive and discriminatory in its use of violence. *The state's excessive reliance on force and oppressive laws* can be called **establishment violence** and contrasted with the state's legitimate use of violence to maintain public order.

The boundary between a crime against society and a crime against the existing political order can blur. In some countries, political actions that oppose the current political leadership are treated as crimes. Thus, political opponents become

Source	Target	
	Individual/Group	State
Individual/ Group	Crime Terrorism Nation-based conflict Class conflict	Riots/Rebellion Separatist violence Coup Revolution
State	Order maintenance Establishment violence	War

FIGURE 12.1
Types of political violence

"enemies of the people" and are subject to constraints on their behavior, deprivation of resources, imprisonment, and death. The state can also institute systematic policies of violence against certain groups that are not overt opponents of the regime but are blamed for problems faced by the state and thus are made scapegoats.

A key instrument of a state's power against its enemies is its security forces, which include official groups such as the regular military and the secret police (e.g., those recently using violence against anti-government demonstrators in Libya, Syria and Yemen), as well as unofficial armed groups (e.g., Colombian paramilitary forces). Another form of state power is judicial systems and prison systems, which punish those whose behaviors displease the state. According to Amnesty International (2011), a nongovernmental organization (NGO) that monitors violations of individual civil rights by agents of the state, political opponents are subjected to establishment violence in two-thirds of all countries. In addition, the state can cause great suffering or even death to individuals through its power to withhold access to rewards such as good jobs, shelter, and welfare services.

In the contemporary world, extensive attention is paid to certain forms of political violence, especially violence between states (war) and individual/group violence (such as terrorism). This attention is understandable because such violence is dramatic and terrifying. Yet an extensive analysis by political scientist R. J. Rummel (2011) of "democide—murder by government"—concludes that the death toll from establishment violence far outweighs the deaths from war during the 20th century. These data are summarized in Table 12.1.

According to Rummel, the deaths of more than 300 million people in the 20th century are directly attributable to government violence and war. The most staggering aspect of these data is that fully 86 percent of those deaths are establishment violence. While about 41 million people were killed in wars, it is estimated

TABLE 12.1

Death by Government and War in the 20th Century

Total Deaths (millions)

	Domestic	Foreign	All	Percentage of Total Deaths
Establishment violence	173	90	262	86%
By communist governments	145	8	153	50
By other totalitarian governments	1	26	28	9
By authoritarian governments	26	53	79	26
By democratic governments	0.2	2	2	1
War	10	31	41	14
TOTAL	182	120	303	100.0%

Note: The totals are rounded to the nearest million.
Source: Adapted from Rummel (2011), Table 1.6; and updates communicated to the author from Professor Rummel by e-mail.

that governments killed more than 260 million of their own citizens (including their colonial subjects)—the people they are supposed to serve. Rummel includes any murder committed by agents of the government, including genocides, politically motivated executions, massacres, and intentional famines. Most deaths through establishment violence have been the work of nondemocratic governments. Half of the deaths (50 percent) are attributable to communist regimes, about 9 percent are the responsibility of other totalitarian governments, and 26 percent are by authoritarian governments (Rummel 2011: Table 4, Figure 1, and later updates provided to the author).

Rummel particularly emphasizes the massive death totals attributable to the 20th century's "bloodiest dictators": Mao Zedong's regime in China killed 76.7 million between 1923 and 1976; Joseph Stalin's Soviet regime killed 42.6 million between 1929 and 1953; more than 20.9 million were eliminated by Hitler and the German Nazi regime (1933–1945); 10 million were killed by King Leopold in his colony of Congo (Focus in 11); and 2.4 million Cambodians died by execution and starvation under Pol Pot's regime (Compare in 10). If you need evidence of the fundamental importance of the state in determining the quality of citizens' lives, the 262 million deaths attributable to the citizens' own governments should be compelling.

Individual Violence Against an Individual

When an individual is the source of violence and another individual is the target, the violence is usually not explicitly political. Most such violence (e.g., murder, robbery, rape, assault, and certain crimes against property, such as burglary and arson) is best characterized as *ordinary crime*. Because only the state (and its agents) has a legitimate right to use violence (this is one definition of the state in Chapter 5 as well as in Hobbes's social contract notion), an individual who does violence without the approval of the state is normally in violation of the law. Even these ordinary crimes have a political element in the sense that the state is usually involved in determining what behaviors are criminal and then in apprehending violators, judging them, and punishing them on behalf of "the people." Notice also that in most societies, members of deprived or subordinate groups tend to engage in violent crimes far more frequently than members of the more advantaged classes. Do you think this pattern might suggest that the commission of some violent crimes and even the nature of the punishment have, in part, a subtle political element?

There are instances where one individual engages in an act of political violence against another individual. For example, U.S. presidents James A. Garfield in 1881 and William McKinley in 1901 were assassinated by individuals who seemed to be acting alone, primarily on political motives. Occasionally, a person's motivation for violence against a political actor is more personal than political. In a famous example from 1804, U.S. vice president Aaron Burr shot and killed distinguished Founding Father Alexander Hamilton in a duel. The two were bitter political enemies from rival political parties, but Burr was also offended by disparaging personal comments that he thought Hamilton had made about him. Burr challenged Hamilton to a duel, and after Hamilton shot in the air as gentlemen normally did,

Burr mortally wounded Hamilton. In 2001, the king and queen of Nepal and six other members of the royal family were shot to death by the king's son, the crown prince, who had quarreled with his mother over his choice of a bride.

Group Violence Against an Individual

Most violence in which a person is targeted for political reasons, including assassinations, is committed on behalf of a group, even if the act is performed by a single individual. Focus in 5 noted the assassinations of two Indian prime ministers, Indira Gandhi and her son Rajiv Gandhi seven years later. Although Indira Gandhi was killed by two guards and Rajiv Gandhi by one woman, in each case the assassins believed they were acting to further the political interests of their nationality group (the Sikhs and the Sri Lankan Tamils, respectively). U.S. president Abraham Lincoln was assassinated in 1865 by one man who was part of a broader group attack on the American political leadership, and some believe that President John F. Kennedy's assassination in 1963 can be attributed to more than one person. And the murders of former Lebanese prime minister Rafik Hariri (in 2005) and former Pakistani prime minister Benazir Bhutto (in 2008) were each the work of a suicide bomber, although organized groups or perhaps even governments were behind the attacks.

Terrorism   An act is usually called terrorism when there is *premeditated, politically motivated violence perpetrated against noncombatant targets by subnational groups or clandestine agents"* (NCTC 2011). Bombs can be planted in public places such as markets or airplanes; civilians can be kidnapped or murdered; harmful chemicals can be placed in food, water, or air. In 2009, there were 11,000 terrorist attacks, 15,000 deaths, and 32,600 serious injuries. The number and severity of terrorist acts in each region changes over time. At present, terrorism occurs more frequently in countries with modest levels of political freedom, in comparison to countries with substantial freedom or minimal freedom (Abadie 2004).

As Figure 12.2 indicates, most of those killed or wounded in terrorist attacks in 2009 were either in South Asia (the location of the largest number of deaths) or the Near East (location of the largest number of injuries). There were more than 1,000 deaths in each of five countries, with the largest number in Iraq (3,654), Afghanistan (2,778), and Pakistan (2,670). Excluding Iraq, the number of terrorist-related deaths and attacks has increased in every region during each of the last five years. Among the 10,867 hostages taken, this act was most frequent in Pakistan and India (NCTC 2011).

Some peoples, such as the Iraqis and Pakistanis, despair of the recurrent terrorist attacks that make their lives feel so much like Hobbes' state of nature. In other countries, people are especially scarred by a particularly traumatic terrorist act. For Norwegians, it is the massacre of 77 mostly teenagers, at a political camp in 2011. For Indonesians, it is the death of 202 people, mostly foreign tourists, in the 2002 bombings of two nightclubs in Bali by Indonesian militants. In Spain, it is the coordinated backpack bombings of Madrid commuter trains in 2004, killing 191 and wounding more than 2,000. And in the United States, it is the most massive terrorist attack in modern history on September 11, 2001. A well-organized

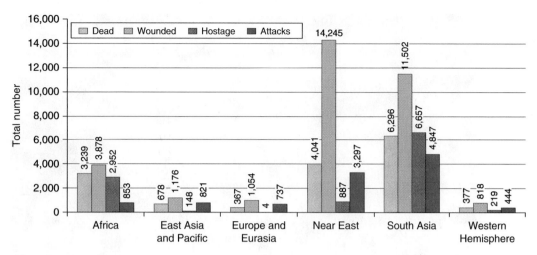

FIGURE 12.2

Terrorist attacks and victims, by region, 2009

Source: NCTC 2011.

group, composed mainly of Saudi Arabians, hijacked four transcontinental passenger airplanes. Two of the planes were flown into the towers of the World Trade Center in New York, one crashed into the Pentagon near Washington, D.C., and the fourth crashed in a field in Pennsylvania after passengers struggled with the hijackers. The carnage was staggering, with almost 3,000 deaths, and the costs of the attack have been estimated at more than $600 billion.

For some, the central question regarding those who engage in terrorism is: Why use violence to harm noncombatants? The motives of political terrorists vary, but some combination of five rationales guide most such acts. First, the terrorists can attempt to punish an existing state (their own or another state) for perceived grievances, even when noncombatants are the victims of their actions. From the terrorists' perspective, no citizens of the targeted state are innocent of their state's misdeeds. (Recall the views of Osama bin Laden in Compare in 4.) Second, terrorists can attack a domestic group whom they wish to subordinate or retaliate against for previous offenses. This characterizes much of the recent violence in Iraq between Shia and Sunnis as well as Sunni attacks on police recruits. Third, the terrorist act can be a means to gain international publicity for the group's cause. Unlike those committing ordinary crimes, terrorists often claim credit for their violent actions and hope for extensive media coverage. Fourth, terrorists may seek to secure financial resources for the group's political activities or may demand the release of imprisoned members. Many acts of violence that involve hostages and ransom demands are of this type. And fifth, an objective of terrorist violence may be to promote revolution—a strategy discussed later in this chapter.

Terrorism is undergoing at least three ominous changes in the early 21st century. First and most important, terrorists have an increased capacity to inflict

People flee from the collapsing towers of the World Trade Center in New York shortly after the shocking terrorist attack on September 11, 2001 that killed almost 3,000 people.

massive damage and disruption. The terrorists' ability to move people, information, and weapons is enhanced by globalization, with its permeable national borders, extensive cross-border travel, and growing immigrant populations. Terrorists also benefit from the rapid expansion of technologies that provide them with far greater destructive capabilities, ranging from digital networks (cyberterrorism) to chemical and biological weapons (bioterrorism), to weapons of mass destruction (WMDs).

A second change is that many terrorists are now operating in very small cells (three to ten people) that are only loosely connected with each other, making penetration and destruction of terrorist "networks" almost impossible. While there is some broad collaboration in training and provision of materials, most terrorist acts are carried out by small, isolated cells. Recall the discussion in Chapter 4 of the rise of the "bunch of guys" (BOGs) who encourage each other to plan and undertake acts of violence (Sageman 2008).

A third change is that some groups, especially religiously motivated terrorists, now seem less constrained regarding the scale of death and destruction they are willing to inflict, even on those who are noncombatants. And an increasing proportion of terrorist acts are committed by individuals who are not only willing to die for the cause but actually intend to die in a suicide act (Council on Foreign Relations 2005; Smelser 2007).

There are ambiguities in the assessment of terrorism. One issue is defining "noncombatants." One attempt to identify combatants states that they are "personnel in the military, paramilitary, militia, and police under military command and control who are [on duty] in … areas … where war zones or war-like conditions exist" (NCTC 2011). Even some who are not terrorists argue that this definition of combatants is too narrow. Are military personnel who are not on duty at the moment really noncombatants? What about attacks on other "repressive agents" of the state, such as police, security guards, judges, or civilians working for the military? While there is agreement about the sheer terror associated with acts of political violence, it is not always clear to everyone whether such acts are best understood as terrorism or just brutal violence against "the enemy" in the service of some political goal.

With the proliferation of groups employing terrorist tactics, it is wryly observed that "one person's terrorist is another person's freedom fighter." The root problem with using terrorism as an analytic concept is that it has become a powerful and negative label in the manipulative language of politics. It is sometimes used regardless of the innocence of the victim, the identity of the actual sponsor of the violence, or the justifiability of the ends. The label communicates a disgust for extreme political violence against innocent individuals, but it can also be used to discredit any group that uses violent means to achieve its political ends or to condemn a group whose political ends, as much as its means, are unacceptable. Ultimately, the issue centers on moral and political values: Are there *any* circumstances in which group political violence against any individuals is justifiable? If so, what kinds of violence are acceptable and under what circumstances? The Debate in 12 considers whether terrorism is ever justifiable.

Group Violence Against a Group

Nation-Based Violence   Nationality groups are increasingly mobilized to demand political autonomy, a process grounded in a deep attachment to the group's identity, described in Chapter 5 as nationalism or ethnonationalism. When these groups clash directly, *the use of force between identity groups* is termed **nation-based violence**. Many of the major armed conflicts during the last several decades have been between nation-based groups within countries, not between countries (Laitin 2007; Miller 2007; SIPRI 2011: Appendix 2A; Taras and Ganguly 2010).

In some cases, groups attempt to establish their own sovereign state based on national identity, a situation discussed later in the chapter as separatist violence. In many instances, however, the nation-based groups are struggling against each other for political and cultural domination or autonomy rather than for separation. The continuing violence between Hindus and Muslims in India (recall the Focus in 5) is a revealing example of how the antipathy between nationality groups can poison their relations as they attempt to share a country or even a remote village. In the southern African country of Angola, more than 1.5 million people died in the prolonged civil war (1975–2002) among three rival groups, each representing a different linguistic/ethnic region, who struggled for control

Throughout history, some individuals and groups have engaged in political violence to achieve their goals. Few would argue that political violence is *never* justified. Most political theorists specify conditions under which people can legitimately engage in political violence to achieve justice and how to define a "just war" (Walzer 2006). However, there are also circumstances in which either the ends to which violence has been used or the means that are employed are unacceptable. In the contemporary world, some of the most serious concerns about political violence relate to attacks labeled "terrorism" because they often victimize people who some claim are "innocent" noncombatants. Is such terrorism ever justified?

SOME TERRORISM IS JUSTIFIED

- Individuals who engage in terrorist acts believe they are acting to defend many people, almost all of whom are "innocents" and "noncombatants." These innocents are themselves a "violated" group who have been the victims of establishment violence or have experienced severe and prolonged oppression, which is also understood to be a form of violence.

- Terrorist tactics are employed as a last resort, but such actions are necessary because the oppressed group is prevented, by establishment violence or by its exclusion from resources, from using nonviolent political means to displace the oppressors. John Locke, in his *Second Treatise of Government* (1690), is among the many theorists who vigorously defend the right of an oppressed people to use violence against unjust governance.

- Innocent people might be harmed by terrorist acts in some instances, but they are the unlucky people who are in the wrong place at the wrong time. They are no different from the individuals that those with power call "collateral damage" when they are killed during state-sponsored violence.

- Many of the targets of terrorism are individuals who sustain and actively support the domination and violence of the oppressors, even if they do not necessarily wear the uniforms of combatants. They are certainly not "innocents."

- Ultimately, there are no true innocents: Those who acquiesce to and enjoy benefits from the policies of the oppressors are also responsible for the harm caused to those who suffer. Those who gain life's advantages while accepting injustice and violence directed against the less advantaged cannot also claim immunity from responsibility and harm.

ALL TERRORISM IS INDEFENSIBLE

- The destruction of *innocent* lives for political gain is morally unacceptable, without exception.

- Only the state has the right to use violence under the conditions of the social contract. Thus, any act of extreme political violence that is not committed by the representatives of the state is illegitimate, regardless of the targeted victim or motivation.

- Terrorism is tactically unwise because it pushes the existing regime to become even more aggressive and less willing to engage in dialogue and compromise (e.g., consider the response of the Israeli government to Hamas in Gaza, which is described in Focus in 12).

- From a pragmatic perspective, terrorism is also tactically unwise because its ultraviolence alienates potential supporters, both within and outside the country. Eventually the terrorist group is isolated and without allies.

- There are considerably more cases where relatively powerless groups were able to replace an oppressive regime with persistent political mobilization than with terrorism.

- If the goal is to achieve social justice, there are effective nonviolent alternatives to terrorism, even for those who lack extensive political resources (e.g., nonviolent resistance to colonialism by

(Continued)

India's Mohandas Gandhi; the use of the electoral process, as in many postcommunist countries).

■ History reveals that terrorism rarely succeeds in achieving the goals desired by the terrorists. Those who do gain power by such brutal violence typically become as oppressive as those they have overthrown. Moreover, they are usually driven from power by further violence before they attain any idealistic outcomes they sought.

■ The use of unrestrained violence for political ends becomes an ethical slippery slope into chaos. It establishes the right of every unhappy group to use "any means necessary" in an attempt to achieve its political ends.

MORE QUESTIONS . . .

1. Are those noncombatants who gain considerable benefits from an unfair political regime truly "innocents" who should not suffer from the consequences of political violence directed against the regime?

2. Do the conditions, motivation, and political goals of the terrorists have any relevance in determining the acceptability of the action, or is terrorism *always* wrong, regardless of conditions, motivation, and goals?

3. Is it possible to make a precise distinction between all terrorists and those who fight for freedom and justice? ◣

of the entire country. The violence in Iraq reveals the deep antagonisms between groups within the Shia, Sunni, and Kurdish nations.

When *group political violence results in the murder of many members of one ethnic group by its rival*, it can be called **genocide** (Weitz 2005). The political system is often a partner in such situations when its machinery of violence is employed by the dominant group. When the state organizes the campaign against an ethnic group, such genocide can also be classified as *establishment violence* (see Figure 12.1). Examples of genocide in the 20th century include the killing of Armenians by the Turks (in 1915), 6 million Jews in Hitler's Germany (1933–1945), the Tutsis by the Hutus in Rwanda (1963–1964), and the Hutus by the Tutsis in neighboring Burundi (1988). Since 1990, the killing of nearly 1 million Tutsis in Rwanda; the Serbs' "ethnic cleansing" of civilian populations, including Bosnians and ethnic Albanians (in Kosovo); and the systematic violence against ethnic groups in Myanmar and Sudan have renewed international concern about preventing genocide and punishing those who are responsible for it.

Many recent conflicts grounded in nation-based hostility can also be a blur of class conflict, separatist violence, revolutionary struggle, and conflict between states, topics addressed below. What is clear is the massive toll that these conflicts levy on their populations. Table 12.2 provides data on just a few conflicts and some of the most visible indicators of human devastation. It lists the number of deaths attributable to political violence. In addition, the toll in disrupted lives is revealed by the number of people who have been forced by the violence to leave their homes and communities—there are currently 27.5 million internally displaced persons worldwide. An additional 15.2 million people have actually fled their country, crossing the border in an attempt to escape the violence. The great majority of these 42.7 million human beings, more than 70 percent of whom are women and children, live in squalor and unremitting hardship; they are homeless or are surviving in miserable refugee camps (IDMC 2011).

TABLE 12.2

Human Devastation from Recent Internal Violence and Ethnic Conflict

Country	Deaths [a]	Refugees [b]	Internally Displaced Persons[c]
Congo, D. R.	3,956,941	361,100	1,700,000
Sudan	3,037,015	387,900	4,580,000
Afghanistan	1,777,964	2,805,100	352,000
Rwanda	846,800	89,300	Undetermined
Burundi	108,068	273,600	100,000
Myanmar	268,916	735,400	446,000
Colombia	67,271	394,700	4,000,000
Iraq	567,321	1,894,600	2,800,000
Former Palestine	Undetermined	3,226,700	160,000
Uganda	32,850	17,600	166,000

[a]Deaths attributable to political violence.
[b]Refugees and asylum seekers who have left their country of origin (as of January 1, 2009).
[c]People driven from their home location due to persecution, armed conflict, or widespread violence (as of January 1, 2010).
Data Sources: Deaths: http://siteresources.worldbank.org; Refugees: http://www.uscrirefugees.org; Internally Displaced Persons: IDMC (2011).

Class Conflict In some cases, intergroup violence might be attributable to an underlying *class conflict* (see Chapter 9), which is often linked to an ethnic or religious cleavage. In recent conflicts in Rwanda, Sudan, and Sri Lanka, for example, one of the groups in the conflict has dominant social, economic, and political power over the others. Thus, class theorists argue that the "real" conflict in many settings is not actually due to religion or language or ethnicity, but to the inevitable class struggle that emerges from stratification and inequality. Of course, class conflict can occur between any strata, such as the peasant class against the landlord class or the capitalist class against the worker class, independent of any nation-based cleavage that might reinforce the class distinctions. The group-based political violence in some Latin American countries, such as Colombia and Guatemala, seems best interpreted as a struggle between deeply unequal classes.

Individual or Group Violence Against the State

Individual or group political violence directed against the political system can have several causes. Be aware that the motivation underlying many acts of terrorism is actually to direct violence against a state, even if the immediate targets are noncombatants. In this section, we examine other forms of violence where the state is the target. At one extreme, such violence might be a person's or a group's spontaneous outburst of frustration with life conditions. At the other extreme, the individual or group might have such deep-seated hostility against the existing political system that it undertakes a lengthy series of violent actions in order to overthrow the system.

Riots And Rebellion   When people find their political, social, or economic conditions intolerable, their frustration can escalate from demonstrations and civil disobedience to riots. *Riots* are usually *spontaneous and relatively disorganized group violence* against property, agents of the political system, perceived opponents in the society, or random targets. Riots are often triggered by a specific incident, such as a police shooting or an economic problem such as a sudden large increase in the price of basic foodstuffs. Once riots start, they can spread or become more organized into violent demonstrations as others are motivated to express their dissatisfaction with the political system or social conditions.

Riots are expressions of frustration in which there is an implicit or explicit demand for redress of grievances. The basic grievances might involve opposition to or support for certain public policies or political leaders. Black South Africans engaged in many riots in their ultimately successful opposition to apartheid during the 1980s. Mass protests and riots have forced many unpopular leaders from power in recent years (e.g., in Bolivia, Egypt, Haiti, Indonesia, Lebanon, Tunisia).

Such political violence turns into **rebellion** when there is *more frequent, premeditated, and widespread violence, involving more people*. At this point, many of those engaged in violence have lost faith in the likelihood that the system will respond to their problems. This deterioration of citizen support and escalation of political action to more intense political violence are at the heart of Samuel Huntington's description of political decay (in Chapter 10).

The violence directed against the Qadaffi regime in Libya is an example of a rebellion. Libyans opposed to his repressive 42-year rule were encouraged by the successes of popular uprisings in neighboring countries such as Tunisia and Egypt in the "Arab Spring" of 2011. Initially, groups of citizens engaged in peaceful protests calling for Qadaffi to step down. These protests were met with violent response from the regime's security forces. As arrests and deaths escalated among the protestors, they begin to increase the violence of their opposition. Groups of rebels took control of some regions, especially in Eastern Libya. The rebellion escalated into a full-scale conflict with extensive casualties between forces loyal to Qadaffi and those committed to ending his rule. The situation was further complicated as other countries, primarily from NATO, entered into an air war against Qadaffi's forces, under the rationale of humanitarian intervention (recall the Debate in 5) to protect rebellious Libyans (and to force Qadaffi out of power). By Qadaffi's overthrow and death, 25,000–35,000 had been killed.

Separatist Violence   At the heart of most nation-based violence is the nationality group's struggle for autonomy—for the right to control its own political and cultural destiny. Some groups engage in **separatist violence** *to achieve substantial or total political autonomy* from the existing political system. If the separatist group is small and lacks political resources, it usually turns to acts of terrorism or attacks against specific individuals within the political system. This characterized the actions of the Irish Republican Army (IRA) throughout much of the 20th century as it attempted to separate Northern Ireland from the United Kingdom and merge it with the Republic of Ireland. Targets of the IRA's bombs and murders were usually the British "occupying army" and members of the Protestant paramilitary groups in Northern Ireland. Separatist violence characterizes recent activities by the Kurds against Turkey, South Ossetians against Georgia, and Kashmiris against India.

Violent uprisings against colonial power were often one element in native people's political struggle for independence. In some cases, organization of the separatist violence was weak or nonexistent. But in others, the separatist violence has been coordinated by an organized group, such as the Mau Mau versus the British in Kenya (1950s) and the Vietminh/Vietcong versus the French and then the Americans in Vietnam (1940s–1970s). The violent resistance (after 2003) to the U.S. military and its allies in postwar Iraq is also characterized by some as native opposition to foreign occupation.

A civil war results when *a significant proportion of the population in a region actively supports a separatist movement, and political violence emerges on a large scale*. In the early 1860s, the political leaders of the slaveholding southern states decided that they no longer wished to be part of the United States federation, and they announced that their states were seceding (withdrawing formal membership). The central government rejected their request to secede, forcing 11 southern states to declare their independence, create a confederation, and initiate a military struggle against the central government. In the bloody U.S. Civil War (1861–1865), the Union forces of the central government ultimately defeated the army of the Confederacy and forced the southern states to remain in the federation.

A similar civil war occurred in Nigeria in 1967–1970. The Igbo tribe, which differed from other major tribes in religion, language, and political traditions, attempted to secede from the Nigerian federation and create a separate state called Biafra. After four years of civil war and nearly a million deaths, the central government's army was victorious, and Biafra was stillborn as a state. In contrast, the Bengalis were successful in their separatist civil war against the central government of Pakistan (recall the Focus in 4), and thus the new state of Bangladesh was created in 1971.

The opening of this chapter described a graphic example of separatist violence—the devastating struggle among the Serbs, Bosnians, Croatians, Kosovars, and other nationality groups after the breakup of Yugoslavia in 1991. These groups' differences in ethnicity, history, language, and religion all reinforced their separate national identities. Widespread separatist violence resulted from the groups' antipathy towards each other and their efforts to determine precisely what states would emerge and where the borders between the states would be.

Coup   A **coup** occurs when *the top leader or part of the leadership group is replaced by violent means or the explicit threat of violence*. Those carrying out the coup have no intention of overthrowing the entire political-economic order, although their opposition to the existing leadership can be based on differences in policy as well as on personal rivalry. Coups are most common in political systems that have no institutionalized procedures for leadership succession. Political violence against the top leadership group is typically organized by other members of the political leadership, by a rival political group, or by the military. An extreme example is Bolivia, where 190 coups occurred over a 156-year period ending in the 1980s. Bangladesh had 21 coups or attempted coups in its first 36 years of existence.

Most coup attempts fail, and the number of successful coups per year has dropped from about 12 to 6 in the last two decades. The coup is typically followed by a period of extremely autocratic rule, but the period until there is a turnover to competitive elections has shortened, particularly due to international pressure for democratic processes (Marinov and Goemans 2008). Among the states where coups have recently ousted leaders are the Central African Republic, Fiji, Guinea, Haiti, Honduras, Madagascar, Mauritania, and Thailand.

Revolution   As John Lennon (of the Beatles) observed, "You say you want a revolution, well you know, we all want to change the world." A revolution is *a rapid and fundamental transformation of the state organization and the class structure* (Skocpol 1979). In contrast to the other forms of political violence against the state, the explicit objective of a revolution is to destroy the existing political system and establish a new one with a fundamentally different distribution of power and value allocations. After a revolution, new leadership takes power, claiming that it will reorganize the state, serve a new ideology, and allocate power and resources to different groups.

However, it can be difficult to specify the precise extent of system transformation that must occur to achieve "revolutionary" changes in the state organization, class structure, or distribution of values (recall the discussion in Chapter 10). When Colonel Muammar Qaddafi overthrew the hereditary king and installed a new revolutionary council committed to creating a "state of the masses" with total egalitarianism (1969), it was clear that there had been a revolutionary change in the Libyan political system. Similarly, when Shah Reza Pahlavi and his "White Revolution" were overthrown and replaced by an Islamic theocracy (in 1979), there was a fundamental transformation in Iran's politics and society.

Although some of the most famous revolutions had occurred earlier (e.g., the American Revolution in 1776, the French Revolution in 1789, the Russian Revolution in 1917), there was a particularly large number of revolutionary movements and revolutions in the period when many colonial territories transitioned to independent countries (especially from about 1950 to 1980). But in many instances, it is not clear whether the essential features of the political system have dramatically changed. This situation can occur either because the attempt to transform the political system is a charade or because it falls far short of its objectives. Can you currently determine whether the recent overthrow of leaders in the "Arab Spring" of 2011 (e.g., in Egypt and Libya) should be characterized as revolutions?

Strategies For Revolution   Four broad strategies can be employed to achieve a revolution.

Strategy 1: Terrorism. As a revolutionary strategy, *terrorism* involves selective acts of violence, usually by small, organized cells of political activists that lack sufficient membership and resources to sustain a direct struggle against the existing state. Violence is used to disrupt public life and to provoke repressive responses from the state, and thus to foster political decay and undermine support for the state. The anticolonial resistance in Algeria is a clear example of the successful use of terrorism. A mixture of random public bombings, disruptions of infrastructure services, and violence against the agents of the colonial French led to a

The Arab Spring. After months of huge demonstrations like this one in Cairo's Tahrir Square and some violence, the populist revolt forced the resignation of Egyptian President Hosni Mubarak and the collapse of his government in 2011.

dramatic decline in the quality of life and provoked repressive responses from the French political and military authorities. As conditions deteriorated, France decided to abandon the ungovernable country, and the anticolonial/terrorist leadership, under Ben Bella, formed a new political system in 1962. (Gillo Pontecorvo's powerful film *The Battle of Algiers* documents this period.)

Obviously, terrorism, like other revolutionary strategies, does not always produce the expected results. Sometimes the terrorists are crushed without achieving any of their objectives, like the terrorist groups in the United States in the 1960s. And sometimes the repression evoked by terrorism merely makes things worse. In Iran, leftist terrorists were successful in destabilizing Shah Reza Pahlavi's regime, but it was the Islamic fundamentalists supporting the Ayatollah Khomeini who succeeded in grasping political power (1979) and forming a new political system even more unappealing to the leftists than the shah's. Nonetheless, terrorism continues to be the preferred strategy for certain revolutionary groups that lack popular support, such as Abu Sayyaf in the Philippines.

Strategy 2: Revolution from above. In a revolution from above (Johnson 1983), violent resistance to the regime occurs primarily in the urban centers, especially the capital city. Usually, the rural areas have minimal involvement in the revolutionary struggle. At least some parts of the political elite and the military are sympathetic to or even supportive of the goals of the revolution. Typically, the final collapse of the old regime is rapid because its leaders are killed or flee. The new political system then penetrates the countryside in an attempt to control the entire country. Examples of revolution from above in the 20th century include Gamal Abdel Nasser's replacement of King Farouk in Egypt (1952), Muammar Qaddafi's victory over King Idris in Libya (1969) and then his violent overthrow (2011), the execution of communist Premier Nicholae Ceauçescu in Romania (1989), and the flight of socialist leaders Mengistu Mariam from Ethiopia and Said Barre from Somalia (1991).

Strategy 3: Guerrilla war. The essence of guerrilla war is *a long, protracted campaign of political violence against the state from rural bases*, although the fighting can be in both rural and urban areas. It is a direct struggle against the military because the guerrilla forces persistently harass the regime's military and authorities by fighting in a hit-and-run style, suddenly attacking an exposed point and then disappearing into the population and the countryside. There is an effort to win the loyalty of the rural population by mixing intimidation and promises of reform. Eventually, the guerrillas gain control of the countryside and then march into the collapsing capital city.

The Chinese revolution, culminating in victory in 1949, is the classic example. Mao Zedong observed that success in the revolution depended on the support of the rural peasants, for "without the poor peasants, there can be no revolution." Many of the successful Third World revolutions after 1950 employed guerrilla warfare, including Cuba under Fidel Castro (1959), Vietnam under Ho Chi Minh (1975), and Zimbabwe (formerly Rhodesia) under Robert Mugabe (1980). This strategy is evident in recent struggles in Afghanistan by the Taliban, Algeria, Colombia, and Congo.

Strategy 4: Democratic revolution. **Democratic revolution** occurs when *legal, generally nonviolent political action is effectively mounted to achieve a fundamental transformation of the political system*. In one form, the population uses the democratic electoral process to select a new leadership elite, which then dismantles the existing political system and creates a new one. Examples of this form are the rise of Hitler and establishment of the Third Reich in Germany (1933) and the election of the anti-Sandinista coalition in Nicaragua (1990).

In a second form, widespread but generally nonviolent citizen resistance to a regime forces the elite to resign (Sharp 2010; Thompson 2003). The new leadership, though not initially elected, implements fundamental transformations in the political system. This occurred in the negotiated "Velvet Revolutions" in Soviet bloc states such as Czechoslovakia, East Germany, and Poland in the late 1980s. More recently, there have been numerous instances of a third form that falls short of revolution but does involve extensive, generally peaceful demonstrations against a leader that result in resignation and the rapid installation of a significantly different political regime. Among the many examples are the Philippines (2001), Georgia's "Rose Revolution" (2003), Ukraine's "Orange Revolution" (2004), and Kyrgyzstan's "Tulip Revolution" (2005). As noted above, the recent "revolutions" in Egypt and Tunisia drove out the old regime leadership through predominantly nonviolent action in the hope of political transformation, but it is not yet clear whether fundamental change will be established.

Conditions for Revolution The conditions under which political revolution occurs is an issue that has fascinated many people, especially those who want to analyze revolution and those who want to lead a successful revolution. The

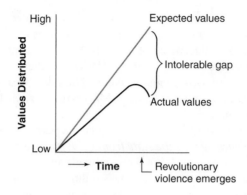

FIGURE 12.3
J-curve description of revolution

Source: Derived from Davies 1971.

most widely cited studies of major historical revolutions include those by Hannah Arendt (1963), Crane Brinton (1957), Chalmers Johnson (1983), Barrington Moore (1966), and Theda Skocpol (1979).

One long-standing explanation of revolution is substantial inequality, a factor emphasized in analyses from Aristotle to Karl Marx to contemporary theorists. A second general approach is the "theory of rising expectations," associated with Alexis de Tocqueville (1835/1945), James Davies (1971), and others. In this view, the key cause of revolution is a sudden increase in the disparity between the values the population expects to enjoy from the government and the actual value distribution the population receives. It is also called the *J-curve theory* because, as indicated in Figure 12.3, the *disparity resembles an inverted J*, and revolutionary violence occurs when the disparity becomes substantial.

Empirical analyses have defined certain conditions that are associated with countries in which revolutions occur: (1) conflicting elites; (2) deep ethnic divisions; (3) rapid economic growth, especially when it is followed by a sharp decline in prosperity; (4) a relatively short history as an autonomous state; (5) divisive interventions by actors in the international system; (6) rapid population growth, especially a high proportion of younger people; and (7) social mobilization. None of these is a "necessary condition" for revolution, and unique events are critically important, but the probability of revolution increases as more of these conditions are present.

USE OF FORCE BETWEEN STATES

12.4 Analyze the nature and causes of war.

⊙─[**Watch** the **Video "The Iran-Iraq War"** at **mypoliscilab.com**

The final box in Figure 12.1 includes those cases in which both the source and target of violence are states. While this form is primarily referred to as a war, there are some situations where the use of violence between states is more limited (Gochman and Maoz 1984):

- In a *blockade*, the military (e.g., ships, troops, munitions) of one state is used to seal off territory (e.g., border crossings, harbors), preventing entry or exit by the rival state.

- In *state-sponsored terrorism*, the state provides financial or material support to groups committing occasional acts of political violence within the rival state.
- A state can engage in a brief, *single use of force*, such as a bombing raid, firing munitions into the enemy state, or rapid invasion for a specific purpose (e.g., the sabotage of a facility).
- In a *clash*, there is a brief engagement between the armed forces of two states, as in a border skirmish.
- In a ***low-intensity conflict (LIC)***, *a group uses conventional weapons in a rival's territory in a sporadic and prolonged manner that does not involve full-scale military conflict*, with the goal of inflicting maximum harm while suffering few or no casualties. (The concept of LIC is also applied to situations in which a government or a powerful external state directs persistent uses of violent force against groups resisting the government, such as guerrillas.) Despite the label, the violence associated with low-intensity conflict *is* intense for those involved, especially the targets.

War

War is *interstate violence that is sustained and organized and (usually) involves hostilities between the regular military forces of the states*. Such violence is the ultimate mechanism for resolving conflict between states. For those who define politics as conflict resolution, war represents the utter failure of politics. But many probably agree with Karl von Clausewitz's famous dictum: "War is regarded as nothing but a continuation of political activity by other means" (Clausewitz 1833/1967: 87). Thus, war is the use of violence by one state to achieve its political goals at the expense of another state.

Robert Ardrey (1966: 27), a well-known ethologist (a person who studies animal behavior to better understand human behavior), wryly observed that "human war has been the most successful of all our cultural traditions." Indeed, the study of world history is usually dominated by wars and recurrent episodes of organized violence among states.

The elimination of war is not among the accomplishments of the modern world. The comprehensive analysis of major interstate wars between 1816 and 1980 found some good news: Wars are less frequent, are considerably shorter, and involve fewer states. But the bad news is that the number of wars "in progress" at any given time has increased substantially since 1900, and the total number of deaths from war has risen astronomically (Sivard 1996). The post–cold war context has possibly reduced the number of interstate wars (Russett 2010). Yet since 1990, about half of the world's countries have suffered the enormous costs of a major armed conflict (SIPRI 2011).

Few of the recent major conflicts are *conventional wars*—that is, wars that entail the direct, sustained confrontation of the military forces of two or more states within a defined space on the soil of one of the combatants. Conflicts that do fit the definition of a conventional war include the Argentina–United Kingdom War (Falklands War, 1982), the Iran–Iraq War (1980–1988), the Iraq–Kuwait War (Persian Gulf War, 1990), the Ecuador–Peru War (1995), the Ethiopia–Eritrea War (1998–2000), the Iraq–U.S.(-led coalition) War (2003) and the brief Georgia–Russia War (2008).

Many contemporary conflicts are more complicated mixes of internal, regional, and transborder combatants. While many are not classic wars, analysts combine them with war into a broader category: *major armed conflicts*. Major armed conflicts have three defining characteristics: (1) the use of armed force between two or more governments or one government and at least one organized, armed group; (2) at least a thousand battle-related deaths in a year; and (3) conflict over control of the government or territory. In the last two decades, 15–30 major armed conflicts were being waged per year. And all 15 such conflicts in 2010 were intrastate, that is, sustained violence within the borders of a country (although combatants from other countries might be participants) (SIPRI 2011: Appendix 2A).

Africa's "world war" in Congo (1998–2003, but the fighting continues; recall the Focus in 11) seems a prototype of the contemporary unconventional war. At one level, it is an internal civil war between the military forces loyal to President Kabila and several large paramilitary groups that rejected his authority to rule. Some of the cleavages underlying the conflict are regional, some are nation-based, and some are based on merely personal animosity and ambition. Other motivations include greed to capture Congo's valuable resources. At its height, the war involved militaries and paramilitaries from eight countries and UN peacekeeping forces and as many as 5.4 million deaths are attributable to the war (Prunier 2008). Another striking example of this type of complex "war" is the bloody conflict in Israel and Palestine, where all forms of political violence collide, characterized in the Focus in 12.

The changing nature of many contemporary wars is evident in the enormous increase in the proportion of civilian deaths. Whereas in World War I there was only one civilian death for every eight military deaths, in World War II there were two civilian deaths for every military death. In the 1990s, nine out of every ten war deaths were *civilians*, and the major armed conflicts going on since 1990 have been killing more than half a million civilians each year. And the remarkable and efficient technologies of modern war are dramatically increasing the casualties. In the 20th century, there were six times as many deaths per war as in the 19th century, and four more times as many war deaths as in the preceding 400 years (Sivard 1996: 7, 17).

Worldwide, the more than $1.6 *trillion* per year that states spend directly on the military to support their security goals could, if reallocated to their prosperity goals, greatly enhance their citizens' quality of life. Total world military spending has increased by fully 50 percent between 2000 and 2010 (SIPRI 2011). The problem, of course, is that many policymakers believe that security goals have the highest priority, and that without security, no other goals can be achieved. Yet in an era of high-tech warfare, almost no one feels truly secure. This insecurity leads every state to push itself and its rivals into an accelerating, unending, and potentially devastating expansion of the capacity for massive political violence.

Do you think some states have a more extensive history of interstate conflict than others? This issue is explored in Compare in 12.

What Causes War?

Can we explain why states go to war? As a partial answer, scholars have attempted to determine whether some states or their populations have particular attributes that result in a greater propensity to engage in war. The findings are inconclusive, since

FOCUS IN 12 | **Ultraviolence among the Children of Abraham: Israelis and Palestinians**

Israelis and Palestinians share a common understanding of their beginnings, yet they split into two nations whose recent history is marked by ultraviolence. Perhaps more than anywhere else in the world, almost every type of political violence in Figure 12.1 occurs with depressing regularity. Helicopter gunships fire missiles at cars to assassinate leaders, suicide bombers kill and maim scores of innocents, bulldozers destroy residential neighborhoods, and bloody wars wreak havoc in several countries. How did things get so bad?

According to legend, the patriarch Abraham settled in and was eventually buried in the land of Canaan, near what is now Hebron, Israel, in about 2000 B.C.E. Abraham developed the foundational principles of a new religion, Judaism. The offspring of one of his two wives (son Isaac and grandson Israel) followed this new religion. The line descending from Abraham's other wife continued to live in the area and did not embrace Judaism. Most family members in this second line were later attracted to the teachings of Mohammed (born in Mecca in 570 C.E.) and another new religion, Islam. Arab military conquests in the seventh to tenth centuries added to the near-total religious domination of Islam in the region.

"The children of Israel" (the Jews) lived in the Canaan area from about 1300 to 700 B.C.E. but ultimately migrated to many countries. Almost everywhere they went, the Jews felt themselves to be a target of discrimination and described themselves as part of a dispersed ("diaspora") nation with no homeland. Thus, in 1897, European Jewish leaders founded the World Zionist Movement, whose central goal was to establish a Jewish homeland and a sanctuary from anti-Semitism. After a debate in which locations in Europe, Africa, Latin America, and the Near East were considered, the Zionists concluded that their homeland should be the "Promised Land" of Abraham's birth, Palestine. They began purchasing land and establishing colonies of Jewish settlers in Palestine. By the outbreak of World War I (1914), they owned 100,000 acres, and 70,000 Jews had migrated to Palestine, living alongside more than 800,000 Arab Muslims (see Figure 12.4).

After the war, the British government, which had a mandate to govern Palestine, agreed under pressure from European Jews that it would assist in establishing a Jewish "home" in Palestine. As discrimination against the Jews in Europe reached horrendous levels with the rise of Nazism, the flow of

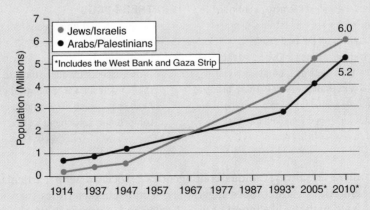

FIGURE 12.4
Population in Palestine/Israel at key dates

(Continued)

Jewish immigrants to Palestine became a flood. By the outbreak of World War II, the number of Jews in Palestine had increased sixfold.

The Muslim Arabs in the Palestine area were increasingly distressed by this massive invasion of Jewish "foreigners." There was violence and guerrilla war between extreme groups of Arabs and Jews. The recently founded United Nations proposed a plan to split Palestine into two states, maintaining Jerusalem as a shared city under UN trusteeship. The Jews accepted this plan in 1947, but the Arabs rejected it, angry that the Jews, who constituted only one-third of the population, would receive the majority (55 percent) of the land. Two hours before the British mandate in Palestine ended in 1947, the Jewish leaders declared a new sovereign state, Israel. The next day, the armies of the surrounding Arab states (Egypt, Lebanon, Syria, and Transjordan) declared war on Israel. The defeat of these armies by the Israeli army resulted in 800,000 homeless Palestinians, many of whom fled to neighboring lands.

Full-scale war erupted three more times between Israel and its Arab neighbors (1956, 1967, and 1973). Each time, Israel defeated the Arab armies and conquered more land, the "Occupied Territories" (especially the West Bank and Gaza). By the late 1960s, these territories were inhabited by 1.2 million Palestinians, who were now an unwelcome nation subjugated within the Israeli state. More than 1 million additional Palestinians were exiles living in Jordan and other Arab states. Jewish settlements continued to expand in the Occupied Territories, establishing new outposts of Jewish control on the best land.

Frustrated Palestinians formed active resistance groups, most notably the Palestine Liberation Organization (1964) and Hamas (1987). These groups were convinced that only political violence and the destruction of the state of Israel would enable them to regain control of their lands. The combination of civil disobedience, armed resistance, and terrorist acts by Palestinian groups, on the one hand, and the strong and often brutal responses by the Israeli military and Jewish militant groups, on the other hand, has resulted in an endless cycle of violence and retaliation. The more militant groups on each side are willing to engage in "whatever means necessary" to protect their land.

The United Nations, the United States, and others have promoted a two-state solution based broadly on the pre-1967 borders in order to achieve stability and peace in the region, but all agreements have collapsed. Some Palestinian groups have renounced terrorism and accepted the continued existence of Israel, and some Israelis agree that there should be a Palestinian state. But after the 2006 election of Hamas as the dominant party in Gaza, there have been new rounds of devastating violence between the Israelis and Palestinians.

Beneath this basic story line there are extraordinarily complex subplots: factional struggles among the Jews and among the Palestinians, disagreements about the legitimacy of violence by each group, and the complicated agendas of external actors (e.g., other Arab states, the United States, MNCs) regarding Islam, oil, terrorism, and so on. The land of Abraham is the cauldron in which this volatile stew of violence boils furiously.

FURTHER FOCUS

1. Should the UN have proposed a land split in 1947 that closely reflected the size of the two populations?
2. If one accepts the idea that "to the victor go the spoils" after a war, do both the Israelis and the Arab states each have a good reason to reject a compromise settlement at this point? ▸

---

there are always unique contingencies associated with particular wars. However, empirical research does suggest seven state characteristics that are generally correlated with the likelihood of war (Kegley and Wittkopf 2004: 411–418):

1. *Newer nations* are more likely to initiate war than are mature states.
2. War is more likely in states that have effectively *socialized their citizens to accept the government's actions* on national security.

3. The most warlike states have *rising prosperity* but are *relatively poor*, though they are not the very poorest states.
4. Countries with *desirable geopolitical features* (i.e., resources and location—recall Chapter 11) have a higher probability of warfare.
5. Countries *not well linked to the global economy* are more likely to engage in war.
6. States that are most *highly militarized*, and especially those that are rapidly expanding their military power, are more warlike.
7. Countries whose political culture reflects a high degree of *nationalism* are more warlike.

COMPARE IN 12 | Levels of War and Peace

How can we compare the extent to which particular countries are more war-prone or more peaceful? One comprehensive study determined the frequency with which more than 100 countries engaged in interstate conflict between 1816 and 1976. The analysis focused on empirical data measuring 14 types of "militarized interstate disputes," including major displays of force and uses of force. A state is considered to be in a dispute whether it is the initiator or the target of the conflict. Because some countries have considerably longer histories as states, the analysis measured disputes per year of the state's existence. The study concluded that less than one-third of the states, primarily major powers, initiated more than 70 percent of all disputes, were the primary targets of more than 60 percent of the disputes, and were also most likely to enter disputes in which other countries were already engaged. Table 12.3 lists the ten most dispute-prone states in the analysis. Notice that the list of most conflict-prone states is topped by Israel, the United Kingdom, India, the United States, and Pakistan, all of whom averaged more than one dispute per year (Gochman and Maoz 1984).

A recent empirical study takes a different approach. It calculates a yearly "Global Peace Index" for 183 countries, using 24 indicators such as external and internal conflicts, military expenditures, and relations with neighboring countries (Vision of Humanity 2011).

In contrast to the earlier study, this index attempts to measure and compare countries' level of peacefulness and nonviolence, although most of the measures in the index do relate to the level of preparation for and engagement in violent activities, both domestic and international. Table 12.3 lists the 10 most peaceful countries, led by New Zealand and Japan. Other rankings in the top half of all countries on peacefulness include Germany (15), the United Kingdom (26), Italy (45), Brazil (74), China (80), and the United States (82). The index can also be examined from the bottom up to identify the *least* peaceful countries in the contemporary world. Table 12.3 indicates that the three least peaceful countries are Somalia, Iraq, and Sudan (183–181). Other countries ranking relatively low on peacefulness include Russia (147), Israel (145), India (135), and Mexico (121).

FURTHER QUESTIONS

1. If you were creating a comparative index of how "peaceful" various countries are, what are the 3–4 most important variables you would include in your index?
2. Is it reasonable that the comparative index for dispute-prone countries makes no distinction among the following three situations: whether a country started a dispute, whether it responded to a violent challenge, or whether it joined a dispute in progress?

(Continued)

TABLE 12.3

Most Dispute-Prone and Most Peaceful Countries

A. Most Dispute-Prone (1816–1976)*	B. Least Peaceful (Current)	C. Most Peaceful (Current)
Israel	Iraq	Iceland
United Kingdom	Afghanistan	New Zealand
India	Somalia	Japan
United States	Israel	Denmark
Pakistan	Sudan	Czech Republic
Germany	Democratic Republic of Congo	Austria
Russia/Soviet Union	Chad	Finland
France	Pakistan	Canada
China	Russia	Norway
Italy	Zimbabwe	Slovenia

*Also highly dispute-prone countries are Zambia, Rhodesia/Zimbabwe, North Vietnam, and Uganda; but these states were independent for only a short amount of the analysis period, thus causing potential measurement error.

Sources: A = Gochman and Maoz 1984: Table 8; B and C = Vision of Humanity 2011.

The contemporary global system has conditions that make many analysts (particularly those with the political idealist perspective described in Chapter 11) optimistic that war is declining. Several forces seem to encourage this optimism. First, democracy has spread to many major countries, and *established democracies rarely fight each other* (the so-called *democratic peace*). In particular, there is a growing "security community" of countries, mainly among the most developed countries in the EU and NATO, among whom an interstate war seems inconceivable. Second, globalization has substantially increased countries' *economic interdependence*. And third, *transnational organizations*, ranging from the UN to NGOS to MNCs, have become more significant and more powerful. Both the second and third factors force countries to recognize their shared interests, create strong inducements for cooperation, and provide institutional support for conflict resolution. Thus, the optimists point to a decrease in the number of interstate wars in recent years and the growing sense that major powers will not fight each other (Jervis 2002; Rasler and Thompson 2005; Russett and Oneal 2001; Russett 2010).

However, others, especially the realists, see the glass half empty. First, if one considers not just the classic interstate wars, but the broader definition of major armed conflicts described above, there has been *no significant reduction in serious conflicts involving states*. And democracies are as likely as nondemocracies to be involved in these conflicts. Even if the democracies rarely fight each other, there are plenty of potential opponents. Second, globalization and development have dramatically intensified the competition for resources, which will provoke more conflict and *resource wars*. And third, global wars are most likely when a dominant power (*a hegemon) weakens* and new challengers rise, and the current hegemon (the United States) seems to be in decline. And even before that occurs, the emerging *multipolar system* is more conflict prone than either the unipolar system or bipolar system that preceded it (Gowa 2000; Klare 2002, 2012; Mearsheimer 2001; Nye 2011; Organski 1968).

At the highest level of abstraction, there are three broad alternative explanations for the causes of war:

1. War can be attributed to *scarcity in nature*. Because the consumption goals of states are greater than the natural resources available, states undertake war to protect or capture resources from other states. Thus, states struggle with each other for the control of resources such as energy, food, minerals, and strategic locations (CNA 2007; Klare 2012).
2. War can be attributed to the *inadequacy of institutions*. In this view, neither the existing sociopolitical structure nor the rules governing the conduct among states are adequate to prevent states from using force to achieve their objectives. Thus, states are guided by self-interest, and there are no conflict-resolution mechanisms that prevent the occasional eruption of large-scale interstate violence.
3. War can be explained by *human nature*. From this perspective, humans are innately aggressive as a biological species. Humans are nearly the only species that engages in widespread killing of its own kind. And humans, it is claimed, are acquisitive, competitive, and selfish by nature rather than by nurture. Thus, war becomes a predictable group-level manifestation of these inherent qualities. A variation on this explanation emphasizes the critical importance of an aggressive leader who draws her country into war (Stoessinger 2010). The gender reference in the previous sentence, while consistent with the alternate chapters referencing in this book, prompts a reminder of the discussion in Chapter 11 of the subfield of international relations theory that asserts female leaders are far less likely than males to resort to violence in interstate disputes (Tickner 2001).

Each of the preceding "ultimate" explanations of war also suggests possible solutions that might eliminate war:

1. If the problem is scarcity of natural resources, one might look to *technological solutions*, as states develop new techniques to use natural resources more efficiently and to develop abundant substitutes for scarce resources.
2. If the problem is inadequate institutions, the need is for *social engineering*—for the creation of organizational arrangements that more effectively structure the relations among individuals and states. In the political domain, this might ultimately entail the creation of a viable world government.
3. If the problem is human nature, the solution is found in *human engineering* by means of a comprehensive political socialization or perhaps even by genetic manipulation to create a population with the "proper" qualities.

There is some evidence to support each of these three general explanations of the causes of war. But there is also sufficient counterevidence so that none of the three positions is compelling as a complete explanation. Neither an abundance of natural resources nor an advanced technology has stopped intergroup violence. And while there are societies whose members have not been driven by human nature into warlike behavior against their neighbors, no set of human institutions or patterns of human learning have been shown inevitably to generate war or perpetuate peace between states.

While the complete elimination of war might be impossible, it does seem that a combination of material abundance, effective institutions, and thorough socialization might reduce the incidence of war. This leads to more questions: Can an effective combination be identified and implemented by political actors? Might the solution produce human conditions nearly as unpalatable as occasional wars?

EVALUATING POLITICAL VIOLENCE: MEANS AND ENDS

12.5 Evaluate the normative implications of political violence.

Watch the **Video "The Crisis in Darfur"** at **mypoliscilab.com**

Study and **Review** the **Post-Test & Chapter Exam** at **mypoliscilab.com**

Political violence can be understood as a failure of institutionalized political action. A strong and persuasive normative perspective contends that political violence, especially within a country, is unacceptable, deviant behavior. Conservative ideology provides the most explicit condemnation of such violence, concluding that the only legacy of violence is to undermine order in the society. The resort to violence is part of an erroneous belief that radical social change can lead to lasting improvements. As Englishman Edmund Burke (1729–1797) observed: "Time is required to produce that union of minds which alone can produce all the good we aim at. Our patience will achieve more than our force" (Burke 1790/1955: 197).

A contrary perspective argues that political violence is often the best or even the only mechanism for liberation from oppression and tyranny. This view contends that many societies are controlled by dominant elites who manipulate the state to serve their interests, not the collective good. If a government and its leaders refuse to be constrained by a limited mandate and are not responsive to the legitimate rights of citizens, then the people have the right to overthrow them by any available means. Although this perspective is mainly associated with class theorists and Marxist ideology, the counterpoint to Burke is provided by another English political thinker, classical liberal John Locke (1632–1704), who argued that citizens create government to protect their rights to life, liberty, and property. If the existing government does not serve these purposes well, argued Locke, the people can and must revolt in order to replace tyranny and create a new and better government (Locke 1690/1963: 466).

Political violence can be a source of either desirable progress or nearly universal suffering and chaos. Clearly, fundamental issues about means and ends are tied up with any assessment of political violence. On one hand, if the maintenance of public order and political institutionalization are valued goals, you must consider whether resorting to political violence undermines long-term prospects for peaceful, orderly governance. Many cynics would share Italian novelist Ignazio Silone's (1937) assessment: "Every revolution begins as a movement of liberation but ends as tyranny." On the other hand, if you value social and political justice, it is important to consider whether the processes of political violence can be a legitimate means of last resort to ensure such justice. Those who justify some forms of political violence might sympathize with African American Eldridge Cleaver's claim that "a slave who dies of natural causes will not balance two dead flies on the scale of eternity."

There are no tidy answers to the question of whether or when political violence is justifiable. Perhaps one way to organize your own assessment of political violence is to reflect on three basic questions:

1. Is political violence unacceptable under *every* possible circumstance?
2. If you answered no to question 1, could an outcome emerge from the use of political violence that is so preferable to the existing situation that establishing the precedent of using political violence is justifiable?
3. If you answered yes to question 2, what specific circumstances would be necessary to justify the resort to political violence?

These issues about the conditions under which political violence might be legitimate are germane on an even larger scale regarding the justification of war. Despite the massive human and financial costs of war, few would support the proposition that there are absolutely no conditions under which war is justified. But what are the circumstances that justify war?

A classic justification is the doctrine of *self-defense*, a position associated with Augustine (354–430 C.E.). A victim of an unprovoked attack has the right to use violence as a means of protection. Apart from total pacifists, few would reject the principle of self-defense as a legitimate rationale for violence. But the application of this principle, whether group versus group or state versus state, might be a subject of considerable disagreement. Here are some examples in the relations between states: Might state A engage in nonviolent actions that are so provocative that state B is justified in responding with violence? What if the initial violence against state B is by an actor from state A who does not have the explicit support of state A? What if the violence by state A was unintentional? What if the initial violence is within the territory of state A but is perceived as directly harmful to citizens or interests of state B? What if state B uses violence to prevent state A from the (expected) use of far more substantial violence? What if the violent response of state B is of far greater magnitude than the violence by state A? Wars sometimes develop because of such patterns of misperception, accident, preemption, and incremental escalation (Schelling 1960).

Frequently, however, violence and war are justified on a more ambiguous rationale associated with Ambrose (339–397 C.E.), as the *defense of universal principles*. In this view, "man has a moral duty to employ force to resist active wickedness, for to refrain from hindering evil when possible is tantamount to promoting it." In accepting the 2009 Nobel Peace Prize, U.S. president Obama cited "just war" principles. Yet the interpretations of "active wickedness" and "evil" are not shared across all cultures. For example, many citizens in most countries believed that Iraq's Saddam Hussein was an evil ruler. However, most did not find this an adequate justification for U.S. president George W. Bush's insistence on a "preemptive" war, especially in the absence of compelling evidence that Iraq endangered other countries with weapons of mass destruction that could not be eliminated except by war. Similarly, what level of evil by a ruling group justifies the resort to violence against that group?

In most cases of political violence, a justification based on universal principles is invoked. Violence is used against others in the name of principles such as freedom, social justice, human rights, self-determination, territorial integrity, egalitarianism, religious freedom, religious orthodoxy, anticommunism, communism, and so on. But all political actors do not accept a single vision of natural law that provides universal principles to govern the relations among states and groups.

When the major actors are states, a core problem is that the international system has not implemented powerful and effective institutional mechanisms that eliminate conflict. Thus, occasional outbreaks of interstate conflict and war are inevitable. The context of international politics is essentially *amoral*. Recognizing this fact is the key to understanding most politics across borders, whether diplomatic activities, alliances, or war. In some instances, a state's actions in the international environment are constrained by the state's views of morality and universal principles. But in other instances, a state's decision makers might conclude that almost any action is acceptable if the action seems to further the state's security, stability, and prosperity goals. What are the chances that contemporary states will ever meet the requirement of the UN Charter to "settle their international disputes by peaceful means in such a manner that international peace and security, and justice, are not endangered"?

In the current technological era, the mechanisms for committing violence are more efficient, powerful, and horrifying than at any time in human history. The implications of this fact are especially evident in the relations between states. But even subnational political groups can now inflict massive and destructive political violence. Thus, in understanding the political world, questions about the use of force and the balance between liberation and destruction are more pressing now than at any time in human history.

KEY CONCEPTS

civil war   330
class conflict   328
coup   330
democratic peace   340
democratic revolution   333
establishment violence   319
genocide   327
guerrilla war   333
J-curve theory   334
low-intensity conflict   335

nation-based violence   325
political society   318
political violence   318
rebellion   329
revolution   331
riot   329
separatist violence   329
terrorism   322
violence   317
war   335

FOR FURTHER CONSIDERATION

1. Is the state more to be feared than its enemies? Assess the implications of the prevalence during the 20th century of "murder by government," in which the state is the actor committing violence and the state's citizens are its target.
2. Summarize the key elements of a three-way debate among an absolute pacifist, a committed revolutionary, and yourself regarding the conditions under which political violence is justifiable.

3. It is suggested that much of contemporary political violence is nation-based. Analyze the nation-based conflicts about which you are aware. Is most of the violence caused by fundamental antipathy between two nationality groups due to differences in ethnicity, religion, language, and so on? Or is the violence primarily motivated by other issues, such as inequality and class conflict, quest for power, geopolitics, or some other cause?

4. Must every revolution end in tyranny (as suggested by Ignazio Silone)? Can you identify a modern revolution that, by the criteria you establish, can be viewed as a success?

5. Which of the characteristics of warlike states on pages 338–339 is most surprising to you? Why? What characteristic did you expect that is not among those listed?

FOR FURTHER READING

Brecher, Michael, and Jonathan Wilkenfeld. (1997). *A Study of Crisis*. Ann Arbor: University of Michigan Press. A comprehensive, usable database from the International Crisis Behavior project that provides valuable information on 412 crises between 1929 and 1992, following the authors' thoughtful analyses of and generalizations about the patterns of interstate crises.

Cimbala, Stephen J. (2000). *Nuclear Strategy in the Twenty-First Century*. Westport, CT: Praeger. In a provocative analysis, Cimbala explains why the danger of nuclear war is increasing and why weaker states and marginal groups are gaining greater advantage from nuclear weapons than the major powers, who will find more benefit from high-tech weaponry.

Cinema of War. Film, in addition to literature, has often been a compelling visual and visceral medium for evoking the heroism and absurdity of war. Among the films that are especially effective are *Apocalypse Now* (Francis Ford Coppola, 1979, 2001); *The Sands of Iwo Jima* (Allan Dwan, 1949); *The Big Red One* (Samuel Fuller, 1980); *In Which We Serve* (David Lean, 1942); *All Quiet on the Western Front* and *Pork Chop Hill* (Lewis Milestone, 1930, 1959); *The Grand Illusion* (Jean Renoir, 1937); and *Platoon* (1986 Oliver Stone,).

Downes, Alexander B. (2008). *Targeting Civilians in War*. Ithaca, NY: Cornell University Press. A blend of case studies and quantitative data are combined to make the controversial argument that democracies are as likely as other forms of government to target noncombatants in interstate conflicts.

Freedman, Lawrence, Ed. (1994). *War*. New York: Oxford University Press. A splendid collection of readings, ranging from the greatest classical treatments of the reasons for and the nature of war to significant contemporary analyses.

Goldstein, Joshua S. (2001). *War and Gender: How Gender Shapes the War System and Vice Versa*. Cambridge, England: Cambridge University Press. This book explores why warfare is dominated by men and concludes generally that it is primarily due to culturally constructed male domination and "militarized masculine stereotypes" rather than genetic differences.

Goldstone, Jack A., Ed. (2003). *Revolutions: Theoretical, Comparative, and Historical Studies*. 3rd ed. Florence, KY: Wadsworth Cengage. A readable set of articles that includes both detailed case studies of revolutions and more analytic work that attempts to develop generalizations about revolutionary violence.

Gourevitch, Philip. (1998). *We Wish to Inform You That Tomorrow We Will Be Killed with Our Families: Stories from Rwanda*. New York: Farrar, Straus and Giroux. A powerful account of the ways in which ethnonationalist rhetoric was used to mobilize the Hutu people to massacre almost one million Tutsis and Hutu moderates in Rwanda in the mid-1990s, while the international community was unwilling to intervene to prevent the genocide.

Gurr, Ted Robert. (2000). *Peoples Versus States: Minorities at Risk in the New Century.* Washington, DC: United States Institute of Peace Press. Based on the valuable Minorities at Risk Project database, the book is an exceptionally rich blend of data-based analyses and case studies of nation-based conflict.

Gutman, Roy, and David Rieff, Eds. (1999). *Crimes of War: What the Public Should Know.* New York: W. W. Norton. Diverse and enlightening discussions on the legal and ethical issues regarding war crimes and international humanitarian law, with powerful commentaries on cases such as Cambodia, Chechnya, and Rwanda, and dramatic illustrations by photojournalists.

Hoffman, Bruce. (2006). *Inside Terrorism.* Revised and updated edition. New York: Columbia University Press. A broad-ranging and troubling exploration of terrorism, with particular attention to the recent evolution of strategies and goals of terrorists.

Jenkins, Philip. (2003). *Images of War: What We Can and Can't Know About Terrorism.* New York: Aldine de Gruyter. A fascinating array of examples is provided to examine how stories about terrorism are transformed in public discussion, especially by the media.

Klare, Michael. (2008). *Rising Powers, Shrinking Planet: The New Geopolitics of Energy.* New York: Henry Holt. This is among Klare's persuasive books (see also Resource Wars, 2001) about the "new geography of conflict," driven by competition for scarce resources, between states in the early 21st century.

Moghadam, Assaf. (2008). *The Globalization of Martyrdom.* Baltimore, MD: Johns Hopkins University Press. The role of al Qaeda and the ideology of Salafi Jihad in almost 1,300 suicide attacks during the past 30 years are analyzed, and suggestions for combating such attacks are offered.

O'Brien, Tim. (1990). *The Things They Carried.* New York: Doubleday Broadway Books. In 22 fictional short stories about a U.S. military platoon in the Vietnam War, the author powerfully conveys universal themes regarding the horror of war from the perspective of the individual soldier.

Parker, Geoffrey, Ed. (2005). *The Cambridge History of Warfare.* 2nd ed. London: Cambridge University Press. An ambitious series of essays examining many aspects of war in the Western world, from ancient Greece through recent wars in the Middle East. A key theme is that Western technology and prosperity produced a dominant military that ensured Western global supremacy.

Prunier, Gerard. (2008). *Darfur: A 21st Century Genocide.* 3rd ed. Ithaca, NY: Cornell University Press. A gripping exploration of the causes and nature of the brutal conflict in Sudan, including a critique of the failure of the international community to prevent the genocide. Equally powerful is his 2008 *Africa's World War: Congo, the Rwandan Genocide, and the Making of a Continental Disaster* (New York: Oxford University Press).

Rasler, Karen and William R. Thompson. (2005). *Puzzles of the Democratic Peace: Theory, Geopolitics and the Transformation of World Politics.* New York: Palgrave Macmillan. A thorough examination of the theories and data regarding the "democratic peace" debate, refining and supporting the concept.

Sassoon, Siegfried. (1968). *Collected Poems: 1908–1956.* London: Faber and Faber. The deeply moving poems about war by a young British intellectual who suffered the horrific experiences of European trench warfare during World War I.

Sharp, Gene. (2010). *From Dictatorship to Democracy: A Conceptual Framework for Liberation.* 4th U.S. edition. http://www.aeinstein.org/organizations/org/FDTD.pdf. First written to help the democracy movement in Myanmar, this remarkable little book provides guidelines for overthrowing a dictatorial regime, and leaders of recent "people's revolutions" indicate they found it very helpful.

Singer, P. W. (2005). *Children at War*. New York: Pantheon. A scholar and former military advisor to the CIA explores the chilling and heartbreaking rise of children as soldiers in many conflict zones. He blends evidence and the actual commentaries of many child soldiers to describe how they are recruited and trained and become ruthless warriors.

Stoessinger, John G. (2010). *Why Nations Go to War*. 11th ed. Boston: Bedford. A readable set of descriptive case studies of modern wars, particularly emphasizing individual behavior and motives, including World War I, Korea, Vietnam, India–Pakistan, Israel–Arabs, Iran–Iraq, the Balkans, and the U.S. wars in the Middle East.

Walter, Barbara F., and Jack Snyder, Eds. (1999). *Civil Wars, Insecurity, and Intervention*. New York: Columbia University Press. Centering on thoughtful case studies of the recent civil wars in Bosnia, Cambodia, Somalia, and Rwanda, important scholars analyze why the international community has not been particularly effective in either preventing the outbreak of or resolving civil wars.

Walzer, Michael. (2006). *Just and Unjust War*. 4th ed. New York: Basic Books. A political philosopher presents a careful argument about the morality of war, grounded in the context of numerous actual wars.

Weiss, Peter. (1965). *Marat-Sade: The Persecution and Assassination of Jean-Paul Marat as Performed by the Inmates of the Asylum at Charenton Under the Direction of the Marquis de Sade*. New York: Atheneum. A brilliant play (and a dazzling film with the same title directed by Peter Brooks) offers a debate about a revolution between Jean-Paul Marat, a leader of the French Revolution who attempts to retain his idealism about revolutionary change despite having become a victim of extremists, and the Marquis de Sade, the ultimate cynic.

Weitz, Eric D. (2005). *A Century of Genocide: Utopias of Race and Nation*. Princeton, NJ: Princeton University Press. A historian offers a compelling and readable comparison of the way in which four major genocides in the 20th century (under Stalin, Hitler, and Pol Pot, and in the former Yugoslavia) drew popular support through the strategic mixture of nationalism and racial identity.

ON THE WEB

http://www.amnesty.org

Amnesty International is the world's leading NGO monitoring establishment violence and human rights abuses and attempting to mobilize citizen support to pressure governments to end such actions.

http://wps.cfc.forces.gc.ca/en/index.php

The Information Resource Centre of the Canadian Forces College provides links to numerous sites detailing current major international conflicts.

http://www.sipri.org

The site of the Stockholm International Peace Research Institute, which conducts research on questions of conflict and cooperation relevant to international peace and security, includes rich databases and significant articles on topics of peace and violence.

http://www.hawaii.edu/powerkills/welcome.html

This site, managed by Professor Rudolf Rummel, an avowed "freedomist," is an exceptionally rich resource of information and links regarding themes of war and peace.

http://www.usip.org

This site for the U.S. Institute of Peace was established and is funded by the U.S. Congress with the goal of preventing conflict, ending current conflicts, and aiding in reconstruction after the hostilities.

http://www.nctc.gov

The National Counterterrorism Center has become the major source of information and data from the U.S. government regarding global terrorism.

http://www.un.org/terrorism

On the official site of the United Nations, one can access information on terrorism and both Security Council and General Assembly resolutions related to political violence.

http://www.ccc.nps.navy.mil/si

The Center for Contemporary Conflict is hosted by the Naval Postgraduate School in California. The site provides information, including many position papers and briefings, regarding current and emerging security concerns in all regions of the world.

http://www.pvtr.org

Centered in Singapore, the International Center for Political Violence and Terrorism offer details and commentaries on current situations of political violence.

http://www.visionofhumanity.org

The Vision of Humanity's Global Peace Index details the components of its yearly rating of the "peacefulness" of every country.

http://www.hrw.org

The electronic home of Human Rights Watch provides access to an extensive database regarding human rights violations taking place throughout the international community.

http://www.sfcg.org

The site of Search for Common Ground, the world's largest NGO working on conflict resolution, is an excellent source for material on this topic.

http://www.historyguy.com

The electronic home of the "History Guy" provides a number of links to detailed information, articles, and news reports related to political conflicts.

http://www.pcr.uu.se

The Conflict Data Project at Uppsala University (Sweden) maintains a rich and current database on armed conflicts in the world.

The Developed Countries of the Global North

The Golden Triangle retail area in Kuala Lumpur is one of Malaysia's many exceptionally modern
and sophisticated zones, despite Malaysia's overall classification as a "developing" country.

LEARNING OBJECTIVES

13.1 Identify the standards used to classify states from a developmental perspective.

13.2 Characterize the types of markets in the Global North and assess their challenges and achievements.

13.3 Identify the obstacles to the political stability of the Global North.

13.4 Trace the development of security challenges to the Global North.

📖 **Read** and **Listen** to **Chapter 13** at mypoliscilab.com

✔ **Study** and **Review** the **Pre-Test & Flashcards** at mypoliscilab.com

The first time you fly into Kuala Lumpur International Airport, you might be surprised. It is stunningly beautiful, modern in every sense. You board the gleaming Aerotrain for a quick, smooth ride from your plane to the main terminal. The terminal is a dazzling structure of glass and steel, with soaring architecture. The use of information and computer technologies (ICTs) pervades every aspect of the airport's systems, from the information boards to the baggage claim processes, to the handling of customs and immigration. When you express surprise, a proud Malaysian tells you that this airport, built in 1998, is ranked as the second best airport in the world.

But it is not just the airport. As you arrive by a sleek train into "KL" (Kuala Lumpur, capital of Malaysia), the night skyline is even more breathtaking—the many towering skyscrapers in a variety of postmodern shapes glow in a kaleidoscope of bright colors. The roads are full of late model cars. You find huge, multistory malls are overflowing with expensive, high-quality goods from all the major brands and labels that you recognize. There are elegant restaurants with every type of cuisine. The teenage Malaysians are using cell phones that have more capabilities than yours does! Except for the differences in dress and language, you might think you were in New York or Paris, except Kuala Lumpur seems more modern and sophisticated. This is the "Third World"?

As you spend more time in Malaysia, you discover more of its complexity. You visit the Petaling Street night market—hundreds of little outdoor stalls hawking everything from T-shirts and cheap jewelry to inexpensive household staples, to a cornucopia of fresh spices, vegetables and fish, to some risky-looking street food. Many of the locals at the market seem very traditional in terms of dress and behavior. You find other parts of KL—slums with old tenement houses, teeming with young kids who seem impoverished in their minimal, worn clothes. You also notice many older buildings from the colonial period under the British.

And as you get away from the major cities and the luxurious hotels along the beautiful tourist-centric beaches, you see more of this other Malaysia. Rural areas where homes and roads are ramshackle and in disrepair, cable TV service and even electricity are pirated from public lines, and trash and decay seem everywhere. Locals travel mainly on foot, bicycle, or in rickety old buses. Most people here do have cell phones, but they do not appear either prosperous or cosmopolitan. Many people don't even look very healthy, with bad teeth and various afflictions. All this more closely matches your image of a less-developed country.

GROUPING THE STATES IN THE CONTEMPORARY WORLD

13.1 Identify the standards used to classify states from a developmental perspective.

Suppose you wanted to include Malaysia in a taxonomy that includes all 180 plus major countries and has a limited number of categories. What categories would you use? Where would Malaysia fit? You might classify Malaysia economically as an upper-middle-income country—given its GDP per capita (PPP) of $14,700—or in a regional group, as part of the countries in East Asia. Or you could utilize a cultural taxonomy in which it is a predominantly Muslim country, although it has substantial minorities of Buddhists and Christians. Ethnically, it is majority Malay, but there is tension with the large number of ethnic Chinese. Historically, it is a postcolonial country, after nearly two centuries of British rule ended in 1963. You might use a political criterion, such as classifying Malaysia as a parliamentary system. Or as a multiparty system, given its governing coalition of fully 13 parties. Or, transitioning after 22 years under a single leader, as an emerging democracy. It is a geopolitically important country, rich in commodities including oil, with a strategic location between the Strait of Malacca and the South China Sea. The list of possible taxonomies is long. Your approach to classification depends on your objectives.

Watch the Video "India's New Middle Class" at mypoliscilab.com

As you discovered in Part One, a central goal of political analysis is to develop general descriptions and explanations of political phenomena. Earlier sections of the book have offered concepts and information about political behavior, political systems, and political processes in a comparative framework. The objective of these final chapters is to draw on these themes and offer broad generalizations about the pursuit of the major goals of prosperity, stability and security by all the countries in the contemporary political world.

To attempt the near-impossible task of generalizing about more than 180 countries, is there an appropriate taxonomy that distinguishes only a few groups? Given the complexity and variations among states, no taxonomy is fully satisfactory. The most commonly used approach for classifying countries uses a single measure of economic development such as GDP/capita. If there is a second dimension, it is usually regional. For example, the World Bank utilizes four economic categories (high income, high middle income, low middle income, and low income) as its main taxonomy and sometimes adds a regional dimension. However, this chapter creates a taxonomy with fewer categories, based on a more nuanced measurement of levels of development. This alternative taxonomy begins with a measure of *economic development*. It then adds a second, *social development* dimension, guided by the broader conception of development defined in Chapter 10. This taxonomy is explained below, and then the rest of this chapter examines the quest for prosperity, stability, and security in the first group of countries, based on the taxonomy. (Malaysia doesn't make this first group, yet . . .)

- **Economic development.** The most widely used measure of economic development is the total value of goods produced in a country divided by the population of the country, typically measured as gross domestic product (GDP) per capita, or GNI per capita. The taxonomy created here utilizes GDP per capita, correcting for purchasing power parity (PPP). As noted in Chapter 8, PPP seems useful for comparing the relative levels of economic development in a manner that reflects the domestic purchasing power of money across countries.

- **Social development.** To enrich the classificatory scheme, this book employs a second dimension, grounded in the types of organizational, technological, and attitudinal development discussed in Chapter 10. Like Malaysia, each country is a unique mix, in terms of the complexity of its organizations, the pervasiveness of high technology, and the blend of traditional and modern attitudes. To measure this mix, an index has been calculated for each country to reflect the pervasiveness of:

  - knowledge (measured as the adult literacy rate);
  - urban lifestyle (measured as percent of population in urban areas);
  - health (measured as longevity and mortality rates to age 5); and
  - communication capabilities (measured as cell phones per capita and computers per capita).

Each country's values on these four components are weighted equally (on 10 point scales) to generate a social development score from 0 to 40. As you assess this social development score, consider whether these four dimensions seem appropriate, whether the operational indicators used to measure each one seem valid, and whether weighting the four dimensions equally seems reasonable. Figure 13.1 locates a selection of countries on the economic development and the social development dimensions and it provides a taxonomy for our analyses, suggesting and naming three clusters of countries.

The Developed Countries of the Global North

The countries in the upper-right quadrant of Figure 13.1 are primarily those usually referred to as the *developed countries*; they are also called the *Global North* and the *First World*. The developed countries group in Figure 13.1 includes most of the countries with the highest levels of GDP per capita in the world, but these states also rank high on the social dimensions of development. Most of these are countries you would probably expect to find in this group, mainly in Western Europe plus Canada, Japan, and the United States, among others. Do any in this group or their relative location surprise you? These countries are generally urbanized and secularized, with highly specialized and institutionalized organizational systems. The population enjoys relatively high levels of health and welfare. Their technological infrastructure is advanced, and most people are frequently and directly involved with advanced technologies of communications, transportation,

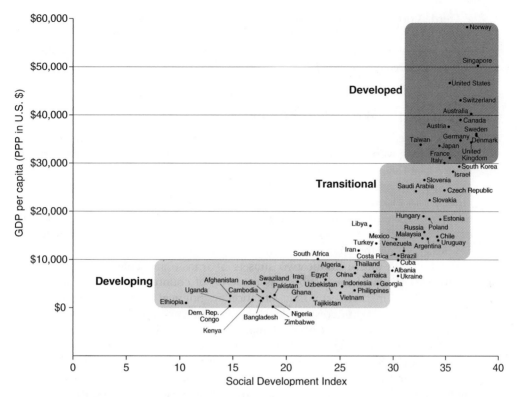

FIGURE 13.1

Classification of selected countries based on economic and social development

Sources: World Bank 2011; UNDP 2011.

and information. These developed countries are also sometimes referred to as *postindustrial societies* because of the growing dominance of the knowledge-based and service-based sectors of their economies.

The Developing Countries of the Global South

Social scientists, political actors, and the media frequently refer to a large group of countries as the *developing countries*, a term used in this book to designate a group of more than 140 countries. As you would expect, these countries have lower levels of economic development and are relatively less developed on the technological, organizational, and attitudinal dimensions than the developed countries. Thus, in Figure 13.1, the developing countries are primarily clustered in the lower-left quadrant.

Beginning in the late 1950s, many of these developing countries were also called the *Third World*. Initially, this term was applied in the context of the cold war (the late 1940s to the late 1980s) to those states that claimed they were "non-aligned": not in the camp of either the United States and its allies (the *First World*) or the Soviet Union and its allies (the *Second World*). Soon, the term was used to refer to almost all developing countries. In the post-cold war era, the concept of a Third World is used less frequently, and another term has emerged: the *Global South*. Nearly all of the developing countries are located geographically south of the developed countries (the *Global North*). This large and diverse cluster of countries will be explored in Chapter 14 as "the developing countries of the Global South."

The Transitional Developed Countries

The developed countries and the developing countries are standard categories in analyses by governmental agencies and social scientists. But there are countries in Figure 13.1, like Malaysia, that seem particularly difficult to classify. At this time, the levels of economic or social development in these countries put them "in the middle." In Figure 13.1 and the final chapters of this book, these countries are called *transitional developed countries* to reflect their middle range on one or both dimensions of development, and in some cases, their high rate of change.

Although all the countries in the world are always in transition, Chapter 15 will distinguish and examine two subsets of transitional countries identified in Figure 13.1. Each of these subsets is made up of countries with some important commonalities in their economic situation or political culture. These countries also face particularly interesting development challenges, and their approaches to achieving their goals are worth studying.

One subset is composed of many of the countries that emerged after the breakup of the Soviet Union as well as its former Eastern and Central European allies. This group of *postcommunist developed countries (PCDCs)* includes states such as Bulgaria, the Czech Republic, Estonia, Hungary, Poland, and Russia. These states are high on most dimensions of social development, especially in the attitudinal and organizational domains, and have moderately high (by world standards) levels of economic development. Most are attempting to transform their economic systems from command-oriented to market-based and to shift their political systems towards democratization. The World Bank (2011) sometimes refers to them as the "transitional economies."

The second group of transitional countries examined in Chapter 15 is called the *newly industrializing countries (NICs)*. The NICs are characterized by rapidly growing, export-centered economies. Most NICs are included in one of two subgroups with distinctive regional and political-cultural differences: East Asia (e.g., Malaysia, South Korea, Thailand) and Latin America (e.g., Argentina, Chile, Mexico). On the economic dimension and increasingly on the social dimension, the leading NICs are reaching levels of development that approach those of some of the developed countries.

Thus, Chapters 13–15 examine the developed countries, the developing countries, and the transitional developed countries. Each chapter describes critical issues for countries in these groups as they attempt to achieve their key goals. General patterns and similarities within each group are emphasized, but you should keep the following points in mind:

- There are substantial differences among states within each group, especially among the large number of states lumped together as the "developing countries of the Global South."

- Each state has unique features that are lost in such generalized discussion.
- In some instances, a trait is more similar among certain states across groups rather than among all the states within one group.

As these qualifications suggest, this method of grouping countries for analysis and generalizations is not perfect. Like any taxonomy (see the Appendix), there is an attempt to create groups that can be distinguished analytically, are based on some specifiable criteria, and seem to make sense. However, not every country fits neatly into a category. Examples of this in the framework in Figure 13.1 include some resource-rich (oil) states in the Middle East and Africa and some PCDCs that have high social development but have had particularly severe economic declines in the transition to market economies. The categories proposed here are acceptable if their use provides clarification and insight and, ideally, if they facilitate the development of generalizations and theory. As a political analyst, *you* should assess the utility of this taxonomy relative to alternative ways of grouping countries for analysis. The remainder of this chapter focuses explicitly on the developed countries of the Global North. It considers their pursuit of their three broad goals—prosperity, security, and stability—within the context of the global system.

GOAL: PROSPERITY

The developed countries pursue the goal of prosperity (and its components of economic development, economic growth, and welfare distribution) with great energy. Based on our classification, these are already the most economically developed countries in the world. Thus, the emphasis in these countries is on sustaining a high level of economic growth under the assumption that this will generate an expanding economic base that provides more material benefits to the population and also enables government to distribute greater welfare to the citizens.

13.2 Characterize the types of markets in the Global North and assess their challenges and achievements.

Mixed Economy

To achieve prosperity, these countries have relied on a mixed political economy, which includes considerable private ownership and control of productive resources (land, labor, and capital). Private actors (firms and households) are encouraged to use their resources aggressively to acquire desired goods, to produce goods, and to maximize their profit. Chapter 8 characterized the state's key roles in the mixed political economy: regulating the free market, providing guidance and incentives for production decisions, and redistributing some money and goods, mainly to less-advantaged individuals in the society.

A central policy debate in most of the Global North countries is the appropriate level of state activity in the political economy. Should the state reduce the taxes and regulations imposed on private actors under the assumption that the market economy is most likely to stimulate greater production and higher economic growth, thus benefiting all? Or should the state capture more resources and redistribute them as welfare to its citizens? This debate is sometimes characterized as "growth versus welfare."

The countries vary considerably in the extent to which the free market dominates in the political economy. Each country's political economy is slowly adjusted

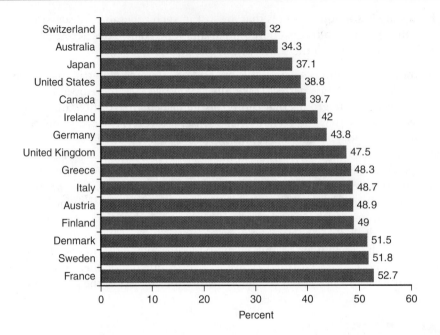

FIGURE 13.2

General government expenditures as a proportion of GDP

Source: OECD (2011): Table 25.

as the balance of political power among key policymakers shifts between those supporting greater economic freedom and limited government, consistent with classical liberal ideology, and those supporting a more active state committed to redistributive and regulatory public policies, consistent with the ideology of democratic socialism. One broad comparative measure of the public–private mix is the percentage of productive capacity (measured as GDP) that is in the public sector. Figure 13.2 indicates that this varies substantially, from more than 50 percent in France, Sweden, and Denmark to less than 35 percent in Australia and Japan. While all of the developed countries have mixed political economies, the break between a more capitalist system and a more democratic-socialist system might be defined loosely as about 45 percent of total GDP.

The more democratic-socialist regimes are usually evident in the Scandinavian countries as well as Austria, Belgium, France, Italy, and the Netherlands. These mixed economies are sometimes called **social market systems** because *the state encourages an extensive free market economy but is also committed to social welfare distribution and economic regulation.* Compared with the more free market–oriented countries discussed below, taxation is higher in these systems, and more revenue is reallocated either as transfer payments or as subsidized goods and services (e.g., health care, housing, educational and cultural opportunities, public transportation) to the citizens. The state is also more active in regulatory policy, protecting individuals and society from the undesirable actions of firms (e.g., price fixing, unsafe working conditions, environmental degradation).

In some of these social market systems, the public sector retains control or ownership of some major productive resources (e.g., energy, transportation) that have strategic importance for the country.

The *developed countries in which most economic activity is in the private sector and the government has a limited role in regulatory and redistributive policies*, designated as **market economies**, currently include Australia, Canada, Japan, Switzerland, and the United States. Social welfare services are limited towards a basic "safety net" with which the state protects individuals from only the harshest consequences of poverty. Government also limits its constraints on private economic activity (e.g., deregulation, fewer antitrust actions, less protection of unions). Private control of the productive system is extended, particularly by **privatization** (i.e., *the selling off of state-owned firms and contracts with private firms to provide public goods and services*). Even in market economies, certain domains, such as basic education, public safety, core infrastructure (e.g., roads, sewers), and national defense, are primarily the responsibility of the public sector. Compare in 13 describes key features of the political economies of Sweden and Switzerland, examples of a social market system and a market economy.

COMPARE IN 13 | Sweden and Switzerland

Sweden and Switzerland have a lot in common besides the first two letters in the Anglicized versions of their names. Relatively small countries with populations between 8 and 9 million, they are among the world's most developed countries on almost every measure. Both are very prosperous, with among the world's best Human Development Index scores (ranking ninth and thirteenth) and very high levels of GDP per capita (PPP). Both are export-oriented economies, with about 70 percent of the workforce engaged in services and about 30 percent in industry jobs. Most citizens in each country enjoy a long life (averaging more than 81 years) filled with high-quality material possessions (CIA 2011).

Public services and the infrastructure of roads and telecommunications are excellent. Nearly the entire adult population is literate and multilingual. The incidence of violent crime is quite low. Each political system is a stable, highly institutionalized multiparty democracy with an efficient administration and independent judiciary. They have a long history of neutrality in international affairs, spend among the world's lowest amounts on the military (as a percentage of GDP), and rank in the top fifteen on the Global Peace Index (visionofhumanity 2011). Yet they do differ notably on their approach to political economy and their political institutions.

Political Economy. Sweden is a social market system. With more than 90 percent of the economy in private hands, the Swedish state is committed to market capitalism. Sweden is ranked second in the world on economic competitiveness (World Economic Forum 2011); yet Sweden has one of the most expansive welfare states in the world. About one-third of the national economic output is spent on social programs. Among the benefits available to all citizens at little or no direct cost are comprehensive health care, higher education, child care, maternity/paternity leave, job training, and public transportation. Those suffering economic hardship receive substantial income supplements and support for amenities such as housing. Sweden has the world's most equal distribution of wealth and income (ranking first on the Gini index). It also has one of the world's highest scores on gender equality, with many women in positions of power and authority in both the public

(Continued)

and private sectors (ranking second in the world, for example, on the percentage [47 percent] of women in the national legislature).

Systems like Sweden's are sometimes termed "cradle to grave" socialism. As one example, the state provides complete nursing home care to any elderly citizen for less than 5 percent of the actual costs. The regulatory policies of the state are also extensive in both economic life (e.g., environmental protection, working conditions, product safety) and also in social life (e.g., the state has even banned parental spanking to protect children against physical abuse). This extensive social welfare is financed by high taxes. Total taxes paid by citizens and firms are about 57 percent of GDP. While this tax burden reduces Swedes' disposable income, most citizens are supportive and proud of their social market system.

In Switzerland, the state follows a model of limited government with regard to the political economy. The state exercises very little regulatory control over its free market economy, which is one of only six countries providing full economic freedom according to the Heritage Foundation (2011), and the country is ranked as the most competitive economy in the world (World Economic Forum 2011). The constitution explicitly emphasizes the role of the private sector in setting economic policy. Switzerland has one of the lowest rates of taxation and the lowest proportion of overall government spending (about 33.3 percent of GDP) among all the developed countries. The Swiss state generally expects citizens to take care of themselves through the private market, with minimal provision of most public services, except education. Recently, there has been considerable opposition among the citizens to increases in the modest level of welfare support that government provides to the least advantaged Swiss.

Political Institutions. Sweden is a constitutional monarchy with a king. A unitary state, all power emanates from the central government. It is a classic multiparty parliamentary system, with political power centering on the prime minister and cabinet, who control a unicameral legislature elected by proportional representation. The progressive Social Democratic Party has held a majority or led a majority coalition for more than 80 percent of the period since 1932. Sweden joined the European Union in 1995, but rejected participation in the euro (currency) zone.

Switzerland's political institutions are quite unique. The executive (Federal Council) is a collective group of seven equal members who each run one major department and cannot veto legislation, with the president of the executive changing yearly. The national legislature has two houses, one elected by proportional representation (PR) and the second by majority vote. There is no judicial review of the laws. Another aspect of Switzerland's limited government is the substantial use of popular voting on policies, based on the view that the people should hold ultimate power. Thus, citizens can use the referendum process to hold a national vote on any piece of legislation passed by the legislature. Switzerland is a confederation composed of 23 cantons (states) with substantial local power and autonomy. This reflects a country with complex nation-based distinctions, including four official languages (German, French, Italian, and Romansch). Switzerland delayed joining the United Nations until 2002 and does not belong to the European Union.

FURTHER QUESTIONS

1. Which of Switzerland's rather unique political institutions do you find most appealing?
2. Is it surprising that two countries with such different political and economic systems could be so similar in prosperity and quality of life? ◣

Performance

The developed countries assess their prosperity primarily in terms of economic activity, usually measured as GDP per capita. Figure 13.3 provides comparative data on GDP per capita (adjusted for PPP) for many developed countries. Measured on

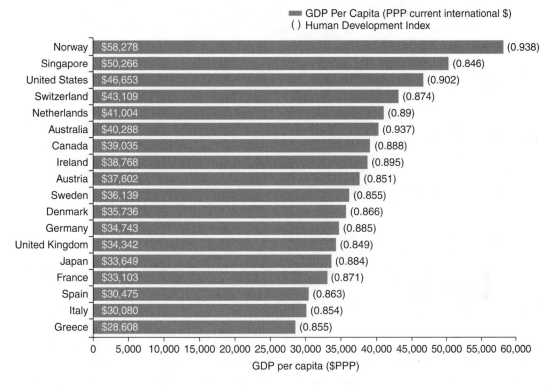

GDP Per Capita (PPP current international $)
( ) Human Development Index

Country	GDP	HDI
Norway	$58,278	(0.938)
Singapore	$50,266	(0.846)
United States	$46,653	(0.902)
Switzerland	$43,109	(0.874)
Netherlands	$41,004	(0.89)
Australia	$40,288	(0.937)
Canada	$39,035	(0.888)
Ireland	$38,768	(0.895)
Austria	$37,602	(0.851)
Sweden	$36,139	(0.855)
Denmark	$35,736	(0.866)
Germany	$34,743	(0.885)
United Kingdom	$34,342	(0.849)
Japan	$33,649	(0.884)
France	$33,103	(0.871)
Spain	$30,475	(0.863)
Italy	$30,080	(0.854)
Greece	$28,608	(0.855)

GDP per capita ($PPP)

FIGURE 13.3

Prosperity measures for selected developed countries

Source: UNDP 2011.

this indicator, all of the countries in the Global North enjoy considerable prosperity. Only a few oil-rich ministates (e.g., Qatar, Kuwait) have higher GDP per capita than most of the developed countries. Most of these countries have been very concerned about their low rates of growth in GDP per capita, especially in the recent period of global recession, because there is an assumption that economic growth is critical to the vitality of the society. Some critics accuse the developed countries of "growthmania," and suggest that quality of life and citizen satisfaction are better measures of performance than an increasing GDP and should be the focus of public policy.

The *Human Development Index (HDI)*, the second measure in Figure 13.3, is computed by the UN Development Programme (2011) to reflect the quality of life enjoyed by citizens in a country. It is a composite index that gives equal weight to three indicators: "a long and healthy life, as measured by life expectancy at birth; knowledge, as measured by the adult literacy rate and...[school] enrollment levels; and a decent standard of living, as measured by GDP per capita (PPP)" (UNDP 2008: 394). HDI scores range from 1.00 to 0.0. A score of 1.00 would indicate that all the country's citizens have attained the most desirable levels of health, education, and living standards. Broadly, a score of .785 or above currently represents a "very high" level of human development (41 countries), scores in the .784–.675 range are "high" levels (44 countries), .674–.485 constitutes a "medium" level of human development (42 countries), and a score below .485 indicates a "low" level (42 countries) (UNDP 2011: Table 1).

Every developed country achieves an HDI score in the "very high" range. Norway currently has the highest HDI score in the world (.938), followed closely by Australia. Thus, on both a basic measure of economic production and a quality-of-life index that adds measures of literacy and health, the developed countries seem relatively successful in achieving their overall prosperity goals. A more comprehensive quality-of-life index might include many other indicators in addition to the three employed by the United Nations. If you were attempting to create a comparative measure of the quality of life across many countries, what indicators would *you* include?

Challenges to Prosperity

Erratic Economic Growth Most Global North countries have periods of solid economic growth (about 4 percent or higher per year). However, there are also extended periods, such as in the early years of the decades of the 1980s, 1990s, 2000s, and 2010s, when many have not sustained the high levels of economic growth that are the basis of their own definition of prosperity. These countries averaged only 2.0 percent annual GDP growth from 2000-2009 (World Bank 2011). And, more seriously, there are periods of recession (a negative change in a key economic growth measure). The worldwide economic decline that began in 2008 has been the most significant period of low or negative growth that developed countries have suffered in more than 70 years. Almost every developed country has struggled with weak economic growth in the period since 2008, and some, such as Greece, Portugal, Spain, and Ireland (recall the opening discussion in Chapter 8) have experienced a deep financial crisis. Analysts disagree on all of the causes of this crisis, but they include risky and often illegal practices in the financial industry, the dramatic deterioration of overinflated stock markets and housing markets, government debt, shrinking consumer demand, and high unemployment. All of these caused huge losses in asset wealth and interacted negatively with each other and with poor economic growth.

The Competitive Globalized Economic System The economic crisis that began in 2008 is a powerful example of the vulnerability that all economies face in the highly interdependent global system. Serious problems in only a few Global North economies can quickly infect the economies of many other countries, especially among those in the EU. Moreover, with the increasing power of multinational corporations and the spread of global markets, a government has less direct control over its own political economy (Chapter 11). As globalization increases the productive capabilities of many countries, every Global North country faces increasing competition from the developing countries, newly industrializing economies, and postcommunist countries, all of which tend to have lower production costs. As more jobs are outsourced and more goods are imported, a developed country must struggle with more structural unemployment and declining economic vitality (Zakaria 2009).

The European Union (EU) and the Others   The developed countries face not only the complexities of international competition and globalization, but also the multiple challenges of sorting out their economic relations with one another. The competition for markets and resources has become very intense between the EU and those Global North countries that are not members of the EU (especially the U.S. and Japan). While the 27 member states within the European Union enjoy substantial economic advantages, some members have resisted its uniform policies (e.g., on agriculture, on government debt, on contributions) and have continued to protect their national economic prerogatives. Moreover, the less prosperous EU members (many of whom are not yet Global North countries in Figure 13.1) drain resources from the wealthier members. And the fragile interdependencies between the stronger and weaker member–states in the euro zone have been highlighted by the economic crises in countries such as Greece and Ireland, which required major bailouts to protect the value of the euro (McCormick 2006).

The Distribution of Prosperity   The governments of the developed countries have a substantial list of goods and services that they want to distribute to their citizens. However, extensive public spending combined with low economic growth results in serious fiscal challenges. An increasing proportion of the population does not work due to unemployment or aging. Despite the high GDP per capita, the proportion of people in poverty is between 10 and 20 percent in the majority of these countries and inequality in the distribution of prosperity among the

In front of the Parliament building in Athens, striking dockworkers express dismay at the extensive privatization and spending cuts by the Greek government as it attempts to respond to the severe economic crisis in Greece and in the entire eurozone.

citizens is growing (CIA 2011). In the market economies, persistent poverty and inequality are especially problematic issues because the state is not very generous in alleviating these hardships and this situation can produce an "underclass" of citizens who are permanently disadvantaged in education, job skills, housing, health care, and most broadly, quality of life (Wilson 1990, 1997). The current situation is also a problem for the social democracies, given their commitment to an extensive role for government in the redistribution of prosperity to all their citizens (Castles 2004, 2010).

Eleven of these countries, mostly the social democracies, are still among the 20 major countries with the world's most equal income distributions (the others are postcommunist developed countries discussed in Chapter 15). As the costs of government continue to rise, there are larger budget deficits and growing resistance to higher taxes. The Debate in 13 considers whether the costly commitments of the social democratic model can be sustained. In the brutally competitive global economy, no developed country has resolved the public policy issues related to sustaining economic growth and distributing prosperity, and the debate over these issues is intense. Nevertheless, the current bottom line is that the developed countries of the Global North have a better overall record than any other set of countries in the world in delivering higher absolute levels of prosperity to most citizens.

▶ THE DEBATE IN 13 | Are the Social Democracies Dying?

Surveys often identify most of Europe's social democracies as the happiest places on earth, where citizens enjoy a high level of services provided by the state (Levy 2010). These services include deeply subsidized or free healthcare, education, and public transportation, as well as unemployment protection, care for the elderly, and many other publicly-provided benefits (such as Sweden, described in the Compare in 13). However, critics suggest that these social welfare states are unsustainable, because this vast array of government services is too expensive for the public sector to afford. Particularly during the global recession, an animated policy debate in the countries in Scandinavia and Western Europe is: Are the social democracies dying?

THE SOCIAL DEMOCRACIES ARE DYING

- The governments of most European social democracies (e.g., Greece, Spain) are running very large deficits as they attempt to provide extensive welfare services. Social welfare goods

substantially drain government resources relative to the revenue they generate. This overspending undermines the country's credit rating, currency strength, and overall fiscal health (Laquer 2009).

- The social democratic model puts an enormous burden on economic growth by aggressively taxing wages and profits. Those funds should be left in the hands of wage earners and entrepreneurs where they will stimulate innovation, encourage investment, and create more incentives for people to work hard.

- The citizens' votes tell the story: There has been a significant decline in voter support for parties (e.g., the Social Democrats in Denmark, Germany, and Sweden, the PASOK Party in Greece, and Britain's Labour Party) that are associated with higher taxes and extensive public spending on social welfare. And the anti-social welfare, anti-tax parties and movements have gained substantial strength in the social democracies (Castles et al., 2010).

(Continued)

- Most citizens agree that generous provision of welfare services produces a significant number of people who become dependent on government support and who lose the initiative to work and take responsibility for themselves (Murray 1984).
- The government can no longer afford the excessive salaries and generous pension plans that have historically supported the large and overstaffed public employee unions who provide most social welfare state services.

THE SOCIAL DEMOCRACIES ARE ALIVE AND WELL

- Citizens of most social democracies enjoy a combination of the world's highest standard of living, greatest prosperity, greatest income equality, and strong democracy. It is this "good life" that produces a population that is generally more satisfied with their lives than the citizens in any other system in the world (Levy 2010).
- The current revenue and deficit problems affect the governments of all developed countries, not just the social democracies. It is the global recession and financial crisis, not social welfare programs, that is the root cause of current fiscal problems in the Global North (Rajan 2010).
- The majority of citizens in social democracies do not support severe and permanent cuts in their governments' policies that provide social welfare

services. Even if social democracies reduce some programs to balance budgets during the recession, reinstatement of those program levels will be in demand when the economy improves and revenues increase (Sandbrook et al. 2007).

- The political and social costs of severe reductions in social welfare programs, such as healthcare or poverty assistance, would be dramatic. Even citizens who support long-term cuts in social welfare services will reconsider their views when they see the actual impacts of such reductions, resulting in a substantial decline in the support for extreme fiscal restraint and anti-tax movements (Castles et al., 2010).
- The political parties most closely aligned with the social democratic ideology have been extremely successful in elections during the past three decades, reflecting broad, long-term citizen support for their policies. As economic conditions improve, a resurgence of support for these parties will occur (Hill 2010).

MORE QUESTIONS

1. Will the strong, sometimes violent resistance to reductions in social welfare programs (e.g., in Greece, Spain, and others) enhance or reduce the overall support for social democracy?
2. What reductions in the social welfare programs do you think are most defensible? Which are least desirable? ▲

GOAL: STABILITY

The developed countries of the Global North have been generally successful in achieving their stability goals of democratization, political institutionalization, and order maintenance.

13.3 Identify the obstacles to the political stability of the Global North.

◉ Watch the Video "EU Reluctance to Admit Turkey" at mypoliscilab.com

Liberal Democracies

All the developed countries are constitutional democracies, and thus leaders and policies are constrained by the rule of law. Extensive political rights and civil liberties are enjoyed by the citizens, as reflected in the world's highest scores from Freedom House (2011), except for Singapore, which is only "partly free." Individuals and groups have substantial freedom to criticize and oppose the government and to engage in a wide variety of nonviolent political actions to change leaders and policies.

Leaders operate with a limited mandate, leadership succession is regularized, and the selection of many public officials is based on citizen elections with genuine alternatives. Chapter 3 indicated that most Global North countries have moderately high political involvement, at least with regard to elections and interest in politics.

Chapters 6 and 7 described the variation in the political structures of these liberal democracies. Most are stable parliamentary governments, with multiparty systems based on coalitions (e.g., Denmark, Germany, Sweden). A few experience instability due to the fragmented nature of the party system (Italy). Many countries have dual executives, often with a constitutional monarch (e.g., the United Kingdom, Japan, Sweden). There are a few hybrids with an elected president in addition to the cabinet and prime minister (e.g., Austria, France [recall Focus in 7]). The United States is an exception as a presidential government with a two-party system, and Switzerland is an exception as a council system.

Political power is distributed rather than concentrated in a single governmental structure. Most are unitary states, although there are several federations (e.g., Canada, Germany, the United States). Even in the unitary states, policy implementation for many human and welfare services is decentralized to local governments. The national legislatures are important actors in the policy process, with about half being unicameral. These countries generally have the world's lowest levels of corruption, and their governments operate with large, efficient bureaucracies and relatively independent judiciaries.

Political Institutionalization

The developed countries have high levels of political institutionalization; that is, substantial capabilities, value and stability support political structures and processes. Some developed countries restructured their political system in the last 60 years. Many created new constitutional systems after World War II had undermined the legitimacy of their previous political regimes, as in Austria, France, Italy, Japan, and Germany. One goal of the restructuring was to distribute power more broadly within the political system and to increase the participation and influence of the citizens. Democratic political processes are now firmly established throughout the Global North.

The governments in many of the developed countries evolved over centuries by means of gradual and generally nonviolent mechanisms of political change. This pattern applies to states such as Belgium, Canada, Denmark, Sweden, Switzerland, the United Kingdom, and the United States. The distribution and uses of political power have changed as new groups gain admission to and influence in the political system, extending participation steadily until mass representative democracy is created. This "politics of inclusion" has drawn important groups into the political process and built their support for the political system, reducing their need to use mechanisms such as violence to achieve their political goals.

In the United Kingdom, for example, evolving political inclusion for more than 800 years has ensured the stability of the regime. The basic story line is that the political system has slowly drawn new groups into the political process, penetrating downward from the most powerful to the least powerful citizens. Starting in 1215, the substantial political powers of the hereditary monarch were limited, and the power of the national legislature was increased. Equally significant, the British electorate expanded steadily, as new classes of the population were granted political rights by lowering barriers based on wealth, gender, and age. Political inclusion also affected the political party system, which adapted to the social and economic composition of the citizenry. For example, at the beginning of the 20th century, a new Labour Party was formed to represent the British working class. In 1945, the Labour Party gained enough seats in the House of Commons to form a government majority and enact significant new public policies that established "the welfare state" and greatly benefited the working class and the poor. Further adaptations in the party system have accommodated the growing national identity in Scotland, Northern Ireland, and Wales. While there are occasional outbreaks of political instability in Britain, the politics of inclusion have been effective in incorporating new political forces into the institutionalized political regime and sustaining a highly stable political system.

Order Maintenance

The developed countries have had varying levels of success in meeting the stability goal of order maintenance. This goal can be interpreted as the *absence of disorder* in the political, social, and personal domains. Disorder includes political violence (e.g., illegal demonstrations, riots, rebellions, coups, and revolutions), social disorders, (e.g., murder, rape, robbery, white-collar crime, and organized crime), and also personal disorders (e.g., suicide, substance abuse). While a few Global North countries have exceptionally high levels of order maintenance, such as Switzerland and Singapore (see Focus in 13), most are neither the most orderly nor the most disorderly in the political world.

▶ FOCUS IN 13 | Welcome to the Brave New World: Singapore

Singapore has used government policy more expansively to achieve order maintenance than any other developed country. A small island of 4.7 million people located off Malaysia, Singapore gained independence from Britain in 1963 and became a republic in 1965. Prime Minister Lee Kuan Yew exercised singular power for 31 years (until 1990) and guided the country to remarkable economic success and he still plays a powerful role, with his son as prime minister. Its annual economic growth rate has averaged 8.3 percent since 1965. Its GDP per capita has risen dramatically, placing it fifth in the world in terms of its overall prosperity.

Singapore is also notable for the remarkable social-control policies first instituted by Prime Minister Lee and the parliament he dominated for three decades. For example, to deal with traffic congestion, the government maintains a strict quota on the number of cars imported. An individual who purchases a new car must pay import duties and registration taxes that triple the car's market price. To reduce the massive yearly automobile registration fee, the driver can save $10,000 per year by purchasing a special red license that allows only nighttime and weekend driving. The high toll-road charges and other auto fees are used to subsidize an efficient mass transit system.

To promote financial responsibility and personal savings by its citizens, the government places 34 percent of each worker's wages in a special fund. The worker can use these forced savings only to buy government stocks, to purchase a house, or for retirement.

The state uses the media and the schools to support extensive campaigns to discourage certain behaviors,

(Continued)

such as spitting in public, long hair on men, and littering. The stiff penalties imposed to enforce its social-control policies received worldwide attention in 1994 with the "flogging" of visiting U.S. teenager Michael Faye for painting graffiti on automobiles. For many offenses, there are heavy on-the-spot fines: in U.S. dollar equivalents, $124 for driving without a seat belt, $250 for littering, $310 for eating on a subway, and $310 for smoking in a restaurant. To prevent speeding, all taxicabs are equipped with a bell that begins to ring loudly as soon as the taxi exceeds the legal speed limit, and there is a yellow light on top of trucks that flashes when the driver goes too fast. Technological surveillance includes computerized camera systems that record the license plates of cars that violate traffic laws, and odor-activated video cameras in elevators that record anyone who urinates in the elevator (the person is also locked in). There is even a law against failing to flush after using a public urinal.

Singapore also instituted a set of unsubtle eugenics/population-control policies. Women with less than a high school education are given a government-subsidized home mortgage, but they lose the subsidy if they have a third child. To increase the low child-bearing rate among college graduates, the government's Social Development Unit offers a computer-matching service for educated singles. One program, eventually discontinued, offered these smart singles a government-funded vacation at a romantic seaside holiday camp.

Because of such extensive policies of social control, Singapore has been subjected to jokes and serious criticism about its limitations on civil liberties. But no one denies that the country is exceptionally orderly, clean, and efficient (Sesser 1992).

FURTHER FOCUS

1. Would you accept Singapore's substantial restrictions on personal freedom in exchange for an exceptionally high level of order, cleanliness, and efficiency in your society?
2. Does Singapore demonstrate that a country with minimal democracy (recall Chapter 7) can sustain high prosperity (a GDP per capita [PPP] greater than every major developed country except Norway)?

Source: By permission of Mike Luckovich and Creators Syndicate, Inc.

The politics of these states is characterized by pluralism (see Chapter 9), with multiple competing elites and groups. The vigorous group politics and the broad opportunities for political action allow for some political turbulence, which does occur, especially in periods of citizen dissatisfaction with economic or social conditions. Although there are occasional outbursts of significant political violence, these states enjoy relatively high levels of political order.

The level and nature of social and personal disorder varies considerably among the states and among different populations within states, and thus it is difficult to generalize. The Netherlands, Norway, and Japan, for example, have relatively low levels of social disorder such as violent crime. Yet Japan has one of the highest suicide rates in the world, alcohol abuse is high in Norway, and drug abuse is high in the Netherlands. France, Italy, and the United States, in contrast, are relatively high on most measures of social and personal disorder and are among the increasing number of developed countries with substantial problems related to substance abuse and drug-related crime, especially among the lower classes. What explanations do you think best account for the fact that some of the developed countries seem to have such high levels of social and personal disorder?

Challenges to Stability

Value Conflicts and Disputes Because the Global North countries allow open group politics, the active disagreements about specific policies and even about fundamental values can produce instability. The political ideologies of classical liberalism, conservatism, and democratic socialism are each embraced by some citizens and, along with numerous other "isms" (e.g., feminism, environmentalism, and religious fundamentalism), shape complex political cultures. There is strong support for the fundamental principles of democracy. However, during the last several decades, most developed countries have experienced a substantial decline in citizens' trust and confidence in political leaders and in key political institutions, including legislatures, political parties, and bureaucracies (Dalton 2008; Pharr and Putnam 2000).

There are ongoing political debates, sometimes quite intense, regarding the degree to which the state should have an active role in the *political economy* and should distribute generous welfare benefits to various groups in the society. This is related to other policy disagreements on the level of taxation and the extent of government regulation of the economy. Both the Compare in 13 on Sweden and Switzerland and the Debate in 13 on social democracy reflect some of these differences.

Another area of enduring value conflicts centers on disputes about the circumstances in which *state regulation of individual behavior* is legitimate. Such regulation might be justified to preserve social peace, promote the collective good, protect the rights and freedom of others, or protect the individual from himself and others. In the United States, for example, state constraints on private behavior generate controversy, political disorder, and occasional violence regarding such areas of public policy as: abortion, free speech (media, internet), gay rights, control of firearms, marijuana legalization.

Multiculturalism and Immigration Most developed countries are struggling with issues arising from their cultural diversity. The desire for regional autonomy has been a source of occasional instability in some countries with a long history of multiple nationalities (e.g., the Quebecois in Canada, the Basques and Catalans in Spain, the Walloons and Flemish in Belgium). And some of the instability is due to clashes between the majority ethnic group and "native-born" minorities, especially people of Afro-Caribbean or Arabic descent. For example, the concern about "home-grown terrorists" in England has soured relations between the Anglo majority and Britain's Muslims (Leiken 2009). However, the main source of recent instability is due to intensifying conflicts related to *immigration*. Legal immigration within the EU, for example, has resulted in large enclaves of "foreigners" from Southern and Eastern Europe whose languages and customs grate on some in the ethnic majority in Western and Northern European countries. And *illegal* immigration is an even more disruptive issue in some Global North countries, as in the United States, where the treatment of nearly 12 million individuals who have entered the country without permission is a major public policy puzzle.

Every country faces policy debates about cultural diversity: The French ban full-face-hiding veils in public and the wearing of head scarves and other "religious symbols" in schools; the Danes reverse their open-door policy and place stringent restrictions on immigration; Italy calls for revision of the EU's open internal borders policy. These kinds of responses have generated counter demands for policies supporting multiculturalism and protecting minority rights (e.g., bilingualism in Canada, a citizenship process for illegal immigrants in the United States). At this point, the conflicts associated with diverse cultures and non-native populations are an issue in almost every developed country.

Political Polarization   The political elites and governments are committed to working within the framework of representative democracy and group politics as they attempt to resolve value conflicts. They are generally successful in establishing compromises on issues that might become highly politicized. However, pluralism is not well suited to situations in which there is substantial *political polarization* as *politics becomes a battleground between large, mobilized groups with conflicting and deeply held values*, and centrist policies and center parties are only weakly supported by the citizens. In such situations of "hyperpluralism," it is extremely difficult for policy makers to make decisions and resolve conflicts because it is often impossible to satisfy the opposing viewpoints. If key groups become dissatisfied with government paralysis and unresponsiveness, they can make increasingly strident political demands, engage in aggressive political actions in support of their policy preferences, and produce high levels of political instability. Some states, such as the Netherlands, Norway, and Switzerland, have limited these problems by nurturing a cultural style of social tolerance or by developing political institutions that accommodate competing groups (Eckstein 1966; Lijphart 1984). However, the governments of most developed countries are currently challenged by increasing polarization and intolerance among political groups.

Domination and Control?   Some analysts offer a far more critical description of how many of the developed countries maintain order. They describe societies in which the state controls its citizens by coercion rather than consensus, combining limited welfare distribution, extensive political socialization, and effective restraints on public life by the state's agents (e.g., the police, the bureaucracy, the judicial system). Some class and elite theorists also argue that most developed countries are controlled by a "hegemonic elite"—a network of extraordinarily powerful, overlapping groups that sustain their domination over a long period of time (Domhoff 2005, 2009; Esping-Andersen 1990; Poulantzas 1973). These theorists insist that politics in the developed countries is not a fair competition among groups, that the state is not a neutral referee, and that most public policies enable certain groups to maintain their advantaged position in society. Thus, privileged groups reap huge benefits from public policy, and most citizens derive minimal gains in the quality of their lives (Chapter 9).

It is clear that the developed countries do have powerful and effective institutions that can shape the political process, control groups, and contain instability. Even the pluralist explanation acknowledges that there are huge inequalities in the political resources available to different groups (Dahl 1961; Parenti 2010). There is no doubt that certain institutions and individuals have extraordinary powers to shape political life in the developed countries (Johnson 2009). Yet most analysts and most citizens see no compelling evidence that these political systems are dominated by self-serving, nondemocratic elites. In response, radical (Marxist) theorists interpret such citizen views as evidence that the state *can* fool most of the people all of the time. One of the great (and perhaps impossible) challenges for political scientists is to develop an indisputable empirical analysis of how political power is exercised, how values are allocated, and how order is maintained in the developed countries.

GOAL: SECURITY

The first half of the 20th century was a period with substantial insecurity, marked by two massive multistate wars among Global North countries. The borders of most of the states survived intact (there are notable exceptions, including Austria-Hungary after World War I and Germany after World War II), but many states were devastated in human, material, and political terms by these wars. Since the end of World War II in 1945, the developed countries have generally enjoyed success in the pursuit of their basic security goals, especially survival and freedom. Arguably, the greatest security victory during the recent period is the collapse in 1990 of the communist state in the Soviet Union, a significant threat. In the early 21st century, these countries are still establishing new arrangements for security in the altered, post–cold war global system.

13.4 Trace the development of security challenges to the Global North.

👁 **Watch** the Video "Bin Laden Killed in Pakistan" at mypoliscilab.com

✳ Explore the Comparative "Foreign and Security Policy" on mypoliscilab.com

The Era of Colonialism

Some developed countries have been extremely successful at extending their influence or control over other states in order to enhance their own security goals. Belgium, France, Germany, Japan, Portugal, Spain, and the United States dominated substantial colonial territories until the mid-20th century. In 1945, Great Britain was the leading colonial power, controlling more than one-fourth of the world's population in its worldwide empire. Colonialism was a means by which many of these countries furthered their security goals. Although their colonial holdings are now independent states, some developed countries continue to exert their power through neocolonialism, as described in Chapter 11.

The Cold War Period

From World War II until the late 1980s, the security-oriented actions of most developed countries were powerfully influenced by *the international struggle between the United States and the Soviet Union*, generally called *the cold war*. During the cold war period, U.S. policy was based on the assumption that the main threat to the security of the developed countries was the Soviet Union, its allies, and the worldwide expansion of communism. In this view, the freedom, influence, and even survival of the developed countries depended on strong military power to counterbalance the Soviet bloc. As the leading country on the Global North's side of this bipolar balance of power system, the United States had a foreign policy based on at least two core elements.

First, the United States maintained extensive military power, including a large nuclear arsenal, in an attempt to deter Soviet military activity outside the Soviet Union and its European satellites. The United States was the key actor in the North Atlantic Treaty Organization (NATO), a mutual security pact among the developed countries, and it was prepared to undertake military actions anywhere in the world where Soviet activities threatened its conception of international stability. Second, the United States applied its considerable military, economic, and political power to influence the actions of many developing countries. It provided support to pro–U.S., anticommunist regimes and to many nonaligned countries, and it attempted to destabilize leftist or pro-Soviet regimes (e.g., in Afghanistan, Cuba, Grenada). This policy was generally successful, but the United States suffered its most costly setback in its direct military involvement and ultimate defeat in Vietnam (1964–1975).

Not all political elites in the developed countries shared the United States' perception of a bipolar struggle between the forces of good and evil. Some states (e.g., Austria, Finland, Switzerland) maintained a position of neutrality during the cold war. Others (e.g., Denmark, France, Greece, Italy, New Zealand, Sweden) emphasized a more conciliatory policy of *détente* ("relaxation" of tensions) with the Soviet bloc, based on the view that both blocs had common interests in maintaining their superior position internationally and preventing a global nuclear war. This latter view became more widespread by the late 1980s due to the conflict-reducing initiatives of Soviet leader Mikhail Gorbachev.

The Post–Cold War Period

By 1990, with a speed that stunned the world, the Soviet bloc countries and even the Soviet Union were transformed (see Chapter 15). These countries moved away from communism and towards democratic politics and market political economies. They sought economic cooperation rather than military conflict with the United States and Western Europe. The cold war seemed to end with the unification of East and West Germany (1990) and particularly with the breakup of the Soviet Union (1991) into 15 countries.

In the *post–cold war period,* six of the world's 10 highest spenders on military are Global North countries, whose combined military spending is more than $1.1 trillion per year, 68 percent of the world total in 2010. The United States alone accounts for 43 percent of this total (SIPRI 2011). The global military power of the United States is unmatched and it projects this power extensively in some cases, as in Iraq and Afghanistan. However, the developed countries now generally emphasize collective security arrangements through the United Nations and NATO (Walt 2006). Most are not conflict oriented. For example, 15 of the Global North countries are among the 18 countries with the highest scores on the Global Peace Index (Vision of Humanity 2011). While there is a general assumption that a major military conflict between any Global North countries is inconceivable, the evolving international system does pose at least four major security challenges, which are described next.

Challenges to Security

Disorder in the Rest of the World   Most major political violence occurs in the Global South, as it did during the cold war period. In Afghanistan, Colombia, Congo, Iraq, North Korea, and Somalia, among others, complex patterns of disorder persist, despite various strategies of intervention by the developed countries and international organizations. In each situation, governments of the Global North must weigh the security benefits from stabilizing a distant part of the international system against the substantial costs of intervening and the difficulty (impossibility?) of maintaining stability in many of those countries (Brzezinski 2004). And Russia has recommitted itself to a strong military presence and a sphere of influence along its very long borders, which could result in disorder and conflict affecting the Global North.

Globalization of Terrorism   The individuals from the Global North who represent its government institutions and multinational corporations in the countries of the Global South are particularly vulnerable to terrorist violence and expect protection. And while the great majority of terrorist acts are committed in developing countries, some developed countries are terrorist targets. Globalization has facilitated the extensive movement of people and information that has placed cells of terrorists in every country in the Global North. Such groups committed the deadly attacks on the U.S. World Trade Center and the Pentagon in September 2001 and on the mass-transit systems in Madrid (2004) and London (2005). The developed countries have never been more vulnerable to terrorist attacks by "home-grown terrorists" and individuals from the Global South.

Proliferation of Weapons   The heavy armaments of Russia and the United States have been significantly reduced by agreements during the post–cold war period (e.g., START II). However, this period is also characterized by the expansion of military power in many states, the ease with which chemical and biological weapons can be acquired, and the spread of nuclear capabilities. Equally serious is the widespread distribution of "light weapons" (e.g., guns, shoulder-fired missiles, land mines) to irregular forces in countries everywhere because such weapons cause most of the casualties from political violence (Klare 1997). The developed countries, which lead the world in the production and sales of military hardware, have failed to implement effective strategies to prevent the further proliferation of all these kinds of weapons. Indeed, the Global North countries (along with Russia) are the suppliers of more than 85 percent of the weapons in the global market (SIPRI 2011).

Competition for Markets and Resources   Earlier discussion emphasized that the global economic competition for markets and resources has become a source of increasing conflict (Chapter 11). Not only do the countries of the Global North compete with each other, but the newly industrializing countries and many developing countries are intensifying this competition. The developed countries can no longer dictate to their advantage where the desirable jobs are, who gets scarce resources (e.g., energy, food), and who garners the maximum benefits and profits in the global marketplace. Fierce economic competition among states, regions, and multinational corporations could be the greatest source of insecurity for the developed countries in the era of globalization (Zakaria 2009).

THE DEVELOPED COUNTRIES OVERALL

✔•⌐Study
and **Review** the
Post-Test &
Chapter Exam at
mypoliscilab.com

In terms of pursuing the broad goals of prosperity, stability, and security, the developed countries of the Global North generally have the highest levels of "success" in the world. These states have the most developed systems of economic production, with evolved political economies based on a mix of capitalism and democratic socialism. The majority of productive resources remain under private control and most states have established a substantial program of welfare distribution to the citizenry. Most of their citizens enjoy a higher standard of living than is available to the majority of people in any other part of the world.

By exercising their considerable economic, military, and political power in the global system, the developed countries have also met their security goals. They have a strong record of survival, influence, and some domination of countries outside the Global North. In their pursuit of security goals, they achieved "victory" in the cold war against the Soviet Union. The leading developed countries still exercise their power energetically to maintain their advantages in the international system.

The developed countries, perhaps because of their prosperity and security, have been able to maintain relatively open, fair, and stable politics. There are tensions between the commitment to individual freedom and limited government, on the one hand, and state intervention to increase equality of outcomes, on the other. Although pluralism is occasionally strained, a wide range of political beliefs and actions are tolerated. Many individuals and groups are able to mobilize their political resources to influence the processes of government and decision making, and citizens have the right to select among leadership elites at regular intervals. In comparison with other countries during the past 50 years, the developed countries of the Global North receive high marks for maintaining constitutional, participatory politics.

The success of the developed countries in achieving prosperity, stability, and security is not unqualified. Some of their citizens live in relative poverty and despair, and increasing inequalities in wealth and income might be the Achilles' heel of their prosperity. The recent economic turbulence has resulted in reduced economic vitality, cuts in the distribution of welfare, and lowered confidence that there is greater prosperity in the future. Also, critics, especially in developing countries, argue that the developed countries have maintained their prosperity by exploitation—of the poor within their own societies and of the populations and resources of other states by means of neocolonialism and military intervention. The countries of the Global North have not reached the top by being passive or generous, but globalization and the emergence of new economic powers might undermine some of their advantages in access to resources and markets.

Security issues have become more complex as the Soviet threat, which encouraged cooperation among the developed countries, has been replaced by more diverse and complex threats. These include increasingly violent regional instabilities in the Global South; the insecurities associated with the current forms of terrorism; and the complex destabilizing impacts of globalization on relations with allies, competitors, and adversaries. All of these pressures present important challenges to Global North countries in their effort to remain dominant in the global system.

KEY CONCEPTS

cold war   370
developed countries   352
developing countries   353
First World   352
Global North   352
Global South   354
Human Development Index
   (HDI)   359
newly industrializing countries
   (NICs)   354

political polarization   368
post–cold war period   371
postcommunist developed
   countries (PCDCs)   354
postindustrial societies   353
privatization   357
social market system   356
Third World   353
transitional developed
   countries   354

FOR FURTHER CONSIDERATION

1. How would you further classify the developed countries into two or more subsets? What criteria would you use?
2. In the current period, what is the greatest threat to the stability of the Global North? What is the most appropriate strategy to reduce that threat?
3. How should the desirable level of distribution of prosperity among citizens in a society be determined? Should the state do anything to ensure that prosperity is distributed more equally among its citizens? What actions by the state are appropriate and might be effective?
4. Write a script or role-play (with others) a situation in which a classical liberal, a conservative, and a democratic socialist discuss the virtues and failings of a particular developed country.

5. If you were to create a quality-of-life index, what measures would you include? Rank the importance you would attach to the various measures, and explain why you have given those rankings.

FOR FURTHER READING

G. Bingham Powell, Kaare Strom, and Russell J. Dalton, Eds. (2012). *Comparative Politics Today: A World View.* 10th ed. New York: Longman. Solid case-by-case studies of selected developed countries (England, France, Germany, Japan, and the United States) as well as Brazil, China, Egypt, India, Mexico, Nigeria, and Russia, employing structural-functional concepts (recall Chapter 5).

Burgess, Anthony. (1970). *A Clockwork Orange.* Harmondsworth, UK: Penguin. A dystopian novel describing a near-future Britain in which youth gangs rule the mean streets of a divided and amoral society. Stanley Kubrick's chilling film of the same title was based on this book.

Castles, Francis G., Stephan Leibfried, Jane Lewis, Herbert Obinger and Christopher Pierson. Eds. (2010). *The Oxford Handbook of the Welfare State.* New York: Oxford University Press. A comprehensive set of more than 50 essays exploring many topics regarding the philosophy, implementation, challenges, and future of the modern welfare state.

Hill, Stephen. (2010). *Europe's Promise: Why the European Way Is the Best Hope for an Insecure Age.* Berkeley, CA: University of California Press. A detailed argument that the social democracies of Western Europe provide the most desirable future course, based on such virtues as their approaches to health care, environmental sustainability, pluralist democracy, trade network, and social market economies

Kennedy, Paul. (1989). *The Rise and Fall of the Great Powers.* New York: Random House. A sweeping analysis of how countries such as the United Kingdom and the United States become the strongest in the world and then decline.

Laquer, Walter. (2009). *The Last Days of Europe: Epitaph for an Old Continent.* New York: St. Martin's Griffin. A strong critique of the current directions of European social democracies, especially due to the problems with sustaining the welfare state, difficulties within the EU framework, and the challenges of immigration.

Marmor, Theodore, Richard Freeman, and Kieke Okma. Eds. (2009). *Comparative Studies and the Politics of Modern Medical Care.* New Haven, CN: Yale University Press. A series of thoughtful essays by experts on the key policy issues facing health care reform in the developed countries, including Canada, Germany, the United Kingdom, and the United States.

Nye, Joseph S. (2011). *The Future of Power.* New York: PublicAffairs. Nye extends his ideas about military, economic and soft power through a rich analysis of how the U.S. can combine these with "smart power" to limit its decline as the dominant power in the world.

Pharr, Susan J., and Robert D. Putnam, Eds. (2000). *Disaffected Democracies: What's Troubling the Trilateral Countries?* Princeton, NJ: Princeton University Press. A strong and diverse set of essays exploring the extent to which citizens in the advanced democracies have lost confidence and trust in their political leaders and political institutions, and even in democratic processes.

Pinder, John, and Simon Usherwood (2007). *The European Union: A Very Short Introduction.* 2nd ed. New York: Oxford University Press. A solid (and brief) exploration of the institutions, processes, and challenges of the European Union as it attempts to extend its roles, power, and effectiveness.

Rawnsley, Andrew. (2010). *The End of the Party: The Rise and Fall of New Labour.* London: Penguin. A spellbinding account of the political machinations among the leaders of the British Labour Party (especially Tony Blair and Gordon Brown) from 2001 to

2010 by an acclaimed journalist. And for a hilarious, rude satire of British politicians in the same era, see the film *In the Loop* (2009).

Schmidt, Vivien. (2006). *Democracy in Europe: The EU and National Policies.* New York: Oxford University Press. The challenges facing the EU, including its limited popular support among citizens, are less due to shortcomings in the institutions of the EU than in the way in which political leaders in EU countries frame national versus European values and priorities.

Tsoukalis, Loukas and Janis Emmanouilidis. (2011). *The Delphic Oracle on Europe: Is There a Future for the European Union?* New York: Oxford University Press. The current debates over the challenges facing the EU during a period of internal disagreements, evolving institutions, and global complexity are explored by scholars and policymakers.

Wilensky, Harold. (2002). *Rich Democracies.* Berkeley: University of California Press. Using case studies, interviews, and quantitative data, a distinguished political scientist offers a comprehensive (at 900+ pages) and compelling perspective on how the 19 "rich democracies" have evolved over the last half-century, with particular attention to social policy and a focus on the interplay among the form of political economy, political institutions, and key political actors.

Zakaria, Fareed. (2009). *The Post-American World.* New York: Basic Books. This provides a readable exploration of the likely reduction in dominance, but also the continuing strengths, of the United States in the emerging global system characterized by "the rise of rest" and especially countries like China, India, and Russia.

ON THE WEB

http://europa.eu/index_en.htm

The official Web site of the European Union provides detailed information about each EU member state.

http://www.oecd.org

The Organization for Economic Cooperation and Development is a cooperative association of 30 member countries, primarily the developed countries plus a few of the most economically advanced countries in East Europe and Asia. The OECD site provides information about its activities as well as data on member states.

http://www.coldwar.org

The home page of the Cold War Museum contains a number of fascinating online exhibits and an online discussion forum regarding this important period.

http://www.osce.org

The electronic home of the Organization for Security and Cooperation in Europe, the world's largest regional security organization, which centers in Europe but now includes 56 member states, provides extensive information regarding issues related to the goal of security.

http://www.usa.gov

The official Web portal for the U.S. government, the site offers many links to the agencies and information associated with the various governmental institutions in the United States.

http://www.canada.gc.ca

The official Web site of the Canadian government, with links to the agencies of the central and provincial governments.

http://ukonline.direct.gov.uk

The Web site for the government of the United Kingdom with multiple links to government agencies, services, and information.

The Developing Countries of the Global South

Giants of the postcolonial era: President Kwame Nkrumah of Ghana greets President Sukarno of Indonesia (right) and Prime Minister Jawarharlal Nehru (center) of India at the United Nations in 1960. All three were leaders in their countries' independence movements and then the first elected political leader, for 14, 22, and 17 years, respectively.

LEARNING OBJECTIVES

14.1 Group the Global South into distinct geographical and political regions and identify the main obstacles they face.

14.2 Outline the strategies the Global South has used to achieve economic development.

14.3 Assess the level of inter-state violence and economic security within the Global South.

14.4 Identify factors that lead to political stability in the Global South.

In ancient times, the Gold Coast of West Africa was home to several flourishing kingdoms and many linguistic groups. The area had sufficient food, rich resources, and land for all. From about the 16th century, the peoples of the Gold Coast developed trade with several European powers, exporting commodities, especially gold and cocoa, and serving as a key location in the extensive slave trade in West Africa. The British conquered the area in the 1870s and ruled it as a colony for 90 years. Then, in 1957, the Gold Coast became the first colonial territory in sub-Saharan Africa to gain its independence, as a country called Ghana.

At independence, there was widespread optimism that Ghana would be the model of political and economic development for many countries emerging from colonialism. Its leader, Dr. Kwame Nkrumah, (in photo on page 376) became an articulate spokesperson for African freedom and development in the postcolonial era. An active multiparty system participated in Ghana's first fair and contested election, won by Nkrumah and his Convention Peoples Party (CPP). GDP per capita was about $1,200 in a predominantly agricultural economy that was also successful in exporting major raw materials, and most Ghanaians had a decent material life.

However, significant problems emerged soon after the election, including economic shortfalls associated with a decline in world cocoa prices, and widespread corruption and inefficiency within the CPP and the government administration. Opposition groups vehemently criticized both the failures of the CPP, calling it "a party of incompetents" and the extensive powers exercised by Nkrumah, whom they labeled "a dictator." Angered by these criticisms, Nkrumah and the CPP passed laws restricting opposition activities. When these restrictions caused opponents to protest verbally and then violently, the government responded with even more repressive measures.

The government became increasingly autocratic. An election in 1960 and a referendum of support for the government in 1964 were rigged. By the 1965 election, legal opposition was nearly eliminated and all CPP candidates were declared elected. With the economy and the social order collapsing, an army-led a coup in

1966 overthrew Nkrumah and installed a "temporary" military junta. From 1966 to 1981, Ghana alternated between civilian governments and military regimes that seized control by further coups in 1972, 1978, 1979, and 1981, justifying their actions on the grounds of civilian incompetence and corruption. A young air force officer, Jerry Rawlings, led the last two coups. By 1981, Rawlings concluded that he was Ghana's best hope and that he should lead the government. Despite several assassination and coup attempts, Rawlings ruled continuously from 1981 until 2000.

Nkrumah had attempted to install a command economy with strong state ownership and control, but there had been minimal economic growth, a declining standard of living for most people, and increasing reliance on neocolonial assistance. Rawlings used political power with equal purposefulness to shift Ghana to a market economy. He collaborated with the International Monetary Fund (IMF) to secure loans, privatized most public enterprises, and radically cut public services. After GDP per capita growth of only about 2 percent per year during the 1990s, Ghana's growth rate has improved to 5.6 percent per year since 2000, and inflation has been "held down" to a yearly average of 18 percent (World Bank 2011).

Under international pressure, Rawlings allowed a free presidential and parliamentary election in 2000. In the first peaceful, democratic transition of power in Ghana's history, opposition leader John Kufuor was elected president. Kufuor was reelected in 2004 and then was replaced by John Mills in a fair, closely contested election in 2008. Freedom House now classifies Ghana as a "free" electoral democracy. However, with GDP per capita/PPP of $1,533, life expectancy at 61 years, and adult literacy at 58 percent, the overall level of development for such a promising, resource-rich country remains disappointing (World Bank 2011; CIA 2011).

The history of Ghana reveals some of the patterns of political, economic, and social development relevant for many of the countries in the Global South. After exploitation during colonial domination, an independent state forms with high hopes of economic and political progress. However, the country has struggled with long periods of low or negative economic growth, a low overall standard of living, continued economic dependence on developed countries and multinational corporations, political authoritarianism, social disorder, and violence. Although the recent improvements remain somewhat fragile, will the optimism about Ghana's development trajectory finally be realized?

This chapter will explore more fully how the countries of the developing world have attempted to make progress in the pursuit of prosperity, security, and stability, given such challenges. These challenges can be huge. As the United Nations (UNDP 2007) observed:

> Many people are poor because they live in countries that are poor. Because they are poor, these countries do not have the resources—finance, technology, and skills—they need to extricate themselves from their predicament. This vicious circle has become more pronounced with globalization. Because they lack the human, financial, physical, and institutional resources required to take advantage of globalization, these countries are unable to reap its benefits and are becoming marginalized in the world economy. Like certain individuals or regions within a country, the countries themselves are, in a sense, caught in a "poverty trap." They therefore require special help to change the conditions in which they find themselves.

GROUPING COUNTRIES IN THE DEVELOPING WORLD

Understanding the developing countries of the Global South is challenging because of their diversity. Developing countries contain dusty villages where poor and uneducated people scrape out a subsistence diet from their small farms. They also have large cities where some people are exceptionally rich; some live and work in modern, technologically advanced settings; and yet many others live in poverty and squalor. Some developing countries are huge states with a billion people while others are small islands with a population of fewer than 50,000. Some developing countries are successfully adopting European political forms of representative democracy, popular participation, and freedom of opposition. Others are run by small governing cliques that ruthlessly eliminate all opposition, and changes in leadership occur only through political violence.

14.1 Group the Global South into distinct geographical and political regions and identify the main obstacles they face.

Developmental Classification

All of these characteristics fit some of the 150+ developing countries of the Global South, with their combined population of more than 5.2 billion people. While there are a variety of ways in which particular countries can be classified as "developing," this book uses the classificatory scheme described in Chapter 13 and illustrated in Figure 13.1. Rather than just using a gross national income (GNI) per capita figure as the World Bank does (any country below $11,455 is a developing country), Figure 13.1 adjusts the income figure for purchasing power parity and then utilizes a second multifaceted dimension measuring the country's overall level of social development, based on key indicators of literacy, urbanization, health, and communications.

Developing countries, *Global South*, Third World, low income countries, least developed countries and similar labels are a useful shorthand for a set of traits attributed to states that, relative to the developed countries (and even to most of the transitional countries discussed in Chapter 15), *are less advanced economically, are less modern, and have a lower overall standard of living.* Most also have high birthrates (sometimes higher than their economic growth rates) and youthful populations (in more than 40 developing countries, at least 45 percent of the population is below age 15). For some of these countries, it is not clear when, if ever, they will reach the levels of political, economic and social development currently enjoyed by the developed countries of the Global North. However, some developing countries will certainly achieve these levels.

This chapter helps you to identify dominant patterns and general trends among the developing countries, although generalizations oversimplify political reality and are subject to qualifications. The countries of the Global South encompass many different histories, traditions, religions, and political ideologies, and they do not share a single political culture. They also have different approaches to politics and strategies of development.

As you read this chapter, and especially as you formulate your own understanding about the developing countries, be sensitive to the variation *across* these states and, in many cases, *within* each state. Just as the most developed countries have some people living in abject poverty and primitive conditions, even the poorest developing countries have advanced technology, and some citizens enjoy enormous wealth and an exceptionally high standard of living.

Regional Classification

Although this chapter generalizes across all developing countries in the Global South, it sometimes uses region as a second element of classification. Before this chapter presents generalizations regarding the pursuit of prosperity, security, and stability, it is illuminating to note some broad regional differences.

East Asia and the Pacific   One regional group includes East Asian developing countries, as well as the few Pacific island states (with a population of at least 300,000). Most of these countries have been traditional, village-based agrarian societies until recently, and most cope with the challenges of multiple ethnicities. China dominates this group in human and historical-cultural terms, given its huge size (1.3 billion people), the dispersion of ethnic Chinese to many of the other countries, the diffusion of Confucian culture, and China's attempts to dominate many of its neighbors. Most of these countries had a late experience with colonialism, which never penetrated too deeply into the societies. China and some of the other East Asian countries (e.g., Cambodia, North Korea, Vietnam) have a recent history of communist political regimes that have been brutal and repressive. This region is also the site of some of the developing world's most successful emerging economies in recent decades, including several "Asian Tigers" that have advanced to developed-country status (e.g., Singapore, Taiwan) and newly industrialized countries (NICs) such as the "Little Dragons" (e.g., Malaysia and Thailand).

South Asia and Central Asia   The Central Asian group is primarily composed of the "Stans"—countries with nomadic, kin- and clan-based social organization, localized power bases and weak central authority, and cultures that have been dominated by Islam for hundreds of years. The primary colonial experience for most of the "Stans" (but not Pakistan) occurred late, when they were annexed by the Soviet Union in the early 20th century and were socialized in its totalitarian social order, if not its command economy model. The South Asian group, composed mainly of the multistate, multiethnic Indian subcontinent (recall Focus in 5), did have considerable colonial penetration from the late 17th century as part of the British Empire. India, Bhutan, and Sri Lanka differ from most other developing countries in the region because of their Hindu culture. While similar to the Islamic societies in reinforcing a rigid, traditional, male-dominated social order, these Hindu cultures are also highly stratified on the basis of caste. Huge India (1.2 billion people) is arguably the only institutionalized democracy in the region. While India's villages remain traditional, some of its urban areas have evolved into sites of substantial economic growth and development, driven by its large sector of well-educated, technology-savvy, English-speaking men and women.

North Africa and the Middle East   This region includes the dozen states and ministates of southwest Asia (e.g., Iraq, Iran, Saudi Arabia) as well as the five North African states that are on the Mediterranean Sea and are dominated by the

Sahara Desert (Algeria, Egypt, Libya, Morocco, Tunisia). Most of the peoples of North Africa and the Middle East are Islamic in religion and culture and mainly Arabic in ethnicity and language (Persian Iran is an exception). The area has major geopolitical importance because of its petroleum resources as well as its strategic location, including its waterways. Much of the region was controlled by the Ottoman Empire between 1453 and 1918. In the 19th and 20th centuries, Europe exercised colonial power mainly through indirect economic and military involvement, but European values and structures did not penetrate deeply into most of these states. Many remain socially conservative and somewhat tribal-feudal. Economically, most of these countries are in the middle-income group, although several of the small oil-rich states are very wealthy (e.g., Bahrain, Qatar, United Arab Emirates).

Sub-Saharan Africa Despite its substantial natural resources, sub-Saharan Africa (the African continent excluding the states of North Africa listed above) is the poorest and least economically developed region in the world. About two-thirds of the world's poorest countries (as measured by GDP per capita) are in this region. After the abolition of the slave trade, the experiences with colonialism in most of these states were late, occurring between the 1880s and the 1950s, and were extremely intensive and exploitative. Currently, many of these countries are generally in a neocolonial situation, with limited control over their own resources and a dependency on foreign financial and technological assistance. A strong sense of national unity is rare because colonial powers created states that arbitrarily merged many nationality groups that had no historical commonality. More than two-thirds of the population in these countries is rural, although increasing numbers of people are migrating to cities. In many countries, the authority of the central, modern state is weak, and national political, social, and economic structures lack institutionalization.

Latin America There are two subsets of countries in Latin America. One subset includes countries that tend to be relatively advanced in both economic and social development, with a substantial technological sector. Most of these states have achieved sufficient development to be classified among the NICs (to be discussed in Chapter 15): Argentina, Brazil, Chile, Costa Rica, Mexico, and Uruguay. After long periods of colonial control most of these states were granted independence before the mid-19th century. In most, there is a strong national identity corresponding to the country's geographic boundaries, and the state has considerable political institutionalization. Other well-institutionalized structures in these societies include the armed forces, the church, and an upper-class elite. Most of these states are highly urbanized (more than 80 percent of the population throughout Latin America now lives in cities).

A second subset of Latin American countries is composed primarily of the small states of Central America and the Caribbean. These small states (e.g., Honduras, Nicaragua) and hundreds of Caribbean islands (e.g., Jamaica, Haiti) are extremely diverse in culture and geography. Compared with the rest of the region, these states tend to have longer colonial legacies and to be less developed and less urban. The Caribbean states have an ethnic-cultural heritage that is African and Asian (and, secondarily, English and French) more than Indian and Hispanic (the heritages that predominate in the rest of Latin America).

ACHIEVING DEVELOPMENT IN THE GLOBAL SOUTH: SOME OBSTACLES

All developing countries strive for the benefits of prosperity, security, and stability. Each country has its own unique bundle of reasons why it has not yet achieved a high level of economic, political and social development. These include its history, geopolitical situation, leadership, culture, and many other factors. When analysts attempt to generalize about some of the most common obstacles to development in the Global South, there are several that seem to be identified most frequently. It is helpful to briefly consider some of these obstacles.

Overpopulation   On average, each woman in the developing world has more than three children. The population of the developing countries more than doubled from 1950 to 2005 and is estimated to grow from 5 billion to about 8 billion by the mid-21st century. Today, 97 out of every 100 births are in countries that cannot meet the needs of their existing population. More people results in even greater demands on existing resources, such as land, fuel, and water, and the poorest countries do not fare well in global competition for these finite resources. The additional people will require more than 1.5 billion new jobs, hundreds of millions of new schools and houses, and a significant expansion in health care just to maintain the current low standard of living (UNDP 2011). A high birth rate also means a high proportion of young people who, especially if they are frustrated with their conditions, increase the potential volatility of social order. Unless resources expand faster than the people to whom they are distributed, development is not possible.

Corruption and Inefficiency   Many countries in the Global South are characterized by high levels of corruption, inefficiency, or both (Bates 2008; Isbister 2006). Inefficiency has many sources, including poor management, the ineffective use of modern technologies and the absence of Weberian bureaucracies (as defined in Chapter 6) in which organizational actors behave in predictable, rule-following ways. And corruption is an even more serious obstacle. Chapter 6 noted that the terms *baksheesh* ("something given"), *chai* ("tea"), and *mordida* ("the bite") describe the private payoffs that organizational personnel (from high-ranking leaders to low-level functionaries) expect to receive before they will assist citizens. Widespread corruption demoralizes the population and drains productive energy from the political economy. Corruption exists in every society, yet it seems especially pervasive in public and private organizations in the Global South. According to Transparency International (2011), a nongovernmental organization that measures levels of corruption in 178 countries, 56 of the 60 most corrupt countries are in the Global South. Among the world's 30 *least* corrupt countries, all are high-income countries of the Global North (except middle-income Chile and Uruguay).

Geopolitical Vulnerability   A developing country's resource base and its strategic location can substantially influence its development trajectory (recall Compare in 11 on geopolitics). Each country's geopolitical situation is different. Some countries are heavily reliant on only one or a few primary commodities (e.g., oil, copper, bananas), and their economic health can be closely tied to how much wealth those commodities generate in the global economy. At least 50 percent of exports are still from primary commodities in two-thirds of all developing countries, especially the least developed countries, where 80 percent of exports are primary commodities (UNCTAD 2011). Some countries are located at strategically important nodes or have such desirable resources that both internal actors and external actors can engage in behaviors that are very damaging to the country (e.g., corruption, group violence) in an attempt to capture the benefits. And some developing countries are so impoverished of basic resources that they struggle to provide their own population with food or water, have few resources to trade in the international marketplace, and have so little strategic importance that they tend to be ignored, even if their circumstances are dire (Collier 2007; Klare 2012).

Internal Disorder   Many countries in the Global South are damaged by various forms of internal disorder, especially due to political violence and insufficient political institutionalization. All of the bottom 40 countries on the "failed state" index are developing countries that are wracked by some combination of civil war, nation-based conflict, terrorism, and high crime rates (Foreign Policy 2011). An associated effect of these disruptions is more than 23 million internally displaced people and 15 million people in refugee camps outside their own country (UNHCR 2011). Many countries in the Global South also suffer from limited citizen support for their government institutions, less-than-legitimate transfers of government authority, and extensive human rights violations. Development is hamstrung in the absence of a governmental system that functions effectively.

Neocolonialism   The discussions of the dependency approach in Chapter 10 and of colonialism and neocolonialism in Chapter 11 (including Focus in 11, on Congo) reveal that a developing country's official independence does not necessarily end its subordination to the developed countries and global institutions. The developed countries, international financial institutions, and multinational corporations are the major sources of the financial capital, advanced technologies, and even the security that many actors in developing countries need to survive in the global system. With this can come neocolonialism—*informal and indirect, but still significant, control of the resources, the economic system, and even the political system of a developing country by powerful external actors* (Wallerstein 2004; Weatherby 2011).

The Compare in 14 briefly considers how some of these obstacles have affected development in two countries. However, before you read the Compare, consider the "acid test" types of indicators in Table 14.1. Which country would you prefer to have been be born into 20 years ago, knowing nothing of your personal circumstances? (Recall Compare in 1).

TABLE 14.1

Select indicators for Nigeria and the Philippines

	Nigeria	Philippines
Population	155 m	94 m
Political rights (1-7, 1 = best)	4	3
Civil liberties (1-7, 1 = best))	4	3
GDP/capita (PPP)	$2,300	$3,600
Human Development Index	.423	.638
Average annual GDP growth, 2000–2009	6.4%	4.9%
Literacy rate	68	94
Economic freedom index (179 countries)	111th	115th
% in poverty	70%	33%
Life expectancy (years)	47.6	71.7
Population growth rate	2.4%	1.9%
Corruption (178 countries) (1st = least corrupt)	134th	134th
Internet users /100	28.3	8.2
Failed state index (1st = most failed)	14th	50th
Global Peace Index (153 countries) (1st = most peaceful)	142nd	136th
Income inequality (136 countries) (1st = most unequal)	44th	36th
Gender inequality index (169 countries) (1st = most equal)	142nd	97th

COMPARE IN 14 | Obstacles to Development: Nigeria and the Philippines

When you examine the indicators for Nigeria and the Philippines in Table 14.1, it is evident that each of these countries has achieved only a modest level of development. These indicators, as well as Figure 13.1, place both countries in the Global South. Each country has a long and rich history, and each was viewed as having great potential for successful development at the time of independence. Yet many decades later, each still has a relatively low GDP per capita, a medium or low score on the Human Development Index, limited political rights and civil liberties, substantial poverty, and so on. Among the many factors that might offer partial explanations for their development trajectories, let's briefly consider the five obstacles to development listed in the previous section. The differences in the scale of some of these obstacles might also help account for the high probability that you selected the Philippines in the acid test.

Population growth has placed significant strains on both countries. In each country, the population has quadrupled since 1950. Just since 1990, the populations have increased by 54 percent in the Philippines (adding 33 million) and by 30 percent in Nigeria (adding 46 million). And, it is estimated that by 2050, the Philippines will add an additional 50 million and Nigeria will add more than 200 million (UNDP 2011). The many extra people and increasingly youthful population in each country during recent decades has created the need for extensive new infrastructure, generated more social disorder, and caused any increases in economic resources to be distributed among far more people.

Corruption is a serious problem in both countries, which share the very high corruption ranking of 134th among all countries. In Nigeria, much of the

(Continued)

considerable wealth generated by oil revenues that does not leak out to the MNCs seems to remain in the pockets of the power elite, and does not benefit the general population or facilitate economic growth. Nigeria has an entrenched culture of corruption in which those with control over almost any action expect a payoff to do their job, whether it is providing a license, recording a document, dealing with a legal infraction, and so on. The Philippines is "the Asian country that has been most hurt by corruption" in a region known for corruption (PERC 2011). The corruption of top government officials in the Philippines became legendary during the rule of President Ferdinand Marcos, from 1965–1986. He, his infamous wife Imelda, and his political cronies drained the country of an estimated $10 billion dollars. Subsequent President Joseph Estrada was convicted of corruption valued at more than $85 million. Estrada was pardoned by his successor, Gloria Arroyo, who is herself now under investigation for corruption. Arroyo's replacement in 2010, Ninoy Aquino, ran on the slogan: "If there is no corruption, there is no poverty" and made the usual promise: "I will not only not steal, but I'll have the corrupt arrested."

Dependence on primary commodities is a key *geopolitical* problem for Nigeria, which gets 95 percent of its foreign exchange capital and 80 percent of its federal government revenue from oil. The heavy reliance on oil has benefitted Nigeria when oil prices are high, but leaves the economy vulnerable to price changes. The huge wealth associated with the oil resources provokes unscrupulous behavior among many who want to capture a piece of the action. Although 70 percent of the labor force is still in agriculture, Nigeria suffers periodic food shortages due to inefficiencies and drought. The Philippines benefits from a more favorable geopolitical situation. The country is a successful producer of foods for domestic consumption and export. As an island with strategic importance in its region, the Philippines receives benefits from the United States, which has located military operations there. These conditions have helped the country diversify its economy, with the service sector generating 55 percent of GDP and the industrial sector adding nearly one-third.

In the 50 years since independence, Nigeria has experienced persistent political *disorder*, due to deep nation-based divisions among regional groups. The struggle to control oil resources and the reins of government are at the base of most of these conflicts. There have been at least six successful coups by military officers who then led oppressive regimes that target opponents with establishment violence. Among the recurrent episodes of violence, the bloodiest (with at least 300,000 deaths) was a civil war from 1966–1970, in which the Igbos failed in the attempt to create an independent state (Biafra). In the Philippines, President Marcos used increasingly repressive tactics to retain power during his 20-year rule. He declared martial law in 1972 and his security forces ruthlessly punished opponents. When Marcos attempted to steal another election in 1986, the citizens had enough of his corrupt and autocratic rule, and through a "people power" mass movement, forced him to flee the country. His successor as president, Cory Aquino, survived at least nine coup attempts. Her successor, Joseph Estrada, was driven from power in 2001 by another populist movement that was orchestrated by the country's power elite. Despite sporadic political violence from indigenous peoples, communists, and political Islamists, there is broad order maintenance (CIA 2011).

Neocolonialism is more evident in Nigeria. After independence from Britain in 1960, Nigerian governments asserted increasing control over oil resources. However, the elite collaborates with multinational companies similar to those that exploited Nigeria's oil during colonialism. Nigeria remains very dependent on financial aid, technological support, and business capabilities from the Global North. The Philippines had a considerably longer experience under Spanish (1521–1892) and U.S. (1892–1946) colonial control. But in recent decades, it has established substantially more autonomy over its economy and is more capable of pursuing its own goals in the global system.

FURTHER QUESTIONS

1. Which obstacle to development is likely to be the most difficult to overcome in each country?
2. If you were the top leader in Nigeria or the Philippines, what one policy might you push hardest to improve the country's overall development trajectory? ▲

GOAL: PROSPERITY

14.2 Outline the strategies the Global South has used to achieve economic development.

◉—[**Watch** the Video "Kenya's Developmental Challenge" at mypoliscilab.com

All developing countries strive for the benefits of prosperity associated with economic growth and development and welfare distribution. While the developing countries employ the same economic strategies as the more developed countries, many of them have had only limited success in achieving prosperity. Indeed, a low level of overall economic performance is the most conventional indicator of a developing country. These countries range from the lowest current GNI per capita (PPP) average of only $290 *per year* (Liberia) to more than $16,000 (Libya). The average income per person for all 40 low-income countries is only $1,199 per year; and even the 103 middle income countries average only $6,357 per year, in comparison to $36,4373 for the high income, developed countries (World Bank 2011).

A very low level of income per capita suggests limited resources within the society, but it does not reveal the additional fact that these resources are often very unequally distributed and that even the most basic goods are minimally available to many people. More than 1.3 billion people in the Global South live on less than $1.25 per day, and 2 billion live on less than $2 per day, conditions of severe poverty. More than 800 million adults are illiterate, and more than 1 billion have no access to clean water (UNDP 2011). At a minimum, developing countries need to feed their own populations. Yet one billion people, including one-third of all children in developing countries, are undernourished. The number of deaths from the effects of hunger is tragic: 10 million per year, including 16,000 children per day (UNWFP 2011).

These stark statistics might be hard to grasp, but they are graphic illustrations of the difficult life conditions that are the daily reality of millions in the Global South. What can be done to improve the conditions of all these people? It is clear that political choices (such as decisions regarding the organization of the political economy, the distribution of prosperity, the education of women, and the form of government) *can* have a powerful impact on the quality of citizens' lives. Let's explore some of the choices that governments must make in the quest for prosperity.

The Quest for Prosperity: Strategic Choices

Each developing country must make choices in at least five key strategic areas in its broad approach to economic development, given the obstacles to prosperity described above, its conditions, and its vulnerability to the many stronger actors in the global system: (1) the balance between state control and the market; (2) the balance between import substitution and export promotion; (3) the mix of manufacturing, services, and commodities; (4) the role of agriculture; and (5) the extent of collaboration with foreign capital.

Statism Versus Neoliberalism A basic policy decision for a developing country is whether to foster economic growth by means of greater state control of the political economy or a more market-oriented approach (see Chapter 8). After independence, many developing countries opted for statism—*more extensive state control of the political economy*—because they assumed that economic dependency and underdevelopment could best be overcome by a strong centralized effort to plan and control the production and distribution of goods in the society. In this approach, the state's role is expansive—it owns major industries and natural resources (via nationalization), controls production decisions, regulates prices and wages, protects domestic producers from foreign competition, and encourages import substitution.

By the late 1980s, most developing countries had rejected statism because of its disappointing results and had shifted to a strategy of neoliberalism (the *market-oriented approach* described in Chapters 8 and 10). With neoliberalism, the state plays a very limited role in owning, controlling or regulating economic resources, it supports globalized free trade, it facilitates foreign direct investment, and it holds down taxes and public spending in order to keep more money in the hands of private entrepreneurs.

Producing for Domestic Consumption or Export Every political economy produces some goods and services for its own population and some for export to other countries. And some products are imported from other countries because of cost and quality considerations. Ideally, a developing country will export goods with greater value than the goods it imports to avoid a "balance of payments" deficit and increased borrowing and debt.

A developing country can use public policy to influence its mix of imports and exports. One policy option is *import substitution—a country decreases the share of goods that are imported by producing more of those goods domestically*. The government can exhort its citizens to buy domestically produced goods (e.g., "Buy Nigerian!") or it can provide subsidies to its firms or consumers in order to lower the prices of those goods. A common tactic is trade protectionism—the use of tariffs and other procedures to discourage imports or make imports more expensive than goods produced in the country. In the current globalized economic system, powerful economic actors (e.g., the World Trade Organization, the International Monetary Fund) apply considerable pressure on developing countries to eliminate such protectionism and allow free trade.

A second policy option is *export promotion—firms are encouraged to produce goods and services that can be exported and sold at a profit in the global economy*. The government can implement policies that provide its domestic firms with an advantage over global competitors. The effect of such policies could be lower taxes on domestic firms, a well-trained labor force, less restrictive environmental policies, subsidized materials, less costly regulations on business practices, and so on. In recent decades, almost all developing countries have enacted policies intended to facilitate export promotion. This strategy has been used very effectively by the Asian NICs and, more recently, by countries such as China and India.

The Role of Agriculture Food is a crucial good in all economies. Globally, 37 percent of all workers are still engaged in agriculture, and the percentage is considerably higher in most developing countries. More than 70 percent of the world's poor live in rural areas, where most small farms produce little more than is necessary for family subsistence (World Bank 2011). Some political regimes attempted to achieve food surpluses through statist control over agriculture. The state organized most arable land into large farms and developed a plan for production

The shift from subsistence farming to cash crops is one key to rural development, as in this field of broccoli in Equador.

based on shared labor and technology. This approach was most fully implemented in command economies, such as Cambodia, China, Cuba, and Tanzania. State-controlled agriculture was not successful because most rural people resisted social restructuring and were not motivated to work as hard for the general welfare as for their own profit.

Consequently, nearly all Global South countries now encourage market-based production of cash crops by private farmers or local collectives (Isbister 2006). In general, the vision is to implement public policies that facilitate: (1) stable and attractive prices within a reliable market, (2) an efficient system of distribution, and (3) increased crop yields. One key strategy is to transition from subsistence farming to *commercial agriculture*, a system where people produce a surplus of food that can be sold in a market. This generates cash for rural people, food to support a growing urban population, and financial capital from food exports. This strategy is especially effective on large farms. However, small farms still produce half of the food grown in developing countries and are especially vulnerable to the complex global food market. Governments have encouraged some agricultural self-help programs through the use of natural farming techniques, have provided loans to small farmers for irrigation projects and soil protection, and have attempted to stabilize market prices, at least in the domestic food market.

Government policies have also facilitated the **green revolution**, which employs *new farming technologies, including hybrid grains, chemical fertilizers, and* *pesticides*. These technologies doubled average yields for rice, corn, and wheat in the Global South between 1960 and 1996. However, the costs of purchasing fertilizers and pesticides have risen dramatically, making profitability more challenging. And unanticipated negative consequences from high-tech farming sometimes emerged. In Indonesia, for example, the green revolution initially increased rice yields dramatically. However, yields soon dropped because pesticides were killing off many good insects and the new hybrid rice breeds were less resistant to the bad insects. So the government implemented policies by the mid-1980s that limited pesticide use and required farmers to return to traditional crop rotation techniques and natural fertilizers.

Despite advances in agriculture, the pressures to provide food and fuel remain intense in many of the least developed countries, especially due to the growing population, social disorder, and impacts of climate change (Klare 2009; von Braun 2008). Many rural people engage in extensive deforestation, overgrazing, and aggressive farming techniques that exhaust the soil, destroy forests, and harm ecologically sensitive areas. During the 1990s, mainly in the Global South, 6.25 million square miles of timberland disappeared, 250 billion tons of arable topsoil vanished from croplands, and deserts claimed 5.3 million square miles (an area about one-and-a-half times the size of the United States) (Worldwatch 2003). Ironically, some of the most successful small farmers are those producing lucrative but illegal cash crops such as coca and opium rather than legal crops, which are less profitable.

An additional challenge is that governments of the Global North pay their own farmers agricultural subsidies (on key crops such as sugar, rice, and cotton) that enable their farmers to make a profit even when selling (below cost) at prices lower than the prices of crops imported from the Global South. The Global North's protectionist trade policies and $360 billion per year subsidizing its farmers in the Global North result in a loss of $50 billion per year for the countries in the Global South (Brown 2002; International Food Policy Research Institute 2003).

The Mix of Manufactured Goods, Services, and Commodities   A political economy is developed most effectively by diversifying its goods. This entails producing and profitably marketing a balanced mix of commodities, manufactured goods and services. Industrialization is a classic strategy for increasing economic development and hence prosperity via *manufacturing*. The aim is to use labor and capital to transform commodities into intermediate goods (e.g., cotton to cloth, trees to lumber, ore to steel, water to electricity) and then into more refined and valuable goods (e.g., clothing, furniture, televisions, trucks). For example, Bangladesh and Indonesia produce an increasing share of the shoes and clothing that are exported. More electronic equipment, furniture, cars, and other relatively sophisticated goods in the global marketplace are now being manufactured in countries such as China, Brazil, and the Philippines.

And in the postindustrial period, there is increasing emphasis on producing *services* (e.g., data entry, tourism) and knowledge-based goods (e.g., banking services, computer software) instead of manufactured goods. For example, India's large population of well-educated, English-speaking technical workers has made it an international center for activities such as writing computer software and staffing call centers. While greater prosperity is a key driver of more service jobs, a government can also stimulate its service sector by improving its educational system and its technological infrastructure.

Diversification can be most difficult for those countries that are particularly rich in primary *commodities* such as energy resources (e.g., oil), foods (e.g., coffee), or minerals (e.g., copper). Under colonialism and neocolonialism, much of the profit from such commodities was exported to other countries or multinational corporations. Governments can take control of their commodities through nationalization or by awarding contracts to domestic entrepreneurs. But it can be difficult to insure that the profits are captured by the state and then invested in national development, rather than being accumulated by a small elite. Some analysts conclude that developing countries with rich commodities are particularly vulnerable to instability as external and domestic actors attempt to exploit those resources, as in Bolivia (mining) and Nigeria (petroleum) (Collier 2007).

Collaboration with Foreign Capital Economic growth in any country requires a stable political and economic environment, a trained and disciplined workforce, effective use of technologies, an efficient infrastructure for distributing goods, and the infusion of financial capital. Most developing countries are challenged on all these dimensions and especially suffer from the absence of sufficient capital to invest in the production system, to purchase imports, and to distribute welfare benefits to a needy population. Because their internal financial resources are often too limited to serve all these needs, many developing countries look to the Global North and its major national and multinational corporations and financial institutions for three types of financial capital: foreign aid, direct foreign investment, or loans.

Foreign aid. Most aid from the Global North has been in the forms of shared technology, grants and loans (with no expectation of repayment), and debt forgiveness on existing loans. Many developing countries argue that the Global North "owes" them such aid as compensation for decades or even centuries of colonial and neocolonial exploitation that left the developing countries with depleted resources and severe underdevelopment. While the provision of aid is sometimes altruistic, the developed countries usually offer such aid with strings attached that serve their own self-interest: economic (to obtain resources, to open markets for their own goods and services), political (to establish alliances or a political sphere of influence, to exclude ideological rivals), or military (to deploy strategic military power in Global South territory).

Foreign direct investment. Consistent with the ideology of neoliberalism described above, most developed countries, MNCs, and financial institutions offer *foreign direct investment (FDI)*, not aid. That is, they *invest in the developing country's firms or set up their own firms within the country.* Such investment is provided by those who expect substantial profits due to the rich resources, cheap labor, tax advantages and minimal regulation in the developing country. Many developing countries accept such foreign involvement in their economy on the assumption that capital, jobs, and other economic benefits will "trickle down" to their population (Maxfield 1997).

Loans. The simplest approach to acquiring financial resources is to borrow funds from the international financial community, composed primarily of major banks and coordinated by the International Monetary Fund and the World Bank. Loans offer an enticing short-term solution for securing funds to finance economic growth and distribute welfare benefits to the population. Eventually, however, resources must be found to repay both the loans and the interest on those loans and many Global South countries are burdened with huge debt service costs.

Microcredit. One reaction to the reliance on foreign capital is an innovative approach to investment that has emerged in developing countries. This strategy recognizes that effective entrepreneurial activities often begin with small, local firms. However, billions of people in developing countries have no capital with which to start their own small enterprises. Therefore, energetic but poor individuals are provided with **microcredit**—*tiny loans* to enable them to launch such ventures. Women, who perform a substantial majority of all work in the developing countries, have been the recipients of 84 percent of this financial assistance. Microcredit approaches are now utilized in more than half of all developing countries, and loans have been extended to more than 150 million poor people. Fully 82 million of these are the world's very poorest, earning less than $1 per day (Microcredit Summit Conference 2006). Focus in 14 describes how this program emerged and has evolved in Bangladesh. Many governments and NGOs are actively expanding their efforts to provide such small-scale, local financial support due to the success of this strategy. Of course, this modest level of internal capital does not substitute for the continuing need for a large-scale infusion of capital from the international community.

FOCUS IN 14 | Poor Women and Development: Microcredit in Bangladesh

Each economic development project requires financial capital. Such funds are typically provided by national or global banking institutions to companies and other major economic actors who have a record of business success. However, a very different approach was crafted by some innovative thinkers in the Third World. Professor Muhammad Yunus in Bangladesh began with a bold and visionary assumption: that "millions of small people with their millions of small pursuits can add up to create the biggest development wonder." Yunus built on the novel concept of "microcredit." That is, he assumed that if motivated individuals in humble circumstances were given access to a small amount of financial capital, they would use their creativity and energy to establish successful small firms.

In 1976, Yunus and his associates established the Grameen Bank in order to test their faith in the untapped entrepreneurial abilities of ordinary women and men. The bank makes small loans to those Bangladeshis who present promising ideas and show willingness to work hard to implement them. These small loans, averaging $160, are extended to people without land or assets—people too poor to qualify for traditional bank loans. Before microcredit, most of these people had no option for borrowing except from intermediaries who charged extremely high interest rates, thus worsening their economic situation. In contrast, the Grameen Bank offers these small loans at a reasonable interest rate and allows an extended time for repayment.

A notable feature of the Grameen Bank's microcredit program is that 97 percent of the 8.4 million borrowers are women. Prior to receiving a loan from the bank, the typical female borrower had never controlled much money. Most of the women

(Continued)

have used these loans effectively, establishing a diversity of small businesses in their communities: enterprises such as paddy husking and lime making; services such as storage, marketing, and transport; and manufacturing activities such as pottery making, weaving, and garment sewing.

Overall, the women have been reliable borrowers and prudent entrepreneurs. Kept on track by peer pressure and peer support, the women repay their loans in tiny weekly payments and use their businesses to move themselves and their families out of poverty. Surprising many in the global financial community, more than 98 percent of the borrowers fully repay their loans from the Grameen Bank. Eventually, many of the women reapply for larger loans as they expand their business enterprises. These loans have provided a rich base of small businesses and economic growth for the country. And, according to the bank, microcredit has "enabled women to raise their status, lessen their dependency on their husbands, and improve their homes and the nutritional standards of their children."

Microcredit has now spread to nearly all of the villages in Bangladesh. More than $10.8 billion has been lent, and more than 10 percent of the Bangladeshi population has benefited directly from microcredit. About 70 other developing countries (and even some developed countries) have replicated the methods of the Grameen Bank, and these loans have assisted more than 150 million clients and more than 465 million family members worldwide. The Grameen Bank remains a remarkable and inspiring model of the capacity of poor women and microcredit to be a powerful source of economic development. In recognition, Yunus and the Bank were awarded the Nobel Peace Prize in 2006. (This discussion is based on Grameen Bank 2011).

FURTHER FOCUS

1. What is your assessment of the granting of microcredit almost exclusively to women?
2. Are there limits to extending microcredit to *billions* of poor people in developing countries? ▲

Current Outcomes

Figure 14.1 presents two prosperity measures for selected developing countries. Although GDP per capita (PPP) is not a perfect measure of prosperity (recall Chapter 8), it is one reasonable indicator for comparative purposes. A striking aspect of Figure 14.1 (as well as Figure 13.1) is the low yearly GDP per capita in many countries, especially in comparison with the developed countries. From an astonishing low of only $187 per capita (in PPP) for Zimbabwe to nearly $17,000 per capita in Libya, the range on this measure is broad across the Global South.

The limited prosperity is also evident in the low Human Development Index (HDI) scores of many developing countries (Figure 14.1), with the very lowest scores predominantly in Africa. It is again Zimbabwe that has the lowest HDI score among these countries, at only .140 and Libya is the highest at .755. There is a broad correlation between GDP per capita (in PPP) and quality-of-life scores, but the relationship is far from perfect. In a striking example, Vietnam, South Africa and Equatorial Guinea have similar HDI scores, but Vietnam's GDP per capita is less than one-third of South Africa's and less than one-tenth that of Equatorial Guinea. The variation between the two measures reinforces the point that quality of life can be based on more than simply the average current economic product of the country and that the policies of government do matter. As the United Nations notes, in considering such differences: "So, with the right policies, countries can advance faster in human development than in economic growth.

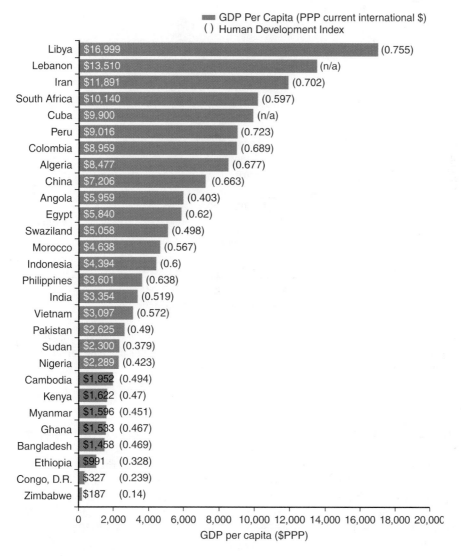

FIGURE 14.1

Prosperity measures for selected developing countries

Sources: World Bank 2011; UNDP 2011: Table 1

And if they ensure that growth favors the poor, they can do much more with that growth to promote human development" (UNDP 2001: 13).

Figure 14.2 offers another way to think about countries' varied success in achieving prosperity, by comparing the rate of recent economic growth (2000–2009) with the proportion of the population that survives on less that $2 per day. Most of the countries in the figure achieved quite good average rates of economic growth, with the majority in the 4–6 percent per year range (until the global recession) and some even higher. However, most also have a large

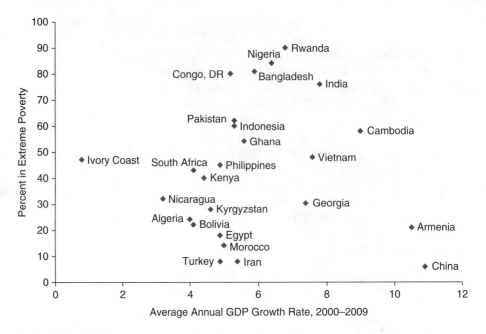

FIGURE 14.2

GDP growth rate and extreme poverty rate (less that $2 per day) for selected developing and transitional developed countries

Source: World Bank (2011):

proportion of very poor people, with the majority having more than 40 percent of their population in extreme poverty.

Regional data provide a different perspective on varying rates of growth. The average annual GDP growth rate between 2000 and 2009 is highest in East Asia (9.4 percent), led by China. The annual growth in South Asia is 7.3 percent, followed by Eurasia (5.8 percent), sub-Saharan Africa (5.1 percent), the Middle East and North Africa (4.7 percent), and Latin America (3.7 percent) (World Bank 2011).

These differences between countries and regions are one aspect of "uneven development." The distribution of prosperity at the *individual* level is also uneven. Most of the countries with huge inequalities in the distribution of prosperity, as measured by the Gini index, are in the Global South (recall Compare in 8). Of the 20 countries with the world's most unequal distributions of income, 18 are in the Global South. These countries have extremely high Gini index scores, ranging from 70.7 in Namibia to 50.1 in Zimbabwe. Nearly all of these countries are in either sub-Saharan Africa (9) or Latin America and the Caribbean (10). Only a small proportion (11 percent) of the quartile of the world's countries with the most *equal* distributions of wealth are in the Global South (e.g., Albania, Ethiopia, Kyrgyzstan, Pakistan).

In many developing countries, both the decisions of the political system and the actions of the international financial community have resulted in an array of policies that have generally increased the economic advantages of the wealthier groups and reduced welfare benefits to the less advantaged sectors of the population. The result is that more than a billion people in the Global South have experienced a substantial *decline* in their standard of living since the late 1980s.

As many developing countries experience decreases in real wages, rising unemployment, and greater income inequality, some leaders, particularly in Latin America (e.g., Hugo Chavez in Venezuela, Evo Morales in Bolivia), have reacted against neoliberalism. Their strategy allows participation in the global economy but shelters the country's economy from global free trade. It also emphasizes public policies that aim to provide substantially more welfare distribution, social services, and jobs for the poor. President Morales (2006) of Bolivia, with the seventh most unequal income distribution in the world, is clear in his condemnation of the neoliberal model: "The worst enemy of humanity is U.S. capitalism. That is what provokes uprisings like our own, a rebellion against a system, against a neoliberal model, which is the representation of a savage capitalism. If the entire world doesn't acknowledge this reality, that the national states are not providing even minimally for health, education and nourishment, then each day the most fundamental human rights are being violated."

GOAL: SECURITY

The developing countries search for security in the face of pervasive insecurity. Their problems are grounded in low levels of political and economic development, which reduce their capacity to control their own population and resources and make the state vulnerable to intervention by other states. Paradoxically, this relative weakness can also lead a state to be more aggressive in its interstate relations, both as a defensive reaction against perceived threats and as a means to divert its citizens' attention from internal problems. Not one of the top 25 countries on the Global Peace Index is a developing country. However, 8 of 10 (Table 12.3) and 23 of 25 states with the lowest scores on the Global Peace Index are developing countries (Vision of Humanity 2012).

14.3 Assess the level of interstate violence and economic security within the Global South.

⊙—[**Watch** the **Video "Iran's Nuclear Ambitions"** at **mypoliscilab.com**

✸—[Explore the Comparative "Violence and Civil Wars" on mypoliscilab.com

Interstate Violence

At any given time, most developing countries are *not* involved in violent interstate disputes. However, most wars since 1950 and most major armed conflicts occur in the Global South, often between neighboring states (SIPRI 2011). The following list offers five reasons for the frequent interstate violence between *adjacent* developing countries:

- The *geographic boundaries* between some states do not correspond to the boundaries of historically established nations, so conflict develops in an attempt to realign states with nations.
- Differences in the *cultures* of two states, especially differences grounded in nationality, political ideology, or religious belief, can produce animosities so strong that violence erupts.
- States look covetously at valuable *resources* in neighboring states and sometimes attempt to gain control of those resources by force.

- States with severe *internal problems* can use neighboring states as scapegoats, redirecting internal frustration into violence against those states.
- Conflict between states can be encouraged by the *actions of other states* that are attempting to serve their own national interests.

Most interstate conflicts between adjacent developing countries involve a combination of reasons. For example, the Iran–Iraq War (1980–1988, with an estimated one million dead) is an example of a conflict resulting from the complex, interrelated impacts of nationality (Persian versus Arab), competition for resources (especially oil in Kurdish areas), religious ideology (Shia versus Sunni), personal animosity between leaders (Saddam Hussein versus Ayatollah Khomeini), internal problems in each country, and external influences from global superpowers with interests in the region. As noted in Chapter 12, interstate conflicts in the Global South only occasionally expand into a war (e.g., Cambodia–Vietnam, China–India, Eritrea–Ethiopia, India–Pakistan). It is more common for the conflict to take the form of a more limited "militarized dispute" short of war (e.g., Cambodia–Thailand, Colombia–Ecuador, India–Pakistan).

Occasionally, there are interstate conflicts between a developing country and a more developed country *on its border*. Most notable have been the five wars and many militarized disputes since 1948 between Israel and the neighboring Arab states, especially Syria, Egypt, and Jordan. In another example, the Soviet Union was concerned about the political decay in neighboring Afghanistan. It dispatched more than 115,000 troops to set up and defend Afghanistan's Marxist government, but it became entrenched in a long guerrilla war (1979–1987) in which 1 million Afghans died and the Soviets retreated in defeat.

When a developing country has been involved in interstate conflict with a *nonadjoining* state during the postcolonial period, the other combatant is usually a country from the Global North that uses force to serve its strategic, economic, or ideological interests. This can involve intervention in an internal war within the developing country (e.g., the United States in Vietnam in the 1960s, France in the Central African Republic in 1996, the NATO-led coalition in Afghanistan since 2001) or a somewhat more conventional war (e.g., between the United Kingdom and Argentina in 1982, and between the U.S.-led coalition and Iraq in 2003).

Some argue that the entire period of colonialism and neocolonialism should be understood as the sustained use of military, economic, and psychological violence by the developed countries against the developing countries. Certain actors in the Global South use this claim to justify their use of political violence against those representing the Global North—as exemplified by the sponsorship of terrorist activities against Europeans and Americans by actors from the Global South (e.g., al-Qaeda).

The search for security can be extremely costly. Many developing countries devote a substantial amount of their limited resources to military expenditure. In 2010, they spent more than $433 billion on their militaries. In the last decade, military spending has been increasing rapidly in *every* region of the Global South: North Africa (94 percent increase), East Asia (56 percent), the Middle East (56 percent), South America (50 percent), South Asia (41 percent), and sub-Saharan Africa (19 percent) (SIPRI 2011). Obviously, these huge military expenditures can enhance security and stability. But empirical analyses suggest that greater military might is actually associated with a *higher* probability that a state will be involved in interstate conflict (Bremer 1980). And expenditures on the military represent resources that are not available for economic development, education, health care, and other forms of welfare distribution.

Economic Security

The fact that many developing countries have such fragile economic systems is also a crucial element in their quest for security because a state's goal of *autonomy*—of controlling its own destiny—depends in part on its *capacity to resist external manipulation of its political economy*. When the developed countries and multinational corporations provide economic and technological assistance, they expect to exert substantial influence and to receive generous benefits such as favorable regulations and advantageous trade relations. And because developing countries owe more than $2 trillion to the financial institutions of the developed world, those institutions expect some control over each country's internal affairs.

This economic intervention has come most explicitly from the *International Monetary Fund (IMF)*, a consortium of financial institutions that sets economic policy and monitors the behavior of global lenders and debtors. To grant additional loans or to reschedule payments on existing loans, the IMF requires "conditionalities"—the debtor state must fulfill specific conditions that the IMF sets. The IMF's conditions (sometimes called "the Washington Consensus") often include requirements that the state implement a *structural adjustment program (SAP)*, which increases the debtor state's openness to the global economy by facilitating free trade and direct foreign investment. Often, the SAPs also require the state to reduce public spending, with particularly severe reductions in the distribution of welfare services to its population, tax cuts, and privatization of state-owned firms (Petrik 2009).

Leaders in some of the major developing countries have recently become more vocal in their opposition to this external manipulation of their internal affairs, especially to the economic and trade policies associated with conditionality. Some developing countries are organizing their own regional free-trade zones to increase their autonomy from the developed countries. For example, Mercosur is comprised of Argentina, Brazil, Paraguay, Uruguay, and Venezuela, representing more than half of Latin America's population (plus five associate members), and there is a trade group of Islamic states with 300 million people, including Iran, Kazakhstan, Pakistan, and Turkey.

However, the political and financial elites in nearly all developing countries seem to believe that their interests are currently best served by cooperation with the developed countries and the international financial community and that loss of some control over their political economy and even over their policy processes is an acceptable cost. This continuing need for support is captured in a paradoxical comment by Kenya's former president Daniel Arap Moi: "No country can maintain its independence without assistance from outside." In the contemporary political world, no state can survive as an independent entity. But the developing countries are particularly dependent on outside assistance in many forms, especially economic and technological. This dependency makes them susceptible to influence, manipulation, or even control by other states. Thus, few of them can escape this economic component of their insecurity.

GOAL: STABILITY

14.4 Identify factors that lead to political stability in the Global South.

Many countries in the Global South find that achieving stability is as elusive as achieving prosperity and security. They have not been able to establish and institutionalize structures that maintain social order and ensure effective functioning of the political system through time. This reduces their capacity to govern, raises the probability of political decay, and increases their vulnerability to outside actors.

👁—⎡**Watch** the
Video
"Nollywood" at
mypoliscilab.com

Inadequate Political Development

Recall from Chapter 10 Kwame Nkrumah's credo: "Seek ye first the political kingdom and all else shall be added unto you." This perspective places primary importance on the political system as the crucial instrument for achieving the developing country's major goals. In many cases, the people who staff the various positions within governmental institutions have good intentions and attempt to perform their responsibilities in a manner that serves the public interest. However, in many developing countries, the political system is a flawed instrument for achieving those goals. And good intentions can be swamped by harsh political realities.

Political development is one of the three pillars in the stability goal of states (recall Figure 5.1). In its essence, this is achieved as the government's capabilities increase and it has greater political institutionalization (Chapter 10). Modern political institutions in most developing countries (South American states are the general exception) have existed for fewer than 60 years. The governments in most countries have increased their political capabilities in that period; but the effective functioning of the various political institutions described in Chapters 6, 7 and 8 such as political parties, judiciaries, center-periphery relations, and so on is still a work in progress. Indeed, many countries have already significantly altered their institutional arrangements and even their constitutions one or more times, making political institutionalization more challenging.

Capabilities analysis emphasizes control of the environment, but from climate change to global economic recessions to the price of oil, there is so much that the government in these countries simply cannot control, especially in the external environment. Globalization has made the difficulties in dealing with the world outside the country's borders even more complex. And within their border, these political institutions are faced with strong and often competing demands from citizens. There are conflicting values and agendas among different groups, based on differences in economic well-being, nationality identity, region, and many other cleavages. Their political economies do not provide an adequate level of material well-being for many within their population, and marked inequality in the distribution of the existing resources can make the situation even more volatile (Collier 2007). Given all these circumstances, it is unsurprising that many citizens have not yet invested the confidence and trust in their political institutions that are among the keys element of political development. And that these political institutions, when subjected to the (inevitable) internal and external pressures, function ineffectively or break down in political decay (Bratton and van de Walle 1997; Sorensen 2007).

The Decline of Order

Political Decay   Order maintenance is another pillar of the stability goal in Figure 5.1. Samuel Huntington's (1968) model of political decay, described in detail in Chapter 10, is based on the problems of achieving political order in developing countries. The postcolonial history of Ghana that opened this chapter, like the case studies of Cambodia, Congo, and India examined in other sections in this book, includes episodes of serious political decay. As the citizens' dissatisfaction with the political system rises, in the absence of political institutionalization, the result is usually an increase in political decay—noncompliance with political authority, protests, strikes, riots, terrorism, nation-based violence. In some cases, authoritarian leadership reestablishes order through repression; in some cases, new leaders are installed who promise democracy; in some cases, order requires external intervention (e.g., by the United Nations or another country); and in some cases, there is a lengthy period of chaos in a failed state where no one is able to maintain order. Rarely is the short-term outcome a dramatic increase in either the capabilities or the democratic processes of the political system (Bates 2008; Sorensen 2008).

Military Regimes   Until recently, the new political leadership that restored order in many developing countries often came from the military. There are three reasons the military emerges under conditions of political decay. First, a key norm within the military is a *commitment to order*, a norm that induces the military to act when the existing leadership has failed to maintain social order. Second, the military has the *capabilities to function effectively* because it is the most highly institutionalized and disciplined organizational structure in most developing countries. Third, the military has the *capacity to subdue disorder* because it usually controls the greatest concentration of force and violence in the society.

As in the examples of Ghana, Nigeria, and Congo, the emergence of strong military leadership has been a recurrent pattern in numerous Global South countries. In the early 1980s, for example, military regimes were in power in 15 of the 22 major Latin American states and in 20 of the 26 major sub-Saharan African states. The military in most developing countries now accepts the professional norm that it should support the civilian regime and prevent political decay, but that it should not seize power. In "protected democracies," the military does not take direct political control but protects the political leadership in exchange for public policies that the military supports, such as maintaining social stability and the military's privileged status in society (Colburn 2002). There are still cases where members of the military take political power in countries experiencing political decay (as in Thailand and Fiji in 2006, Bangladesh in 2007, Guinea and Mauritania in 2008, Honduras in 2009, and Egypt in 2010). The military actors typically claim that they are restoring order, honesty, and democracy, but they usually establish an authoritarian regime.

Internal War When political decay becomes so extensive that no groups, not even the military, can maintain order, a country is likely to become embroiled in internal war—either civil or revolutionary. Conflict is often shaped by identity politics—some combination of ethnonationalist, class, religious, and regional cleavages (Laitin 2007). In the past decade, rival groups competing for power and control of resources reduced Afghanistan, Burundi, Colombia, Congo, Haiti, Iraq, Ivory Coast, Liberia, Libya, Sudan, Sierra Leone, Sri Lanka, and Somalia to near anarchy. In a few countries (e.g., Cambodia, India, Nepal, Peru, the Philippines), variations of Marxism continue to appeal to frustrated groups that are persuaded their situation fits Marx's revolutionary call that the people have nothing to lose but their chains (recall the Debate in 8).

Major internal violence in Global South countries is almost always supported by other states. While different rationales are offered for intervention, these other states are usually pursuing their own national interests while providing financial or military assistance to combatants. Indeed, a key element in the pervasive inse-curity *and* instability of developing countries is the ease with which other states can pursue their own policy goals within the context of internal violence in these states. Syria and Israel invade Lebanon; Uganda, Rwanda, Burundi and then the U.N. send troops into Congo's civil war; the Soviet Union and then the United States are major participants in the internal war in Afghanistan; NATO enters the internal war in Libya. Almost all recent uses of UN peacekeeping forces (14 of 15 active operations in 2011) have been attempts to maintain *internal* stability in a developing country (United Nations Peacekeeping 2011).

Democratization

The trend towards democratization, the third pillar of the stability goal, is evident in the Global South (Chapter 10). Most developing countries are under consider-able pressure to shift away from authoritarian and military regimes towards re-gimes with an elected leadership; a multiparty system; and open, pluralist politics. Two key sources of this pressure are citizen groups demanding political rights and the governments and financial institutions of the Global North.

Figure 14.3 summarizes the levels of freedom in Global South countries, according to Freedom House (2011). A "free" country grants its citizens exten-sive political rights (e.g., to form political parties that represent a significant range of voter choice, to engage in vigorous political opposition) and civil liberties (e.g., protection of religious, ethnic, economic, linguistic, and other rights). A country that is "not free" substantially limits these rights and liber-ties. "Partly free" means that there are significant political restrictions and violations of civil liberties, even though the country might be an electoral de-mocracy (recall pages 170–176).

The spread of democratization is most extensive in *Latin America*. In 2011, every country in the Western Hemisphere had an electoral democracy except Haiti, Venezuela, and Cuba, which is the only "not free" country in the region. Recently, some countries, such as Bolivia and Ecuador, weathered serious episodes of politi-cal decay that earlier would almost certainly have resulted in a military coup. Some, including Argentina, Haiti, and Venezuela, defeated coup attempts. Freedom House

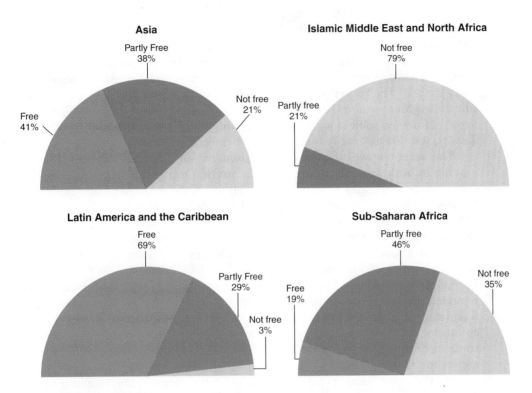

FIGURE 14.3

Levels of freedom in the developing countries, by region, circa 2010

Source: Freedom House (2011)

(2011) classifies two-thirds of the Latin American countries as fully "free" democracies (including Argentina, Brazil, Chile, Costa Rica, and Uruguay). Among the nine "partly free" countries are Colombia, Mexico, Nicaragua, and Venezuela.

In *Asia*, the spread of democratization is mixed. China emphatically crushed the prodemocracy movement in Tiananmen Square in 1989. Cambodia, Myanmar, North Korea, and Vietnam are also among the Asian developing countries that are classified as "not free." Twelve more (including Bangladesh, Malaysia, Pakistan, and the Philippines) are only "partly free." The "free" countries include Indonesia and India, still the world's largest democracy, although it has been battered occasionally by political decay, including parliamentary deadlock, assassination, and extensive violence among Hindus, Muslims, and Sikhs. Electoral democracies are functioning in 59 percent of the Asian countries, although some are fragile and under persistent pressure from dissatisfied groups.

Although less than two-fifths of the countries in sub-Saharan Africa are electoral democracies, this is the region's highest level on this measure since independence. Freedom House (2011) classifies 8 of the 48 countries as "free," led by Botswana, Ghana, and South Africa, while 23 are "partly free" (e.g., Kenya, Nigeria) and 17 are "not free" (e.g., Angola, Congo, Zimbabwe).

Many of the developing countries of the *Islamic Middle East* and *North Africa* have introduced elements of democratic politics. The pressure for democratization increased substantially with the "Arab Spring" of 2011. Most countries now have multiple political parties and elect their political leadership (e.g., Egypt, Iran, Morocco), while others at least have a democratically elected legislature (e.g., Jordan). The region is in considerable flux, as are the Freedom House classifications. Many countries remain "not free" (e.g., Bahrain, Iran, Saudi Arabia, Syria). However some countries (e.g., Egypt, Iraq, Libya, Tunisia) might, like Turkey, stabilize as "partly free" electoral democracies.

The recent wave of democracy (discussed in Chapter 10) seems to be moving in both directions in the Global South. On the one hand, increases in overall prosperity and in education levels in many countries have improved the conditions for the consolidation of democracy. Most regimes have granted some political rights to individuals and groups and have raised the level of elite accountability through elections. Legitimate elections have occurred in additional countries such as Kenya, Philippines and Tanzania. Also, in the aftermath of questionable elections, leaders have been driven from power by popular uprisings. Such "soft coups" demanding greater democracy have removed leaders from power recently in Bolivia, Egypt, Georgia, Haiti, Kyrgyzstan, Paraguay, Peru, Ukraine and Yemen, and forced concessions in countries such as Morocco and Myanmar. While such "people power" has some virtues, it offers citizens a mixed message about the range of legitimate tactics for replacing leaders.

On the other hand, Freedom House describes recent setbacks and a global "pushback" against democracy and groups advocating political freedom and human rights (Puddington 2011). Some regimes have increased their repression in response to popular uprisings. There are still occasional military coups. And many recent elections lack legitimacy. For example, in Afghanistan, after a U.N.-backed investigation concluded that tens of thousands of fraudulent votes were counted in the 2009 presidential election, the rival candidate withdrew before a revote on the grounds that the repeat election could not be free or fair, and Hamid Karzai retained the presidency without a legitimate mandate.

Political Approaches

Given all these challenges, what political approach will increase the likelihood of prosperity, security, and stability? Developing countries pursue these goals within various political frameworks. One method for categorizing these frameworks is to consider the political approach taken regarding two basic issues: resource equality and democratic participation.

Resource equality concerns the extent to which the political system attempts to produce an equal distribution of key economic and social values (e.g., wealth, income, status, housing, health care, education, jobs). The state's policies can result in either greater equality or greater inequality. *Democratic participation* concerns the extent to which the people are mobilized into active and meaningful involvement in the political process. As discussed in Chapter 7, at the nondemocratic theoretical extreme, one person has all the political power in a country and

Keen to learn! Education is a policy priority in many countries that are attempting to achieve both social and economic development.

all others are prevented from any political action. At the democratic extreme, every citizen has an equal role in political decisions and actions.

Obviously, there is no actual political system on extreme end of the continuum for either resource equality or democratic participation. Figure 14.4 indicates four ideal-type political approaches that have different orientations towards the desired mix of equality and democracy. The next sections describe features of each.

Conservative Authoritarianism *Conservative authoritarianism* describes regimes that *attempt to preserve the traditional socioeconomic order and culture* and have little or no commitment to resource equality or democratic participation. Certain groups, defined by lineage, ethnicity, class, religion, military power, or some other trait, enjoy great advantages in the distribution of economic and social power. This socioeconomic elite, with support from the government apparatus, exercises substantial control over the political economy. Most people are allowed little or no role in the political process. Political repression of the populace can be based on traditional practices, especially those associated with religion, or on state actions, especially those implemented by agents of the state such as the police and the military.

Greater political stability tends to occur in conservative authoritarian states that have minimal commitment to egalitarianism and where those groups engaged in order maintenance are well organized and loyal to the elite.

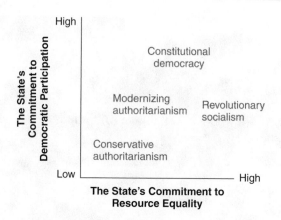

FIGURE 14.4
Ideal-type political approaches

Contemporary examples of such political systems are Iran, Nepal, Saudi Arabia, Somalia, and Tajikistan.

Modernizing Authoritarianism *Modernizing authoritarianism* characterizes a regime dominated by an elite group that *desires to preserve culture and tradition,* but the elite *accepts that some development is inevitable and perhaps even desirable.* These states can have well-institutionalized organizational structures in the public sector, and technocratic elites within the bureaucracy can be a key group within the ruling coalition. Typically, most of the political economy is under private control, and the state works cooperatively with economic actors.

Substantial economic and social inequalities remain, and the elites make no major attempt to reduce them. Rather, there is an assumption that economic development will have an indirect, trickle-down effect and will eventually raise the absolute level of economic and social power of the less advantaged. Many of these states claim to be evolving slowly towards democracy, but popular political participation is limited and opposition is restrained. Political leaders put a strong emphasis on stability and allocate considerable state resources to order maintenance, especially for the military and security forces. Modernizing authoritarianism characterizes regimes such as China, Indonesia, Kenya, Morocco, Nigeria, and Syria.

Revolutionary Socialism *Revolutionary socialism* refers to a regime with *a strong commitment to economic and social equality and to use political power to achieve this goal.* The leadership contends that a small, unconstrained political elite is essential to reduce the massive inequalities in the society. This leadership acts on behalf of the population, asserting totalitarian control over the political economy and the society. The citizens are mobilized, but only to support the policies of the elite, and there is no effort at genuine democratization. Extensive state-controlled political socialization, through the educational system, social groups, culture, and the media, indoctrinates citizens to serve collective interests. These states also employ repression and sanctions to induce desirable behavior. China under Mao Zedong is a clear example of revolutionary socialism. Few current regimes follow this approach, although North Korea and the military regime in Myanmar display aspects of revolutionary socialism. Cambodia, Cuba, Laos, and Vietnam also operate with regimes that generally support the goals of egalitarianism.

Constitutional Democracy A *constitutional democracy* promotes *open politics in which citizens are allowed considerable political rights and civil liberties*. The leaders are directly accountable to the citizens and accept a limited mandate by means of an electoral system with genuine alternatives. The state engages in some welfare distribution, particularly to those in greatest need, but there is no attempt to use public policy to achieve substantial economic equality. Botswana, India, and Jamaica are among the states that have generally maintained constitutional democracies in the last 30 years. As noted, many countries in the Global South have evolved towards constitutional democracy since the mid-1990s. These countries still face substantial pressure to limit democratic processes when they undergo the inevitable problems and disorder in the pursuit of prosperity, security, and stability.

Which Route? Every state attempts to attain prosperity, security, and stability. But in terms of the dimensions depicted in Figure 14.4, leaders must make fundamental choices about the approach they use to pursue these goals. The rhetoric of political leaders in most developing countries (but not in conservative authoritarian regimes) includes a vision in which their society ultimately achieves both a high level of political democracy and considerable social and economic equality— the upper-right corner in Figure 14.4. The key question is: What is the most effective route to reach that "ideal location"?

The route the state takes will be influenced by many factors that its leaders cannot control in the short run: a country's political culture, its geopolitical situation, its nationality composition, its history of political institutions and leaders, its relations with other states, and so on. Within these constraints, political choices *can* be made. One set of major policy choices concerns the structure of the political economy, especially the level and nature of state involvement in the economic system. And Figure 14.4 reflects two other key choices regarding the emphasis on attaining political democracy and on achieving social and economic equality.

IS IT GETTING BETTER ALL THE TIME?

In the pursuit of prosperity, the overall balance sheet for the developing countries is complicated. On the positive side, there is greater economic diversification, with manufactured goods now accounting for two-thirds of exports (excluding oil). The annual economic growth rate from 2000 to 2009 was a strong 6.4 percent (World Bank 2011). The "average person in the developing world" is living longer (on average, 16 years longer than in 1960), is healthier,

✓•⟮**Study** and **Review** the **Post-Test & Chapter Exam** at **mypoliscilab.com**

better educated, and has more material possessions than at any prior time (UNDP 2005: 25). However, most Global South economies are still net importers of capital, technology, manufactured goods, oil and even food, and there is continued dependency on the developed countries and multinational corporations. Prosperity is very uneven, with some countries, especially in East Asia, enjoying tremendous economic growth while many other developing countries languish. Moreover, inequality in the distribution of prosperity is increasing within most Global South countries, particularly those with rapid growth. There are serious shortcomings in the pursuit of prosperity when 2 billion Global South people live on less than $2 per day.

Developing countries are spending more each year to achieve greater security, but there is little evidence that most citizens in the Global South feel more secure from violence than in the past. The spread of more deadly weapons, the increasing movements of populations across borders and within countries, the propensity of external actors to intervene within the borders of many Global South countries have somewhat altered the nature of insecurity, but certainly not reduced it fundamentally.

Economic underdevelopment is the main factor distinguishing the countries of the Global South from those of the Global North, but *political* underdevelopment is the pivotal problem if the political system is to be used as the crucial instrument for social and economic change. Regardless of their political approach, nearly all developing countries face difficult challenges as they attempt to use the political system to achieve prosperity, security and stability. Most have valuable natural resources and a population that is willing to apply its energies to achieve these goals. However, their underdevelopment places them at an enormous disadvantage in the contemporary world, with its patterns of political, military, and economic inequality.

The Debate in 14 asks whether there will always be a Third World. For many of these states, especially the low-income developing countries, it is possible that *no* political approach and *no* form of political economy can simultaneously achieve all their major goals (a claim first put forth in the Compare in 1 "acid test"). The leaders of any developing country must make very difficult decisions about how to gain partial success on some of their goals. Some objectives will have to be sacrificed in the quest for others, and there is no assurance that *any* objective can be fully attained.

For the developing countries, the obstacles are formidable, and determining the best strategy for achieving desired outcomes is baffling. At every turn, the underlying political choices are fundamental: freedom versus security, economic development versus welfare, political equality versus economic equality, democracy versus efficiency, aid versus independence, neoliberalism versus statism, guns versus butter. Yet there are grounds for some optimism. Since 1990, even the low-income countries have achieved some improvements: Life expectancy has increased by 1.8 years, adult illiteracy has declined from 45 percent to 37.7 percent, debt service has been reduced from 23 percent to 9.7 percent of exports, and the number of "free" countries has increased. Perhaps it is getting better, even if not in every developing country and not all the time.

THE DEBATE IN 14 | Will There Always Be a Third World?

While other terms are more favored today, "**Third World**" is still widely used to characterize a large number of *countries that have a relatively low level of economic development*, measured as GDP per capita. The label might encompass as many as 150 countries that are not yet "developed" to the level of countries in the Global North; but a more limited classification might include the 40 "low-income countries" and some or most of the (56) "lower-middle-income" countries (World Bank 2011). Some analysts predict that these less developed countries will close the gap with the more developed countries, given the homogenizing dynamics of globalization (see Chapter 11). Others claim that substantial inequality between countries is an essential feature of the global system, and that continuing economic inequality is inevitable in a world of limited resources, free trade, disparities in technology, and hegemonic power relations. The poor countries, it might be said, will always be with us. Will there always be a Third World?

THE THIRD WORLD IS ON A PATH TO DEVELOPMENT

- Numerous social indicators reveal significant recent improvement in the life conditions of those living in the Third World. Life expectancy has increased from 55.6 years to 66.1 years (1970–2005); the literacy rate has increased from 68.8 percent to 76.7 percent (1990–2005); the mortality rate for children under 5 (per 1,000) has decreased from 167 to 72 (1970–2008) (UNDP 2008; UNMDG 2011).
- The number of people living in severe poverty in the Third World decreased from 46 percent in 1990 to 27 percent in 2005 and is projected to decline to 15 percent by 2015 (UNMDG 2011).
- Overall, the Third World achieves higher economic growth rates than the high-income countries. Since 2000, low-income countries have grown at an annual rate of 5.5 percent and lower middle-income countries have grown

at 8.5 percent, compared with only 2.0 percent annual growth in the high-income countries (World Bank 2011).
- The mobility of capital, the transfer of technology across borders, and the extensive outsourcing of economic activity associated with globalization are producing substantial and increasing economic and social benefits for most citizens in the Third World (Baghwati 2007; Wolf 2004).
- The huge growth in international trade nearly tripled the volume of trade generated by low-income countries between 1970 and 1990, to $203 billion (World Bank 2005). The external debt service (as a percentage of exports) that burdened most developing countries has been reduced from 16 percent in 1990 to only 3 percent in 2008 (UNMDG 2011).
- If "Third World" is merely a label for those countries that are *relatively* poor, even while the absolute standard of living rises to a reasonable level for most of the population in most developing countries, then there will always be a Third World, but only because some countries will continue to be less rich than others.

THE THIRD WORLD WILL NEVER DISAPPEAR

- It is likely to take generations before the "average person in the Global South" will catch up with even the current social statistics of the average Global Northerner. The Global Southerner lives 19 fewer years, has one-twentieth the yearly income, and is ten times more likely to be illiterate. In the last two decades, 1 billion people have experienced a deterioration in their standard of living (UNDP 2010).
- There are more people in the Third World living in extreme poverty today than there were in 1981. And among the poorest 60 percent of families in the Third World, one-half of girls and one-third of boys do not attend secondary school (UNWDG 2011).

(Continued)

- Despite higher growth rates and claims of convergence, the absolute differences between the Third World and the developed countries remain huge. For example, even if economic growth in the developed countries were to stop from this moment forward, it would take Latin America until 2177 and sub-Saharan Africa until 2236 to catch up (World Bank 2005: 37).

- The developed countries continue to enjoy enormous competitive advantages over the Third World, in terms of their control of capital flows, their greater technological capacity and innovativeness, and their military and political power. These advantages helped generate the current vast inequalities between rich and poor countries, and there is no reason to assume that the rich countries will allow these advantages to wither.

- Powerful global institutions such as the WTO and multinational corporations generally operate in ways that favor the developed countries over the Third World. Globalization has resulted in increasing inequality between the world's rich and poor countries (Khor 2011).

- Since 1970, the value of international trade for countries in the Global North has increased significantly more than that for the Third World, despite a population that is less than one fifth as large. And in real terms, the external debts of Third World countries have actually increased by more than 25 percent between 1990 and 2003 (World Bank 2005).

- A few developing countries will successfully reach a high level of development. However, there are few data or trends to suggest that there will be any dramatic reduction in the dependency or overall quality of life for the majority of people in most Third World countries, relative to developed countries.

MORE QUESTIONS ...

1. Might globalization generate some hardships and greater inequalities for some Third World populations in the short run but ultimately have very positive impacts on productivity, trade, and prosperity in their countries?

2. Is it a satisfactory situation if most people in Third World countries are increasingly better off in terms of life expectancy, literacy, caloric intake, and so forth, yet the relative disparities in quality of life between the Global North and the Third World increase?

KEY CONCEPTS

conservative authoritarianism 403
constitutional democracy 405
democratization 400
export promotion 387
foreign direct investment (FDI) 390
Global South 379
green revolution 388
import substitution 387

International Monetary Fund (IMF) 397
microcredit 391
modernizing authoritarianism 404
neocolonialism 383
neoliberalism 387
revolutionary socialism 404
statism 386
Third World 407

FOR FURTHER CONSIDERATION

1. Assess the claim that the label "Third World" has no meaning, either analytical or political, in the globalized, post–cold war world.

2. Are the problems in achieving economic development in the developing countries attributable primarily to the actions of the developed countries, or are they better explained by domestic circumstances in these countries?

3. Choose a real (or imaginary) developing country, and specify its conditions. Given your country's conditions, what arrangements (especially political institutions and political economy) make the most sense for progressing towards the key development goals you emphasize?

4. Is political violence in the developing countries likely to be greater or less during the next 10 years compared with the past 10 years? Why?

5. Other than greater economic prosperity, what conditions seem most likely to sustain the shift to democratization in many developing countries? In particular, what forms or arrangements of political structures are most important?

FOR FURTHER READING

Andersen, Roy, Robert Seibert, and Jon Wagner. (2012). *Politics and Change in the Middle East.* 10th ed. New York: Pearson. A multidisciplinary, comparative introduction to the political systems in this important region, focusing particularly on current challenges.

Collier, Paul. (2007). *The Bottom Billion: Why the Poorest Countries are Failing and What Can be Done about It.* New York: Oxford University Press. A compelling analysis and set of policy prescriptions regarding the severe problems, particularly grounded in corruption, resource wealth, and subordination in the global economy, that cripple the 50 poorest, failing countries in the Global South. Also worthwhile is Collier's *Wars, Guns and Votes* (2010).

Dominguez, Jorge I. and Anthony Jones, Eds. (2007). *The Construction of Democracy: Lessons from Practice and Research.* Baltimore, MD: Johns Hopkins University Press. Scholars and major political officials from numerous countries, mainly in the developing world, explore the necessary conditions for creating and sustaining democracy, with particular emphasis on the fit between the sociocultural nature of the country and the fostering of associational behavior and trust among the citizens.

Isbister, John. (2006). *Promises Not Kept: Poverty and the Betrayal of Third World Development.* 7th ed. Bloomfield, CT: Kumarian. A sensible and balanced analysis of the difficulties that have prevented most developing countries from achieving sustained development, exploring both the external and the internal obstacles to prosperity.

Meadows, Donella, Jurgen Randers and Dennis Meadows. (2004). *Limits to Growth: The 30 Year Update.* White River, VT: Chelsea Green Publishing Company. Updating the earlier arguments in their *Limits of Growth* studies, the authors provide a powerful case that overpopulation and overuse of resources, and the failure to respond effectively to these phenomena, are dangerous challenges to prosperity and stability in all countries, with particular risks for those in the developing world.

Moyo, Dambisa. (2009). *Dead Aid: Why Aid Is Not Working and How There Is a Better Way for Africa.* New York: Farrar, Straus and Giroux. A controversial argument that development in many African countries has actually been harmed by the more than $1 trillion in aid, which has caused aid dependency and worsened corruption, and that different approaches are necessary to facilitate development.

Nugent, Paul. (2004). *Africa Since Independence: A Comparative History.* New York: Palgrave Macmillan. A richly comparative discussion of the evolution of many important African countries covering the entire postcolonial period.

Onwumechili, Chuka. (1999). *African Democratization and Military Coups.* Westport, CT: Praeger. A sobering and occasionally encouraging characterization of 40 years of struggle to establish democracy in African countries and to limit the tendency towards violent takeovers and authoritarian rule by the military.

Schedler, Andreas, Ed. (2006). *Electoral Authoritarianism: The Dynamics of Unfree Competition.* Boulder, CO: Lynne Rienner. These articles examine authoritarian regimes that hold elections, which the book contends are the most common form of political regimes in the developing world. They focus on the impacts of elements such as elections, the military, constitutions, and external actors.

Simon, Julian. (1998). *The Ultimate Resource 2*. Princeton, NJ: Princeton University Press. A powerful critique of those, like the Limits to Growth group, who predict disaster due to overpopulation and environmental degradation. It argues that the ultimate resource (people producing knowledge and then applying it as technology) will outstrip problems.

Skidmore, Thomas, Peter Smith and James Green. (2009). *Modern Latin America*. 7th ed. New York: Oxford University Press. A helpful comparative introduction to society, politics, and economic development in Latin America, with numerous interesting case studies.

Weatherby, Joseph N., et al., Eds. (2011). *The Other World: Issues and Politics of the Developing World*. 9th ed. New York: Longman. Thoughtful general chapters on neo/colonialism, women and development, and political economy precede informative chapters focusing on each region of developing countries.

Wiarda, Howard J., Ed. (2004). *Authoritarianism and Corporatism in Latin America—Revisited*. Gainesville: University Press of Florida. The book argues that the apparent shift towards democratization in many Latin American countries is illusory. Rather, these countries still have strongly entrenched authoritarian and corporatist power structures.

World Bank. (Yearly). *World Development Report*. New York: Oxford University Press. Systematic yearly statistics on the economic, financial, and demographic aspects of development for more than 180 states. Each annual issue also emphasizes a key theme (e.g., 2001 on poverty, 2003 on sustainable development, 2007 on climate change, 2009 on economic geography, 2011 on conflict, security and development), with a strong emphasis on the developing countries.

Yunus, Muhammad. (2008). *Creating a World Without Poverty: Social Business and the Future of Capitalism*. New York: Public Affairs Publishing. A remarkable vision from the inspiring Nobel Prize winner who established the Grameen Bank (Focus in 14), in which he sketches a business model that would enable every family to live with dignity and security.

ON THE WEB

http://allafrica.com
This site links to hundreds of current, Africa-focused newspaper articles as well as more than 900,000 articles in a searchable archive.

http://english.aljazeera.net
An Arab world perspective (in English) on the news from arguably the most influential regional news source in the Middle East.

http://lanic.utexas.edu/index.html
The Latin American Network Information Center, hosted at the University of Texas, Austin, provides a vast number of Internet-based information sources about all countries in Latin America.

http://www.undp.org
The Web site for the United Nations Development Programme, a key unit of the United Nations that specializes in issues of economic and political development.

http://www.unohrlls.org/en/home

The site for the United Nations' Office of the High Representative for the (48) "Least Developed Countries," (31) "Landlocked Developing Countries" and "Small Island Developing States" provides details of the challenges and opportunities for this almost entirely Global South group.

http://www.aseansec.org

On the official Web site of the Association of Southeast Asian Nations are information and documents relevant to ASEAN, news about countries in the region, and somewhat self-serving Web pages constructed by each member state.

http://www.unctad.org

This part of the home page of the United Nations Conference on Trade and Development focuses on issues regarding the world's least developed countries.

http://www.un.org/womenwatch

This French-based bilingual site provides links to various research, documents, organizations, and activities that concern the role of women in the development process.

http://www.twnside.org.sg

Based in Malaysia, the Third World Network provides a strong perspective through a diverse array of analyses, policy papers, and information on the full range of issues facing developing countries, including trade and development, environment, human rights, and globalization.

The Transitional Developed Countries

Hungarians in Budapest enjoy the freedom and prosperity associated with the democratic politics
and market-based economy that replaced a repressive communist regime.

LEARNING OBJECTIVES

15.1 Trace the historical, political, and economic development of the postcommunist states.

15.2 Evaluate the attempts by the postcommunist states to achieve prosperity through a transition to market economies.

15.3 Assess the efforts by postcommunist states to balance democratic freedoms and political stability.

15.4 Analyze the impact of the fall of the Soviet system on the security of postcommunist states.

15.5 Identify the attributes of newly industrialized countries.

15.6 Distinguish between Asian and Latin American development strategies and assess their successes.

15.7 Analyze factors that encourage political stability in newly industrialized countries.

15.8 Characterize the types of security threats that newly industrializing countries in Asia and Latin America face.

15.9 Predict the success of the development strategies of the postcommunist states and the newly industrializing countries.

It was not easy being Hungary in the 20th century. As a landlocked country in the center of Europe, Hungary was drawn into every continental drama. It was the junior partner in the Austro-Hungarian empire, but was on the losing side in World War I. As a result of the war, Hungary lost two-thirds of its land, and more than 5 million ethnic Hungarians found themselves living within the new borders of other countries. Communists and right-wing fascists fought for Hungary's soul between the wars. Hungary then sided with Germany during World War II, and by the end of the war, the country was physically and psychologically devastated. At this point, troops from the Soviet Union helped the communist leaders take control of the Hungarian government. By the late 1940s, Hungary was part of the Soviet bloc of states and had one of the most repressive communist regimes in Europe. Huge numbers of the regime's critics were killed or imprisoned, and there was minimal prosperity under the rigid command political economy.

Frustrated citizens took to the streets in a 1956 rebellion and tried to set up a more democratic government; but the Soviets invaded with more than 150,000 troops and brutally crushed the "freedom fighters." Although the near-totalitarian government ruled firmly, there were experiments in the 1970s and 1980s with more private enterprise in the economy and expanded rights for workers, and

Read and **Listen** to **Chapter 15** at mypoliscilab.com

Study and **Review** the **Pre-Test & Flashcards** at mypoliscilab.com

Hungary was said to have established "goulash communism" (that is, combining some of every approach into the political economy pot).

Hungary was among the leaders when the peoples of East European countries were finally able to throw off the communist yoke in 1989. Hungary shifted immediately to democratic politics, holding its first open and competitive multiparty election in 1990. It also abandoned the command political economy, quickly privatizing almost half of the state-owned enterprises. Between 1990 and 1998, the share of GDP generated by the private sector rose rapidly, from 25 percent to 80 percent. The state also withdrew many of its communist-era human and social services to citizens.

This combination of changes resulted in a few difficult years of transition and financial hardship for most people in the society. But foreign direct investment flowed in, and Hungary became a poster child for the remarkably rapid transformation of some former communist-bloc countries into relatively prosperous, market-based economies. It joined the European Union (EU) in 2004 and became a member of the North Atlantic Treaty Organization (NATO). Hungary's 10 million citizens enjoy strong political rights and civil liberties, as the former Communist Party has alternated with the center-right parties in controlling the parliament.

Unfortunately, extensive borrowing and the dead weight of the many state enterprises that were not sold off became a serious drag on the economy, especially when the global economic meltdown occurred in 2007 onward. As economic conditions have again become very difficult for many citizens, confidence in political leaders and political parties has dropped significantly. Nonetheless, Hungary has made a quite impressive transition from the oppressive life and underachieving economy of the communist era to its current state. Freedom House rates it as a free, liberal democracy with its highest score (1.0). Hungary has a GDP per capita (PPP) of nearly $19,000, is in the "very high" group on the Human Development Index (.805), has averaged more than 3 percent growth per year, and has the second most equal income distribution in the world. It looks promising to be Hungary in the 21st century (World Bank 2011).

As suggested in the discussion of Figure 13.1, Hungary is among a group of countries termed "*transitional developed countries.*" They are characterized by levels of economic and social development that are notably higher than that of countries in the Global South. Most are transitioning towards levels of development that could result in their classification as developed countries but they have not yet achieved those levels. Many have also experienced substantial change in the past several decades. Chapter 13 proposed two subgroups of transitional developed countries for particular attention, the postcommunist developed countries (PCDCs) and the newly industrialized countries (NICs).

In a fitting homage to a contemporary political world that seems characterized by rapid and often dramatic upheaval, this final chapter focuses on these two subsets of countries where the forces of change seem strong. Currently, they are revealing case studies of "countries in the middle" within our framework of analysis. Hopefully, you will be able to apply the concepts and political knowledge you have learned in earlier chapters to explore the broad patterns of change these groups are encountering and make your own assessments of how these transitional countries will cope with the challenges they face in their quest for prosperity, stability and security. Let's examine the postcommunist developed countries first.

THE POSTCOMMUNIST DEVELOPED COUNTRIES

After the Soviet bloc broke up in the late 1980s and early 1990s, 29 new national political systems emerged, including 15 states carved out of the former Soviet Union. Many NGOs treat this set of 29 countries as a group. Freedom House (2011) clusters these countries as "Nations in Transit," and the World Bank (2011) refers to the entire group as "Europe and Central Asia" (Western Europe is part of another group of "high-income economies"). However, based on the classification scheme in Figure 13.1, our analysis excludes from the transitional group those 11 postcommunist countries that still seem to have the characteristics of other developing countries (e.g., Albania, Armenia, Georgia, Moldova, Tajikistan, Ukraine, Uzbekistan).

Thus, this chapter focuses on only the 18 countries from this group that are at moderate levels on economic and social development in Figure 13.1. This group is designated the *postcommunist developed countries (PCDCs)*. These PCDCs include some of the states that emerged from the Soviet Union (e.g., Belarus, Estonia, Kazakhstan, Latvia, Lithuania, Russia) and most of the states that evolved from the Soviet Union's previous allies in Central and Eastern Europe (e.g., Bulgaria, Croatia, the Czech Republic, Hungary, Poland, Romania, Serbia, Slovakia, Slovenia). These countries have a combined population of about 240 million.

Some of the PCDCs, particularly those in Central and Eastern Europe, are currently engaged in a process of substantial economic and political transformation. Until the late 1980s, these countries were communist states and were trying to achieve prosperity, stability, and security under the structure of a command political economy and totalitarianism (for 60 years in the Soviet Union and 40 years in Central and Eastern Europe). Since about 1990, these states have abandoned their communist ideologies and attempted to transform themselves into more market-oriented political economies and to implement democratic politics. These sweeping changes were the watershed events in the shift in the international system to the post–cold war period (described in Chapter 13). However, some of the PCDCs that emerged from the former Soviet Union have resisted the strongest currents of change, especially in their political regimes, which remain authoritarian.

Figure 13.1 reflects that these countries are relatively advanced on the social development dimension. Their populations are well educated and mainly urban, and they are incorporating advanced technologies into their economies and their private lives. The states have adopted democratic political processes and are institutionalizing them in varied degrees. The political economies in most states were significantly depressed during the economic transitions in the 1990s, but their GDP per capita measures are now increasing and five have reached the level of high-income countries (World Bank 2011). Some citizens in these countries

15.1 Trace the historical, political, and economic development of the postcommunist states.

Watch the Video **"Russian Political Reform"** at **mypoliscilab.com**

TABLE 15.1

Acid Test II

	Kappa	Lambda	Mu
Governmental type	Nondemocracy	Electoral Democracy	Nondemocracy
Political rights (1–7, Freedom House)	7	4	6
Civil liberties (1–7, Freedom House)	6	4	5
Press freedom	Not free (15th percentile)	Free (72nd percentile)	Not free (16th percentile)
Legitimate political parties	1	54	28
% females in legislature	37%	12%	14%
Life expectancy	71	67	65
Human Development Index	.912	.770	.817
Literacy rate	99%	98%	99%
% below poverty line	2%	44%	31%
Serious crimes/100,000	687	5,490	4,950
GDP/capita annual growth	2.7%	6.1%	8.1%
Inflation	3%	68%	13%
Gini index of income inequality	21.5	48.7	41.1
Top: Bottom 20% of income distribution	5.4:1	12.6:1	7.6:1
GNI per capita (not PPP)	$3,200	$1,600	$7,560

support the shift to a market economy, although others are dissatisfied with the effects of this change on themselves and on their society. Thus, the next sections explore their current quest for prosperity, stability, and security. But before you explore the details of these countries in transition, you are invited to examine Table 15.1 and then take one more "acid test" in Compare in 15.

COMPARE IN 15 | Acid Test II

Here is another acid test. Before reading further, examine Table 15.1 closely. As in the Compare in 1, assume that you were born in one of these three countries 20 years ago, but you do not know your life conditions at birth (e.g., gender, ethnicity, family wealth, educational opportunities, and so on). *Into which of these three countries would you prefer to have been born? Why?*

Each of the three countries seems to offer a different bundle of virtues and shortcomings, and you are forced to make trade-offs. If you especially value economic and social stability, safety, and equality, you might choose Kappa. Lambda might be your choice if individual rights and freedoms are given highest priority. And the economic vibrancy and potential of Mu might lead you to prefer to be

(Continued)

a young adult there, despite its political and social negatives.

In this acid test, the three alternatives actually characterize the *same* country at three recent time periods. Kappa is the Soviet Union in 1989, just before it broke into multiple countries; Lambda is the Russian Federation in 1999, after 10 years of postcommunist adjustments; and Mu is the Russian Federation in 2009. Over this brief period, Russians have experienced a roller-coaster ride from a rigid and repressive totalitarian system that did provide basic economic and personal security (Kappa) to a free but impoverished, dangerous, and chaotic system of democracy and free enterprise (Lambda), and then an economically dynamic society with a subtler form of authoritarianism and growing inequality (Mu).

Kappa: The Russian people lived for seven decades under a system guided by the principles of Marxism-Leninism, where a commitment to equality promised everyone a decent standard of living; access to affordable education, jobs, and health care; and a safe, secure life. The political system did generally deliver on these goals, although the level of prosperity and the quality of goods were modest at best, and life was relatively dull under a repressive, one-party state that substantially limited personal freedoms. The Soviet Union was one of the world's two great military superpowers and had substantial international influence. However, shortcomings in the envisioned prosperity and quality of life led (then) president Mikhail Gorbachev to begin loosening restrictions on the political and economic systems in the late 1980s, facilitating the collapse of the Soviet Union by 1991.

Lambda: The 1990s was a period of complex transitions as the new state of Russia abandoned communism. There were efforts to establish a competitive, multiparty democracy, privatize the political economy, and severely cut the provision of communist-era services by the state. These changes were generally successful in producing a free society and market economy; but the transition also resulted in surging unemployment, hyperinflation, (e.g., prices increased twenty-six-fold in 1992 alone), a drastic increase in poverty and hardship (e.g. an increase from 2 percent in 1989 to fully 50 percent

in 2000), a vast and widening gap between the rich and the poor, and skyrocketing crime. Two-thirds of the lucrative enterprises moved into the hands of insiders (especially powerful entrepreneurs called "oligarchs"), whose agenda was to acquire the society's economic assets at bargain prices and then exploit those assets ruthlessly. This *crony capitalism—the tendency for members of the old (Communist Party) elite to use their connections to prosper as the new economic elite*—did produce a small proportion of very wealthy people.

Mu: In the first decade of the 21st century, Russia began to stabilize. The 2000 election for president was won by Vladimir Putin, a former KGB (secret police) officer who was popular among the Russian people for his aggressive approach to law and order. The economy recovered rapidly (aided by record high oil prices), with strong economic growth, inflation under control, and a major decline in unemployment. Crime rates have been falling as law enforcement and security services have reestablished their traditional, heavy-handed approach. However, Putin, still the dominant power, has also reasserted strong authoritarian control, jailing rivals, stifling political opposition, and muffling the media, and Russia is again "not free" according to Freedom House. The Russia-in- transition of 2009 seems to offer its citizens, especially those with entrepreneurial zeal, the promise of substantial opportunities for economic advancement, but at the cost of political and personal freedoms. And many citizens who have suffered substantial declines in their quality of life because of these huge economic transitions and the end of extensive service provision by the government look back with some longing at the old days under communism (CIA 2011; Goldman 2003, 2008; McFaul, Stoner-Weiss and Bunce 2010).

FURTHER QUESTIONS

1. Did the judgments that guided your choice seem to be based on the same priorities you applied on Compare in 1 (Acid Test I)?
2. Is it reasonable that many Russians now say they prefer the Russia of the 1980s (Kappa) to the current conditions (Lambda)? ◣

GOAL: PROSPERITY

Strategy

15.2 Evaluate the attempts by the postcommunist states to achieve prosperity through a transition to market economies.

When they were communist regimes, the principal strategy for achieving the goal of the equal distribution of abundant goods and material welfare to the entire population was the *command political economy*, as detailed in Chapter 8. The state and the Communist Party, guided by a comprehensive plan, attempted to control nearly all of society's valued resources. As in "Kappa" (in Compare in 15), these countries did reach relatively high levels on most quality-of-life measures (such as the Human Development Index). Most citizens had access to inexpensive or free health care, education, food, and shelter, and most had economic security against problems such as illness and old age. However, these countries' economic performance (on measures such as GDP per capita) was disappointing. As described in Chapter 8, the rigid planning and limited incentives in these command economies resulted in low productivity, poor-quality products, and a serious mismatch between demand and supply.

Since the early 1990s, most of the PCDCs have attempted to achieve a rapid transition to a market political economy. Private firms produce goods for profit, and the prices of most goods are determined by supply and demand. Central planning has been abandoned, and most state-owned enterprises have been sold to private actors ("privatized") or shut down. In 1990, the proportion of GDP in the private sector ranged from only 5 percent in Russia to 30 percent in Poland, and the average was less than 15 percent. By 2006, GDP in nearly all PCDCs was between 75 and 80 percent private (although Russia was only 65 percent) (Estrin et al. 2009). Twelve of the 18 PCDCs are now among the top half of all (180) countries in economic freedom, led by Estonia at fourteenth (Heritage Foundation 2011).

Performance

During the initial years of transition, most PCDCs experienced a substantial decline in GDP and hyperinflation (inflation averaged higher than 100 percent per year in all but two of the PCDCs) (World Bank 1996: Table A3). The real income of most people dropped substantially, cuts in welfare services were deep, and unemployment soared. The number of people in absolute poverty increased enormously in less than a decade—from about 14 million people just prior to the "fall of communism" in 1988 (4 percent of the region's population) to 147 million in 1996 (40 percent of the population). This is the period of Russia-as-Lambda in Compare in 15.

Since the late 1990s, the economies and the living standards of many people in the PCDCs have improved steadily. Ten of the PCDCs are now among the 27 member states of the EU, and seven others are in various stages of potential membership. As Figure 15.1 indicates, the prosperity of some PCDCs, especially those in Central Europe such as Slovenia, the Czech Republic, Hungary, and Poland, is at a relatively high level, as measured by GDP per capita and HDI figures that place them in the range of some Global North countries. Others are improving more slowly, due to a combination of preexisting conditions and less effective transition to market political economies. This characterizes parts of the former

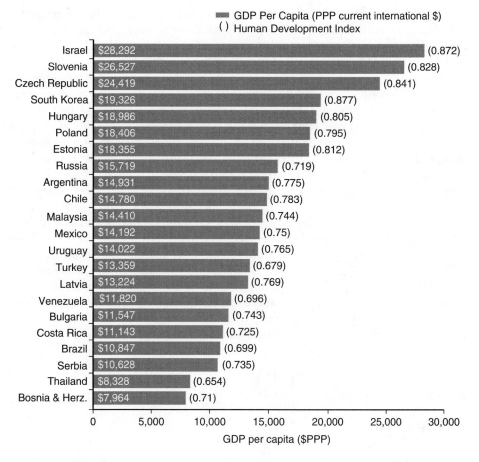

FIGURE 15.1

Prosperity measures for selected transitional developed countries

Source: UNDP (2011)

Soviet Union, including Azerbaijan, Belarus, and Russia ("Mu" in Compare in 15), as well as the PCDCs of Eastern Europe (e.g., Bulgaria, Romania, Serbia). In general, prosperity and optimism about the economic future are more evident among the population living in major cities and among the younger cohorts; poverty and disillusionment are more common for many in nonurban areas and among the older generations, who have lost nearly all the social services and welfare they received under communism.

Challenges

Because their political economies now function like other market systems in the global economy, the postcommunist developed countries face all the formidable challenges to sustaining prosperity that confront the developed countries of the

Global North, as detailed in Chapter 13. Competition for markets and resources is ruthless, flows of capital and labor are difficult to manage, and nonstate actors are hard to control. The PCDC economies have struggled like those in the Global North in the global recession that began in 2008.

Moreover, the ongoing transitions of their political economies generate additional challenges for the PCDCs. First, the state and key economic actors must continue to *streamline their regulatory systems* and *institutionalize free market mechanisms* (e.g., capital markets, business contracts, business law), which did not exist under the command economy. Second, these states must *establish an appropriate level of welfare distribution* for the many people whose material living conditions have declined significantly. These populations were socialized to believe in their right to cradle-to-grave support from the state. Now many face the dual hardship caused by both economic transition and by their governments' drastic reductions of the large state subsidies for food, shelter, health care, education, transportation, and other benefits. Third, the PCDCs must *ensure that the vigorous new group politics does not undermine economic policy making*. Many citizens have used their new democratic rights to vote out of power each set of incumbent leaders and parties, whom they blame for the negative impacts from economic transitions and from the harsh effects of a turbulent global economy. This repeated turnover of government control results in substantial political instability and makes it difficult for any political leadership to implement tough economic policies and retain popular support (Bonker 2006).

GOAL: STABILITY

Strategies

15.3 Assess the efforts by postcommunist states to balance democratic freedoms and political stability.

👁 Watch the **Video** **"The Litvinenko Affair"** at **mypoliscilab.com**

As communist political regimes, a basic assumption in Soviet bloc countries was: prosperity + equality = stability. That is, social and political stability would result because the people were satisfied with the relatively equal distribution of abundant goods and services. Although these countries did have among the world's most equal distributions of wealth and did provide many inexpensive goods and services to all citizens, the major shortcoming in the stability equation was that the systems were unable to produce goods in abundance. The failure of the economy to provide adequate goods was a major source of citizen dissatisfaction.

To ensure stability in the absence of prosperity, these authoritarian, one-party states utilized four key instruments of social control over many aspects of people's lives: (1) the *Communist Party*, whose active members, 10 percent of population, were a watchdog against dissidents; (2) a huge *governmental apparatus* of administrators, police, and others who enforced obedience; (3) *rewards* (e.g., desired jobs, better housing) were allocated to those who were obedient, and *sanctions* (loss of benefits, prison) were imposed on those who resisted; and (4) extensive use of the agents of *political socialization* (e.g., schools, mass social organizations, the media) to drill in communist ideology. Overall, these social controls created a highly stable but oppressive environment for most people.

During the 1980s, opposition to the Communist Party became more open and personal freedoms expanded significantly, with an enormous boost from then Soviet premier Mikhail Gorbachev's policy of *glasnost*—a tolerance of public discussion and criticism of the political, economic, and social systems. Then, in 1989, the citizens in every East European country filled the streets, demanding political and human rights. After decades of repression, the Communist Party leadership capitulated in country after country, lacking either the will or the capacity to retain power. A signal moment was November 9, 1989, when the Berlin Wall, the most notorious symbol of the Iron Curtain, was opened, allowing a joyous reunion of 1 million East and West Berliners. Except in Romania (where events corresponded to a violent revolution from above), the dramatic changes occurred in these countries with so little violence that they are best described as "democratic revolutions" (see Chapter 12). By December 1991, even the Soviet Union "died" and was replaced by 15 independent countries.

These countries adopted new constitutions that established hybrid governments, with a president and a legislature–plus–prime minister selected through (mixed-member) proportional representation electoral systems (see Chapter 7). In most of the hybrids, the president has substantial power, including the right to dismiss the prime minister and cabinet. The presidents have occasionally dismissed governments in response to citizen dissatisfaction with the governments' handling of the major economic and political transitions. These hybrid systems do not have well established traditions yet and the new constitutions are somewhat ambiguous. Thus, there are situations where the power relationships between president and prime minister have become very strained (Schleiter and Morgan-Jones 2009). And in the Russian hybrid, when Putin was forced (by term limits) to leave the presidency, he managed to shift considerable power to his new role as prime minister.

There has been a "freedom divide" among these countries (Puddington 2011). Most of the PCDCs seem to have institutionalized the political structures and processes of democracy. Elections are fair, open, and very competitive, multiple parties hold seats in the legislature, and there are smooth leadership turnovers. The citizens' political rights and civil liberties are extensive, and there is a vigorous political discourse. Table 15.2 shows that 13 of the PCDCs are now classified as "free" by Freedom House (2011), including eight that have already been rated as "consolidated democracies." Macedonia is only "partly free" and is among the six PCDCs characterized as "semi-consolidated democracies" at this point.

In contrast, four (Azerbaijan, Belarus, Kazakhstan, and Russia) are "consolidated authoritarian regimes" that have reverted to state repression and control mechanisms similar to those of the communist era. All are classified as "not free." including several whose ratings have dropped. Since Vladimir Putin's regime began in 2000 and has been extended under Dmitry Medvedev (2008–2012), Russia has steadily reduced democratic practices, political rights, and civil liberties. The three other authoritarian regimes have each had only one or two entrenched leaders since 1990, Soviet-era restrictions on democratic practices such as free speech, freedom of the press, and political opposition, and strong state control of the economy (Freedom House 2011; Shkolnikov 2009).

TABLE 15.2

Democracy Rankings of Postcommunist Developed Countries

Consolidated Democracies	Freedom House Ranking and Score
Estonia	Free: 1.0
Slovenia	Free: 1.0
Latvia	Free: 2.0
Czech Republic	Free: 1.0
Poland	Free: 1.0
Lithuania	Free: 1.0
Slovakia	Free: 1.0
Hungary	Free: 1.0
Semi-Consolidated Democracies	
Bulgaria	Free: 2.0
Romania	Free: 2.0
Croatia	Free: 1.5
Serbia	Free: 2.0
Macedonia	Partly Free: 3.0
Montenegro	Free: 2.5
Consolidated Authoritarian Regimes	
Russia	Not Free: 5.5
Kazakhstan	Not Free: 5.5
Azerbaijan	Not Free: 5.5
Belarus	Not Free: 6.5

Source: Freedom House (2011)

Challenges

Currently, most of the PCDCs face significant destabilizing forces related to social disorder, nationality issues, and globalization. Many of these countries, including Slovenia, Belarus, the Czech Republic, Slovakia, Kazakhstan, and Hungary, still have among the highest levels of income equality in the world (measured by the Gini index of inequality; recall Table 8.1). However, *economic and social inequality* are increasing in almost all of these transitional countries in the absence of communist controls, and the gaps between the rich and poor have become substantial and apparent to everyone in these societies.

Social Disorder

The combination of freewheeling capitalism, the decline in communist-era social controls, and increases in inequality has resulted in a rise in *social disorder*. This is reflected in a decline in citizens' obedience to laws and rules and is particularly evident in the high incidence of crime. In Russia, more than 4,000 mafia crime groups are engaged in widespread extortion, auto theft, drug peddling, burglary, and other criminal activities. In the first five years of postcommunism, for example, reported serious crimes increased 270 percent in Romania, 222 percent in Bulgaria, and 105 percent in Poland (Murphy 1995). While crime rates have now stabilized, countries that were accustomed to almost no violent crime under communism are now attempting to cope with distressing levels of crimes against both people and property. In many regions, the police are either ineffective or corrupt, and citizens live in fear of organized crime, random criminal violence, and even the police (McFaul 1998).

Nationality Conflicts

A few nationality groups, such as the Poles and the East Germans (who were reunited with their West German brothers and sisters in 1990), now live in ethnically homogeneous states. In 1993, Czechoslovakia broke peacefully into two states based on its two main ethnic groups (Czechs and Slovaks). However, *identity politics and ethnonationalism* (recall Chapter 5) threaten the stability of many PCDCs because they have significant minority populations. Marginalized nationality groups are increasingly active in demanding greater autonomy, and the majority group has often responded by aggressively asserting its domination.

Thus, internal nation-based conflict has produced disorder in many PCDCs. Yugoslavia, a complex multiethnic state under communism, became a brutal battleground as different nation-based groups killed more than 250,000 of their neighbors during the 1990s and still struggle with interethnic hostilities despite the breakup of the Balkans into six countries (recall the opening section of Chapter 12). Current nation-based hostility in several countries is particularly directed against the Roma (gypsies) and against those of Russian heritage who live in other PCDCs (because Russians were transplanted to control other parts of the Soviet bloc during communism). Other conflicts that have exploded into separatist violence include several in highly multinational Russia (e.g., Chechnya and Ingushetia). Russia also invaded Georgia in support of the demands for autonomy by the South Ossetians.

Entry into Europe and Global Society

After decades of relative isolation, most PCDCs are now fully engaged with global society. The Iron Curtain had kept the population in, and it had also buffered the people from many of the complex cultural changes that were occurring outside. Unrestricted travel, unlimited media exposure, and the open borders of the 10 PCDCs that joined the European Union have exposed the people to a dizzying and somewhat destabilizing set of new ideas and cultural norms. Many of the younger citizens now identify as "Europeans" rather than giving first loyalty to their country. This can affect their attitudes towards their national political institutions. Ironically, while the authoritarian regimes have maintained substantial control over the flow of people and ideas into their societies, they are also facing destabilizing pressures from the unstoppable influences of globalization, resulting in increasingly strident demands for liberalization among frustrated segments of their populations.

Chechen rebels threaten Russian prisoners of war captured during a bloody battle in Grozny, part of the Chechens' two decade violent struggle for independence. The Chechens are among the nationality groups that have attempted to gain autonomy from Russia after the breakup of the Soviet Union.

GOAL: SECURITY

15.4 Analyze the impact of the fall of the Soviet system on the security of postcommunist states.

In Halford John Mackinder's (1996) famous 19th-century geopolitical analysis, Eastern Europe and western Russia were the essential "heartland": control of that region would ensure world dominance. The region has been a battlefield for the last 200 years, including devastating invasions by the French under Napoleon, during World War I, and by the Germans under Hitler during World War II.

Given this history, the Soviet Union perceived itself to be surrounded by increasingly hostile, anticommunist threats to its survival after World War II. To the east, Japan, a historical military adversary, evolved into a major capitalist world power. To the southeast, China, with its huge population and alternative vision of communism, displayed growing combativeness. To the southwest, the militancy of Islamic fundamentalism presented a clear danger, given its antipathy to communism and the large population of Muslims in the Soviet Union's southwestern regions. To the west were the major capitalist powers, with their deep animosity to the communist systems and with NATO's devastating military (including nuclear) capabilities stretched along almost half of the Soviet bloc's border.

As a consequence, the Soviet Union placed exceptionally high importance on security goals and aimed for unchallengeable military power. To create a buffer zone, the Soviet Union gained control over territory on all sides, annexing some areas and creating a bloc of subservient states in Central and Eastern Europe. The Soviet bloc built the world's most powerful military for conventional warfare, and the Soviet Union had near parity with NATO allies in air power and nuclear capabilities. From the late 1940s until the late 1980s, the cold war rivalry between the Soviet Union and the United States dominated the bipolar international system, spawning a huge military buildup on each side. Soviet leaders from Stalin to Gorbachev opted for guns over butter, spending 9 to 15 percent of national income on defense. This high military expenditure substantially reduced the resources available for economic growth and the distribution of welfare, and is a key reason for the demise of the Soviet system.

The postcommunist period has fundamentally altered the security situation for the PCDCs. Many of the old sovereign states did not even maintain their core security goal, survival. East Germany disappeared, having merged with West Germany in 1990. Yugoslavia fractured into multiple states, and Czechoslovakia split in two. Then in December 1991, the Soviet Union itself disappeared, replaced by 15 states that are based on historical ethnic and regional boundaries.

Ten former members of the Soviet security bloc switched sides, joining their old enemy NATO, despite strong opposition from Russia. Thus most PCDCs are now part of a reliable collective security system led by the United States. In response, Russia has actively rebuilt its military under Putin's leadership, and only the United States and China spend more on total military expenditures (SIPRI 2011). Although diminished from its cold war strength, Russia's military machine still includes a huge standing army and the largest number of stockpiled (14,000) and operational (5,192) nuclear weapons in the world (Federation of American Scientists 2011). Russia's military resurgence, its assertive foreign policy, and its brief war with Georgia in 2008 are viewed with alarm by most of its geopolitical neighbors, including many PCDCs (Aslund and Kuchins 2009; McFaul, Stoner-Weiss and Bunce 2010).

In retrospect, the international system had become relatively secure under the strong bipolar security regime dominated by the United States and the Soviet Union. According to balance-of-power analyses, the current evolution towards a more diffuse, multipolar international system will increase insecurity in the relations among states (see Chapter 11). Relations between Russia (and its allies) and the other PCDCs (and their NATO allies) is one of the new security concerns in the multipolar system.

For the PCDCs in the EU, the ruthless competition in the global marketplace and their economic niches among EU countries require different strategies than those during their previously protected status in the Soviet bloc. And the formidable military and economic power of China, the rise of other countries like India, and the turbulence emanating from the Islamic "Stans" and Middle East all create new security issues for the western-oriented PCDCs. For Russia and its allies, these same factors are a challenge, but they also constitute opportunities to reduce the imbalance of power with the Western bloc. All of the postcommunist developed countries are attempting to adapt to this new security environment.

THE NEWLY INDUSTRIALIZING COUNTRIES

During the past several decades, one group of countries has been particularly successful in attempting the transformation from developing towards developed countries. These countries have been labeled the ***newly industrializing countries (NICs)***.

15.5 Identify the attributes of newly industrialized countries.

✳—Explore the
Comparative
"Development" on
mypoliscilab.com

Some international organizations (e.g., the World Bank) also refer to them as the newly industrializing economies (NIEs). A NIC is distinguished by its economic *transition to a major exporter of manufactured goods and services and by its sustained high economic growth rate.*

The NICs have risen higher than other countries in the Global South on the economic (vertical) dimension in the analytic framework presented in Figure 13.1. To this point, two NICs in Asia (e.g., Singapore, Taiwan) have been so successful in advancing on both the economic and social dimensions that they were "promoted" to the developed countries group in Figure 13.1. Several other Asian NICs (e.g., Malaysia, South Korea) have persistent high levels of economic growth and it is possible that several others (Thailand, China) will soon enter this NIC group in the figure.

A larger group of Latin American countries also are located in the transitional group in Figure 13.1. This includes Argentina, Brazil, Chile, Costa Rica, Mexico, Uruguay, and Venezuela. The discussion below will suggest that these countries are characterized by spurts of strong growth followed by declines and even negative growth. But their overall economic profile fits the NIC model and their levels of social development certainly place them in the transitional country group. A few countries outside these two regions (e.g., Israel, Saudi Arabia, and Turkey) are currently difficult to classify but are arguably NICs based on their location in Figure 13.1. This section focuses primarily on the key political and economic transitions that are occurring in the NICs of Asia and Latin America. Although some commonalities are identified, these two groups are discussed separately.

GOAL: PROSPERITY

Approach

15.6 Distinguish
between Asian
and Latin
American
development
strategies and
assess their
successes.

Asian NICs   The most successful NICs, particularly those in Asia, have pursued prosperity by employing variations on the *developmental state approach* described in Chapter 10: (1) an export-oriented market political economy, but with an activist state whose policies enable firms to be more profitable; (2) close cooperation between firms and government to target niches in which export goods can be sold; and (3) government support of the agrarian sector, including the redistribution of land and encouragement of commercial agriculture.

This approach, adapted from Japan, emphasizes the primacy of economic development relative to political or social development (Fallows 1995; Johnson 1996; Simone 2001). State expenditures are directed towards improving the economic infrastructure (e.g., transportation systems, communications networks) and educating the labor force. Government policy encourages savings and investment rather than consumerism, and it limits wage rates for workers. Only as economic development reaches high levels is there a shift towards policies that enable citizens to acquire more consumer goods and that increase the state's welfare distribution to less-advantaged citizens. Many analysts conclude that the success of the developmental state strategy in the Asian NICs is associated with a social and political culture that is influenced by ethical-religious philosophies such as Buddhism, Taoism,

👁—Watch the
Video
"The Mexican
Peso Crisis" at
mypoliscilab.com

and most notably Confucianism (Compton 2000; Fallows 1995; Focus in 4). These norms emphasize hard work, acceptance of authority, and subordination of personal needs to collective goals.

While the broad strategy of the Asian NICs is similar, there are significant differences among these states. For example, the South Korean government has supported and protected a few very large national firms called *chaebols* (e.g., Hyundai, Goldstar, Samsung), which produce a broad diversity of manufactured goods. In contrast, Malaysia (recall the opening of Chapter 13) has encouraged small domestic firms, has allowed more extensive involvement of foreign multinational corporations, especially from the United States and Japan, as it has focused on manufacturing, particularly electronics components, and has balanced this with exports of commodities, particularly petroleum and wood.

Latin American NICs Government economic policies in most Latin American NICs have been less interventionist than those in Asia. Many Latin American countries adopted a version of the developmental state or neoliberal approach only in the last several decades, after abandoning statist strategies (Compare in 8 on Mexico; Triesman 2004). The majority are in the top one-third of countries on economic freedom rankings. The governments have generally been less involved in firms' production decisions, less active in agrarian reform and rural land redistribution, and less controlling regarding the role of multinational corporations in their economies than the Asian NICs. The vast economic system of the United States, the dominant power in the hemisphere, has had considerable impact on economic development in Latin America for generations, and especially on Mexico, an impact that became even greater when Mexico joined Canada and the U.S. in NAFTA in 1994.

Most Latin American NICs have a substantial endowment of natural resources and farmlands. Thus, their governments have generally attempted to balance their development policies to support not only manufacturing and service industries but also the extraction and processing of commodities (e.g., foods, oil, minerals). The long history of active electoral politics in the Latin American NICs has had numerous consequences for economic policy, including more extensive distribution of social welfare goods by the state to secure votes and fewer restrictions on trade union activities.

Performance

Asian NICs The high rates of economic growth are a distinguishing feature of the Asian NICs. The steady upward trajectories of their economies are reflected in Figure 15.2. Malaysia and Thailand, for example, have increased per capita income by a factor of five between 1970 and 2010 and South Korea's rate is even more remarkable (UNDP 2011). Since 1980, they are among the fastest growing economies in the world. All achieved positive trade surpluses and high levels of capital accumulation, as their firms became competitive in the international marketplace across a wide range of goods (Mahbubani 2008). Although the Asian economic crises of the late 1980s, late 1990s and then the global economic

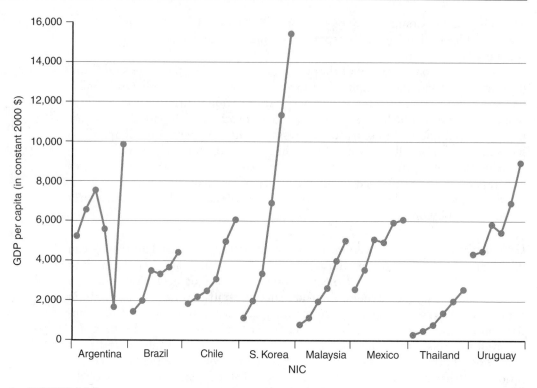

FIGURE 15.2

Changes in prosperity measures for selected NICs, 1960–2009

Source: indexmundi.com

slowdown since 2008 did dampen growth of these NICs somewhat, South Korea still has the highest growth rate among the NICs and Malaysia trails only Chile (Table 15.3).

High growth has translated into substantial improvements in the wealth and quality of life in the NICs. South Korea currently has the highest GDP per capita (PPP) among all the transitional developed countries. It also has the highest Human Development Index score and Malaysia's HDI has increased rapidly in the recent period. The recent phenomenal growth rates in China and Vietnam have led some to classify them among the Asian NICs; but their overall national levels of development (measured as GDP/capita and social development) still place them below the transitional developed countries group in Figure 13.1. The severe declines in currency and asset value and in investment that the Asian NICs suffered during the regional and global recessions have debunked the "magic" of the Asian NICs as invulnerable engines of economic growth; but many developing countries in other regions continue to emulate the Asian NICs strategy, although without similar sustained success (Winters 1998).

TABLE 15.3

Economic Growth and Inflation in Selected Transitional Developed Countries, 1995–2009

	GDP Growth, 1995–2009*	Inflation, 1995–2009*
Belarus	6.44	104.33%
Estonia	5.69	7.8
Kazakhstan	5.43	22.69
Poland	4.69	7.84
Slovakia	4.51	6.27
Croatia	3.87	3.65
South Korea	3.84	3.56
Bulgaria	3.83	88.74
Russia	3.61	34.21
Romania	3.37	32.96
Hungary	3.09	10.38
Chile	3.02	N/A
Czech Republic	2.79	4.49
Malaysia	2.76	2.63
Turkey	2.47	42.66
Costa Rica	2.4	12.31
Thailand	2.33	3.34
Uruguay	2.23	12.85
Argentina	2.04	5.98
Israel	1.72	4.07
Brazil	1.54	11.04
Venezuela	1.01	32.1
Mexico	1.0	11.64
Postcommunist Developed Countries	Newly Industrializing Countries	Others

*Average annual rate

Source: World Bank (2011)

Latin American NICs Most Latin American NICs range from $11,000–$15,000 in GDP/capita (PPP) (Figure 15.1). Figure 15.2 and Table 15.3 help reveal the general pattern that the Latin American NICs, apart from Chile, have not been able to sustain rates of economic growth comparable to the Asian NICs since 1960. In the last two decades, most Latin American NICs have tamed hyperinflation but economic growth has been more up and down, averaging less than 3 percent annually. Chile and Costa Rica have the highest growth rates, but most averaged only 1.0–2.5 percent per year (Table 15.3).

Many Latin American NICs experience recurring periods of economic decline and inflation, rather like their less-developed regional neighbors (recall Chapter 14). Mexico suffered a "peso crisis" in 1994, Brazil's economy has been highly volatile (see Focus in 15), and the economies of Argentina and Uruguay dropped precipitously in 2002. Argentina is indicative of the up-down pattern. In 2002, Argentina was in a severe period of negative growth and unemployment, defaulted on $130 billion in bonds, devalued its currency and was in deep economic crisis. After a bumpy decade, the economy exploded in 2010 and 2011, driven by manufacturing and food exports, and has averaged about 9 percent growth. However, high inflation (25 percent) and the end of various government subsidies could lead to another steep decline (Kraul 2011).

The core causes of these economic problems in the Latin American NICs are disputed, but many analysts attribute them to the same sorts of weaknesses listed above for PCDCs such as Russia. Privatization, corruption, international competition, and exploitation by multinationals and "crony capitalists" have taken a severe toll on the political economies of Latin America (Weintraub 2009). As the Latin American NIC economies have been buffeted by the forces of globalization and high economic volatility, their governments have implemented structural adjustment programs required by the International Monetary Fund. Cuts in government spending and restrictions on the money supply have resulted in increased unemployment and reductions in government services.

Some citizens in the Latin American NICS enjoy an extremely high standard of living, many material possessions, and quality services (e.g., health care, education). Argentina, Chile, and Uruguay have HDI scores above .750. However, many people in most Latin American NICs have suffered a serious reduction in their standards of living over the last three decades. Those who are very poor experience a life as harsh as that in many of the developing countries. In addition, the inequalities of income and wealth in several of the NICs are among the most severe in the world and are getting worse. Brazil, Panama, and Chile are among the 20 countries with the world's highest levels of wealth inequality, and every Latin American NIC except Argentina and Venezuela is among the world's one-third most unequal countries (CIA 2011).

These are some of the reasons for the concern for citizens' social welfare and the active opposition to neoliberalism and globalization that are increasingly evident in Latin America and are voiced by many major leaders in the region. Its most prominent leader, Venezuela's Hugo Chavez, has promoted "twenty-first-century socialism" as an alternative development path for Latin America. It emphasizes stronger state engagement in the political economy, with increased state ownership of major resources, more extensive redistribution of benefits to the less advantaged, and a resistance to key aspects of economic globalization. The issues associated with economic liberalization policies pervade not only the strategies of industrialization but also the dynamics of political stability and democratization in the Latin American NICs (Wiarda and Kline 2007).

FOCUS IN 15 | Order and Progress in Brazil: Sometimes

The motto on the Brazilian flag is "Order and Progress." The vision of order and progress has guided much of Brazilian policy since the founding of the republic in 1889, but recent history has cast doubt on its ability to sustain this vision. Brazil is the fifth largest country (in area) in the world, with a population of 200 million and vast natural resources. In many ways, Brazil reflects the promise of development in the 21st century—but it also epitomizes the troubles associated with that quest.

PROGRESS

From the mid-1960s to the mid-1970s, the state took the lead in guiding Brazil's industrialization, emphasizing import substitution and promoting exports. The involvement of international capital and foreign corporations was encouraged. The results were impressive. Brazil's economic development was praised worldwide as a "miracle," with yearly growth averaging 10 percent. Brazil's economy is now larger than that of all the rest of South America and is the tenth largest in the world. Since 2000, its average annual growth has been a respectable 3.6 percent, with strong performance in recent years. It is a leader among the developing countries in the production of many goods, including agricultural exports such as coffee, sugar, and cocoa; minerals such as tin, gold, iron ore, and bauxite; and industrial goods such as textiles, cement, automobiles, weapons, and machinery. Since 1970, life expectancy has increased 12 years (to age 72), infant mortality has dropped to one-third its former level, and adult literacy has risen to 90 percent.

ORDER

Politically, Brazil is a constitutional democracy. The government is a federal republic, with an elected president who has dominant power over the bicameral National Congress. It has a multiparty system, universal and compulsory voting, an independent judiciary, and a partly free press. Its Freedom House

President Dilma Rousseff has continued the conditional aid programs begun by Lula da Silva that provide substantial government support to poor Brazilian families who keep their children in school and participate in regular health care visits and disease immunization.

rating is "free," and its citizens enjoy relatively high levels of political rights and civil liberties. There have been two decades of competitive and fair elections, including the smooth transition to the presidency of Dilma Rousseff in 2011 after 79 percent voter turnout. The large state bureaucracy has maintained social and political order, with minimal class-based conflict, and Brazil is often cited as one of the

(Continued)

world's most successful multiracial societies. A strong military ensures Brazil's security and sovereignty.

PROGRESS?

The economic miracle in the 1970s was built on a weak base of economic statism; fueled by debt-led growth; and deeply dependent on external support for finance capital, technology, and markets. Much of the growth was in the 600 state-owned companies, many of which were extremely inefficient and eventually went bankrupt. The emphasis on industrial development has had many negative consequences, including a decline of the agricultural sector resulting in 2 million landless peasants and the need to import basic foods.

After years of miracle growth, the economy came close to collapse in the early 1980s and again in the mid-1990s. The average annual growth rate from 1995 to 2009 has been only 1.5 percent per year, which is actually an improvement on the entire period since 1975. During the 1990s, hyperinflation was also a problem (reaching a staggering high of 2,864 percent in 1990). Brazil's foreign debt is the third largest among the transitional countries and Global South—more than $310 billion. Under structural adjustment pressures from the international banking community, reductions in social spending leave almost half of Brazil's huge population with a very low standard of living. Brazil has the world's tenth most unequal distribution of income, with wealth heavily concentrated in the urban upper and upper-middle classes.

ORDER?

Since 1930, the military has deposed six top political leaders. The military, supported by the middle class, seized power most recently in a 1964 coup against an elected government that was judged too sympathetic to the needs of the many rural and urban poor. The military government was repressive and ruthless, crushing leftist opposition, censoring the press, and compiling one of South America's worst records of human rights abuses. An elected president took office in 1985 after 21 years of authoritarian military rule, and a new constitution was implemented in 1988. Since that time, the recurrent economic problems have provoked a huge rise in social disorder. Crime rates are extremely high; urban riots are frequent, especially in the huge *favelas* located in the cosmopolitan cities; and there is violence between peasants and landholders, who are disputing the government's announced but unfilled promises of land reform.

One recent president (Collor de Mello) was forced to resign due to a massive corruption scandal. When the next president (Fernando Henrique Cardoso) was elected in 1995, the citizens reflected their disgust with government: One in three Brazilians abstained from voting in the presidential election, and blank (protest) votes outnumbered votes cast for any senate candidate in 22 of the 26 states. Brazil scores only 3.7 on a 10-point corruption scale (where 10 is very clean). Like prior administrations, President Rousseff's government was immediately embroiled in corruption scandals, and five Cabinet ministers were among those fired in her first nine months.

Policy making is stymied by a fractious legislature composed of more than a dozen major political parties, many of whose members actually change parties between elections and are primarily loyal to their regional political bosses. The Brazilian flag's proud announcement of "Order and Progress" flaps ironically over the building where these politicians attempt to govern (CIA 2011; Goodwin 2008; Transparency International 2011; and World Bank 2011.)

FURTHER FOCUS

1. Based on this account, what might be the main reason why less than one in three Brazilians is satisfied with how democracy works in their country?
2. What policies might help Brazil achieve the GDP per capita and HDI score of a developed country?

GOAL: STABILITY
Asian NICs

The governments of the Asian NICs have been particularly concerned about maintaining a highly stable and orderly social system. Political conflicts, social disorder, and labor agitation are viewed as serious impediments to economic development and contrary to the Confucian cultural norms about harmonious social relations that continue to be influential in these countries. Thus, from independence until recently, governments in the Asian NICs were illiberal democracies—centralized, authoritarian, and repressive (Simone 2001). For example, South Korea was dominated by three autocratic presidents for 40 years, between 1948 and 1987. Malaysia's Mahathir Mohammed retired in 2003 after 22 years in power. The remarkable public policies to promote stability in former-NIC Singapore were described in Focus in 13. Some countries in the region have been less successful in maintaining order. Thailand has suffered nearly 20 successful or attempted coups since 1932. The most recent military coup occurred in 2006, after an election boycotted by all major opposition parties.

> **15.7** Analyze factors that encourage political stability in newly industrialized countries.

Latin American NICs

Strong political leaders and a hegemonic class elite were also characteristic of most Latin American NICs in the second half of the 20th century, apart from consistently democratic Costa Rica. Argentina, Chile, Uruguay, and Venezuela alternated between periods of rule by a civilian government and by authoritarian military regimes that, in most cases, came to power by violence and ruled repressively. Mexico was dominated nationally by a single, socially conservative political party, PRI, from 1929 until 2001.

Broadly, this political authoritarianism in Latin America has been linked with a traditional social structure that was based on hierarchical class strata and a dominant ruling class whose members controlled the economic and political systems. Political-cultural norms also included popular acceptance of leaders, often with a military background (*caudillos*) in an earlier era, who exert extremely strict control over the political system. Thus, the political cultures have typically assumed that there would be electoral democracies, but that the regime would be hegemonic, involving the alternation between elites rather than open competition among truly opposing groups (Castenada 2010; Lozada 2003).

Democratization?

By the late 1980s and early 1990s, most NICs had begun a process of democratization that is proceeding at varying rates in different countries. Vigorous and competitive democratic politics reemerged in the 1990s in place of repressive regimes in Argentina, Chile, Malaysia, and Uruguay. With the 2000 election of Vicente Fox, even PRI in Mexico lost its one-party dominance of the national political system (recall Chapter 7). In 1992, South Korea held its first fair and actively contested presidential election with a genuine multiparty system. Freedom House (2011) classifies South Korea and all the Latin American NICs except Venezuela as "free." Malaysia's strict censorship laws and restraints on oppositional politics are some of the reasons it is only "partly free." Thailand is also "partly free" after a controversial military coup in 2006, but elected its first women prime minister, who intends to lead a broad coalition government, in a generally fair election in 2011.

Along with positive effects, the combination of democratization, greater prosperity, and economic volatility has generated forces of instability in many NICs. One specific source of instability comes from those groups that have been most negatively affected by cutbacks in government welfare and by the recurring periods of economic crisis. A second source is the minority ethnic groups in many of these countries, who also tend to be the poorest citizens. Thus frustration and political violence are evident from the large numbers of poor and politically marginalized groups, such as the peasants in the Chiapas region of Mexico, students and labor union members in South Korea, and the Indian populations in Brazil and Chile (recall the Maputo in Chapter 9). Criminal groups have also created very high levels of violence in such NICs as Brazil and Mexico. Instability that occurs just outside the borders of a NIC can spill over into disruption and violence inside that NIC, as in Malaysia (from Indonesia), South Korea (from North Korea), and Venezuela (from Colombia). The mix of economic volatility, inequality, and widespread political disillusionment continues to generate serious challenges to the stability of many of the NICs.

The probability of instability increases where the dissatisfaction of the poor is not counteracted by the middle classes who, in many Latin American NICs in particular, offer little support for their political systems (Colburn 2002; Torcal and Montero 2006). There are numerous examples of this instability: an attempted coup is part of the continuing middle class unrest regarding the authoritarian style of populist President Hugo Chavez in Venezuela (2002); two recent Costa Rican presidents have been jailed for corruption; rioting in Argentina (2002) resulted in the succession of five "presidents" in less than three weeks; and the middle classes display little enthusiasm for the political regime, as evident in Mexico and Brazil (Focus in 15; Castenada 2010; Lozada 2003). Thus, in 2011, less than half of those surveyed in Argentina, Brazil, Mexico, and Venezuela indicated they were "satisfied" with the way democracy was working in their country (Latinobarometro 2011).

GOAL: SECURITY

Asian NICs

15.8 Characterize the types of security threats that newly industrializing countries in Asia and Latin America face.

Despite their effective policies to promote internal stability, the Asian NICs operate in a region where there are significant external threats to security. Japan brutally occupied most of these countries during World War II (and, in the case of Korea, from 1905). South Korea has the particular challenge of huge differences in political economy and ideology in dealing with its militaristic brothers and sisters in North Korea, a conflict that exploded into the Korean War (1950–1953). Despite recent discussion of reunification, tensions remain high, especially with the development of North Korea's nuclear weapons capabilities.

Malaysia (like Thailand) is an active member of the Association of Southeast Asian Nations (ASEAN), a collective security agreement among most countries in the region, including many that are adjacent to it. From a broader perspective, the Asian NICs perceive China, Russia, and Japan as major powers in the region that might have geopolitical designs on them. These three countries rank second, third, and sixth, respectively, in the world in total military expenditures. With the exception of South Korea, none of the Asian NICs has sufficient military power to resist the advances of a strong country. Yet Malaysia and even South Korea also rely on the protection of an interested "big brother" (e.g., Great Britain, the United States) or the international security regime (e.g., the United Nations) to provide sufficient military power to protect their borders. The Asian economic crisis of the late 1990s and the recent worldwide recession are clear indicators that these transitional countries are all extensively connected to the global economy, resulting in considerable economic dependence on key actors such as China, the European Union, Japan, the United States, and the International Monetary Fund.

● Watch the Video "Drug Policy in Mexico" at mypoliscilab.com

Latin American NICs

The borders of Latin American states were established in the 19th century and have been relatively stable for more than 150 years. While there have been occasional border issues and political disagreements between the Latin American NICs and their neighbors in recent decades, these rarely reach the level of militarized disputes. Interstate war involving these states was rare in the 20th century. While the NICs' considerable military strength could be deployed for protection against neighboring states, it has been more actively engaged in maintaining internal order, either by supporting the political leadership or by overthrowing it and seizing political power. (Costa Rica is the exception, in that it has no standing military).

Some of the most significant threats to security have been from the former colonial powers that limited the Latin American NICs' autonomy and freedom of action, particularly the United States, Spain, and Great Britain. The NIC's relationship with the powerful United States, which has a strong economic and political presence over the entire hemisphere, has dominated the security concerns of many of these NICs. Venezuela's Chavez has taken the lead in promoting new directions in foreign policy that involve ties with countries that are antagonistic to the United States, such as Cuba and Iran. The most notable conventional war since 1950 that involved a NIC is the Falklands War between Argentina and Great Britain in 1982. This conflict resulted from the Argentine military government's attempt to seize islands off its coast that remained under the colonial dominion of Britain. Argentina's defeat in a short war, like the deep penetration into Latin American economies by the developed countries and their financial institutions, was a reminder that dependency and subordination can persist in the postcolonial period, even for relatively strong NICs.

THE FUTURE OF THE TRANSITIONAL DEVELOPED COUNTRIES

While the two sets of countries discussed in this chapter are quite different from each other, most of these countries-in-transition share both optimism and uncertainty about their futures. These countries have experienced substantial political, social, and economic development in recent decades, yet these development dynamics could disrupt the relative stability and prosperity they have enjoyed.

15.9 Predict the success of the development strategies of the postcommunist states and the newly industrializing countries.

The Postcommunist Developed Countries

Most PCDCs are attempting to make dramatic transformations, having abandoned political institutions, a political culture, and a political economy that provided generations of citizens with stability and security, although with disappointing levels of prosperity. Unlike the Asian NICs, where economic development preceded political democratization, most of the PCDCs are engaged in a simultaneous transition to both democratic politics and a market economy. Coping with both forms of change at once can be especially disruptive. The citizens in the postcommunist developed countries have high expectations about the standard of living their governments should provide. Thus, there is a particular risk of an intolerable gap emerging between expectations and reality in the achievement of prosperity, stability, and security (recall the J-curve theory in Chapter 12).

Shifts to a market political economy and a democratic political system require extensive institutional adaptation and citizen tolerance. The PCDCs that began the process with the highest levels of economic development and the greatest population homogeneity are in Central Europe or the Baltics. They have been particularly successful in "harmonizing" their systems with other countries in the European Union. In most of these countries that are now part of the EU, liberal democracy and civil society are functioning well, the private economy has grown relatively strong, and the probability of further improvements in prosperity and quality of life seems high. Some are on a trajectory to rise into the most developed country group in Figure 13.1 within a decade.

Political leadership and the political system are generally under more pressure in Russia and other PCDCs outside the EU, where the levels of prosperity and stability have been disappointing in the postcommunist period. The economic decline has been so severe that some European postcommunist countries (e.g., Albania, the Ukraine) that still remain relatively high on social development have dropped into the developing world range in Figure 13.1, at least temporarily. Despite some economic surges, Russia and several other countries have drifted back into authoritarianism. Inequality and economic hardships, combined with weakened economic safety nets, further heighten the challenges facing these countries, where the upward transition is uncertain. The direction of the transition of Russia—huge, resource rich, influential, assertive—is of critical importance for the region and even for the international system.

The NICs

Several of the NICs (e.g., South Korea, Chile), rather like the leading PCDCs, seem to be on a promising trajectory to close the gap with the more developed countries in achieving prosperity, stability, and security. However, for most of the emerging NICs, current efforts at transition to a consistently healthy economic system and to full political democracy will result in a mix of positive and negative outcomes. Economic growth and development offer the possibility of rising standards of living for a larger proportion of the population as the market generates more products.

To the extent that their political economies become more diversified and resilient, the emerging NICs should also have increased control over their destiny in the global economy. Yet the uncertainties and speed of change in the global economy are extremely high, and thus the transitions in the NICs might be favorable or unfavorable. The sudden and precipitous decline in the economic fortunes of many Asian NICs in the late 1990s and the ups and downs of the economies of many of the Latin American NICs are compelling evidence that economic growth is reversible and that its foundations can be substantially less solid than they appear. Few of these transitional countries have escaped crony capitalism, dependency, and overspeculation in currencies, property, and stocks, and thus they have suffered setbacks, especially during the recent global recession.

Deepening democratization and stronger civil societies now exist in many NICs. These factors provide increased resistance to a return to authoritarian politics, although the traditional appeal of such politics remains among key sectors in these societies. Among the greatest challenges facing policy makers in the NICs are sustaining solid economic growth and responding to the aspirations of the population, especially where poverty is widespread and inequality remains high.

Next?

There are promising signs that democratic practices are becoming more deeply institutionalized and that economic growth can be achieved in many of the transitional developed countries. However, the transitions to full democratization and economic development are complex and entail considerable disruption and dislocation. It is evident that no one fully understands how to sustain solid economic growth in the current international environment, and thus prosperity in the transitional countries is vulnerable to many forces that their leaders cannot control. Most of the countries examined in this chapter are likely to confront periods when false steps, political decay, disruptions from the external environment, or bad luck could severely challenge their pursuit of prosperity, security, and stability. Some will achieve the high levels of economic and social development of the developed countries. Each of these transitional countries strives to be in that group, sooner rather than later, later rather than never.

SO . . .

We have explored complex questions about politics in this book, and sometimes, despite our desire for clarity and closure, there is no straightforward answer. It is quite possible that this is both the best and worst of times in the political world, and that there are grounds for both hope and despair. That is our Final Debate.

Many people look to their political system and its leaders to provide effective solutions in a complex world. But many also seem to think that political acts are a major source of obstacles preventing their achievement of goals. This book's central objective has been to increase your understanding of the political world through the discussions and many examples that, hopefully, have helped you (to use Popper's expression from Chapter 1) "to see more clearly than before."

Voltaire observed, "If we believe absurdities, we shall commit atrocities." The political world is full of disagreement, hyperbole, and ruthless competition. Political science cannot necessarily make the world a better place; its primary role

✓•⎯ Study and **Review** the **Post-Test & Chapter Exam** at **mypoliscilab.com**

is to increase our understanding about how politics works. Such understanding can be the basis of insights: about different conceptions of how politics should be organized, about the basis of any real political disagreements that require response, about mechanisms for conflict resolution, and about how to organize ourselves in the pursuit of specific (private, group, national, or global) interests within a framework of the common good.

As individuals, we often feel powerless in the face of the massive power mobilized in the political world. But every individual—even you!—can affect what happens. The widely-celebrated democratic ideals are based on the assumption that people, individually and collectively, can make a difference. First, if you approach political questions with knowledge, insight, and sensitivity, you can better understand how to think and act in the political world. Second, you can communicate your own political demands and supports in order to influence the policies that are made by actors in the political system. Third, you can become a political activist—as a shaper of public opinion, a leader of a political group, or a public official. What is your personal strategy to act in ways that increase the likelihood that this really does become "the best of times"? The American novelist F. Scott Fitzgerald observed: "One should be able to see that things are hopeless and yet be determined to make them otherwise." In the political world, things are not hopeless unless people like you fail to think, to understand, and to act.

▶ THE FINAL DEBATE | What Time Is It?

Novelist Charles Dickens opens *A Tale of Two Cities* with his famous observation: "It was the best of times, it was the worst of times. It was the age of wisdom, it was the age of foolishness. . . . It was the spring of hope, it was the winter of despair." Many people might consider this an apt description of the political world early in the second decade of the 21st century. As you reach the end of this book, it is reasonable for you to consider what *you* now think about the political world. How would you characterize the political world today? How does it affect *you*?

IT IS THE WORST OF TIMES

- There is now far greater possibility of the use of weapons of mass destruction than at any point in human history. Our weapons arsenals have far more power and efficiency than ever before, and a few of the 4,800 operational nukes could

literally end most life on Earth. Not only is there a proliferation of governments that can deploy dangerous weapons, but now other, more reckless actors, including rogue states and terrorist groups, are also able to either steal or manufacture nuclear, chemical, or biological weapons that can do massive harm.

- Our applications of technology are out of control. The development and uses of many technologies are often driven by self-serving motives, short-term thinking, and indifference to their negative impacts. It is no coincidence that the huge expansion of technological capacity has occurred during a period in which humans have killed far more of their race than at any other time in history, environmental degradation has reached frightening levels, the loss of community and social trust is severe, and global inequalities are at their starkest levels.

(Continued)

- Many governments seem incapable of effective governance—that is, they seem unable to make and implement wise policy decisions that respond to the complex demands presented by diverse groups with conflicting agendas and different ideologies. Governments are increasingly constrained by insufficient global resources to satisfy all needs. While more countries are democracies, this situation has not led to beneficial increases in political knowledge, participation, or commitment to democratic principles. And contemporary political institutions have not changed the underlying reality that power corrupts.
- The complexity and interdependency of national economic systems have created a volatility and fragility that have resulted in economic downturns that are more rapid, deeper, and more difficult to correct. The new global economy makes it almost impossible for a government to manage its own economy or to protect it from severe disruptions.
- Globalization has also undermined the capacity of governments to protect their economies from manipulation by global capital and multinational corporations, to protect their workers from the loss of jobs, or even to protect their national cultural norms and values from being undermined by outside influences that are alien and undesirable. Both the clash of civilizations between hostile worldviews and the intolerance among nation-based identity groups seem to be generating more and more dangerous conflicts.
- *The bottom line: We live in a world of uncertainty and insecurity where the general welfare of humankind is not nurtured or protected.*

IT IS THE BEST OF TIMES

- The danger of a catastrophic nuclear war between the United States and the Soviet Union, whether intentional or accidental, is no longer a grave risk. All the major nuclear powers have actually reduced their stockpiles. Since the end of the cold war, the United Nations has been much more active in collective peacekeeping operations, and there are now comparatively few interstate wars.

The fact that democracies do not fight with each other is another positive factor as an increasing majority of countries embrace democracy.
- Technology (i.e., applied knowledge) in its many forms has vastly expanded human powers of control and production. With wise policies from our governments to guide the development and application of technologies, we have the capacity to provide sufficient resources to ensure that every human being has the food, health, knowledge, and material goods for a long and satisfying life.
- Democracy and political institutionalization have spread to more political systems than ever. As citizens experience the value of open political discussion and of selecting their leaders in fair and competitive elections, they become more engaged and take more responsibility for dealing with the political issues in their country and the world. They demand more effective governance from political actors, and they support leaders who further the goals of prosperity, stability, and security.
- The new global economy has increased the quality, affordability, and accessibility of almost every good and service that people need. Worldwide, today's "average person" enjoys a material standard of living that far surpasses that of any previous era.
- Globalization has increased richness and breadth of our experiences and broadened our identity as citizens of the world. We share information and ideas, trade goods and services, and recognize that what happens everywhere has consequences for our own welfare. The incentives and interdependency encouraging us all to get along have never been greater.
- *The bottom line: More people live longer and with a higher quality of life than at any point in history.*

MORE QUESTIONS . . .

1. If you were to judge this debate, what would be your decision on which side is more compelling?
2. *How about you?* Given the political world described in this Debate, throughout this book, and in your broader experience, do you expect that things will be better or worse for *you* over the next several decades? Why?

KEY CONCEPTS

crony capitalism   417
developmental state approach   426
newly industrializing countries
   (NICs)   425

postcommunist developed countries
   (PCDCs)   415
transitional developed countries   414

FOR FURTHER CONSIDERATION

1. Why has Russia not followed the path towards democracy that seems so successful in most of the other postcommunist developed countries?
2. Under what, if any, conditions might the cold war be revived?
3. Develop an argument for including any of the NICs in the group of more developed countries considered in Chapter 13.
4. Is there any element in the NIC development strategy that seems particularly difficult to implement in countries outside Asia?

FOR FURTHER READING

Alexander, James. (2000). *Political Culture in Post-Communist Russia: Formlessness and Recreation in a Traumatic Transition*. New York: St. Martin's. From detailed studies of two Russian towns, the author offers an illuminating explanation of the difficulties associated with the "traumatic transition" from authoritarianism to a more liberal democratic political culture and the continuing impacts of broader Russian cultural traditions.

Fallows, James. (1995). *Looking at the Sun: The Rise of the New East Asian Economic and Political System*. New York: Pantheon. A readable and insightful analysis of the interplay among political culture, politics, and political economy in the Asian NICs during their takeoff period.

Flynn, Norman. (2000). *Miracle to Meltdown in Asia*. New York: Oxford University Press. The rise and sudden crisis in the Asian NICs are thoughtfully analyzed, with particular attention to the balance of power among the market, cronyism, and authoritarianism in governing the state and guiding the political economy.

Freedom House. (2011). *Nations in Transit 2011* http://www.freedomhouse.org. Each year, Freedom House publishes a book with chapter-length descriptions of the politically-relevant developments in each PCDC, as well as the other countries that emerged from the Soviet Empire.

Goldman, Marshall. (2008). *Petrostate: Putin, Power and the New Russia*. Oxford: Oxford University Press. An analysis of the clever actions by Vladimir Putin and other Russian leaders to renew the country's power and global position, primarily by exploiting its oil resources.

Lie, John. (1998). *Han Unbound: The Political Economy of South Korea*. Stanford, CA: Stanford University Press. A sociology professor born in South Korea offers a personal and academic exploration of the remarkable social, economic and political developments during the transformation of South Korea, one of the original Asian Tigers.

Mahbubani, Kishore. (2008). *The New Asian Hemisphere: the Irresistible Shift of Global Power*. New York: Public Affairs. A carefully developed and rather persuasive argument that the 21st century, like most earlier centuries before the last several, will be dominated by the countries of Asia.

Mankoff, Jeffrey. (2009). *Russian Foreign Policy: The Return to Power Politics.* Lanham, MD: Rowman & Littlefield. The author explores the evolving and increasingly aggressive strategy of Putin and Russia to reassert itself in its region and then globally through diplomacy, trade, and military strength.

McFaul, Michael, Kathryn Stoner-Weiss, and Valerie Bunce. (2010). *Democracy and Authoritarianism in the Postcommunist World.* New York: Cambridge University Press. Three leading scholars of the region provide a rich analysis of the patterns of political and social transition in the PCDCs.

Oppenheim, Lois Hecht. (2007). *Politics in Chile: Socialism, Authoritarianism and Market Democracy.* 3rd Ed. Boulder, CO: Westview Press. The transitions in politics and political economy in Chile, arguably the most successful Latin American NIC, are described for the period since 1970, from Allende's socialism through Pinochet's authoritarianism to the current rise towards developed country status.

Simone, Vera. (2001). *The Asian Pacific: Political and Economic Development in a Global Context.* 2nd ed. New York: Longman. A thorough comparative study of the political and economic development of the 15 countries of East and Southeast Asia, with particularly strong treatment of China, Japan, and the Asian NICs.

Thomas, Robert. (1999). *The Politics of Serbia in the 1990s.* New York: Columbia University Press. An interesting approach to understanding the political dynamics and power struggles in Serbia, the key protagonist in the chaotic Balkans, with an analysis of what was being said (as well as done) by the key actors, especially the late Slobodan Milosevic.

True, Jacqui. (2003). *Gender, Globalization, and Postsocialism: The Czech Republic After Communism.* New York: Columbia University Press. A rich combination of the study of the dynamics of change in a postcommunist society with the way in which gender roles are affecting those changes and being changed by them, all within the context of globalization.

Wiarda, Howard J. and Harvey Kline. (2007). A Concise Introduction to Latin American Politics and Development. 2nd Ed. Boulder, CO: Westview Press. A very solid book covering exactly what the title suggests, including political culture, political parties and interest groups, class and politics, political economy, and so on with a primary focus on the Asian NIC countries.

ON THE WEB

http://www.aseansec.org/index.asp

On the official Web site of the Association of Southeast Asian Nations, there are information and documents relevant to ASEAN, news about the Asian NICs, as well as other countries in the region, and somewhat self-serving Web pages constructed by each member state.

http://lanic.utexas.edu

The Latin American Network Information Center, hosted by the University of Texas, Austin, provides a vast number of Internet-based information sources about the politics, economics, culture, and other areas of the Latin American NICs as well as other countries in the region.

http://www.tol.cz

Transitions Online provides detailed information regarding political and cultural issues relevant to these postcommunist developed states.

http://www.themoscowtimes.com/index.php
An online daily English-language newspaper published in Moscow that provides a perspective on the politics and society of Russia.

http://www.europeanforum.net
The European Forum for Democracy and Solidarity offers country-by-country information on politics and economics for various social democratic parties, including the postcommunist developed countries.

Political Analysis

The mind rests in explanation.

—Aristotle

Chapter 1 suggested that you are often exposed to knowledge claims about the political world. Focus in 1 explained how you might develop a political analysis to assess the claim that younger adults have less political knowledge than older adults. Suppose you heard the claim that "in a democracy, men are more likely to vote than women." If the 1976 data in Table 1 were presented as evidence, would you be satisfied that the claim is correct?

The United States is a democracy, and a presidential election seems like a legitimate instance of voting. The table indicates that a higher proportion of men than women voted in the 1976 presidential election. But you would probably want more data from more election years in the United States, for example. So Table 1 provides a second election for comparison. Now what do

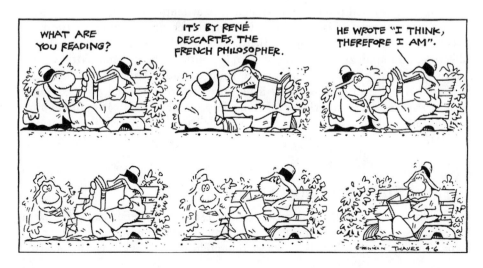

Source: Frank & Earnest reprinted by permission of Newspaper Enterprise Association, Inc.

TABLE 1

Participation of Eligible Voters in the 1976 and 2008 U.S. Presidential Elections, by Gender

	1976	
	Men	**Women**
Voted	a. 77%	b. 67%
Did not vote	c. 23%	d. 33%
Yule's $Q = +.24$		

	2008	
	Men	**Women**
Voted	a. 62%	b. 66%
Did not vote	c. 38%	d. 34%
Yule's $Q = -.09$		

---

you think of the claim? Because the data from 2008 are not consistent with the pattern from 1976, you would recognize that the analysis of this knowledge claim is not straightforward. You might decide to analyze data from even more U.S. elections. You would discover that women voted at a lower rate than men in every U.S. presidential election through 1976, and that women have voted at a higher rate than men in every subsequent election. Now what? Perhaps you would decide that, to better assess the claim, it would be appropriate to examine data for other democracies, too. Or you might attempt to explain why the relationship between gender and voting in the United States seems to have changed.

When you explore these kinds of issues, you are engaged in political analysis. Chapter 1 defined political analysis as the attempt to describe and explain political phenomena. This Appendix will introduce you to some of the basic tools political scientists use for political analysis—that is, for conceptualizing, collecting, and analyzing data about actual political phenomena. After a brief discussion of various types of data, we shall consider how to read data like those in Table 1 and how to draw a tentative inference based on those data. Most of the Appendix describes four broad approaches used for political analysis: taxonomic analysis, formal analysis, functional analysis, and relational analysis.

DATA IN POLITICAL ANALYSIS

Many political analyses rely on data assessment. *Data* can be defined as any observations, facts, statistics, or other forms of information that attempt to measure or represent some aspect of reality. The data used in political analysis can be characterized on different dimensions, including the style of measurement, the level of analysis, the composition, and the time dimension.

1. *Style of measurement.*
   a. **Nominal data** *measure by applying names to phenomena that have some common characteristic.* Examples: male voters or female voters; Conservative, Labour, or Liberal Democrat parties in Britain; democratic, authoritarian, or totalitarian governments.
   b. **Ordinal data** *rank phenomena in an order,* such as from higher to lower, bigger to smaller, greater to lesser. Examples: developed countries or developing countries; voters who are older than 65, voters between ages 35 and 65, or voters younger than age 35; Australia ranked 13th in the world on GDP per capita (PPP, excluding ministates).
   c. **Interval data** *are like ordinal data, but they also have a numerically equal distance between any two adjacent measures*—the distance from 5 to 6 is the same as the distance from 81 to 82. Example: the difference on an opinion scale between 1 (= strongly agree) and 2 (= agree) is the same as the difference between 4 (= disagree) and 5 (= strongly disagree).
   d. **Ratio data** *are like interval data, but they also have a real zero point.* Examples: Australia's GDP per capita PPP is $41,000; the percentage of citizens participating in boycotts for political or ethical reasons; the number of seats in the legislature held by a particular political party.
2. *Level of analysis.* Political data can be measured at different levels of combination. Examples: at the *individual* level, the strength of a particular individual's loyalty to a political party; at the *group* level, the percentage of Canadians who believe that terrorism is never justifiable; the average number of correct political knowledge answers for young adults; at the system level, the total number of operational nuclear weapons worldwide. (In international relations theory, the three levels are individual, state, and global system).
3. *Composition.* Data can measure a single phenomenon, such as a political leader's age or a country's rate of inflation in a particular year, or they can be measures that aggregate phenomena, such as the percentage of total votes cast for all conservative political parties in an election or a country's average annual rate of inflation over ten years.
4. *Time dimension.*
   a. **Cross-sectional data** *measure a single point in time.* Example: a country's GDP per capita in 2012.
   b. **Longitudinal data** *measure several points through time.* Example: a country's GDP per capita in 1970, 1990, and 2010.

The example of voting in the 1976 and 2008 presidential elections uses data that are nominal (men versus women), ratio (percentages), and aggregated (for many people) in a longitudinal analysis (two comparable elections). You might think of data as dry statistics, but the data in political analysis are rooted in real-world events. If properly analyzed, relevant data can increase our political knowledge on an endless list of questions. Examples: Are countries that spend the greatest amount on military preparedness more likely to avoid war? Is religion or social class a better predictor of whether a Scot will vote for the Labour Party?

What characteristics of a country are most associated with the level of citizen support for democracy?

ON READING TABLES

Does Table 1 help you to clarify the relationship between gender and voting level in democracies? Because political analysis often includes data presented in tables, it is useful to know the basic steps for reading them. When you examine a table such as Table 1, you should first establish precisely what the data are about. The title of the table and the names given to the variables (the key concepts measured in the table) indicate what the analyst who created the table thinks it reveals. But the analyst can be misleading or mistaken, so it is worthwhile to assess whether the phenomena measured by the data correspond to the labels given to the variables, whether the data seem relevant to the analytic question, and whether the data seem accurate.

Next you should examine the data in the table. What do the data measure? Table 1 provides data on the percentage of men and women who did or did not vote in the election of the U.S. president in 1976 and 2008. How are such tabular data read? Is either one of these two statements supported by the 2008 data in the table?

1. Thirty-eight percent of those who did not vote were men.
2. Thirty-four percent of the women did not vote.

It is useful, especially when there are percentages in a table, to examine how the columns (up and down) and the rows (across) are formed. In the case of percentages, find any direction(s) in which the data add to 100 percent. In this table, the columns add to 100 percent. Thus, statement 2 is supported by the table and statement 1 is not. Can you see why this is so?

In many cases, the analyst uses more sophisticated techniques than tables in order to assess the relationships between variables. Focus in the Appendix discusses the relational modes of analysis and considers the use of statistical techniques to examine these relationships. It also explains the meaning of the Yule's Q statistics in Table 1.

You can look at simple arrays of data, like those in Table 1, and draw your own conclusions. Graphical representations (like the four scattergrams in Figure 1) are another straightforward way to assess data. Each point in the figures represents one case, located at its appropriate value on each of the two variables in the analysis. This visual mapping of cases can provide useful insights about the nature of the relationship between two variables.

As the data become more complex, statistics can help inform your judgment. Table 1 indicates that the correlation between gender and voting in the 1976 election data is $\pm.24$, using a very simple correlation statistic for 2×2 tables called "Yule's Q." The correlation of $\pm.24$ suggests that in these data, there is a moderate, systematic relationship between male gender and higher probability of voting. In the 2008 data, the relationship between gender and voting appears less pronounced, and this judgment is supported by the Yule's Q of $-.09$, which indicates that there is almost no systematic relationship between gender and turnout rate.

FOCUS IN THE APPENDIX | Assessing Relationships between Phenomena

To interpret most quantitative analyses in political science (and most other social sciences), you need to understand a bit about the meaning of the most commonly used statistics (e.g., Pearson's *r*, regression analysis, factor analysis). Ideally, you will take some statistics coursework so that you understand the logic and assumptions of the statistics being employed.

The simplest relational statistics (e.g., Pearson's *r, tau beta*, Spearman's *rho*) usually range in value between +1.00, which indicates a perfect positive relationship between the variables, and –1.00, which indicates a perfect negative relationship between the variables. These simple statistics (as well as more

sophisticated ones) also have a *significance* level— an indication of how likely it is that the observed relationship between the variables might have occurred by chance. This is normally measured in terms of this chance probability: .05, .01, .001. The smaller the probability of a chance relationship, the greater the analyst's confidence that the variables are actually associated.

In the case of two variables, a +1.00 correlation would look like graph *A* in Figure 1: As one variable increases one unit in value, the other variable increases at a corresponding rate. For example, you would find a +1.00 correlation if each $100,000 spent on congressional political campaigns increased

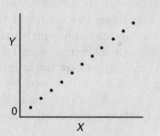

Perfect Positive Correlation:
$r = + 1.0$

A

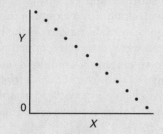

Perfect Negative Correlation:
$r = - 1.0$

B

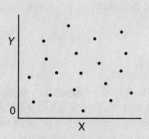

Virtually No Correlation:
$r \cong .00$

C

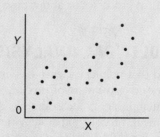

Mild Positive Correlation:
$r \cong + .30$

D

FIGURE 1

Correlation relationships between two hypothetical variables, *X* and *Y*

(*Continued*)

voter turnout by 1 percent. A –1.00 correlation would look like graph B. Rarely do real-world phenomena in political science come even close to a perfect positive or negative correlation.

A correlation statistic close to .00 means that there is almost no linear relationship between the two variables, as in graph C. For example, you might find that campaign expenditure levels have no consistent relationships with voter turnout rates. Political phenomena are often extremely complex and subject to many influences, so they typically have little or no systematic relationship with other factors that you might consider. Thus, in many political analyses, the statistical associations are low or statistically insignificant. The strongest statistical relationships for interesting political data are usually at moderate levels of correlation, in the range of ±.10 to ±.35, as in graph D. ▲

While most statistics of association require a calculator or a computer, you can calculate Yule's Q yourself for any 2×2 table: (1) multiply the values of the two cells on each diagonal: $a \times d$ and $b \times c$; (2) subtract the two products: $ad - bc$; (3) add the two products: $ad + bc$; (4) divide $ad - bc$ by $ad + bc$; (5) the result of this division should be a correlation score, ranging between +1.00 and –1.00. The formula for Yule's Q is thus $(ad - bc)/(ad + bc)$. (Unlike the case for most correlation statistics, a positive Yule's Q means that the ad diagonal is stronger than the bc diagonal.)

Beyond simple statistics and graphs, political scientists use an array of sophisticated data-analysis techniques to examine questions involving quantitative data. Most of the techniques are elaborations on the basic idea of examining whether the values on phenomena seem to be systematically related to each other, although the techniques can involve extremely complex computations that analyze the interrelated effects of many **independent variables** (*the variables that in a cause-and-effect explanation produce change in another variable*) that account for changes in the value of the **dependent variable**—*the variable whose changing value the analysis is attempting to explain.*

The use of statistics and other quantitative techniques can be helpful in political analysis. The more demanding task for the analyst is to use careful judgment to decide whether the relationship identified by such techniques has *substantive* significance. The key question is: Do the tables, statistics, and other data provide useful insights about political processes or about how political phenomena are associated?

MODES OF POLITICAL ANALYSIS

Chapter 1 indicated that political science has little theory in the strictest sense of the term; that is, it does not have a set of precise, systematically related generalizations. However, most contemporary political analysis does strive to make our understanding of politics more general, precise, and systematic by ordering empirical data with one of these four modes of political analysis: taxonomic, formal, functional, or relational.

Taxonomic Analysis

Aristotle (384–322 B.C.E.), the father of political analysis, was interested in distinguishing different types of Greek city-states. He classified them by using a concept

> **TABLE 2**
>
> **Aristotle's Taxonomy of Political Systems**
>
> | How Many Rule? | In Whose Interest? | |
> | --- | --- | --- |
> | | **General** | **Self** |
> | One | Monarchy | Tyranny |
> | A few | Aristocracy | Oligarchy |
> | Many | Polity | Democracy |

derived from earlier work by Herodotus (ca. 484–425 B.C.E.): the size of the ruling group. Aristotle defined three categories: the city–state might be ruled by one person, by a few people, or by many people.

This is an example of taxonomic analysis: *the orderly arrangement of some political phenomena by developing a set of distinct categories.* Most political analysis begins with a taxonomy—a set of categories that classify data into different types. The categories within a taxonomy establish the crucial concepts that define the analysis. The criteria for naming the types and for classifying phenomena into each type are arbitrary in the sense that they are established by the analyst on the basis of substantive concerns. But the categories ought to be exhaustive (all cases are classified), mutually exclusive (no case fits into more than one category), and comparable (all categories are distinguished by the same criteria). Relevant data might be of any type, although they are usually nominal or ordinal.

Aristotle's three categories of city–states are sufficient to create a taxonomy. But to enrich his analysis, Aristotle also employed a second concept: the group(s) whose interests the ruler serves. His two categories were: (1) the ruler(s) could rule in the general interest, or (2) the ruler(s) could rule in self-interest. Thus, Aristotle's taxonomy of governments had two central concepts, each based on nominal data, resulting in the six categories displayed in Table 2. Aristotle then provided names for each category in the taxonomy. He labeled as a monarchy any city–state in which one person ruled in the general interest; if a few ruled in their own interests, the system was called an oligarchy. Notice that Aristotle labeled the most perverse case, where many attempt to rule in their self-interests, a democracy!

Aristotle used his taxonomy for political analysis by placing each Greek city–state in one of the six categories. Athens, for example, was classified as an aristocracy. Notice that a taxonomy organizes data, but it does not answer the *how* and *why* questions. To explore such questions (e.g., Is a prosperous middle class more likely in an oligarchy? Under what conditions does a polity transform into a democracy?), the analyst must move beyond taxonomic analysis.

Formal Analysis

Suppose you want to travel around New York City on the subway. If you are unfamiliar with New York, you will probably use a subway map, which indicates the spatial relationships among different subway stations and identifies the stations where one subway line connects with another.

A subway map is an example of the product of formal analysis. A formal analysis *specifies abstract forms that correspond to the reality in which the analyst is interested.* The analyst attempts to "model" reality by defining and interrelating concepts so that the linkages among the concepts in the formal analysis reflect the dynamics and interactions among the actual phenomena. Some formal analyses have the same physical form as the actual phenomena being modeled, such as a miniaturized version of an automobile engine. But most formal analyses use symbol systems as abstract representations of the phenomena, such as a subway map, a schematic drawing of the circuitry in a radio, or a mathematical formula for the trajectory of an object moving through space.

Most formal analyses of political phenomena are recent. Some political scientists have attempted to devise schematic diagrams that represent how some aspect of politics works. In one well-known example, David Easton (1965) developed an abstract diagram, composed of boxes and arrows, that attempts to characterize the flow of activities by which decision makers in the political system establish public policies. Their decisions are influenced by the resources available in the environment and the pressures they experience from various groups. This "political system model" is explained in detail in Chapter 5.

An array of formal analyses called rational choice theory (or *public choice theory*) has become an important approach in political science. Applications of rational choice theory can be quite complex, but they share two basic features. First, they attempt to represent political processes primarily by means of mathematical formulations or systems of symbolic notation. From the perspective of advancing a science of politics, such formal theories are given special prominence because they aim to be general, systematic, abstract, and testable in actual settings.

Second, it is assumed that political actors (e.g., voters, legislators, political parties) behave purposefully. The approach does not assume that all political actors behave with complete rationality all the time, but it does assume that their behavior is goal-oriented and calculating. Both their preferences for various outcomes and their calculations of the costs, benefits, and likely success of different strategies to achieve those outcomes can be formulated as quantified indicators or as systems of symbols (Mueller 2003).

Rational choice theory is applied to a variety of topics in the study of politics. The question of whether to vote in an election allows for a brief and simplified example. The rational choice approach suggests that a person will/should calculate whether to vote by the following sort of analysis: First, how much will it cost (in time, energy, etc.) to figure out what each candidate will do, assess how it will affect outcomes that I value, and then actually go and vote? Second, how much will I benefit if a particular candidate wins? Third, what is the probability that my vote will determine if my candidate wins? By comparing the costs and benefits outlined above, I can decide whether it is worth it to vote. Rational choice theorists identify a "paradox of voting"—in their analytic framework, it is almost never rational to vote because the costs will far outweigh the benefits, particularly because of the extraordinarily small chance that my vote will make the difference in who wins (Riker and Ordeshook 1973). Of course, someone might reply that there are good reasons to vote: if everyone who supports my candidate follows the same logic and decides not to vote, our candidate would lose; voting is an expression of citizenship and group solidarity; and sometimes elections are close and a few votes do make a difference (ask Al Gore about Florida in 2000).

Functional Analysis

Suppose someone asks you how a car works. You are likely to discuss the key structural components of a car's engine and power train, such as its carburetor, pistons, and driveshaft. You might then detail the processes of the internal combustion engine, noting how an ignited fuel expands in an enclosed area, pushing a series of mechanisms into directed motion. This style of description and explanation is the basis of functional analysis. *Functional analysis describes the contributions of a certain element (process or structure) to the activities of the phenomenon under study.*

In political science, one widely used form of functional analysis identifies certain functions (i.e., processes) that occur within a political system, and it describes how and by what structures the functions are performed. Some scholars (Powell, Dalton and Strom 2012) have defined certain functions, including political communication, rule adjudication, and interest articulation, that must be performed in every political system.

Applications of functional analysis are described in Chapters 5, 10, and 11. As a brief example here, we can consider the interest articulation function. Individuals might want their government to protect their right to own handguns. The processes by which individuals communicate this specific interest to others in the political world are called *interest articulation.* According to functional analysis, this communication of political needs and wants is a necessary function in every effective political system. Most functional analysts also describe and explain how structures perform these types of functions. Thus, interest groups emerge to amplify the shared interests of many individuals. For example, the National Rifle Association uses various strategies to promote many individuals' concerns about gun ownership to those who make and implement government policies on firearms.

Related to functional analysis is constitutive analysis. *Constitutive analysis assumes that political functions can be explained primarily in terms of one fundamental concept.* (Indeed, every scientific discipline strives to discover, ultimately, the fundamental structure or process that accounts for more complex phenomena.) Among the concepts that have been proposed as the central one to explain politics are the interactions between groups, classes, or roles. Constitutive theories are discussed in various chapters, especially in Chapter 9, which presents the elite, class, and pluralist approaches to explaining politics. As an example, Karl Marx's (1867) theory of politics pivots on one key concept: class. In every historical period, society is divided into a set of classes based on the distribution of economic power. The structure of classes determines political and social relations as well as economic relations. In political terms, the class structure determines who wields political power, for what purposes, and for whose benefit. The role of the state and the dynamics of political change are also explained in terms of class relations.

Relational Analysis

Table 1 considers the question of voting differences between men and women: Is there some relationship between an individual's gender and the likelihood that she or he votes? This is typical of the kinds of questions addressed by relational analysis.

The central goal of relational analysis is to *discover and explicate the systematic connections between phenomena*. The basic question is always: Are political phenomena linked? For example, Are democratic countries more stable than nondemocratic countries? Are older people more politically knowledgeable than younger people? Is Confucian culture associated with higher national economic growth more than is Muslim culture? What characteristics are associated with states more likely to participate in interstate wars?

Both formal analysis and functional analysis also assume connections, but relational analysis tries merely to identify the connections between phenomena. It does not attempt to model or schematize the connections, as does formal analysis. And it does not focus on crucial functions, as does functional analysis. There are two levels of relational analysis: (1) correlational analysis and (2) causal analysis. To determine whether there is a systematic association between variables, most correlational and causal analyses use various statistical techniques. These statistics provide a mathematical appraisal of the extent to which change in one phenomenon is systematically related to changes in one or more other phenomena. Focus in the Appendix provided further information about a few such statistics.

Correlational analysis. Correlational analysis *determines whether there is a statistically probable relationship between two variables*. It does not presume, as does causal analysis (discussed in the next section), that one variable actually is the agent that causes change to occur in another variable. It merely assesses the strength and direction of an association between variables. Many empirical attempts to understand politics begin with the establishment of a correlation between political phenomena.

For example, evaluating the linkage between gender and voting in Table 1 is an example of correlational analysis. The table and the Yule's Q statistic both seem to support the tentative conclusion that, for 1976 at least, there is a modest *correlation* (i.e., *a systematic, statistically probable association*) between gender and voting. However, the correlation statistic for the 2008 election is considerably weaker (closer to .00), and it is in the opposite direction (women's participation is higher). Any generalization could also take into account empirical comparative analyses of many countries that do not find a strong correlation between gender and voting rates in most democracies (Inglehart and Norris 2003). The need for more data and more subtle analyses seems clear.

Causal analysis. Causal analysis goes beyond correlational analysis because it *explicitly identifies one phenomenon as the effective agent that brings about changes in another phenomenon*. Much of the language in political analysis is loosely causal, implying that there is a cause-and-effect relationship between two variables. However, causal analysis is the only approach that attempts an explicit empirical test of cause and effect. Causal analysis presents the "If X, then Y" mode

> ### TABLE 3
>
> **Relationship between Number of Political Parties and Type of Electoral System**
>
> | Number of Parties† | Electoral System* | |
> | --- | --- | --- |
> | | Plurality | Other |
> | Two | 23 | 4 |
> | More than two | 7 | 73 |
> | Yule's $Q = +.97$ | | |
>
> *Note:* Based on data from 20 Western democracies in elections of legislative representatives between 1945 and 1965.
>
> *In plurality or "first-past-the-post" systems, the party/candidate with the largest number of votes wins a seat in the legislature, and all other parties/candidates gain no seats. In "other" systems, there is some form of proportional representation or vote transfer.
>
> †Number of political parties with at least 5 percent of the seats in the legislature.
>
> *Source:* Rae 1971.

of explanation described in Chapter 1. Here X is the *independent variable* that, given a certain value, actually causes Y, the *dependent variable*, to change in a particular way.

An example of causal analysis links the electoral system and the number of political parties. In his landmark book *Political Parties*, French political scientist Maurice Duverger (1954) contends that the type of electoral system *causes* the number of effective parties to increase or decrease. In particular, he offers two hypotheses:

1. Plurality electoral systems (in which the candidate who receives the most votes wins) reduce the number of major political parties toward two.
2. Electoral systems with proportional representation (in which candidates are elected to the legislature in proportion to their party's share of the total vote) and with multimember districts (more than one legislator per district) allow more than two major parties (recall Focus in 6).

Political analysts (e.g., Riker 1982; Taagepera and Shugart 1989: Ch. 13) have tested Duverger's hypotheses using data from various electoral systems. Table 3 presents data from 20 democratic countries for the period from 1945 to 1965 (Rae 1971). Do you think the data in Table 3 support Duverger's hypothesis? Why?

DRAWING CONCLUSIONS FROM EMPIRICAL ANALYSES

The purpose of empirical analysis is to increase our knowledge about politics. It is especially important that the analyst draws appropriate conclusions. In political analysis, as in politics, things are often not what they seem. Let us consider some of the potential problems, using the causal analysis of electoral systems and party systems as an example. You probably concluded that the data in Table 3 support Duverger's hypothesis. The relationship seems very strong and the correlation statistic (+.97) is extremely high. Do we now know that the electoral system causes different types of party systems? Yes, maybe.

Yes: There is certainly some persuasive empirical evidence for such a conclusion, such as this very high correlation. And, on logical grounds, it does seem reasonable that the electoral system might cause variations in the number of parties that survive over time.

Maybe: The political analyst must always be cautious in drawing conclusions and making generalizations. Several questions should be considered:

1. Are the data and methods appropriate? Did the analysis use accurate, relevant data and the correct analytic techniques? Is the sample of nations or the time period examined typical? Does this generalization also hold for non-European nations? Were systems divided between "plurality" and "other" in a manner consistent with Duverger's hypothesis?

2. Are the analyst's inferences about cause and effect persuasive? Might the dependent variable (in this case, the number of political parties) actually have a significant effect on the presumed independent variable (the electoral system)? That is, because the parties in most legislatures have the power to establish the electoral system, certain parties might try to implement an electoral system that perpetuates their power via the existing party system.

3. Are there plausible rival hypotheses? Is there another independent variable, not considered in this analysis, that might better account for the pattern of values on the dependent variable? It is possible that both the number of parties and the electoral system are related primarily because each is correlated with the third variable? For example, the number of fundamental issues that divide the electorate might have the greatest effect on the number of major parties if one party emerges for each pattern of positions on the fundamental issues (Taagepera and Shugart 1989).

When political scientists use the scientific method, other analysts might raise any of these kinds of "problems" with a conclusion. The data, the methods, or the inferences might not stand up to such scrutiny. In our examination of Duverger's claims about the causal relationship between electoral systems and the number of parties, none of the three problems just listed seems to undermine the analysis. Until one of these types of criticisms is supported persuasively, we can have some confidence that the generalization about the causal relationship is correct—that electoral systems do seem to cause certain types of party systems to evolve over time.

The gender and voting analysis based on the 1976 election data in Table 1 can serve as an example of how an initial causal inference can be challenged. There is clearly a correlation in 1976 between gender and voter turnout. The three potential problems must be considered in an assessment of whether the data reveal that gender differences do *cause* a different probability of voting:

1. The data and methods do seem appropriate. However, a generalization (even limited to the United States) certainly requires more than a single case.

> ### TABLE 4
>
> **Participation of Eligible Voters in the 1976 U.S. Presidential Election, by Gender and Education Level**
>
> | | Percentage Who Voted | |
> | Education Level | Men | Women |
> | --- | --- | --- |
> | Grade school | 72 | 50 |
> | High school | 69 | 64 |
> | College | 86 | 84 |

2. The posited cause-and-effect relationship seems reasonable. This is the only possible direction of causality because voting certainly cannot "cause" gender. Also, there are reasonable explanations for why men might vote at higher rates than women. Can you think of at least one?

3. However, to make a compelling argument that the data reveal causality, it would be necessary to ensure that there is no other causal agent (i.e., no plausible rival hypothesis) that better explains voting levels or that creates the apparent relationship between gender and voting. While the analyst can never disprove every competing hypothesis, it is important to examine and reject the most plausible ones.

Let us reexamine the 1976 voter turnout data in Table 1. Can you propose another explanation for the incidence of voting in the United States that is as plausible as gender? Among those you might suggest are age, social class, occupation, interest in politics, identification with a political party, and education level. Table 4 provides the relevant data on one of these alternative explanations—education level—for our analysis of voting in 1976. Do these data alter your judgment about the importance of gender?

One reasonable interpretation of Table 4 is that the 1976 election revealed a considerable difference between men and women in the incidence of voting among those with minimal education, but almost no difference in the levels of voting between men and women who have a college education. In the absence of further analysis (and many further analyses could be attempted), these data about education seem to reduce the power of gender as an adequate causal explanation of voting. One might infer, at least on the basis of Table 4, that both education and gender were important in 1976 but that the impact of gender was powerfully altered by education level. Perhaps the gender gap had closed by 2008 because the proportion of men and women with college educations had equalized. Perhaps. This closer look should suggest to you that if you were developing a causal theory of voter turnout, you would need to consider many variables and diverse data.

This example reveals a common challenge for most of the interesting questions addressed by causal analyses of politics: There are almost always clusters of plausible explanatory factors that seem interrelated. For example, What accounts for a person's decision to vote for the conservative National Action Party (PAN) in Mexico—class, education, family experiences, occupation, wealth, beliefs about society, attitudes toward governmental leaders, or something else? What factors lead a group to undertake revolutionary violence—political oppression, poverty, corrupt government officials, charismatic leadership, unequal distribution of wealth, foreign domination, or something else? Working on these kinds of puzzles is the stuff of political analysis.

KNOWLEDGE AND POLITICS REVISITED

Chapter 1 suggested a number of ways it is possible to know things about the political world. Your understanding of politics does not need to be grounded in the scientific method and in empirical analysis. Insight and understanding about politics might be based on the method of authority or the method of personal thought, or they might be derived from other sources such as literature, films, or art.

In the attempt to develop precise and valid generalizations about politics, however, most contemporary political scientists use some form of the scientific method and some of the modes of political analysis described in preceding sections. Whatever types of data and modes of analysis they use, political scientists generally accept the notion that all aspects of their research should be subject to scrutiny and challenge by other analysts. Most also agree that their hypotheses, inferences, generalizations, and theories must be subject to some empirical test of validity. Although various sources of knowledge can provide you with insights about politics, this book emphasizes the modes of political analysis described in this Appendix as the best means for broad understanding of the political world.

KEY CONCEPTS

causal analysis   452
constitutive analysis   451
correlation   452
correlational analysis   452
cross-sectional data   445
dependent variable   448
formal analysis   450
functional analysis   451
independent variable   448
interval data   445

longitudinal data   445
monarchy   449
nominal data   445
oligarchy   449
ordinal data   445
political analysis   444
ratio data   445
rational choice theory   450
relational analysis   452
taxonomic analysis   449

GLOSSARY

adjudication   Every society creates and enforces rules and laws regarding the proper forms of behavior for individuals and groups. The adjudication function attempts to interpret and apply the relevant rules or laws to a given situation. Most political systems have established judicial structures (e.g., criminal courts) whose primary role is adjudication.

administration   The general term used to describe the machinery and processes through which rules and policies of an organization are applied and implemented. It is a core function of political systems and is usually one of the four basic institutional structures (along with executives, legislatures, and judiciaries). (*See also* bureaucracy.)

assembly system   A form of collective leadership in which a large group, usually constituted as a legislature, is clearly dominant over the executive. Examples: the United Nations; the European Parliament.

associational interest group   A type of political interest group organized specifically to further the political objectives of its members. Examples: the British Medical Association; Common Cause. (*See also* interest group.)

authoritarianism   (1) A political system generally characterized by little or no commitment to equality or democratic participation and by a strong emphasis on order and stability. The political behavior of the population is severely constrained. In many countries, authoritarian regimes are dominated by a military elite. (2) A personality syndrome, associated particularly with political and social attitudes and behavior, in which the individual tends to revere strong leadership, draw sharp boundaries between the identity group and all others, be intolerant of unconventional behaviors, and exhibit considerable hostility toward minority groups.

authority   (1) A source of knowledge about the political world. The method of authority involves the appeal to any document, tradition, or person that is believed to possess the controlling explanation regarding a particular issue. (2) The legitimacy attached to the decisions of the political system, in the sense that people will willingly accept those decisions as binding, independent of their own self-interest.

balance of power   A configuration of power among a set of states in which there is a broad equality in the power resources (political, economic, and especially military) that can be exercised by competing states. Through a system of shifting alliances, no state or group of states is able to achieve a preponderance of power. Thus, stability and the status quo are usually sustained because states will intervene to prevent a serious imbalance that might lead to domination.

bureaucracy   Though often used as a synonym for administration, bureaucracy has been defined, especially by Max Weber (1958a), as a particular structure and style through which administration can operate. Structurally, bureaucracy is characterized by hierarchical organization and a highly specialized division of labor. Members of the bureaucracy behave according to specific rules of action so that treatment of each case is relatively predictable and nondiscriminatory. (*See also* administration.)

capitalism   One of the great "isms," explicitly linking politics to political economy, capitalism is a system that corresponds loosely to a market economy. In this system, private economic actors are generally free from state constraints and the state engages in only limited efforts to shift resources among private actors. Capitalism is founded on the philosophy of laissez-faire economics. There is no assumption that capitalism requires a particular form of political processes to function efficiently.

causal analysis A type of relational analysis, causal analysis goes beyond correlational analysis because it explicitly identifies one phenomenon as the effective agent that brings about changes in another phenomenon. Causal analysis presents the "If *X*, then *Y*" mode of explanation, where *X* is the independent variable that, given a certain value, actually causes *Y*, the dependent variable, to change in a particular way.

civil law A system of law in which the central principle is to apply a very precise, detailed set of existing legal codes to the current case. Sometimes termed "scholar-made law," it evolved from Roman law and the Napoleonic codes and is common in many countries influenced by continental European legal forms.

civil war A form of political violence that occurs when a significant proportion of the population within a region actively supports a separatist movement, and political violence emerges on a large scale. Examples: Libya (2011); U.S. Civil War (1861–1865).

class approach An analytic explanation of the value allocation process (politics) based on a core notion of stratification—structured inequality in the distribution of key values in society. The class approach centers on an examination of the tactics of class domination and the dynamics of class struggle. Class theory is particularly associated with the writings of Karl Marx (1867/1981) and later forms of Marxist theories.

classical liberalism One of the major Western political ideologies. In classical liberalism, the highest value is placed on each individual's natural rights to life, liberty, and property and the freedom of the individual to pursue these rights as an independent

actor. Government plays a very limited role under classical liberalism, which celebrates a laissez-faire economy and discourages government attempts to create material equality (although equality of opportunity is important). Political thinkers associated with classical liberal thought include John Locke (1632–1704), Adam Smith (1723–1790), and John Stuart Mill (1806–1873).

colonialism A situation of dominance and subordination in the relations between two states. One state asserts substantial power and control over the other, based on military, economic, and/or political power. The goals of the dominant state might include: to extract resources, to control a market for its products, to use the strategic location, to instill its own values into members of the subordinate state, or to obtain international prestige. Most areas that were colonial holdings became independent in the decades after 1945. (*See also* neocolonialism.)

command economy An ideal type political economy in which the state assumes total control of almost all significant factors of production. The state replaces or eliminates the role of private owners of land, labor, and capital; makes all production decisions; and determines the value of all goods. The state owns, plans, controls, and regulates all major economic activity. (*Compare with* market economy.)

common law A legal system that is grounded in general laws that have been promulgated over time. It relies on precedents, based on earlier judicial decisions, to guide current adjudication. Sometimes referred to as "judge-made law," it is the dominant form of jurisprudence in the U.S., Great Britain, and numerous other countries.

communism One of the major "isms" linking politics and political economy, communism is a system that is closely associated with the command political economy. Based on the theories of Karl Marx (1867/1981) and others, the key to communism is the socialization of resources—the notion that the state must maintain control of society's land, labor, and capital. Although it is primarily an economic system, communism also emphasizes an ideological commitment to economic and social equality among all of its citizens. It also posits that until such equality is achieved, government and politics must be guided powerfully by a unified leadership. Examples: Cuba; the former Soviet Union.

confederation A loose association of states. In a confederation, each state delegates some power to a supranational central government but still retains primary power, and its compliance is always conditional. Confederations are usually created when states decide that the performance of certain functions is enhanced by structured cooperation with other states. Example: the United Nations.

conservatism One of the major Western political ideologies, at the core of conservatism is the commitment to sustain traditional values and forms of behavior and to maintain social order. Tradition and religion, rather than reason, are viewed as the most reliable sources for guiding society. There is loyalty to the nation and antipathy to egalitarianism. The writings of Edmund Burke (1790/1955) provide a good example of conservative thought.

constitution A set of statements that describes the fundamental rules of a political system, including a characterization of the core activities of major political structures. Most constitutions are a single, written document, such as the U.S. Constitution, but some are embedded primarily in major statutes, precedents, and legal decisions.

constitutional regime A political system that operates in terms of the rule of law, as defined in the constitution, and that ensures effective restraints on the power holders. The defining feature of a constitutional regime is that the state does attempt to fulfill the provisions of its constitution.

core Refers to the set of states, firms (especially multinational firms), and financial institutions that have enormous power and influence in the global system and the international political economy. The core, primarily located in the developed countries, dominates the world's "periphery," composed of institutions and peoples that have minimal power and are primarily located in the developing countries. Core is a crucial concept of the dependency approach, which is an explanation of both the relations between states and the development process.

corporatism A corporatist state is characterized by extensive economic cooperation between an activist state and a set of large organizations that represent actors who control major productive resources. In the hope that there will be cooperation and consultation (rather than conflict) among the state, big capital, big owners, and big labor, the leaders of these groups are given great influence in working with the state to make and implement policy on key political economy issues.

correlational analysis A form of relational analysis that determines whether there is a statistically probable relationship between two variables. The analysis does not conclude that one variable is actually the agent that causes change to occur in another variable (as in causal analysis) but merely assesses the strength and direction of the association between variables. Correlational analysis is often a key step in any empirical attempt to understand politics.

council system A political system in which a small group shares collective leadership and is responsible for both executive and legislative functions. All members of the council have relatively equal power, so decisions and actions are based on the will of the council majority or council consensus. Examples: mayor-council systems and boards of supervisors in many U.S. local governments.

coup Occurs when the top political leader or leadership group is replaced by violence or the explicit threat of violence. A coup is a common form of leadership turnover in political systems that have no accepted and enforceable procedures for leadership succession. Examples: ouster of Aristide in Haiti (2004); elimination of Qaddafi in Libya (2011).

democracy   A political system in which governance is accomplished by leaders whose authority is based on a limited mandate and who are elected by a universal electorate. Such an "electoral" democracy becomes a "liberal" democracy when the population selects among genuine alternatives and also has significant rights to political participation, expression, and opposition.

democratic socialism   A variation of socialist ideology that treats greater egalitarianism as its primary goal but also assumes that its goals can and should be implemented by a government that comes to power and rules by democratic means, not by violence and repression. Under democratic socialism, the government might own some of the major economic resources and regulate much of the economy, but it does not attempt to plan and control all aspects of the economic system. (*See also* socialism.)

democratization   The effort to institutionalize democratic political regimes more fully and deeply, especially in countries with limited democratic processes. Analyses often try to measure the extent of democratic consolidation and to specify the political, economic, and social conditions conducive to further democratization.

dependency approach   This claims that an economic and political hierarchy exists in which many actors take advantage of those with less power and resources. At the top are the most developed countries, and the poor people and the villages of the developing countries are at the bottom. Some analysts claim that many of the difficulties facing the less developed countries stem from their vulnerability to, and dependence on, the more highly developed countries and the transnational institutions they control.

dependent variable   The Y variable whose value changes as a result of changes in some other specified (independent) variables. Causal analysis presents the "If X, then Y" mode of explanation, where X is the independent variable that, given a certain value, actually causes Y, the dependent variable, to alter in value in a particular way.

dictatorship   A political system in which political leaders are not subject to a limited mandate but have absolute power and authority. The citizens have no regular and realistic opportunity to replace such political leadership in a nonviolent manner.

dual executive   A political system in which one actor, the head of state, performs the more ceremonial aspects of top leadership and embodies the nation, while another actor, the head of government, is responsible for the more political aspects of the executive role. (*See also* executive.) Example: The United Kingdom has Queen Elizabeth II (head of state) and Prime Minister David Cameron (head of government).

economic development   This occurs as more and more households and firms within a country are engaged in ever-higher levels of production and consumption. Based on greater control of the environment and resources, more (and more complex) goods are produced and exchanged, and the gross domestic product (GDP) gets larger relative to the number of people sharing in the market.

electoral system   The framework by which the votes of citizens are converted to specific selections of candidates who have a mandate to hold office. There are many variations, some based on selection proportional to votes cast (forms of PR) and others based on the selection of the candidate with most (plurality) or at least half (majority) of the votes.

elite approach   An analytic explanation of the value allocation process (politics) in which the political world is characterized by political stratification, the segmentation of the population into separate groups with greater or less power. There are only two major strata—those that do more of what there is to do (in the policy process) and that get more of the resources that are available, and those that do less and get less. These two groups are called the political elite and the mass, respectively. Key elite theorists include Gaetano Mosca (1896/1939) and C. Wright Mills (1956).

executive The branch of the political system composed of a leader or group of leaders who are responsible for defining and managing the implementation of public policy. A broad definition of the executive includes not only the chief executive (e.g., mayor, governor, prime minister, president, queen) but also the entire administrative system.

fascism A political ideology that places fundamental importance on the unity and harmony of government and society and is defined particularly by its opposition to forces that might weaken that collective unity. It further assumes that the top leader is the embodiment of the natural will and that all individuals and groups must obey the will of the leader. It is both antisocialist and antidemocratic. Fascism had a major impact on twentieth-century history and is particularly associated with regimes such as those of Adolf Hitler ("Nazism") in Germany (1932–1945) and Benito Mussolini in Italy (1922–1943).

federation A political system in which there is a constitutional division of power and functions between a central government and a set of regional governments, usually known as states, provinces, or cantons. Power is shared among the levels of government, and no level has legal power to dominate any other level in all policy domains. Examples: Brazil; Canada; Mexico; the United States.

formal analysis Specifies abstract forms that correspond to the reality in which the analyst is interested. The formal analyst attempts to "model" reality. Most formal analyses use symbol systems as abstract representations of the phenomenon under study, such as a subway map or David Easton's (1965) political system model.

functional analysis Describes the contributions of a certain element (process or structure) to the activities of the phenomenon under study. For example, one form of functional analysis identifies certain functions or processes (e.g., political communication, rule adjudication) that occur within a political system and describes how and by what structures the functions are performed.

geopolitics An analytical method that assumes that the geography of a state—its particular geographical location and also its physical characteristics, natural resources, and human resources—can significantly affect the domestic and foreign policy actions of the state.

globalization The increasing integration of diverse economic, sociocultural, military, and environmental phenomena by means of dense networks of action and information that span vast distances around the world. These networks dramatically increase interdependence among actors within the international system and within environments such as the economic system and the environmental system.

guerrilla war Violent opposition to an existing regime by means of a long, protracted campaign primarily from rural bases. Fighting is typically in a hit-and-run style, with extensive efforts to win the support of the peasants and the creation of new political institutions prior to collapse of the old regime. Example: FARC's lengthy campaign against the Colombian government.

hegemony The existence of an extraordinarily powerful group (a "hegemonic elite") or country ("hegemon") that sustains its domination over other actors for a long period of time.

hybrid system A political system that attempts to blend the desirable aspects of both the presidential and cabinet systems of government. Hybrid systems have a prime minister and an elected legislature that can both enact and implement policies, but they also have a president who may have relatively equal power with the cabinet or may have key specific, but limited, powers. Examples: France; Russia.

ideal types An analytic construct that defines "pure forms" of a phenomenon (e.g., ideal types of political economies). These forms are distinguished by the configuration of key characteristics. Few, if any, real-world cases are identical to an ideal type, which is a means to facilitate comparative analysis.

independent variable   The variable in a cause-and-effect hypothesis or explanation that produces change in another variable. In the "If X, then Y" mode of explanation, X is the independent variable that, given a certain value, actually causes Y, the dependent variable, to change in a particular way.

interest group   A group that directly attempts to influence the allocation of public values or other actions of those in the political system. It may undertake political action, provide goods or services to political actors, or provide data and information to those within the political system in its attempts to achieve its political objectives. It may also exert influence through compliance or non-compliance with the government policy process.

intergovernmental organizations (IGOs)   A political actor whose members are states, not private groups or individuals. IGOs can shape the cooperative relations among states, some or all of whom are their members. States form IGOs to provide a forum of communication among states, to enact multinational laws and treaties, and to intervene in disputes between states. Examples: European Union; NAFTA; NATO.

international law   A broad attempt to establish principles and rules that formalize and constrain the interactions among states. Positivist law, or written agreements between states in the form of international treaties or conventions, is the basis for international law.

international organization   A broad term that refers to many of the cross-national institutions whose objectives are to influence the behavior and policies of states. The two primary forms are nongovernmental organizations (NGOs) and intergovernmental organizations (IGOs). Examples: Amnesty International; the United Nations.

international regime   A set of norms, rules, and procedures that are accepted by many countries and guide their behavior with each other in a particular issue domain. Examples: the World Trade Organization on trade relations; the Nuclear Nonproliferation Treaty.

international relations   One of the four major subfields within political science that examines the interactions among states and other transnational actors as they pursue political goals. Subjects of analysis include foreign policy, interstate conflict, globalization, and international law.

judicial review   In political systems where the judiciary is relatively independent, the judiciary can interpret or even revoke the policy decisions and actions taken by the other political structures, thus exercising the power of judicial review. In the United States, for example, the Supreme Court exercises the power of judicial review when it decides whether a law passed by Congress is unconstitutional.

judiciary   An important branch of most political systems, the system of courts and personnel that determine whether the laws of the society have been transgressed, and if so, whether and what type of sanctions ought to be imposed on the transgressor.

legislature   The political structure in which, typically, policy issues are discussed and assessed and public policies are enacted by a set of elected or appointed legislators. Although a particular legislature may not exercise these powers, most have three broad roles: (1) enacting legislation, (2) representing the citizenry, and (3) overseeing the executive.

liberal democracy   A political system that not only is an electoral democracy (periodic elections, limited mandate) but also ensures extensive political rights (e.g., parties promoting genuine alternatives, opposition) and civil liberties (e.g., freedom of expression, religion, and the media).

market economy   An ideal type political economy in which there is near-total private control of land, labor, and capital. Every actor has direct control over his or her own factors of production, and production decisions are essentially the sum of all private actors' decisions. The exchange value of goods is decided by the market. The state is generally quite passive in a market economy, simply enforcing rules and providing minimal protection to economic actors. (*Compare with* command economy.)

Marxist-Leninist socialism   A variant of socialist ideology heavily influenced by the writings of Karl Marx and the interpretations by V. I. Lenin. It begins with three assumptions regarding the changes necessary to produce the key goals of equality and social justice: (1) it might be necessary to use violence to overthrow the old economic order, (2) a powerful government is necessary to restructure the economic system, and (3) a small dictatorial leadership group must manage the government and effect the economic and social changes. This group will be unnecessary when equality is achieved and can be replaced by decentralized citizen-run politics. (*See also* socialism.)

micropolitics   An analytic focus on individual and small-group political processes, with a particular emphasis on how the individual understands the political world and how the individual acts politically.

mixed economy   A political economy that attempts to combine the strengths of both market and command economies while also minimizing their shortcomings. Control of the means of production is shared between the state and private actors. The state's rules, actions, and direct involvement in the economic system guide some production, distribution, and pricing decisions and also moderate and limit the market behavior of private households and firms.

monarchy   (1) A political system with a hereditary sovereign, often called a king or queen, as in United Kingdom of Great Britain and Northern Ireland. (2) Analytically, a political system in which one person exercises a very large proportion of political control, which can also be termed an "autocracy."

nation   A sociopolitical unit defined by a deeply shared fundamental identification among a set of people based on shared ethnicity, language, descent, culture, religion, and/or geographic space. The nation is a major group, beyond the family, with whom the individual identifies very powerfully.

nationalism   A strong affection and commitment to the wellbeing of the nation with which one identifies, in comparison with minimal concern for those outside the nation. Nationalism can become the underlying principle shaping people's loyalty and willingness to make sacrifices for the protection and enhancement of the nation and its collective interests.

natural law   Sensible, widely accepted (universal?) norms of behavior that direct us to act with goodness and are recognizable through human reason. They should guide the relations among states and individuals and should restrain hostile or destructive interactions.

neocolonialism   New forms of domination and dependence between states that have emerged in the decades since the end of colonialism (after World War II). Although direct occupation by colonial powers was ended at independence, domination has been extended in some cases by the manipulation of power resources such as economic aid, technology transfer, military support, and economic intervention. (*See also* colonialism.)

neoliberalism   An approach to economic development that emphasizes a reliance on a local and global free market that is guided by entrepreneurs who shape decisions about the production and distribution of goods. The state plays a minimal role in the political economy, and public spending is focused on infrastructure support (e.g., transportation, education) rather than welfare distribution.

nonconstitutional regime   A political system in which there is persistent nonenforcement of crucial limits on the rulers and/or protection of the rights of the ruled, especially those limits and rights specified in a constitution and other key legal documents. Most authoritarian or totalitarian regimes are nonconstitutional.

nongovernmental organizations (NGOs) National or transnational associations that are not part of the governmental/state apparatus but are committed to the promotion of an issue with national or international policy dimensions. (In the latter case, the association is called an international nongovernmental organization.) Members are groups and individuals who combine their knowledge and financial and political resources to pursue a shared objective. Examples: Amnesty International's monitoring of human rights; Médecins sans Frontières (Doctors Without Borders) provisions of medical assistance.

normative political knowledge Answers questions about what ought to be rather than simply providing descriptions and explanations of what is. Examples of normative questions: What are the appropriate domains of state action? Should there be limits on free speech? How much and what types of health care should the state provide?

oligarchy Literally, rule by the few. Hence, a political system in which a small number of actors dominate the resource allocation process, usually serving their own interests.

parliamentary government A political system in which the executive and legislative functions and structures are fused. The people elect the legislature (parliament), whose majority empowers a cabinet, which then empowers one of its members to be the chief executive, usually called a prime minister or premier. The cabinet devises, drafts, and implements most policies, although they must be enacted by the legislative majority. Examples: Italy; the United Kingdom.

participatory democracy Democracy in its classic sense as government of and by all the people. There is active, direct participation by all citizens in the policy process.

party system The configuration of political parties in a political system. Party systems are generally classified according to the number of political parties and the nature of the interactions among the parties in the governing process.

pluralism An analytic explanation of the value allocation process (politics) that is grounded in the concept of the group—any aggregate of individuals who interact to pursue a common interest. Within this approach, politics can be understood as the interaction among groups that are pursuing their political interests, and policy decisions are the outcome of that group process. It is assumed that any particular individual can belong to many different groups and has some political resources that can be used in an attempt to influence policy decisions.

political analysis The attempt to describe and explain political phenomena that strives to make understanding of politics more general, precise, and systematic, and ultimately to generate and test theories.

political belief system The configuration of an individual's political orientations across an array of political issues. Many political beliefs are evaluative orientations, which synthesize facts (cognitive orientations) and feelings (affective orientations) into a judgment (evaluative orientation) about some political phenomena.

political culture The general configuration of a particular people's (e.g., a nation's or a country's) political beliefs. It characterizes those cognitive, affective, and evaluative orientations that are dominant among those people. Many explanations of political behavior and political processes are grounded in interpretations of political culture.

political decay The phenomena that occur when there is a decline in the capacity of the political system and especially its effectiveness in maintaining order. It can be manifest in collective behavior such as demonstrations, protests, rebellion, and other forms of political violence. It is often associated with extensive demands that the political system cannot meet and with the loss of citizen support for the political system.

According to Samuel Huntington (1968), the probability of political decay increases as a state has a lower level of political institutionalization.

political development   The specifically political aspects of development and modernization. It can refer either to a set of characteristics of the political system or to the process through which those characteristics are increased. The key characteristics of more developed political systems can include: (1) the concentration of power in the central state; (2) "modern" forms of political organization, such as institutionalized party systems and effective bureaucracies; (3) complex and extensive forms of individual and group political behavior; and (4) expanded capabilities of the political system to maintain order, manage the environment, meet the demands of the citizens, and so on.

political economy   The combination, in theory or in practice, of politics and economics. The political system and the economic system are inextricably intertwined because many of the decisions made by the political system have significant effects on the economy, and activities within the economic system have major effects on the state. Two ideal-type political economies are the market economy and the command economy.

political elite   A general term for those individuals who have relatively high levels of power, influence, interest, knowledge, and involvement in political life. It is the stratum of the population that does more of what there is to do (in the policy process) and gets more of what there is to get (in the allocation of values).

political idealism   A perspective, especially in international relations theory, that posits that human nature is basically good and thus states have a natural tendency to be cooperative and even altruistic. Political institutions can then be shaped to facilitate the emergence of these cooperative, nonviolent tendencies in the relations among states.

political ideology   A comprehensive set of beliefs about the political world, including a specification of desirable political goals and the best way to achieve those goals, based on particular assumptions about human nature, the relation of the individual to the state and society, and the desirability of equality.

political institutionalization   The extent that political organizations and procedures have acquired value in the eyes of the population and the stability to withstand significant pressure. It is measured by the political system's capacity to regulate its citizens, respond flexibly to citizen demands, extract and distribute resources efficiently, and adapt to changing circumstances.

political participation   The term applied to all modes of the political actions by individuals and groups. The broad goal is to influence the actions or selection of political rulers. Modes of political participation for an individual range from listening to political discourse to voting, to taking part in a demonstration, to holding political office.

political party   An organized group that attempts to capture political power directly by placing its members in government office. The political party is the broadest institution in most political systems that links individuals and groups to the state, and it can organize the activities of those participating in government. It also aggregates political interests into a comprehensible set of policy goals.

political realism   A perspective, especially in international relations theory, that assumes that people are naturally disposed to behave selfishly and that this self-interested orientation extends to the behavior of states. The fundamental goal of each state is to ensure its own security and survival by maximizing its power. Interstate conflict is likely to be a recurring event, and states sometimes use balance-of-power strategies to limit the frequency of major conflicts.

political resources   Something that can influence the actions and decisions of political actors, such as social status, money, legality, special knowledge or skills, ability to mobilize large numbers of people, visibility in the media, and control of productive capabilities. According to the pluralist approach, political resources are of many forms and widely distributed. According to the class and elite approaches, one or a few types of political resources are critical, and control of those resources tends to be concentrated in a limited group.

political science   A set of techniques, concepts, and approaches whose objective is to increase the clarity and accuracy of understandings about political phenomena. This academic discipline is labeled a "science" in many countries because most political scientists use the scientific method to establish shared knowledge about the political world.

political socialization   The process through which individuals acquire their cognitive, affective, and evaluative orientations toward the political world. Some of the most important agents (sources) are the family, the schools, peer groups, the media, and culture.

political society   Formed when individuals cede to the state a monopoly over the legitimate use of violence, sacrificing their own right to do violence to others in exchange for a similar sacrifice from others. Thomas Hobbes (1651) called this agreement among individuals the *social contract*.

political system   A (formal) theoretical concept that attempts to model the fundamental structures, processes, and institutions of politics. According to David Easton (1965), the defining feature is its authoritative allocation of values for the collectivity.

political violence   The use of physical violence, or very serious threats of such violence, to achieve political goals. The modes range from nuclear war to assassination to riots. Some analysts define as political violence other activities that do not entail physical violence, such as racial epithets or ethnic discrimination.

politics   The processes through which power and influence are used to promote certain values and interests and to determine who gets what, when, and how in a given social system.

positivist law   Explicit written agreements, often enacted by legislatures and interpreted by judiciaries, that specify appropriate and unlawful behaviors as well as the sanctions for the latter. In the form of treaties or conventions between states, positivist law is the basis of international law.

power   Exercised when A (one actor) induces B (another actor) to behave in a manner in which B would not otherwise behave. One taxonomy classifying the forms of power includes force (coercive power), exchange (economic power), and mutuality (integrative power).

presidential government   A political system in which there is a separation of executive and legislative power and structures. This is meant to ensure a system of checks and balances in the policy process, with the legislature taking primary responsibility for policymaking and the president (the executive) taking primary responsibility for policy implementation (although in practice these distinctions may be blurred). The president and the members of the legislature are elected independently, for fixed terms. Examples: Mexico; the United States.

privatization   The selling off of state-owned firms to private actors and/or the use of private firms to provide public goods and services.

prosperity   A fundamental goal for a state and its citizens, with key subgoals including the capacity of the political economy to control resources in order to produce and distribute desired goods and to provide for adequate material well being for its population (see Figure 5.1).

public policy   Any decision or action by a governmental authority that results in the allocation of a value. A taxonomy of public policies could be based on the functional area of the policy (e.g., environmental, trade), the overall effects of the policy (e.g., redistributive, symbolic), or the stages of the policy process (e.g., problem definition, evaluation).

rational choice theory   An array of formal analyses that share two basic features: (1) they are attempts to represent political processes primarily by means of mathematical formulations or systems of symbolic notation, and (2) it is assumed that the behavior of political actors is goal-oriented, based on self-interest, and calculating. Examples: game theory; minimum winning coalition theory.

relational analysis   Approaches to political analysis that specify the systematic connections between sets of phenomena, revealing either patterns of association (correlation) or causality.

representative democracy   A form of electoral democracy in which citizens elect people to represent them in the governing process and to allocate values on their behalf for the collectivity. Also known as a republic.

revolution   A rapid and fundamental transformation of the state organization and of the allocation of values in a society. A revolution often involves the use of force and violence to destroy the existing political system.

security   A fundamental goal of a government and society, with key subgoals including the capacity to survive and to protect its borders from unwanted external intervention (see Figure 5.1).

security dilemma   The situation in the politics across borders where every state is concerned about its security goals because there is no overarching authority that can necessarily enforce a violation of a state's sovereignty.

socialism   One of the major Western political ideologies in which the most important goal is to provide a high-quality, relatively equal standard of living for all. Each individual is encouraged to enhance the collective good of all in an environment that encourages cooperation and sharing. Government plays a crucial role as it attempts to use its allocation of values and control of resources to increase the material, social, and political equality of all citizens. Two major variations are Marxist-Leninist socialism and democratic socialism.

social market system   A political-economic system in which the state encourages the operation of an extensive free-market economy but is also committed to social welfare distribution and some income redistribution, within the context of a democratic political process. Contemporary examples: Germany; Sweden.

soft power   A form of power exercise in which actor B is persuaded to agree to what another actor (A) wants because B greatly admires A's qualities, culture or ideals, even if the agreement is not in B's evident self-interest. In this situation, there is no explicit use of either force or economic inducement, the "hard" forms of power.

sovereignty   The premise that each state has complete authority and is the ultimate source of law within its own borders. It assumes that all states are equal before the law and that each state has the right to protect its territory against any aggression or intervention.

stability   A fundamental goal of a government, with key subgoals including the capacity to maintain public order and to manage public institutions with adequate capabilities to function effectively in pursuing its policy objectives (see Figure 5.1).

state   (1) The legal notion of the state is that it is a "territorially bound sovereign entity." (2) In the general language of political science, the word *state* usually refers to the organizational units, institutions, and individuals that perform the political functions for a national territorial entity, such as France or Nigeria. (3) The state can also be defined as the entity with a monopoly on the legitimate use of violence to enforce the laws and decisions of the society.

statism   A state-centered strategy for facilitating economic development. The statist approach emphasizes the importance of strong state action to support and guide the production and distribution of goods by the political economy. The state typically plans and regulates major aspects of the political economy and might own and operate key economic sectors.

taxonomic analysis   Approaches to political analysis that establish the orderly arrangement of phenomena into a set of categories that classify those phenomena/data into different types. Categories should be exhaustive, mutually exclusive, and differentiated by consistent criteria. The categories of a taxonomy establish the crucial concepts that structure the analysis.

territorial integrity   A concept closely associated with sovereignty, it is a premise of international law that holds that a state has the right to resist and reject any aggression, invasion, or intervention within its territorial borders.

terrorism   Premeditated violence serving an underlying political objective, in which the target of violence is a "noncombatant." Those engaged in terrorism can have a variety of political objectives, such as promotion of a cause, revenge, or extraction of resources. As a revolutionary strategy, terrorism involves selective acts of violence, usually by small, organized cells of political activists.

totalitarianism   A political regime that demands complete obedience to its extensive rules regarding not only politics but nearly all aspects of life, including culture, economics, religion, and morality. It might prescribe and proscribe the behavior and thoughts of its population in every domain of existence. Examples: contemporary North Korea; the Soviet Union under Joseph Stalin.

transnationalism   A system of institutions and relationships in which key actors' loyalties and identities are not linked to any particular country. Many of these powerful actors are multinational corporations (MNCs) such as General Motors, Exxon, and Sony, and other important transnational actors include the International Monetary Fund, OPEC, NATO, and other IGOs and NGOs.

Increasingly, MNCs and other transnational actors hold international economic power, shape global culture and communications, and operate outside the legal control of states.

treaty   A formal agreement between states that they will cooperate or assist each other militarily, economically, and/or politically. A treaty carries a stronger expectation of compliance than an alliance. Examples: NATO; Nuclear Nonproliferation Treaty.

unitary state   A political system in which the central government holds all legitimate power. The central government may delegate power or functional responsibilities to territorial units (often called departments, regions, or prefectures), but those delegated powers and functions can be revoked at any time. Examples: China; France; Japan; the United Kingdom.

war   Interstate violence that is sustained, organized, and usually involves hostilities between the regular military forces of the states. War is the ultimate mechanism for attempting to resolve power struggles and conflict between states. Examples: Iran–Iraq War (1980–1988); Korean War (1950–1953).

welfare state   A system of state interventions in the political economy whose goal is to implement public policies that provide all citizens with an adequate quality of life in domains such as education, health care, housing, and employment pportunities. Usually characterized by relatively high taxes, more extensive resource allocations (e.g., transfer payments or subsidized goods and services), and more active state intervention to protect citizens against the behaviors of those firms or others whose actions reduce the quality of life. Example: Sweden.

REFERENCES

Abadie, Alberto. (2004). "Poverty, Political Freedom, and the Roots of Terrorism." Cambridge, MA: KSG Working Paper 04-043 (October).

Abdallah, Saaman, Sam Thompson, Juliet Michaelson, Nic Marks, and Nicole Steuer. (2009). *The Happy Planet Index.* www.happyplanetindex.org

Acemoglu, Daron and James A. Robinson. (2009). *Economic Origins of Dictatorship and Democracy.* New York: Cambridge University Press.

Agnew, John. (2003). *Geopolitics: Re-Visioning World Politics.* London: Routledge.

———— (2009). *Globalization and Sovereignty.* Rowman and Littlefield.

Almond, Gabriel, and Sidney Verba. (1963). *The Civic Culture.* Princeton, NJ: Princeton University Press.

Amnesty International. (2011). *Amnesty International Report 2011,* http://web.amnesty.org/report2011.

Anderson, James E. (2011). *Public Policy making: An Introduction.* 7th ed. Boston, MA: Wadsworth.

Ardrey, Robert. (1966). *The Territorial Imperative.* New York: Atheneum.

Arendt, Hannah. (1963). *On Revolution.* New York: Viking Press.

Aslund, Anders and Andrew Kuchins. (2009). *The Russia Balance Sheet.* Washington, DC: Peterson Institute for International Economics.

Bachrach, Peter, and Morton Baratz. (1962). "The Two Faces of Power." *American Political Science Review* 56 (December): 947–952.

Bagdikian, Ben. (2004). *The New Media Monopoly.* Boston, MA: Beacon Press.

Baghwati, Jagdish. (2007). *In Defense of Globalization.* New York: Oxford University Press.

Bala-Gbogbo, Elisha. (2010). "Nigeria to Charge Dick Cheney in Pipeline Bribery Case." *Blomberg.com (December 1, 2010).* http://www.businessweek.com/news/2010-12-01/nigeria-to-charge-dick-cheney-in-pipeline-bribery-case.html

Barber, Benjamin R. (1995). *Jihad Versus McWorld.* New York: Random House.

————. (2004). *Strong Democracy: Participatory Politics for a New Age.* 20th anniv. ed. Berkeley: University of California Press.

Barbour, Sara (2008). "Takin' It to the Web." *Miller-McCune Journal.* October 2008: 20–23.

Bardach, Eugene. (2008). *A Practical Guide for Policy Analysis: The Eightfold Path to More Effective Problem Solving.* 3rd ed. Washington, DC: CQ Press.

Barnet, Richard J., and John Cavanagh. (1994). *Global Dreams: Imperial Corporations and the New World Order.* New York: Simon and Schuster.

Barnett, Michael N. and Martha Finnemore. (2004). *Rules for the World: International Organizations in Global Politics.* Ithaca, NY: Cornell University Press.

Bates, Robert H. (2008). *When Things Fell Apart: State Failure in Late Twentieth Century Africa.* Cambridge: Cambridge University Press.

Baumol, William and Alan Blinder, Alan. (2011). *Economics.* 12th ed. Belmont, CA: Thompson.

Baumgartner, Frank, Jeffrey Berry, Marie Hojnacki, David Kimball and Beth L. Leech. (2009). *Lobbying and Policy Change: Who Wins, Who Loses and Why.* Chicago: University of Chicago Press.

Baumgartner, Frank, and Beth Leech. (1998). *Basic Interests: The Importance of Groups in Politics and Political Science.* Princeton, NJ: Princeton University Press.

Bennett, W. Lance. (2012). *News: The Politics of Illusion.* 9th ed. New York: Longman.

Bentley, Arthur. (1908/1967). *The Process of Government.* Cambridge, MA: Harvard University Press.

Berenskoetter, Felix and M.J. Williams, eds. (2007). *Power in World Politics.* New York: Routledge.

Berrebi, Claude. (2007). "Evidence About the Link Between Education,

Poverty, and Terrorism Among Palestinians." *Peace Economics, Peace Science, and Public Policy* 13 (1): article 2.

Berry, Jeffrey. (2000). *The New Liberalism: The Rising Power of Citizen Groups*. Washington, DC: Brookings Press.

Betts, Richard K. (2010). "Conflict or Cooperation?: Three Visions Revisited." *Foreign Affairs 89 (November/December):* http://www.foreignaffairs.com/articles/66802/richard-k-betts/conflict-or-cooperation?page=show

Bill, James, and Robert Hardgrave. (1981). *Comparative Politics: Quest for Theory*. Lanham, MD: University Press of America.

Bimber, Bruce. (2003). *Information and American Democracy: Technology and the Evolution of Political Power*. New York: Cambridge University Press.

Birnbaum, David (2005). "The Road to Riches is Called K Street," *Washington Post* (June 22, 2005): A01. http://www.washingtonpost.com/wp-dyn/content/article/2005/06/21/AR2005062101632.html

Black, Cyril. (1966). *The Dynamics of Modernization*. New York: Harper and Row.

Bloomberg.com (2009). http://www.bloomberg.com/apps/news?pid=20601109&refer=home&sid=aH3aDwXXnvqc

Blustein, Paul. (2006). *And the Money Kept Rolling In (and Out): Wall Street, the IMF, and the Bankruptcy of Argentina*. New York: Public Affairs.

Bonker, Frank. (2006). *The Political Economy of Fiscal Reform in Central-Eastern Europe*. Northampton, MA: Edward Elgar Publishing.

Boulding, Kenneth E. (1989). *Three Faces of Power*. Newbury Park, CA: Sage.
——— (1993). "Power." In *The Oxford Companion to Politics of the World*, ed. Joel Krieger, pp. 739–740. New York: Oxford University Press.

Boulianne, S. (2009). "Does Internet Use Affect Engagement? A Meta-Analysis of Research." *Political Communication*, 26(2), 193–211.

Bratton, Michael, and Nicolas van de Walle. (1997). *Democratic Experiments in Africa: Regime Transitions in Comparative Perspective*. New York: Cambridge University Press.

Brecher, Michael, and Jonathan Wilkenfeld. (2000). *A Study of Crisis*. Ann Arbor: University of Michigan Press.

Bremer, Stuart. (1980). "National Capabilities and War Proneness." In *Correlates of War, II*, ed. J. David Singer, pp. 57–82. New York: Free Press.

Brinton, Crane. (1957). *The Anatomy of Revolution*. Rev. ed. New York: Vintage.

The Brookings Institution. (2011). "How Social Networking can Reinvigorate American Democracy and Civic Participation." Washington, D.C. (June 28, 2011). http://www.pewinternet.org/Presentations/2011/Jun/~/media/Files/Presentations/2011/Jun/Brookings_social_media.pdf

Brown, Mark Malloch. (2002). The Millennium Development Goals and Africa: A New Framework. Address at Makerere University, Uganda. November 12, 2002. http://content.undp.org/go/newsroom/2002/november/mmb-uganda.en;jsessionid=axbWzt8vXD9

Brzezinski, Zbigniew. (2004). *The Choice: Global Domination or Global Leadership*. New York: Basic Books.

Bueno de Mesquita, Bruce, and George Downs. (2005). "Development and Democracy." *Foreign Affairs 84* (September/October): 77–86.

Burke, Edmund. (1790/1955). *The Works of Edmund Burke*. New York: Harper and Row.

Calderisi, Robert. (2007). *The Trouble with Africa: Why Foreign Aid Isn't Working*. New York: Palgrave.

Castells, Manuel. (2009). *Communication Power*. New York: Oxford University Press.

Castenada, Jorge G. (2011). *Manana Forever?: Mexico and the Mexicans*. New York: Alfred Knopf.

Castles, Francis G. (2004). *The Future of the Welfare State: Crisis Myths and Crisis Realities*. New York: Oxford University Press.

Castles, Francis G., Stephan Leibfried, Jane Lewis, Herbert Obinger and Christopher Pierson. Eds. (2010). *The Oxford Handbook of the Welfare State*. New York: Oxford University Press.

Center for Responsive Politics. (2009). http://www.opensecrets.org.

Central Intelligence Agency. (2011). *World Factbook 2011*. http:// www.odci.gov/cia/ciahome.html

Chadwick, Andrew and Philip Howard. (2009). *Routledge*

Handbook of Internet Politics. New York: Routledge.

Cheibub, Jose Antonio. (2007). *Presidentialism, Parliamentarianism, and Democracy.* New York: Cambridge University Press.

Clausewitz, Karl von. (1833/1967). *On War.* Ed. and trans. Michael Howard and Peter Paret. Princeton, NJ: Princeton University Press.

CNA Corporation. (2007). *National Security and the Threat of Climate Change.* CNA Corporation: Alexandria, VA.

Cohen, Saul Bernard. (2008). *Geopolitics of the World System. 2nd ed.* Rowan & Littlefield.

Colburn, Forrest. (2002). *Latin America at the End of Politics.* Princeton, NJ: Princeton University Press.

Coles, Robert. (2003). *Bruce Springsteen's America: The People Listening, a Poet Singing.* New York: Random House.

Collier, Paul. (2010). *Wars, Guns and Votes: Democracy in Dangerous Places.* New York: Harper.

Compton, Robert W. (2000). *East Asian Democratization: Impact of Globalization, Culture, and Economy.* Westport, CT: Greenwood.

Connor, Walker. (1994). *Ethnonationalism: The Quest for Understanding.* Princeton, NJ: Princeton University Press.

Converse, Philip. (1964). "The Nature of Belief Systems in Mass Publics." In *Ideology and Discontent,* ed. David Apter, pp. 224–240. Glencoe, IL: Free Press.

Cortright, David, and George Lopez, Eds. (2002). *Smart Sanctions: Toward Effective and Humane Sanctions Reform.* Lanham, MD: Rowan and Littlefield.

Costanza, Robert. (2008). "Stewardship for a 'Full' World." *Current History* (January): 30–35.

Council on Foreign Relations. (2005). *What Is Terrorism?* http:// cfrterrorism.org/ terrorism/introduction.html.

Cutright, Phillips. (1963). "National Political Development: Measurement and Analysis." *American Sociological Review* 20: 253–264.

Cropf, Robert A. and William S. Krummenacher. Eds. (2011). *Information Communication Technologies and the Virtual Public Sphere: Impacts of Network Structures on Civil Society.* Hershey, PA: IGI Global.

Crouch, Colin and Wolfgang Streeck. Eds. (2006). *The Diversity of Democracy: Corporatism, Social Order and Political Conflict.* Cheltenham, UK: Edward Elgar.

Dahl, Robert. (1961). *Who Governs? Democracy in an American City.* New Haven, CT: Yale University Press.

———. (1971). *Polyarchy: Participation and Opposition.* New Haven, CT: Yale University Press.

———. (1991). *Democracy and Its Critics.* New Haven, CT: Yale University Press.

———. (2006). *A Preface to Democratic Theory.* Expanded ed. Chicago: University of Chicago Press.

Dahl, Robert, and Bruce Stinebrickner. (2003). *Modern Political Analysis.* 6th ed. New York: Pearson.

Dahrendorf, Ralf. (1959). *Class and Class Conflict in Industrial Society.* Stanford, CA: Stanford University Press.

Dalby, Simon. (2008). "Imperialism, Domination, Culture: The Continued Relevance of Critical Geopolitics" *Geopolitics* 13.3 http://www.informaworld.com/ 10.1080/14650040802203679

Dalton, Russell. (2008). *Citizen Politics: Public Opinion and Political Parties in Advanced Industrial Democracies.* 5th ed. Washington, DC: CQ Press.

———. (2009). *The Good Citizen.* Washington, DC: CQ Press.

Davies, James C. (1971). "Toward a Theory of Revolution." In *When Men Revolt and Why,* ed. James C. Davies, pp. 134–147. New York: Free Press.

Davis, Winston. (1987). "Religion and Development: Weber and the East Asian Experience." In *Understanding Political Development,* ed. Myron Weiner and Samuel Huntington, pp. 221–280. Boston: Little, Brown.

Delli Carpini, Michael X., and Scott. Keeter. (1996). *What Americans Know about Politics and Why it Matters.* New Haven: Yale University Press.

Demick, Barbara. (2003). "U.S. Gets a Bad Name in South Korea." *Los Angeles Times,* July 12, A3.

Derbyshire, Denis, and Ian Derbyshire. (2000). *Encyclopedia of World Political Systems.* New York: M. E. Sharpe.

Diamond, Larry. (2008). *The Spirit of Democracy: The*

Struggle to Build Free Societies Throughout the World. New York: Holt.

Diamond, Larry, and Mark F. Plattner. (2009). *Democracy: A Reader.* Baltimore, MD: Johns Hopkins University Press.

Dolan, Julie Ann, Melissa Deckman, and Michele Swers. (2007). *Women and Politics: Paths to Power and Influence.* New York: Prentice Hall.

Domhoff, G. William. (2005). "Social Cohesion & the Bohemian Grove: The Power Elite at Summer Camp." http://sociology.ucsc.edu/whorulesamerica/power/bohemian_grove.html

————. (2009). *Who Rules America? Power, Politics, and Social Change.* 6th ed. Boston: McGraw-Hill.

Doyle, Michael W., and Nicholas Sambanis. (2000). "International Peacebuilding: A Theoretical and Quantitative Analysis." *American Political Science Review* 94 (December): 779–801.

Drezner, Daniel. (2007). *All Politics Are Global.* Princeton, NJ: Princeton University Press.

Duverger, Maurice. (1954). *Political Parties.* New York: Wiley.

Easterlin, Richard. (2006). "Building a Better Theory of Well-Being." In *Economics and Happiness: Framing the Analysis,* eds. Luigino Bruni and Pier Luigi Porta, pp. 29–64. New York: Oxford University Press.

Easton, David. (1965). *A Framework for Political Analysis.* Englewood Cliffs, NJ: Prentice Hall.

Ebenstein, William and Alan O. Ebenstein. (2001).

Introduction to Political Thinkers. 2nd ed. Florence, KY: Wadsworth.

Eckstein, Harry. (1966). *Division and Cohesion in Democracy: A Study of Norway.* Princeton, NJ: Princeton University Press.

Economic Policy Institute. (2011). *The State of Working America.* http://www.stateofworkingamerica.org/

Edwards, George, Martin Wattenberg, and Robert Lineberry. (2008). *Government in America.* 13th ed. New York: Longman.

Elgie, Robert. (2004). "Semi-presidentialism: Concepts, Consequences and Contesting Explanations," *Political Studies Review, Vol. 2, No. 3.*

Elkington, John, and Seb Beloe. (2003). *The 21st Century NGO: In the Market for Change.* London: Sustain-Ability.

Enloe, Cynthia. (2001). *Bananas, Beaches and Bases: Making Feminist Sense of International Politics.* Berkeley, CA: University of California Press.

Eriksson, Mikael, Peter Wallensteen, and Margareta Sollenberg. (2003). "Armed Conflict, 1989–2002." *Journal of Peace Research* 40:593–607.

Erikson, Erik. (1958). *Young Man Luther.* New York: W. W. Norton.

————. (1969). *Gandhi's Truth.* New York: W. W. Norton.

Esping-Andersen, Gosta. (1990). *The Three Worlds of Welfare Capitalism.* Princeton, NJ: Princeton University Press.

Estrin, Saul, Jan Honousek, Evzen Kocenda and Jan Svejnar. (2009). "Effects of Privatization and Ownership in Transition Economies." *Policy*

Research Working Paper 4811. New York: World Bank.

Europa: Gateway to the European Union. (2011). http://europa.eu.int/index_en.htm

Evans, Gareth. (2008). *The Responsibility to Protect: Ending Mass Atrocity Crimes Once and For All.* Washington, D.C.: Brookings.

Fagen, Richard. (1964). *Cuba: The Political Content of Adult Education.* Stanford, CA: Hoover Institute.

Fallows, James. (1995). *Looking at the Sun: The Rise of the New East Asian Economic and Political System.* New York: Random House.

Federation of American Scientists. (2012). http://www.fas.org/.

Fendrich, James. (1993). *Ideal Citizen: The Legacy of the Civil Rights Movement.* Albany, NY: SUNY Press.

Foreign Policy. (2011). "Failed State Index." *Foreign Policy: June 1, 2011.* http://www.foreignpolicy.com/articles/2010/06/21/2010_failed_states_index_interactive_map_and_rankings

Fowler, James, and Christopher Dawes (2009). "Partisanship, Voting, and the Dopamine D2 Receptor Gene." *Journal of Politics* 71 (3): 1157–1171 (July 2009).

Frank, Robert. (2001). Luxury Fever: Money and Happiness in an Era of Excess. Princeton, NJ: Princeton University Press.

Franko, Patrice. (2003). *The Puzzle of Latin American Economic Development.* 2nd ed. Lanham, MD: Rowman & Littlefield.

Fraser, Matthew. (2005). *Weapons of Mass Distraction: Soft Power and American*

Empire. New York: St. Martin's Press.

Freedom House. (2011). *Freedom of the World*. http://www .freedomhouse.org

Friedman, Thomas L. (1999). "DOScapital." *Foreign Policy* 113 (Fall): 110–127.

———. (2007). *The World Is Flat: A Brief History of the Twenty-first Century*. 2nd revised ed. New York: Farrar, Straus and Giroux.

Fukuyama, Francis. (1992). *The End of History and the Last Man*. New York: Free Press.

———. "Confucianism and Democracy." (2009). In Putnam, Robert and Marc Plattner. Eds. *Democracy: A Reader*. Baltimore, MD: John Hopkins University Press.

———. (1999). *The Great Disruption: Human Nature and the Reconstitution of Social Order*. New York: Free Press.

Garrett, R. Kelly and James N. Danziger. (2011). "The Internet Electorate." *Communications of the ACM* 54: 3 (March): 117–123.

Givan, Rebecca Kolins, Sarah Anne Soule and Kenneth Roberts. Eds. (2010). *The Diffusion of Social Movements: Actors, Mechanisms and Political Effects*. New York: Cambridge University Press.

Gladwell, Malcolm. (2010). "Why the revolution will not be." *The New Yorker*. (October 4, 2010). Retrieved from http://www.newyorker .com/reporting/2010/10/04/ 101004fa_fact_gladwell

Gleditsch, Nils Petter, Lene Siljeholm Christiansen and Håvard Hegre. (2007).

Democratic Jihad? Military Intervention and Democracy. World Bank Policy Research Working Paper 4242.

Global Exchange. (2009). "Top Reasons to Oppose the World Trade Organization." http:// www.globalexchange.org

Gochman, Charles S., and Zeev Maoz. (1984). "Militarized Interstate Disputes, 1816–1976." *Journal of Conflict Resolution* 18 (December): 588–615.

Goldman, Marshall I. (2003). *The Piratization of Russia*. New York: Routledge.

———. (2008). *Petrostate: Putin, Power and the New Russia*. Oxford: Oxford University Press.

Goodin, Robert, and Philip Pettit Eds. (2006). *Contemporary Political Philosophy: An Anthology*. 2nd ed. Oxford: Blackwell.

Goodwin, Paul. (2008). *Latin America*. 13th ed. New York: McGraw-Hill.

Gowa, Joanne. (2000*). Ballots and Bullets: The Elusive Democratic Peace*. Princeton, NJ: Princeton University Press.

Graber, Doris A. (2009). *Mass Media and American Politics*. 8th ed. Washington, DC: CQ Press.

Grameen Bank. (2011). http:// www.grameen-info.org

Grotius, Hugo. (1625/1957). *De Jure Belli et Pacis [On the Laws of War and Peace]*. New York: Macmillan.

Hamilton, Alexander, James Madison and John Jay (2007). *The Federalist Papers*. Minneapolis, MN: Filiquarian Publishing, LLC.

Happy Planet Index (2011). www.happyplanetindex .org

Harm, Marie and Hermann Wiehle. (1942). *Lebenskunde für Mittelschulen. Fünfter Teil. Klasse 5 für Mädchen* (Halle: Hermann Schroedel Verlag), pp. 168–173. http://www .calvin.edu/academic/cas/gpa/ textbk01.htm

Haynes, Jeffrey. Ed. (2010). *Religion and Politics in Europe, the Middle East and North Africa*. London: Routledge/ECPR Studies in European Political Science.

———. (2007). *An Introduction to International Relations and Religion*. Essex: Pearson.

Hearnshaw, F. J. C. (1933). *Conservatism in England*. London: Macmillan.

Heilbroner, Robert. (1993). "The Multinational Corporation and the Nation-State." In *At Issue: Politics in the World Arena*, ed. Steven L. Speigel, pp. 338–352. New York: St. Martin's Press.

———. (1994). *Twenty-First Century Capitalism*. New York: W. W. Norton.

Heritage Foundation. (2011). *Index of Economic Freedom 2011*. http://www.heritage .org/research/features/index/ countries.cfm

Heyne, Paul, Peter Boettke, and David Prychitko. (2010). *The Economic Way of Thinking*. 12th ed. New York: Prentice Hall.

Hibbing, John, Douglas R. Oxley, Kevin B. Smith, John R. Alford, Matthew V. Hibbing, Jennifer L. Miller, Mario Scalora, and Peter K. Hatemi. (2008). "Political Attitudes Vary with Physiological Traits," *Science* 321(5896): 1667–1670.

Hibbing, John, and Kevin Smith (eds.). (2007). *The Biology of*

Political Behavior. The Annals of the American Academy of Political and Social Science, 614 (1).

Higley, John and Michael Burton. (2006). *Elite Foundations of Liberal Democracy*. Lanham, MD: Rowman & Littlefield.

Hill, Stephen. (2010). *Europe's Promise: Why the European Way Is the Best Hope for an Insecure Age*. Berkeley, CA: University of California Press.

Hobbes, Thomas. (1651/1958). *Leviathan*. Oxford, England: Clarendon.

Hoffman, John and Paul Graham. (2009). *An Introduction to Political Theory*. 2nd ed. Essex, England: Pearson Educational.

Hoover, Kenneth, James Marcia and Kristen Parris. (1997). *The Power of Identity: Politics in a New Key*. Chatham, NJ: Chatham House.

Horowitz, Donald L. (1990). "Comparing Democratic Systems." *Journal of Democracy*, Vol.1, No.4: 73–79.

Hunter, Floyd. (1953). *Community Power Structure*. Chapel Hill: University of North Carolina Press.

Huntington, Samuel P. (1968). *Political Order in Changing Societies*. New Haven, CT: Yale University Press.

———. (1991). *The Third Wave: Democratization in the Late Twentieth Century*. Norman: University of Oklahoma Press.

———. (1998). *Clash of Civilizations and the Remaking of the World Order*. New York: Simon and Schuster.

Huxley, Aldous. (1932). *Brave New World*. London: Chatto and Windus.

IDMC (Internal Displacement Monitoring Center). (2011). http:// www.internal-displacement.org

Ikenberry, G. John. (2011). *Liberal Leviathan: The Origins, Crisis and Transformation of the American World Order*. Princeton, NJ: Princeton University Press.

Inglehart, Ronald and Pippa Norris. (2003). *Rising Tide: Gender Equality and Cultural Change Around the World*. New York: Cambridge University Press.

Inglehart, Ronald, and Christian Welzel. (2005). *Modernization, Cultural Change, and Democracy: The Human Development Sequence*. New York: Cambridge University Press.

Inkeles, Alex. (1997). *National Character: A Psycho-Social Perspective*. New Brunswick, NJ: Transaction.

Inkeles, Alex, and David Smith. (1999). *Becoming Modern: Individual Change in Six Developing Countries*. Cambridge, MA: Harvard University Press.

International Institute for Democracy and Electoral Assistance. (2011). www.idea .int/vt

International Food Policy Research Institute. (2003). www.ifpri.org/

International Social Survey Program. (2004). http://www .gesis.org/en/services/data/ survey-data/issp/modules-study-overview/citizenship/

Isbister, John. (2006). *Promises Not Kept: Poverty and the Betrayal of Third World Development*. 7th ed. Bloomfield, CT: Kumarian Press.

Iyengar, Shanto and Jennifer McGrady. (2006). *Media Politics*. New York: Norton.

Jackson, Robert. (2007). *Sovereignty: The Evolution of an Idea*. Malden, MA: Polity Press.

Jenkins, Barbara. (1993). "Multinational Corporations." In *The Oxford Companion to Politics of the World*, ed. Joel Krieger, pp. 606–608. New York: Oxford University Press.

Jennings, M. Kent, Gregory Markus, and Richard Niemi. (1991). *Youth-Parent Socialization Panel Study, 1965–1982*. Ann Arbor, MI: Interuniversity Consortium for Political Research.

Jensen, Jane. (2008). *Women Political Leaders: Breaking the Glass Ceiling*. New York: Palgrave Macmillan.

Jensen, Michael. (2010). "Local Democracy and the Internet." Irvine, CA: CRITO Working Paper.

Jervis, Robert. (2002). "Theories of War in an Era of Leading-Power Peace." *American Political Science Review* 96 (1): 1–14.

Johnson, Chalmers. (1983). *Revolutionary Change*. 2nd ed. London: Longman.

Johnson, Simon. (2009). "The Quiet Coup." *The Atlantic*. (May 2009). http://www .theatlantic.com/doc/200905/ imf-advice

Johnston, Michael. (2006). *Syndromes of Corruption: Wealth, Power and Democracy*. New York: Cambridge University Press.

Juergensmeyer Mark. (2003). *Terror in the Mind of God: The Global Rise of Religious Violence*. Rev. ed. Berkeley: University of California Press.

Juergensmeyer, Mark. (2008). *Global Rebellion: Religious Challenges to the Secular*

State. Berkeley, CA: University of California Press.

Kahler, Miles. (2002). "The State of the State in World Politics." In *Political Science: State of the Discipline,* ed. Ira Katznelson and Helen Milner. New York: W. W. Norton.

Kaplan, Robert D. (2009). "The Revenge of Geography." *Foreign Policy* (May/June): 96–105.

Karatnycky, Adrian and Peter Ackerman. (2006). "How Freedom Is Won: From Civic Struggle to Durable Democracy." http://www.freedomhouse.org/template.cfm?page=137

Karlekar, Karin. (2009). "Freedom of the Press." http://www.freedomhouse.org

Katz, E. and Paul Lazarsfeld. (1955). *Personal Influence.* New York: Free Press.

Kegley, Charles W., Jr. (2011). *World Politics: Trend and Transformation.* 13th ed. New York: Thompson Wadsworth.

Kegley, Charles W., Jr., and Eugene Wittkopf. (2004). *World Politics: Trend and Transformation.* 9th ed. New York: Thomson Wadsworth.

Kennedy, Paul. (2006). *The Parliament of Man: The Past, Present, and Future of the United Nations.* New York: Random House.

Keohane, Robert O. (2005). *After Hegemony: Cooperation and Discord in the World Political Economy.* Princeton, NJ: Princeton University Press.

Keohane, Robert O. and Joseph Nye. (2000). "Globalization: What's New. And What's Not. (And So What?)" *Foreign Affairs* (Spring): 104–119.

———. (2011). *Power and Interdependence: World Politics in Transition,* 4th ed. New York: Longman.

Khor, Martin. (2011). "Developing a Global Partnership for Development: Critical Issues and Proposals for Trade and Finance." http://www.twnside.org.sg/crisis_2.htm

King, Gary, Kay Scholzman, and Norman Nie, Ed. (2009). *The Future of Political Science: 100 Perspectives.* New York: Routledge.

Klare, Michael T. (1997). "The New Arms Race: Light Weapons and International Security." *Current History* 96 (April): 173–178.

Klare, Michael. (2002). *Resource Wars: The New Landscape of Global Conflict.* New York: Henry Holt.

———. (2007). "Global Warming Battlefields: How Climate Change Threatens Security." *Current History* (November): 355–361.

———. (2009). *Rising Powers, Shrinking Planet: The New Geopolitics of Energy.* New York: Holt.

———. (2012). *The Race for What's Left: The Global Scramble for the World's Last Resources.* New York: Metropolitan Books.

Klein, Naomi. (2008). *The Shock Doctrine: The Rise of Disaster Capitalism.* New York: Metropolitan Books.

Klingemann, Hans Dieter. (2009). *The Comparative Study of Electoral Systems.* New York: Oxford University Press.

Koopmans, Tim. (2003). *Courts and Political Institutions: A Comparative View.* Cambridge, England: Cambridge University Press.

Kraul, Chris. (2011). "Are Argentina's Good Times an Illusion?" *Los Angeles Times,* August 2, 2011: B1, B5.

Kuhn, Thomas. (1996). *The Structure of Scientific Revolutions.* 3rd ed. Chicago: University of Chicago Press.

Kurian, George, James E. Alt, Simone Chambers, Geoffrey Garrett, Margaret Levi, and Paula D. McClain. Eds. (2011). *The Encyclopedia of Political Science.* Washington, D.C.: CQ Press.

Kurlantzick, Joshua. (2007). *Charm Offensive: How China's Soft Power is Transforming the World.* New Haven, CN: Yale University Press.

Laitin, David. D. (2007). *Nations, States and Violence.* New York: Oxford University Press.

Lanchester, John. (2010). *I. O. U.: Why Everyone Owes Everyone and No One Can Pay.* New York: Simon & Schuster.

Laquer, Walter. (2009). *The Last Days of Europe: Epitaph for an Old Continent.* New York: St. Martin's Griffin.

Larkey, Edward. (1990). "Rock Music and Cultural Theory in the German Democratic Republic." In *Politics in Familiar Contexts,* ed. Robert L. Savage and Dan Nimmo, pp. 215–224. Norwood, NJ: Ablex.

Layard, R. (2005). *Happiness: Lessons from a New Science.* New York: Penguin.

Lasswell, Harold. (1960). *Psychopathology and Politics.* New York: Viking.

Latinobarometro. (2011). http://www.latinobarometro.org

Leiken, Robert S. (2009). "The Menace in Europe's Midst." *Current History* 108 (717): 186–188.

Lenski, Gerhard. (1966). *Power and Privilege: A Theory of Social Stratification*. New York: McGraw-Hill.

Levi, Margaret. (2002). "The State of the Study of the State." In *Political Science: State of the Discipline*, ed. Ira Katznelson and Helen Milner. New York: W. W. Norton.

Levy, Francesca. (2010). The World's Happiest Places. *Forbes.com*. http://www.forbes.com/2010/07/14/world-happiest-countries-lifestyle

Lijphart, Arend. (1984). *Democracies: Patterns of Majoritarian and Consensual Government in Twenty-One Countries*. New Haven, CT: Yale University Press.

Lindblom, Charles E. (1977). *Politics and Markets: The World's Political-Economic Systems*. New York: Basic Books.

———. (2003). *The Market System: What It Is, How It Works, and What to Make of It*. New Haven, CT: Yale University Press.

Linz, Juan J. (1990a). 'The Perils of Presidentialism,' *Journal of Democracy*, Vol.1, No.1, pp. 51–69.

———. (1990b). 'The Virtues of Parliamentarism', *Journal of Democracy*, Vol.1, No.4, pp. 84–91.

———. (1993). "Authoritarianism." In *The Oxford Companion to Politics of the World*, ed. Joel Krieger, pp. 60–64. New York: Oxford University Press.

———. (1994). "Presidential or Parliamentary Democracy: Does it Make a Difference?" In *The Failure of Presidential Democracy*. ed. Juan J. Linz and Arturo Valenzuela.

Baltimore: The Johns Hopkins University Press: 3–87.

Linz, Juan J., and Alfred Stepan. (1996). *Problems of Democratic Transition and Consolidation: Southern Europe, South America, and Post-Communist Europe*. Baltimore, MD: Johns Hopkins University Press.

Lipset, Seymour Martin Lipset. 1959. "Some Social Requisites of Democracy: Economic Development and Political Legitimacy." *American Political Science Review 53* (March): 69–105.

Little, Richard. (2007). *The Balance of Power in International Relations: Metaphors, Myths and Models*. New York: Cambridge University Press.

Locke, John. (1690/1963). *Two Treatises on Government*. New York: New American Library.

Love, Nancy S., Ed. (2010). *Dogmas and Dreams: A Reader in Modern Political Ideologies*. 4th ed. New York: Seven Bridges Press.

Lozada, Carlos. (2003). "Think Again: Latin America." *Foreign Policy* 135 (March/April): 18–26.

Lukes, Steven. (2005). *Power: A Radical Review*. 2nd ed. London: Palgrave-Macmillan.

Lupia, Arthur, and Mathew McCubbins. (1998). *The Democratic Dilemma: Can Citizens Learn What They Need to Know?* Cambridge, England: Cambridge University Press.

Machiavelli, Niccolò. (1517/1977). *The Prince*. Trans. and ed. Robert M. Adams. New York: W. W. Norton.

Mackinder, Halford John. (1996). *Democratic Ideals and Reality*. Washington, DC: U.S. Government Printing Office.

Mahbubani, Kishore. (2008). *The New Asian Hemisphere: The Irresistible Shift of Global Power*. New York: PublicAffairs.

Mainwaring, Scott and Matthew S. Shugart. Eds. (1997). *Presidentialism and Democracy in Latin America* Cambridge: Cambridge University Press.

Mander, Jerry. (1999). "Regarding the WTO." *International Forum on Globalization*. http://www.ifg.org/media.html

Mandelbaum, Michael. (2004). *The Ideas that Conquered the World: Peace, Democracy and the Free Markets in the Twenty-first Century*. New York: PublicAffairs.

March, James G., and Johan P. Olsen. (1989). *Rediscovering Institutions: The Organizational Basis of Politics*. New York: Free Press.

———. (2006). "Elaborating the 'New Institutionalism.'" In *The Oxford Handbook of Political Institutions*, ed. R. A. W. Rhodes, Sarah Binder, and Bert Rockman. Oxford: Oxford University Press.

Marinov, Nikolay, and Goemans, Hein. (2008). "What Happened to the Coup d'Etat?: International Responses to the Seizure of Executive Power." Paper presented at the Midwest Political Science Association Annual Conference, Chicago, IL, April 3, 2008.

Marshall, Monty G. and Jack Goldstone. (2009). *The State Fragility Index*.

http://www.systemicpeace.org/polity/polity4.htm

Marx, Karl. (1867/1981). *Capital*. Trans. David Fernbach. New York: Vintage.

Marx, Karl, and Friedrich Engels. (1848/1978). "The Communist Manifesto." In *The Marx-Engels Reader*, 2nd ed., ed. Robert Tucker, pp. 482–500. New York: W. W. Norton.

Maslow, Abraham. (1954). *Motivation and Personality*. New York: Harper and Row.

Maxfield, Sylvia. (1997). *Gatekeepers of Growth: The International Political Economy of Central Banking in Developing Countries*. Princeton, NJ: Princeton University Press.

McCormick, John. (2006). *The European Superpower*. New York: Palgrave.

McFaul, Michael. (1998). "Russia's Summer of Discontent." *Current History* 97 (October): 307–312.

———. (2007). "New Russia, New Threat." *Los Angeles Times*, September 2, M8.

McFaul, Michael, Kathryn Stoner-Weiss and Valerie Bunce. (2010). *Democracy and Authoritarianism in the Postcommunist World*. New York: Cambridge University Press.

McLellan, David. (1983). "Marx in England." *History Today* 33: 3. http://www.historytoday.com/MainArticle.aspx?m=12568&amid=12568

———. Ed. (2007). *Marxism After Marx*. 4th ed. New York: Palgrave.

Mearsheimer, John J. (2001). *The Tragedy of Great Power Politics*. New York: W. W. Norton.

———. (2011). *Why Leaders Lie: The Truth about Lying in International Politics*. New York: Oxford University Press.

Meisner, Maurice. (1999). *Mao's China and After*. 3rd ed. New York: Free Press.

———. (2006). *Mao Zedong: A Political and Intellectual Portrait*. London: Polity Press.

Meyer, Josh. (2007). "Small Groups Now a Large Threat," *Los Angeles Times*, August 16, A1, A10.

Microcredit Summit Conference. (2006). http://www.microcreditsummit.org

Miller, Benjamin. (2007). *States, Nations and the Great Powers: The Source of Regional War and Peace*. New York: Cambridge University Press.

Miller, Roger LeRoy. (2011). *Economics Today*. 16th ed. New York: Prentice-Hall.

Mills, C. Wright. (1956). *The Power Elite*. New York: Oxford University Press.

Moisi, Dominique. (2009). *The Geopolitics of Emotion: How Fear, Humiliation and Hope are Reshaping the World*. New York: Random House.

Moore, Barrington. (1966). *The Social Origins of Dictatorship and Democracy*. Cambridge, MA: Harvard University Press.

Morales, Evo. (2006). *Quoted in La Prensa (September 10, 2006)*. http://en.wikipedia.org/wiki/Domestic_policy_of_Evo_Morales

Morgenthau, Hans J. (2005). *Politics Among Nations*. 7th Brief ed. Revised by Kenneth W. Thompson with David Clinton. New York: McGraw Hill.

Mosca, Gaetano. (1896/1939). *The Ruling Class*. Trans. Hannah Kahn. New York: McGraw-Hill.

Mossberger, Karen, Caroline Tolbert, and Ramona McNeal. (2008). *Digital Citizenship: The Internet, Society, and Participation*. Cambridge, MA: MIT Press.

Mueller, Dennis. (2003). *Public Choice III*. New York: Cambridge University Press.

Murphy, Dean. (1995). "East Europe P.D. Blues." *Los Angeles Times*, February 28, 1995: pp. H1, H4.

Murray, Charles. *Losing Ground: American Social Policy, 1950–1980*. New York: Basic Books.

Nadiri, Khalid. (2007). "Of Note: China's Peasant Populism: A Look Inland." *SAIS Review* 27 (1) (Winter-Spring): 125–126.

NCTC (National Counterterrorism Center). (2011). *A Chronology of Significant International Terrorism for 2009*. http://www.NCTC.gov

Nelson, Joan. (1993). "Political Participation." In *The Oxford Companion to Politics of the World*, ed. Joel Krieger, pp. 720–722. New York: Oxford University Press.

Niemi, Richard G., and Herbert Weissberg. (2001). *Controversies in Voting Behavior*. 4th ed. Washington, DC: CQ Press.

Nimmo, Dan, and James E. Combs. (1990). *Mediated Political Realities*. 2nd ed. White Plains, NY: Longman.

Norris, Pippa. (2004). *Electoral Engineering: Voting Rules and Political Behavior*. Cambridge,

England: Cambridge University Press.

———. (2003). *Institutions Matter*. London: Cambridge University Press.

Norris, Pippa, and Ronald Inglehart. (2004). *Sacred and Secular: Religion and Politics Worldwide*. New York: Cambridge University Press.

———. (2009). *Cosmopolitan Communications: Cultural Diversity in a Globalized World*. New York: Cambridge University Press.

Nugent, Neill. (2008). *The Government and Politics of the European Union*. 6th ed. Durham, NC: Duke University Press.

Nye, Joseph S. (2004). *Soft Power: The Means to Success in World Politics*. Washington, DC: Public Affairs.

———. (2011). *The Future of Power*. New York: PublicAffairs.

O'Connor, Karen, and Larry Sabato. (2007). *The Essentials of American Government*. 8th ed. New York: Longman.

OECD. (2011). Organization of Economic Cooperation and Development. *Main Economic Indicators*. http://www .oecdilibrary.org/economics/ main-economic-indicators _22195009

Organski, A.F. K. (1968). *World Politics*. New York: Alfred Knopf.

Orwell, George. (1945/1964). *Animal Farm*. Middlesex, England: Penguin.

———. (1949/1967). *1984*. Middlesex, England: Penguin.

Packenham, Robert. (1998). *The Dependency Movement: Scholarship and Politics in Development Studies*.

Cambridge, MA: Harvard University Press.

Panitch, Leo. (2009). *Renewing Socialism: Democracy, Strategy and Imagination*. London: Merlin Press.

Pattison, James. (2010). *Humanitarian Intervention and the Responsibility to Protect: Who Should Intervene?* New York: Oxford University Press.

PERC [Political and Economic Risk Consulting]. (2011). http://www.asiarisk.com/

Parenti, Michael. (2010). *Democracy for the Few*. 9th ed. New York: Wadsworth.

Peterson, Scott. (2001). "Jaded Hope: Russia 10 Years Later." *Christian Science Monitor*, August 17, 1, 7–8.

Petrik, Will. (2009). "International Monetary Fund and the Inter-American Development Bank: A History of Limited Choices and Broken Promises." Council on Hemispheric Affairs. http:// www.coha.org/2009/04/ international-monetary- fund-and-the-inter-american- development-bank-a- history-of- limited-choices- and-broken-promises/

Pew. (2011). *Pew Internet and American Life Project*. http:// www.pewinternet.org/

Pharr, Susan J., and Robert D. Putnam, Eds. (2000). *Disaffected Democracies: What's Troubling the Trilateral Countries?* Princeton, NJ: Princeton University Press.

Phillips, Kevin. (2003). *Wealth and Democracy: A Political History of the American Rich*. New York: Broadway Books.

Pickering, Jeffrey and Mark Peceny. (2006*)*. "Forging Democracy at Gunpoint."

International Studies Quarterly 50, 3, 539–60.

Plasser, Gunda. (2002). *Global Political Campaigning*. Westport, CN: Greenwood Publishing.

Popper, Karl. (1963). *The Open Society and Its Enemies*. Vol. 2. New York: Harper and Row.

Posen, Barry. (2003). "Command of the Commons: The Military Foundation of U.S. Hegemony." *International Security* 28 (Summer 2003): 5–46.

Post, Jerrold. (2008). *The Mind of the Terrorist: The Psychology of Terrorism from the IRA to al-Qaeda*. London: Palgrave Macmillan.

Poulantzas, Nicos. (1973). *Political Power and Social Classes*. London: Sheed and Ward.

Powell, G. Bingham, Kaare Strom, and Russell Dalton, Eds. (2012). *Comparative Politics Today: A World View*. 10th ed. New York: Longman.

Prunier, Gerard. (2008). *Africa's World War: Congo, the Rwandan Genocide, and the Making of a Continental Disaster*. New York: Oxford University Press.

Przeworski, Adam. (1985). *Capitalism and Social Democracy*. Cambridge, England: Cambridge University Press.

———. (1993). "Socialism and Social Democracy." In *The Oxford Companion to Politics of the World*, ed. Joel Krieger, pp. 832–838. New York: Oxford University Press.

———. (2004). "Democracy and Economic Development." In *The Evolution of Political Knowledge*, ed. Edward

D. Mansfield and Richard Sisson. Columbus: Ohio State University Press.

Przeworski, Adam, Michael Alvarez, Jose Antonio Cheibub, and Fernando Limongi. (2000). *Democracy and Development: Political Institutions and Well-Being in the World, 1950–1990.* New York: Cambridge University Press.

Puddington, Arch. (2011). "Democracy under Duress." *Journal of Democracy 22 (2):* 17–31.

Putnam, Robert. (1993). *Making Democracy Work: Civic Traditions in Modern Italy.* Princeton, NJ: Princeton University Press.

———. (2000). *Bowling Alone: The Collapse and Revival of American Community.* New York: Simon & Schuster.

Putnam, Robert and Marc Plattner. Eds. (2009). *Democracy: A Reader.* Baltimore, MD: John Hopkins University Press.

Pye, Lucian W. (1962). *Politics, Personality, and Nation-Building.* New Haven, CT: Yale University Press.

———. (1985). *Asian Power and Politics: The Cultural Dimensions of Authority.* Cambridge, MA: Belknap Press.

Rae, Douglas. (1971). *The Political Consequences of Electoral Laws.* New Haven, CT: Yale University Press.

Rajan, Raghuram. (2010). *Fault Lines: How Hidden Fractures Still Threaten the World Economy.* Princeton, NJ: Princeton University Press.

Rasler, Karen and William R. Thompson. (2005). *Puzzles of the Democratic Peace: Theory, Geopolitics and the Transformation of World Politics.* New York: Palgrave Macmillan.

Reynolds, Andrew, Ben Reilly and Andrew Ellis. (2005). *Electoral System Design: The New International IDEA Handbook.* http://www.idea.int/publications/esd/

Reppy, Susan. (1984). "The Automobile Air Bag." In *Controversy,* 2nd ed., ed. Dorothy Nelkin, pp. 161–174. Beverly Hills, CA: Sage.

Richards, Andrew. (2007). "Economic Challenges for New Democracies." In *The Construction of Democracy: Lessons from Practice and Research.* Ed. Jorge Dominguez and Anthony Jones, pp. 45–76. Baltimore, MD: Johns Hopkins University Press.

Riker, William. (1962). *The Theory of Political Coalitions.* New Haven, CT: Yale University Press.

———. (1982). "The Two Party System and Duverger's Law." *American Political Science Review 76 (4):* 753–766.

Riker, William, and Peter Ordeshook. (1973). *An Introduction to Positive Political Theory.* Englewood Cliffs, NJ: Prentice Hall.

Ritholtz, Barry. (2009). *Bailout Nation: How Greed and Easy Money Corrupted Wall Street and Shook the World Economy.* New York: Wiley.

Ritter, Daniel and Alex Trechsel. (2011). "Revolutionary Cells: On the Role of Texts, Tweets and Status Updates in Nonviolent Revolutions." Paper presented at the Conference on the Internet, Voting and Democracy.

Laguna Beach, CA. May 15, 2011.

Robinson, Matthew (2009). *Justice Blind? Ideals and Realities of American Criminal Justice.* 3rd ed. Upper Saddle River, NJ: Prentice-Hall.

Robinson, Simon. (2003). "Iraqi Textbooks: X-ing Out Saddam." *Time,* July 21: 18.

Robinson, William I. (1998). *Promoting Polyarchy: Globalization, US Intervention, and Hegemony.* Cambridge: Cambridge University Press.

Rodrik, Dani. Ed. (2003). *In Search of Prosperity: Analytic Narratives on Economic Growth.* Princeton, NJ: Princeton University Press.

———. (2011). *The Globalization Paradox: Democracy and the Future of the World Economy.* New York: W. W. Norton.

Rosenau, James, and Ole Holsti. (1993). "The Structure of Foreign Policy Beliefs Among American Opinion Leaders— After the Cold War". *Millennium,* 22: 235–278.

Rosenberg, Shawn. (1988). *Reason, Ideology, and Politics.* Cambridge, England: Polity.

———. (2002). *The Not So Common Sense: Differences in How People Judge Social and Political Life.* New Haven, CT: Yale University Press.

Rostow, W. W. (1960). *The Stages of Economic Growth: A Non-Communist Manifesto.* Cambridge: Cambridge University Press.

Rotberg, Robert I., Ed. (2003). *When States Fail: Causes and Consequences.* Princeton, NJ: Princeton University Press.

Roubini, Nouriel and Stephen Mihm. (2011). *Crisis*

Economics: A Crash Course in the Future of Economics. New York: Penguin.

Rubenfeld, Samuel. (2011). "Egypt Requests Freeze on Mubarak's Assets." *Wall Street Journal* (February 22, 2011).

Rueschemeyer, Dietrich, Marilyn Rueschemeyer, and Bjorn Wittrock. (1998). *Participation and Democracy East and West: Comparisons and Interpretations.* Armonk, NY: M. E. Sharpe.

Rummel, R. J. (2011). *Death by Government.* http://www .hawaii.edu/powerkills/

Russett, Bruce. (2010). "Peace in the Twenty-first Century." *Current History* 109 (January 2010): 11–16.

Russett, Bruce, and John R. Oneal. (2001). *Triangulating Peace: Democracy, Interdependence, and International Organizations.* New York: W. W. Norton.

Russett, Bruce, John R. Oneal and Michaelene Cox. (2000). "Clash of Civilizations, or Realism and Liberalism Déjá Vu?: Some Evidence." *Journal of Peace Research,* 37: 583–608.

Russett, Bruce, Harvey Starr, and David Kinsella. (2009). *World Politics: The Menu for Choice.* 9th ed. New York: Thomson Wadsworth.

Rustow, Dankwart. (1967). *A World of Nations: Problems of Political Modernization.* Washington, DC: Brookings Institution.

Safran, William. (2008). *The French Polity.* 7th ed. London: Longman.

Sageman, Marc. (2008). *Leaderless Jihad: Terror Networks in the Twenty-First Century.* Philadelphia:

University of Pennsylvania Press.

Said, Edward. (2001). "The Clash of Ignorance." *Nation.* (October). http://www.the-nation.com/doc/20011022/said

Salisbury, Robert H. (1990). "The Paradox of Interest Groups in Washington, D.C.: More Groups and Less Clout." In *The New American Political System,* Rev. ed. Ed. Anthony King. Washington, DC: American Enterprise Institute.

Salisbury, Robert H., John P. Heinz, Robert L. Nelson, and Edward O. Laumann. (1991). "Triangles, Networks, and Hollow Cores: The Complex Geometry of Washington Interest Representation." In *The Politics of Interests,* ed. Mark P. Petracca, pp. 130–149. Boulder, CO: Westview.

Sandbrook, Richard, Marc Edelman, Patrick Heller and Judith Teichman. (2007). *Social Democracy in the Global Periphery: Origins, Challenges, Prospects.* New York: Cambridge University Press.

Sassen, Saskia. (1996). *Losing Control? Sovereignty in the Age of Globalization.* New York: Columbia University Press.

Schain, Martin, Aristide Zolberg and Patrick Hossay. (2002). *Shadows Over Europe: The Development and Impact of the Extreme Right in Europe.* New York: Palgrave Macmillan.

Schedler, Andreas, Ed. (2006). *Electoral Authoritarianism: The Dynamics of Unfree Competition.* Boulder, CO: Lynne Rienner.

Schelling, Thomas. (1960). *The Strategy of Conflict.*

Cambridge, MA: Harvard University Press.

Schleiter, Petra and Edward Morgan-Jones. (2009). "Constitutional Power and Competing Risks: Monarchs, Presidents, Prime Ministers and the Termination of East and West European Cabinets." *American Political Science Review* 103 (3) August: 496–512.

Schmalleger, Frank J. (2011). *Criminal Justice: A Brief Introduction.* 9th ed. Englewood Cliffs, NJ: Prentice Hall.

Schmidt, Eric and Jared Cohen. (2010). "The Digital Disruption: Connectivity and the Diffusion of Power." *Foreign Affairs* 89 (November/December): 75–85.

Schmitter, Philippe C. (1993). "Corporatism." In *The Oxford Companion to Politics of the World,* ed. Joel Krieger, pp. 195–198. New York: Oxford University Press.

Schneider, Carsten. (2009). *The Consolidation of Democracy: Comparing Europe and Latin America.* London: Routledge.

Schumpeter, Joseph. (1950). *Capitalism, Socialism, and Democracy.* 3rd ed. New York: Harper and Row.

Sen, Amartya. (2006). *Identity and Violence: The Illusion of Destiny.* New York, NY: W.W. Norton.

Sesser, Stan. (1992). "A Nation of Contradictions." *New Yorker,* January 13, 37–68.

Sharp, Gene. (2010). *From Dictatorship to Democracy: A Conceptual Framework for Liberation.* 4th U.S. edition. http://www.aeinstein.org/organizations/org/FDTD .pdf

Shayo, Moses. (2009). "A Model of Social Identity with an Application to Political Economy: Nation, Class and Redistribution." *American Political Science Review* 103: 147–174.

Shirky, C. (2011). "The political power of social media". *Foreign Affairs. (January/February).* http://www .foreignaffairs.com/ articles/67038/clay-shirky/ the-political-power-of-social-media

Shkolnikov, Vladimir. (2009). "Nations in Transit: Democracy's Dark Year." Pp. 1–9 in *Nations in Transit.* 13th ed. New York: Freedom House.

Shugart, Matthew and John M. Carey. (1992). *Presidents and Assemblies: Constitutional Design and Electoral Dynamics.* New York: Cambridge University Press.

Silone, Ignazio. (1937). *Bread and Wine.* Trans. Gwenda David. New York: Harper and Row.

Simone, Vera. (2001). *The Asian Pacific: Political and Economic Development in a Global Context.* 2nd ed. New York: Longman.

Singh, Inderjit. "China and India: Comparative Transition to Modernization." Paper presented at the annual meeting of the International Studies Association, Hilton Hawaiian Village, Honolulu, Hawaii, March 5, 2005, http://www .allacademic.com/meta/ p71394_index.html

SIPRI (Stockholm International Peace Research Institute). (2011). *The SIPRI Yearbook.* http://www.sipri.org

Sivard, Ruth Leger. (1996). *World Military and Social Expenditures 1996.*

Washington, DC: World Priorities.

Skinner, B. F. (1948). *Walden Two.* New York: Macmillan.

Skocpol, Theda. (1979). *States and Social Revolutions: A Comparative Analysis of France, Russia, and China.* New York: Cambridge University Press.

Smelser, Neil. (2007). *The Faces of Terrorism: Social and Psychological Dimensions.* Princeton, NJ: Princeton University Press.

Smick, David. (2008). *The World is Curved: Hidden Dangers to the World Economy.* New York: Penguin.

Smith, Adam. (1776/2009). *An Inquiry into the Nature and Causes of the Wealth of Nations.* http://www.adam-smith.org/smith/won-intro.htm

Smith, Jackie. (2007). *Social Movements for Global Democracy.* Baltimore: Johns Hopkins University.

Sniderman, Paul M., et al. (1991). "The Fallacy of Democratic Elitism: Elite Competition and Commitment to Civil Liberties." *British Journal of Political Science* 21 (August): 349–370.

Sniderman, Paul. (1975). *Personality and Democratic Politics.* Berkeley: University of California Press.

Sophocles. (1967). *Antigone.* Trans. E. F. Watling. Middlesex, England: Penguin.

Sorensen, Georg. (2008). *Democracy and Democratization: Processes and Prospects in a Changing World.* 3rd ed. Boulder, CO: Westview.

Spagnoli, Filip. (2003). *Homo-Democraticus: On the Universal Desirability and the*

Not So Universal Possibility of Democracy and Human Rights. Cambridge, England: Cambridge Scholars.

Stein, Howard. (2006). "The World Bank and the Application of Asian Industrial Policy to Africa: Theoretical Considerations." *Journal of International Development* 6 (3): 287–305.

Steans, Jill. (2006). *Gender and International Relations.* 2nd ed. Malden, MA: Polity Press.

Stepan, Alfred. (2009). "Religion, Democracy and the 'Twin Tolerations.'" In Putnam, Robert and Marc Plattner. Eds. (2009). *Democracy: A Reader.* Baltimore, MD: John Hopkins University Press.

Stiglitz, Joseph. (2006). *Making Globalization Work.* New York: W. W. Norton.

———. (2003) *Globalization and Its Discontents.* New York: W. W. Norton.

———. (2010). *Free Fall: Free Markets and the Sinking of the US Economy.* New York: W. W. Norton.

Stoessinger, John G. (2010). *Why Nations Go to War.* 11th ed. Boston: Wadsworth.

Stone Sweet, Alec. (2004). *The Judicial Construction of Europe.* Oxford: Oxford University Press.

Strøm, Kaare. (2004). "Parliamentary Democracy and Delegation." In Kaare Strøm, Wolfgang C. Müller, and Torbjörn Bergman (eds.), *Delegation and Accountability in Parliamentary Democracies.* Oxford: Oxford University Press: 55–106.

Strauss, Leo. (1959). *What Is Political Philosophy?* New York: Free Press.

Stone, Clarence. (1989). *Regime Politics*. University of Kansas Press.

Sunstein, Cass. (2001). *Designing Democracy: What Constitutions Do*. New York: Oxford University Press.

———. (2009). *On Rumors: How Falsehoods Spread, Why We Believe Them, What Can be Done*. New York: Farrar, Straus & Giroux.

Szabo, Stephen. (2011). "Welcome to the Post-Western World." *Current History* 110 (January 2011): 9–13.

Taagepera, Rein, and Matthew S. Shugart. (1989). *Seats and Votes*. New Haven, CT: Yale University Press.

Taras, Raymond, and Rajat Ganguly. (2010). *Understanding Ethnic Conflict: The International Dimension*. 4th ed. New York: Pearson-Longman.

Tawney, R. H. (1938). *Religion and the Rise of Capitalism: A Historical Study*. Middlesex, England: Penguin.

Thompson, Leonard. (1966). *Politics in the Republic of South Africa*. Boston: Little, Brown.

Thompson, Mark R. (2003). *Democratic Revolutions: Asian and Eastern Europe*. London: Routledge.

Thoreau, Henry David. (1849/1981). *Walden and Other Writings*. Ed. J. W. Krutch. New York: Bantam.

Thurow, Lester C. (1997). *The Future of Capitalism*. New York: Penguin.

Tickner, J. Ann. (2001). *Gendering World Politics*. New York: Columbia University Press.

Tilly, Charles. (2007). *Democracy*. Cambridge University Press.

Tocqueville, Alexis de. (1835/1945). *Democracy in America*. New York: Knopf.

Torcal, Mariano, and Jose Ramon Montero. (2006). *Political Disaffection in Contemporary Democracies: Social Capital, Institutions, and Politics*. London: Routledge.

Transparency International. (2011). http://www.transparency.org

Triesman, Daniel. (2004). "Stabilization Tactics in Latin America: Menem, Cardosa, and the Politics of Low Inflation." *Comparative Politics* 36 (July): 399–419.

True, Jacqui and Brooke Ackerly. (2010). *Doing Feminist Research in Political and Social Sciences*. New York: Palgrave.

Truman, David. (1951). *The Governmental Process*. New York: Knopf.

Tsebelis, George. (2002). *Veto Players. How Political Institutions Work*. Princeton, NJ: Princeton University Press.

Turner, Thomas. (2011). "Kabila's Congo: Hardly 'Post-Conflict'." *Current History* 110 (May 2011): 196–201.

Union of International Associations. (2011). http://www.uia.be/

UNCTAD (2011). *Commodities at a Glance*. http://www.unctad.org/en/docs/1suc20112_en.pdf

UNDA (2011). *The United Nations Development Agenda: Development for All-Goals, Commitments and Strategies Agreed at the United Nations World Conferences and Summits since 1990*. New York: United Nations.

UNDP (United Nations Development Programme). (2001). *Human Development Report 2001*.

———. (2005). *Human Development Report 2006*. http://www.hdr.undp.org/reports

———. (2006). *Human Development Report 2006*. http://www.hdr.undp.org/reports

———. (2008). *Human Development Report 2008*. http://www.hdr.undp.org/reports

———. (2011). *Human Development Report 2010/2011*. http://www.hdr.undp.org/reports.

UNMDG. (2011). *United Nations Millenium Development Goals*. http://www.un.org/millenniumgoals/11_MDG%20Report_EN.pdf

UNHCR. (2011). *United Nations High Commissioner for Refugees*. www.unhcr.org

United Nations Peacekeeping Operations. (2011). http://www.un.org/Depts/dpko/dpko/home.shtml

UNWFP (2011). United Nations World Food Programme. http://www.wfp.org

Verba, Sidney, Norman Nie, and Jae-on Kim. (1978). *Participation and Political Equality: A Seven-Nation Comparison*. Cambridge, England: Cambridge University Press.

Verba, Sidney, Kay Schlozman, and Henry Brady. (1995). *Voice and Equality: Civic Voluntarism in American Politics*. Cambridge, MA: Harvard University Press.

Vision of Humanity (2011). http://www.visionofhumanity.org/gpi/home.php

Victoroff, Jeff. (2005). "The Mind of the Terrorist: A Review and Critique of Psychological Approaches." *Journal of Conflict Resolution* 49 (February): 3–42.

von Braun, Joachim (2008). "Food and Financial Crises: Implications for Agriculture and the Poor." International Food Policy Research Institute: *Food Policy Report No. 20.* http://www.ifpri.org/pubs/fpr/pr20all.asp

Waldron, Jeremy. (2006). "The Core of the Case Against Judicial Review." *Yale Law Journal* 115 (2006): 1346–1406.

Wallerstein, Immanuel. (1974). *The Modern World System.* New York: Academic Press.

———. (1980). *The World System II.* New York: Academic Press.

———. (2004). *World-Systems Analysis: An Introduction.* Raleigh, NC: Duke University Press.

———. (2005). "After Developmentalism and Globalization, What?" *Social Forces* 83 (3) March: 1263–1278.

Walt, Stephen M. (1997). "Building Up a New Bogeyman." *Foreign Policy* 106: 176–89.

———. (2006). *Taming American Power: The Global Response to U.S. Primacy.* New York: W. W. Norton.

Weatherby, Joseph. (2011). "The Old and the New: Colonialism, Neocolonialism, and Nationalism and the War on Terror." In *The Other World: Issues and Politics of the Developing World,* 10th ed., Ed. Joseph Weatherby et al., Ch. 2. New York: Longman.

Weatherby, Joseph, et al. (2011). *The Other World: Issues and Politics of the Developing World.* 10th ed. New York: Longman.

Weber, Max. (1951). *The Religion of China: Confucianism and Taoism.* Ed. Hans H. Gerth. New York: Free Press.

———. (1958a). *From Max Weber: Essays in Sociology.* Ed. Hans H. Gerth and C. Wright Mills. New York: Oxford University Press.

———. (1958b). *The Religion of India: The Sociology of Hinduism and Buddhism.* Trans. Hans Gerth and Don Martindale. New York: Free Press.

Weintraub, Sidney. (2009). "An Economic Storm Hits Latin America." *Current History* 108: 58–64.

Weiss, Thomas, Ed. (1996). *NGOs, the UN, and Global Governance.* Boulder, CO: Lynne Rienner.

Weiss, Thomas and Sam Daws. Eds. (2009). *The Oxford Handbook on the United Nations.* Oxford: Oxford University Press.

Weitz, Eric D. (2005). *A Century of Genocide: Utopias of Race and Nation.* Princeton, NJ: Princeton University Press.

Welzel, Christian. (2007). "A Human Development View on Value Change." http://margaux.grandvinum.se/SebTest/wvs/articles/folder_published/article_base_83

Wendt, Alexander. (1995). "Constructing International Politics." *International Security* 20:1: 71–81.

Wendt, Alexander. (1999). *Social Theory of International Politics.* Cambridge, England: Cambridge University Press.

Wiarda, Howard J. (1997). *Corporatism and Comparative Politics: The Other Great "Ism."* Armonk, NY: M. E. Sharpe.

———. (2003). *Political Development in Emerging Countries.* Belmont, CA: Wadsworth.

———. Ed. (2004). *Authoritarianism and Corporatism in Latin America—Revisited.* Gainesville: University Press of Florida.

Wiarda, Howard J. and Harvey Kline. (2007). *A Concise Introduction to Latin American Politics and Development.* 2nd Ed. Boulder, CO: Westview Press.

Wilensky, Harold. (2002). *Rich Democracies.* Berkeley: University of California Press.

Williams, Michelle. (2008). *The Roots of Participatory Democracy: Democratic Communists in South Africa and Kerala, India.* New York: Palgrave Macmillan.

Wilson, William Julius. (1990). *The Truly Disadvantaged.* Chicago: University of Chicago Press.

———. (1997). *When Work Disappears.* New York: Knopf.

Wolf, Martin. (2004). *Why Globalization Works.* New Haven, CN: Yale University Press.

World Economic Forum. (2011). *Global Competitiveness Report 2010–2011.* http://www.weforum.org/issues/global-competitiveness

Winters, Jeffrey A. (1998). "Asia and the 'Magic' of the Marketplace." *Current History* 97 (December): 418–425.

Woo-Cumings, Meredith, Ed. (1999). *The Developmental State*. New York: Cornell University Press.

World Bank. (1996). *World Development Report 1996*. New York: Oxford University Press.

———. (2005). *World Development Report 2004–2005*. New York: Oxford University Press.

———. (2011). *World Development Report 2011*. New York: Oxford University Press.

World Trade Organization. (2011). *What Is the World Trade Organization?* http://www.wto.org.

World Values Survey. (2006). http://www.worldvaluessurvey.org.

Worldwatch. (2003). *State of the World 2003*. Washington, DC: Worldwatch Institute.

Woshinsky, Oliver. (1995). *Culture and Politics*. Englewood Cliffs, NJ: Prentice Hall.

Wright, Erik Olin. (1998). *The Debate on Classes*. London: Verso.

Wrong, Dennis. (1996). *Power: Its Forms, Bases, and Uses*. Brunswick, NJ: Transaction.

Yan, Zhang. (2010). "Bribery Cases on Rise in China".

China Daily (September 8, 2010). http://www.chinadaily.com.cn/china/2010-09/08/content_11271378.htm

Zakaria, Fareed. (2007). *The Future of Freedom: Illiberal Democracy at Home and Abroad*. Rev. ed. New York: W. W. Norton.

———. (2009). *The Post-American World*. New York: W. W. Norton & Company.

Zaller, John R. (1992). *The Nature and Origins of Mass Opinion*. New York: Cambridge University Press.

Zukin, Cliff, et al. (2006). *A New Engagement? Political Participation, Civic Life, and the Changing American Citizen*. New York: Oxford University Press.

PHOTO CREDITS

INDEX